NetWare User's Guide

Covers versions 3.11 and 3.12

NetWare User's Guide

Covers versions 3.11 and 3.12

Edward Liebing

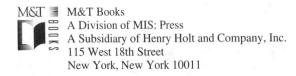

M&T Books
A Division of MIS: Press
A Subsidiary of Henry Holt and Company, Inc.
115 West 18th Street
New York, New York 10011

Limits of Liability and Disclaimer of Warranty
The Author and Publisher of this book have used their best efforts in preparing the book and the programs contained in it. These efforts include the development, research, and testing of the theories and programs to determine their effectiveness.

The Author and Publisher make no warranty of any kind, expressed or implied, with regard to these programs or the documentation contained in this book. The Author and Publisher shall not be liable in any event for incidental or consequential damages in connection with, or arising out of, the furnishing, performance, or use of these programs.

Library of Congress Cataloging-in-Publication Data

Liebing, Edward
    NetWare user's guide: covers versions 3.11 and 3.12 / by Edward Liebing.
      p. cm.
    Includes index.
    ISBN 1-55851-318-3 : $29.95
    1. Operating systems (Computers) 2. NetWare (Computer file) I. Title.
    QA76.76.063L5293   1993
    005.7'1369--dc20   93-4987
                             CIP

Trademarks:
The Coordinator is a trademark of Action Technologies. IBM PC DOS, IBM PCs, IBM PS/2s, and IBM ProPrinter are trademarks of IBM Corp. MS-DOS, Microsoft Word, and Microsoft Windows are trademarks of Microsoft Corp. DESQview 386 is a trademark of Quarterdeck Office Systems Corp. Compaq is a trademark of Compaq Corp. AT&T is a trademark of AT&T. WordPerfect is a trademark of WordPerfect Corp. HP LaserJet is a trademark of Hewlett-Packard Corp. Epson Action Printer is a trademark of Epson Corp. dBASE III PLUS is a trademark of Ashton-Tate Corp. Revelation is a trademark of Revelation Technologies. NetWare, NetWare shell, Transaction Tracking System (TTS), and NE-1000 are trademarks of Novell, Inc. Brief is a trademark of UnderWare, Inc. Lotus is a trademark of Lotus Corp. All other products, names, and services are trademarks or registered trademarks of their respective companies.

Publisher: Steve Berkowitz
Associate Publisher: Brenda McLaughlin
Project Editor: Mike Welch
Development/Technical Editor: Dave Doering

Copy Editor: Kristen Little
Cover Design: Mark Masuelli
Production Editor: Eileen Mullin

96 95 94 93   4 3 2

Contents

CHAPTER 4 — PRINTING UP A STORM 367

xiv

Acknowledgments

To my family, Maddy, Rachel, Marie, Becky, and Sarah and Anne.

To my editors, Dave Doering and Mike Welch, who kept me thinking that updates aren't so bad after all.

To Vince Sondej and Rich Hillyard for their technical expertise on Windows and NetWare menus.

To Novell for the NetWare operating systems, to Thomas-Conrad for use of an Ethernet topology, and to Compaq for a really nice SystemPro.

Thank you one and all for making this book possible.

Foreword

In the first edition of this book, I said you were never sure of the best place to begin with user's guides. Yet due to the success of the first edition, I think I've hit the right audience with the right kind of material.

NetWare User's Guide is designed to serve two purposes: to acquaint new users with NetWare services, and to provide a reference for the experienced NetWare user. The introduction and the first four chapters are for the novice user, explaining how NetWare works and how to use NetWare's utilities. Chapter 5 and the appendices are for those of you who are familiar with both DOS and NetWare and want a quick reference for the utilities as well as for troubleshooting your workstation.

The introduction gives a basic overview of network operation and briefly explains the services and utilities available on a NetWare network. Chapter 1 shows you how to log in to a server, how to understand the login scripts you may see, how to use DOS and network commands for directory management, and how to log out of the server. Chapters 2 and 3 present detailed explanations of each NetWare utility and NetWare service and list the tasks you can perform in each utility. Each explanation is followed by a simple example and, where appropriate, a more complex example. Chapter 2 explains the menu utilities and shows you how to use them; Chapter 3 discusses the command-line utilities that work from your network prompt.

Chapter 4 is about printing. This chapter explains the use of NetWare's many printing utilities, as well as the concepts behind the NetWare print server. Throughout the chapter, you'll see examples of when, why, and how to print on a NetWare network using these utilities.

Chapter 5 is designed to give experienced users enough information to be able to take care of themselves. Specifically, Chapter 5 presents hands-on information on how to set up your CONFIG.SYS and AUTOEXEC.BAT files, as well as the NET.CFG file, which complements the NetWare shell or DOS Requester.

Chapter 6 gives you troubleshooting skills by presenting the NetWare shell error messages and how to respond to them, as well as calling attention to other problems you may encounter.

The appendices are for your reference. Appendix A compares and contrasts the DOS environment and NetWare. Appendices B and C give you a quick reference to the tasks you can perform from either a menu or a command-line utility. Appendix D covers the tasks you perform when given the additional responsibilities of a workgroup manager, object manager, print queue operator, and print server operator. Appendices E and F are for 3.12 users as they cover NetWare 3.12's NMenu and FirstMail utilities.

While this book looks at the manager and operator responsibilities, it doesn't go into the duties and responsibilities of the NetWare supervisor. That topic fills volumes by itself. However, Chapters 5 and 6 on the NetWare shell error messages does go into some detail on what a supervisor or an experienced user can do to solve the problems indicated by various error messages.

This book is based on what happens on a network using MS DOS version 3.3, 4.01, 5.0, and 6.0 and DR-DOS version 6.0 as the workstation operating systems, and NetWare versions 3.11 and 3.12 as the network operating system. The author has tried to represent the capabilities of the versions of DOS and NetWare, but oversights will occur and are unintentional.

While this book describes many ways to execute a command, other possibilities may exist in some cases. Get one sequence down and stick with it for familiarity's sake—but once you become familiar with one method of implementing a command, try some new ways and expand your working knowledge of NetWare. That's when it starts to be fun!

Edward A. Liebing
August 1993

Why This Book Is for You

Anyone working on a NetWare network will find in this book a wealth of information on how to better use NetWare in day-to-day activities.

➤ If you are a new NetWare user, you will learn how NetWare works and how to log in, work in its directory structure, set up and maintain login scripts, print efficiently, and use NetWare's many menu and command-line utilities.

➤ More experienced NetWare users will find this book a quick reference for the utilities as well as for troubleshooting workstations.

➤ NetWare supervisors will benefit from practical advice on setting up users and their working environments, and gain much of the author's experience through numerous tips and tricks on how to better manage and delegate responsibilities to workgroup managers, console operators, print server operators, and others.

➤ Consultants will find this book indispensable for troubleshooting and maintaining a NetWare environment, especially because workstation setup and error messages are covered in detail.

Whatever your NetWare experience, you will find *NetWare User's Guide, Covers versions 3.11 and 3.12,* is an invaluable reference for setting up, maintaining, navigating, and working efficiently in NetWare.

1

A Primer for Users of NetWare 3.11 and 3.12

What's in an Operating System?

If you've ever been to the theater, you've probably noticed at least two basic elements for putting on a production: the stage and the backdrops. The stage is a platform for performing the play itself, and the backdrops accentuate the action on the stage. Without the stage, actors would be without a necessary platform from which to project their skills; without the backdrops, the actors themselves would have to carry the entire mood and tone of the play. The stage and backdrops become tools to assist the actors in presenting the play.

An operating system also includes two elements: *services* and *utilities*. The operating system is the platform that allows you to perform important functions on a computer. If you're at all familiar with IBM's or Microsoft's Disk Operating System (known as DOS), you'll recognize that DOS provides you with a platform for performing certain services, such as accessing applications, databases, utilities, modems, and printers. DOS also provides you with a number of utilities—that is, tools to help you do your work, such as DIR (show me the directory's contents), CLS (clear the screen), and DEL (delete files).

Using the DOS platform, thousands of applications and utilities have been written and are still being written to help you to do your job more efficiently. Each application takes advantage of DOS's file access and format standard so you can bring up the application while using DOS and print the documents accordingly. The same can be said of the utilities built on the DOS platform; these utilities make the operating system more useful by enhancing its functionality.

Like DOS, OS/2, and the Macintosh's System 7, NetWare offers a number of utilities that make getting around in the operating system easier. For instance, what do you do if you forget where you stored a file? How can you find an application on the network? How do you "map" a drive letter to the application? When you do, how do you know if you have enough "rights" to use the application? By becoming familiar with

NetWare utilities, you can learn how to get around the network and make the best possible use of your time.

What Services Does the NetWare Operating System Provide?

Network computing has been equated with the ability to share information. Many companies are "downsizing" their minicomputer and mainframe platforms to include local and wide area networks; this trend means that LAN/WAN popularity is growing. Many companies are using LANs to handle important tasks more efficiently than their minicomputer and mainframe counterparts can. These tasks include word processing, spreadsheet updates, desktop publishing, and so forth. Workers also have a growing need to access information, wherever that information may be stored—on minicomputers or mainframes, other LANs, or even other personal computers (PCs).

With these changes in a company's work habits, LANs have proven themselves a more effective and flexible method of getting information to the place where the work gets done—your desktop PC (also known as a workstation). LANs offer the means to connect these PCs into a network and perhaps to another PC network by means of a product known as a "bridge" or "router." Then, through hardware/software products known as "gateways," your desktop can even gain access to minicomputer and mainframe environments to retrieve the information you need to in order to do your job.

Using PCs on the desktop has become a widespread and effective means of managing the tasks necessary to a business. But what does a network operating system such as NetWare have to offer its users over and above the advantages offered by the PCs themselves?

Think of NetWare as a bundle of network services and utilities that help you work more efficiently. NetWare does for the network what DOS, OS/2, and Macintosh's System 7 do for the workstation. A single-user workstation operating system, such as DOS, allows you to access applications, databases, modems, and printers. It allows you to take data from certain resources and change that data into information; then it allows you to print that information in the form of presentations, surveys, studies, and so forth.

NetWare expands on this concept by making it possible for many people in a working environment to share services and resources. Instead of each workstation having a hard disk, modem, applications, utilities, and printers, NetWare centralizes these services for everyone attached to the network. With a network operating system, even diskless workstations can access available services and network resources.

Looking Around Your Workplace

Let's take a look at your workplace and identify the many elements of a network. The network is made up of several components, with each component performing its own specific duty. These components include:

- ➤ Server
- ➤ Workstations
- ➤ Network interface boards
- ➤ Cabling scheme
- ➤ Printers
- ➤ Disk subsystem
- ➤ Uninterruptible power supply (UPS)
- ➤ Bridges, routers, and gateways
- ➤ Modems

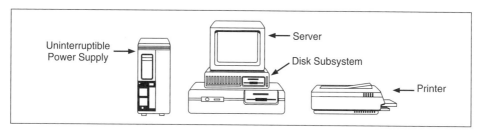

Figure I-1. Look around your office and see how many of these components you can find.

It isn't necessary for your workplace to have every component on this list. Actually, all you need in your workplace is a server, workstations, network interface boards, a cabling scheme, and most likely a printer. However, each component offers an added service to your working environment. As your office grows, these elements, as well as others, may become more and more familiar to you.

Somewhere in your workplace is the server (also known as the file server)—an important piece of equipment, for the server centralizes many of the services we are talking about. The server is a personal computer similar to the one you use as a workstation if your PC runs DOS or OS/2. Physically, however, the server probably has more memory than your workstation. It can also have a number of hard disk drives, a tape drive for backup purposes, an uninterruptible power supply (UPS), and a printer or two attached to it.

Sometimes you'll see another server-like box connected to the server. This is called a disk subsystem, and its purpose is to increase the amount of disk space available to network users. With the advent of multimedia and imaging, disk subsystems can contain many gigabytes of disk storage. The disk subsystem or the server might also have a tape backup unit, which the system supervisor uses to back up the server's data onto tapes. If you accidentally erase a valuable file or if a server's hard disk drive doesn't work properly, your supervisor can use the information stored on the tapes to restore the server to its previous state.

You may also see another important box near the server: the uninterruptible power supply (UPS). The UPS makes sure that your server gets enough straight voltage by preventing power fluctuation and by protecting the server against power spikes, which can seriously damage the server's hard disks. Some UPSs are intelligent enough to automatically shut down your server when its reserve power gets low. Often UPSs are built into the office or building, offering added protection.

If your server is out in the open, go to the back of it. Among all the cables back there you'll see some type of cable attached to a board (known as a network interface board) in one of the slots in the back. Similarly, the board and cabling you have in your workstation allows it to communicate with the servers on the network and provide your connection to the network's services and utilities.

You may have also noticed that the server has a printer or two attached to it. With the first version of NetWare, each printer had to be attached directly to the server. System managers had to make sure that the printers were in an accessible location; therefore, the server was usually nearby. An added feature of the NetWare 3.x operating systems, however, is the ability to support printers that are either attached to your workstation or to another strategically located computer known as a print server. The printer, therefore, can be more accessible, while the server can be placed away from traffic and away from possible tampering or damage.

Many companies actually have "bridges" installed over modems although you can't actually see these bridges. A bridge or router allows your LAN to communicate with other LANs in an architecture known as a wide area network (WAN). Another popular configuration involves a workstation or server communicating with a minicomputer or mainframe over a modem. Because your workstation is communicating with a different kind of network, you are using "gateway" software and hardware for this capability.

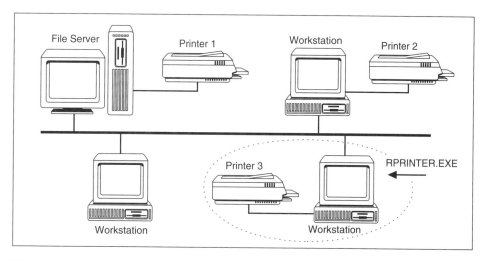

Figure I-2. With NetWare 3.11, printers can be attached to the file server, to the print servers, or to workstations across the network.

At the Workstation

As you read this, you're probably sitting in front of your workstation, which, in many cases, is as powerful as the server. You may or may not have your own hard disk, but a local area network lets you share the hard disk space on the server.

Your workstation is different from a stand-alone PC because the workstation has a network interface board or card. You also run some software that helps the workstation talk to the network board, communicate across its attached cable, and access services on the network. One piece of this software, called the NetWare shell or DOS Requester, enables you to communicate with network servers. Chapter 1 deals more extensively with this software.

Local area networks use the processing power of every computer on the network. Once your workstation receives an application from the server, all processing for that application is done on your workstation's processor. Using your workstation's processing power allows your server to do what it does best: coordinate file access, application access, and directory and disk access, as well as coordinate printing services and security and maintain communications between workstations and the network.

NetWare—The Network Operating System Software

The server in a local area network runs software known as the *network operating system*. When you request an application from the server, your workstation performs all of the processing for the application. But it's the server that makes sure the application and accompanying data files get to you. The same is true for utilities; your workstation does the processing, but the server delivers the utility.

The server software also makes sure that you have the proper rights to use an application in the first place, and that your data files are protected when you're using them as well as when they're stored on the server.

The server software offers *file services, communications services, and queue management.* File services mean your files are properly "locked" when you're in them and accessible when they're not in use. Coupled with security, file management also protects your personal files from others on the network. Communications services mean that with the proper security and access, you can access information on servers and mainframes from across the hall, across the street, or across the globe. Queue management is a store-and-forwarding procedure that first stores jobs at a queue (location) and then forwards those jobs to some service, such as a print server or a printer.

The multiuser world provides some additional challenges to the network operating system. In order to perform file services in a multiuser environment, NetWare has to "lock" each file during its update cycle. The update cycle includes reading the data file, modifying the file's contents, and then writing the updated file back to disk. When many users access databases regularly, such protection becomes imperative.

A classic example of early multiuser systems without file locking is Jim and Jane's shared word processing directory and data files. Jim opens a data file and does some minor modifications before he is called away from his desk. Jane opens the same file at her workstation and furiously modifies the file during Jim's absence. Contented with her changes, Jane closes the file and goes on to another project. Meanwhile, Jim returns and simply closes the file without ever looking at it again. Whose changes are saved to the disk? Jim's are. Since Jim closed the file last, only Jim's changes are saved and all of Jane's work has been undone. This example is just one potential problem that NetWare addresses and overcomes.

The methods of file locking are important for applications, for through file locking in network applications, a number of other users can access the application you're in at the same time. With such applications as databases, NetWare makes certain that the database file record you're in is sufficiently protected against access by other users. This doesn't mean that others can't access the database; networking databases take into account multiple users—only the file record that you're currently in is inaccessible to other users until you're finished with that record.

8

Think of an office using stand-alone computers. The work area may contain a printer for every one or two workstations. As many of you have had occasion to notice, stand-alones don't share printers well, so you have to run your data files over to the workstation with the printer in order to print the file. A network, on the other hand, allows you to share printers by placing your printing jobs in a storage place known as a print queue to wait their turn to print out. When you print a file, NetWare places that file in a queue in an order determined by when the job was sent (queue management).

NetWare looks at hard disks on the server in two ways: *physically* and *logically*. The physical disk is the hard disk itself, and your NetWare supervisor can designate certain areas of the disk as sections known as volumes. Each of these sections is a logical (meaning non-physical) volume. NetWare always has a SYS (for system) volume—the SYS volume is where NetWare stores and looks for the operating system and its utilities. In these volumes, your supervisor sets up directories and subdirectories which contain applications and data files; in these volumes, you can set up directories and subdirectories to store your data files. You can also have CD ROMs as read-only volumes.

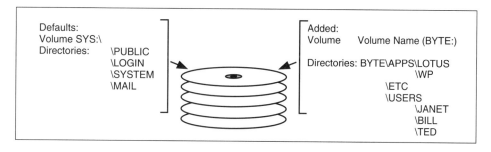

Figure I-3. On the server's hard disk drives, Netware stores files and directories for NetWare 3.11. One hard disk can be single volume, or a volume can span multiple hard disks. Directories are created and stored under volumes and files are created and stored in directories.

The directories you create in a designated volume area constitute your home area on the network. They contain much of the information you'll be able to access. These directories and other shared directories, along with the applications and utilities you access, form the basis for your workstation environment when you're working on this server. The SYSCON utility described in Chapter 2 will show you how to set up a login script so you'll have immediate access to your most frequently used directories every time you log in.

Data Protection

Novell has worked hard to incorporate a data protection design. This design includes the addition of extra hardware (known as disk mirroring or disk duplexing), as well as certain software protections such as Hot Fix, duplicate directory tables, and NetWare's Transaction Tracking System (TTS). Before NetWare 2.2, your company had to buy SFT NetWare to get disk mirroring/duplexing and TTS. However, these features now come with NetWare 3.11 and 3.12 and may be incorporated into your data protection scheme. Let's look at what this protection means.

NetWare's software protection includes the use of more than one directory table and the use of Hot Fix. Directory tables tell where your data files are located; redundant directory tables exist so that if one directory table goes bad, NetWare will go to the other table (placed on a different sector of the disk) so you can access your files. Hot Fix checks to see if the information written to the disk is correct; if it isn't, NetWare marks that area as bad and then writes the data to another part of the disk. If that write is successful, NetWare continues its work.

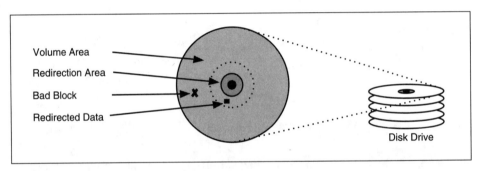

Volume Area
Redirection Area
Bad Block
Redirected Data

Disk Drive

Figure I-4. Hot Fix keeps track of bad block areas on hard disks and rewrites data to known good block areas.

For hardware data protection, NetWare 3.11 and 3.12 allow for redundant hardware. NetWare 3.11 allows for a second disk drive or a collection of drives, containing the same information as the first, to run in concert with the original. If one hard disk in a collection goes bad, another disk can take over—and you'll never know the difference. Currently available redundant hardware includes hard disks, connector cables, and controller boards. But since the change from the damaged component to the good one takes place without your knowledge, you needn't worry about it.

SFT III NetWare takes hardware redundancy to a new level by mirroring actual file servers. This is done through high-speed network interface boards and mirroring information from the primary server to the secondary server. If the primary server goes down, the secondary server automatically takes over. Aside from a brief pause, users often will never know the switch occurred.

Another service NetWare 3.11 provides is the protection of the information on your hard disks against data corruption. Data corruption occurs when the power fails as you are sending information to the server. While that information is being written to disk, only part of the data gets written. To prevent data corruption, NetWare includes a software feature called Transaction Tracking System, as previously mentioned. TTS treats a block of data as a "transaction." Either the transaction is entirely written to disk, or the transaction is aborted and nothing is written to the disk. Whether all of your data within the transaction is updated or none of the transaction data is saved, your database is preserved from corruption.

How Security Affects What You Can Do on the Server

It's important for you to have a basic understanding of how security works so you'll know why you're able to access an application or data in one directory but not in another directory.

Security is like going to an amusement park: What you can do at the park depends on the tickets you buy. You can think of tickets as permissions to do something. For example, you can buy tickets to give you access to the amusement sights and shows, but not to let you go on the rides. Or you can buy ride tickets, which won't let you in to see the shows. You can also buy tickets to access certain parts of the amusement parks. And, of course, you can buy the all-day pass to see and do everything.

NetWare also has a set of permissions that give you access to applications, utilities, and the information available on the server. You basically need three permissions in NetWare: permission to access the *server* through passwords, permission to access a *directory* through the basic security rights, and permission to access a *file* through the basic security rights as well as through file flags.

Passwords. Security begins with your login name and password, which allow you to log in to a server. If security has been enforced at all, you'll need a login name, or username, and a password just to get on a NetWare server. These passwords should be unique to each person, and intruders shouldn't be able to guess what they are. Don't make your password predictable by using the name of a relative, friend, offspring, spouse, or pet. With NetWare 3.1x, passwords are stored encrypted on the server as well as sent to the server in an encrypted fashion for further protection.

Once you're logged in to the server, you'll be able to access various directories. What you can do in these directories depends on a security structure based on security rights.

Basic Security Rights

To keep directories and files secure, NetWare 3.1x uses eight basic security rights. Your supervisor uses these rights to determine what you can see and do in the network directories and subdirectories. These rights include Read, Write, Create, Erase, Modify, File Scan, Access Control, and Supervisory. Here's what each right offers on the file and directory levels:

Supervisory. The Supervisory right allows you to have all rights to the assigned directory, its subdirectories, and the files within the directory. This right overrides all other restrictions placed on subdirectories as well as files. And this right can't be masked out through the directory or file IRM (Inherited Rights Mask). It must be revoked through trustee assignments or equivalences at the directory level in which it is initially given.

On the file level, the Supervisory right gives you all rights to the file. For example, if you have the Supervisory right on a file, you can grant rights to other users and modify the other rights at the file level.

Read. This right allows you to open and read in files in a directory and to open and read information contained in a file. You will normally use it in conjunction with Read and File Scan (RF) rights. The combination of these two rights allows you to read a file or to execute a *.COM, *.BAT, or *.EXE file in a directory.

Write. This right allows you to open a file and place new information into it (write to a file); with NetWare security, you need Write, Create, Erase, and sometimes Modify (WCEM) rights to actually write to a closed file in a network directory. (You have all rights to local drives, such as a floppy drive like drive A:.)

File Scan. This right allows you to search directories for filenames as well as see the filenames in a given directory. If you don't have this right in a directory or at the file level, you will see the "File not found" message when you type DIR. You also need this right when you copy files to and from a directory.

Create. The Create right allows you to create and write to new files. You also need this right to copy files to a directory, to write to a closed file, and to recover deleted files. The Create right allows you to make new subdirectories as well.

Erase. The Erase right allows you to delete existing files; you also need this right to add information to an existing closed file. You can also delete subdirectories with the Erase right.

12

Modify. The Modify right allows you to change the attributes of a directory and a file. (Setting these attributes is known as *flagging files*). You can read about file flags under the heading "Directory and File Flagging Utilities" in Chapter 3. You also need the Modify right when you want to rename a file or a directory.

Access Control. This right allows you to grant and revoke trustee rights to users and groups. For security purposes, you may have Access Control rights only to your own home directory. You also need this right to change the inherited rights mask.

These basic security rights apply to the directories themselves (where they are known as the *inherited rights mask*), to users and groups (where they are known as *trustee assignments*), and to files. Your supervisor assigns a combination of these rights to each directory, user or group, and file. These assignments can give you total access to the directory, or restrict you so that you can't even see which files are in a directory.

You don't have any trustee assignments in a directory until you are assigned those rights by your supervisor. However, individual trustee rights are not the only way you can receive trustee rights to a directory. A supervisor may place several users in a group and give the group trustee rights in a directory, or your supervisor may assign all of one person's or group's trustee rights to another person or group. Such assignments are called *security equivalences*. Whichever way you receive rights to a directory—as a trustee assignment, a group assignment, a security equivalence, or a combination of all three—the rights contained in these trustee assignments are compared to the inherited rights mask that directory has, giving you *effective rights*—the rights you can effectively use in a directory. The inherited rights mask settings block out any other rights at that directory or file level. NetWare 3.1x adds another set of security at the file level, allowing for a file's inherited rights mask. But since the file directory rights mask is often used in a limited manner, let's look at how trustee, group, and directory rights work first.

In order to put the trustee, group, and directory rights into perspective, imagine yourself in a directory created especially for you. As an example, say your name is Ted, you have a directory called TED (with all rights) under the directory USERS, and you're logged in to server ADMIN. Also imagine that when you type MAP F: <Enter> at the network prompt, you see a drive mapping with this structure: "Drive F: = ADMIN/ VOL1: USERS\TED." When you go into drive F (by typing F: <Enter>) and type RIGHTS <Enter>, you see what follows.

```
F:\USERS\TED> rights
ADMIN/VOL1:USERS/TED Your Effective Rights for this directory
are [RWCEMFA]:

*    May Read from File.                          (R)
```

```
    *    May Write to File.                       (W)
         May Create Subdirectories and Files.     (C)
         May Erase Subdirectories and Files.      (E)
         May Modify File Status Flags.            (M)
         May Scan for Files                       (F)
         May Change Access Control                (A)

    * Has no effect on directory

    Entries in Directory May Inherit [RWCEMFA] Rights.

    You have ALL RIGHTS to this directory area.
```

In this instance, you have all rights to the directory TED. In order to determine this, NetWare first looked at your trustee assignments in the USERS/TED directory, and then looked to see if you also have any trustee rights to that directory from other users or groups to which you are security equivalent. If you do have other security equivalences, NetWare first adds your user trustee rights to the rights of those groups or users. This gives you your potential rights, or the rights you can potentially have in that directory.

Then NetWare compares your combined group and user rights to the rights the directory itself contains (the *directory rights mask* or IRM). At this point, NetWare takes away from your user and group rights anything you haven't been granted on the directory level. These rights have been "masked out" of your potential rights in the directory. This masking gives you your effective rights, or the rights that you can effectively use in the directory.

To take this example a bit further, let's say you have all rights (RWCEMFA) through your trustee assignments to the directory TED/REPORTS, but the directory itself has only Read, Write, Create, and Erase (RWCE) rights available. Your effective rights in that directory are only RWCE.

The Final Permission—File's Inherited Rights Mask and File Attributes

After you have figured out your effective rights at the directory level, you still may find that certain files won't let you access or modify them. Your inability to access certain files in a directory may mean the file's inherited rights mask (IRM) is being used to modify how you access the files.

Supervisors normally invoke a file's IRM and file flags in directories where a lot of users have common access to the files. You may also use this extra security when sharing access to data in your own personal directories. The file's IRM is the same as a directory IRM, only it is invoked at the file level.

14

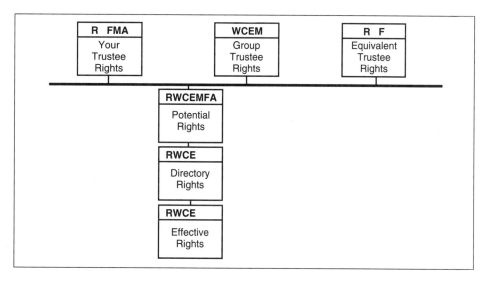

Figure I-5. Inherited Rights Mask gives you your effective rights in a directory.

File flags are also an effective means of preventing accidental changes to, or deletions from, a particular file. From the network prompt or from within the FILER utility, you can mark a file Shareable, Read/Write or Read/Only, Indexed, Transactional, Hidden or System, and Archived. You can also flag a file for a Read or Write Audit to prevent the file from being copied, deleted, or renamed. Files can also be flagged as purgeable, archivable, or executable only (Execute Only). For example, if you have modify rights, you can flag on-screen memos Shareable Read/Only, and coworkers can share the message without being able to modify the message itself.

When you want to access an application, NetWare looks at the files you wish to access and how those files are flagged. If those files are flagged Read/Only, you won't be able to write to them. File flags are not figured into your effective rights, but you can see how a particular file is flagged by going into the appropriate directory and typing FLAG with the desired filename and extension <Enter> at the network prompt. For example, if you have a file called ROGET.ART in your present directory, you can type FLAG ROGET.ART <Enter> at the network prompt. You can also see how files are flagged in the FILER utility in Chapter 2.

In NetWare 3.1x, directories can also have attributes, just as files do. However, they do not have as many. For example, in directories where you have Supervisory or Access Control Rights, you can set the directories with a Delete or Rename Inhibit attribute to prevent directories from accidently being deleted or renamed. You can also hide directories through the Hidden or System attributes, or continually purge deleted files within the directory through the Purge attribute. These are done through the FILER menu utility or through the ALLOW command-line utility.

Security That Supervisors Can Affect

In addition to the permissions for file access described previously, you may have other restrictions placed on you. Your supervisor is usually the one who sets up your initial trustee rights, your directory and file access, and your directory and file flags. But with NetWare 3.1x, system supervisors can also enforce restrictions on your account. To tell you how extensive these restrictions can be, here's a list of the things your supervisor can do to you in a single option found in the SYSCON utility:

➤ Disable your account entirely, which means that you simply can't log in, as if you'd never been created on the network;

➤ Set an expiration date, after which time you won't be able to log in;

➤ Limit the number of workstations that you can have logged in to the server;

➤ Set your system up so that only the supervisor can change your password or edit your login script (more on login scripts in Chapters 1 and 2);

➤ Establish a rule that your password must be a certain length (the default is five characters);

➤ Make you change your password every certain number of days;

➤ Limit the number of times you can try unsuccessfully to log in before NetWare disables your account;

➤ Require you to use a unique password;

➤ Limit your disk space (this restriction is set during the installation procedure);

➤ Limit not only the number of your connections, but also the procedure workstations you can log in from;

➤ Limit the times of day when you can be logged in to the server.

Security in a Nutshell

To get a feel for what all this means to you, type RIGHTS <Enter> at the network prompt to see your effective rights in a given directory, or go to your home directory (where you have at least RF effective rights) and type NDIR /SUB <Enter>. You will see all the files in your present directory as well as in the subdirectories beneath, like this:

```
NTS1/BYTE:USERS\TED
      Files:       Size       Last Updated      Flags         Owner
      ----------   -------    ---------------   ----------    -----
      EQUIP LOG    4,986      7/14/93 10:04a    [Rw-A——]      TED
      GIMIC ART    6,100      7/14/93 11:56a    [Rw-A——]      TED
      LASTCALL     49,456     7/14/93 7:13p     [Rw-A——]      TED
      RINDP TXT    9,345      7/14/93 9:07p     [Rw———]       TED

                   Inherited   Effective
      Directories  Rights      Rights       Owner    Created/Copied
      ----------   ---------   ---------    ------   ---------------
      386          [-RWCEMFA]  [——]         TED      3-20-93 2:06p
      REPORTS      [-RWCEMFA]  [——]         TED      3-18-93 8:06a
      REPORT90     [-RWCEMFA]  [——]         TED      5-05-93 1:38p
      ST           [-RWCEMFA]  [——]         SUPER    3-18-93 8:07a
      ARTICLES     [-RWCEMFA]  [——]         PAUL     3-21-93 7:42a
```

You can also type FLAG *filename.ext* <Enter> at the network prompt to see how individual files are flagged. For a running list of every directory on the server in which you have trustee rights, type WHOAMI/A <Enter> at the network prompt. You may even want to chart all your trustee assignments.

But the quick way to find out what your rights are is to type the filename of the program you want to open and see if it opens. If it does, you probably have enough rights to use the program; if it doesn't, you don't. If you're supposed to have enough rights but can't open the program, go to the directory, type RIGHTS at the network prompt, and see if one of the basic components to opening a program—Read and File Scan—has been taken away. If you don't have RF rights in the directory, ask your supervisor to give you the proper rights. You can also type FLAG *filename.ext* <Enter> to ensure no file attributes are preventing you from opening the file.

You can cause yourself much frustration if you don't pay enough attention to security. For example, you may be able to open a program, but find yourself unable to open any data files in that program in order to edit them. Or you might open a program and work on a file for hours, and then discover you can't save to that filename or to that directory. Those are the times you'll wish you'd checked your security.

You may also experience occasional problems because of the way different applications interpret NetWare security. When problems arise, applications that are not aware of NetWare's security features may send you inaccurate or misleading error messages. For example, an application may send you an error message saying the file cannot be found, when NetWare is really trying to let you know that you don't have rights in that directory or to that file.

Even DOS can create this kind of confusion. For example, if you try to rename a file in a directory where you don't have Create or Modify rights, DOS won't tell you that you don't have those rights; DOS doesn't even know about those rights. So you'll get the error message, "Duplicate filename or File not found." If you start getting these error messages when you know you have files out there, start checking your rights.

Security plays an important part in what you can do on a server. But even in the tightest security environment, you can still perform many functions and explore many menus and utilities while in NetWare. The rest of this book will help you understand what you can do on the network and how you can use NetWare's utilities to make your job run smoother and easier.

CHAPTER 1

Getting on the Network

Many system supervisors create a customized menu screen for their users to see as soon as they log in to the network. This menu screen gives the users an instant overview of what's available to them on the network. It also protects users from having to deal with the particulars of the command line. (For in-depth information on how to create your own menu through NetWare's MENU utility, see the "The MENU Utility" in Chapter 2, and NetWare 3.12's NMenu Utility in Appendix E.) But if you don't have a menu interface, this chapter covers some information on logging in and managing your directories. If you do go directly into a menu when you log in, ask your supervisor for permission to have a network prompt while you learn about NetWare.

This chapter assumes you have a working connection to the server. If this isn't the case, you may need to start in Chapter 5's troubleshooting section. Chapter 5 is written for the advanced user who may already be familiar with much of the material in this chapter. Chapter 5 also shows you how to make a new boot disk containing CONFIG.SYS, AUTOEXEC.BAT, and NET.CFG files, as well as the necessary NetWare files.

Getting on the Network: The Preliminaries

To access the applications and data on the network, your workstation needs certain software programs to enable your network interface board to communicate with the server. Your supervisor should have already placed those files on your boot disk or hard disk. These files include:

    CONFIG.SYS
    AUTOEXEC.BAT
    IPX.COM
    NETX.COM

Your workstation loads initial information about your workstation environment from two files: CONFIG.SYS and AUTOEXEC.BAT. The CONFIG.SYS file sets up configuration parameters for your workstation—for example, by loading drivers to better use high memory or by loading a mouse driver. The workstation then loads the

AUTOEXEC.BAT file. (The AUTOEXEC.BAT is a file that allows you to set up other environmental parameters; it does not contain data.)

The AUTOEXEC.BAT file can also load any number of programs or utilities for the DOS and network environments. In the DOS environment, the AUTOEXEC.BAT and CONFIG.SYS files let you customize your working environment and add the little touches that make working in the DOS environment more tolerable. For example, you can add memory managers in the CONFIG.SYS and temporary paths in the AUTOEXEC, allowing you to maintain a Windows environment. AUTOEXEC.BAT lets you keep your customized features in the network environment as well.

The IPX.COM and the NETX.COM files are NetWare programs. IPX establishes communication between your network interface board, the LAN cable, and the network. NETX.COM is the NetWare shell and serves as a coordinator between your workstation and the server you wish to access. The NetWare shell sends to DOS information meant to execute locally and to the network information meant for the network. NETX.COM works for all versions of DOS.

Because of the size of IPX and the NetWare shell, workstations stand to lose 64KB or more of valuable memory needed to run DOS applications. (Most DOS versions still works from 640KB of conventional memory.) With NetWare 3.1x and 80386- or 80486- type workstations, you have two other NetWare shells that can be loaded into extended or expanded memory. You can use the EMSNETX.COM NetWare shell for placing approximately 32KB of the NetWare shell into expanded memory, leaving approximately 8KB of shell in conventional memory. If you're using extended memory, you can use the XMSNETX.COM file for additional conventional memory gains. Each method gives you back approximately 32KB of conventional memory for running applications. Also, MS DOS 5.0 or 6.0 and DR-DOS 6.0 come with memory managers that allow you to load IPX and NETX into upper memory. We'll tell you more about using memory managers and memory extenders with NetWare shells in Chapter 5.

With more recent versions of NetWare 3.11 and 3.12, you may see different NetWare communications files instead of IPX and NETX. These include the ODI communications drivers and the DOS Requester. An example of an AUTOEXEC.BAT file containing these files would be the following:

```
LSL.COM
NE2000.COM
IPXODI.COM
VLM.EXE
```

ODI stands for Open Data-link Interface and includes the LSL.COM, NE2000.COM, and IPXODI.COM files. ODI allows you to have more than one communications protocols running, such as IPX and TCP/IP. The NE2000.COM file is the network interface board driver, and is specific to the network board your workstation has installed. (You set the board driver through the NET.CFG file—more on this in Chapter 5.)

The VLM.EXE file is the NetWare DOS Requester, which comes with NetWare 3.12; however, it also works with NetWare 3.11 and replaces the NetWare shell—NETX.COM. VLM stands for Virtual Loadable Modules, and the DOS Requester is a collection of individual modules that covers what NETX.COM does, and adds other capabilities as well. The DOS Requester works with DOS version 3.1 or later.

Briefly, here's a list of the loadable modules that come with the DOS Requester and what the modules do.

VLM.EXE. This is the VLM manager for the DOS Requester. VLM.EXE directs incoming requests and outgoing replies through every stage of the DOS Requester. It oversees where the VLM modules are loaded into memory and the order in which they are initially loaded. Having loaded the VLM modules, VLM.EXE then directs each step of requests to their proper destination. Other application vendors may also write VLM modules that can plug into the VLM manager for use as extended resources to the client workstation.

CONN.VLM. The Connection Table Manager is a critical piece of the DOS Requester that spans all the layers of the DOS Requester. CONN.VLM keeps track of and allocates the number of connections the DOS Requester can have (defaults to 8), and presents connection table information to other module tasks.

REDIR.VLM. This is the DOS Redirector portion of the VLM architecture. The DOS Requester now takes advantage of DOS's Int 2Fh redirection capabilities and DOS internal tables. This allows NetWare to handle requests for DOS that DOS can't perform locally. This capability became available in MS DOS and PC-DOS version 3.1. Incorporating this feature in the DOS Requester reduces a lot of redundancy between NetWare and DOS.

GENERAL.VLM. This module contains a number of functions used for other modules, such as creating and deleting search drive mappings, getting connection information, last print queue and server information, search modes, and long and short machine names.

NETX.VLM. This module is used in conjunction with Bindery Services to ensure compatibility with the utilities that come with NetWare 3.x and below. You'll also need to load NETX.VLM if you are running applications that are written to take advantage of the NetWare shell's specific API functionality. Otherwise, you won't need this loaded.

TRAN.VLM. This is the transport protocol multiplexor, as explained earlier. The NetWare DOS Requester initially comes with the IPXNCP module for using IPX. Other protocols are planned for future releases.

IPXNCP.VLM. The IPXNCP transport module is a child process module of TRAN.VLM. It is not a replacement for the IPX communications drivers (IPXODI.COM or IPX.COM). The IPXNCP module takes care of building packets with a proper NCP header and so forth, and hands the packets to the IPX protocol for transmission over the cable.

NWP.VLM. This NetWare protocol multiplexor module coordinates requests to the right network module. The NWP module will connect to the available services, perform logins and logouts, and handle broadcasts through its child modules.

NDS.VLM and **BIND.VLM.** The NetWare DOS Requester comes with two network service modules: the NDS.VLM module for NetWare 4.0 Directory Services, and the BIND.VLM module for Bindery services found in NetWare 3.x and earlier. The DOS Requester works with all versions of NetWare and by running the BIND.VLM, takes the place of the NetWare shell.

FIO.VLM. This is the DOS Requester's File Input/Output module, which is used when accessing files on the network. This module incorporates the File Cache, Packet Burst, and Large Internet Packets capabilities.

PRINT.VLM. This module takes care of printer redirection capabilities for both Directory Services and Bindery Services. The print module also uses FIO.VLM to speed up printing services.

NMR.VLM. This is the NetWare Management Responder module. It is designed to load at the same time as the DOS Requester modules, but it isn't really a part of the DOS Requester. When loaded, the NMR.VLM module acts as a workstation agent compatible with Novell's Windows and OS/2 Network Management Responder. The module gathers and communicates workstation configuration information and statistics, as well as ODI information and statistics.

SECURITY.VLM. This module is used for NetWare's enhanced security feature and provides additional security as needed. The SECURITY.VLM module resides at the transport layer of the DOS Requester, and offers additional NCP session protection through a message digest algorithm. The first several bytes in a request packet are preceded by this digest algorithm. If you use this for security reasons, you may see performance degradation.

AUTO.VLM. The Auto-reconnect module reestablishes its connection with the server after it detects the loss of the NCP connection. As downed servers become available again, the AUTO.VLM module reconnects to the server and then rebuilds your environment, including connection status, drive mappings, and printer connections. Open files are restored, which means your recovery from the connection loss depends on how the application you were running recovers from a connection loss and reestablishment.

To load the module, you must specify VLM = AUTO.VLM in the NET.CFG file and load NDS.VLM or BIND.VLM. If you are using VLM.EXE's default module loading list, you only need to place VLM =AUTO.VLM somewhere under the "NetWare DOS Requester" heading in NET.CFG. See the heading "NET.CFG Parameters for the Dos Requester" in Chapter 5.

Some programs have been written to use other communications languages, such as TCP/IP and NETBIOS. When this happens, you may see additional communications files loaded as well as NetWare's communications files in your AUTOEXEC.BAT file. If you are using the TCP/IP communications protocol, you will load TCP/IP and TELAPI files along with IPXODI. If you are loading NetBIOS, you will load the NETBIOS.COM and INT2F.COM files.

You can use the AUTOEXEC.BAT file to load the programs that are necessary for your computer to talk to the network. Otherwise, you'll have to load each program by hand—a tedious procedure. If your name is defined as Ted on server ADMIN, your typical AUTOEXEC.BAT file for establishing a NetWare connection will include at least the following statements and in the following order (the PROMPT command—PROMPT PG, which causes your current directory path to display at the network prompt—is optional but useful):

```
PROMPT $P$G
IPX
NETX
F: LOGIN ADMIN/TED
```

If you're already on the network and curious as to what you have in your AUTOEXEC.BAT file, and if you boot from a boot disk, type TYPE A:AUTOEXEC.BAT <Enter> at the network prompt line. If you boot from a hard disk, type TYPE C:AUTOEXEC.BAT <Enter>. To learn how to make your own AUTOEXEC.BAT file, or edit the one you use, go to the "Setting Up Your AUTOEXEC.BAT file" heading in Chapter 5.

What You See When You Log In

When you turn on your workstation, it first performs a self-check to make sure all the hardware it thinks it has is in place. Next, it loads the CONFIG.SYS file and then your AUTOEXEC.BAT file. Since what you see on your screen depends on the commands in your AUTOEXEC.BAT file, this book can't pinpoint exactly what you will see. But, for example, if you're booting from a disk containing the AUTOEXEC.BAT, IPX.COM, and NETX.COM files, and if you're using the AUTOEXEC.BAT file shown above, you'll see the following boot process fill your screen:

```
A:PROMPT $P$G
A:>
A:>IPX
Novell IPX/SPX V3.26 rev A
(C) Copyright 1985, 1992 Novell Inc. All Rights Reserved.
LAN Option: NetWare NE-1000 V3.02 EC (900831)
Hardware Configuration: IRQ=3, I/O Base=300h, No DMA or ROM
A:>NETX
NetWare V3.26 rev. A-Workstation Shell for PC DOS V3.x
(C) Copyright 1992 Novell Inc. All Rights Reserved.
Attached to server NTS3
Tuesday, June 22, 1993 11:55:21 am
A:> F:
F:\LOGIN>LOGIN ADMIN/TED
Enter your password:
```

The first line on this list gives the PROMPT command, which tells DOS to display the directory path, including the directory you're currently in at the DOS prompt. On a stand-alone computer, you normally get a bare A:> or C:> for a prompt. That wouldn't be informative in a network environment where you can have twenty-six drive letters to choose from, each of which might contain several directories and subdirectories in the directory path. The PROMPT command isn't mandatory, but it's helpful because it lets you know at all times where you are in the directories.

After telling DOS to give you your directory path at the prompt, the AUTOEXEC loads IPX. IPX or IPXODI establishes your communications with the network and displays the LAN driver information, telling you what type of network interface board is installed in your workstation as well as telling you about the board's interrupt settings.

With connections established, the example AUTOEXEC next executes the NETX (or VLM.EXE) file. NETX or VLM.EXE attaches you to the first server that answers the "Is there anyone out there I can talk to?" broadcast. (You can also specify a "preferred" server, which then becomes the server you automatically log in to first—see the heading "Parameters That Affect the NetWare Environment" in Chapter 5.) In this example, Ted's workstation is initially attaching to Server NTS3, followed by NTS3's network date and time.

The next series of items shows the AUTOEXEC changing the A: prompt to the first network prompt, which is defaulted to C: (for a DOS version 2.x with no internal hard disk) or F: (for DOS version 3.x and above). The F: default drive takes into account that your workstation may have two floppy disk drives, two hard disk drives, and a virtual disk drive, which covers the drive letters A: to E:. Of course, some of you won't need that many local drives, and others may need more to accommodate local drive mappings. (You can also specify a first network drive in the NET.CFG file—see the heading "Parameters That Affect the NetWare Environment" in Chapter 5.)

Next, you see the login command, followed by the name of the server and the name of the person logging in. In this example, you are logging in to server ADMIN. If the login procedure is successful, you will receive an "Enter your password:" command if your supervisor has set up your system so you need one.

At this point, if you type in your password correctly and press <Enter>, you're on the network. Once you're logged in, NetWare will run a login script. The login script sets up your network environment: for example, it creates drive mappings to the data directories of your most-used applications. Once the login script runs, and providing you don't go directly into a menuing system or application, you will be left at a network prompt (a fancy term for the DOS prompt once you are logged in to the network and are at a network drive letter).

If your supervisor has set up a NET.CFG file, the list of items in the initial display will also include a number of network parameters that your supervisor has designated for you. These parameters include such items as IPX sockets, cache buffers, file handles, and local printers, as the following example illustrates.

```
Novell IPX/SPX V3.22
(C) Copyright 1985, 1990 Novell Inc. All Rights Reserved.
LAN Option: NetWare Ethernet NE-2000 V1.05 EC
Hardware Configuration:IRQ=3, I/O Base=300h, No DMA or ROM

NetWare V3.26 rev. A—Workstation Shell for PC DOS V5.0
(C) Copyright 1983, 1992 Novell Inc. All Rights Reserved.
    Attached to server NTS3
    Friday, November 15, 1992 11:55:21 am
    A:> F:
```

```
F:\LOGIN> LOGIN ADMIN/TED
Enter your password:
```

To see the DOS Requester running, the next example uses the following commands in the AUTOEXEC.BAT:

```
CD\NWCLIENT
LOADHIGH LSL
LOADHIGH NE1000
LOADHIGH IPXODI
VLM
CD\
F:
LOGIN UP/TED
```

This AUTOEXEC.BAT file first changes to the NWCLIENT directory, then it loads the ODI communications drivers—LSL, NE1000, and IPXODI. In this example, the communications drivers are being loaded into the Upper Memory Block (UMB) area using the LOADHIGH command, thereby giving the workstation more conventional memory to work with. The AUTOEXEC.BAT next loads the DOS Requester (VLM), then goes to drive F: and logs in to Server UP. Listing 1-1 is an example of what you can see on the screen by using such commands:

Listing 1-1. This example uses the ODI communications drivers as well as the DOS Requester.

```
NetWare Link Support Layer v2.01 (921105)
(C) Copyright 1990, 1992 Novell, Inc. All Rights Reserved.

Novell NE1000 Ethernet MLID v1.27 (930114)
(C) Copyright 1991 - 1993 Novell, Inc. All Rights Reserved.

Int 5, Port 300, Node Address 1B096A61 L
Max Frame 1514 bytes, Line Speed 10 Mbps
Board 1, Frame ETHERNET_802.3, LSB Mode

NetWare IPX/SPX Protocol v2.10 (930122)
(C) Copyright 1990-1993 Novell, Inc. All Rights Reserved.
```

```
VLM.EXE        - NetWare virtual loadable module manager v1.0
                 (930210)
(C) Copyright 1993 Novell, Inc. All Rights Reserved.

The VLM.EXE file is pre-initializing the VLMs...........
The VLM.EXE file is using extended memory (XMS).
CONN.VLM       - NetWare connection table manager v1.0 (930210)
IPXNCP.VLM     - NetWare IPX transport module v1.0 (930210)
TRAN.VLM       - NetWare transport multiplexor module v1.0
                 (930210)
BIND.VLM       - NetWare bindery protocol module v1.0 (930210)
NWP.VLM        - NetWare protocol multiplexor module v1.0
                 (930210)
FIO.VLM        - NetWare file input-output module v1.0 (930210)
GENERAL.VLM    - NetWare general purpose function module v1.0
                 (930210)
REDIR.VLM      - NetWare DOS redirector module v1.0 (930210)
PRINT.VLM      - NetWare printer redirection module v1.0
                 (930210)
NETX.VLM       - NetWare workstation shell module v4.0 (930210)
You are attached to server UP
Enter your password:
```

What you see on your screen depends on how verbose you allow the message screens to be and what parameters you load through the NET.CFG file. You may see something similar to Listing 1-1, or you may see much more or less information.

The first three segments are what you can see when LSL, the network board driver, and IPXODI load into memory. The rest of the listing shows the many modules that the DOS Requester loads into memory. This is followed by the DOS Requester attaching to a file server, and then asking the user for a password.

Again, what you see on the screen depends upon what you have in your AUTOEXEC.BAT and the other configuration files you may access. The above example only shows the essentials the AUTOEXEC uses for establishing a connection with a server, and these are the files your supervisor will normally set up. You can also add your Terminate-and-Stay-Resident (TSR) programs and other DOS utilities, which enhance working in the DOS environment. (For a more detailed discussion of using your AUTOEXEC.BAT and CONFIG.SYS to help set up your workstation environment, see Chapter 5.)

Logging In and Attaching to Servers

You can access NetWare servers on the network in two ways: You can log in to a server, or you can attach to a server. Each method offers a different degree of accessibility. You can have no more than eight server connections at any time, and you can only log in to one server at a time. However, once you're logged in, you can then attach to as many as seven other servers. The eight server connections limit also applies with 3.12's DOS Requester. While the DOS Requester can have more connections, NetWare 3.1x utilities do not support more than eight server attachments.

As you type LOGIN *servername/username* <Enter> to get into a server and then enter the correct password, NetWare looks in a small database called the bindery to get information about you. But to log in to a server, you must either be established as a user on the server or log in as someone who is. Many servers have a GUEST account with no password for people who need to access certain limited utilities, data, or other services, such as printers and modems.

When you log in to a server as an established user, NetWare reads your bindery information and executes the system login script, then your personal login script before leaving you at the network prompt. When you attach to a server, NetWare establishes a connection with that server and reads your bindery information, but does not execute the network or personal login scripts. You can try out the ATTACH command by typing ATTACH *servername/username* <Enter> at the network prompt. For example, if your name is Ted and you're set up as a user on server NTS3, type ATTACH NTS3/TED <Enter>.

When you just want to see if you can attach to another server, type SLIST <Enter> at the network prompt to see what servers are available, choose an interesting server name, and then type ATTACH *servername/*GUEST <Enter>. Some servers have passwords for their guest accounts, so you'll need to know the password before you can log in or attach to those servers. Servers with a guest account that has no password allow you to attach to them; however, getting around on strange servers can be quite difficult if you don't know that server's directory structure. But for the sake of exploring new frontiers, go ahead. Later on, log in to those servers as user GUEST and see what directories and utilities are available to the guest account.

Successful attachment to a server will cause your screen to display a "Your station is attached to server *servername*" message. Then, if you want to know which servers you're connected to, type WHOAMI <Enter> at the network prompt. Among other things, WHOAMI will show you the name of the server you're logged in to and the names of all the servers you're attached to. If you want to see what directories you have available to you, type WHOAMI /A <Enter>. (For a full explanation of WHOAMI, turn to the "User Identification Utilities" heading in Chapter 3.)

As mentioned before, you can have no more than eight server connections at any time. If you try to attach to more servers than the connection limit and you are using the NetWare shell, you'll see the message, "The limit of 8 server connections has been reached," and you won't be allowed to attach. To attach to another server, you'll have to log out of one of your connections by typing LOGOUT *servername* <Enter> for the server you need to detach from, and then typing ATTACH *servername/username* <Enter> for the server you want to add.

With the DOS Requester you won't see the preceding message if you have changed the Connections=8 parameter in the NET.CFG file. While you can have more than eight connections active in NetWare 3.11 or 3.12, you will only see eight connections when you use the NetWare utilities. In the end, you will find the confusion with utilities isn't worth the problems you face, so use the default setting of eight.

Note that nice but unnecessary server attachments can affect performance. So, if your performance becomes sluggish when you're attached to several servers, drop the servers you need the least. Then set up a batch file to attach to and log out of those least-used servers when you need to. You can also set up a way to attach to these seldom-used servers through the login script. (See "Login Script Functions and Their Examples" in "The SYSCON Utility" section found in Chapter 2.)

What You See When You Are There—The System Login Script and Your Personal Login Script

Now that you've successfully logged in to a server (and attached to some others as well), let's look at the login script. The login script is a tool that primarily sets up network drive mappings to the directories you need to access when you first log in. The login script does this by assigning a letter to the designated directory path.

If you've played around in DOS at all, you may have used the SUBSTITUTE command to give a particularly long directory path a single-letter name. For example, suppose you often use a subdirectory called ACCOUNTS that resides at the end of the SPREAD\COAST\WEST directory path. You don't want to change directories (CD) down to the ACCOUNTS subdirectory every time; so instead you can put the SUBSTITUTE command in your AUTOEXEC.BAT file: SUBST E:=SPREAD\COAST\WEST\ACCOUNTS. Then, to get to the ACCOUNTS subdirectory, you simply type E: at the DOS prompt and press <Enter>.

When NetWare was new, DOS didn't have the capability of substituting letters for network drives. So NetWare engineers created the MAP utility. The MAP utility is a network version of DOS's SUBSTITUTE command; it allows network users to map up to twenty-six different directory and subdirectory extensions for use. (For a full explanation of MAP, turn to the "MAP" heading in Chapter 3.) But the MAP command only lasts as long as you're logged in. As soon as you log out, all of your mapped drives go away. Then the next time you log in, you have to type them in again.

Since typing in directory mappings can be rather tedious, NetWare engineers created a login script where you can store network and DOS commands, load menuing programs, and set up your network environment. This login script, stored in your personal mail directory, is where you also keep your most commonly accessed directory mappings, as well as other DOS and NetWare commands that you want invoked each time you log in. In this way, the login script is very similar to DOS's AUTOEXEC.BAT file.

There are three kinds of NetWare login scripts: the default login script, the *system* login script, and the *personal* login script. Each of these login scripts assists your system supervisor in setting up users and directories in NetWare. (The personal login script sets up your personal touches to the NetWare environment once the other login scripts run.)

When the server is first installed and the supervisor logs in, NetWare executes a default login script so that the supervisor can access the NetWare utilities. The supervisor's default login script mappings look similar to the following (the user's default login script will not have drive G: mapped to the SYS:SYSTEM directory):

```
Drive A maps to a local disk.
Drive B maps to a local disk.
Drive C maps to a local disk.
Drive D maps to a local disk.
Drive E maps to a local disk.
Drive F:= ADMIN/SYS:LOGIN
Drive G:= ADMIN/SYS:SYSTEM
-------
SEARCH1 :=Z:. [ADMIN/SYS:PUBLIC]
```

Drives A: through E: are all mapped to local drives. Drive F: is mapped to the LOGIN directory of volume SYS on server ADMIN. Drive Z: is a search drive, mapped to the PUBLIC directory on volume SYS:. (More on search drives later.)

From the default login script, the supervisor can go into the SYSCON utility and add users, groups, applications, databases, or anything else the system needs, as well as define directories and security for those users, groups, and directories. Supervisors also have access to the SYS:SYSTEM directory, where NetWare stores the supervisor utilities necessary for maintaining and troubleshooting the server.

While adding applications and utilities to NetWare, the system supervisor can make those tools available to all users through a search path. If you're familiar with DOS's PATH command, you know how handy this command can be. On a stand-alone computer running DOS, you don't have to go into each directory in order to use an application or a utility. For instance, suppose you often use your word processor, spreadsheet, games, and utility directories. Instead of going into each directory to access the program, you can use the PATH command in your AUTOEXEC.BAT file and link those directories into a searching pattern, such as:

```
PATH=C:\UTIL;C:\SPREAD;C:\WP;C:\GAMES <Enter>.
```

Then you can access your programs from whatever directory you're presently in.

NetWare's search drives work much like the PATH command, except that you don't need to link the directory names together in a single line. In the default login script example, you'll see the SEARCH1 :=Z:. [ADMIN/SYS:PUBLIC] drive mapping. Login scripts can contain up to twenty-six drive mappings, one for each letter in the alphabet. You can also define up to sixteen of those drive mappings as search drives. Once your application directory is marked as a search drive and you have the proper rights to use that application (at least Read and File Scan rights—see the Introduction on security), you can access the search drive from any directory by typing the name of the application at the network prompt. Here is a small example of a typical system login script:

```
MAP S1:=SYS:PUBLIC
MAP S2:=SYS:PUBLIC/MSDOS/V5.00
IF MEMBER OF GROUP "WP51" THEN BEGIN
    MAP S3:=SYS:PUBLIC/WP51
END
IF MEMBER OF GROUP "WS" THEN BEGIN
    MAP S3:=SYS:PUBLIC/WS
END
MAP S4:=SYS:PUBLIC/UTIL
```

Briefly, this system login script says that search drive 1 is the SYS:PUBLIC drive (the "S" stands for search drives). For its search drives, NetWare counts backwards from the letter Z, so the SYS:PUBLIC drive (S1) appears as the Z drive. Your system supervisor will make sure you have a SYS:PUBLIC drive as one of your search drives; since the PUBLIC directory contains all the NetWare menus and utilities, you need access to SYS:PUBLIC to get around on NetWare.

The next search drive is a DOS directory that allows users to format disks and perform other DOS functions from the network.

The next two statements are a little different. The IF MEMBER command means that users who belong to a particular group will get to use the application they like best. So if you belong to the WP51 group, you will have access to the WP51 directory and applications. END means this is the end of the command statement. Search drive 4 is mapped to a subdirectory called UTIL, which can contain small applications, batch files, and utilities for everyone or for designated groups to use.

As a point of reference, let's look at the first two login scripts in perspective. Suppose your server is named ADMIN. Your supervisor has set up a system login script like the one just described, but hasn't set up personal login scripts for any users. If you're a newly defined user who has just logged in to server ADMIN, and you type MAP <Enter> at the network prompt, you'll see that NetWare has added the search drives to the default user login script:

```
Drive A maps to a local disk.
Drive B maps to a local disk.
Drive C maps to a local disk.
Drive D maps to a local disk.
Drive E maps to a local disk.
Drive F:= ADMIN/SYS:LOGIN
  ――

SEARCH1: = Z:. [ADMIN/SYS:PUBLIC]
SEARCH2: = Y:. [ADMIN/SYS:PUBLIC/IBM_PC/MSDOS/V5.00]
SEARCH3: = X:. [ADMIN/SYS:PUBLIC/WP51]
SEARCH4: = W:. [ADMIN/SYS:PUBLIC/UTIL]
```

Now that you've been defined as a user on the network and if given the ability, you can set up the third type of network login script—your own personal login script. The personal login script is exactly that: a personalized script containing the drive mappings to the directories and applications you use most often. Here's an example of a personalized login script user Ted might see upon typing MAP:

```
Drive    A: maps to a local disk.
Drive    B: maps to a local disk.
Drive    F: = ADMIN/VOL1:USERS/TED
Drive    G: = ADMIN/VOL1:USERS/TED/SPSHEET
Drive    H: = ADMIN/SYS: REPORTS/AUG
         - - - - - - - - -
SEARCH1: =  Z:. [ADMIN/SYS:PUBLIC]
SEARCH2: =  Y:. [ADMIN/SYS:PUBLIC/IBM_PC/MSDOS/V5.00]
SEARCH3: =  X:. [ADMIN/SYS:PUBLIC/WP]
SEARCH4: =  W:. [ADMIN/SYS:PUBLIC/UTIL]
SEARCH5: =  V:. [ADMIN/VOL1:USERS/TED/ST]
```

Drives F: and G: contain the same server name (ADMIN), volume name (VOL1), user directory (USERS), and Ted's subdirectory (TED); drive G:, however, goes one subdirectory level deeper than drive F:. Drive H:, mapped to volume SYS:, is a group directory where Ted and his cohorts share files. The search drives are mainly what Ted sees from the system login script. However, drive V: is Ted's personal search drive, one he mapped himself; this is where Ted can place his own favorite utilities and batch files.

The Three Faces of the Login Script

Once you've set up your own personal login script, what you normally see when you log in is a conglomeration of your personal login script and the system login script. If as a new user you don't yet have a personal login script, NetWare will supply you with a default script. If your supervisor has created a system login script but not your personalized login script, you'll see a mixture of the default login script and the system login script.

Clear as mud? Wait, it gets better. If you put in a drive mapping at the same drive letter where your supervisor put a system drive mapping, your personalized script will overwrite the system drive mapping.

Now that the mud is sufficiently stirred, let's look at the place where you create a personal login script.

Getting to Your Login Script

To change your personal login script so the same directories display every time you log in, you need to go into the SYSCON utility. To do this, type SYSCON at the network prompt and press <Enter>. You'll see a screen similar to the one shown in Figure 1-1:

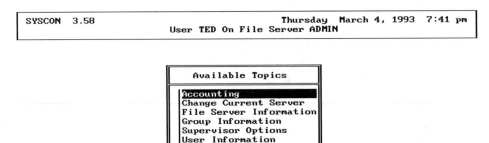

Figure 1-1. The initial SYSCON screen

Getting around in the menus is simple. Pressing <Enter> on a highlighted option brings you to the next screen available under that option, and pressing <Esc> brings you to the previous screen. For example, from the "Available Topics" window, select the "User Information" option by pressing the <PgDn> (3) key on the numeric keypad. (Be sure the NumLock key is off or nothing will happen and you will hear a beep.) Once that option is highlighted, press <Enter>. The <PgDn> key brings you to the bottom of the list of selections, and the <PgUp> (9) key brings you to the top of the list. You can also use the Up (8) and Down (2) arrow keys to highlight and select an option, or you can type the first letters of the option you wish to select and the selector bar will move to that option.

The "User Information" option will present the "User Names" window. Highlight your login name and press <Enter>. You will see a "User Information" window with all kinds of options, one of which is the "Login Script" option.

Highlight the "Login Script" option by typing the letter L or by moving the selector bar to the "Login Script" option with the Down arrow key. Press <Enter>. This will bring up the "Login Script" window, shown in Figure 1-2.

You've arrived at your personal login script. If you plan to modify your script, turn to the "Setting Up Your Login Script" heading under the SYSCON Utility discussion in Chapter 2. If you aren't going to modify your script, take a look at what's there, then press the <Alt-F10> keys simultaneously. You will see the "Exit SYSCON Yes/No" window with the "Yes" option highlighted. Press <Enter> and you'll return to the network prompt.

```
 SYSCON   3.58                            Thursday  March 4, 1993  7:44 pm
                          User TED On File Server ADMIN

┌──────────────────────────────────────────────────────────────────────────┐
│                       Login Script For User TED                            │
├──────────────────────────────────────────────────────────────────────────┤
│map *1:=admin/vol1:users\ted                                                │
│map h:admin/vol1:users\ted\articles\july                                    │
│map i:=vol1:users\ted\reports\jan                                           │
│map j:=admin/vol1:users\ted\tech                                            │
│map k:=admin/vol1:users\ted\reports                                         │
│                                                                            │
│attach up/ted                                                               │
│map o:=up\sys:reports                                                        │
│map s16:=admin\vol1:users\ted\st                                            │
│                                                                            │
│map                                                                         │
│drive j:                                                                    │
│                                                                            │
│                                                                            │
└──────────────────────────────────────────────────────────────────────────┘
```

Figure 1-2. Example login script

How to Use DOS Commands at the Network Prompt

Since NetWare allows a workstation to use DOS (as well as OS/2 and Macintosh System/ Finder) for its workstation operating system, on the network, most DOS commands function just as they do at a stand-alone workstation. When you turn on your machine, it loads CONFIG.SYS, then the COMMAND.COM file into the workstation's memory and initiates the AUTOEXEC.BAT file.

However, a number of DOS commands don't behave the same way on the network as they do locally. There's a trick to using COMP (DOS's file-compare utility), COPY and XCOPY, DIR, ERASE or DEL(ete), and MKDIR and RMDIR commands across different volumes. DOS commands don't know anything about NetWare servers or volumes, so you will have to use NetWare's MAP command to designate a drive letter in order for certain DOS commands to work.

Let's say you're logged into server ADMIN and you want to copy the REGAL.RPT file from server ADMIN's SYS:REPORTS/JUNE directory to your ADMIN/ VOL1:USERS/TED/SPSHEET directory. Let's further suppose you have sufficient rights in both directories to copy the file. Since DOS can't make sense out of NetWare volumes, you can help the procedure by typing MAP H:=SYS:REPORTS/JUN <Enter>, then by typing MAP I:=VOL1:USERS/TED/SPSHEET <Enter>. Since DOS understands drive letters being substituted for long directory paths, it thinks this is just another instance of the SUBSTITUTE command. With the drive mappings in place, type COPY H:REGAL.RPT I: <Enter>, and DOS will copy the file into your SPSHEET directory.

Other DOS commands also work differently in a NetWare environment than they do in a stand-alone environment. These commands include ASSIGN (you must use NetWare's MAP command to assign drive equivalences) and BACKUP and RE-COVER (which won't pick up OS/2 or Macintosh extended filenames or resource forks), as well as DISKCOMP, FORMAT, and DISKCOPY (NetWare uses a bigger block structure, so these won't work on network drives or directories).

Don't use the LABEL command on the network; it can erase the files in the directory root on a volume (if you have sufficient rights). The SUBST command works only for local drives; use MAP for mapping network drives. And while the PATH command will work on the network (the PATH directory designations become search drive mappings), it works best locally. PATH designations are searched last in NetWare's search drive hierarchy, even if you see them scattered through your drive mappings when you type MAP <Enter> at the network prompt, and are only searched for executable files (such as *.COM, *.EXE, or *.BAT files).

You will also find that the PRINT command with some versions of DOS won't work unless you type in ENDCAP before PRINT (this ends any CAPTURE statements to network printers—see the "Using the CAPTURE Command" heading in Chapter 4) and have a local printer attached. MS DOS 6.0 and DR-DOS 6.0 with the DOS Requester will allow you to designate a printer port, which can tie into the CAPTURE command you have running. Since DOS knows little of the NetWare server, and depending on your DOS version, you may need to use NetWare's NPRINT to print out text files on a network printer (see "Using the NPRINT Command" heading in Chapter 4). See Appendix A for more details on NetWare and DOS differences.

And as one last note on DOS commands, if you're using the COMSPEC command locally, (COMSPEC=C:COMMAND.COM or A:COMMAND.COM), and the system supervisor has set up a COMSPEC command in the system login script, you may find that your workstation hangs when you leave certain applications. A simple way to see if the supervisor has set up a COMSPEC command is to place an REM statement on the same line and in front of COMSPEC, log in to the network, and type SET <Enter> at the network prompt. If you see that you have a COMSPEC set to a network drive, leave REM before your COMSPEC statement and use the network's COMSPEC.

For the most part, however, NetWare works well with workstation operating systems, and the NetWare shell or DOS Requester does a good job of sorting through local and network requests. When you work from the network prompt and update a data file to disk, the NetWare shell looks at the requests to determine if you're saving the file to a local destination or to a network destination. For example, when you press F10 (Save) while you're in WordPerfect and the data file is on your hard disk, the shell determines that you're requesting to update a file to a local destination and sends the update there. However, if the update is to a file in a network directory, the shell sends the update in the form of a write request to the server.

Setting Up Directories and Copying Files

Some of the most basic tasks you perform on the network are driven by DOS commands. These commands include those for manipulating directories—MD (make a directory), RD (remove a directory), and CD (change directory), as well as those for copying (COPY) and deleting (DEL) files. As mentioned earlier, some of these elements can have a network twist, such as using the NetWare MAP utility to help in copying files. You can also use NetWare's SALVAGE utility to retrieve newly deleted files—with some stipulations—see "The SALVAGE Utility" heading in Chapter 2 when you need to.

(For those of you unfamiliar with the DOS directory-manipulation commands mentioned above, here's a brief explanation of CD; later paragraphs in this chapter explain MD and RD. More detailed information on these and other DOS commands is available in the DOS manual.)

CD, for Change Directory, is one of the most frequently used DOS commands. CD allows you to move between all the directories and subdirectories on a volume. For example, to move from directory G:USERS to the TED subdirectory below G:USERS, type in CD TED <Enter>. To move to the REPORTS subdirectory of directory TED when you're in G:USERS, type CD TED\REPORTS <Enter>. To go back up the directory tree, say from G:USERS\TED\REPORTS to G:USERS\TED, type CD .. <Enter>. (When you're changing directories, it's very important to have a PROMPT command similar to PROMPT PG; otherwise, you won't be able to tell which directory you're actually in when you type CD at the network prompt.)

You must have the proper rights to be able to create and copy files as well as to create directories. For example, to copy files from a directory, you must have at least Read and

File Scan (RF) effective rights in the directory you're copying from. You must also have Write, Create, and sometimes Modify (WCM) effective rights in the directory you're copying to. With NetWare 3.1x, you need only Create and Erase effective rights in your current directory in order to create and delete a subdirectory. To see your effective rights in the current directory, type RIGHTS <Enter>.

From a user's perspective, NetWare uses DOS to create, delete, and change directories. For example, suppose your drive G: is mapped to VOL1:USERS/TED. Suppose also that directory TED is getting too cluttered and you want to create a REPORTS directory under TED. (There are different levels of directories, with subdirectories under directories, and subdirectories under those subdirectories. This can get confusing in a hurry; so for simplicity's sake, let's refer to all levels as directories.) You can type G: <Enter> at the network prompt to get to the TED directory, then you can type MD (Make Directory) REPORTS <Enter>, creating the directory REPORTS below directory TED.

A word of warning here. DOS doesn't tell you whether or not your directory creation is successful; all you see is that the network prompt returns to you. But if you try to create the directory again, you'll see a message like "Directory already exists." (The type of message you receive depends on the DOS version you're running.) This gets to be a bit confusing, so take your time and make a couple of extra directories until you get the hang of it.

Now that you've created the REPORTS directory, you can map a drive to that directory to copy files. For example, if drive I: is available, you can type MAP I:=VOL1:USERS/TED/REPORTS <Enter>. It's then a simple matter to copy files from G: to I:. (For a further explanation of the MAP command, see the "MAP" heading in Chapter 3.)

Let's suppose you're in drive G: and you want to copy several files with an .RPT extension, such as MAYTIME.RPT and JUNTIME.RPT. With an I: drive mapping to the REPORTS directory, you can use DOS's COPY command or NetWare's NCOPY command to copy files. To copy these files from drive G: to drive I:, type NCOPY G:*.RPT I: <Enter>. (The asterisk [*] is a global wild card; it tells the system to copy all files in that directory with the .RPT extension. A question mark [?] is a single-character wild card; for example, if you're in the G: directory and you type NCOPY ?FILE I: <Enter>, you're telling the system to copy AFILE, BFILE, CFILE, and all files with any letter in that position.) When using the NCOPY command, you'll see something like this:

```
From ADMIN/VOL1:USERS/TED
```

```
To ADMIN/VOL1:USERS/TED/REPORTS
    MAYTIME.RPT to  MAYTIME.RPT
    JUNTIME.RPT to  JUNTIME.RPT
    JULTIME.RPT  to  JULTIME.RPT
3 files copied.
```

You can then delete the files from the G: directory by typing DEL *.RPT <Enter> while in the G: directory. Or, if you're in a directory other than G:, you can type DEL G:*.RPT <Enter>.

But what if you decide you don't like the directory name REPORTS and you need something more specific, like REPORTS91? You can run the NetWare RENDIR (REName DIRectory) program and rename the directory. From the TED directory, type RENDIR REPORTS REPORT91 <Enter>. The name of the REPORTS directory will change to REPORT91. If you type MAP <Enter> at the network prompt, you'll see that the directory entry for drive I: has also changed to REPORT91. However, you'll have to change the drive mapping in the login script to reflect the name change if you want that directory to appear every time you log in. (For a further explanation of the RENDIR utility, see the "Directory and File Management Utilities" heading in Chapter 3.)

To use the RD command to delete or remove a directory, you must first delete the files from within that directory. Do this by typing DEL *.* <Enter> or simply DEL. <Enter>, depending on the DOS version you're using. You'll see a confirmation question like "Are you sure? N" at the prompt. Type "Y" and press <Enter> to delete all the files. You can also type ERASE *.* <Enter> instead of DEL to get the same effects.

With the directory now empty, you can proceed to delete the directory itself. But before you do, it's best to remove any drive mappings to the directory you wish to delete; otherwise, the drive mapping will become invalid when the directory is deleted. The simplest way to do this is to go to the directory above the directory you want to remove by typing CD .. <Enter>. Now that you're one directory above the one you wish to remove, you can delete the directory itself. For example, to delete a directory like TED\TIMES, type RD TIMES <Enter> from the TED directory, and directory TIMES is gone. (The FILER utility will let you delete both directories and files simultaneously—see "The FILER Utility" heading in Chapter 2.)

Let's suppose you don't need the REPORT91 directory after all. Since you've already deleted the *.RPT files from the G: directory (VOL1:USERS/TED), you can either recopy the files back from the REPORT91 directory on the I: directory path, or you can run the SALVAGE utility. If you haven't done any file copying, creating, or deleting since you deleted files from the G: directory, you can go to the G: directory and type SALVAGE <Enter>, and watch your files restore. The SALVAGE utility has had a menuing facelift, so all you need to do now to select the "Recover deleted files" option and press <Enter>. You will see a screen similar to this one:

```
Salvaging file on volume ADMIN/VOL1:
    MAYTIME.RPT recovered.
    JUNTIME.RPT recovered.
    JULTIME.RPT recovered.
3 file(s) recovered.
```

If you've modified, created, deleted, or copied files since you deleted those *.RPT files from drive G:, you can still restore them through SALVAGE. You can also copy the files from the I: directory. Do this by simply going to I: and typing COPY *.RPT G: <Enter>.

Now that you've either salvaged or recopied the *.RPT file back into the G: directory, go to the REPORT91 directory by typing I: <Enter> at the network prompt. Once at the REPORT91 directory, type DEL *.* <Enter> to delete the files. Then type CD .. <Enter> to move up to the TED directory. At the TED directory, type RD (Remove Directory) REPORT91 <Enter> and the REPORT91 directory will be erased. If you type MAP <Enter>, you'll see that the drive has been removed from your drive mappings.

The Backslash Symbol (\) and NetWare Shortcuts

When you use the MAP command, it doesn't matter whether you use a frontslash (/) or a backslash (\). NetWare will turn your backslashes into frontslashes for you. For example, if you type MAP I:=VOL1:USERS\TED\REPORTS at the network prompt, NetWare will display Drive I: = ADMIN/VOL1:USERS/TED/REPORTS. But when you work with DOS's CD, RD, MD, and other commands, use the backslash or you'll receive an invalid parameter error. In fact, it's just easier to get in the habit of always using the backslash key.

DOS uses the .. and \ parameters to change directories, and NetWare gives these parameters a distinct twist. For example, to move up a directory in DOS, you type CD .. <Enter> at the prompt. To move down a directory—for example, to directory REPORT—you type CD REPORTS <Enter>. If you want to move to the root of a DOS (or NetWare) directory, you can type CD\ <Enter>. In NetWare, this brings you to the volume root (for example, ADMIN/SYS:). In NetWare 3.11 and as part of the MAP ROOT command, you can now designate any directory to act as if it were the volume root.

40

In NetWare, you can be six or seven subdirectory levels deep in no time, and using the CD command to get around can become cumbersome. Where DOS only allows you to move up the directory path one directory at a time by using CD .. for one directory or CD ..\.. for two, NetWare allows you to add another dot for each directory you wish to move up, using two dots for the initial directory and one dot for each additional directory. For example, if drive I:'s directory path is VOL1:USERS/TED/REPORTS/MAY, and you want to move up to VOL1:USERS/TED, type CD ... <Enter> at the prompt. If you want to move up to the USERS directory, type CD .... <Enter>, or type CD \USERS <Enter>. Typing CD .... <Enter> on local drives won't work; you'll need to use the DOS equivalent command, which is CD ..\..\.. <Enter>. Or you can type CD \USERS <Enter> if you have a similar directory path on a local drive.

This capability allows for all sorts of interesting gyrations. As an example, if you're in I:'s VOL1:USERS/TED/REPORTS/MAY directory, and you want to change to the VOL1:USERS/TED/REPORT93 directory, you can type CD ...\REPORT93 <Enter>. If you're in VOL1:USERS/TED/REPORTS directory and you want to copy your *.RPT files to the TED directory, you can type NCOPY *.RPT .. <Enter> at the prompt. If you want to copy your *.RPT files from the REPORTS directory to the MAY subdirectory, you can type NCOPY *.RPT MAY <Enter>. (But make sure you type it in correctly; some unexpected things can happen if you don't.)

NCOPY looks first for a directory by the name you designate—in this case, directory MAY. If NCOPY can't find a directory by that name, it creates a file by that name and copies the source files into it. So be sure you have a directory by the name you designate in the command. Also, don't put a slash in the command, such as \MAY; NetWare or DOS will try to create a file at the designated root in the same fashion as described above.

Again, what you can copy depends on your rights in the directory you are copying from and in the directory you are copying to. If you're in the VOL1:USERS/TED/REPORTS/MAY directory, and you want to copy the *.RPT files to the REPORT93 directory that is on the same directory level as MAY (directly beneath REPORTS), you can type NCOPY *.RPT ..\REPORT92 <Enter>. If you're in the MAY directory and you want to create a JUNE directory beneath REPORTS, you can type MD ..\JUNE <Enter> at the prompt. Experiment—find out how to get around in NetWare's directories, and then settle on a method that best suits your way of doing things. These hints have only scratched the surface!

Accessing Applications and Utilities

For the most part, the applications and utilities you access are those set up by your supervisor. And since your supervisor has set them up, the applications accessible to you are most likely found in your current search drives. I said earlier that a search drive is similar to DOS's PATH command in that it lets you access applications without having to be in the application's directory to do so. NetWare automatically comes with the SYS:PUBLIC search directory, which contains most of NetWare's utilities. (SYS:SYSTEM contains a set of supervisor utilities.)

By typing MAP <Enter>, you will see all the search drive directories presently available to you. To know which applications and utilities these drives contain, go into each of them by typing the drive letter and then typing DIR <Enter>. If there are so many files that they scroll past you, type DIR/W <Enter>, or, if your DOS version allows this, type DIR/P <Enter>. The /W parameter lists the files and their extension across the screen horizontally, and the /P parameter will pause the file listings when the screen is full. You can then press the space bar to see the next screenful of file listings.

Three kinds of extensions indicate programs that will perform something for you; these are the *.COM, *.EXE, and *.BAT extensions. If you want to know which files are executable (in other words, which files will allow you to perform some activity such as word processing or creating spreadsheets) in these directories, type DIR *.COM <Enter>; then type DIR *.EXE <Enter>; then type DIR *.BAT <Enter>. DOS doesn't let you type the three DIR commands together. However, you can use NetWare's NDIR command and put all three commands together by going into the directory you wish to look at and typing NDIR X:*.EXE,*.COM,*.BAT <Enter> at the network prompt. (For a full explanation of the NDIR utility, see the "NDIR" subheading in Chapter 3.) You can also use the SMODE command if you only want to see *.COM and *.EXE files; go to the directory in question and type SMODE <Enter>.

Then at one of your directories where you store data files (usually one where you have at least Create, Erase, and Write rights), you can type the name of the program before the period and the extension (.EXE), and that program will execute (provided you have Read and File Scan rights in that search directory).

If some of your own utilities don't have search drive mappings to them, you'll have to be in the directory where those utilities are located in order to execute them. For example, suppose you use the CED command editor located in your USERS/TED/ST directory. You can either go into the USERS/TED/ST and type CED <Enter> to initiate the editor, or you can set up a search drive. The personalized login script shown in Figure 1-2 shows Ted with the SEARCH5:= W:.[ADMIN/VOL1:USERS/TED/ST] drive mapping. Through similar search drives, you can make it easy to access all of your favorite programs and utilities whenever you need to. You'll simply need to type the network letter at the directory, then type the name of the program or utility—and you're on your way.

How to Log Out of a Server

Logging out is simple. All you have to do is type LOGOUT <Enter> at any network prompt. Depending on how many server attachments you have, you will see something like this:

```
TED logged out from server ADMIN connection 11
Login Time: Thursday July 22, 1993 9:05 am
Logout Time: Thursday July 22, 1993 5:05 pm

TED logged out from server NTS1 connection 87
Login Time: Thursday July 22, 1993 9:05 am
Logout Time: Thursday July 22, 1993 5:05 pm
```

In the above example, if your name is Ted, you've logged out of both ADMIN and NTS1 servers. Typing LOGOUT <Enter>, with no server designation, logs you out of every server you're logged in or attached to. If you only want to log out of NTS1, type LOGOUT NTS1 <Enter> at the prompt.

After the server name in the above example, you see the connection number. This number corresponds to the connection number you see if you type USERLIST <Enter> at the network prompt. (See "The USERLIST Command" in Chapter 3 for a further explanation.) The connection information is followed by the time you logged in to the server and the time you logged out from the server.

When you type LOGOUT, NetWare normally retains an attachment to the server you were logged in to. NetWare also remaps the drive you logged out from to become a LOGIN drive. The next time you log in (if you haven't turned off your machine in the interim), simply type LOGIN *servername/username* <Enter> at that drive prompt, and you'll be asked for your password. If the server you just logged out from is the same server you wish to log in to again, you don't even need to type in the server name. You can just type LOGIN *username* <Enter>, and you will be prompted for your password. And, of course, once you log in, NetWare will present you with the login scripts' drive mappings and network settings and you're back on the network.

If you move to your local drives after you've logged out, you may have a difficult time remembering which network drive contains the LOGIN prompt. If you often work on your local drives after leaving the network, you may wish to designate a drive, such as F:, from which you always exit NetWare. That way, you'll always be able to remember your LOGIN prompt location.

When Users Manage

While this book has been written primarily for NetWare users, many users are taking on more managerial responsibilities. In NetWare 3.11 and 3.12, these managerial responsibilities have more than doubled from earlier versions. The five areas of managerial responsibility in which users can participate without becoming a supervisor or equivalent include:

- ➤ Workgroup manager
- ➤ User account manager
- ➤ Console operator
- ➤ Print server operator
- ➤ Print queue operator

Here's a brief look at each of these titles. Take a look at their responsibilities to see if you want to resign from the title before it's too late.

Workgroup Manager

A workgroup manager is the closest thing to being a supervisor or equivalent, for it includes the ability to create other users or groups as well as manage directories on a selected volume. As a workgroup manager, you can manage your newly created or assigned user accounts. You can make other users who are a part of your responsibility a user account manager, who can then manage the users or groups you assign to them. You also have the ability to delete user and group accounts that are under your responsibility.

Many users become incredibly proficient in a particular application, to the point where other users turn to that person for help much more than to the supervisor. Because of this, a supervisor may defer questions about that application to the user and allow that user to manage the application and the application's directories, as well as be a workgroup manager. So a workgroup manager can also be a person who has been given the rights necessary to access, update, or modify a given application directory. These managers may also maintain printing for that application, which may include becoming a print queue or a print server operator.

User Account Manager

The user account manager has many of the same responsibilities explained under the workgroup manager heading. However, user account managers cannot create new users or group accounts, they can only manage existing user and group accounts. That is, they can assign users to groups, delete the user and group accounts they manage, as well as assign other users to be user account managers.

Console Operator

The console operator (also known as the file server console operator) is allowed rights to manage the file server through the FCONSOLE utility. Within FCONSOLE, the console operator can view connection information, prevent users from logging in, set the server date and time, and broadcast console messages. However, one function a console operator cannot do in FCONSOLE is down the file server.

Print Server Operator

While print server operators cannot create new print servers or assign other users as a print server operator, they can do pretty much everything else to ensure that printers, print queues, and print servers are working. Some of the duties a print server operator must perform are adding printers to printer queues, changing queue priorities, changing printer forms, attaching to file servers for queue access, and downing the print server. Because print server operators must also manipulate print queues, they are often print queue operators as well.

Print Queue Operator

A print queue operator can make print queues available or unavailable for use, create print queues, and manage print jobs in the print queues by changing print job priorities. You can also delete print jobs from within a print queue. You can allow print servers to access a queue, and you will either work in conjunction with a print server operator, or will have that added responsibility.

In the event you have been "duly dubbed" any of these titles, Appendix D discusses in detail the functions, duties, and responsibilities of each position. However, since this is a user's book, Appendix D won't go into the functions, duties, and responsibilities of supervisors or those who are supervisor equivalent.

CHAPTER 2

NetWare Services: The Menu Utilities

NetWare comes with two kinds of utilities to help you better get around on the network: *menu utilities* and *command-line utilities*. Menu utilities, of course, have what's known as a "graphical user interface," or GUI, which keeps you from having to run utilities from the network prompt. Novell uses the C-Worthy library to create its GUI; if you're familiar with other windowing interfaces, you'll find that C-Worthy has its own method for getting you around in its menu structure. We'll cover this method in detail under the "How to Use the Menu Interface" heading a few pages later in this chapter.

You run the command-line utilities, on the other hand, from the network prompt, much like running DOS utilities from the DOS prompt. While there are exceptions, NetWare menus and command-line utilities give you similar functionality, so your choice is more a matter of preference than anything else.

The Menu Utilities

For those of you who don't like to use the utilities run from the command line, NetWare 3.11 offers nine menu utilities to help you get around: SYSCON, FILER, SALVAGE, NBACKUP, SESSION, COLORPAL, DSPACE, VOLINFO, MENU, and HELP. NetWare 3.12 uses a different menu utility than 3.11, and offers an electronic mail package, First Mail. Three other menu-driven utilities—PCONSOLE, PRINTCON, and PRINTDEF—all deal with printing on a network and are explained in Chapter 4. Here's a brief description of the utilities covered in this chapter.

SYSCON—the SYStem CONfiguration utility. (See the section of "The SYSCON Utility" in this chapter for more information.) SYSCON enables you to set up your login scripts and passwords and to view your trustee assignments, account restrictions, time restrictions, and the groups you belong to. It also lets you change to other servers, then view your trustee and group assignments, passwords, login scripts, and account and time restrictions on those other servers. With NetWare 3.11 and 3.12, supervisors can set up volume managers (better known as workgroup managers) and account managers. You may find yourself being duly designated one of these managers.

FILER—the File Maintenance utility. FILER allows you to manipulate files and directories on the network. Through FILER, you can see directory and file information on your current directory, as well as change directories or volumes. You can also look at volume information. With NetWare 3.11, you will find that FILER has undergone a complete facelift from its earlier versions.

SESSION—the Session Manager utility. This utility is a session manager, which means that any drive mappings you create while in the utility will last only for the duration of the session and will go away when you log out. Use this utility when you want to create a temporary setup. SESSION allows you to set up drive mappings, change drive mappings, display search mappings, list groups and users, and send messages to those users or groups.

SALVAGE—the File Salvage utility. SALVAGE recovers recently and not so recently deleted or erased files. There are several expanded features in NetWare 3.11 over earlier versions of NetWare, so read closely before using it.

NBACKUP—the NetWare Backup utility. NBACKUP replaces earlier versions of network backup utilities, by combining NBACKUP, LARCHIVE and LRESTORE, and NARCHIVE and NRESTORE. NBACKUP has both backup and restore procedures for users and managers who want to ensure that their data is protected. Some supervisors also use SBACKUP.NUM, but since this book is a user's guide, we'll only cover NBACKUP.

VOLINFO—the VOLume INFOrmation utility. VOLINFO provides information on the number of kilobytes and directories contained in volumes on the network server. This utility allows you to change to different servers as needed to look at their volume information.

COLORPAL—the COLOR PALette Editor utility. If you have a color monitor, the COLORPAL utility lets you choose the colors for NetWare menus or the menus that you create. COLORPAL doesn't affect any other network applications.

DSPACE—the Disk Usage utility. The DSPACE utility shows you if you have disk space restrictions in place as well as how much disk space is available to you.

MENU—the Menu Execution utility. MENU lets you set up a menu-driven program to give you a menu interface to NetWare. Through MENU, you can access other NetWare utilities and applications without going to the command line. NetWare 3.12 comes with a new MENU program called NMENU. Details about this utility can be found in Appendix E. NetWare 3.12 also adds an electronic mail package called First Mail. See Appendix F for more details about this program.

HELP—The Help utility. This is NetWare's on-line help for all utilities found in NetWare. You can look up the functionality of any menu or command-line utility by typing HELP at the network prompt.

Note: NetWare 3.12 does not have the HELP utility that I discuss here. Instead, NetWare 3.12 comes with a product called Electrotext that allows you to call up the NetWare manuals on-line. You access Electrotext through Windows 3.1. Ask your supervisor if the NetWare manuals have been installed on-line for use with Electrotext. If not, you'll be grateful for having this book since there isn't a HELP utility in 3.12. (However, most 3.12 utilities do come with a basic set of Help screens.)

Before actually going into the menu utilities, let's first look at how to get around in them.

How to Use the Menu Interface

As mentioned earlier, Novell uses the C-Worthy library to create its graphical user interface. The menu interface can be tricky at first, but once you catch on it's easy to get around in. Go into a menu and try these suggestions as you read this explanation. You should be an expert with the menus by the end of this tutorial.

To begin a menu session, simply type the name of the menu utility—for example, SYSCON—at the network prompt, and press <Enter>. When the menu comes up, the first screen you see is the "Available Topics" window, listing the utility's options.

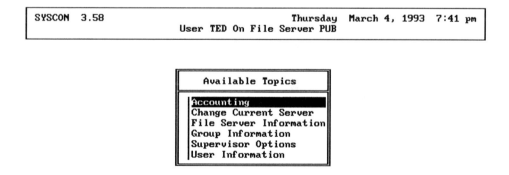

Figure 2.1. The initial SYSCON utility screen

Look first at the top of the screen. Notice the long, rectangular area with a border around it. That's the screen header, and each menu utility has one. The top-left corner of the screen header tells which utility you're in and its version number. This information is followed by the date and time, updated every minute, according to your file server. It's up to the system supervisor to set the correct date and time on the server; if your server is giving you the wrong time, tell the supervisor about it. The next line of the screen header shows your user name and the name of the server the utility will affect. Keep an eye on this line, for when you attach to other servers to look at their information, this second line will change accordingly to help you track which server you're in at a given moment.

When moving around in the menus, pressing <Enter> on a highlighted option brings you to the next screen available under that option, and pressing <Esc> returns you to the previous screen. For example, from the "Available Topics" window, select the "User Information" option by pressing <PgDn> on the numeric key pad and pressing <Enter>. <PgDn> moves the cursor to the bottom of the windowed selections; <PgUp> moves the cursor to the top of the selections. You can also use the Up (8) and Down (2) arrow keys to highlight an option, or you can type the first letters of the option you want and the selector bar will move to that option. Select an option by pressing <Enter>. Try these different options and find the method you prefer for getting around in a window.

Using the Menu Help Screens

You never need to feel stranded in the menus; pressing <F1> at any time will provide an explanation of the menu options currently on the screen. Many of these help screens are quite useful and informative; others merely tell you how to move from one screen to the next. Here's an example of a SYSCON help screen explaining each option from the "Available Topics" window.

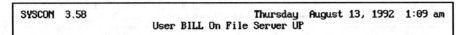

```
SYSCON  3.58                              Thursday  August 13, 1992  1:09 am
                          User BILL On File Server UP
```

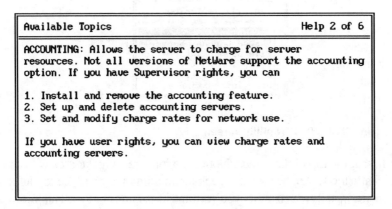

```
Available Topics                                        Help 2 of 6

ACCOUNTING: Allows the server to charge for server
resources. Not all versions of NetWare support the accounting
option. If you have Supervisor rights, you can

1. Install and remove the accounting feature.
2. Set up and delete accounting servers.
3. Set and modify charge rates for network use.

If you have user rights, you can view charge rates and
accounting servers.
```

Figure 2-2. By pressing <F1>, you can see help screens relating to the screen you are viewing.

Each help screen gives you information specific to the option choice currently on the screen. Once you've chosen a different menu option by pressing <Enter>, pressing <F1> will usually bring you a different set of help screens relating to the newly selected option. You can thumb through the help screens by pressing <PgDn> to go to the next screen, or <PgUp> to look at the previous screen. You can also press <TAB> to go to the next screen. The help screens are numbered in the bottom-right corner. When you get to the end of the set of help screens, pressing <PgDn> brings up a little screen that says, "This is the last help screen." Instead of pressing <PgUp> several times to get back to the beginning of the help screens, you can press <Tab>, which returns you to the first help screen.

The Function Key Help Screens

Several function keys provide help in performing tasks in the menus. To get a list of these functions when you're in a help screen, press <F1> again. If you're not in the help screens, bring up the function key assignment menus by pressing <F1> twice. Although not numbered like the other help screens, the function key help menu contains three screens. Here, all three function key help screens are lumped into one screen.

Try each function several times to get a feel for what it does. Then press <PgDn> to go to the next screen and try those functions. Some of these functions work the same in every NetWare menu utility, while others are specific to the particular utility you're in. In any case, you'll use some of these functions often; others you may never use again.

Let's go through each of the functions. A few computers use a different keyboard layout; consequently, your function keys may not match the functions described below. If this is true in your case, go into a menu and press <F1> twice to see how your function keys are listed.

Escape. <Esc> takes you back to the level previous to your last selection. For example, if you want to get out of the help screen, press <Esc>. You also use <Esc> to return to the menu after any error messages. When you want to exit a menu, press <Esc> until you return to the "Available Options" window, followed by the "Exit menuname Yes/No" window with the "Yes" option highlighted. Then simply press <Enter> to return to the network prompt.

Exit. You can also leave the menu utilities from any level by pressing the <Alt> and <F10> keys simultaneously. This will bring you to the "Exit menuname" window with the "Yes" option highlighted; to exit, simply press <Enter>. However, use <Alt>-<F10> only after you have saved your changes; the <Alt>-<F10> sequence doesn't save them for you. To make changes to your login script, for example, press <Esc>; NetWare will ask you if you wish to save the changes. Select the "Yes" option and press <Enter>, and you will be returned to the previous level. You can then press <Alt>-<F10> to exit the utility.

```
┌─────────────────────────────────────────────────────────────────────┐
│ SYSCON  3.62                    Friday September 20, 1991  11:58 am   │
│                       User TED On File Server ADMIN                   │
└─────────────────────────────────────────────────────────────────────┘

┌─────────────────────────────────────────────────────────────────────┐
│ The function key assignments on your machine are:                     │
│                                                                       │
│ ESCAPE          Esc              Back up to the previous level.        │
│ EXIT            Alt F10          Exit the program.                     │
│ CANCEL          F7               Cancel markings or edit changes.      │
│ BACKSPACE       Backspace        Delete the character to the left of   │
│                                  the cursor.                          │
│ INSERT          Ins              Insert a new item.                    │
│ DELETE          Del              Delete an item.                       │
│ MODIFY          F3               Rename/modify/edit the item.          │
│ SELECT          Enter            Accept information entered or select   │
│                                  the item.                            │
│ HELP            F1               Provide on-line help.                 │
│ MARK            F5               Toggle marking for current item.      │
│ CYCLE           Tab              Cycle through menus or screens.       │
│ MODE            F9               Change Modes.                         │
│ UP              Up arrow         Move up one line.                     │
│ DOWN            Down arrow       Move down one line.                   │
│ LEFT            Left arrow       Move left one position.               │
│ RIGHT           Right arrow      Move right one position               │
│ SPECIAL UP      Ctrl PgUp        Move to the very beginning.           │
│ SPECIAL DOWN    Ctrl PgDn        Move to the very end.                 │
│ SPECIAL LEFT    Home             Move to the left-most position on the │
│                                  line.                                │
│ SPECIAL RIGHT   End              Move to the right-most position on    │
│                                  the line.                            │
│ PAGE UP         PgUp             Move up one page.                     │
│ PAGE DOWN       PgDn             Move down one page.                   │
│ FIELD LEFT      Ctrl Left arrow  Move left one field or word.          │
│ FIELD RIGHT     Ctrl Right arrow Move right one field or word.         │
│ F1              Shift F1         Special function 1.                   │
│ F2              F2               Special function 2.                   │
│ F3              Shift F3         Special function 3.                   │
│ F4              F4               Special function 4                    │
│ F5              Shift F5         Special function 5.                   │
│ F6              F6               Special function 6.                   │
│ F7              Shift F7         Special function 7.                   │
│ F8              F8               Special function 8.                   │
│ F9              Shift F9         Special function 9.                   │
│ F10             F10              Special function 10.                  │
└─────────────────────────────────────────────────────────────────────┘
```

Figure 2-3. Available function keys and their assignments

Mark. This feature, or the F5 key, lets you mark options highlighted by the selector bar, allowing you to perform an operation on several items at one time. For example, if you want to mark for deletion a number of files in the FILER "Directory Contents" window, highlight the names of those files one at a time with the selector bar and press <F5> to mark each one, then press <Del>. You'll see the "Delete All Marked Files Yes/No" window with the "Yes" option highlighted. Pressing <Enter> will delete the files. Pressing <F5> twice unmarks a file. The Mark key works only in those options where you are allowed more than one selection.

Cancel. The F7 key is also handy if you change your mind after marking things up. <F7> cancels either your <F5> markings, or your edits to something, such as your login script. In this respect, <F7> is like pressing <Esc> and then <Enter>. Either sequence will return you to an unmarked screen, ready for you to mark it up again.

Backspace, Insert, and Delete keys. The Backspace key deletes the character to the left of the cursor. The Insert, or <Ins>, key works in conjunction with the Delete, or <Del>, key and the Mark (F5) key, mainly for supervisor functions. But as a user, you can operate these keys for certain purposes of your own. Suppose, for example, you want to move two search map lines in your login script, which looks like this:

```
map e:=admin/vol1:users/ted
map f:=admin/vol1:users/ted/93/jan
map S4:=admin/vol1:users/ted/st
map S5:=admin/sys:public/util
map g:=admin/vol1:users/ted/tech
map h:=admin/vol1:users/ted/code
```

Instead of retyping the lines, press <F5> at the beginning of the "map S4" line, then press the Down arrow key twice to include the "map S5" line, and drop to the beginning of the "map g" line. Then press <Del>; the Delete key works as a "cut-and-paste" feature by placing the search map lines in a memory buffer until you paste them somewhere else. Go to the line beneath the "map h" line and press <Ins>. <Ins> then invokes the memory buffer and places the data at the cursor prompt, so you get:

```
map e:=admin/vol1:users/ted
map f:=admin/vol1:users/ted/93/jan
map g:=admin/vol1:users/ted/tech
map h:=admin/vol1:users/ted/code
map S4:=admin/vol1:users/ted/st
map S5:=admin/sys:public/util
```

Modify. Another key on the function assignment screen is <F3>, which you can use to rename, modify, or edit a highlighted item. This function is particularly helpful when you're in the FILER utility and you want to rename files and directories. If you're in FILER and you press <Enter> with the selector bar on the "Directory Contents" option from the "Available Topics" window, you'll see a list of filenames and subdirectory names from the "Directory Contents" window.

Select a file with the up/down arrow keys and press <F3>. You'll see a little "Edit Filename" window with the name of the file you selected. Press the backspace key until the filename is gone; then rename the file and press <Enter>. For example, to change the name of the DATE.SCR file to DATE.DAT, press the backspace key to erase the SCR extension and type DAT; press <Enter> and you'll return to the "Directory Contents" window. Note that the filename now reads "DATE.DAT." Remember, security plays a big part in your ability to rename files and directories. If you try this feature and find that you can't rename the file, check your effective rights or the file flags for possible reasons.

Moving Around in the Menus

<PgDn> moves the cursor to the bottom of the first screen containing selections, and <PgUp> brings you to the top of the first screen containing selections. You can also use the Up (8 on the numeric keypad) arrow key to move up an option, and the Down (2 on the numeric keypad) arrow key to move down an option.

When you're in your login script, or in menu screens where you can type in entries, you have still other ways of moving around. The left arrow (6) key moves you one cursor position to the left, and the right arrow (4) key moves you one cursor position to the right. To move a full word to the left, press the <Ctrl>-left arrow keys; to move one word to the right, press the <Ctrl>-right arrow keys. If your login script occupies more than a single screen and you want to move to the beginning, press <Ctrl>-<PgUp>; to move to the end of your script, press <Ctrl>-<PgDn>. (These same combinations get you to the top or to the bottom of a user, group, or file list.) When you modify your login script, you can use the Home (7) key to go the far left position, and the End (1) key to go to the far right of the line you're on.

Patterns

The FILER utility defines two function keys that you won't find in the other utilities. <F6> lets you mark files that contain a pattern in common and allows you to give those files the same file attributes without changing each filename separately. For example, you can use <F6> to mark all files with the same extension, such as .SCR, and give all those files Shareable Read/Only attributes. To mark the .SCR files, press <F6> and then <Enter>. The "Mark Pattern" screen will appear, with the asterisk (*) already in place. Type .SCR <Enter> in at the cursor. All filenames with the .SCR extension will then be highlighted, which means that they're now marked for deleting, renaming, or having new attributes set for them. (To learn how to perform these functions, see the section on "The Filer Utility" in this chapter.)

<F8> pulls up an "Unmark Pattern" box that allows you to unmark the filenames you marked with <F6>. (Simply pressing <Esc> to leave the screen also unmarks the files.) If you want to be selective on your marked *.SCR files, you can unmark all files starting with the letter S. After marking all the .SCR files, press <F8> and the "Unmark Pattern" screen will appear, with the asterisk (*) already in place. Type S*.* <Enter> in at the cursor. Then all filenames with the .SCR extension except those starting with the letter S will be highlighted.

The rest of the function keys are for supervisor functions.

Getting Back to Basics—Changing Your Password

As an experiment, go in and change your password. If you're not already in SYSCON, type SYSCON at the network prompt and press <Enter>. At the "Available Topics" window, select the "User Information" option. At the "User Names" window, highlight your network user name. Then press <Enter>.

You're now at the "User Information" window. Select the "Change Password" option. If you already have a password, you'll see a small window at the bottom of the screen which says, "Enter Old Password:." Type in your old password and press <Enter>. Next, the screen will say, "Enter New Password," to which you type in your new password and press <Enter>. (This is the first screen you'll see if you don't already have a password.) You will then be prompted to retype your new password. (The system has you do this to make sure you know what you typed, since the password doesn't appear on the screen.) Reenter the new password and press <Enter>, and you'll return to the "Change Password" option. Because of your particular security scheme, your password may need to be a certain length. (NetWare's default is five characters long.) Once you've changed your password, exit SYSCON.

Getting Around in the Menu Utilities

This book is designed to show you every available option in each menu window, such as the "Available Topics" window. After discussing one option, the book will move to the next option without explaining the exit process all over again. To exit any menu utility entirely from any level, press <Alt> and <F10> simultaneously and you will see the "Exit *menuname*" window with the "Yes" option highlighted. Press <Enter> to return to the network prompt.

The SYSCON Utility

The term SYSCON stands for SYStem CONfiguration. The system supervisor uses SYSCON to set up groups, users, directories, and accounts, and to perform other supervisory functions. Right now we'll discuss what you can do in SYSCON as a user.

What Users Can Do in SYSCON—Setting Up Your Login Script and Changing Your Password

Depending on your rights, you as a user can use SYSCON to set up your individual login script and change your password. The rest of SYSCON is a large viewing screen, revealing the setup of the server's environment.

Let's look first at the actual functions you can perform in SYSCON: setting up your login script and changing your password. This is the information you'll use the most in setting up your personal NetWare environment. Don't worry—we'll come back and discuss the other options afterwards.

Setting Up Your Login Script

The main feature SYSCON offers you is the ability to set up your own login script. Setting up a login script is as simple or as intricate as you want it to be. To begin, type SYSCON at the network prompt and press <Enter>. You'll see a screen similar to the one shown in Figure 2-4:

```
SYSCON  3.58                              Thursday  March 4, 1993  7:41 pm
                      User TED On File Server PUB
```

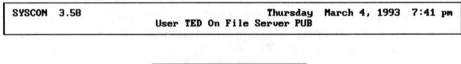

```
┌─────────────────────────┐
│    Available Topics      │
├─────────────────────────┤
│ Accounting               │
│ Change Current Server    │
│ File Server Information   │
│ Group Information        │
│ Supervisor Options       │
│ User Information         │
└─────────────────────────┘
```

Figure 2-4. The initial SYSCON utility screen

By way of review, to get around in SYSCON, pressing <Enter> on a highlighted option brings you to the next screen available under that option; pressing <Esc> brings you to the previous screen. For example, from the "Available Topics" window, select the "User Information" option by pressing <PgDn> on the numeric keypad. Once that option is highlighted, press <Enter>. <PgDn> brings you to the bottom of the list of selections, and <PgUp> brings you to the top of the list. You can also use the Up (8) and Down (2) arrow keys to highlight and select an option, or you can type the first letters of the option you wish to select and the selector bar will move to that option.

Never feel stranded in the menus—pressing <F1> at any time will provide an explanation of the menu options currently on the screen. Each help screen gives you information specific to the option choice currently on the screen. Once you've chosen another menu option by pressing <Enter>, pressing <F1> will bring you a different set of help screens relating to the newly selected option.

From the "Available Topics" window, select the "User Information" option. The "User Information" option will then present the "User Names" window. Select your user name. You'll see a "User Information" window that contains the "Login Script" option.

Select the "Login Script" option to bring up the "Login Script" window. An example of Ted's login script on server ADMIN is shown on the following page.

Available Map and Login Script Functions

To set up your login script, you need to understand three functions: the *map functions*, the *login script functions*, and *DOS commands*. The map functions are much like the basic MAP commands you can perform at the network prompt (MAP is actually a command-line utility), in the SESSION utility, and in the login script. However, your script mappings will last after you log out, because once you place them in the login script, NetWare will remap the drives each time you log in. You can also perform other login script functions, which are very similar to what you do at the network prompt. But again, placing them in the login script means they'll be initiated every time you log in. The login script can also run DOS commands in order to better assist you in setting up your workstation environment.

```
SYSCON   3.58                          Thursday  March 4, 1993  7:44 pm
                      User TED On File Server ADMIN
```

```
                        Login Script For User TED

map *1:=admin/vol1:users\ted
map h:admin/vol1:users\ted\articles\july
map i:=vol1:users\ted\reports\jan
map j:=admin/vol1:users\ted\tech
map k:=admin/vol1:users\ted\reports

attach up/ted
map o:=up\sys:reports
map s16:=admin\vol1:users\ted\st

map
drive j:
```

Figure 2-5. An example login script for user Ted

MAP Functions and Their Examples

Examples of the MAP functions for the login script include:

MAP. Use this command to tell the system to show your drive mappings.

MAP DISPLAY ON. This command displays your drive mappings as the login script designates them. MAP ON is the default, meaning that if you don't put in either of these first two commands, NetWare will assume you want to display your drive mappings as they are defined. This command is used in conjunction with MAP DISPLAY OFF, which turns off displaying the drive mappings and other login script commands.

MAP DISPLAY OFF. This command hides your drive mappings as they are created, much like DOS's ECHO OFF command for batch files. Some people put a MAP DISPLAY OFF command at the top of their login script and a MAP DISPLAY ON at the bottom before running the MAP command. If you do this, you won't have to watch the login script work through its commands.

MAP ERRORS ON. This command shows you if you have any errors in your login script. (This command is the default.)

MAP ERRORS OFF. If you don't want to see your login script errors, use this command.

58

MAP NEXT. NetWare 3.1x offers two additional MAP commands that you can use in the login script or at the network prompt. These new commands are MAP NEXT and MAP ROOT. The MAP NEXT command allows NetWare to select the next available drive letter for a new drive mapping, but it works only from the command line. See "The MAP Command" heading in Chapter 3.

MAP ROOT. The network supervisor will probably use it more than you will. You use this command when you have an application that must have its directory at the root level in order to read from its files or write to its files. (The root level is at the beginning of the volume where the colon resides, such as W:= ADMIN/VOL1:GLIP rather than W:= ADMIN/VOL1:WINDOWS\APPS\GLIP.) This application requirement can create a mess if you don't have rights at the root directory, yet your application must write to a file in the root directory. To solve the problem, the MAP ROOT command makes the application believe that it's at the root level.

Look at this example of setting up drive mappings:

```
map *1:=admin/vol1:users/ted
map h:=admin/vol1:users/ted/articles/july
map I:=vol1:users/ted/92/aug
map j:=admin/vol1:users/ted/tech
map root k:=admin/vol1:users/ted/code

attach nts1/ted
map o:=nts1/sys:spsheet/aug
map S16:=admin/vol1:users/ted/st
drive j:
```

For the sake of this explanation, suppose you're Ted and these are your drive mappings.

MAP *1:=ADMIN/VOL1:USERS/TED. When working with NetWare drive mappings, you can designate a drive letter by using the letter itself, or you can use an asterisk (*) followed by a number. With the asterisk method, the *1 mapping tells NetWare to go to the first available network drive letter and make that the first drive mapping.

However, using the asterisk and number procedure can mean that when you log in from a different workstation, you may see your drives mapped to different letters than the ones you're used to. For example, if your workstation is set up for you to use drive E: as your first drive mapping, you may see C: or G: when you log in from another workstation. This depends on the workstation's CONFIG.SYS file setting, which

59

normally defaults to F: but which you can modify. (See the "Creating the CONFIG.SYS File" heading in Chapter 5). So if you like variety, or if you never use anyone else's workstation, use the asterisk and number sequence.

MAP H:=ADMIN/VOL1:USERS/TED/ARTICLES/JULY. If you prefer your login scripts always to map to the same drive letters, you can put in drive letters such as those listed on line 2 in the example above. By using a drive letter, you're essentially telling NetWare, "Map drive H: to be equivalent to this directory path." Line 2 maps drive H: to the JULY directory found on server ADMIN's VOL1 volume; every time you type H: at the network prompt, you'll be mapped to the JULY directory. The other maps, drives I: through K:, show basically the same information the H: drive map shows. However, drive I: doesn't show the servername. If you're mapping to a directory on the same server where this login script is stored, you don't need to put in the servername.

MAP ROOT K:=ADMIN/VOL1:USERS/TED/CODE. As mentioned earlier, the ROOT command option allows you to set up directory paths which looks as if it were at the volume root. And while this is more geared for installing applications, users will find this command useful if a particular application has problems with incredibly long directory paths. If you use this as it is typed above and you have the PROMPT PG command in place so you can see subdirectories, you will see K:\> as the network prompt. However, if you type MAP at the network prompt, you'll see K: = ADMIN\VOL1:USERS\TED\CODE\ as part of your drive mappings. So the directory CODE acts as if it were at the root level. With the ROOT command in place, you can go down to the directories below, but not up (because you're at the top). Then if you go into a directory below, such as CD OUTPUT <Enter>, your prompt will show K:\OUTPUT> for the network prompt.

ATTACH NTS1/TED. To attach to other servers each time you log in to your regular server, put an ATTACH command inside the login script. Put in the ATTACH command before designating a drive on another server; since this server is not your default, you must also designate the servername in the map designation, as shown in the "MAP O:" line. The command you see in the login script pictured in the example gives the servername and your user name. As you log in to server ADMIN and NetWare scans your bindery information for your drive mappings, NetWare will see that you want to attach to server NTS1 and that you've given your user name.

You can also put in the ATTACH NTS1 command without your name; NetWare will then ask for a user name as well as the password (if you have one). Only after you enter your name and the correct password will you be mapped to server NTS1's directory. Or you can put in your name, to which NetWare will ask for your password only. However, if you're defined as a user on more than one server, and your username and passwords are synchronized across the servers, you won't be asked for your password when you attach to those servers in your login script. (Synchronized passwords became part of NetWare with version 2.15; you synchronize them at the network prompt through the SETPASS utility. See the "SETPASS" subheading under "Server Access Utilities" in Chapter 3.)

MAP S16:=ADMIN/VOL1:USERS/TED/ST. The example also shows that you have one search drive mapped to the ST directory. When you type the name of an executable file (such as SYSCON), NetWare first searches the directory that you're currently in. If NetWare can't find that name in your current directory, NetWare begins searching through directories designated as search drives until it finds the name you typed in. (If NetWare can't find that name, you'll see "Bad command or filename.") Search drives start at the letter Z: (usually designated as SYS:PUBLIC) and work back through the alphabet. By mapping a search drive to this directory, you can have your favorite utilities and created batch files in an area you can call upon from any directory you are in.

Notice, too, that the prefix for this search drive is S16. This prefix means, "Insert this search drive after all other search drives have been mapped." S16 is the maximum number of search drives you can have; if you designate an S16 drive, NetWare will automatically map that directory to the next available search drive number. The S16 designation prevents your drive from overwriting any of the system search drives the supervisor has set up in the system login script.

For example, if you already have search drive mappings S1 to S4, and then you map a drive to S16, NetWare will change that search drive number to S5. This is similar to the asterisk and number (*1) designation in the regular login mappings. You can also type MAP at the network prompt to call up your list of drive mappings, count the number of search drives already taken, and then give your personal search drive a number, such as MAP S5:=ADMIN/VOL1:USERS/TED/ST.

If you are having problems with losing local drive designations from the PATH statement, see "Search Drive Mappings and the PATH Statement" in Appendix A.

DRIVE=*drive letter* or *drive number*. The DRIVE command allows you to specify which network drive you want as your network prompt when you exit the login script. Setting up a default drive letter allows you to begin in the same directory on any workstation you log in from. Be aware that you can create a problem for yourself if you change your CONFIG.SYS file to bring you up on a drive letter other than F: if you are using the NetWare Shell. (Remember, if you're running DOS 3.*x* or above, your system assumes that A: through E: are local drives.)

For example, suppose you change your CONFIG.SYS to read LASTDRIVE = C:, and you use the letter method instead of the asterisk method for mapping drives. If you don't map a drive to D:, NetWare may map a drive to the D: drive letter and there's a good chance the drive will be SYS:LOGIN, where you may have no rights. You won't be able to do anything worthwhile in NetWare until you change to another directory. So if you do map a drive to D:, you won't have that problem. Or you might put DRIVE J: <Enter> on a line in your login script (a legitimate drive mapping) to avoid this problem.

You will also avoid this problem if you use the asterisk sequence (MAP *1:=etc.), for *1 will go to the first available drive (D:). Then if you enter all your drives as asterisk mappings, and you want *4 to be your default drive as you exit the login script, simply type in DRIVE *4: <Enter>. Just be sure you have the default drive mapped to a directory; otherwise, the system ignores your request and puts you in the original default drive.

For workstations running the DOS Requester, the CONFIG.SYS file will automatically have the line LASTDRIVE = Z in it. Because of this, the DOS Requester looks at the workstation's local drive table and maps the first available drive letter as the first network drive. You can make the first network drive F: by placing First Network Drive = F in the NET.CFG file. (See the "NET.CFG Parameters for NetWare" heading in Chapter 5.) You can then place DRIVE = F: in your login script to specify your network drive when you leave the login script.

Login Script Functions and Their Examples

You can perform quite a list of DOS and login script functions:

ATTACH	FIRE PHASERS
BREAK	INCLUDE
COMSPEC	MACHINE
[F]DISPLAY	PAUSE
GOTO	DOS BREAK
PCCOMPATIBLE	DOS SET
REMARK	DOS VERIFY
WRITE	EXIT
IF...THEN...ELSE	
# (EXTERNAL PROGRAM EXECUTION)	

Here's a login script using some of these commands:

```
SYSCON  3.58                              Thursday  March 4, 1993  7:47 pm
                         User TED On File Server ADMIN
```

```
                        Login Script For User TED

map display off
fire phasers 7 times

attach up/ted
map o:=up\sys:spsheet\aug
map s16:=admin\vol1:users\bill\st

display vol1:users\ted\heyyou
SET WPC="/nt-1 /u=teb

rem the next lines for Coordinator use
set usr="bthomas"
set pwd="grumpy"

*Y:COMMAND /C cls
```

Figure 2-6. More login script examples

ATTACH *servername/username.* To use the ATTACH command, type the ATTACH command into the login script box:

```
ATTACH NTS1/TED
MAP O:=NTS1\SYS:SPSHEET\AUG
```

Use the ATTACH command before you designate a drive on another server. Include the servername in the map designation as shown. If your name is Ted, and you want to attach to server NTS1, type ATTACH NTS1/TED in your login script. This gives the servername and your username to server NTS1. As mentioned earlier, you can also put in the ATTACH NTS1 command without your name.

When you're thinking about attaching to another server, find out whether or not the supervisor has attached you to the server under the guise of GUEST. In times past, when supervisors wanted a particular group to send print jobs to a queue and printer, the supervisors would attach you to that server as GUEST. This action meant you would usually end up having no rights to any of your personal directories, since user GUEST had no rights to your directories.

To get around this problem, you need to first log out of the server so you can log back in under your username. To do this, type LOGOUT *servername* <Enter>, then ATTACH *servername/yourname* <Enter> in your personal login script. So you can do this without losing whatever the supervisor has set up, find out all the supervisor has set up for the ATTACH GUEST session. Then incorporate those settings as part of your personal login script, along with the set up you need when you attach to the server.

BREAK ON/OFF. The next command is the network BREAK ON and BREAK OFF. Where DOS offers BREAK ON/OFF functionality for batch files (particularly the AUTOEXEC.BAT file), this command keeps you from being able to interrupt an executing login script. However, if for some reason you want to interrupt your login script procedure, you can type in the BREAK ON command at the beginning of your login script. (Keep in mind, though, that interrupting the login script as it executes is usually not a good idea, for you may not have your network environment completely set up before you interrupt its process.) The login script defaults to BREAK OFF.

COMSPEC *directory path/filename.* Every time you load an application, DOS loads COMMAND.COM for you. When you exit from a program, you'll sometimes see your workstation drive A: light come on, or your drive C: light flicker. That means your workstation is reloading COMMAND.COM so the system will be ready to accept your next command. Setting up COMSPEC in the login script allows DOS to call on COMMAND.COM from the network rather than from your boot disk or hard disk.

Note: Unless you are having problems with a particular application, you don't need to have COMSPEC set when using MS DOS 6.0. The COMSPEC is set through the SHELL= command in the workstation's CONFIG.SYS file.

Your supervisor may already have this command in place in the system login script, so before you put COMSPEC in your personal login script, consult your supervisor. If your supervisor has COMSPEC in the system login script, chances are it's already set up so that you'll access the right DOS directory for the DOS version you're running. However, if you see "Invalid or missing COMMAND.COM" messages when you exit your applications, try setting the COMSPEC command in your login script as is shown next. Then log in again and retry the program that gave you the error message. If that doesn't work, talk to your supervisor.

If you need to set the COMSPEC command in your own login script, be sure you know which DOS version your workstation is running (to find out, type VER at the network prompt); then ask your supervisor the location of the directory where your version of DOS resides so you can map to that directory. For example, if you're running DOS version 4.01 on your workstation, make sure that DOS version 4.01 is somewhere on the network and you can map to it, as shown:

```
MAP INS S2: = SYS:PUBLIC/MSDOS/V4.00
COMSPEC = S2:COMMAND.COM
```

The "MAP INS S2:" parameter means, "Insert this search drive mapping at search drive 2 and map the drive to DOS version 4.01." (NetWare only accepts the directory called 4.00 for 4.01 DOS.) The COMSPEC command then tells DOS to look on search drive 2 anytime it needs to reload COMMAND.COM. When you use this insert parameter (INS S2), you don't overwrite another drive mapping that your supervisor has set up in the system login script; you only bump previous search drives to the next available number. But consult your system supervisor before you use this command. Your supervisor may have put an application on the network that expects to find something at a particular search drive number. If you put something else at that drive number, the application may not work properly for you. (This is especially true when using Windows 3.1.)

(F)DISPLAY *(directory path/filename).* Next is the DISPLAY (or FDISPLAY) command, which lets you display data from a text file on the screen when you're logging in. You can use this command to call up any reminder messages you left for yourself in a text file. That way, instead of modifying your login script, you only have to modify a text file to remind you of things you need to do. If NetWare can't find the directory path or the file, you won't see an error message; you simply won't see any message displayed.

The (F) parameter stands for a filtered display; the DISPLAY command shows you everything, including the printing and word processing codes, but FDISPLAY shows only the text. If you're saving your file with a word processor, use FDISPLAY; if you're saving your file with a text editor, use DISPLAY. You'll have to experiment, however, for not all word processor files can be displayed with FDISPLAY, and you may have to save the file as a DOS text file from within the word processor. For example, in WordPerfect 5.1, you can save WP's formatted files to a DOS file by pressing <Ctrl>-<F5>, then selecting 1 (DOS Text), 1 (Save), and typing in the DOS text filename.

When you use DISPLAY, you must specify the directory path; drive letters won't work here. For example, suppose you have an important interview coming up. You have the date circled on the calendar, but you still want to be extra sure not to forget the interview. You can create a little text file using DOS's COPY CON command (in one of your regular directories where you have Create rights). For example:

```
COPY CON HEYYOU <Enter>
HEY YOU! Don't forget that important <Enter>
```

65

```
INTERVIEW for the VICE PRESIDENCY POSITION! <Enter>
Keep CALM and use plenty of mouthwash. ^Z (Ctrl-Z)
```

Then type in the command along with the directory path and filename, such as DISPLAY VOL1:USERS\TED\HEYYOU in your login script. NetWare will follow the directory path and display the message. You can also keep such a file in a group area where you can pass important messages to group members who also have the DISPLAY command in their login scripts. Or your supervisor may use such a file to send important short memos to everyone. Remember, NetWare scrolls through these messages without stopping, so if the message is long, use the PAUSE command (covered later in this section).

DOS SET name = *value* **or** *parameter*. The DOS SET command lets you specify parameters to the programs you are loading. For example, you can use the DOS SET command when you load such programs as WordPerfect or The Coordinator, an electronic-mail application. To avoid having to type in your initials every time you go into the network version of WordPerfect or WordPerfect Office, put the following parameters in your login script:

```
SET WPC="/nt-1 /u=teb"
```

The /NT-1 chooses the type of network you will run on; the /U=TEB puts in your network initials. There are also several other parameters you can type in for WordPerfect. Or instead of typing in your Coordinator name and password every time you go into The Coordinator, put in the following parameters:

```
set usr="tbeara"      (your username on The Coordinator)
set pwd="grumpy"      (your password on The Coordinator)
```

Then every time you type WP at the network prompt, you'll go directly into WordPerfect without having to type in the network you're on or your initials, and every time you type ATC to access The Coordinator, you'll go directly into the opening menu. Please note that these parameters may change in the product's new releases; consult each product's documentation for the correct parameters to use with the SET command.

Another handy SET command sets up your DOS prompt and your color if you have a color monitor. You can put SET PROMPT="$P $G" in your login script to show directory paths (or you can put PROMPT in your AUTOEXEC.BAT file). You can extend your prompt command to include different parameters if you like. For information on color monitors, see Chapter 5. Also, see your DOS manual for details on PROMPT and the ANSI.SYS file.

DOS VERIFY ON/OFF. You don't really need to use this command, since NetWare performs an automatic read-after-write verification of all files you copy through DOS's COPY or NetWare's NCOPY (short for the network copy) command. The DOS VERIFY command only verifies that the file was written correctly, which NetWare does anyway.

EXIT. This command allows you to interrupt the login script so you can run a particular program, such as a batch file. As an example of the EXIT command, if during the login process you want to go into a menu when you leave the login script, you can type EXIT "MENU GOOD" on the last line in your login script. This command says, "run my menu GOOD for me."

However, the EXIT command is tricky; if you place the EXIT command in the middle of your login script, EXIT leaves and doesn't execute the rest of your login script. If you do put in the wrong parameter, you'll receive the following message:

```
Illegal identifier ...
Remainder of login script ignored.
WARNING: Due to a serious error in your LOGIN script, further
initialization of your network environment can not be accom-
plished successfully. Drive F: has been mapped to the SYS:PUBLIC
directory to give you access to the network utilities. Use the
SYSCON menu utility to fix the error in your script (as indi-
cated above) and then run LOGIN again.
```

Then you can go back into SYSCON and fix your problem. With NetWare 3.1x, you may only see a string of errors rather than the above warning message. The EXIT command puts the command you put in quotation marks directly into the keyboard buffer. So if you run EXIT and it doesn't work, your workstation's BIOS may not be IBM PC-specific, and you may need to run the PCCOMPATIBLE command before using EXIT. However, even with PCCOMPATIBLE, the EXIT command may not work correctly, and it may be better to run your menu at the network prompt.

(PC)COMPATIBLE. NetWare has an intimate knowledge of where the workstation's BIOS (Basic Input/Output System) stores certain information in the keyboard and screen buffers. When you run the EXIT command, NetWare takes advantage of your workstation's BIOS knowledge to place the command you designate into the keyboard buffer. The PCCOMPATIBLE command allows people using a machine name other than "IBM" to use the EXIT command. And with the growing number of AT clones in the workplace, this command becomes more and more important.

Before typing the EXIT filename command, type PCCOMPATIBLE. Then, as EXIT looks at the machine's name and says, "It's not IBM; I can't do this," the PCCOMPATIBLE command says, "Trust me; it's a PC compatible, so go ahead and stuff the keyboard buffer." For example, if you're running a Compaq computer and you want to run the MENU program from your login script, you can type PCCOMPATIBLE on one line and EXIT "MENU menuname" on the next line.

To set up your workstation environment so you can run the EXIT command on a PC compatible, type SHORT MACHINE TYPE = CMPQ as the short machine name parameter in your NET.CFG file. This option will allow PC compatibles, such as AT&T and Compaq, to use the CMPQ$RUN.OVL file found in the SYS:PUBLIC directory. For more information on the NET.CFG file, see Chapter 5.

EXTERNAL PROGRAM EXECUTION *(#directory path/filename)*. If you want to execute a DOS command from your login script, use the EXTERNAL PROGRAM EXECUTION command. Although EXTERNAL PROGRAM EXECUTION is the name of the command, you don't have to type all that; to execute this command, just type a pound sign (#). Let's say you want to know as soon as you log in if you have any mail in The Coordinator. In your login script, put #NEWMAIL *servername/volumename: username* (for example, #NEWMAIL ADMIN/SYS: TBEARA), and NetWare will check to see if you have any mail. (Note the space following the colon in this particular command.) If you have new mail, you'll see "You have new mail from The Coordinator system!" displayed on your screen when you log in. Place this command after your map assignments in your login script so NetWare will know where to look for the command.

You need to know a few things about the EXTERNAL PROGRAM EXECUTION (#) command. You must write out the entire directory path or it won't work; and if you wish to add DOS parameters, you must do so after the filename. You must begin the command with a pound sign (#); when NetWare sees this sign, it will understand that you want to execute something outside your login script. Remember, this is a program execution command, so you must use programs that are executable. You can run .COM or .EXE files, and there is a way to run batch files as well.

When you want to run batch files, you need to run COMMAND.COM with the /C parameter along with the batch filename (the /C parameter spawns another command process so you can go back to the login script after you run the batch file). For example, suppose you want to run a batch file named GO.BAT that clears your screen and pauses before returning you to the login script. First, go to the directory where you want to store the batch file (such as G:\USERS\TED) and type:

```
COPY CON GO.BAT     <Enter>
CLS                 <Enter>
PAUSE ^Z
```

Then in your login script, type:

```
#Y:COMMAND /C G:\USERS\TED\GO
```

The Y: designates the directory where your DOS files and COMMAND.COM is stored. COMMAND allows you to run the batch file, and G:\USERS\TED\GO shows the directory path to the GO.BAT file. Remember, this is a DOS call, so you must use the backslash when writing out the directory path. As another example, if you just want to clear the screen, you don't need a batch file. Type #Y:COMMAND /C CLS in your login script and your script will clear the screen at the place where you put in the command.

Don't load Terminate-and-Stay-Resident (TSR) programs through the EXTERNAL PROGRAM EXECUTION command. If, for instance, when you start up your computer, you load COMMAND.COM, IPX, and the NetWare shell programs that stay in memory for as long as your computer is on. Then you load a lot of transient memory programs, such as LOGIN, which pop into memory long enough for you to use and are then discarded. If you stick a TSR program out there while you're in one of these transient programs, the TSR is going to end up in memory beyond your transient programs. When you leave LOGIN, you end up with a big memory hole that can't be accessed because of the TSR program. Instead of your TSR taking 12KB of memory, it now takes about 30KB–40KB—and you may find yourself unable to access large applications.

FIRE PHASERS (*n* times). This command creates a sound reminiscent of the laser noises in "B" science fiction movies. Type FIRE PHASERS and the number of times you want the phasers to fire; if you want to hear the phasers fire seven times, type FIRE PHASERS 7. If you want the phasers to fire when you receive new mail, type IF NEW_MAIL = "YES" THEN FIRE PHASERS 7. You're actually using the command to tell you when events occur in your login script.

MACHINE = *name*. Use the MACHINE command if you're running machine-specific programs, or if you want to use the name in a search drive designation. For example, if you want to display a full directory path designating your machine type, your workstation operating system, and the operating system version, you can type the following code:

```
MAP S2:=SYS:PUBLIC\%MACHINE\%OS\%OS_VERSION
```

You usually designate this directory path when you want to set up COMSPEC to find the COMMAND.COM file. (Supervisors often use the above command in the System login script.) If you're running machine-specific programs, such as the CLEAR program for the IBM PC, you can type this command:

```
IF MACHINE = "IBM_PC" THEN #PUB/SYS:PUBLIC\UTIL\CLEAR
```

NetWare will leave the login script, run the CLEAR program, and then return and finish the login script.

PAUSE or WAIT. Use this command to put a pause in the login script. For example, if you're running a lengthy text from the DISPLAY command, or if you want a message to sink in rather than merely scroll by, type PAUSE at any point where you want the pause to occur. Then you'll see the "Strike a key when ready..." message at the bottom of the DISPLAY file's information. When you press any key, the rest of the login script will execute.

REMARK *text*. A remark is just a comment you write to yourself inside the login script. The comment is never displayed on the screen; it's a personal note to you. There are several ways to use the REMARK command. For example, you can type:

```
REMARK Check with supervisor before setting up search drives!
```

or you can type

```
REM Check with supervisor before setting up search drives!
```

or you can use an asterisk (*) and type

```
* Check with supervisor before setting up search drives!
```

or you can use a semicolon (;) and type

```
; Check with supervisor before setting up search drives!
```

Whichever way you do it, only you will see the remark in the login script.

Getting into Serious Stuff—The WRITE, IF/THEN, AND/OR /NOR ELSE, and INCLUDE Utilities

Probably only the most zealous NetWare user will use these last three commands. But if you're up for some interesting login scripts, take a look at the next three commands: WRITE, IF/THEN, and INCLUDE. (AND/OR/NOR/ELSE are parameters you can use with IF/THEN statements.)

```
 SYSCON   3.58                        Monday  August 16, 1993  10:43 am
                         User TED On File Server ADMIN

                        Login Script For User TED

map display on
WRITE "Good %GREETING_TIME, %FULL_NAME, it's \n %DAY_OF_WEEK, %MONTH_NAME,
%YEAR \n at %HOUR:%MINUTE:SECOND %AM_PM."

WRITE "And how are your today?"

WRITE "Your machine type is %MACHINE, your server is %FILE_SERVER,"
WRITE "your OS is %OS_VERSION, your network address is %NETWORK_ADDRESS,"
WRITE "you are at workstation %P_STATION, and NetWare knows you as %USER_ID."

if day_of_week="TUESDAY" and hour24<"14" then begin
   write "\7Meeting with marketing at 2:00!"
end
if day_of_week="THURSDAY" and hour24<"10" then begin
   write "\7Conference meeting at 10:30. Be there!"
end
```

Figure 2-7. An example of IF/THEN statements in user Ted's login script

WRITE *text strings; variables.* The WRITE command allows you to write messages to yourself that will appear on your screen when you log in. There are two basic elements to the WRITE command: the text strings and the variables that NetWare supplies. When you write out strings of text, you must place the text itself inside quotation marks; for example:

```
WRITE "How do you do today?"
```

The WRITE command comes with four symbols, known as supercharacters, to help you compose your prose:

   \r   returns the cursor to the beginning of the same line

\n   moves the cursor to the next line

\"   embeds quotation marks within the text

\7   sounds a beep

You may not ever use the \r symbol, as it tends to overwrite the message you've just written. The WRITE command automatically moves the cursor to the beginning of the next line at the proper time. Remember that the \r supercharacter doesn't move the cursor to the next line; it moves it to the far left of the line you're on. Using the \r can cause you to overwrite your text if you're not careful. (You'll see these supercharacters at work in upcoming examples of the WRITE command.)

WRITE comes with several variables to help you identify objects and call information from NetWare. These variables can help you write to yourself information such as the kind of machine you're running on, the DOS operating system you're using, the date and time, and your full login name. Following is a list of the variables you can use and what these variables display on the screen.

Table 2-1. Variables you can use in the login script

Variables	What You See Displayed
HOUR	Hour of the day or night (1 to 12)
HOUR24	Hour on a 24-hour clock (00 to 23)
MINUTE	Minutes (00 to 59)
SECOND	Seconds (00 to 59)
AM_PM	A.M. or P.M., depending on day or night
MONTH	Number of the month (01 to 12)
MONTH_NAME	The month's name (January, July, etc.)
DAY	Number of the day (01 to 31)
NDAY_OF_WEEK	Weekday number (1 to 7; Monday is 1)
YEAR	Year in full format (1989, 1990, etc.)

SHORT_YEAR	Year in short format (89, 90, etc.)
DAY_OF_WEEK	Day of the week (ex. Monday, Tuesday)
LOGIN_NAME	The name you log in with
FULL_NAME	Your full name (as defined in SYSCON)
STATION	Workstation number
P_STATION	Physical station number (12 hex digits)
GREETING_TIME	Morning, afternoon, or evening
NEW_MAIL	See if any new mail arrived; you'll see a YES or NO
SHELL_TYPE	Shell type number (0, 26, 4, etc.)
OS	Workstation operating system (for example, MS DOS)
OS_VERSION	Workstation DOS version (for example, 3.3)
MACHINE	Machine type the shell is written for (for example, IBM_PC)
SMACHINE	Short name for the machine type (IBM)
ERROR_LEVEL	No errors equals 0, errors equals any other number
MEMBER OF "group"	Returns TRUE for IF/THEN statements if it is a member of a "group"; otherwise it's false
ACCESS_SERVER	When server is working, displays TRUE; otherwise displays false
<DOS ENVIRONMENT>	The definition of DOS names and strings to pull into the Login script using brackets
PASSWORD_EXPIRES	Displays a number value
NETWORK_ADDRESS	The last eight hex digits of your network address
FILE_SERVER	The name of a file server
USER_ID	The number NetWare assigns you when your name was created

Using the WRITE Variables

To give you an idea of how to use these variables, in this section I have included a few examples of WRITE commands and what they produce. You can write them all on one line—NetWare will break to a new line when necessary. However, lines that are more than 128 characters can produce error messages, and lines that are more than 75 characters can be hard to troubleshoot and read when written to the screen. You'll have to experiment; when you start producing error messages, end a troublesome line with a quotation mark and start another line with the WRITE command and a quotation mark.

You can write variables in two ways: by prefacing them either with a percent sign (%) or with a semicolon (;). You can put all the commands inside the WRITE quotation marks if you put a percent sign in front of the variable and put the variable in uppercase. Try putting the following message into your personal login script. When you make the entry, don't use the <Enter> key at the ends of your lines; let NetWare break the lines for you, or you'll get an error message. Here's an example with the \n supercharacter:

```
WRITE "Good %GREETING_TIME, %FULL_NAME, it's \n %DAY_OF_WEEK,
%MONTH_NAME %DAY, %YEAR \n at %HOUR:%MINUTE:%SECOND %AM_PM."
```

With this entry in your login script, the next time you log in you should see displayed on your screen:

```
Good morning, Ted E. Beara, it's
Monday, August 24, 1992
at 8:47:44 am.
```

Without the \n (new line) supercharacter, the WRITE command will string out the message on one line, and then drop to the next line on its own, as follows.

```
Your machine type is IBM_PC, your OS version is 4.00, and you
are at workstation 0000D800F53E.
```

This was done by entering the following command:

```
WRITE "Your machine type is %MACHINE, your OS is %OS_VERSION,
and you are at workstation %P_STATION."
```

If you don't want to fuss with maximum character lines, you can type:

```
WRITE "Good %GREETING_TIME, %FULL_NAME,"
```

```
WRITE "it's %DAY_OF_WEEK, %MONTH_NAME %DAY, %YEAR"
WRITE "at %HOUR:%MINUTE:%SECOND %AM_PM."
```

This WRITE command will produce:

```
Good morning, Ted E. Beara,
it's Monday, August 24, 1992
at 8:47:44 am.
```

Here's yet another example:

```
WRITE "Your machine type is %MACHINE, your OS is %OS_VERSION,"
WRITE "you are on %FILE_SERVER at address %NETWORK_ADDRESS"
WRITE "your workstation is %P_STATION, and NetWare knows you as
%USER_ID."
```

With this WRITE command, you'll see:

```
Your machine type is IBM_PC, your OS is 4.00,
you are on NTS1 at address 00000002,
your workstation is 00001B308B52, and NetWare knows you as
12005D.
```

You can do the same thing by using the semicolon instead of the percent sign, except that in this case you put the variables in lowercase and place only the text inside quotation marks. The spacing is trickier with the semicolon than with the percent sign; use the semicolon only for small variable strings, if at all. An example follows.

```
WRITE "Good "; greeting_time; ", it's time to water the lawn."
```

With this WRITE command, you'll see this greeting:

```
Good morning, it's time to water the lawn.
```

Choose some of the WRITE variables and experiment with them in your login script. When you experiment, don't be upset if you see an error message or two, they'll tell you when you put in the wrong syntax. (The error messages begin at the point of infraction, so you can use this information to help fix the syntax problem.)

Since the login script ignores line spacing, you can type WRITE <Enter> to give you space between commands in the login script. But remember that the login script scrolls;

you may not see all of your WRITEs if you have too many line spaces. However, you can use the PAUSE command to prevent the login script from scrolling.

IF *conditionals*...**THEN** *command.* The IF/THEN statement is fun to use. It includes all the parameters from the WRITE command as well as a few of its own. IF/THEN statements function by seeing if certain conditions are in place so you can perform a certain task. When the IF condition is met, the THEN command is executed; IF "something" is happening, THEN "perform this action."

In order to find out if a condition is met, you can often equate the condition to something that already exists or is going to happen at a certain time (like a day of the week). For example, you can say "If DAY_OF_WEEK = "WEDNESDAY", then WRITE "Hooray!!"; so if the day is Wednesday, you'll see Hooray!! on your workstation monitor. In NetWare, you can use conditionals like group members or workstation addresses to see if what you are designating actually exists on the server, or you can use days of the week or hours to show a certain time. You'll see how this works a little later on.

You can present the conditional relationships of the IF statement in several ways: equal, not equal, greater than, less than, greater than or equal to, and less than or equal to. NetWare gives you four ways to say something is "equal" and six ways to say something is "not equal." Any way will work fine, but for the sake of familiarity and efficiency, choose one way to work with, at least for a while. The equals/not equals relationships include:

Equals	Not Equals
IS	IS NOT
=	!=
==	<>
	#
EQUALS	DOES NOT EQUAL
	NOT EQUAL TO

There are only two ways to write out the other conditional relationships: Either write it out in all caps, or use the symbol that stands for the conditional.

Conditional Written Out	Conditional Symbol
IS GREATER THAN	>
IS LESS THAN	<

IS GREATER THAN OR EQUAL TO   >=
IS LESS THAN OR EQUAL TO   <=

As examples of some of these conditional statements, here are the IF/THEN statements from the last example:

```
If day_of_week="TUESDAY" and hour24<"14" then begin
write "\7Meeting with marketing at 2:00!"
end
If day_of_week="THURSDAY" and hour24<"10" then begin
write "\7Conference meeting at 10:30. Be there!"
end
If day >= "16" and day <="20" then begin
write "\7Car \"extortion\" due!"
end
```

The first line of the previous example says, "If the day of the week is equal to Tuesday, and the hour is before 2 p.m. (1400 hours), then write the message 'Meeting with marketing at 2:00!' and beep once (\7) when you write this to the screen." If you log in after 2 p.m. on Tuesday, you won't see the message because the time condition wasn't met; if it's any other day of the week, you won't see the message. The BEGIN command allows you to write on more than one line; otherwise, the whole IF/THEN statement has to be on one line. The END command means, "This is the end of the command statement."

The second IF/THEN statement says pretty much the same thing. The third statement says, "If the day of the month is greater than or equal to the 16th, or if it's less than or equal to the 20th, then write Car 'extortion' due! and beep once (\7) when you write this to the screen." The IF conditionals are being mixed with the WRITE variables to give you a statement.

One important note about writing numbers: whenever you refer to a number less than 10, be sure to put a zero (0) before it (except for NDAY_OF_WEEK). For example, write 05 rather than just 5. Otherwise, if you write something like "If day >= "6" and day <="20"," NetWare will interpret this to mean, "If conditional is greater than or equal to 6, but less than or equal to 2, then perform something." In this case, nothing will be performed. But if you say, "If day >= "06" and day <="20"," then your conditional will work fine. You need to compare the same number of digits to the same number of digits.

You can also use the predefined variables explained in the WRITE command; when the IF condition is met, the login script will run the THEN command. For example:

```
if "%P_STATION" == "0000D800E2BA" then begin
    set bfile="sld.rst"
    set bflags=""
    set bbackup="."
    set bpath="Y:\\public\\brief\\macros"
    set bhelp="Y:\\public\\brief\\help"
    set dirstack = "pub\\byte:users\ted"
    set usr="TBeara"
end
```

In this case, if the physical station equals 0000D800E2BA, then login will set up your Brief environment (a command editor, like WordPerfect is a word processing editor). But when you're at a workstation that doesn't have 0000D800E2BA as its physical station number, you'll see your regular login script without the Brief environment. This way, when you go to someone else's workstation, you won't mess up your host's workstation environment, or possibly leave confidential information on that workstation. (Since the login script uses the backslash to mean something, you need to put in two backslashes in your SET command to designate a single slash in the command.)

To set up the DOS environment for DR-DOS, perform the following:

```
IF <OS> <> "DRDOS" THEN BEGIN
    DOS SET OS="%OS"
    DOS SET VER="%OS_VERSION"
END
```

For this example to work, place the following in your AUTOEXEC.BAT file:

```
SET OS=DRDOS
```

As the AUTOEXEC.BAT creates a DOS SET variable of "DRDOS," the IF/THEN statement in the login script checks to see if the workstation's operating system is DRDOS. (You can do the same for MS DOS as well.) The login script then uses DOS SET commands to match the login script's %OS and %OS_VERSION variables. Supervisors can then use these variables to find the correct OS version on the network.

To get a glimpse of how long before your password becomes invalid, type the following command:

```
IF PASSWORD_EXPIRES < VALUE "7" THEN
    WRITE "You have %PASSWORD_EXPIRES days until your password
        expires."
END
```

The %PASSWORD_EXPIRES variable displays how many days before the password's expiration date. The above example begins displaying to the screen when the expiration date is less than seven days.

As you've probably realized by now, you need to experiment a lot to get a full understanding of all you can do with the login script.

Some Information on Command-Line Parameters

Command-line parameters correspond to anything you may have typed after your login name when you log in to the server. You can have as many as nine parameters, and you can use names or key words to designate the parameters you wish to use. Let's look first at what you put in the login script, then we'll talk about what you type in at the login prompt.

You can define up to nine different parameter names to call up different environments in your login script. In the login script, these names use the percent sign for identification and are followed by a number, such as 1, 2, 3, etc. One of these names is already taken up, for the first parameter (%1) is your login name; %2 is whatever name you choose to give it; (the same is true for the other parameters). These names can be the names of directories, abbreviations of programs, or the names of programs themselves. For example, when you want to use the PFIX program, you can use PFIX as the second parameter and then designate the PFIX environment in your login script, which can look like this:

```
If "%2" == "PFIX" then begin
    attach pub/ted
    map ins s1:=pub/byte:users/ted/pfix20
    map s4:=pub/sys:public
end
```

Once you set up these parameters in your login script, it's a simple matter to call them up; just type in the names of the parameters after your username when you log in. For example, to create the PFIX environment, type this statement:

79

```
Login ADMIN/TED PFIX
```

So when you type in your login name (the first parameter) and add the second parameter, PFIX, after your login name, the login script will run this IF statement and set up your login script according to the information found in the THEN command. In this case, you'll attach to server PUB and map two search drives. In the next example, you're not only setting up a search drive through the second parameter, but you're also having that parameter designate the name of the directory you wish to set up in the search drive:

```
IF "%2" = "UTIL" THEN MAP S16:=PUB/BYTE:USERS/TED/%2
```

This example shows that when you log in and add the second parameter UTIL after your login name (LOGIN ADMIN/TED UTIL), the login script will set up a search drive to the UTIL directory. So if you have a UTIL directory at the end of the PUB/BYTE:USERS/TED directory path, NetWare will map the search drive; if no such directory exists, you'll receive an error message. This statement also assumes that server PUB is your default server or that you're already attached to it. You can also combine these two examples by changing this last example into a %3 statement:

```
IF "%3" = "UTIL" THEN MAP S16:=PUB/BYTE:USERS/TED/%3
```

Then when you log in, you can add the second and third parameters, such as LOGIN ADMIN/TED PFIX UTIL at the login prompt. The login script will first run the second command-line parameter, attaching you to server PUB and mapping out two search drives so you can use PFIX. Then the login script will set up a third search drive to the UTIL directory. In this example, the third parameter is based upon the success of the second parameter; the second parameter isn't valid, you won't be able to run %3 because you won't be attached to server PUB.

However, you don't have to set up your parameters so they are dependent on one another. For example, you could put a login parameter like LOGIN ADMIN/TED LOVES GRAPE GRAVY in your AUTOEXEC.BAT file. In this instance, you would only set up a %4 parameter for the GRAVY designation, which could look like:

```
If "%4" == "GRAVY" then begin
    attach pub/ted
    map ins s1:=pub/byte:users/ted/reports
    map s4:=pub/sys:public/utils
end
```

When you run your workstation's AUTOEXEC.BAT file, you'll create your REPORTS environment. Otherwise, when you type in your login name at a different workstation (or even at your own workstation) and you don't want the REPORTS environment, you don't have to include the parameter.

You can also use AND/OR/NOR/ELSE as parameters to extend your IF/THEN statements. For example, to ensure you can invoke a particular program when you use the %2 parameter, type the following:

```
IF "%2" = "c" OR "%2" = "C" THEN BEGIN
    map k:=admin/sys:clipper5
    map s16:=admin/sys:clipper5\bin
    map s16:=admin/sys:clipper5\ng
    map s16:=admin/sys:clipper5\lib
  ELSE
    WRITE "You do not have Clipper loaded for this login."
END
```

In this example, the OR parameter allows you to check for both an uppercase and lower case letter C, which then sets up the Clipper program. If you don't use the "%2" option to set up Clipper, you will see the message telling you that the program isn't loaded.

If you type in command-line parameters and they don't work, first check your syntax. If that doesn't work, try typing in the commands in all capital letters in the login script. Have fun with the IF/THEN and WRITE commands. They can add a lot of variety to what you see when you log in.

INCLUDE *directory path/filename.* The INCLUDE command is different from the DISPLAY command. The DISPLAY command works like DOS's TYPE command—it displays a file's contents on the screen. INCLUDE is a file that contains parts of your login script and can be used as an extension of your login script commands. For example, suppose you wanted to set up a LOTUS environment that you occasionally access. Instead of cluttering up your login script with IF/THEN routines that you occasionally use, you can create a file, such as the NOW file in the TED directory, containing these routines. Then you set up your login script to use the INCLUDE command:

```
IF "%2" = "LOTUS" THEN INCLUDE VOL1:USERS/TED/NOW
```

The line is saying, "Include the NOW file found at the VOL1:USERS/TED/NOW directory path." Then in the NOW file in the TED directory, you can put in:

```
attach pub/ted
map *4:=pub/byte:users/ted/reports
map INS S3:=pub/sys:public/lotus
```

You can create and edit the NOW file with any text editor or word processor (if you use a word processor, be sure to save the file in text format). Now when you log in to your normal default server and you add the parameter LOTUS after your login name (such as LOGIN ADMIN/TED LOTUS), the login script will pick up your parameter designation in the IF...THEN statement, go out to the NOW file, and run the login specifications you have in that file. In this instance, it's attaching to server PUB and mapping two drives: one to the LOTUS directory and one to your REPORTS directory.

You can put INCLUDE commands into the NOW file as well and call up another login script file and execute those parameters. You can do this kind of nesting up to ten levels deep; in other words, your login script file can include another login script file and that file can include another—up to ten times. However, there really isn't a need for this. Since you've pulled this routine out from the login script, it'll be easier to write it out in one file. But the functionality is there, nonetheless.

You can also use INCLUDE to perform tasks similar to tasks you can perform with the (F)DISPLAY command. However, you need to keep consistent with the login script format. So if you're going to just put in messages to yourself or to a group, it would be easier to use (F)DISPLAY.

When you finish changing your login script, press <Esc>. You will see the "Save Changes Yes/No" window with the "Yes" option highlighted. If you want to save your changes, press <Enter>; if you don't, highlight the "No" option and press <Enter>. Either way, you'll return to the "User Information" window.

Changing Your Password

You can change your password through the "Change Password" option in SYSCON, or you can use the SETPASS command at the network prompt. (See the "SETPASS" subheading in Chapter 3.) To change your password in SYSCON while you're at the network prompt, type SYSCON <Enter>, select the "User Information" option <Enter> at the "Available Topics" window, then select your login name from the "User Names" window and press <Enter>. Next, select the "Change Password" option at the "User

Information" window and press <Enter>. You'll see a small window at the bottom of the screen that says, "Enter Old Password:"

```
Enter Old Password:
```

Figure 2-8. When you choose the "Change Password" option, you'll need to fill out the Old Password and New Password screens

Type in your old password and press <Enter>. Next, the screen will say, "Enter New Password," to which you type in your new password and press <Enter>. You'll then be prompted to retype your new password. Re-enter the new password and press <Enter>, and you'll return to the "Change Password" option.

Because of your particular security scheme, you may need your password to be a certain length. (NetWare's default is five characters long.) If you don't make your password long enough, you'll see a screen that says, "The new password is not long enough. Press ESCAPE to continue." When you press <Esc>, you'll return to the "Change Password" option without any changes having been made. NetWare remembers your last eight passwords; if you type in a password you've used before, you'll see, "The new password is a duplicate of a previously used password. Press ESCAPE to continue."

To see how your password restrictions are set up, press <Esc> at the password error and choose the "Account Restrictions" option at the "User Information" window. There you'll be able to see if you're required to have a password and what length that password is supposed to be. You can also see if you're required to have a unique password. (You can find a more complete description of account restrictions under the "Information You Can See About Yourself and Others" heading in the discussion of the SYSCON utility later in this chapter.) If you've checked your "Account Restrictions" option and you're still having problems changing your password, ask your supervisor, or workgroup or account manager for assistance. With this information in mind, change your password.

With NetWare 2.1 and above, supervisors can no longer see your password. If you forget your password, the supervisor will have to give you another so you can log in. You can then change your password again so that even your supervisor won't know what it is. To exit the "User Information" window, press <Esc>; to exit SYSCON, press <Alt>-<F10>. You'll see the "Exit SYSCON Yes/No" window with the "Yes" option highlighted. Press <Enter> to return to the network prompt.

One other point: Sometimes, after you've changed your password in SYSCON, the next time you log in NetWare will tell you that your password has expired and that you need to change it again. Then, when you use up your "grace logins," you'll need to change your password once again. If you have the same login name on multiple file servers and you are using SETPASS, NetWare will ask if you wish to synchronize those passwords to reflect this password change. If you choose "Yes," all servers you log in to will now reflect the password change, making your life a little easier. This synchronization aspect is probably why you're asked to change passwords again in the first place. NetWare sees that your passwords are not synchronized and has you rectify the situation.

What Users Can Do in SYSCON—Looking Around

In SYSCON, you can see how the server environment is set up. This information can help you figure out what you can and can't do on the server. In SYSCON, the "Available Topics" window gives you a list of options:

➤ Accounting

➤ Change Current File Server

➤ File Server Information

➤ Group Information

➤ Supervisor Options

➤ User Information

Each option gives you valuable information about your server. The "Accounting" option shows how the server charges for its resources. (We'll save the "Change Current Server" option until last; you need to look around your present server before jumping all over the network.) The "File Server Information" option allows you to look at basic information about your server or any server on the internet. Selecting the "Group Information" option will show you which groups are available, the names of those groups, and the member list for each group. The "Supervisor Options" can be accessed only by someone with supervisory rights or supervisor equivalence; however, since it's important for you to know which restrictions the supervisor can set up, we'll take a look at those functions. The "User Information" option provides information about the users on the server.

Let's look at each option on the "Available Topics" window.

Accounting

You'll see the accounting information only if your supervisor has set up the server to take advantage of the accounting feature. If you choose the "Accounting" option from the

"Available Topics" window and you see "Accounting not installed on file server *servername*" on your screen, go to the next option.

Accounting allows a server to track and, if necessary, charge for the services that it offers. Suppose, for example, that Ted is using a lot of disk space on server COMM. Since ADMIN is actually Ted's default server, server COMM's supervisor may be annoyed by the number of megabytes Ted is taking up on COMM. Instead of simply limiting Ted's disk space or disabling Ted's account, COMM's supervisor charges Ted for his disk storage space. When Ted gets the bill, he'll work harder to keep his disk space down.

To look at the accounting restrictions, select the "Accounting" option at the "Available Topics" window. You'll see an "Accounting" window displaying the following options: Accounting Servers, Blocks Read Charge Rates, Blocks Written Charge Rates, Connect Time Charge Rates, Disk Storage Charge Rates, and Service Requests Charge Rates.

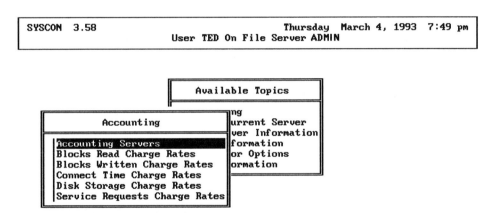

Figure 2-9. The initial Accounting screen

The "Accounting Servers" option displays the names of all servers that have charge accounts for their services. Only those servers named in the screen can charge for their services. Supervisors can insert the names of other servers into the "Accounting Servers" window, signifying that those servers can now charge for their services as well. Figure 2-10 shows an example of the "Accounting Servers" window.

85

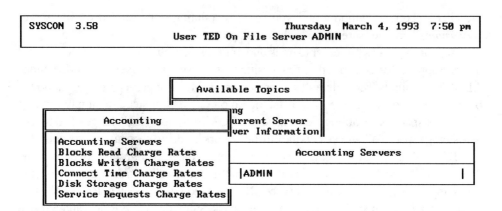

Figure 2-10. Choosing an Accounting Server

After seeing which servers are authorized to charge for their services, press <Esc> and choose one of the rate options to get a feel for how this is set up. For example, select "Connect Time Charge Rate" and press <Enter>. You'll see a screen similar to the one in Figure 2-11.

As you can see, you can be charged for just about anything. The screen shows how much you can be charged for your connection to COMM. The right side of the screen shows the time and the day, as well as the rate defined for each entry. This example has Rate 2 from 8 a.m. to 12 p.m. for Monday through Friday and Rate 1 for all other hours and days. The "Rate" entry shows the different types of rates a supervisor can set up; the "Charge" entry shows the ratio that can be charged at each of the rates.

The charge ratio becomes any number the supervisor needs it to be in order to cover network costs. If connection time is worth ten cents per minute, for example, the system supervisor sets up a ratio to determine the overall charge. The supervisor multiplies the charge by the number of minutes of connection time, then divides that number by the second part of the equation to determine what you owe. For example, if your account balance shows that you connected to server COMM for 500 minutes and you have a 1/10 charge ratio, you owe $50.00 (500 min/$0.10 per minute) for your connection time.

Each rate option has a similar screen, and they all work the same way. Take a look in each of them by pressing <Esc>, then highlighting the next option and pressing <Enter>. To get out of the rate options, press <Esc> until you reach the "Available Topics" window.

```
┌─────────────────────────────────────────────────────────────────────────┐
│ SYSCON  3.58                          Thursday  March 4, 1993  7:55 pm    │
│                     User TED On File Server ADMIN                         │
├─────────────────────────────────────────────────────────────────────────┤
│                                          Sun  Mon  Tue  Wed  Thu  Fri  Sat│
│        Connect Time Charge Rates    8:00am   1    2    2    2    2    2    1│
│                                     8:30am   1    2    2    2    2    2    1│
│                                     9:00am   1    2    2    2    2    2    1│
│                                     9:30am   1    2    2    2    2    2    1│
│                                    10:00am   1    2    2    2    2    2    1│
│                                    10:30am   1    2    2    2    2    2    1│
│  Rate   Charge      Rate   Charge  11:00am   1    2    2    2    2    2    1│
│   1   No Charge     11              11:30am   1    2    2    2    2    2    1│
│   2   1/10          12              12:00pm   1    2    2    2    2    2    1│
│   3                 13              12:30pm   1    2    2    2    2    2    1│
│   4                 14               1:00pm   1    1    1    1    1    1    1│
│   5                 15               1:30pm   1    1    1    1    1    1    1│
│   6                 16               2:00pm   1    1    1    1    1    1    1│
│   7                 17               2:30pm   1    1    1    1    1    1    1│
│   8                 18               3:00pm   1    1    1    1    1    1    1│
│   9                 19               3:30pm   1    1    1    1    1    1    1│
│  10                 20               4:00pm   1    1    1    1    1    1    1│
│          (Charge is per minute)      4:30pm   1    1    1    1    1    1    1│
└─────────────────────────────────────────────────────────────────────────┘
```

Figure 2-11. Looking at charge rates for connect time

Looking at Your Server Information

(The next option under SYSCON's "Available Topics" window is actually "Change Current Server". But we've deferred discussion of that option until later in this chapter so you can see everything that your default server has to offer first. Right now, we'll move on to the next option after "Change Current Server"—"File Server Information.")

The "File Server Information" option on the "Available Topics" window gives you such information as which NetWare version and operating system (OS) revision you're running, the date of the operating system revision, and the level of System Fault Tolerance (SFT) software the server is running, as well as the transaction tracking information you have available. You can also see information on the number of connections this version of NetWare supports and which of those connections are currently in use, the number of volumes version 3.11 supports, and the network and node address of the network interface board servicing your connection in the server.

Select the "File Server Information" option from the "Available Topics" window. You'll see another window listing the names of all the NetWare servers on your company's internetwork.

```
SYSCON  3.58                           Thursday  March 4, 1993  7:56 pm
                        User TED On File Server ADMIN
```

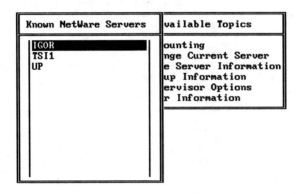

```
┌─────────────────────────┬──────────────────────┐
│ Known NetWare Servers   │ vailable Topics      │
├─────────────────────────┼──────────────────────┤
│ IGOR                    │ ounting              │
│ TSI1                    │ nge Current Server   │
│ UP                      │ e Server Information │
│                         │ up Information       │
│                         │ ervisor Options      │
│                         │ r Information        │
│                         └──────────────────────┘
│                         │
│                         │
│                         │
│                         │
└─────────────────────────┘
```

Figure 2-12. Looking at the available file servers

To see all the servernames in the "Known NetWare Servers" window, press <Ctrl>-<PgDn> to go to the bottom of the listing, or <Ctrl>-<PgUp> to go to the top of the listing. To move a screenful at a time, press <PgDn> to go down a screenful, or <PgUp> to move up a screenful. To highlight the name of your server, begin typing your server's name until the correct servername is highlighted and press <Enter>. (The name of the server you're presently in is displayed in the second line of SYSCON's top screen.) To see your server information, press <Enter> and you'll see a screen like the following one.

The first line shows your servername. The second line tells you which version of NetWare this server is running. NTS1 is not running Transaction Tracking Service, or TTS. How the server is being used will reflect the level of SFT and TTS you see.

"OS Revision Number" displays the date of the operating system version. "Connections Supported" shows the maximum connections that this version of software can have active at one time (250 connections in this case). The next entry, "Connections In Use," shows how many (6) of those connections are currently being used.

"Volumes Supported" shows that this version of the software can have up to 64 volumes on your server. To see how many volumes you have, you'll need to go into the VOLINFO utility. The last two entries, "Network Address" and "Node Address," give you this server's network and node addresses for the LAN A network interface card. Since file servers can have up to four network interface cards, with each card having a different LAN letter name (A, B, C, and D), all you see is LAN A's network and node address.

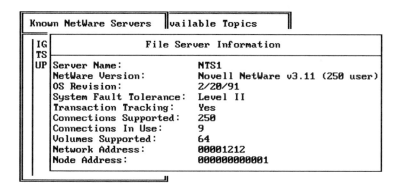

Figure 2-13. Looking at file server information

If you are supervisor or equivalent, you'll see two additions—Serial Number and Application Number. The Serial Number shows the number for the NetWare operating system, while the Application Number entry shows the numbers for certain applications that have been written specifically to display numbers in this entry (which presently aren't many).

There's not a whole lot you can do with this information; however, now you know which version of NetWare your file server is running. To return to the "Available Topics" window, press <Esc> twice.

Group Information

The next option displayed on the "Available Topics" window is "Group Information." Supervisors and workgroup managers use this option to create groups, add users, and give those groups trustee assignments in directories on the network. Users access this option to see the groups that have been created on their servers, the full names of the groups, and the members of those groups. The "Group Information" option also shows you your trustee rights for the groups you belong to and indicates which directories those rights affect.

Select the "Group Information" option from the "Available Topics" window. You'll see a window listing all the groups that have been defined on the server.

89

Place the selector bar on one of the group names and press <Enter>. You'll see a "Group Information" window. If you're a member of the group, you'll see four entries: "Full Name," "Member List," "Other Information," and "Trustee Assignments." However, if you're not a part of the group, the "Group Information" window will display only two options: "Full Name" and "Member List." You can see which groups you belong to through the "Groups Belonged To" option in the "User Information" window in SYSCON, or you can type WHOAMI/G at the network prompt when you're not in a menu utility.

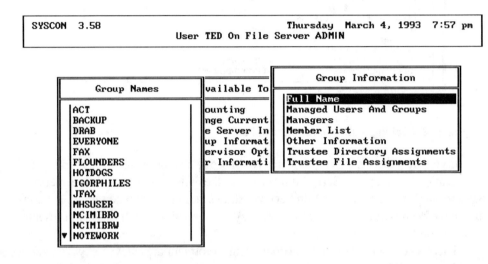

Figure 2-14. The Group Information's initial screen

The "Full Name" option is the full name of the group. If the group name hasn't been fully defined, you'll see a screen saying, "No full name specified. Press ESCAPE to continue." Supervisors can set up users as well as groups to assist in server management. If the group that you highlight is one of those groups, you'll see which users or groups are being managed. If, on the other hand, the group is being managed by another user or group, you can highlight the "Managers" option to see who it is. For more on workgroup and account managers, turn to the "When Users Manage" heading at the end of Chapter 1 and Appendix D..

The "Member List" option displays the names of all members of this group; from this option, supervisors and workgroup managers can add or delete you as a user of a group. The "Other Information" option shows you the group ID number; you'll see a little screen down at the bottom that says something like, "Group ID: 078D0295," which is the identification number by which the bindery knows the group. The "Trustee Directory Assignments" option shows you in which directories this group has been given assignments. The "Trustee File Assignments" option shows you which files have been given specific attribute assignments to the group. This display is the only place where you can directly see which trustee assignments you have through this group. Press <Esc> until you return to the "Available Topics" window.

Looking at What Supervisors Can Do for You

Although this is a user's guide, it's important for you to know what options are available to your supervisor; the network setup directly affects what you can do. So let's look briefly at the "Supervisor Options" selection at the "Available Topics" window. If you aren't interested in looking at the supervisor options, skip to the last option in SYSCON, "User Information."

If you have supervisor equivalency, you can select "Supervisor Options"; otherwise you'll see a window which says, "No supervisor privileges on file server ADMIN (*servername*)."

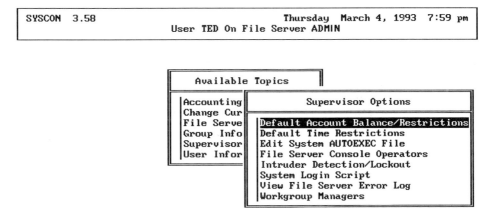

Figure 2-15. Available supervisor options

Supervisors have eight options that directly affect what you can and can't do on the network. These options include: "Default Account Balance/Restrictions," "Default Time Restrictions," "Edit System AUTOEXEC File," "File Server Console Operators," "Intruder Detection/Lockout," "System Login Script," "View File Server Error Log," and "Workgroup Managers."

Default Account Balance/Restrictions. With this option, the supervisor sets up blanket restrictions for all network users added after the defaults were set up. These restrictions include expiration dates on accounts, the number of times you can be logged in, password restrictions, and how much credit you have for accounting purposes. If you need your personal account modified, your supervisor can do so by changing your account restrictions or balance through the "User Information" option. The supervisor can also set up unlimited credit for new users through the Allow Unlimited Credit entry. Through the Low Balance Limit entry, supervisors can adjust how much credit new users can have before they lose the services they are being charged for.

Default Time Restrictions. This alternative shows the time of day when network users (who were added after the defaults were set up) can log in to the server. Those times marked with an asterisk on the matrix are the times you can log in. If you need access to a server at different times, your supervisor can change your time access in your personal time restriction option under your "User Information" window.

Edit System AUTOEXEC File. This option allows supervisors to enter console commands into the AUTOEXEC.SYS file that will be executed every time the file server is brought up. Console commands are commands that supervisors run at the server console so they can see how the server is running. These commands can also assign print queues for the network printers. Instead of having to tell the server which printer is attached to which queue every time the server comes up, the supervisor can place those commands in this file to be automatically executed.

File Server Console Operators. This feature allows supervisors to give certain users added access to server information by making them file server console operators. If certain users need access to server information for maintenance purposes, but the supervisor doesn't want these users to be supervisor equivalent, the supervisor can make these users *console operators*. This means these users can run the FCONSOLE utility, which contains pertinent information on how the file server is running. That is the added privilege they receive.

Intruder Detection/Lockout. With this option, supervisors can prevent potential intruders from trying to guess their way into the system by locking that workstation for a specified time. The specifics include setting up how many times a person can try to guess a login password and how many days, hours, and minutes must pass before the account becomes active again.

System Login Script. This alternative is used by the supervisor to set up directory and application paths for the entire server. These drive mappings can then be used by everyone who accesses the network, or the supervisor can set them up for specific groups of users instead. Supervisors can also use the system login script to make default system settings that will affect everyone who logs into the server. I've covered login script capabilities in detail under the "Setting Up Your Login Script" heading earlier in this chapter.

View File Server Error Log. This is the next option in the "Supervisor Options" window. When supervisors press <Enter>, NetWare reads from a file all the errors that have been logged since the last time the supervisor cleared out the error log messages. These messages are also shown at the file server console.

Workgroup Managers. This option allows supervisors to add or remove users or groups from the designation of workgroup manager. Once you've been granted this title and given proper directory rights to a volume, you can then govern the users and groups assigned to you as well as those you create.

Perhaps this gives you a better idea as to what your supervisor can do to keep your system running smoothly.

Information You Can See about Yourself and Others

The "User Information" option in SYSCON's "Available Topics" window is probably the best place to get information on what you can and can't do on the network. At the "Available Topics" window, select the "User Information" option, press <Enter>, then select your login name from the "User Names" window and press <Enter>. You'll see a screen like the one shown in Figure 2-16:

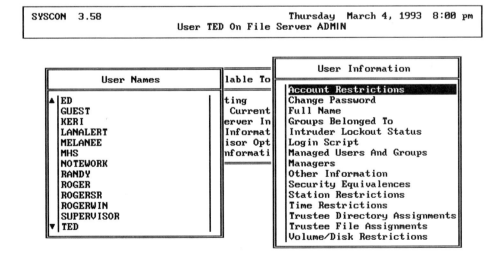

Figure 2-16. The User Information screen contains most of what you do in SYSCON

The "User Information" window contains most of your functionality in SYSCON. From this window you created your login script and changed your password. You can also choose another user's name from the "User Names" window; however, unless you have supervisor equivalence, the information you can see is limited to that user's full name and the groups he or she belongs to.

The first option from the "User Information" window is the "Account Balance" option. (You'll see this option only if the accounting feature is installed on your server. Otherwise, your first option will be "Account Restrictions.")

```
┌─────────────────────────────────────────────┐
│                                             │
│      Account Balance For User TED           │
│                                             │
├─────────────────────────────────────────────┤
│ Account Balance:          ▌421▐             │
│ Allow Unlimited Credit:    No               │
│    Low Balance Limit:      5                │
│                                             │
└─────────────────────────────────────────────┘
```

Figure 2-17. To see your account balance, select the Account Balance option

If you recall, your supervisor can set up restrictions on which services you can access from those servers that charge for their services. Here, you see what those restrictions are. The "Account Balance" option shows your account balance, whether or not you have unlimited credit, and what your low balance limit is. In this example, Ted has an account balance of 421 from the 500 credits that the supervisor set up in the "Default Account Balance/Restrictions" option. Each time Ted uses a service on this server and is charged for that service, his account balance decreases. If Ted needs a bigger balance, he will have to negotiate for it. The supervisor can then change Ted's account balance in the "User Information" screen.

If Ted were allowed all the credit in the world on this server, the "Allow Unlimited Credit" entry would say "Yes." The "Low Balance Limit" entry shows Ted's cutoff point; when Ted reaches 5, he will no longer be able to receive any charged services. This number could also be a negative number, meaning that Ted is allowed to go "in the hole" before his services are revoked.

Next on the "User Information" window is the "Account Restrictions" option. This option shows many restrictions that your supervisor can place on your account. If you'll recall, I briefly discussed the "Account Restrictions" option in the Introduction. Select the "Account Restrictions" option and press <Enter>. You'll see a screen like following one:

```
SYSCON  3.58                        Thursday  March 4, 1993  8:01 pm
                      User TED On File Server ADMIN
```

```
                   ┌──────────────────────────────────────────┐
                   │       Account Restrictions For User TED   │
    ┌──────────────┤Account Disabled:            ▓No▓          │
  ▲ │ED            │Account Has Expiration Date:   Yes         │
    │GUES          │   Date Account Expires:       September 17, 1993
    │KERI          │Limit Concurrent Connections:  Yes         │
    │LANA          │   Maximum Connections:        2           │s
    │MELA          │Allow User To Change Password: Yes         │
    │MHS           │Require Password:              Yes         │ps
    │NOTE          │   Minimum Password Length:    5           │
    │RAND          │Force Periodic Password Changes: Yes       │
    │ROGE          │   Days Between Forced Changes: 30          │
    │ROGE          │   Date Password Expires:      August 1, 1993
    │ROGE          │   Limit Grace Logins:         Yes         │
    │SUPE          │      Grace Logins Allowed:    6           │gnments
  ▼ │TED           │      Remaining Grace Logins:  6           │ts
    └──────────────┤Require Unique Passwords:      Yes         │ns
                   └──────────────────────────────────────────┘
```

Figure 2-18. The Account Restrictions screen contains many security parameters that help build your security framework

If you were Ted, here is what the previous example would mean to you.

Account Disabled. Through the "Account Restrictions" option, your supervisor can disable your account entirely. That means you can't log in, as if you had never been created on the network. This feature is useful for the supervisor, because once you've been created on the network, even when you've been disabled, you can easily be reenabled; the supervisor won't have to set everything up for you from scratch.

Account Has Expiration Date and **Date Account Expires.** Your account can also be given an expiration date, which means you won't be able to log in after the date specified in the "Date Account Expires" entry. This feature is extremely handy in managing college and educational environments where class turnaround can reach gigantic proportions.

Limit Concurrent Connections and **Maximum Connections.** Your supervisor can limit the number of workstations you can have logged in to the network. In our example, you're limited to having only two different machines logged in at the same time.

Allow User to Change Password. Your supervisor can allow you to change your password, or instead, set the "Allow User To Change Password" entry to "No," in which case the supervisor will have to change your password and then tell you what your new password is. In addition, you won't be able to edit your login script. For the most part, the "Change Password" entry was designed for people who share the same account together; that way, one person can't change the password or login script on the other users of the account.

Require Password *through* **Remaining Grace Logins.** These eight entries are interrelated. Designating "Yes" at the "Require Password" entry requires you to have a password of a certain length. While this entry defaults to five characters, the supervisor can set this entry anywhere from one to twenty characters in length, so hope you have a merciful supervisor. The "Force Periodic Password Changes" entry gives the super-visor the option of having you change your password every certain number of days; NetWare will prompt you when it's time to change your password.

You can be given a limited number of "grace" logins in connection with the "Force Periodic Password" changes. When the "Limit Grace Logins" entry is set to "Yes" and your password has expired, you'll be able to log in without changing your password for only the number of times that appears in the "Grace Logins Allowed" entry. In our example, you have a grace login of 5, which means that after your password has expired, you'll have to change your password during one of the next five times you log in or you won't be able to log in at all. Then you'll need to have the supervisor change your password.

Require Unique Passwords. "Require Unique Passwords" means that NetWare will remember your last few passwords and will require you to use a different password. This is for security reasons, so it's for your own good.

Change Password. This option is explained fully under the subheading "Changing Your Password" covered earlier in this chapter.

Full Name. This option displays the user's full name as defined by the supervisor. You can see this information on any other user you select from the "User Names" window. If your supervisor has entered your full name and you select the "Full Name" option, you'll see a screen like this one:

```
Full Name:  Ted E. Beara_
```

Figure 2-19. Where to see your full name on this server

The "Full Name" window will appear in the lower-right corner of your screen and gives your full name as your supervisor has written it. If it's spelled incorrectly, have your supervisor type it in correctly.

Groups Belonged To. This option displays the names of all the groups of which you are currently a member. Your supervisor or workgroup manager can use this option to make you a part of other groups as well. Other group tasks, such as making group trustee assignments, are performed at the "Group Information" option in the "Available Topics" window.

Select the "Groups Belonged To" option. You'll see a screen like the one shown in Figure 2-20.

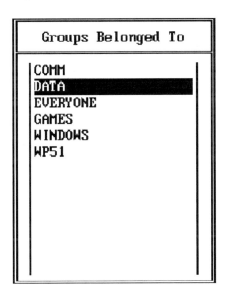

Figure 2-20. Select the Groups Belonged To option to see which groups you are a part of

This example shows that Ted belongs to a number of groups, including group EVERYONE and group WP51. Being a part of a group gives you the group's trustee assignments and therefore the group's security equivalences. You can see a group's trustee assignments by pressing <Esc> three times, then highlighting the "Group Information" option on the "Available Topics" window, pressing <Enter>, choosing one of the groups that appear on your "Groups Belonged To" window, and choosing the "Trustee Directory Assignments" or the "Trustee File Assignments" option. To exit the "Groups Belonged To" window, press <Esc>.

Intruder Lockout Status. If someone were logging into the network using your user name, the system supervisor or workgroup manager could go into this option under you name and see your lockout status. The first entry, Account Locked, shows if it is presently locked. Supervisor or workgroup managers could then change the entry to "No" to let you try to log back in to the server.

Incorrect Login Count. This shows how many times you, (if you forget your password), or intruders have tried guessing your password before the account locks. You will see zero in this entry when you log in correctly or when the entry reaches the time specified in the Account Reset Time.

Account Reset Time. This is normally blank unless your account has reached its incorrect login count threshold; in which case, the Account Reset Time entry shows you how long of a lockout period has been designated. The next entry, Time Until Reset, shows how much longer this account will remain locked unless the supervisor or workgroup manager resets the Account Locked entry to No.

Last Intruder Address. This entry shows you from which workstation address the "intruder" was using to attempt logging in. If you forgot your password, the network and node address will be your own workstation's. If you type in your password wrong but eventually log in, you'll see the workstation's address display because you typed in an incorrect password at least once. To leave the "Intruder Lockout Status" option, press <Esc>.

Login Script. This is the next option on the "User Information" window. I discussed the login script extensively earlier in this chapter.

Managed Users and Groups. If you have been duly dubbed a workgroup manager, you can select this option and see those users and groups that have been assigned to you or have been created by you. From the "User Information" window, you can set up or modify those user's account balance and restrictions, change their passwords, give them a full name, and make them part of the groups that you have assigned to you or that you create. You can also create or modify those users' login scripts, add certain security equivalences (within your user/group arena), add station and time restrictions, and give trustee directory and file assignments. This effectively makes you a miniature supervisor to assist in user management.

Managers. If you have been assigned to a workgroup or to an account manager, you can see who they are by selecting this option.

Other Information. This option shows you some basic information about you as a user—the last time you logged in, whether or not you're a console operator, how much disk space you're currently using, and your user ID (how you're known to the bindery). If you're in the "User Information" window and you want to select the "Other Information" option, type the letter O on the keyboard and press <Enter>. Figure 2-21 shows an abbreviated version of the window you'll see:

```
Last Login:                       August 13, 1992  1:36:44 am
File Server Console Operator:     No
Disk Space In Use:                     72 KBytes
User ID:                          2B000007
```

Figure 2-21. The Other Information option shows basic statistics about you as a user

This window appears at the bottom-right of your screen. If your supervisor has designated the amount of disk space you can have, you'll see your maximum disk space (in kilobytes) listed as well.

Security Equivalences. This is the next option on the "User Information" window. Security equivalences are the rights you receive when you're made equivalent to other users or groups. For example, you can be made supervisor equivalent, and therefore have rights to everything on the server. Select the "Security Equivalences" option, and you'll see a screen like this one:

```
              Security Equivalences

   COMM                    (Group)
   DATA                    (Group)
   ED                      (User)
   EVERYONE                (Group)
   GAMES                   (Group)
   SUPERVISOR              (User)
   WINDOWS                 (Group)
   WP51                    (Group)
```

Figure 2-22. To see whose security you are equivalent to, select the Security Equivalences option

When a supervisor adds you to a group, you're considered equivalent to that group in security, which means you have the same trustee privileges as the group does. (To see what your group trustee assignments are, find out which groups you are a part of by selecting the Groups Belonged To option. Select the Group Information option from SYSCON's main screen, one of the group's names that you belong to, and then the Trustee Directory Assignments option.) In our example, Ted is equivalent to a number of groups, including EVERYONE and WP51. You can be made equivalent to another user, giving you that person's trustee assignments. You can also be made equivalent to the supervisor, which means you have all rights to every volume on the server. It also means you have responsibilities to other users—don't abuse your privileges.

A little information on inherited rights, directory paths, and security equivalences: Sometimes you'll type RIGHTS at the command line and see all sorts of rights in a directory you know you don't have access to through your individual trustee assignments. Let's say that your directory path is DEPT\PR\REPORTS and you have Read and File Scan rights as your trustee assignment to subdirectory REPORTS. Let's also say that you belong to a group called PR that has the rights RWCEMFA to directory DEPT. Let's also say that no directory or file rights have been taken away, (all directory assignments are still intact).

When you type RIGHTS at the subdirectory REPORTS command line, you'll see that you have the effective rights RWCEMFA to subdirectory REPORTS. This is because groups are viewed as a security equivalence, which means that you have all the rights of the group itself. This also means that you have all the group's trustee assignments for the directory in which they were defined as well as through the subdirectories beneath. This is true until you reach a level where the supervisor has given a different trustee assignment to the group or defined a different directory- inherited rights mask. In that case, you will only have the rights granted to all subdirectories that were granted at the directory level.

When NetWare figures your effective rights for subdirectory REPORTS, it looks at the directory's inherited rights mask. If you want to experiment, type WHOAMI/A at the network prompt; you'll see the name you've been defined as, your security equivalences, the groups you're a member of, and the trustee assignments for the directories you have rights to.

So your effective rights are determined by your trustee assignments, your group trustee assignments, and the trustee assignments of whoever you are made security equivalent to minus the rights taken away by the directory and file inherited rights mask. If you're supervisor-equivalent or have been given supervisory directory assignment at a volume level, you'll have all rights to all directories at the volume level and beneath the volume level, even if you have trustee assignments to directories that are flagged otherwise.

Station Restriction. Through this option, your supervisor or workgroup manager can limit the number of workstations you can log in from by entering your workstation's network address. To see if your workstation has such a restriction, go to the "User Information" window and select the "Station Restriction" option.

Figure 2-23. Select this option to see if this restriction is being enforced on you

As you can see by the screen, Ted has one station restriction. This entry means Ted can log in to a particular network address (the first part of the screen) and a node address, which is his own personal workstation. If you don't have any station restrictions and you select this option, you'll see, "User Ted has no station restrictions. <Press Escape to continue>," or you may see the "Allowed Login Addresses" window with nothing in it. This means you can log in to the file server from anywhere on the internetwork. If you're curious as to what other addresses look like, type USERLIST/A <Enter> at the network prompt. The /A parameter on the USERLIST utility calls up the network and node addresses for all the users currently logged in to the server. Your own login name will have an asterisk by it.

Time Restrictions. Select this option from the "User Information" window. You ill see a table such as this one:

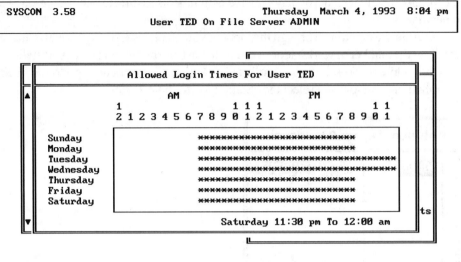

Figure 2-24. You can check to see if there is any time you won't be allowed to access this server

The preceding figure shows the restrictions that the supervisor set up in the "Default Time Restrictions" option in the "Supervisor Options" window. But if you work later than 8 p.m. on Tuesday and Wednesday, ask your supervisor to extend your personal time restrictions on those days—for the sake of the example in the above figure, let's say to 11 p.m.

Each asterisk stands for a half-hour time allotment. If you happen to work late on another day, at the designated restriction time you'll receive a message saying, "Connection time has expired. Please log out." Then at five minutes after your logout time, you'll see a message saying, "ADMIN connection terminating in 1 minute." If you don't respond to that message, you'll see the message, "Network error on Server ADMIN: Connection no longer valid. Abort, Retry?" and your connection to the file server will be terminated.

Be warned—this is not a gentle process! If you're in a program that doesn't save your data to a backup file, you'll lose data. What's more, you won't be able to press "Retry" to regain your connection, and when you press "Abort," you'll be left at a LOGIN prompt. If you try to log in during a time restriction, you'll see:

Attempting to login during an unauthorized time period. The
supervisor has limited the times that you can login to this
server.
Access to server denied and you have been logged out. You are
attached to server NTS1.

If you're attached to more than one server and you're in a directory on the server that
has logged you out, you'll see a message that says, "Current drive no longer valid," and
you'll have to go to a drive mapping on one of the other servers you're attached to. Know
your time restrictions; if you're working beyond those restrictions regularly, talk to your
supervisor about extending your personal time restrictions. To exit the "Time Restrictions" option, press <Esc>.

Trustee Directory Assignments. Trustee and group assignments are the second
level of security that NetWare provides. (A login password is the first.) *Trustee
assignments* are the rights given to your network name along with the directories that you
can access. These assignments affect not only the directory they're assigned to, but all
the subdirectories beneath it, or until you reach a subdirectory level where you've been
given a different directory assignment.

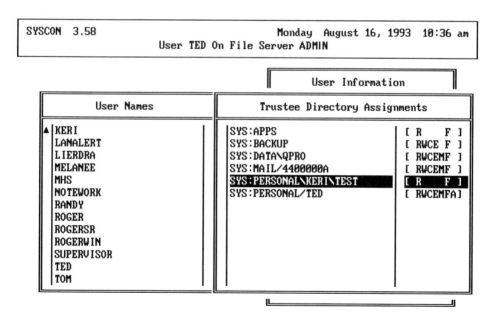

Figure 2-25. This option shows the directories you have personally assigned to you

Trustee assignments contain the basic security rights; these rights affect you and the groups you belong to, as well as the directories and files you wish to access. Suppose again that you are Ted, and that the previous figure is your screen. You have all but Supervisor rights to your home directory, located at the directory path BYTE:USERS\TED. You also have been given Read and File Scan rights to the TEST subdirectory under USERS\KERI. This means the supervisor gave you a trustee assignment to the subdirectory TEST and if there are any subdirectories beneath TEST, those rights will apply to them as well.

The next two entries in the "Trustee Directory Assignments" window show that you have all rights except Supervisory and Access Control to directories DATA\QPRO and 28000007, which means you won't be able to manipulate the directory rights mask and control other people's access to those directories and the directories below them.

From the "Trustee Directory Assignments" option, you can't see how a direc-tory's rights mask is set up, so you can't tell what your effective rights will eventually be in a directory. Again, you can find out your effective rights through the NDIR utility discussed under the "Directory and File Management Utilities" heading in Chapter 5, the RIGHTS utility covered under the "Directory and File Security Utilities" heading also in Chapter 5, the FILER utility covered under "The FILER Utility" section in this chapter, or the WHOAMI utility with the /A parameter discussed under the "User Identification Utilities" heading again in Chapter 5.

Trustee File Assignments. This option shows you to which files you have been given specific file assignments. For example, user Ted has two file assignments given him in the DATA\QPRO directory: BRKEVEN.WQ1 and GROWTH.WQ1. For the BRKEVEN.WQ1 file, Ted has Read and File Scan rights only, which means he can't modify the data in the file but can look at that data.

No matter what his other trustee and directory assignments have been, Ted has Read and File Scan rights to the file. However, Ted must have at least Read and File Scan rights as a directory assignment in order to find this file in the first place. For the GROWTH.WQ1 file, Ted has Read, Write, Erase, Modify, and File Scan rights, which allow him to modify this file.

If you are a workgroup manager or supervisor equivalent, you can grant users trustee file assignments by highlighting their name in the "User Names" option, selecting the "Trustee File Assignments" option, and pressing <Ins>. You can then type in the directory path along with the filename. If you don't know the directory path, press the Insert key again, and work your way through the volume and directory selections presented to you. To do this, highlight the proper volume and directory using the up/down arrow keys, and press <Enter>.

Once you have selected the proper directory, press <Esc> then <Enter>. You will see the "Enter a file for editing trustees, or press <Insert> for a list of files" window in the upper part of the screen. Here you can type in the filename or press Insert to see which files are available in a window just below the "Enter the file" window.

When you have selected or typed in the filename, press <Enter> to place the file in the "Trustee File Assignments" window and give it RF rights. To modify the rights, press <Enter> then Insert to bring up the "Trustee Rights Not Granted" window. There you can highlight the rights through the F5 key and press <Enter> to add the rights to the "Trustee Rights Granted" window.

Press <Esc> to return to the "Trustee File Assignments" window, press <Esc> again to return to the "User Information" window.

Volume/Disk Restrictions. The Volume entry refers to NetWare 3.x and the Disk entry refers to NetWare 2.2.

Selecting the "Volume/Disk" option shows you a "Select A Volume" window with the server's volumes listed. Selecting a volume and press <Enter> brings you to a "User Volume/Disk Restrictions" window with three entries. The Limit Volume Space? entry shows you whether or not you have been given a restriction. If the entry says Yes, you will see how many disk blocks in Kilobytes you are allowed. If the entry says No, you will see zero in the Volume Space Limit entry.

The Volume Space Limit: entry shows you how many Kilobytes you have been allotted on the volume selected. The Volume Space In Use entry shows you how much of your volume space you already have in use. You can subtract the space in use from the space limit to see how much disk space you have left.

If you run out of space on this volume, you can either delete or back up to floppy disks some of your least used data, negotiate for more disk space, or move data to a volume where you do have more disk space. But when you run out of disk space, you won't be able to save the data you are working on to the network directory and you will see a message similar to "Out of disk space." When you know you have enough rights and you see this type of error, check your volume restrictions.

To leave the "User Volume/Disk Restrictions" window, press <Esc>.

This finishes our discussion of the options available in the "User Information" window. This information should give you a better idea of what you can and can't do in the network directories on this server.

Changing Your Current Server

If you want to browse around the servers and see what you can see, choose the "Change Current Server" option from SYSCON's "Available Topics" window. You can change to any other server you're a user on, or you can log in as GUEST to server guest accounts. However, if you come in as GUEST, you'll only be able to see how a guest is set up. Some guest accounts may require a password, so you may not see anything.

Go into SYSCON. At the "Available Topics" window, select the "Change Current Server" option and press <Enter>. You'll see a list of all the servers you're currently attached to. To add another server to the list, press <Ins>. You'll see an "Other File Servers" window listing all available servers on the network.

```
SYSCON  3.58                           Saturday  January 9, 1993  6:19 pm
                        User TED On File Server ADMIN
```

Figure 2-26. Choosing other file servers to look at

To see the names of all the servers on the network, press <Ctrl>-<PgDn> to go to the bottom of the listing, or <Ctrl>-<PgUp> to go to the top. To move a screenful at a time, press <PgDn> or <PgUp>. Select the name of the other server you want to look at and press <Enter>.

The "Change Current Server" option attaches you to the other servers and prompts you for your username and, when appropriate, for your password. When you log out from the network, you'll log out of these other server attachments as well. (Or you can be specific and log out of certain servers anytime you wish.)

If one of the servers you're trying to log in to as GUEST asks for a password and you try to fake it, you'll see a little screen that says, "Access to file server denied. Press ESCAPE to continue." Press <Esc> and you'll get another shot at the password. But once you realize your chances of guessing the password are pretty slim, press <Esc> again to return to the "Other File Servers" window.

SYSCON doesn't really change your servers; if you've been looking at another server's environment, when you exit SYSCON you'll be on the same server you were on when you entered SYSCON. Now that you're attached to another server, choose to view that server's information by highlighting the servername and pressing <Enter>. Notice that the servername has changed at the top of your menu; your username may have as well. This way you can track which server's information you are seeing.

Once you've chosen another server, you can take a look at all the options on the "Available Topics" window just as you did for your default server. The only restrictions depend on how you're defined on that server. For example, if you attach to another server as GUEST, you'll be limited to what GUEST can do on that server. But take the time to look at a few servers so you can get a feel for the network and the resources available to you.

You can also detach from the extra servers in SYSCON by highlighting the servername in the "File Server/User Name" window and pressing <Del>. You'll see a "Logout from server. Yes/No" window with the "Yes" option highlighted. Press <Enter> to log out from that server. If you attach to several servers and you want to log out of them, use <F5> to mark the servers you wish to log out of and then press <Del>. You'll see the "Log out from all marked servers. Yes/No" window with the "Yes" option highlighted. Press <Enter> to log out of those servers. If you accidentally mark the server you're logged in to, you'll see a screen which says, "You cannot log out from your default server. Press ESCAPE to continue."

To exit SYSCON, press <Esc> until you come to the "Exit SYSCON Yes/No" window with the "Yes" option highlighted. Press <Enter> and you'll return to the network prompt.

The FILER Utility

FILER, the file maintenance utility, allows you to look at information about your directories and files. In FILER, you can delete, rename, and copy files (as well as the subdirectories they're in) to other directories (if you have the proper rights). With effective rights that include Access Control, you can also manipulate the inherited rights mask of the directory you're in, and you can assign other users trustee assignments to your directories. You can also add, delete, and rename subdirectories if you have Create, Erase, and Modify rights.

Let's go in and start playing. Because you can do many things in FILER (as opposed to SYSCON), we'll just go straight through the screens, emphasizing the fine points as we go.

Before entering FILER, go into a directory in which you have Access Control rights. If you're unsure where you have Access Control rights, go to any directory and type WHOAMI/A <Enter> at the network prompt. The /A parameter will show you the rights you have in directories on all the servers you're attached to. You may wish to copy the information to a file, then print that file. You can do this by going to your home directory and typing WHOAMI/A >TEST1 <Enter>, then typing NPRINT TEST1 Q=*queuename* NFF NB <Enter>.

If you can't find a directory in which you have Access Control effective rights, go to a directory where you have the most rights and a large number of files so you can practice FILER commands. At the directory's network prompt, type FILER <Enter>. You'll see the "Available Topics" window with five options: "Current Directory Information," "Directory Contents," "Select Current Directory," "Set Filer Options," and "Volume Information."

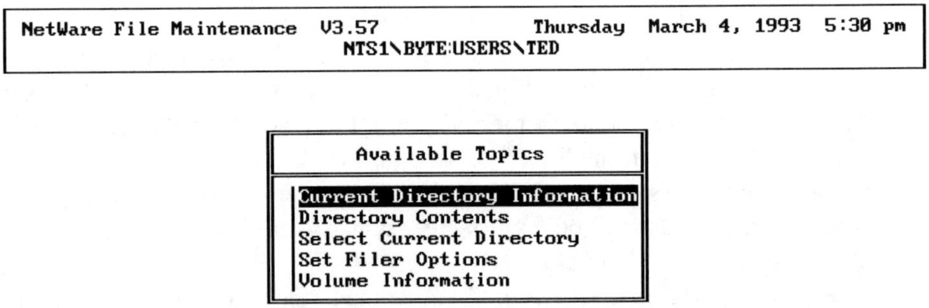

```
┌─────────────────────────────────────────────────────────────────────┐
│ NetWare File Maintenance   V3.57         Thursday  March 4, 1993  5:30 pm │
│                       NTS1\BYTE:USERS\TED                             │
└─────────────────────────────────────────────────────────────────────┘
```

```
        ┌────────────────────────────────┐
        │        Available Topics        │
        ├────────────────────────────────┤
        │ Current Directory Information  │
        │ Directory Contents             │
        │ Select Current Directory       │
        │ Set Filer Options              │
        │ Volume Information             │
        └────────────────────────────────┘
```

Figure 2-27. The initial FILER utility screen

As with other NetWare menu utilities, to get around in FILER, pressing <Enter> on a highlighted option brings you to the next screen available under that option, and pressing <Esc> brings you to the previous screen. For example, from the "Available Topics" window, select the "Directory Contents" option by pressing the Down arrow key on the numeric keypad. Once that option is highlighted, press <Enter>. <PgDn> brings you to the bottom of the screen's list of selections and <PgUp> brings you to the top of the screen's list. At a menu window, you can also use the Up (8) and Down (2) arrow keys to highlight and select an option, or you can type the first letters of the option you wish to select and the selector bar will move to that option.

Never feel stranded in the menus: pressing <F1> at any time will provide an explanation of the menu options currently on the screen. Each help screen gives you information specific to the option choice currently on the screen. Once you've chosen another menu option by pressing <Enter>, pressing <F1> will bring you a different set of help screens relating to the newly selected option.

Now, back to FILER's "Available Topics" window. The second line in the screen header shows ADMIN/VOL1:USERS/TED and displays the entire directory path of the directory you're currently in, including the name of the server. If you change directories, the screen header will change accordingly, giving you a running indicator of which directory you're in at any given time. From the "Available Options" window, select the first option—"Current Directory Information."

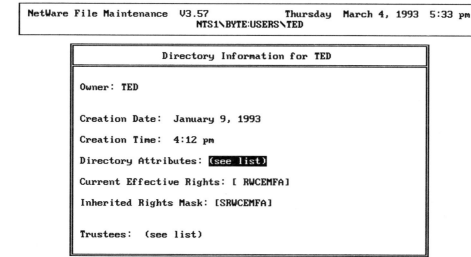

Figure 2-28. Information about the directory you are currently in

The "Directory Information for *username*" window contains seven entries, which you may or may not be able to change, depending on your rights. The seven entries include the directory's owner, its creation date and its creation time, the directory attributes, the directory's current effective rights, the inherited rights mask, and the list of trustees to whom you have given access rights.

What you can do with each of the entries depends on what rights you have in the directory. The first three entries—"Owner," "Creation Date," and "Creation Time"— are mainly for supervisors or workgroup managers to use; users can only look at them. If given Access Control rights, you can change the directory's inherited rights mask, which affects your current effective rights to that directory and all directories thereafter (unless again assigned). You can also assign trustee privileges to your directories if you wish. Then, with Modify rights, you can add the directory attributes. Let's look at the first three entries: "Owner," "Creation Date," and "Creation Time."

The Directory's Owner, Creation Date, and Time

The "Owner" entry is first in the "Directory Information" window. As a user, you can't make changes to this entry. The name in the screen designates the owner of this directory. For the most part, it doesn't matter who creates a directory, for a supervisor can assign you ownership of a directory with its subdirectory structure to better keep track of the files or directories you're creating or using. (Some software will look at directory/file ownership as a means to see how much disk space is in use). So directory ownership is initially assigned when you create a directory or when your supervisor defines who owns a directory.

The creation date and time show you when the directory was created. While supervisors can edit a directory's creation date and time, you can only look at the information displayed on the screen.

Directory Attributes, Current Effective Rights and the Inherited Rights Mask

With NetWare 3.1x and with Read, File Scan, and Modify rights, you now have the ability to add directory attributes just as you can add file attributes. You have five directory attributes from which to select: Delete Inhibit, Hidden and System Directory, Purge Directory, and Rename Inhibit.

Delete Inhibit. This option prevents you or others from accidentally deleting the directory. Then, in order to delete the directory, you then need to reset the directory attribute without the "Delete Inhibit" option in the "Current Attributes" window. To do this, highlight the option and press <Del>.

Hidden and **System Directory.** Since these attributes are essentially the same (both hide the directory), it's best to stay with one choice for simplicity's sake. You can choose Hidden Directory when you wish to hide a directory from FILER or from DOS's DIR command. However, you can go into the directory if you know its name. For example, to hide directory MEMO under directory TED, you first choose the "Select Current Directory" option from the "Available Topics" window. Next, type in the directory path to include the directory you wish to hide: in this case, MEMO. Press <Enter>, and the second line in the FILER screen should now reflect the directory change.

Select the "Current Directory Information" option, then select the "Directory Attributes" entry and press <Enter>. You'll see the "Current Attributes" window with nothing in it; press <Ins>, highlight the "Hidden Directory" option, and press <Enter>.

110

That selects the option. Then press <Esc> again to return to the "Directory Information" window.

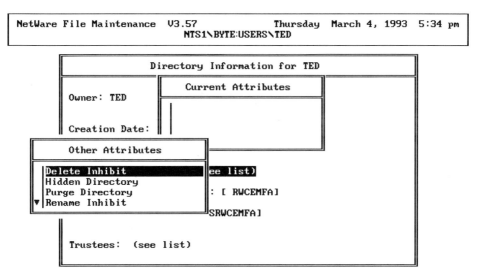

```
NetWare File Maintenance   V3.57           Thursday  March 4, 1993  5:34 pm
                          NTS1\BYTE:USERS\TED

              Directory Information for TED

                     Current Attributes
    Owner: TED

    Creation Date:

        Other Attributes
    ┌─────────────────────────┐
    │ Delete Inhibit          │ee list)
    │ Hidden Directory        │
    │ Purge Directory         │: [ RWCEMFA]
  ▼ │ Rename Inhibit          │
    └─────────────────────────┘SRWCEMFA]

    Trustees:  (see list)
```

Figure 2-29. Setting directory attributes

If you hide the directory VOL1:USERS\TED\MEMOS, you won't see the directory listed if you're in directory TED and you type DIR <Enter>. However, if you know the MEMOS directory exists, you can type CD MEMOS <Enter> from directory TED and be in the MEMOS directory. You can also use NetWare's NDIR command (as well as a number of file managers) and see hidden or system directories.

If you've hidden a directory and you want to unhide it, include the directory in the directory path you type in for the "Select Current Directory" option. It will show up if it's there. Then follow the procedures explained earlier to find the "Current Attributes" window, but now press <Del> on the highlighted option. You'll be asked if you want to delete the attribute. Press <Enter> over the "Yes" option; you'll be able to see the directory normally. Again, you need Read, File Scan, and Modify rights to add the Hidden attribute.

Purge Directory. This attribute allows you to purge the files in the directory as soon as you delete them. This is useful when you have an application that performs backups every five or ten minutes.

111

With NetWare 3.x, deleted files are still salvageable through the SALVAGE utility. Once you delete a file, the file is still kept track of by NetWare and is protected from overwrites for 1 minute and 59 seconds.

NetWare keeps writing new files past the deleted files until the entire volume is filled with deleted and present files. Once the volume is full, and you need create or delete another version of your data files, NetWare takes the least recently accessed file(s) and purges them so it can use their disk space. This means that at any given time, you may have a lot of deleted files. However, if everyone is doing this, NetWare volumes can remain full of deleted files, which can degrade performance.

To get around this situation, you can set the Purge Directory attribute on the directories where you save your backup files. This way, you will still have your backup file saved as a real file if the server goes down, but you won't be needlessly filling the disk with every five-minute version of the backup file. To set this attribute, highlight the "Purge Directory" option and press <Enter> to add it to the "Current Attributes" window.

Rename Inhibit. This option prevents you or others from accidentally renaming the directory. To set this attribute, highlight the "Rename Inhibit" option and press <Enter> to add it to the "Current Attributes" window. Then in order to rename the directory, you'll need to reset the directory attribute without the "Rename Inhibit" option in the "Current Attributes" window. To do this, highlight the option and press <Del>. To leave the "Directory Attributes" window, press <Esc>.

The "Current Effective Rights" entry shows your effective rights for this directory. Depending on your site's security scheme, it's a good idea to have full rights (but without supervisory rights) in your home directory. As the introduction to this book points out, your effective rights are a combination of basic security rights as they apply to you as a trustee of that directory, menus, and the directory inherited rights mask. To get your effective rights, NetWare looks at the trustee rights your supervisor, workgroup, or account manager may have assigned to you as a user or group member and through your security equivalences. NetWare then compares these rights to the directory rights (the Inherited Rights Mask), displaying the rights you can effectively use in that directory.

If the directory's inherited rights mask gives you only Read and File Scan (RF) rights at the directory level, but you have the rights RWCEMFA from your trustee assignments, you'll still have only RF rights in that directory. However, if you have Access Control rights in this directory or in its parent directory, you can redefine the directory's inherited rights mask, as I'm going to explain next.

To find out what your trustee assignment rights are, go into SYSCON and check your trustee assignments as well as your security equivalences and your group trustee

112

rights. You have several ways to find out all your rights, but to see your effective rights, trustee assignments, security equivalences, and groups, type WHOAMI/A <Enter> at the network prompt. See Chapter 3 for more information about the WHOAMI command.

Depending on your security scheme, you probably have Access Control rights in at least one directory. If you do, go to that directory and follow along during this discussion. You can always change things back before you exit FILER. (Follow along even if you don't have Access Control rights in any directory. But you'll only be able to view a directory's inherited rights mask rather than change it, and you won't see the "Trustees" option in the "Directory Information" window at all. In fact, that's one easy way to find out if you have Access Control rights.)

"Inherited Rights Mask" is a fancy term for the rights a user, including yourself, can have in a directory. With Access Control rights, there are two ways to limit users' rights in a directory: through the inherited rights mask and through trustee assignments. The inherited rights mask affects everyone, including yourself, while trustee assignments affect only those you give access to. If you have Access Control rights and you want to limit everyone's activities in a specific directory, you can choose which rights you want to allow. Use <F5> to mark the options you want to exclude in the "Inherited Rights Mask" window. Press <Del> and you'll see a window asking you if you want to delete those rights. Press <Enter> and users no longer have those rights in your directory.

A word of caution: it is possible to delete your own rights. If you delete Access Control rights, leave FILER and go into another directory, then return to the directory where you deleted Access Control rights, you won't be able to restore your Access Control rights from FILER. So be careful when deleting directory rights. It's much safer to use the trustee rights entry; trustee rights affect only the person you designate. Another word of caution: What you can do in FILER depends largely on the version you use. Some versions give you erroneous information on your rights. If all else fails, leave FILER and type RIGHTS at the network prompt to see what you really have. Then use Grant to grant and revoke rights.

If you wish to add rights to a directory, press <Ins> when the "Inherited Rights" window is displayed. You'll see another window listing the rights that are not part of the current rights mask. Use <F5> to mark the rights you wish to put back. Press <Enter>. Those rights are now restored.

From a user's perspective, there's really no need to edit the inherited rights mask. The directory rights mask affects the directory you're presently in and all subdirectories until you redefine the inherited rights mask.

What You Can Do with Access Control Rights—Granting Trustee Assignments

You can use the "Trustees" entry to grant rights in a directory to which you have Access Control rights. (You can give trustee assignments here in FILER or at the network prompt through the GRANT or ALLOW utilities. Supervisors and workgroup managers can also use the FILER, GRANT, ALLOW, or SYSCON utilities.)

From the "Directory Information" window, select the "Trustees" entry. The resulting window shows who you have given trustee rights to, whether those rights are given to a user or group, and what those rights are.

To add other trustees, press <Ins>. You'll see the names of the other users and groups on the server. Highlight the name of each user or group you're allowing access to your information and press <Enter>, or use <F5> to mark as many names as you want. Then press <Enter>.

A new user given a trustee assignment in FILER receives only Read and File Scan rights with that assignment; you might want to modify those rights if you also want the user to write files to your directory. Do this by selecting that user's name and pressing <Enter>, thereby bringing up the "Trustee Rights" window with all the rights that user presently has.

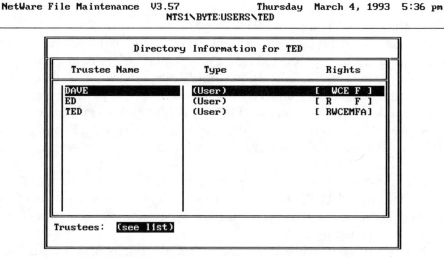

Figure 2-30. The Trustees option shows who you have assigned rights to in the directory you are currently in

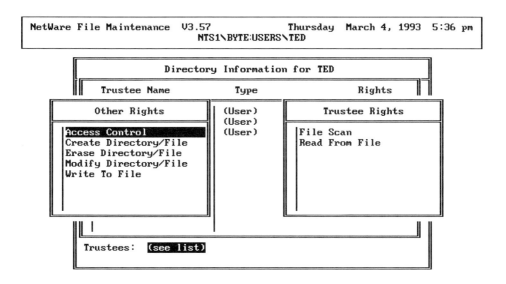

Figure 2-31. With Access Control Rights, you can select a user, and grant or revoke rights within the current directory

The rights you give depend on what you want that user or group to do in your directory. For example, if you want the other users to be able only to copy files into the directory, give them Write, Create, Erase, and sometimes, Modify rights. To add that capability, press <Ins> when at the "Trustee Rights" window, then use <F5> to mark those rights you wish that user or group to have—Write, Create, Erase, Modify, and File Scan. To add the additional rights, press <Enter>.

If you decide later to revoke any rights, use <F5> to mark all the rights you wish to delete, then press <Del>. You'll see a window that says "Revoke All Marked Rights" with the "Yes" option highlighted. Press <Enter> and the rights are gone. When you define trustee rights for other users or groups, they'll see that they've gained or lost a trustee assignment the next time they try to perform something or when they look at their trustee or group assignments in SYSCON.

You can view information from the "Directory Information" window for every directory on the server. However, if you don't have rights in a given directory, you'll see that you don't have any trustee assignments or effective rights. And if you have RF rights (probably the most common combination), all you'll see is the directory's creation date and time, your effective rights in that directory, its inherited rights mask, and the name of the directory's owner. Press <Esc> until you return to the "Available Topics" window.

Looking at the Directory Contents Option

Next on the "Available Topics" window is the "Directory Contents" option. From this option you can change several filenames, copy multiple files, and set the attributes (usually known as file flags) of those files all at once. Or you can copy a single file to another directory on this, or another, file server; view and change a file's attributes; view the last time the file was accessed, archived, or modified; view the file's owner and its size; and view the file's contents. You can also perform a number of subdirectory procedures, so let's first look at what you can do at the subdirectory level, then we'll drop into the file level. Highlight "Directory Contents" from the "Available Topics" window and press <Enter>.

```
NetWare File Maintenance   V3.57            Thursday  March 4, 1993  5:52 pm
                            NTS1\BYTE:USERS\TED
```

```
                        Directory Contents

        . .                             (parent)
        \                               (root)
        ACCT                            (subdirectory)
        LETTERS                         (subdirectory)
        CVR-SHT.FAX                     (file)
        FAX.CFG                         (file)
        FAX.LOG                         (file)
        IBM$RUN.OVL                     (file)
        JETERLOG                        (file)
        JETQUEUE                        (file)
        JFPOP.$$$                       (file)
        MODEM.BAT                       (file)
        PCPLUS.DIR                      (file)
        PCPLUS.KEY                      (file)
```

Figure 2-32. Use this option to see which files and directories are available from your current directory

At the "Directory Contents" window, you can see entries such as "Parent," "Root," "Subdirectories," and "Files." The "Parent" entry allows you to move up the directory path until you reach the volume designation (:); to use it, highlight the "Parent" entry and press <Enter>. You'll see the "Would you like to make the parent directory the current directory?" window with the "Yes" option highlighted. Press <Enter> and you'll move one directory level up the directory path.

Unless you're supervisor-equivalent or have trustee assignments at the volume level, you'll eventually run out of rights in this directory path. If you select the "Parent" entry and you don't have at least RF rights, you'll see a window that says "You have no search rights for this directory. You'll only be able to view subdirectories, not files. <Press ESCAPE to continue>." While you can view the subdirectory names, FILER does respect the Hidden or System directory attributes, which can also hide the directory names from your view.

The next entry is "Root." This entry brings you to the volume level and not to any false root levels you might have created through the MAP ROOT command. (See the "MAP" subheading in Chapter 3.) When you select the "Root" entry, you'll see the "Would you like to make the root the current directory?" window with the "Yes" option highlighted. Pressing <Enter> then brings you to volume level, where you probably won't have any rights, and you'll have the same restrictions as when you moved too high up the directory path using the "Parent" entry.

Looking At Multiple Directories At Once

Next in the "Directory Contents" window are your subdirectory listings (if you have any). These are followed by any files you might have in this directory. For multiple subdirectories, FILER lets you copy the subdirectory files themselves or the entire subdirectory structure to another directory path or to another server. You can also set the Directories' Inherited Right Mask all at once instead of one directory at a time. If you highlight and select a single subdirectory, you'll see five options, including those selections discussed for multiple subdirectories, and an option to make the subdirectory your current directory as well as view or set directory information.

Let's first go through the multiple subdirectory options. To see the "Multiple Subdirectory Operations" window, use <F5> to highlight two or more subdirectories and press <Enter>. You'll see the "Multiple Subdirectory Operations" window with three options: "Copy Subdirectories Files," "Copy Subdirectories Structure," and "Set Inherited Rights."

Copy Subdirectories Files. If you want to copy just the files in the marked subdirectories, choose this option and press <Enter>. You'll see the "Copy Subdirectory To:" window, allowing you to type in the directory path. So if you know the path, type it in; otherwise, press the Insert key to see the "File Server/Local Drives" window.

This window contains local drive specifications as well as all the servers you're currently attached to. For example, let's say you want to make a quick-and-dirty backup on files in two directories whose files will fit on a floppy disk. (This situation is quite hypothetical).

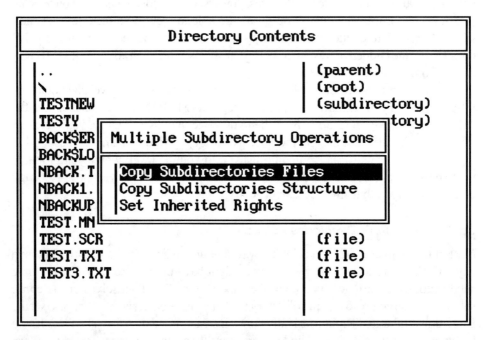

Figure 2-33. Use this option to copy all the subdirectory's files at once

Select the two directories as outlined, then select the "Copy Subdirectories Files" option <Enter>, press <Ins> to bring up the "File Servers/Local Drives" window. From there, highlight the "Drive A:" option, press <Enter>, then <Esc> to bring you again to the "Copy" window. Pressing <Enter> now begins the copying function, and you'll see a small "Copying Files" window, showing the files that are being copied. If there's enough room on the floppy disk, you'll then return to the "Multiple Subdirectory Operations" window. If there's not enough room, you'll see an error to that effect.

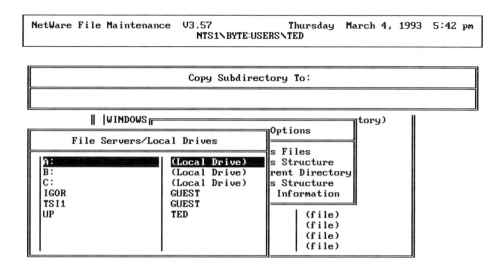

Figure 2-34. Once you select which files to copy, you need to designate a directory path to copy them to

This file copying routine works a lot like DOS's XCOPY command; when the routine runs out of room in the area it's copying to, it stops. However, unlike the XCOPY command, FILER has no method to copy files marked as needing to be archived, so you're stuck copying all the files. You must also remember that if you flag a file or directory with the Hidden or System attribute, you won't be able to delete or copy that file until you change the file's attribute back to Normal.

Copy Subdirectories Structure. Now let's suppose you want to copy the files and the subdirectory structure to another file server. For this example, be sure you're attached to the server you wish to copy to, and be sure you have at least Write, Create, Erase, Modify, and File Scan rights in the directory where you plan to create the subdirectory structure. With the subdirectory highlighted, choose the "Copy Subdirectories Structure" option and press <Enter>. Then press Insert at the "Copy Subdirectory To:" window and you'll see a list of local drives as well as a listing of the servers you're attached to.

Let's further suppose you wish to copy these files and directories to NTS3, which you're currently not attached to. By pressing <Ins>, you'll see the "Other File Servers" window, which lists all the servers on the internetwork. You can choose another server by typing the servername and pressing <Enter>.

If you happen to type your username incorrectly, or if you mistype your password, you'll see a screen that says, "Access to file server denied. Press Escape to continue." Press <Esc> to try typing in your password again, or press <Esc> twice to return to the "Other File Servers" window. When you want to return once more to the "File Servers/ Local Drives" window, press <Esc>. You can also log out from an attached server by highlighting the name of that server with the selector bar and pressing <Del>. You'll see a "Logout from server Yes/No" window with the "Yes" option highlighted. Press <Enter> to log out from the designated server.

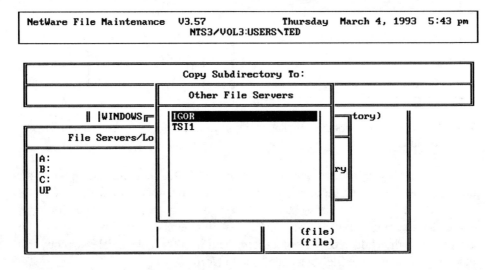

Figure 2-35. You can copy files to other file servers

For this example, suppose Ted wants to copy TAXES and CALLS directories (with files) to the NTS3/VOL3:USERS\TED directory path. First Ted selects the file server by pressing <Enter> on its highlighted name. You next see a "Volumes" window; highlight the correct volume where the files go and press <Enter>. At the "Network Directories" window, select the appropriate directory path where you wish to put the directories and files, pressing <Enter> for each directory confirmation along the way. Then when you've reached your directory destination (USERS\TED for our example), press <Esc> to return to the "Copy" window, then press <Enter>. FILER will now copy over the directories and files.

If the same directories already exist on the destination file server, you see an error message telling you so and FILER halts the copy process. You then need only to copy the files—one directory at a time if you wish to perform the copy from FILER. Be sure that you don't leave duplicate directories and files lying around all over the place. Unless your copying is for backup purposes, once you copy directories/files to another place, delete them from their original location. Most network managers make at least one full backup copy of all network directories—and those who don't should be fired! Duplicate copies can lead to using the wrong file or copying over the most current version, so if you copy files and subdirectory structures, clean up your originals.

Set Inherited Rights. This is the last option on the "Multiple Subdirectory Operations" window. Earlier in this chapter I discussed in detail how, with Access Control rights, you can change a directory's inherited rights mask (IRM). With this option, you can change the inherited rights mask for all selected directories. The same methods and warnings apply here as were explained earlier. Press <Enter> to select this option.

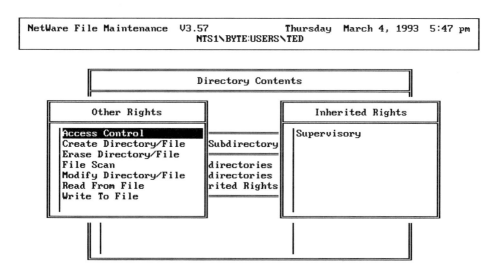

Figure 2-36. You can use FILER to set the IRM in directories and subdirectories

The "Inherited Rights" window appears with nothing or with "Supervisory" in it. To modify the inherited rights mask, press <Ins> to bring up another window with the rights you wish to select for the directories you've highlighted. You can use <F5> to mark the rights you wish to give the directories, then press <Enter> and the rights will hop over

121

to the "Inherited Rights" window. Then as you press <Esc> to exit the window, you'll see the "Set marked subdirectories to specified inherited rights" window with the "Yes" option highlighted. Pressing <Enter> saves the new inherited rights, while highlighting "No" and pressing <Enter> allows you to leave without changes to the inherited rights mask for those directories.

Remember, you need Read and File Scan rights to read files from a directory, and you need Write, Create, Erase, Modify (sometimes), and File Scan rights to write to a directory. Also remember that whatever you set at the directory rights mask level also affects you. So whatever rights you take away, *you* lose those rights as well. Again, if you wish to allow other users rights to your directories, it's best to set up individual trustee assignments than use the directory rights mask as a means to screen rights.

You can also delete subdirectories and their structure by highlighting the subdirectories and pressing the Delete key. You'll see the "Delete Subdirectory Options" window that will allow you to delete the entire subdirectory structure (directories and files) or to delete only the files in the marked subdirectories. If you choose to delete the entire subdirectory structure, you'll receive a second confirmation window asking if you wish to delete all marked subdirectories, which includes any subdirectories they may have, as well as all files. Answering "Yes" deletes the structure. (If you made a big mistake on your deletion, exit FILER and run the SALVAGE utility.) If you select the "Files Only" option, you'll also receive a second confirmation window, asking if you wish to delete all files in the marked directories. Answering "Yes" deletes the files.

You can also rename a single subdirectory or a group of subdirectories after selecting the "Subdirectory Information" option. To rename a single subdirectory, highlight the subdirectory name and press <F3>. You'll see an "Edit Directory Name:" window where you can rename the subdirectory.

Renaming a group of subdirectories requires that they have similar names. For example, suppose you have three subdirectories—JUNE91, JUNE92, and JUNE93— whose names you want to change to JULY91, JULY92, and JULY93. You'll need Create, Erase, and Modify rights to perform this function. Highlight these three subdirectories with either <F6> (pattern-finder) or <F5> (mark).

To use the pattern-finding function, press <F6>, then press the Backspace key over the asterisk in the Mark Pattern window. Type JUN* in the window and press <Enter> to highlight the three subdirectories. FILER will mark only those subdirectories that match the pattern as it is described, so be sure to put in the asterisk (*) wild card, or use the question mark wild card by typing JUN???. Press <F3> and you'll be asked for the original name pattern that all three directories have in common. In our example, you would type in JUNE* and press <Enter>. You'll see the "Rename Patterns" window, where you type in JULY* and press <Enter>. The directory names will change from JUNE91, JUNE92, and JUNE93 to JULY91, JULY92, and JULY93.

These changes will also be noted in SYSCON. If you've given trustee assignments for those directories to other users, their "Trustee Assignment" options will modify to show your changes.

Options for Single Directories

If you simply highlight one subdirectory from the "Directory Contents" window, you'll see five options. These options include "Copy Subdirectory's Files," "Copy Subdirectory's Structure," "Make This Your Current Directory," "Move Subdirectory's Structure," and "View/Set Directory Information." The first two options work the same as described in the multiple directory section and will be covered briefly here. We'll cover the last three options in more detail.

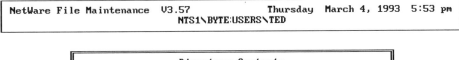

```
NetWare File Maintenance   V3.57          Thursday  March 4, 1993  5:53 pm
                          NTS1\BYTE:USERS\TED
```

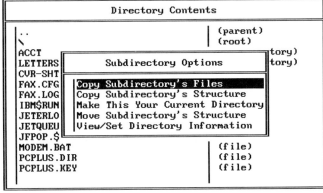

Figure 2-37. FILER comes with a number of options for single subdirectory modification

Copy Subdirectory's Files. If you want to copy just the files in a subdirectory, choose this option and press <Enter>. You'll see the "Copy Subdirectory To:" window, allowing you to type in the directory path. If you know the path, type it in; otherwise, press the Insert key to see the "File Server/Local Drives" window. This window contains local drive specifications as well as a listing of all the servers you're currently attached to.

For this example, let's suppose you need to copy and send a disk with invaluable data to Rhodes, Italy. Select the subdirectory containing the files and press <Enter>, then select the "Copy Subdirectory's Files" option and press <Enter>. Press <Ins> to bring up the "File Servers/Local Drives" window. From there, highlight the "Drive A:" option, press <Enter>, then press <Esc> to bring you again to the Copy window.

Pressing <Enter> now begins the copying function, and you'll see a small "Copying Files" window, showing the files that are being copied. If there's enough room on the floppy disk, you'll then return to the "Subdirectory Options" window. If there's not enough room, you'll see an error message to that effect.

Again, you can perform the same function from the network prompt through NetWare's NCOPY or DOS's COPY or XCOPY commands. If you only want to copy files that need to be archived, use XCOPY or NCOPY, for FILER has no method to copy files marked as needing to be archived, so you're stuck copying all the files (not just files needing to be archived). If you flag a file with the Hidden or System attribute, you won't be able to delete or copy that file until you change the file's attribute back to Normal.

Copy Subdirectory's Structure. Now let's suppose you want to copy the files and any subdirectories that lie beneath the selected directory to another server. You'll need at least Write, Create, Erase, and Modify rights in the directory you want to copy to. This time, choose the "Copy Subdirectory's Structure" option and press <Enter>. Then press <Ins> at the "Copy Subdirectory To" window and you'll see a list of local drives as well as the servers you're attached to, as shown in Figure 2-38.

Let's further suppose you wish to copy these files and directories to NTS3, which you're currently not attached to. By pressing <Ins>, you'll see the "Other File Servers" window, which lists all the servers on the internetwork. You can choose another server by typing the servername and pressing <Enter>. You'll then be asked for your username on that server, and in many instances, for a password. The correct answer brings you back to the "File Server/Local Drives" window with name of the additional server highlighted. Press <Enter> to add the server to the "Copy" window.

For this example, suppose Ted wants to copy the directory BIGTAXES and its subdirectory JAIL (with files) to the NTS3/VOL3:USERS\TED\TAXES directory path. First Ted selects the file server by pressing <Enter> on its highlighted name. You next see a "Volumes" window; highlight the correct volume where the files go and press

<Enter>. At the "Network Directories" window, select the appropriate directory path where you wish to put the directories and files, pressing <Enter> for each directory confirmation along the way. Then when you've reached your directory destination (USERS\TED\TAXES for our example), press <Esc> to return to the "Copy" window, then press <Enter>. FILER will now copy the directories and files over to NTS3.

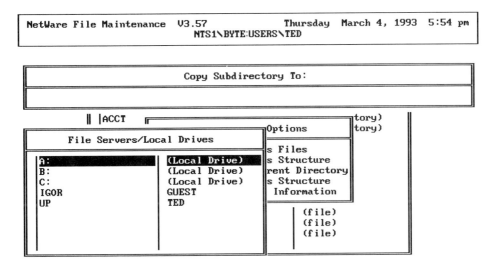

Figure 2-38. You can copy a subdirectory from one server to another server through the "Copy Subdirectory's Structure" option

If the same directories already exist on the destination file server, you see an error message telling you so, and FILER halts the copy process. You then need only copy the files—one directory at a time if you wish to perform the copy from FILER.

Make This Your Current Directory. With this option you can browse through the files in any subdirectory. To do so, highlight the subdirectory, <Enter>, choose this option, <Enter>, and the selected subdirectory now becomes the current directory. You can then peruse the files or select another subdirectory through the same means through which you selected this one. If you're down the wrong directory path and you want to backtrack, choose the "Parent" entry <Enter>, then press <Enter> again to go to the next level up.

Move Subdirectory's Structure. This option allows you to move the highlighted directory and files under another directory on the network. To do this, highlight the "Move" option and press <Enter>. You will see the "Destination Directory" window with your present server and volume listed in it.

Type in the directory path where you wish it to move and press <Enter>. You will see a "New Name:" window with the present directory name listed. If you wish to rename the directory, you can do so by pressing the backspace key to delete the name, typing in a new directory name, and pressing <Enter>. Then when you press <Esc> to leave the "Subdirectory Option" window, you will see the directory move under its new directory destination.

You can move directories and their files to floppy disks or other file servers on the network.

View/Set Directory Information. This last option on the "Subdirectory Options" window shows the same window as the first option I covered in the "Available Topics" window—"Current Directory Information." Instead of presenting that information again, we'll just refer you to the explanation under Figure 2-29 if you want to learn what you can do in that directory. You can also delete subdirectories and their structure by highlighting the subdirectory names and pressing <Del>. I also covered this process earlier, so instead of presenting that information again, we'll send you to the "Copy Subdirectories Structure" subheading under Figure 2-34 for directions on subdirectory deletion.

With multiple and singular subdirectories operations covered, let's now turn to the files themselves. Let's first look at the options you have when highlighting multiple files in a directory; then we'll look at single file options.

Performing Multiple File Operations

From the "Available Topics" window, choose the "Directory Contents" option. You'll see a list of subdirectories and files on the screen. To select a group of files, either use <F5> to mark those files, or use <F6> to mark a file pattern. <F6> will call up a "Mark Pattern" window.

For example, if you want information on some files that all have the same extension, you can specify in the "Mark Pattern" window all the files that have that extension. The figure below indicates that all files with an .SCR extension, regardless of the filename, are highlighted. (The asterisk * wild card indicates any filename.)

```
Mark Pattern: *.SCR
```

Figure 2-39. You can use wild cards to mark files in the "Mark Pattern" window

You can designate other file patterns as well. For example, if you want to set the file attributes on files that begin with the letter S, put S*.* in the pattern box. You can also use the question mark (?) wild card in FILER. Suppose you want to mark files that start with the letter S, specifically the SL_}SYS.* files. You can enter the file pattern as ????SYS.*, and FILER will designate the SL_}SYS.* files. Of course, in this case it's probably easier just to use <F5>, and <F6> might be easier under different circumstances. The advantage of <F5> is that your files don't have to be in any pattern, although the file marking may get tedious.

Once you've marked your files, put the selector bar on one of them and press <Enter>. You'll see the "Multiple File Operations" window with three options—"Copy Marked Files," "Set Attributes," and "Set Inherited Rights."

```
NetWare File Maintenance   V3.57          Thursday  March 4, 1993  5:55 pm
                              NTS1\BYTE:USERS\TED
```

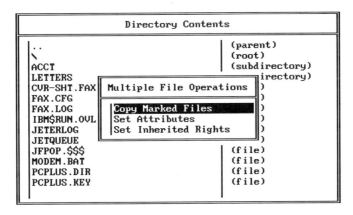

```
                      Directory Contents
  ..                                    (parent)
  \                                     (root)
  ACCT                                  (subdirectory)
  LETTERS                       ┌───────irectory)
  CUR-SHT.FAX  Multiple File Operations )
  FAX.CFG                               )
  FAX.LOG     ┌─────────────────────┐   )
  IBM$RUN.OVL │Copy Marked Files    │   )
  JETERLOG    │Set Attributes       │   )
  JETQUEUE    │Set Inherited Rights │   )
  JFPOP.$$$   └─────────────────────┘(file)
  MODEM.BAT                            (file)
  PCPLUS.DIR                           (file)
  PCPLUS.KEY                           (file)
```

Figure 2-40. In the "Multiple File Operations" window, you can select and copy marked files to designated directories, servers, or disks

Copy Marked Files. This option brings up a "Copy Files To:" window with your present directory path in the window. You can modify the directory path with the Backspace key to erase some or all of the directory path, then type in the directory path where you wish to copy the files. Or you backspace over the present directory path, then press <Ins> to call up the "File Server/Local Drives" window. This window contains local drive specifications as well as a list of all the servers you're currently attached to. For example, let's say you simply want to back up three files.

At the "File Servers/Local Drives" window, highlight the "Drive A:" option, press <Enter> then press <Esc> to bring you again to the "Copy" window. Pressing <Enter>

now begins the copying function, and you'll see a small "Copying Files" window, showing the files that are being copied. If there are files with the same filename in the directory you're copying to, you may be asked if you wish to overwrite the existing file. Selecting "Yes" then overwrites the file, and selecting "No" skips that file in the file copying process. Again, you need at least Read, File Scan, Write, Create, and Erase rights in the directory you're copying to for the files to copy.

You can perform the same copying functions from the network prompt through NetWare's NCOPY or DOS's COPY or XCOPY commands. If you only want to copy files that need to be archived, use XCOPY, for FILER has no method to copy files marked as needing to be archived, so you're stuck copying all the files. If you flag a file "Hidden," "System," or "Delete Inhibit," you won't be able to delete or copy that file until you change the file's attribute back to Normal (Nonshareable, Read/Write). You also can't delete Hidden or System flagged files (unless you change the flag first).

Set Attributes. With Modify rights, this option allows you to assign attributes to all the files you have highlighted without having to perform this function on an individual level. If you have only Read and File Scan rights in this directory, you can copy the files from the directory, but not set any file attributes.

To look at file attributes, mark a few files and press <Enter>. You'll see the "File Attributes" window showing you how those files are presently flagged. (If the files aren't flagged at all, you'll see an empty screen.) To look at the "Other File Attributes" window, press <Ins>.

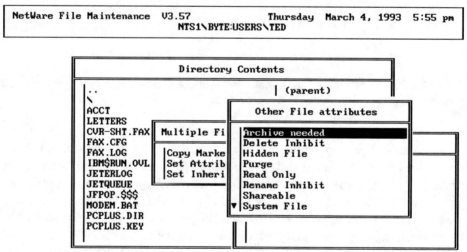

Figure 2-41. With this option, you can set multiple file attributes at once

You'll need at least Modify rights to change a file's attributes, and Read and File Scan to see the files in the first place. The default flags for files are Nonshareable and Read/Write. Other available attributes are Archive Needed, Delete Inhibit, Hidden File, Purge, Read Only, Rename Inhibit, Shareable, System File, and Transactional. The Archive Needed attribute is automatically set whenever you modify a file. The next time you go into the file and make changes, your system's backup procedures will know to back up the file again. If you flag a file as Hidden, you won't see that file listed when you type DIR at the System prompt. But if you know it's there, and you know the filename, you'll be able to access the file. FILER is also unable to see a file that you flag as Hidden.

The Delete Inhibit attribute prevents you or someone else from accidentally deleting the marked files, even though you have Erase rights in the directory or file. If the application accessing the file deletes the file before modifying it, the appli-cation won't be able to modify the files contents either. So use this attribute on execu-table files rather than data files. The Indexed flag is automatically placed on database files that have grown past 10MB in size, so you probably won't need to use this flag Unless you go into Set FILER Options and set FILER to recognize these files.

The Purge attribute allows NetWare to immediately purge the marked files after they are deleted. The Read Only flag means you'll be able to read and copy the file, but not modify it. So if you have files that you only want to read, but not modify, flag them Read Only. The Rename Inhibit attribute prevents you from renaming the file even though you have Modify rights in the directory. The Shareable flag means the file can be opened by more than one person at a time; you'll most likely use this flag for your programs or utilities in an area that other people are accessing. The System file attribute is reserved for the operating system files themselves.

The Transactional attribute marks a file as transactional. Files marked transactional are treated in a special way by the server. Updates to these files are grouped together in what's called a transaction, which means that either all the updates in the transaction are written to the disk, or none of the updates are written to the disk. Database files are typically flagged transactional; the transactional element protects the database from being corrupted by a partial write. Your supervisor normally takes care of files that are flagged as transactional, so consult your supervisor before doing so.

Now that you've learned about setting file attributes, highlight an attribute you want to give a file through the up/down arrow keys and press <Enter>. The safest flag you can perform is the Archive Needed flag. Highlight this flag and press <Enter>. You can also use <F5> to mark as many other attributes as you wish. Press <Enter>. The marked attributes are transferred to the "File Attributes" window as well as added to the file. When you press <Esc>, you'll see the "Set marked files to specified attributes. Yes/No" window, with the "Yes" prompt highlighted. Press <Enter> to keep these new flag settings and you'll return to the "Multiple File Operations" window.

Set Inherited Rights. This is the final option in the "Multiple File Operations" window. These are the files' inherited rights mask, which are the same IRM you find at the directory level that is applied now to the file level. The IRM includes Supervisory, Access Control, Create, Erase, File Scan, Modify, Read, and Write.

When you select the Set Inherited Rights, you may see the Supervisory right already in the "Inherited Rights" window. This is because the Supervisory right can't be filtered out by the IRM. So if you have the Supervisory right from a trustee assignment, you can't take it away using file or directory rights. The Supervisory right can only be revoked by the supervisor or workgroup manager at the directory level in which it is initially given.

The Access Control right allows you to give other users trustee assignments and change the file and directory IRMs for files, directories, and subdirectories. Highlight the option and press <Enter> to add this right to the selected files.

The Create right allows you to salvage the file after the file is deleted. You do this through the SALVAGE utility (see "The SALVAGE Utility" heading later in this chapter). The Erase right gives you the ability to delete the marked files. The File Scan right allows you to see the specified files when you type DIR at the network prompt in this directory.

You need the Modify right to change any of the files' attributes as well as rename the marked files. However, you'll need Create, Write, and Erase rights to actually modify the data written in the files. The Read right allows you to open and read the marked files, while the Write right allows you to open and write to the marked files.

To add these rights to the marked files, press Insert to bring up the "Other Rights" window, then highlight the rights with the up/down arrow keys and press <Enter>, or use the F5 key to highlight a number of rights, then press <Enter>. The marked rights are added to the "Inherited Rights" window.

To delete a right (except Supervisory), highlight the option and press <Del>. You will see the "Revoke Right" window with the "Yes" option highlighted. Press <Enter> to delete the right.

Once you are finished setting the marked file's IRM, press <Esc> and you'll see a "Set marked subdirectories to specified inherited rights" window with the "Yes" option highlighted. Press <Enter> to set the IRM and return to the "Multiple File Operations" window. Again, setting the IRM affects everyone—including yourself.

Press <Esc> again and you'll return to the "Directory Contents" window.

Looking at Options for a Single File

Now let's look at what you see with a single file selection. At the "Directory Contents" window, highlight a file and press <Enter>. You'll see four options in the "File Options" window: "Copy File," "Move File," "View File," and "View/Set File Information." (If you have no rights in a directory, you'll see a window that says, "You have no rights in this directory. Press Escape to continue.")

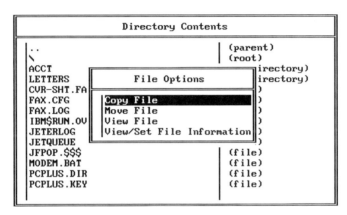

Figure 2-42. The "File Options" window allows you to copy, move, view, and manipulate files in the designated directory

Copy File. This is the first option in the "File Options" window. You need at least Read and File Scan rights to copy a file from a directory; you need at least Write, Create, Erase, and Modify rights in the directory to which you're copying the file. To copy the file you're looking at, highlight the "Copy File" option and press <Enter>. A "Destination Directory" window will appear just beneath the screen header information.

There are two ways you can specify the destination directory path. If you know the whole directory path, you can type it in. For example, if you want to copy a file to directory REPORTS beneath the directory you're currently in, NTS2/BYTE:USERS/ TED, type PUB/BYTE:USERS/EDLIE/REPORTS in the "Destination Directory" window and press <Enter>. The directory path on the second line of the FILER header screen shows your present directory path. If you want to go to the REPORTS/APRIL directory, type PUB/BYTE:USERS/EDLIE/REPORTS/APRIL and press <Enter>.

131

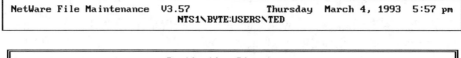

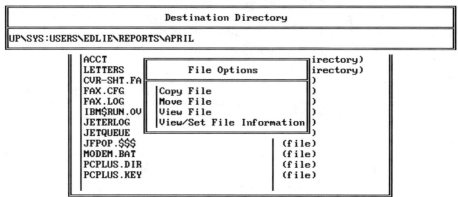

Figure 2-43. Once you select a file, you need to designate a directory to copy it to

If you're attached to another file server and you know your directory path, you can put in that directory path as well. A wrong directory path entry will cause a "Specified directory does not exist" message, which means you typed in the wrong path. If you try to copy the file to a directory in which you haven't sufficient rights, you'll see a window that says, "You have no rights to copy to the specified directory. Press ESCAPE to continue." Press <Esc> to return to the "Destination Directory" window for another try.

Once you've typed in the proper directory path, press <Enter> and you'll see a window that says, "Destination Filename:" and the name of the file you wish to copy. You can change the filename by pressing the Backspace key until the presented filename is gone, typing in a new filename, and pressing <Enter>. If the file already exists in the directory, you'll see the "Overwrite the existing file (filename) Yes/No" window with the "Yes" option highlighted. Press <Enter> if you wish to copy over the file, or choose the "No" option and rename the file.

The second method for putting in the directory path is by first erasing the path in the "Destination Directory" window and pressing <Ins>. This will display a list of all the file servers you're currently attached to. For example, suppose you're attached to server ADMIN and want to copy a file to a directory on server NTS2. Choose the "Copy File" option and press <Ins>. The "File Servers/Local Drives" window will appear.

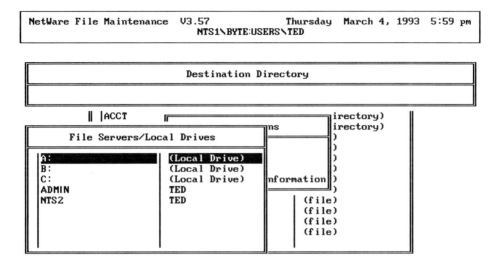

Figure 2-44. You can copy the file to other file servers or local drives

To indicate where you want to copy the file to, highlight either an available local drive or the name of the server you wish to send to. Press <Enter>. Suppose, for example, you want to send a file to the NTS2/BYTE:USERS/TED/REPORTS/APRIL directory. First choose server NTS2. The selected server becomes a part of the "Destination Directory" window, and you'll see the volumes on that server displayed in a "Network Volumes" window. Highlight the volume you want, BYTE, and press <Enter>. A "Network Directories" window with the directories in volume BYTE will appear. Choose the desired directory—USERS, in our current example.

As you continue to specify directories from the "Network Directories" window, the subdirectories under your specified directory continue to appear in the window. If you wish to look at one of those directories, highlight the desired directory name and press <Enter>. Once you reach the desired directory, press <Enter>. You'll see a window that says, "Destination Filename:" and the name of the file you want to copy. You can change the file's name by pressing the Backspace key over the presented filename, then typing in a new filename and pressing <Enter>.

You can add other servers when you need to copy files to their directories. At the "File Information" window, select the "Copy File" option <Enter>; then, at the "Destination Directory" window, press <Ins> to get to the "File Servers/Local Drives" window. By pressing <Ins> again, you'll see a list of all the servers on the network. You can choose another server by typing in the servername and pressing <Enter>. Enter your login name and password for that server, and the servername will be added to the "File Servers/Local Drives" window. You can then select that servername and press <Enter>. Follow the procedures described above to copy a file to a directory on that server.

Move File. This option is the same as the "Copy File" option, only the whole file is moved to the designated location rather than simply being copied to the other location. To do this, highlight the "Move File" option and press <Enter>. You will see the "Destination Directory" window with your present server and volume listed in it.

Type in the directory path where you wish to move the file and press <Enter>. You will see a "New Name:" window with the present filename listed. If you wish to rename the file, you can do so by pressing the backspace key over the present name, typing in a new filename, and pressing <Enter>. Then when you press <Esc> to leave the "File Option" window, you will see the file move under its new directory destination.

You can move files to other directories, floppy disks, or other file servers on the network.

View File. This option lets you look at the file's contents. However, files that are not straight text files (files created through word processing or database functions) will appear on the screen with DOS's interpretation of those functions—in other words, quite an interesting display of graphic characters. Select the "View File" option and you'll see a screen similar to the following:

```
NetWare File Maintenance   V3.57              Thursday   March 4, 1993   6:02 pm
                           NTS1\BYTE:USERS\TED

   TED.MNU                                                            ↓   93

%Main Menu,0,0,3
1. Session Management
        Session
2. File Management
        Filer
3. Volume Information
        VolInfo
4. System Configuration
        SysCon
5. File Server Monitoring
        FConsole
6. Print Queue Management
        PConsole
7. Print Job Configurations
        PrintCon
8. Printer Definitions
        PrintDef
```

Figure 2-45. Use the View option to see what is in a file

134

At the top of the file, you see the file's name and a Viewing Offset line, which indicates the percentage of the file you've seen presently displayed on the screen. As you peruse a file, you'll see the offset change accordingly to reflect where you are in the file. If you wish to go to the end of the file, press <Ctrl>-<PgDn> simultaneously. You can use <PgUp/PgDn> as well as the up/down arrow keys to home in on a section of the file. To exit the "View File" option, press <Esc>.

View/Set File Information. The "View/Set File Information" window contains 13 entries: "Attributes," "Owner," "Inherited Rights Mask," "Trustees," "Current Effective Rights," "Owning Name Space," "File Size," "EA Size," "Short name," "Creation Date," "Last Accessed Date," "Last Archived Date," and "Last Modified Date." Highlight the "View/Set File Information" and press <Enter>.

```
NetWare File Maintenance   V3.57            Thursday  March 4, 1993  6:08 pm
                           NTS1\BYTE:USERS\TED

          ┌──────────────────────────────────────────────────┐
          │           File Information for INTRO.DOC          │
          │                                                   │
          │  Attributes: [RoS------------DR]                  │
          │  Owner: TED                                       │
          │                                                   │
          │  Inherited Rights Mask: [SRWCEMFA]                │
          │  Trustees:  (see list)                            │
          │  Current Effective Rights: [ RWCEMFA]             │
          │                                                   │
          │  Owning Name Space: DOS                           │
          │  File Size: 318 bytes                             │
          │  EA Size: 0 bytes                                 │
          │                                                   │
          │  Short Name: TED.MNU                              │
          │                                                   │
          │  Creation Date:       March 3, 1993              │
          │  Last Accessed Date: March 4, 1993               │
          │  Last Archived Date: (NOT ARCHIVED)              │
          │  Last Modified Date: March 4, 1993               │
          └──────────────────────────────────────────────────┘
```

Figure 2-46. The File Information screen shows a lot of information about a file

The first entry is the "Attributes" option. This option is the same for a single file as it is for multiple files, and you must have Access Control rights in order to change a file's attributes (Modify rights may not be enough); otherwise, you can view the attributes in the "File Attributes" window, but you can't change them. At the "File Information for filename" window, select the "Attributes" entry; you'll see a "Current File Attributes" window listing the attributes already assigned to the file. To see the "Other File Attributes" window, press <Ins>.

For a discussion of the different options, see the "Performing Multiple File Operations" heading earlier in this chapter. To choose your options, highlight the attributes you wish to give to a file and press <Enter>. The safest flag you can perform is the Archive needed flag. Highlight this flag and press <Enter>. If you wish, you can use <F5> to mark a series of attributes. Pressing <Enter> will add those attributes to the file. When you press <Esc>, you'll return to the "File Information" window.

The next entry is "Owner." The name in the screen designates the owner of this file. It doesn't really matter who created the file, but you can use this information to keep track of who owns files in your directories and how much space their files are using. However, the supervisor can change the file owner (as well as the directory owner).

The Inherited Rights Mask entry is the same as the entries you see under the "Set Inherited Rights" option when selecting multiple files. When you select the Inherited Rights Mask, you may see the Supervisory right already in the "Inherited Rights" window. This is because the Supervisory right can't be filtered out by the IRM. The Supervisory right can only be revoked by the supervisor or workgroup manager at the directory level in which it is initially given.

The other rights in the IRM include Access Control, Create, Erase, File Scan, Modify, Read, and Write. The Access Control right allows you to give other users trustee assignments and change the file and directory IRMs for files, directories, and subdirectories. Highlight the option and press <Enter> to add this right to the selected file.

The Create right allows you to salvage the file after the file is deleted. You do this through the SALVAGE utility. The Erase right gives you the ability to delete the file. The File Scan right allows you to see the specified file when you type DIR at the network prompt in this drectory.

You need the Modify right to change any of the file's attributes as well as rename the file. However, you'll need Create, Write, and Erase rights to actually modify the data written in the file. The Read right allows you to open and read the file, while the Write right allows you to open and write to the file.

To add these rights to the file, press Insert to bring up the "Other Rights" window, then highlight the rights with the up/down arrow keys and press <Enter>, or use the F5 key to highlight a number of rights, then press <Enter>. The marked rights are added to the "Inherited Rights" window.

To delete a right (except Supervisory), highlight it and press <Del>. You will see the "Revoke Right" window with the Yes option highlighted. Press <Enter> to delete the right.

Once you are finished setting the file's IRM, press <Esc> to return to the "File Information for filename" window.

Next is the "Trustees" entry. You can use the Trustees entry to grant rights to a file to which you have Access Control rights. (You can give trustee assignments here in FILER or at the network prompt through the GRANT utility. Supervisors and workgroup managers can also use the FILER, GRANT, or SYSCON utilities.)

Select the "Trustees" entry. The resulting window shows who you have given trustee rights to, whether those rights are given to a user or group, and what those rights are.

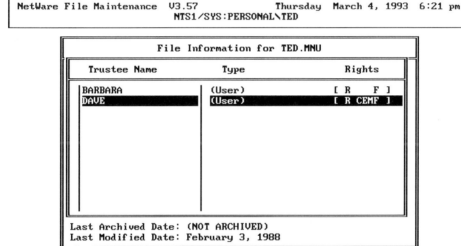

```
NetWare File Maintenance    V3.57            Thursday  March 4, 1993  6:21 pm
                        NTS1/SYS:PERSONAL\TED

              ┌─────────────────────────────────────────────────┐
              │           File Information for TED.MNU           │
              │ ┌─────────────────────────────────────────────┐ │
              │ │  Trustee Name         Type            Rights │ │
              │ │                                              │ │
              │ │ BARBARA              (User)       [ R    F ] │ │
              │ │ DAVE                 (User)       [ R CEMF ] │ │
              │ │                                              │ │
              │ │                                              │ │
              │ │                                              │ │
              │ │                                              │ │
              │ │                                              │ │
              │ │                                              │ │
              │ └─────────────────────────────────────────────┘ │
              │  Last Archived Date: (NOT ARCHIVED)              │
              │  Last Modified Date: February 3, 1988            │
              └─────────────────────────────────────────────────┘
```

Figure 2-47. You add trustees to a file by pressing <Ins>, selecting a user, and granting the proper rights

To add other trustees, press <Ins>. You'll see the names of the other users and groups on the server in the "Others" window. Highlight the name of each user or group you're allowing access to the file and press <Enter>, or use <F5> to mark as many as you want. Then press <Enter>.

A new user given a trustee assignment in FILER receives only Read and File Scan rights with that assignment; you might want to modify those rights if you also want the user to write to the file. Do this by selecting that user's name and pressing <Enter>, thereby bringing up the "Trustee Rights" window with all the rights that user presently has.

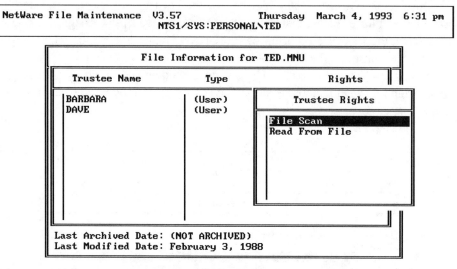

Figure 2-48. You can add other trustee rights by pressing the <Ins> key

The rights you give depend on what you want that user or group to do in the file. For example, if you want the other users to be able only to copy the file into another directory, give them Write, Create, Erase, File Scan, and sometimes Modify rights. To add that capability, press <Ins> when at the "Trustee Rights" window, then use <F5> to mark those rights you wish that user or group to have—Write, Create, Erase, Modify, and File Scan. To add the additional rights, press <Enter>.

If you decide later to revoke any rights, use <F5> to mark all the rights you wish to delete, then press <Del>. You'll see a window that says "Revoke All Marked Rights" with the "Yes" option highlighted. Press <Enter> and the rights are gone. When you define trustee rights for other users or groups, they'll see that they've gained or lost a trustee assignment the next time they look at their trustee or group assignments in SYSCON.

Once you are finished setting the trustee assignments, press <Esc> to return to the "File Information for filename" window. When you are finished, the "Current Effective Rights" entry will show the effective rights you have assigned to that file.

The "Owning Name Space" entry shows if the file is owned by DOS, Macintosh, or OS/2. The "File Size" entry shows how large the file is in bytes. The "EA Size" entry shows the extended attributes size, in particular, this applies to OS/2 and Macintosh files.

If the file is DOS owned, the "Short Name" entry matches the DOS filename. If the file is owned by OS/2 or Macintosh, you'll see a "Long Name" entry, which if you select, will display a "Long Name" window with the name of the file in it.

The next four entries in the File Information window—"Creation Date", "Last Accessed Date", "Last Archived Date", and "Last Modified Date"—provide date information for the file you're in. The "Creation Date" entry shows when the file was created, or the date your supervisor chose when modifying the date. The "Last Accessed Date," "Last Archived Date," and "Last Modified Date" options are similar, each showing the last time you performed those functions. "Last Accessed Date" shows the last time you opened the file; "Last Archived Date" is used by an archiving server (which your network may not be using). Files that haven't been archived will display "Not Archived." "Last Modified Date" shows the date the file was last updated—the same date listed when you type DIR in the directory the file is in. Press <Esc> until you return to the "Available Topics" window.

The last option, "Who Has Rights Here," gives a list of everyone who has rights to the file you have selected. In it, you will see which users can access the file and which rights they have to access it with. Remember that security equivalences play an important part in the rights users have to particular files within a directory. Also coming into play are effective rights and the directory's and file's inherited rights masks.

Changing to Another Directory

While you can get around fairly easily from within the "Directory Contents" option, you can also use the "Select Current Directory" option. If you'd like to look at the file and directory information in another directory, choose the "Select Current Directory" option in the "Available Topics" window. You can use the "Select Current Directory" option to bring up a different directory, but this option doesn't actually change your current directory. When you exit FILER, you'll be in the same directory from which you entered FILER.

To change to another directory from the "Available Topics" window, choose the "Select Current Directory" option. A "Current Directory Path" window will appear just below the screen header information, along with the directory path of the directory you're currently in.

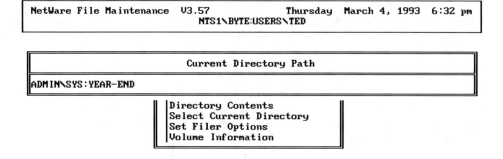

```
NetWare File Maintenance    V3.57          Thursday  March 4, 1993  6:32 pm
                            NTS1\BYTE:USERS\TED

┌─────────────────────────────────────────────────────────────────────────┐
│                      Current Directory Path                               │
├───────────────────────────────────────────────────────────────────────────┤
│ADMIN\SYS:YEAR-END                                                         │
└─────────────────────────────────────────────────────────────────────────┘
                            ║Directory Contents         ║
                            ║Select Current Directory   ║
                            ║Set Filer Options          ║
                            ║Volume Information          ║
```

Figure 2-49. Use the Select Current Directory option to view other directories and their information

There are two ways to specify a new directory path. You can enter the new directory extension by typing in a slash and the name of the new directory. For example, if you want to get to directory REPORTS, directly beneath the directory you're currently in, type /REPORTS in the "Current Directory Path" window and press <Enter>. If you want to go to the REPORTS/APRIL directory, type /REPORTS/APRIL and press <Enter>. If you want to go to a directory above the one you're in, use the backspace key to erase the present directory path until you reach the desired level. Then type in the new directory path. For example, if your directory path is ADMIN/VOL1:USERS/TED/REPORTS/APRIL and you want to go to ADMIN/SYS:YEAR-END, press the backspace key until you reach ADMIN/. Then type in SYS:YEAR-END.

Once you've typed in the proper directory path, press <Enter>. The second line on FILER's header screen will change to reflect the new current directory. If you type the directory name incorrectly, you'll see a window that says, "Specified directory does not exist. Press ESCAPE to continue." Press <Esc> to return to the "Current Directory Path" window for another try. You can also change your directory path by using the backspace key to go to the proper directory level and then pressing <Ins>. This will list all subdirectories beneath the directory displayed in the "Current Directory Path" window.

Selecting one of the directories in the "Network Directories" window makes the selected directory a part of the "Current Directory Path" window. The subdirectories of your new directory path will appear in the "Network Directories" window. Select any subdirectory that's part of the directory path you want. Continue until you reach the desired directory, press <Esc>, then press <Enter>. The second line on FILER's header will change to reflect your new current directory. If you mess up, simply press <Esc> to return to the "Select Current Directory" option with no damage done.

The "Insert" option also lets you choose other servers. Suppose, for example, you're attached to server ADMIN, but you want to see a directory on server PUB. Choose the "Select Current Directory" option and erase the entire directory path that appears in the "Current Directory Path" window. Press <Ins> and you'll see a "File Servers/Local Drives" window.

If server PUB appears in the window, you can select that server directly. Then you can follow the above instructions to get to your designated directory path. If server PUB doesn't appear in the "File Servers/Local Drives" window, press <Ins> again to see a list of all the servers on the network. Select server PUB, then enter your login name for that server and your password. Server PUB will appear in the "File Servers/Local Drives" window. Highlight and select that server; then you can get to your designated directory path by following the above instructions.

Once you reach the desired directory, press <Esc>, then press <Enter>; you'll see the second line on FILER's header change to reflect your new current directory. You'll also return to the "Available Topics" window so that you may perform other FILER functions in that directory.

With NetWare 3.11 and with the "Macintosh" option installed, your supervisor can flag all the directories on a volume as Private, which means that if you don't have at least File Scan rights in a directory, you won't see that directory. Suppose you want to copy a file into the directory path ADMIN/VOL1:DEPT/GUIDE/REPORTS. Let's also say you don't have any rights in the DEPT directory. You can choose server ADMIN and then choose volume VOL1:, but since you have no rights to the directory DEPT, that directory won't appear in the "Network Directories" window. You'll have to press <Esc> to return to the "Destination Directory" window and type in the directory on the keyboard. Then if you have rights to the GUIDE directory below DEPT, you can press <Ins> again and add the GUIDE/REPORTS directory specification, or you can complete the directory path by typing it in at the keyboard. Once the directory path is complete and you've copied the file to it, you'll return to the "File Information" window.

As an interesting aside, suppose when you step out of the Insert mode by pressing <Esc> and begin typing ADMIN/VOL1:DEPT/GUIDE, without noticing you misspell GUIDE as GUILDE. When you press <Enter>, you'll see the window that says, "Specified directory does not exist. Press Escape to continue." If you press <Esc> and then <Ins>, you'll see the message displayed again; however, when you press <Esc> again, the misspelled directory name disappears and you get a list of the available directories in the "Network Directories" window. Then you can highlight the directory you want and press <Enter>. If you misspell the name of a volume, or even the servername, you can do the same thing: press <Esc>, then <Ins>, then <Esc>, and the computer will take you to the place of the spelling infraction.

Setting Up Your FILER Options

If you use FILER often, you may want to set up certain parameters for the files and directories you look at. But remember these parameters last only as long as you're in FILER; if you exit FILER and go back in, you'll have to reset the parameters. The parameters include confirming deletions, confirming file copies, and confirming file overwrites. Other DOS parameters allow you to either include or exclude certain directory and file patterns and to set up file search attributes for Hidden or System files. OS/2 users can be notified if the file attributes or a long name is not preserved during a file copy.

To set up your FILER options from the "Available Topics" window, choose Set Filer Options. You'll see a screen similar to the one shown in Figure 2-50.

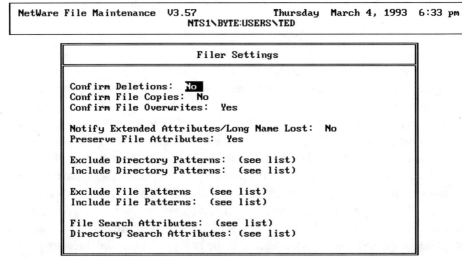

```
NetWare File Maintenance   V3.57            Thursday  March 4, 1993  6:33 pm
                          NTS1\BYTE:USERS\TED


                             Filer Settings

          Confirm Deletions:   No
          Confirm File Copies:   No
          Confirm File Overwrites:   Yes

          Notify Extended Attributes/Long Name Lost:   No
          Preserve File Attributes:   Yes

          Exclude Directory Patterns:   (see list)
          Include Directory Patterns:   (see list)

          Exclude File Patterns    (see list)
          Include File Patterns:   (see list)

          File Search Attributes:   (see list)
          Directory Search Attributes: (see list)
```

Figure 2-50. You can select what files and directories you want to see during this session of FILER

Confirm Deletions, Confirm File Copies, and **Confirm File Overwrites.** These first three entries require Yes/No answers. The default for the "Confirm Deletions" and "Confirm File Copies" entries is "No," meaning you're not prompted to confirm file deletions or copies. The "Confirm Deletions" entry is useful when you delete several files at once. If you want to confirm each individual file deletion before it happens, change the "Confirm Deletions" entry to "Yes."

Confirm File Copies. Since you can copy multiple files to another directory in FILER with NetWare 3.1x, the "Confirm File Copies" entry can be important if you're trying to copy multiple files in data-sensitive directories. If you set this entry to "Yes," you'll be asked to confirm each copy individually; otherwise, the default asks you once if you wish to copy the files, then performs the task if you answer "Yes." The "Confirm File Overwrites" entry is defaulted to "Yes," so when you copy a file to another directory that has a file with the same name, you'll see a little window that says, "Overwrite The Existing File filename Yes/No." If you don't want to see this screen every time you overwrite a file, set the entry to "No."

If you want to change the default setting for any of these three entries, go to the entry you wish and type "Y" for Yes or "N" for No to reflect what you type in.

Notify Extended Attributes/Long Name Lost and **Preserve File Attributes.** These two entries are for OS/2 users. If set to "Yes," the "Notify Extended Attributes/ Long Name Lost" entry will tell you the files using OS/2's extended attributes (that have a name longer than DOS's 8.3 file-naming scheme) what they are saved as when they are translated to the DOS naming scheme. Files copied are reflagged to Normal (NonShareable Read/Write with the Archive bit set). If this is set to "No," OS/2 files will be dropped to NetWare's default without your being notified.

Preserve File Attributes. If you want to preserve your file attributes when you copy files from an OS/2 system, you need to set the "Preserve File Attributes" entry to "Yes." Otherwise, all files transferred are copied and reset to Normal if the entry is set to "No."

Exclude/Include. Next in the "Filer Settings" window are these pattern entries for directories and files. While the entries may be handy for files, there are few reasons for excluding directories. The entries, however, are there nonetheless. Since these entries make more sense for files, we'll use files for our example; apply the same principles to directories.

File Exclude. The "File Exclude" entry allows you to specify a file pattern that you don't want to see in the directories you're in. Suppose you have an abundance of files with an .SCR extension that you don't want to wade through when you list that directory. Select the "File Exclude Pattern" entry from the "Filer Settings" window <Enter>, then press <Ins>. Type in *.SCR to exclude all files with the .SCR extension. Press <Enter> and the .SCR exclude parameter will be added to the "Exclude File Patterns" window. Remember that the same principles apply to directories.

The next time you look at the "Directory Contents" option (providing you don't leave FILER beforehand), you'll see only the files in that directory that don't have the .SCR extension.

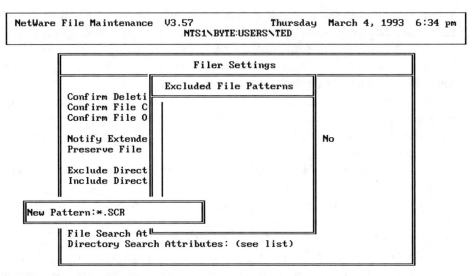

```
NetWare File Maintenance   V3.57          Thursday  March 4, 1993  6:34 pm
                           NTS1\BYTE:USERS\TED
```

```
                            Filer Settings

                       Excluded File Patterns
        Confirm Deleti│
        Confirm File C│
        Confirm File O│

        Notify Extende│                           No
        Preserve File │

        Exclude Direct│
        Include Direct│

New Pattern:*.SCR

        File Search At
        Directory Search Attributes: (see list)
```

Figure 2-51. You can exclude certain file patterns so you won't have to see them when viewing a directory's contents

The "File Include" pattern is similar. If you want to see only the files that begin with the letter S in a directory, go to the "File Include Pattern" entry and press <Enter>. NetWare 3.11 comes with an asterisk (*) in the "Include File Patterns" window, which lists all files in the directory. You need to delete the asterisk before adding new patterns; otherwise, FILER will still look for all files in the directory. Highlight the asterisk and press <Del>; you'll see the "Delete Pattern" window with the "Yes" option highlighted. Press <Enter>. Then to add the include pattern to the "Include File Patterns" window, press <Ins> and type in S* to list all files that begin with the letter S. Press <Enter> and the S* parameter will be added to the "Include File Patterns" window.

You can use wild cards to look for any group of files that have a pattern in their names. For example, if you have many files, but want to see only three—GLSYS.FDM, DLSYS.FED, and SLSYS.FDM—you can put in a pattern using the question mark and asterisk wild cards (like ??SYS*.*). FILER will display only the files with that pattern. However, if you have more than one include pattern in the "Include File Patterns" window, FILER will display a file if it matches any of the patterns.

Note that *exclude patterns* will overwrite *include patterns* if they conflict. So if you have an include pattern of S*, and an exclude pattern of ??SYS*.*, you won't see any files that begin with S and have SYS two letters into their filename.

This procedure also applies to directories. To limit the number of directories you have to view, follow the same steps you followed in the "File Exclude/File Include Pattern" options, but perform them in the "Directories Exclude/Include Patterns" options.

Remember, if you don't like the way you've set up your defaults, press <Del> over a pattern you don't like, answer "Yes" to the "Delete Pattern" window, and everything will be back to normal. Or just exit FILER. When you go back in, the FILER default settings will be there again.

Next in the "Filer Settings" window is the "File Search Attributes" entry. This entry affects only those files flagged as either Hidden or System files. Hidden and System are DOS file attributes that hide your files from standard directory listings such as DIR. Both attributes protect files from being copied or deleted. The System attribute was created to hide files that show up when you look for files with the Hidden attribute. However, NetWare looks at both of them as equal, so with Modify rights, you, too, can flag a file as a System or a Hidden file. You won't be able to see those files in the "Directory Contents" window. But if you want to look at your hidden files, select the "File Search Attributes" entry and press <Enter>. You'll see the "Search File Attributes" window. Press <Ins> to reach the "Other Search Attributes" window.

Since the "Hidden File" option is already highlighted, press <Enter> and the option will be added to the "Search File Attributes" window. Then you'll see all your hidden files while you're in this session of FILER. If you've flagged files as System, you can choose the "System File" option as well, but since NetWare looks at them equally, stick with one flag choice, such as Hidden, for convenience.

The last entry is "Directory Search Attributes," which works exactly like the "File Search Attributes" except that you use it for directories. For an explanation on using this option, simply follow the explanation just given for the "File Search Attributes" entry and substitute "directory" for "file."

Looking at Your Volume Information

The last option on FILER's "Available Topics" window is "Volume Information." This option shows information about the volume where your current directory is located. Here you see the volume's name and type, its total size, how much space is left, the maximum number of directory entries on the volume, and the number of directory entries available.

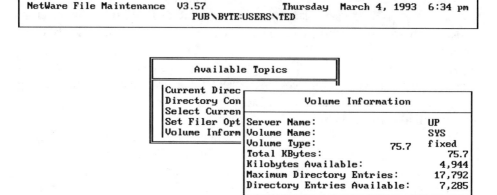

Figure 2-52. You can select and view volume information on the server

The first entry is your servername, followed by the name of the volume your directory is currently on. The "Volume Type" entry indicates whether the hard disk containing this volume is fixed or removable. (An example of a removable disk is a Bernoulli Box or a CD ROM, which is one of the selections you can have with NetWare 3.12.) The "Total Bytes" entry shows how big the volume is in kilobytes. The volume in our example is 75.7 megabytes (MB). (One megabyte is 1,024 kilobytes in size, a kilobyte is 1,024 bytes in size, and a byte is eight bits in size. A word processor uses these bits to form characters and to store data.)

The "Kilobytes Available" entry shows how much space is left on this volume; our example shows that 4.8MB are left. Next is the "Maximum Directory Entries" display, which your supervisor can change if the "Directory Entries Available" figure gets too low.

To exit the "Volume Information" option, press <Esc>. To leave FILER, press <Esc> again. You'll see the "Exit Filer Yes/No" window with the "Yes" option highlighted. Press <Enter> and you'll return to the network prompt.

The SESSION Utility

SESSION is NetWare's session manager. It allows you to set up your drive mappings from a menu and to send messages to users and groups. Because this utility is valid only during your current login session, any drive mappings you set in SESSION will be lost when you log out. SESSION allows you to choose servers to look at (within SESSION) to see how your search and regular drive mappings are mapped, to see your effective rights in the mappings, and to send messages to both users and groups.

To go into the SESSION utility, type SESSION at the network prompt and press <Enter>. The "Available Topics" window will appear with six options: "Change Current Server," "Drive Mappings," "Group List," "Search Mappings," "Select Default Drive," and "User List."

```
Session Manager  3.52                Thursday  March 4, 1993  7:27 pm
                   User TED On File Server ADMIN
```

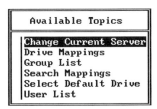

```
 Available Topics
┌──────────────────────┐
│Change Current Server │
│Drive Mappings        │
│Group List            │
│Search Mappings       │
│Select Default Drive  │
│User List             │
└──────────────────────┘
```

Figure 2-53. The SESSION utility's initial screen

To get around in SESSION, press <Enter> on a highlighted option to bring you to the next screen available under that option, and press <Esc> to go to the previous screen. For example, from the "Available Topics" window, select the "User List" option by pressing <PgDn> on the numeric keypad. Once that option is highlighted, press <Enter>. <PgDn> brings you to the bottom of the list of selections, and <PgUp> brings you to the top of the list. You can also use the Up (8) and Down (2) arrow keys to highlight and select an option, or you can type the first letters of the option you wish to select and the selector bar will move to that option.

Never feel stranded in the menus—pressing <F1> at any time will provide an explanation of the menu options currently on the screen. Each help screen gives you information specific to the option choice currently displayed on the screen. Once you've chosen another menu option by pressing <Enter>, pressing <F1> will bring you a different set of help screens relating to the newly selected option. (A word of warning, however: SESSION isn't noted for its informative help screens.)

The first option on the "Available Topics" window is "Change Current Server." SESSION looks at the drive mappings on only the server you're logged in to; however, if you wish to perform a task involving another server—for example, send a message to someone on another server or map a drive to another server—select the "Change Current

Server" option. You'll see the "File Server/User Name" window listing the names of all the servers you're currently attached to. Note that the name of the server from which you entered SESSION is highlighted by the selector bar. To change to a different server, highlight the name of the server you wish to look at and press <Enter>. You'll return to the "Available Topics" window, and the second line on the screen header will indicate your new server.

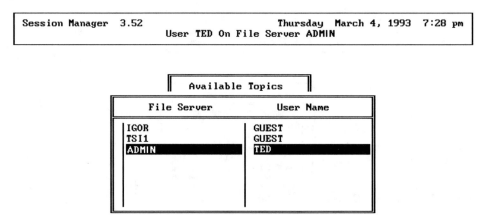

Figure 2-54. You can add servers or you can delete servers that you are attached to

If you wish to add a drive mapping to another server that doesn't show up in the "File Server/User Name" window, press <Ins>. This will display the "Other File Servers" window, which lists all the servers on the internetwork. You can choose another server by typing the servername and pressing <Enter>. Or you can use the usual means for getting around in a NetWare window to choose another server. If you happen to type your user name incorrectly, or if you mistype your password, you'll see a screen that says, "Access to file server denied. Press Escape to continue." Press <Esc> to try typing in your password again, or press <Esc> twice to return to the "Other File Servers" window. When you want to return once more to the "File Servers/Local Drives" window, press <Esc>. You can also log out from an attached server by highlighting the name of that server with the selector bar and pressing <Del>. You'll see a "Logout from server Yes/No" window with the "Yes" option highlighted. Press <Enter> to log out from the designated server. (However, you cannot log out of your default server.)

148

Looking at Your Drive Mappings

The next option on the "Available Topics" window is "Drive Mappings." This option shows the local and network drive mappings that you see from the login script on your default server; if your login script attaches you to other servers and maps drives to those servers, you'll see those drive mappings as well. However, you can't go into the "Change Current Server" option, select another server, and view the drive mappings on that server from this option.

When you select the "Drive Mappings" option, you'll see a screen similar to the one on the following page.

From this screen you may add another drive mapping, or you may delete one of the current mappings (but not local drives). Suppose, for example, you want to delete the G: drive mapping. To go to the G: mapping, type the letter G on the keyboard and press <Del>. The "Delete Drive Mapping Yes/No" window will appear in the center of your screen with the "Yes" option highlighted. Press <Enter> to delete the drive mapping. When you exit SESSION and type MAP at the network prompt, you'll see that you no longer have a drive G: mapping. However, as is the case with all changes made in SESSION, this change only lasts during this session with the server. If you log out and then log back in, the drive mapping will be back. To make a permanent change, you must use the SYSCON utility to change your login script. (See "The SYSCON Utility" heading earlier in this chapter.)

```
Session Manager  3.52                    Thursday  March 4, 1993  7:34 pm
                       User TED On File Server ADMIN
```

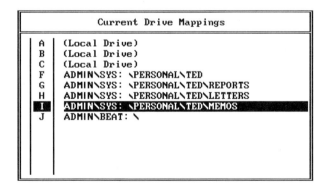

```
            Current Drive Mappings
  A  │  (Local Drive)
  B  │  (Local Drive)
  C  │  (Local Drive)
  F  │  ADMIN\SYS: \PERSONAL\TED
  G  │  ADMIN\SYS: \PERSONAL\TED\REPORTS
  H  │  ADMIN\SYS: \PERSONAL\TED\LETTERS
  I  │  ADMIN\SYS: \PERSONAL\TED\MEMOS
  J  │  ADMIN\BEAT: \
```

Figure 2-55. The Drive Mappings option shows your current mappings (but not your search mappings)

To add another drive to the "Current Drive Mappings" window, press <Ins>. SESSION will present the next available drive letter in a little "Drive" window. However, if you don't like that drive letter, you can change it. If you change a drive letter to one you're already using, you'll see a window that says, "Drive already in use. Press ESCAPE to continue." After you select a drive letter, press <Enter>. A "Select Directory" window will appear just beneath the SESSION screen header.

There are two ways to enter a directory path at the "Select Directory" window. If you know the full directory path, you can type it in. So if you want to map a drive to NTS3/BYTE:USERS/ED/REPORTS, simply type NTS3/BYTE:USERS/ED/REPORTS in the "Select Directory" window and press <Enter>. You'll see "Do you want to map root this drive? Yes/No" with the "No" option highlighted. The MAP ROOT command makes the directory look as if it's at the root level. This function is handy for certain applications that don't cope well with extremely long directory paths. So if your application has a hard time writing to a long directory path, such as NTS3/BYTE:USERS/ED/REPORTS/SOUTHWST/1991/SEPT, you can select "Yes" in the map root window, and that whole directory path will be designated by drive letter G:. You will also see that the directory path now has a backslash at its end, signifying that the path has been duly dubbed a root directory.

Whether you choose "Yes" or "No," the new drive mapping will appear in the "Current Drive Mappings" window. If you're attached to another server and you know the directory path, you can put in that directory path as well. If you type in the wrong directory name, you'll see a window that says, "Specified directory does not exist. Press ESCAPE to continue."

If you can't remember what the correct directory name is, you can also put in the directory path by pressing <Ins> at the "Select Directory" window. The Insert key will list the names of all the servers you're currently attached to. Let's say you're logged in to server ADMIN, but you want to map a drive to a directory on server NTS3. Press <Ins>, choose the drive letter you want, press <Enter>, then press <Ins>. You'll see the "File Servers/Local Drives" window.

To choose server NTS3, highlight the servername and press <Enter>. Suppose, for example, that you want to map a drive to the NTS3/BYTE:USERS/ED/REPORTS/APRIL directory. First choose server NTS3. The selected server becomes a part of the "Destination Directory" window, and you'll see the available volumes on that server; highlight volume BYTE and press <Enter>. You'll see the directories of that volume appear in the "Network Directories" window. Highlight directory USERS and press <Enter>. Continue to choose directories until your desired directory path is complete.

Press <Esc> and then <Enter>, and the drive mapping will be added to the "Current Drive Mappings" window (after you choose whether or not the drive mapping is to be a root drive).

With NetWare for Macintosh installed, your supervisor can flag all the directories on a volume as Private, which means if you don't have at least File Scan rights in a directory, you won't see that directory. Suppose you want to map a drive to ADMIN/ VOL1:DEPT/GUIDE/REPORTS, although you don't have any rights in the DEPT directory. You can choose server ADMIN, then choose volume VOL1, but since you have no rights to directory DEPT, that directory won't appear in the "Network Directories" window. You'll have to press <Esc> to return to the "Destination Directory" window and type in DEPT from the keyboard. Then, if you have rights to the GUIDE directory below DEPT, press <Ins> again and add the GUIDE/REPORTS directory specification, or complete the directory path by typing it in at the keyboard.

You can add other servers to the "File Servers/Local Drives" window by pressing <Ins> again; you'll see a list of all the servers on the network. Select the server you want, then enter your login name and your password for that server. The server will appear in the "File Servers/Local Drives" window. You can then select that server and press <Enter>.

You can also modify a drive mapping by highlighting the drive mapping, then pressing the F3 Modify key. Let's say you want to go to the APR subdirectory in the directory path NTS3/BYTE:USERS/ED/REPORTS. Highlight the drive mapping in the "Current Drive Mappings" window and press <F3>. The drive you highlight will pop up into the "Select Directory" window, where you can type in your directory modification. Or you can press <Ins> to list the directories beneath the REPORTS directory, highlight the APR directory, press <Enter>, <Esc>, then <Enter> again. After you answer the map root question, the directory path will now include the APR directory. This change will last until you log out or log back in again.

A final task you can perform in the "Current Drive Mappings" window is viewing your effective rights in each of the drive mappings. To display the effective rights, highlight the drive option you wish to look at and press <Enter>.

You'll see a window in the center-right side of your screen, showing the effective rights you have in the directory at the bottom of the drive mapping. For a local drive, you'll see a window that says "Directory effective rights do not apply to local drives. Press ESCAPE to continue." If you have no rights in a network directory, you'll see no rights displayed.

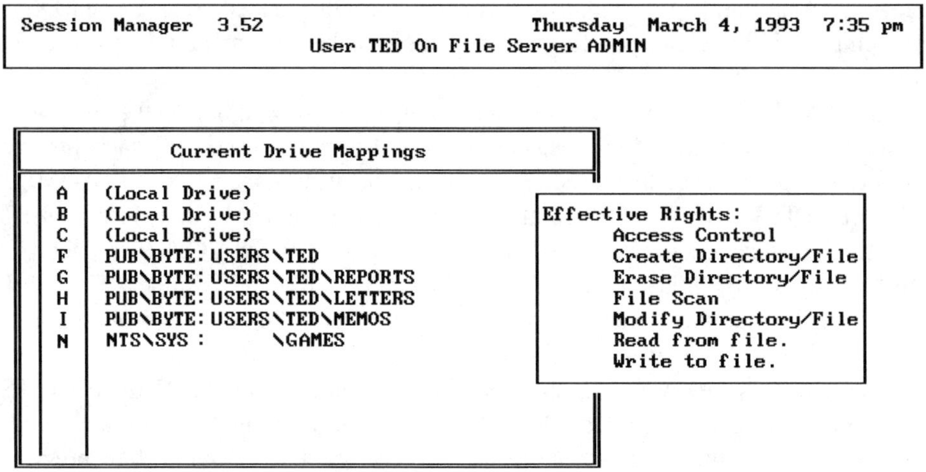

```
Session Manager  3.52                    Thursday  March 4, 1993  7:35 pm
                      User TED On File Server ADMIN
```

```
              Current Drive Mappings
  A  |  (Local Drive)
  B  |  (Local Drive)                    Effective Rights:
  C  |  (Local Drive)                       Access Control
  F  |  PUB\BYTE: USERS\TED                 Create Directory/File
  G  |  PUB\BYTE: USERS\TED\REPORTS         Erase Directory/File
  H  |  PUB\BYTE: USERS\TED\LETTERS         File Scan
  I  |  PUB\BYTE: USERS\TED\MEMOS           Modify Directory/File
  N  |  NTS\SYS :        \GAMES             Read from file.
                                            Write to file.
```

Figure 2-56. You can also see your effective rights in network directories

To exit the "Effective Rights" window, press <Esc>; to exit the "Current Drive Mappings" window, press <Esc> again and you'll return to the "Available Topics" window.

Looking at the Group List Option

About all you can do from the "Group List" window in the "Available Topics" window is send messages. You can send a message to one group or to several groups. A list of the groups on the server appears when you select the "Group List" option. To send a message to a single group, highlight the group's name and press <Enter>. You'll see a "Message" window across the center of your screen.

To send a message to several groups, use <F5> to mark the names of all the groups you want to send the message to. Press <Enter>; you'll see the "Message" window across the center of your screen.

You can have a maximum of forty-five characters (including spaces) in your message, but that count includes your name, as the figure above shows. In NetWare 3.11, Novell took out the ability to erase your name, but you can write to the end of the message window. To edit your message, use <Del> to delete characters from the right and the Backspace key to delete characters from the left. You can also use the Ctrl-Left arrow key to move one word to the left, and the Ctrl-Right arrow key to move one word to the right.

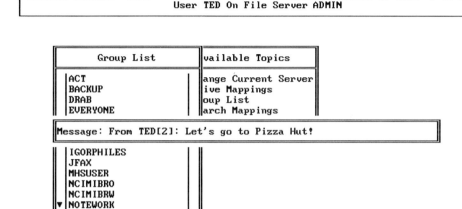

```
Session Manager  3.52                Thursday  March 4, 1993  7:35 pm
                      User TED On File Server ADMIN
```

```
        Group List          │vailable Topics
    │ACT                     │ange Current Server│
    │BACKUP                  │ive Mappings
    │DRAB                    │oup List
    │EVERYONE                │arch Mappings

│Message: From TED[2]: Let's go to Pizza Hut!

    │ IGORPHILES
    │ JFAX
    │ MHSUSER
    │ NCIMIBRO
    │ NCIMIBRW
  ▼ │NOTEWORK
```

Figure 2-57. Through the SESSION utility, you can send messages to users and groups

Once you've typed your message, press <Enter> and the message will be on its way. A sent message appears along the bottom of the receiver's screen. To remove a message you've received, press the <Ctrl> and <Enter> keys simultaneously. If the messages are bothersome, you can avoid receiving most of them with the CASTOFF command. (See the "Message Utilities" heading in Chapter 3.)

Once you've sent your message, you'll return to the "Group List" window. To return to the "Available Topics" window, press <Esc> again.

Seeing What Your Network Search Mappings Are

The next option in the "Available Topics" window is "Search Mappings." The "Search Mappings" option is similar to the "Drive Mappings" option, except that it shows your search paths. Search paths make it simple for NetWare to find a particular application or utility for you. To find an application or utility you've asked for, NetWare first searches the directory you're currently in; if the application or utility isn't there, NetWare then searches the search drive mappings. This process is similar to the way the DOS PATH command works.

With a search drive mapped to the directory where a certain application is, and with the proper rights (at least Read and File Scan rights), you can type the application's execute name (such as WP <Enter> for WordPerfect) from any directory, and you'll be in that application.

153

You should always leave alone the SEARCH1:=Z:. [ADMIN/SYS:PUBLIC] search mapping, because the PUBLIC directory is where you find the NetWare user utilities. Login scripts can contain up to twenty-six drive mappings—one for each letter in the alphabet. You can have up to sixteen of those drive mappings defined as search drives. Search drive designations are assigned starting backwards from Z:.

```
Session Manager  3.52                 Thursday  March 4, 1993  7:36 pm
                      User TED On File Server ADMIN
```

```
                Current Search Mappings

     1   Z:=NTS1\SYS:  \PUBLIC
     2   Y:=NTS1\SYS:  \PUBLIC\IBM_PC\MSDOS\V5.00
     3   X:=NTS1\SYS:  \APPS\WP51
     4   W:=NTS1\SYS:  \PUBLIC\BATCH
     5   V:=NTS1\SYS:  \PUBLIC\UTIL
```

Figure 2-58. You can add, delete, or modify search drive mappings with this option

Select the "Search Mappings" option, and you'll see the "Current Search Mappings" window. You can add another search drive mapping to this screen or delete one of the current mappings. To add another search drive, press <Ins> at the "Current Search Mappings" window. SESSION will present you with the next available search drive in a little "Search Drive Number" window. You can change that number if you don't like it.

If you change it to a drive number you already have, you'll be able to add the drive at that search drive number, and the search drive path that you "borrowed" will move to the next available search drive number. After you've selected a drive letter, press <Enter>. A "Select Directory" window will appear just beneath the SESSION screen header.

You can input a new search path in two ways. If you know the whole directory path, you can type it in. For example, if you want to map a drive to NTS3/SYS:PUBLIC/LOTUS, simply type NTS3/SYS:PUBLIC/LOTUS in the "Select Directory" window and press <Enter>. The new search drive mapping will appear in the Current "Search Mappings" window. This also works when you want to add a search drive to another server to which you are attached. Be sure to include the server in the directory path that you type at the "Select Directory" window. (If you type in the wrong directory name, you'll see a window that says, "Specified directory does not exist. Press Escape to continue.")

If you can't remember the correct directory path, you can put in the search drive by pressing <Ins> at the "Select Directory" window. The Insert key will bring up a list of all the servers you're currently attached to. For example, suppose you're logged in to server NTS1, but you want to map a drive to a directory on server PUB. Press <Ins>, choose the drive number you wish, press <Enter>, then press <Ins>. You'll see the "File Servers/Local Drives" window.

Highlight file server PUB and press <Enter>. Suppose you want to map a search drive to the PUB/SYS:PUBLIC/LOTUS directory. (First, find out if you have any rights to that directory, or your drive-mapping efforts will be in vain.) When you choose file server NTS3, it becomes part of the "Destination Directory" window, and you'll see a list of NTS3's available volumes. Highlight volume SYS and press <Enter>; you'll next see the directories of your directory path appear in the "Network Directories" window. Highlight directory PUBLIC and press <Enter>. Continue until you reach the desired directory, press <Enter>, and the search drive mapping will be added to the Current "Search Mappings" window.

As mentioned earlier, suppose that you step out of the Insert mode by pressing <Esc> and begin typing NTS3/SYS:PUBLIC/LOTOUS, without noticing you misspell LOTUS as LOTOUS. When you press <Enter>, you'll see the window that says, "Specified directory does not exist. Press Escape to continue." If you press <Esc> and then <Ins>, you will see the message displayed again; however, when you press <Esc> again, the misspelled directory name disappears and you get a list of the available directories in the "Network Directories" window. Then you can highlight the directory you desire and press <Enter>. If you misspell the name of a volume, or even the servername, you can do the same thing: press <Esc>, then <Ins>, then <Esc>, and the program will bring you to the place of the spelling infraction.

You can add other servers to the "File Servers/Local Drives" window by pressing <Ins> again; you'll see a list of all the servers on the network. Highlight the name of the server, then press <Enter>. Next, enter your login name and password for that server, and the server will be added to the "File Servers/Local Drives" window. You can then select that server from the "File Servers/Local Drives" window.

You can also add a local drive as a search drive mapping by highlighting the local drive (instead of a server) from the Current "Search Mappings" window. A word of warning: if you do add a local drive this way, the local drive won't go away when you log out or log back in again. And because it's a local drive, that search drive will stay with you even if you log in to other servers from this workstation. This makes SESSION a great PATH editor, for you can add and delete local directories to the PATH command without having to type out the entire PATH command with your designated changes. Then when you exit SESSION and type SET <Enter>, you'll see your changes in the PATH command.

You can also delete a search drive mapping from the Current "Search Mappings" window of SESSION. Suppose you want to delete search mapping number 5 (S5:). To go to the number 5 mapping, use the up/down arrow keys until search drive mapping 5 is highlighted; press <Del>. The "Delete Drive Mapping Yes/No" window will appear in the center of your screen, with the "Yes" option highlighted. Press <Enter> and the search drive will be deleted. You can get rid of local search drives the same way, from whatever server you're presently logged in to. Simply highlight the mapping and press <Del>.

When you exit SESSION and type MAP at the network prompt, you'll see that you no longer have a number 5 search drive or the local search drive. However, this change lasts only for the duration of this session with the server (except local drive modifications, which last until you again modify the PATH command). When you log out and then log back in, you'll have your original drive mapping back. To make a permanent change, you must go into the SYSCON utility and change your login script.

You can also change a drive mapping by highlighting the drive mapping and pressing the Modify (F3) key. Suppose you want to go to the BACKUP directory in the directory path NTS3/SYS:PUBLIC/LOTUS. Highlight the drive mapping in the Current "Search Mappings" window and press <F3>. The drive you highlighted pops up into the "Select Directory" window where you can type in your directory modification. Or you can press <Ins> to list the directories beneath the LOTUS directory, highlight the BACKUP directory, press <Enter>, then <Esc>, and then <Enter> again, and the directory path now includes the BACKUP directory. This change will last until you log out or log back in again.

A final task you can perform in the "Current Search Mappings" window is viewing your effective rights in each of the drive mappings. To display the effective rights, highlight the drive option you wish to look at and press <Enter>. A window in the center-right side of your screen shows the effective rights you have in the directory. For a local search drive mapping, you'll see a window that says "Directory effective rights do not apply to local drives. Press ESCAPE to continue." The window won't show any effective rights for network directories in which you have no rights.

```
Session Manager  3.52                    Thursday  March 4, 1993  7:37 pm
                         User TED On File Server ADMIN


  ┌──────────────────────────────────────────────────────────────────┐
  │                         Select Directory                           │
  ├──────────────────────────────────────────────────────────────────┤
  │NTS1\SYS:APPS\                                                       │
  └──────────────────────────────────────────────────────────────────┘
    ┌──────────────────────────────────────────────────────────┐
    │  2 │ Y:NTS1\SYS:   \PUBLIC\IBM_PC\MSDOS\V5.00              │
    │  3 │ X:NTS1\SYS:   \APPS\WP51                              │
    │  4 │ S:NTS1\SYS:   \APPS\DATA                              │
    │  5 │ W:PUB \SYS:   \PUBLIC\NOTEWORK                        │
    │  6 │ V:NTS1\SYS:   \PUBLIC\UTIL                            │
    │  7 │ U:NTS1\SYS:   \APPS\POP                               │
    │  8 │ T:PUB \SYS:   \APPS\WIZ                               │
    │                                                           │
    └──────────────────────────────────────────────────────────┘
```

Figure 2-59. When you press <F3> on drive mapping, you can change the directory path to another directory

To exit the "Effective Rights" window, press <Esc>; to exit the "Current Search Mappings" window, press <Esc> again and you'll return to the "Available Topics" window.

Choosing a Default Drive

The next item on the "Available Topics" window is "Select Default Drive." It lets you choose which directory you exit to when you leave the SESSION utility.

As you can see, network and search drive mappings are listed together, with no indication of their status. The highlighted drive is the present default drive. To change the default drive, highlight the drive you want to be in when you exit SES-SION and press <Enter>. For example, if drive E: is your default and you want to exit to drive G:, highlight drive G: and press <Enter>. You'll return to the "Available Topics" window, and when you exit SESSION, you'll be at the drive G: prompt.

157

```
┌─────────────────────────────────────────────────────────────────┐
│ Session Manager  3.52                 Thursday  March 4, 1993  7:38 pm │
│                   User TED On File Server ADMIN                    │
└─────────────────────────────────────────────────────────────────┘
```

```
        ┌─────────────────────────────────────────────┐
        │            Select Default Drive             │
        ├───┬─────────────────────────────────────────┤
        │ A │ (Local Drive)                           │
        │ B │ (Local Drive)                           │
        │ C │ (Local Drive)                           │
        │ F │ NTS1\SYS:  \PERSONAL\TED                 │
        │ G │ NTS1\SYS:  \PERSONAL\TED\REPORTS         │
        │▓H▓│▓NTS1\SYS:▓▓\PERSONAL\TED\LETTERS▓▓▓▓▓▓▓▓▓│
        │ I │ NTS1\SYS:  \PERSONAL\ ED\MEMOS           │
        │ J │ NTS1\BEAT: \                             │
        │ U │ NTS1\SYS:  \PUBLIC\UTIL                  │
        │ W │ NTS1\SYS:  \PUBLIC\BATCH                 │
        │ X │ NTS1\SYS:  \APPS\WP51                    │
        │ Y │ NTS1\SYS:  \PUBLIC\IBM_PC\MSDOS\V5.00    │
        │ Z │ NTS1\SYS:  \PUBLIC                       │
        └───┴─────────────────────────────────────────┘
```

Figure 2-60. With SESSION, you can choose which drive you wish to be in when you leave the utility

Look Who's Logged In to the Server

The last option on the "Available Topics" window is "User List." Through the "User List" option you can look at some connection information about a user, or you can send messages to one or more users. Select the "User List" option and you'll see a listing of the users currently available on your default server, or on the server you've changed to through the "Change Current Server" option.

To see connection information about a user, highlight the name of that user and press <Enter>. A small "Available Options" window will appear, listing two options: "Display User Info" and "Send Message." Since "Display User Info" is highlighted, press <Enter> and you'll see a window similar to the one shown in Figure 2-61.

The first line lists the user's full name as defined by the supervisor in SYSCON. If that user's full name hasn't been defined, this line will say, "No Full Name Speci-fied." The "Object Type" entry is how the bindery categorizes the "objects" that use network resources (the bindery is NetWare's special database that keeps track of you and your security rights). In our example, Marti is of the object type User. If you have a print server presently attached, you can see Print Server in its object type.

158

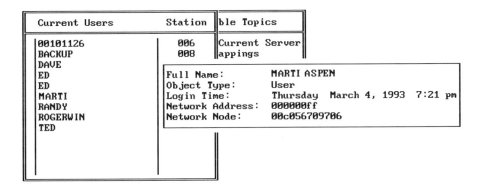

Figure 2-61. You can see information about who's logged in to the server through the "User List" option

The third entry, "Login Time," shows when that user (object) logged in last. "Network Address" shows the network address that your workstation uses to talk to the server. The "Network Node" entry shows the physical network interface board address of Marti's workstation. To hop back to the "Available Options" window, press <Esc>.

If you want to send a message to Marti, select the "Send Message" option. You'll see a "Message" window across the center of your screen. You can have a total of fifty-five characters, including spaces, in your message, but that total includes your name. That means that the length of your name directly affects the length of the message you can send.

If you need to edit your message, <Del> will delete characters from the right, and the Backspace key will delete characters from the left. You can also use the <Ctrl>-<Left arrow key> combination to move one word to the left, and <Ctrl>-<Right arrow key> to move one word to the right.

Once you've typed your message, press <Enter> and the message will be on its way. (NetWare won't send a message if you simply press <Enter> at the message window without typing in anything.) Messages appear on the bottom line of the receiver's screen. To get rid of messages sent to you, press the <Ctrl>-<Enter> keys simultaneously. If someone's sending you a lot of dumb messages and you don't want to get them any more, you can block reception through the CASTOFF command. (See the "Message Utilities"

159

heading in Chapter 3.) Once you've sent your message, you'll return to the "Available Options" window. To abandon a message before you send it, press <Esc>, which returns you to the "Available Options" window.

You can send a message to several people at a time by returning to the "Current Users/Station" window and marking with <F5> the names of all the people to whom you wish to send the message. Press <Enter> and you'll see a "Message" window across the center of your screen. Then follow the steps described above.

From the "Current Users/Station" window, you can either select the name of another user you'd like to view information on or send messages to, or you can press <Esc> and return to the "Available Topics" window. To exit SESSION, press <Esc> again and you'll see the "Exit SESSION Yes/No" window with the "Yes" option highlighted. Press <Enter>, and you're back at the network prompt.

The VOLINFO Utility

As you may recall from the Introduction, a volume is the highest measurable portion of disk space that can span one or more hard disk drives. You start with the server, on which there are physical hard disks; these disks can be divided into volumes, or an entire disk or more than one disk can be designated as a volume. Within volumes, you define directories and subdirectories. NetWare 3.11 and 3.12 allows volumes to span more than one physical disk, as well as allows disks to be divided into up to sixty-four volumes.

Volumes are the second designation in a directory path. For example, in the directory path NTS3/BYTE:USERS/TED/REPORTS, BYTE is the volume. When you map a drive using the MAP utility, you first designate the drive letter, then you type the name of the server (NTS3), followed by the volume on the server (BYTE). The volume name is followed by a colon (:), which indicates that everything below the colon is a directory and, with the proper rights, is accessible. (Since volumes are a logical portion of the disk, they are therefore not accessible.) Below the colon in our example, then, are listed the directory and subdirectory structures: USERS/TED/REPORTS.

The VOLINFO utility lists the names of the volumes on a server and how many kilobytes and directories those volumes contain. In VOLINFO, you can also change to other file servers to see their volume information. You'll probably use VOLINFO only for affirming an error message telling you the system can't perform some file creating/writing or printing task because it has run out of disk space.

Type VOLINFO at the network prompt and press <Enter>. You'll see a screen listing the names of all the volumes on your file server. VOLINFO shows the volume information for the server whose directory you're currently in. For example, suppose you have drive G: mapped to a directory on server UP, and drive F: mapped to a directory on server NTS3. If you enter VOLINFO from drive G:, you'll see the volumes on server UP; if you enter VOLINFO from drive F: you'll see the volumes on server NTS3. Figure 2-62 shows the VOLINFO screen for our sample server, UP.

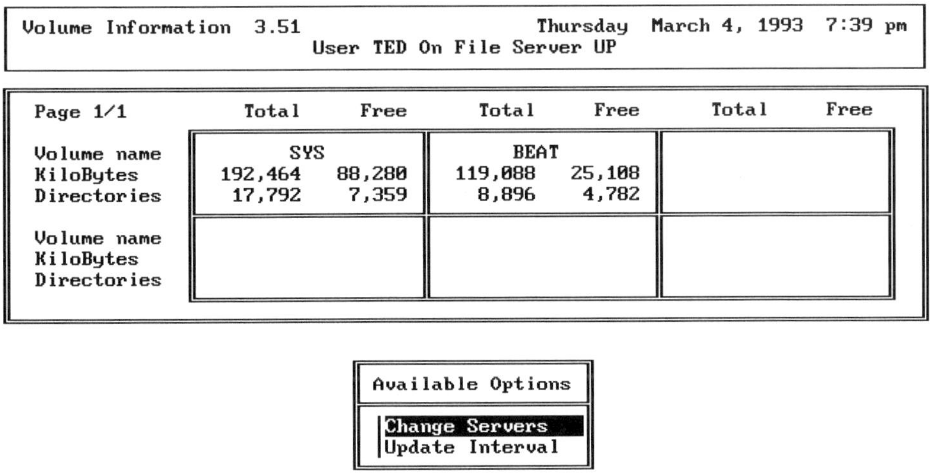

```
Volume Information  3.51                    Thursday  March 4, 1993  7:39 pm
                         User TED On File Server UP

Page 1/1           Total     Free      Total     Free      Total     Free
Volume name          SYS                 BEAT
KiloBytes        192,464   88,280     119,088   25,108
Directories       17,792    7,359       8,896    4,782
Volume name
KiloBytes
Directories
```

```
Available Options
Change Servers
Update Interval
```

Figure 2-62. VOLINFO's initial screen

VOLINFO displays information on eight volumes at a time. Because you can have up to thirty-two volumes, VOLINFO can contain four pages of this initial screen. If you have more than eight volumes, a "Next Page" option appears in the "Available Options" window. Highlight the option and press <Enter> to see those additional volumes. When you select a second page, a "Previous Page" option will appear in the "Available Options" window, allowing you to return to the previous page. You can use the "Next Page" option to toggle through all the pages as well as to return to the first page.

What You See in VOLINFO

The second line on the VOLINFO header screen shows which server you're looking at. The next line down (the first line in the option screen) shows which page you're on, followed by columns headed, "Total" and "Free." Down the left side of these columns are the headings "Volume Name," "KiloBytes," and "Directories." In our example,

Volume SYS has 192,464 kilobytes (192.4 megabytes) total, and 88,280 kilobytes (88.2 megabytes) still free to be used. Volume SYS also has 17,792 total directories defined, with 7,359 directories still available. But note that the entries labeled "Directories" include not only directories, but also every subdirectory, file, and trustee assignment on that particular volume. Every time someone makes a trustee assignment in a directory, it uses an entry from the "Directories" listing. The total number of directories indicates how many directories, subdirectories, files, and trustee assignments your installer allowed for during installation. Volumes that are removable (in other words, volumes on a removable medium, such as a Bernoulli Box) have an [R] next to their volume names.

Notice that between "Page" and "Volume Name" is an entry flashing the word, "Checking." This means that VOLINFO is having NetWare check every five seconds to see if the information displayed has changed. When the information does change, little arrows appear beside the numbers in the "Free" column. These arrows point in the direction of the change, up or down. So if you're watching the information about volume SYS when someone transfers a directory (or other things that VOLINFO counts as a directory) to SYS, the "Kilobytes" and "Directories" entries will drop in the "Free" column and the arrow will point down to reflect the change. If someone deletes a whole directory on the volume, the "Kilobytes" and "Directories" entries will rise in the "Free" column and the arrows will point up to reflect the change. The arrows last until the "Checking" sequence refreshes the screen and no more changes are occurring on the volume.

If the numbers in the "Free" column are blinking, they've reached a minimum level. When the "Free" column reaches zero, you'll start getting error messages when you try to perform tasks, such as transferring or modifying files or directories, on the server. The "Kilobytes" entry flashes when you have less than 1 megabyte (1024 kilobytes) free. The "Directories" entry won't blink until it reaches, or is below, twenty free directories.

But remember that the "Directories" entry entails directories, files, and trustee assignments to a directory—when either of these numbers starts flashing, it's a good idea to do a little housecleaning by deleting unused or unnecessary files, directories, or assignments from the volume.

The Available Options in VOLINFO

You see a "Next Page" option in the "Available Options" window only if you have more than eight volumes. The two permanent options in the "Available Options" window are "Change Servers" and "Update Interval." Use the first of these to look at volume information on other servers; use the second to change how often the VOLINFO screen is updated.

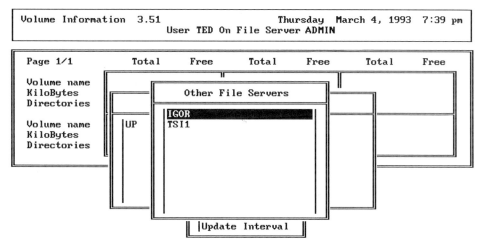

Figure 2-63. You can change to other servers to see their volume information

Select the "Change Servers" option. You'll see a "File Server/User Name" window listing all the servers you're currently attached to. The name of the server whose information you're currently viewing is highlighted by the selector bar. To view volume information for another of the listed servers, highlight the name of the server you wish to look at and press <Enter>.

When you return to the VOLINFO screen, you'll notice that the second line on the screen header reflects the name of the new server. To view volumes on a server whose name doesn't appear in the "File Server/User Name" window, press <Ins> at the "File Server/User Name" window. You'll see an "Other File Servers" window listing the names of all the servers on the internetwork.

Highlight the name of the new server you want to view in VOLINFO and press <Enter>. The "Change Current Server" option will attach you to the other server, prompt you for your user name, and when appropriate, prompt you for your password. The next time you log out from the network, you'll log out of these other server attachments as well. If you haven't been defined as a user on a server, try logging in as GUEST. (Sometimes the GUEST account on a server doesn't require a password.)

You can also detach from servers in VOLINFO by highlighting the servername in the "File Server/User Name" window and pressing <Del>. You'll see a window that

163

says, "Logout From Server Yes/No," with the "Yes" option highlighted. Press <Enter> and you're logged out from that server. If you're logged in to several servers and you want to log out from some of them, use <F5> to mark the servers you wish to log out from and press <Del>. You'll see a window that says, "Logout From All Marked Servers Yes/ No," with the "Yes" option highlighted. Press <Enter> and you'll log out of those servers. If you accidentally mark your default server, a screen that says, "You Cannot Logout From Your Default Server. Press ESCAPE to continue" will prompt you.

Once you've added a new server to the "File Server/User Name window," highlight the name of the new server and press <Enter>. You'll return to the VOLINFO screen, where the second line of the screen header will display the new *servername*, and the columns will display information on the selected server's volumes.

The other permanent option in the VOLINFO "Available Options" window is "Update Intervals." With this option you can change the frequency with which VOLINFO refreshes the volume statistics and shows any changes. Select the "Update Intervals" option and you'll see a screen similar to the one shown in Figure 2-64.

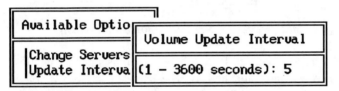

Figure 2-64. You can change the length of the interval VOLINFO's information is updated to the screen

The default setting in the "Volume Update Interval" window is five seconds; you can change the interval from one second to one hour (3600 seconds). You probably won't ever be in VOLINFO long enough to warrant the maximum update interval. Shorter update intervals increase the server's workload; on the other hand, longer intervals mean you may not be seeing the most current numbers available. So it's probably best to leave the intervals at five seconds.

To exit the "Volume Update Interval" window, press <Esc>. To exit the VOLINFO utility, press <Esc> again. You'll see the "Exit VolInfo Yes/No" window with the "Yes" option highlighted. Press <Enter> to return to the network prompt.

The COLORPAL Utility

COLORPAL affects the color schemes of NetWare's menu utilities, including the ones you make using the MENU utility. If you have a color monitor and you like the color scheme you see when you go into the menus, skip COLORPAL. But if you want to add a little variety to your NetWare menus, you can change the color scheme with this utility.

COLORPAL is a bit trickier than the other utilities in that it takes some preparation before you can use it. With the proper rights, you can make changes in COLORPAL's default parameters in the SYS:PUBLIC directory that will affect not only you, but everyone on the network. Everyone will be affected, for example, if you have Write, Create, and Erase rights to the SYS:PUBLIC directory and happen to be in that directory when you change COLORPAL's parameters. While this isn't too likely for most users, it can happen most often through security equivalences.

Setting Up the IBM$RUN.OVL File

When you change the colors of your monitor in COLORPAL, your changes are saved in a file named IBM$RUN.OVL. This file is created and stored in the directory from which you call COLORPAL. So pick a directory where you have at least Read, Write, Create, Erase, File Scan, and Modify rights (and where you wouldn't mind having the IBM$RUN.OVL file stored). Then go into COLORPAL from that directory and change some colors. NetWare will automatically copy the IBM$RUN.OVL file into that directory for you.

Make sure that when you access the menu utilities, you use your personal IBM$RUN.OVL file so you can see your nifty new changes instead of the old default colors from the SYS:PUBLIC IBM$RUN.OVL file. If you have a personal search drive mapped for yourself, put the IBM$RUN.OVL file in that directory.

However, since NetWare starts at the first search drive when looking for the IBM$RUN.OVL file, and the first directory containing the IBM$RUN.OVL file is SYS:PUBLIC, you may still end up with the old default colors. While you can get around this problem by making your directory path search drive number 1, it's not a good idea. Bumping SYS:PUBLIC and your DOS directories out of their station can mean you lose other parameters your supervisor has set up. You may also lose your ability to access the COMMAND.COM file from the network. In the system login script, supervisors often set up the COMSPEC=Y:COMMAND.COM command and attach it to a drive letter they know won't change. By inserting a drive mapping at the beginning, you may bump the COMSPEC setting out of order, causing your workstation to hang while you're in applications or as you leave them.

An easier method is to go into the directory that is storing your personal IBM$RUN.OVL file and call the menus from that directory only. You can accomplish this best through the MENU utility, which allows you to set up your personal menu options, which is discussed under "The MENU Utility" heading in this chapter.

What COLORPAL Can Do to Your Monochrome Monitor

For the most part, COLORPAL doesn't affect monochrome monitors. But if you have a monochrome monitor and you start changing the COLORPAL palettes, your menu screens may not be as readable as they were before. You might overwrite some of the windows, or make the screens unreadable, or maybe hide the highlight bar by making it the same shade as the background screen. So be careful—the changes you can make in COLORPAL usually aren't wonderful enough to justify messing up your monochrome display.

Some monitors emulate color monitors by using gray scales instead of actual colors. These monitors, particularly some from AT&T and Compaq, can use an alternate overlay file named CMPQ$RUN.OVL. This file is also found in the SYS:PUBLIC directory, but it has a black-and-white default palette. If you have one of these types of monitors and you find that your menus are hard to read, you can go into your NET.CFG file and put in SHORT MACHINE TYPE = CMPQ as the short machine name parameter. Then your workstation will use CMPQ$RUN.OVL with its black-and-white palette instead of IBM$RUN.OVL with its color palette. (Adding parameters to the NET.CFG file gets a more in-depth explanation in Chapter 5.)

If you set your workstation to use the CMPQ$RUN.OVL file as described above, things get trickier when you want to use COLORPAL to change the black-and-white default palette. COLORPAL only recognizes the IBM$RUN.OVL file. So if you want your workstation to use the CMPQ$RUN.OVL file with COLORPAL, don't change your short machine type in the NET.CFG file. Instead, go into the SYS:PUBLIC directory and copy the CMPQ$RUN.OVL file into the directory from which you will run COLORPAL. Then, in that directory, rename the CMPQ$RUN.OVL file to IBM$RUN.OVL so you can change the color scheme. Change the name by typing RENAME CMPQ$RUN.OVL IBM$RUN.OVL <Enter> at the network prompt. Once you've done this, you can follow the rest of the procedure described below.

Changing COLORPAL to Match Your Tastes

With the preliminaries out of the way, let's have some fun. Go into the directory to which you want NetWare to copy the IBM$RUN.OVL file. Type COLORPAL at the network prompt and press <Enter>. You'll see a screen showing the color palettes that come defined in COLORPAL.

166

IBM Color Palette Editor   V1.01b   Thursday March 4, 1993 5:19 pm

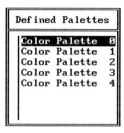

Figure 2-65. The COLORPAL utility's initial screen

To get around in COLORPAL, pressing <Enter> on a highlighted option brings you to the next screen available under that option, and pressing <Esc> brings you to the previous screen. For example, from the "Defined Palettes" window, select the Color Palette 4 option by pressing <PgDn> on the numeric keypad. Once that option is highlighted, press <Enter>. <PgDn> brings you to the bottom of the list of selections; <PgUp> brings you to the top of the list. You can also use the Up (8) and Down (2) arrow keys to highlight and select an option.

The first five color palettes (0–4) come predefined in NetWare. These are the palettes you need to change to get colors different from the default. NetWare uses Color Palette 0 for lists, menus, and for displaying normal text. Palette 1 is used for the main headers and the screen backgrounds; Palette 2 affects the help screens. Palette 3 is used for error messages, and Palette 4 affects your exit and alert windows. You can't delete the default color palettes that come with NetWare, but you can change their colors.

If you press <Enter> when the "Color Palette 0" option is highlighted, you'll see two additional windows: "Edit Attribute" and "Current Palette." The "Edit Attribute" window shows five attributes that can be changed: Background Normal, Background Reverse, Foreground Intense, Foreground Normal, and Foreground Reverse. Each attribute affects some part of the menu display itself. For example, "Background Normal" changes the menu titles and text aspects of the screen. The "Background Reverse" option affects the color of the selector bar itself.

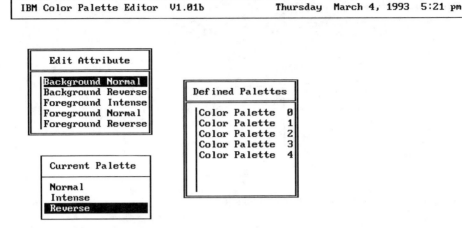

Figure 2-66. Use the COLORPAL utility to change the foreground and background colors to NetWare menuing utilities

"Foreground Intense" affects the border colors that are highlighted when you are in a particular menu window—for instance, the yellow border around the "Defined Palettes" window. The "Foreground Normal" option affects the border colors for menus you're not currently in. For example, when you pull up the "Edit Attribute" window, that border becomes yellow and the border for the "Defined Palettes" window is intense white. The "Background Reverse" option affects the selector bar itself, while "Foreground Reverse" is for the text covered by the selector bar.

Note: You can affect the colors you see on the screen more in Palettes 1, 2, and 3 from Background and Foreground Reverse options, while the colors in Palettes 0 and 4 work more from the Background Normal and Foreground Normal options.

The "Current Palette" window shows how the present colors look and how the color changes you make will affect the screen. This window comes with Normal, Intense, and Reverse options. As you make a change in the "Edit Attributes" window and press <Enter>, that change will appear in the "Current Palette" window. That way, if you don't like what you see, you can press <Enter>, change the color again, and see if the new choice is better.

To change a color, highlight one of the options in the "Edit Attribute's window and press <Enter>. A "Select Color" window will appear with a list of colors in it. You have two types of color schemes for the color palettes: foreground colors and background colors. There are sixteen foreground and eight background colors to choose from. The sixteen foreground colors include:

168

Black	Light Cyan
Blue	Light Green
Brown	Light Magenta
Cyan	Light Red
Dark Gray	Magenta
Green	Red
Intense White	White
Light Blue	Yellow

The eight background colors include:

Black	Green
Blue	Magenta
Brown	Red
Cyan	White

Choose the "Background Normal" option. Highlight the option and press <Enter>. Your screen will look like the following one:

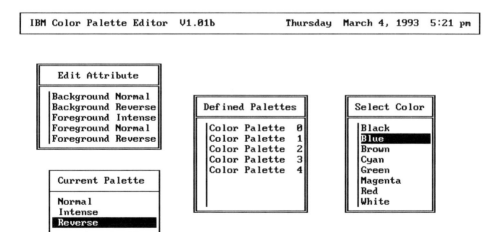

Figure 2-67. You can change colors on presently defined palettes, or you can define your own palettes

If you're in Color Palette 0 and have chosen the "Background Normal" option, you'll see that the default color is Blue. To select another color, highlight a different selection and press <Enter>. The color you choose will be displayed in the "Current Palette" window so you can see if you like the color scheme. If you don't like the color scheme, press <Enter> again and make another selection. If you do like the color scheme, select another option in the "Edit Attribute" window; press <Enter>. Do the same for each selection. Or, if you like the color scheme, press <Esc> to return to the "Defined Palettes" window where you can highlight and select another "Color Palette" option.

[The selections you make in COLORPAL may appear different from your initial tryouts. For example, most of what you see in help screens, main headers, and error messages (Palettes 1, 2, and 3) are actually the colors you set using the Background and Foreground Reverse options. Palettes 0 and 4 work more from the Background Normal and Foreground Normal options.]

Following is a rundown on the predefined colors that come with Color Palette options 0 through 4.

For Color Palette 0: (List Menus and Normal Text)

➤ Background Normal is Blue

➤ Background Reverse is White

➤ Foreground Intense is Yellow

➤ Foreground Normal is Intense White

➤ Foreground Reverse is Blue

For Color Palette 1: (Main Headers and Screen Background)

➤ Background Normal is Blue

➤ Background Reverse is Cyan

➤ Foreground Intense is Light Cyan

➤ Foreground Normal is Cyan

➤ Foreground Reverse is Blue

For Color Palette 2: (Help Screens)

➤ Background Normal is Black

➤ Background Reverse is Green

➤ Foreground Intense is Light Green

➤ Foreground Normal is Green

➤ Foreground Reverse is Black

For Color Palette 3: (Error Messages)

➤ Background Normal is Black

➤ Background Reverse is Red

➤ Foreground Intense is Light Red

➤ Foreground Normal is Red

➤ Foreground Reverse is Yellow

For Color Palette 4: (Exit and Alert Screens)

➤ Background Normal is White

➤ Background Reverse is Magenta

➤ Foreground Intense is Yellow

➤ Foreground Normal is Magenta

➤ Foreground Reverse is Intense White

Experiment until you find the color scheme you want for your menus. Once you finish, press <Esc> to return to the "Defined Palettes" window, then press <Esc> again. You'll see the "Save Changes Yes/No" window with the "Yes" option highlighted. Press <Enter> and the "Exit ColorPal Yes/No" window will appear with the "Yes" option highlighted. Press <Enter> and you'll return to the network prompt.

You might want to add your own color palette to use for the MENU utility. (See the next heading for more information.) MENU allows you to use Color Palettes 0 through 4 that come with COLORPAL, as well as any color palettes that you create in the "Defined Palettes" window.

To create a new color palette, type COLORPAL <Enter> at the network prompt; or, if you're still in COLORPAL, return to the "Defined Palettes" window and press <Ins>. COLORPAL will add and highlight the Color Palette 5 Option. (Option 5 and any other option additions default to the same colors as you see in the Color Palette 0 option.) Press

<Enter> on Option 5 and define the colors to your tastes, just as you did when you edited the other color palette options.

When you're satisfied, press <Esc> until you reach the "Save Changes Yes/No" window with the "Yes" option highlighted. Press <Enter> and the "Exit ColorPal Yes/No" window will appear with the "Yes" option highlighted. Press <Enter> and you'll return to the network prompt. Don't use the <Alt>-<F10> sequence to exit COLORPAL; the utility won't save your changes if you do. That sequence sends you instead to the "Exit ColorPal" window where, if you press <Enter>, all your changes will be lost.

Note: When you first create a copy of the IBM$RUN.OVL file by saving COLORPAL in your present directory, that file is copied with the Hidden file flag. This means that when you type DIR <Enter> at the network prompt in that directory, you won't see the file. However, if you again make changes to COLORPAL and save those changes, the IBM$RUN.OVL file may then be reflagged Normal, (which includes the attributes Shareable, Read/Write, and sometimes Archived).

If you end up really hating all your changes and you just want to go back to colors you've grown to love, simply go into the directory storing the IBM$RUN.OVL file and delete it. To do so, type DIR <Enter>. If you don't see the file, type FLAG *.OVL N <Enter> to reflag the file without Hidden. You can then type DEL IBM$RUN.OVL <Enter> to delete the file.

The MENU Utility

NetWare's MENU utility allows you to set up your own menu program so you can use a menu to easily access programs and utilities you use all the time. If you're adventurous, you can create quite an extensive menu to assist you in your work.

The examples given here are by no means an exhaustive listing of what you can accomplish in MENU; rather, they only hint at the possibilities. With a little ingenuity, you can set up marvelous environments, calling up different menus for each day of the week or for different occasions.

Looking at the MAIN Menu Program

A good place to begin discussing MENU is with a menu that's already created, so let's first look at a file called MAIN.MNU. This file is located in the SYS:PUBLIC directory; to look at its contents, you call it up with the actual menu utility called MENU. Type MENU MAIN <Enter> at your network prompt and you'll see MAIN's "Main Menu" window.

```
┌─────────────────────────────────────────────────────────────────┐
│ Novell Menu System  V2.1          Thursday August 13, 1992 2:34 am │
└─────────────────────────────────────────────────────────────────┘
```

```
        ┌───────────────────────────────┐
        │           Main Menu           │
        ├───────────────────────────────┤
        │ ▊1. Session Management▊        │
        │  2. File Management            │
        │  3. Volume Information         │
        │  4. System Configuration       │
        │  5. File Server Monitoring     │
        │  6. Print Queue Management      │
        │  7. Print Job Configurations   │
        │  8. Printer Definitions        │
        │  9. Logout                     │
        └───────────────────────────────┘
```

Figure 2-68. The default menu screen that comes with NetWare

NetWare's main menu lists eight menu options and a logout sequence. The menu options it displays are for NetWare's SESSION, FILER, VOLINFO, SYSCON, FCONSOLE, PCONSOLE, PRINTCON, and PRINTDEF utilities. These utilities work just as they do when you run them from the network prompt, except that as you exit a utility, you return to this menu. The "Logout" option will log you out of all your attached servers and leave you in the LOGIN directory at the network prompt.

You get around in your or NetWare's menu creations the same way you do any other menu utility. To select an option, use the Up arrow key to move the selector bar up an option; use the Down arrow key to move it down an option. To go to the top of the options, press <PgUp>; to go to the bottom of the options, press <PgDn>. You can also select an option by typing the initial letter(s) (or numbers) of the option. To choose the selected option, press <Enter>. <Enter> brings up the next screen available under that option and <Esc> returns you to the previous screen. To exit the menu, press <Esc> from the main level, or press <Alt>-<F10> simultaneously from lower MENU levels. You'll see an "Exit Menu Yes/No" window with the "Yes" option highlighted. Unless you're set up to return to the login script or to logout, pressing <Enter> will return you to the network prompt.

Looking at the Guts of Menu MAIN

Now that you've seen what the MAIN.MNU file looks like when you run it, let's take a look at what the actual file contains. In order to make your own menu, first download the MAIN.MNU file to your main user directory or your personal search drive directory. Then rename the file and use it to make your own menu program.

To use the MENU utility, you need Read, File Scan, Write, Create, and Erase rights in the directory from which you invoke the program. To rename the file, you'll also need Modify rights. So go either to your home directory (where you probably have all rights) or to your personal search drive directory. Whichever you choose, type NCOPY Z:MAIN.MNU <Enter> at the command line, and the MAIN.MNU file will download to your directory if Z: is your SYS:PUBLIC directory. If you get a message that the file can't be found, go to drive Z and type RIGHTS <Enter> to make sure you have at least Read and File Scan rights to SYS:PUBLIC. If you do have RF rights, type NDIR MAIN.MNU <Enter> to see if the file is there. If it isn't, ask your supervisor to put MAIN.MNU in the SYS:PUBLIC directory or copy the file to your personal directory.

Once you have the MAIN.MNU file in your working directory, rename the file so you can play around with it. If you want to rename the file NEWMENU.MNU, for example, type RENAME MAIN.MNU NEWMENU.MNU <Enter>. (Remember that you must have Modify rights to rename an existing file.) Because you copied this file from the SYS:PUBLIC directory, the file might be flagged Read Only; you might need to flag the file Read/Write before renaming it. If you try to rename the file but receive an error message like "Duplicate filename or file not found," type FLAG MAIN.MNU N <Enter>. Then rename the file.

With the file renamed, go into your text editor or word processor and pull up the renamed file. (It will be in DOS text form.) The file structure of the NEWMENU.MNU file looks like the one shown in Listing 2-1:

Listing 2-1. How NetWare's default menu is structured

```
%Main Menu,0,0,3

1.  Session Management
       Session

2.  File Management
       Filer

3.  Volume Information
       VolInfo

4.  System Configuration
       SysCon
```

```
5. File Server Monitoring
      FConsole

6. Print Queue Management
      PConsole

7. Print Job Configurations
      PrintCon

8. Printer Definitions
      PrintDef

9. Logout
      !Logout
```

The first line—%Main Menu,0,0,3—begins with a percent sign and ends with a listing of numbers. The percent sign indicates that a menu name that follows is the title of the menu. You'll see this name the next time you pull up the menu. For the other menu utilities you see in NetWare, this title is usually "Available Options." You also use the percent sign to begin submenus, as the next example will explain.

The first two numbers in the first line indicate the menu's position. The first number is for the vertical position and the second number is for the horizontal position. The numbers 0,0 tell MENU to place this menu window in the middle of the screen. The third number defines which color palette from COLORPAL you want for the menu; you can give each submenu a different color if you so wish. (See "The COLORPAL utility" heading earlier in this chapter.)

The second line—1. Session Management—begins one of the options that you can select from the menu itself. The commands to invoke the option are always indented beneath the option itself, as the third line of our example shows. In the Session Management example, the command you invoke when you select the option is the name of the utility itself—in this instance, SESSION. You see this structure throughout the NEWMENU.MNU file. (Options can have many more commands than you see in this example. The following examples deal with other commands to set up the environment the way you want it.) The last option in this example, 9. Logout, uses !LOGOUT as its command. The !LOGOUT command immediately logs you out from all your attached servers.

When creating your own menu utility, remember to:

➤ Start the names of the main menu and all submenus with a percent sign (%);

➤ Designate the menu's position and color palette using numbers after the menu name;

➤ Write option names to the left margin and indent two or more spaces the commands for executing the options;

➤ Be sure to save the file as a DOS text file.

You can put the .MNU extension on the menu files you create to identify them as menu files, or you can give your menu file any other extension. But then when you call up the menu file with an extension other than .MNU, you must include the name and the extension. For example, you can call your personal menu NEWMENU.TXT, but you'll have to type MENU NEWMENU.TXT <Enter> to call the menu. If you keep the .MNU extension, as in NEWMENU.MNU, you only need to type MENU NEWMENU <Enter> because the MENU utility recognizes the .MNU extension.

Creating Your Own Menu

Now that you have the basics of creating a menu utility, it's time to create your own menu. Let's call it the "What I Use" menu. In this example, you'll create the "What I Use" menu with four options. The first option accesses a word processing program. The next option will enable access to the network prompt and DOS. The third option takes the MENU that NetWare supplies (MENU MAIN) and makes it a submenu of the "What I Use" window. The fourth option moves the "Logout" option from the NetWare Utilities submenu to your "What I Use" menu window. When you're finished, the "What I Use" menu utility will look like this:

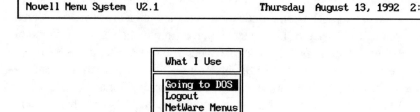

Figure 2-69. A working sample menu

From any DOS text editor or word processor that allows you to save files in the DOS text format, bring in the NEWMENU.MNU file. The first window of our new menu is the "What I Use" window, and it will be centered in the middle of the screen. For the time being, let's go with regular NetWare menu colors. Above the %Main Menu,0,0,3 line in NEWMENU.MNU, type the following:

```
%What I Use,0,0
```

The options you want to see in the "What I Use" window include "Going to DOS," "WordPerfect," "NetWare Utilities," and "Logout." So beneath the %What I Use line, type in the following parameters:

```
%What I Use,0,0
Going to DOS
WordPerfect
NetWare Utilities
Logout
```

It doesn't matter in what order you type in the options—MENU will rearrange them in alphabetical order when they appear on the screen (unless you number the options, in which case MENU puts them in numeric, rather than alphabetic, order). Note that the options in the "What I Use" window go completely to the left margin. Now, with the options in place, it's time to put in the commands to run the options.

The command format is exactly the same as the one for creating batch files; if you need to brush up on creating batch files, consult your DOS manual. To set up commands in MENU, you must indent the entire command format 2 to 5 spaces so MENU can distinguish the command from the option. For example, under the "Going to DOS" option that you created, you can type the following:

```
%What I Use,0,0
Going to DOS
   CLS
   prompt=Type "EXIT" to return to the Menu
   COMMAND
```

The "Going to DOS" option can be invaluable for accessing the network prompt from the menu. The first command clears the screen, then DOS sets your prompt to "Type 'EXIT' to return to the What I Use Menu." The actual command is COMMAND, which spawns a child COMMAND.COM process so you can run another application or utility. Then, when you're through in DOS, simply type EXIT <Enter> to return to the menu.

The only drawback to the above example is that it leaves your DOS prompt at "Type 'EXIT' to return to the What I Use Menu." See the example and its explanation under the heading "An Explanation of Rich's Menu" and under the "MAP Y:=PRUFROCK\SYS:WP386 <Y" subheading to get around this problem.

Next, you want to set up access to your word processor—WordPerfect in this example. Under the "WordPerfect" option, type the following:

```
%What I Use,0,0
Going to DOS
    CLS
    prompt=Type "EXIT" to return to the Menu
    COMMAND
WordPerfect
    cls
    echo Loading WordPerfect 5.1 (or whatever version you use)
    wp
    cls
    echo Exiting to the What I Use menu
```

Under the WordPerfect entry, the CLS command clears the screen, after which you will see, "Loading WordPerfect 5.1" flash on your screen. The WP command calls up WordPerfect itself. Then as you exit WordPerfect, the CLS command again clears the screen and you see, "Exiting to the What I Use menu." If you want to put in just the execution command, simply put WP beneath the WordPerfect option; you can skip the CLS and ECHO commands. When you exit the application, you'll simply return to this menu.

Next, you want to make the original MAIN.MNU file a submenu of your "What I Use" window. To do this, place a call for the submenu beneath the "NetWare Utilities" option.

```
%What I Use,0,0
Going to DOS
    CLS
    prompt=Type "EXIT" to return to the Menu
    COMMAND
WordPerfect
    cls
```

```
    echo Loading WordPerfect 5.1
    wp
    cls
    echo Exiting to the What I Use menu
NetWare Utilities
    %NetWare Utilities
```

The percent sign tells MENU to look for the "NetWare Utilities" option as a submenu known as "NetWare Utilities." Submenus are listed after all the options of the "What I Use" window have been defined. So go ahead and define the "Logout" option, then put in the "NetWare Utilities" menu, similar to the following one:

```
NetWare Utilities
    %NetWare Utilities
Logout
    !logout
%NetWare Utilities,0,80
1.  Session Management
    Session
2.  File Management
    Filer
3.  System Configuration
    SysCon
4.  Print Queue Management
    PConsole
5.  Print Job Configurations
    PrintCon
```

This example uses only the NetWare menu utilities you might use most often. Set your options according to your preference, or leave them all in. Moving the "Logout" option to the "What I Use" menu means you won't have to go to a submenu to log out.

Also notice that the window is positioned at 0,80, which places the submenu at center right on your screen. For more information on positioning your menu windows, see the next section.

Defining a Window Position

The first two numbers after the name of the window will position your windows. The first number sets the vertical placement and can range from 1 to 25, with 1 being the top of the screen and 25 the bottom. The second number sets the horizontal placement and can range from 1 to 80, with 1 being the screen's far left and 80 the screen's far right. So if you want a menu to appear in the left-bottom on your screen, select 25,1 settings; if you want center-bottom of your screen, select 25,40; if you want right-bottom, select 25,80. The bottom-left corner of the menu will be placed in a position in relation to those coordinates.

The following diagram lists the settings you can use to put your menus in different places on the screen. Because of the rather puzzling setup of designating the center lines as 0 and 0, even though they are really 12 for the vertical axis and 40 for the horizontal axis, you end up being able to use various number combinations to place a screen in the same place. The best thing to do—in this instance as well as elsewhere in NetWare—is learn one way and stick with it.

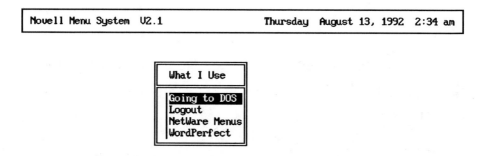

Figure 2-70. Example menu for explanation of positioning

MENU uses line 12 as the center of vertical placement in the screen (see the center window in the previous figure), and allows you to use 0 for that vertical center. For horizontal placement, MENU considers line 40 to be the horizontal center, and allows you to use 0 to center your menus horizontally. Thus MENU considers 0,0 the center of your screen, and 0,0 is the default if you don't put in any positions after your window name; your windows will always pop up in the center of the screen.

Another important factor is that windows try to synchronize to the center of wherever you place them. In other words, if you create a large window and choose 25,80 (right-bottom), MENU leaves one space on all sides of the created window—so it places the bottom of the window at position 24 and the far-right side of the window at line 79.

Setting Up Command-Line Utilities in Your Menus

You can also define the command-line utilities that you wish to run from the menu. Let's add another option, "Command Line Utilities," to the NEWMENU.MNU file. This option will set up another submenu so that a command-line utility can run in the menu environment. From any DOS text editor or word processor that allows you to save files in the DOS text format, bring in the NEWMENU.MNU file. Beneath the other options, place the following command:

```
%What I Use,0,0
Going to DOS
    COMMAND
WordPerfect
    wp
NetWare Utilities
    %NetWare Utilities
Logout
    !logout
Command Line Utilities
    %Command Line Utilities
```

Go to the end of the "NetWare Utilities" submenu in this file and type the following:

```
%NetWare Utilities,0,80
1. Session Management
    Session
.  .
%Command Line Utilities,0,1
NCOPY
    NCOPY @1"Enter Drive and Filename" @2"Enter Destination"
    dir @2/w
    pause
RIGHTS
    RIGHTS @"Enter Drive Letter"
    pause
NDIR
    NDIR @"Parameters?"
    pause
MAP
```

181

```
MAP @"Drive Letter or 'Enter' for All Mappings"
pause
```

Command Parameters in MENU

It usually takes more than simply typing the name of the command to use most DOS and NetWare utilities. For example, to use COPY, you need to know which files in which directories you wish to copy to which other directory, and you need to include that information when running the command. MENU allows you to designate those inputs by using @ (the "at" sign). Any message you give must be in quotation marks, and those quotation marks must be set directly against the @ sign. Messages aren't necessary, but they serve as prompts so you know where you are during command execution. The pause command allows you to view what's being done before you return to MENU.

In the NCOPY example above, NCOPY @1 designates which drive and filenames you wish to copy from. The "Enter Drive and Filename" prompts you to type in which directory you wish to copy from and which file you wish to copy. The @2 prompt asks which drive letter you wish to copy the file to. If you just want to type in the command without any prompts, type NCOPY @"". MENU will display a line at the bottom of the screen for you to enter NCOPY's parameters.

The command parameters also allow you to use numbers along with the @ sign. These numbers allow you to reuse a name or letter at another place. Once you've defined a parameter using the @ sign, you can reuse the parameter within the same command. For example, in the NCOPY command itself, if you answered the first parameter as G:*.RPT and the second parameter as H:, from then on NCOPY copies all the *.RPT files from G: to H:. Then the DIR @2 command under the NCOPY option says, "Whatever drive letter you designate for the second parameter (H), display files in that directory using the DOS /Wide parameter (DIR H:/W)." That way, you can see if you've copied the desired files to the designated directory.

The NDIR command in this example allows you to enter any NDIR parameters you wish. The "at" (@) sign simply asks for the parameters you wish to enter before pressing <Enter>. Since NDIR has quite a list of parameters, it doesn't make too much sense to list all the parameters. Again, if you don't like the prompts, just put in the command as NDIR @"" <Enter>, and you can then type in the command as if it were on the command line.

When you put in a string of @ signs and prompts, you need to keep those prompts on the same line; otherwise, the prompts on the second line will be misinterpreted as either an option of the menu or as a separate command.

182

MENU reserves certain symbols for its own use. Some of the more prevalent ones are double quotes (""), the "at" sign (@), the percent sign (%), the comma (,), and the backslash (\). If you use any of these symbols in anything you write within the command parameters, be sure to precede each symbol with a backslash—for example, "Print 15\%\@ home." However, you can't offset internal quotation marks with the backslash; use single quotation marks ('Enter') instead when you need quotes within the parameter quotation marks. With that in mind, experiment to see what you can do with the command-line utilities in the MENU program.

When you finish editing your script, exit your editor and save the file as a DOS text file. Then type MENU NEWMENU <Enter>, or whatever name you called the file. Your own menu will appear on the screen. You can then see if you made any mistakes that need correcting once you get out of the menu.

One of the biggest problems you can face in MENU is leaving the directory in which you initiated the menu. When this happens, MENU doesn't always know how to get back to the menu window or which screen to display, so it locks up on you. Depending on how well you've set your menuing system, you might wish to place the .MNU file into your personal search directory and see if that gets rid of some problems.

Menu for the Advanced User

If you've played around with MENU before, you'll probably appreciate an advanced example of menuing. Here's a menu from Rich Hillyard, a technical writer at Novell who tinkers a lot and who has added some special features to his menu program. The lines in bold are discussed at the end of the program listing.

Listing 2-2. Example menu (for advanced users)

```
%FROGGER Menu 1,12,40
Music
%Music Menu
Paintbrush
    @echo off
    cls
    systime gadfly
    cls
    echo Loading MicroSoft Paintbrush
    newmail prufrock/boom: rhillyar
    q:
    cd gadfly\sys:home\rich\pbrush
```

```
        mouse
        FRIEZE EPSONMX P1 0 1CNQ 640 480 4
        PBrush M 1CNQ 640 480 4
        mouse off
        q:
        cd gadfly\sys:home\rich\dept
        f:
        cd gadfly\sys:home\rich
        cls
        echo Exiting to FROGGER menu
        newmail prufrock/boom: rhillyar
Rolex Watch
        @echo off
        cls
        f:
        systime gadfly
        cls
        echo Loading the Rolex watch
        newmail prufrock/boom: rhillyar
        rolex
        cls
        echo Exiting to FROGGER menu
        newmail prufrock/boom: rhillyar
BackMeUp
        @echo off
        cls
        backmeup
Calculator
        @echo off
        cls
        f:
        systime gadfly
        cls
        echo Loading the calculator
        newmail prufrock/boom: rhillyar
        y:\appl\office\calc /u-rlh
        cls
        echo Exiting to FROGGER menu
Login Message
        @echo off
        cls
```

```
    f:
    newmail prufrock/boom: rhillyar
    type gadfly\sys:dept\message\message.dat
    pause
WordPerfect 5.1
    @echo off
    cls
    systime gadfly
    cls
    echo Loading WordPerfect 5.1
    newmail prufrock/boom: rhillyar
    f:
    cd sys:home\rich
    map y:=prufrock\sys:wp386 <y
    wp
    f:
    cd sys:home\rich
    cls
    echo Exiting to FROGGER menu
    newmail prufrock/boom: %usr%
DOS (Temporary)
    @echo off
    set temp=%prompt%
    prompt=Type "EXIT" to return to FROGGER Menu$_%temp%
    cls
    command
    prompt=%temp%
    set temp=
GWBASIC
    @echo off
    cls
    g:
    echo Checking for Coordinator mail
    newmail prufrock/boom: rhillyar
    gwbasic
    cls
    f:
    newmail prufrock/boom: rhillyar
Coordinator
```

```
    @echo off
    cls
    f:
    systime gadfly
    cls
    map e:=prufrock/boom:atc\exe <y
    cls
    echo Loading the Coordinator
    newmail prufrock/boom: rhillyar
    if not exist e:tutor1.exe goto done
    e:
    set mv=prufrock/boom:
    e:atc2 -v
    f:
    map del e:
    goto end
    :done
    echo PRUFROCK is not on line.
    :end
    cls
    echo Exiting to FROGGER menu
    newmail prufrock/boom: rhillyar
NetWare Menu
    %NetWare Menu
Games
    %Games Menu
%Games Menu,12,16
Jeopardy!
    @echo off
    cls
    echo Loading Jeopardy!
    newmail prufrock/boom: rhillyar
    f:
    cd sys:home\rich\games\j
    menu
    cd sys:home\rich
    Echo Exiting to FROGGER Games menu
    cls
Bricks
    @echo off
    cls
```

```
echo Loading Bricks
if exist s:avail.exe goto itsthere
echo Mapping drive to PRUFROCK\SYS:GAMES\GRAPHICS
map s:=prufrock\sys:games\graphics
if errorlevel 1 goto notthere
:itsthere
s:
cd sys:games\graphics
bricks
cd sys:public
goto finish
:notthere
echo PRUFROCK\SYS:GAMES\GRAPHICS could not be found
:finish
f:
Echo Exiting to FROGGER Games menu
```

```
%NetWare Menu,12,22
1.  SESSION
    @echo off
    cls
    f:
    session
2.  FILER
    @echo off
    cls
    f:
    filer
3.  PRINTCON
    @echo off
    cls
    f:
    printcon
4.  PCONSOLE
    @echo off
    cls
    f:
    pconsole
5.  SYSCON
    @echo off
    cls
    f:
```

```
      syscon
6.    LOGOUT
%LOG OUT NOW?
%Music Menu ,15,57
Happy Birthday
      @echo off
      cls
      z:gwbasic g:birthday
Great White North
      @echo off
      cls
      z:gwbasic g:gwnorth
Twilight Zone
      @echo off
      cls
      z:gwbasic twilight
Jetsons
      @echo off
      cls
      z:gwbasic g:jetsons
%LOG OUT NOW?,21,,3
<Enter> to Log Out; <Esc> to Return to Menu
      !logout
```

An Explanation of Rich's Menu

SYSTIME and **NEWMAIL prufrock/boom: rhillyar** or **%usr%.** Two commands you see throughout Rich's menu are SYSTIME and NEWMAIL. MENU offers a no-effort means to perform such tasks as synchronizing your workstation's internal clock to network time and keeping an eye on your mailbox.

    MOUSE application parameters MOUSE OFF. This example shows you how to set up application parameters in MENU—actually the same process as setting up parameters in batch files. In this example, Rich calls up his mouse program, whose drivers are installed at boot-up time. (Don't load TSR programs from the MENU utility; see the subheading "Menu and Terminate-and-Stay-Resident (TSR) Programs" later in this section.) Rich next loads the program's parameters and then unloads the mouse when he exits the program.

    @ECHO OFF and **ECHO Loading Microsoft Paintbrush.** These commands help you keep your screen uncluttered. The @ECHO OFF command (the @ parameter is used in DOS 3.3 and above) keeps the commands themselves from appearing on the screen. You can then use the ECHO command to put messages on the screen, offering an alternative to a blank screen.

But if you want a blank screen, you can place >NUL at the end of lines containing commands. The >NUL command is sort of DOS's "black hole" which tells the command to write to the black hole instead of the screen. If you want to save the executed part of a command to a file, simply replace the NUL sign with a filename, such as >SAVE. You can use the >NUL sign with any command that makes you type in CLS to clear the screen from unwanted messages. In many places where Rich uses CLS, you can place >NUL at the end of the command previous to the CLS command. It's just another way to keep your screen looking tidy.

BACKMEUP. See the heading "Using Batch Files in MENU" later in this section.

Y:\APPL\OFFICE\CALC /U-RLH. Here Rich writes out the entire directory path for the application. You need to do this only if the directory path hasn't been assigned a drive letter through the MAP utility. Again, you can place these small utilities in your personal search drive directory.

TYPE GADFLY\SYS:DEPT\MESSAGE\MESSAGE.DAT and **PAUSE.** This command types out the MESSAGE.DAT file from the MESSAGE directory. This can be the same file that you can read using the INCLUDE command in your login script. (See the subheading "Login Script Functions and Their Examples" under "The SYSCON Utility" heading in this chapter.) Or it can be any DOS text file that you or your group uses to pass on messages to one another. The PAUSE command is necessary so you can read the message instead of having the message flicker on the screen and disappear as you return to the menu.

MAP Y:=PRUFROCK\SYS:WP386 <Y. This is a rather interesting command. Rich is mapping drive Y: to the WP386 directory on an already-existing search drive path. When you overwrite a search drive mapping, you'll see:

```
Drive Y: is in use as a search drive.
Do you want to reassign this search drive? (Y/N) Y
```

In order to answer the "Yes" prompt without having to interrupt your menu routine to physically type a "Y" and press <Enter>, you can create a little input file to supply the answer. The < parameter at the end of the mapping tells NetWare to interject the information found in the Y file. You create the Y file like this:

```
COPY CON Y <Enter>
Y <Enter>
^Z
```

Then when you overwrite existing search drives, the Y file will answer, "Do you still want to change it?" You can put the Y file out in your personal search drive directory to answer the question and keep the menu flowing. You can actually name this file anything you want; just be sure to put the same filename after the redirection arrow.

```
SET TEMP=%PROMPT%
PROMPT=Type "EXIT" to return to FROGGER Menu$_%temp%
COMMAND
PROMPT=%TEMP%
SET TEMP=
```

This sequence initially sets up your regular prompt as a temporary prompt and sets the prompt for this command sequence as "Type 'EXIT' to return to FROGGER Menu$_%temp%." The $_ parameter is a line feed, so what you see on your screen is the "Type 'EXIT'" prompt, followed by your normal prompt. COMMAND initiates a child COMMAND.COM sequence so you can run another command or utility from the network prompt. The PROMPT=%TEMP% and SET TEMP= commands reset your prompt to the way it was before you used this menu option. (To avoid problems with this sequence, you'll need to make some changes in the SHELL parameter of your CONFIG.SYS file. See Chapter 5.)

```
IF NOT EXIST E:TUTOR1.EXE GOTO DONE
...
:DONE
```

ECHO PRUFROCK is not on line. This batch file command says, "If you can't find the TUTOR1.EXE file, then go to the :DONE parameter and write PRUFROCK is not on line." This is another example of using batch file parameters in the menu utility. (See your DOS manual for more information on setting up batch files.)

```
NetWare Menu
    %NetWare Menu
Games
    %Games Menu
```

%Games Menu,12,16. Use the percent sign (%) to set up submenus that you call from your main menu screen. Then when you start the submenu, use the percent sign and the submenu name at the beginning of what you wish to put in the submenu. For example, the main menu has the NetWare Menu and Games options, but in order to create submenus (such as Games) beneath the main menu, you need to place the percent sign (%) in front of the submenu name and also give the submenu its name. Then use the percent sign and menu name to define the options in the submenu.

The **Bricks** option in the **Games** Menu. The BRICKS game has some interesting parameters in it. From the "IF EXIST S:AVAIL.EXE GOTO ITSTHERE" to the "MAP S:=PRUFROCK\SYS:GAMES\GRAPHICS" command, you have two conditions that must be met before the BRICKS game can run. The first condition is that directory S: must have the AVAIL.EXE file. If this condition is not met, the error level equals 1 and the BRICKS option goes to the :NOTTHERE condition and tells you that the graphics "could not be found." The second condition tries to map a drive to the GRAPHICS directory, and if that condition isn't met, you'll also see the "could not be found" message. If you don't receive an error level message, you can run the BRICKS program.

%LOG OUT NOW?,21,,3 ... <Enter> to Log Out; <Esc> to Return to Menu ... !logout. Rich also does something interesting here. Instead of simply being logged out of the server, Rich set up an "Are you really sure?" menu. This menu has only one parameter so you can't choose anything else, and you can either press <Enter> to invoke the !LOGOUT command, or the Escape key to return to menu.

Using Batch Files in MENU

BACKMEUP. The BACKMEUP utility is a small batch file (BACKMEUP.BAT) that Rich uses to back up his home directory and subdirectories. The batch file looks like this:

```
@echo off
cls
echo Attaching to server ADMIN
attach admin/rich
if errorlevel 1 goto end
map k:=admin\vol1:users\rich
cls
f:
echo Backing up GADFLY\SYS:HOME\RICH and subdirectories
cd GADFLY\SYS:HOME\RICH
XCOPY f:*.* k: /s /m
logout admin
:end
^Z
```

In this batch file, Rich attaches to the server (server ADMIN) on which he wants to back up his directory, and then maps a drive to the directory where he wishes to store his files. If the batch file receives an error while attaching to server ADMIN, the IF/GOTO statement will take the batch file to the :END statement and back to the menu.

If the batch file can attach to server ADMIN, Rich maps a drive to K:=ADMIN\VOL1:USERS\RICH, maps F: to GADFLY\SYS:HOME\RICH, and runs DOS's XCOPY command using the /S(ubdirectories) /M(odify) parameters. XCOPY then copies all modified files since the last backup, as well as those modified files found in Rich's subdirectories. When XCOPY is finished, the batch file logs out from ADMIN and returns to the menu. This is another example of a batch file you can place in your personal search drive directory. (With NetWare 3.11, you can use NCOPY's command with /S and /M or /A parameters—see the "Directory and File Management Utilities" heading in Chapter 3.)

You can also have a batch file call other batch files by using DOS's CALL command (in DOS version 3.3 and above) before the next batch filename. The CALL command creates another child COMMAND.COM for the second batch file and then returns you to the first batch file when the second batch file completes. The MENU program itself takes about 14KB, and each COMMAND.COM takes about 3KB, depending on which version of DOS you're using. Also, some versions of DOS won't allow you to run a batch file from within a batch file.

MENU and Terminate-and-Stay-Resident (TSR) Programs

Don't invoke terminate-and-stay-resident (TSR) programs from MENU. MENU begins by creating a working copy of COMMAND.COM and by loading itself into memory. When you choose an option in your MENU, you also create a "child" copy of COMMAND.COM to run the program. These copies of COMMAND.COM and the invoked program stay in memory long enough for you to use and are then discarded. If you load a TSR program as well, the TSR will sit in a memory location beyond the programs that are already in memory. Then, when you leave MENU and the transient programs leave memory, you end up with a big memory hole that can't be accessed because of the TSR program. Instead of your TSR taking 12KB of memory, it can now take up to 70KB, and you end up unable to access your larger applications.

If you want to use TSR programs, load them from your AUTOEXEC.BAT file or after your login script and before entering MENU. Then when you want to use them, simply press the proper keys to invoke the program, even if you're in MENU. Some TSRs work well; others don't. Sometimes it's the order in which you load the TSRs that conflicts with other programs you're using, so it's a good idea to experiment on the order in which you load your TSRs.

Other Information

After you create your own menu utility, you may also want to set up a specialized version of MENU to run on a stand-alone workstation. To use MENU on your stand-alone workstation, you need the following files:

SYS$MSG.DAT	MENUPARZ.HLP
SYS$ERR.DAT	MENU.EXE
IBM$RUN.OVL	MENUPARZ.EXE
SYS$HLP.DAT	

NetWare documentation suggests you run the menus from a hard disk—on the hard disk, put all the files in the same directory. You can run MENU from a local disk, but keep all the files on the same disk if you do.

To run MENU on a stand-alone workstation, rename the IBM$RUN.OVL to $RUN.OVL. Go to the directory where you downloaded the above files and type RENAME IBM$RUN.OVL $RUN.OVL <Enter>. You must also set up a CONFIG.SYS file with the minimum parameters of BUFFERS=20 and FILES=30.

Use the same methods for creating your stand-alone version of MENU. However, you must specify in your AUTOEXEC.BAT file where files such as COMMAND.COM are found. You must also specify your directory paths to applications or files, or make heavy use of the PATH command. Sometimes MENU gets confused in a stand-alone environment and hangs after running a utility, so it's best to spell out the exact steps necessary to run a program and return to the directory storing MENU. For example, suppose you have the menu files stored in C:\MENU and you want to access a calculator in C:\UTIL\CALC. Under the Calculator option in your menu script, type:

```
Calculator
    cd \util\calc
    calc
    cd \menu
```

Experiment; have fun.

Exiting from your personal menu is the same as exiting other menus—press <Esc> (or <Alt> and <F10> simultaneously) until you reach the "Exit Menu" window with the "Yes" option highlighted. Press <Enter> and you'll return to the network prompt.

The SALVAGE Utility

Use the SALVAGE utility to recover files you've deleted through the FILER utility or through DOS's DELETE or ERASE commands.

NetWare 3.x has been specifically designed to retain deleted files on its hard disks by not copying over the files until the entire disk is full. Until that point, you can run SALVAGE in your directories where you have Read, File Scan, Create, Erase, and Modify rights, and pull up the deleted files. Deleted files are dated when you delete them; consequently, you can choose which version of the deleted file you wish to retrieve. If you delete the directory, your deleted files are stored in a hidden directory called DELETED.SAV, which every volume has as one of its root directories. You'll need supervisory rights or be supervisor equivalent to see this directory and recover deleted files from it.

As new disk blocks are needed, NetWare 3.1x writes over the earliest deleted file(s), thereby purging those deleted files from accessibility. How many versions of a deleted file you see depends on the size of your volume. Version 3.1x supervisors can also disable this feature through a console SET command, or supervisors can place the Purge flag on a given directory or file, thereby purging all files in the directory as they are deleted.

Using the SALVAGE Command

At the network prompt, type SALVAGE and press <Enter>. You'll see a screen offering the options "Salvage from Deleted Directories," "Select Current Volume," "Set Salvage Options," and "View/Recover Deleted Files."

```
NetWare File Salvage Utility  V3.53          Thursday  June 3, 1993  4:37 pm
                      TED on UP/SYS:PERSONAL/TED
```

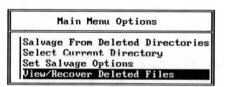

```
              Main Menu Options
      ┌──────────────────────────────────┐
      │ Salvage From Deleted Directories │
      │ Select Current Directory         │
      │ Set Salvage Options              │
      │ View/Recover Deleted Files       │
      └──────────────────────────────────┘
```

Figure 2-71. The initial SALVAGE screen

194

Use the "Select Current Directory" option to choose which directory you want to recover deleted files from if you aren't already in that directory. (You can also highlight the directories marked ".." and "/" to move up the directory tree while in the file listings.) This also allows you to restore those deleted files to that directory. Choose the Select Current Directory option and press <Enter>. You'll be in the "Current Directory Path" windows showing the current directory you're in.

This window works like any of the other Current Path windows in the other utilities. You press the Backspace key to erase the name of your current directory, then type in the name of the directory you want. If you can't remember the directory name or path, press <INS>. You'll see a listing of the available directories. You can then highlight the one you want and press <Enter> to add it to the path. If you backspace over the volume name and press <INS>, you'll see a listing of the available volumes on that server. If you backspace over the servername and press <INS>, you'll see a listing of the available servers you are logged into or attached to. Press <INS> again and you'll see a listing of any other servers on the network that you can attach to. Choose one, press <Enter>, and you can type in a valid user name to attach to that server. (Make sure you choose another NetWare 3.x server. This aspect of Salvage does not work with NetWare 2.2 and earlier.) Once you choose your path, press <Enter>.

Use the "Salvage From Deleted Directories" option to view the files in the DELETED.SAV hidden directory at the root level. You'll need to be a supervisor, supervisor equivalent, or have the supervisory trustee right at the root level to use this option. If you are one of these, or have the supervisory trustee right, you'll next type in a pattern for the filename you want to recover.

This window has the default "*" which means shows all files. You can use both wildcards, * and ?, in this window. After you type the pattern in, press <Enter>. Salvage shows you all files from your deleted directories. It does not preserve the directory structure, only the files themselves. You can highlight the names you want, using the F5 key to mark them, then press <Enter> to recover them. Press <Enter> again to say Yes, perform the recovery. The files are restored to the DELETED.SAV directory at the root with their original trustee rights. You then copy the files to the directory you want them in. Use the "Set Salvage Options" to sort the lists you view of deleted files. You can sort by Deletion Date, Deletor, File Size, or Filename. The default is filename.

Highlight the type of sorting you want and press <Enter>. Now when you view lists of recoverable files, you'll see the list in the order of Deletion Date, or alphabetically by the Deletor's name, by File Size, or alphabetically by Filename.

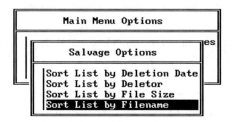

```
NetWare File Salvage Utility  V3.53        Thursday  June 3, 1993  4:41 pm
                     DAVE on UP/SYS:PERSONAL/DAVE
```

Figure 2-72. You can sort the type of files you wish to recover by using this option

To view or recover deleted files, highlight the "View/Recover Deleted Files" option and press <Enter>. You then type in a pattern for the names you want to view or recover. The windows shows a "*," meaning show all deleted files. You can type in specific extensions, such as .TXT, .PCX, .WP. You can also use the "?" wildcard to stand for a single character in the name.

For example, if you had deleted all the daily reports for june, Labeled REPORT1.JUN, REPORT2.JUN, REPORT3.JUN, etc., you could see and recover these by typing REPORT?.JUN in the window. You could also type *.JUN if you used the .JUN extension only for the reports.

After you type in the pattern, press <Enter>. You'll then see a list of those files matching the pattern. You'll see a screen similar to e one on the next page.

Highlight the name of the file you want to recover and press <Enter>. You'll see a window listing information about this file. You can use this information to determine if this is the file you want.

You have the choice of recovering this file or not. Press <ESC> to back out, or highlight NO and press <Enter>. Your list of recoverable files reappears.

If you highlight YES and press <Enter>, Salvage recovers the file and restores it to the current directory. If you recover a file with the same name as an existing file, then the program asks you to rename the recovered file. Type in a new name and press <Enter>. The recovered file now appears in the directory with the new name.

You can also use <F5> to mark and recover multiple files at once. Once you mark the files, press <Enter>, you see the "Recover ALL Marked Files" window with the "Yes" option highlighted. Pressing <Enter> then recovers all marked files to the directory from which they were deleted or to the DELETED.SAV directory if the directory was deleted.

```
NetWare File Salvage Utility  V3.53        Thursday  March 4, 1993  7:26 pm
                     TED on ADMIN/SYS:PERSONAL/TED
```

```
                         28 Salvageable Files

 ..               6-09-92  4:44:14pm <DIR>     SUPERVISOR
 /                0-00-80 12:00:00am <DIR>
 ACCT             3-04-93  5:47:40pm <DIR>        TED
 LETTERS          3-04-93  5:47:28pm <DIR>        TED
 $_TSTF_$.000     3-04-93  7:04:10pm      0  TED
 $_TSTF_$.000     3-04-93  7:04:02pm      0  TED
 $_TSTF_$.000     3-04-93  7:03:40pm      0  TED
 $_TSTF_$.000     3-04-93  7:02:18pm      0  TED
 $_TSTF_$.000     3-04-93  7:00:50pm      0  TED
 $_TSTF_$.000     3-04-93  7:00:46pm      0  TED
 $_TSTF_$.000     3-04-93  7:00:12pm      0  TED
 $_TSTF_$.000     3-04-93  6:58:56pm      0  TED
 $_TSTF_$.000     3-04-93  6:58:50pm      0  TED
 $_TSTF_$.000     3-04-93  6:58:48pm      0  TED
 $_TSTF_$.000     3-04-93  6:58:14pm      0  TED
 $_TSTF_$.000     3-04-93  6:57:12pm      0  TED
▼$_TSTF_$.000     3-04-93  6:55:44pm      0  TED
```

Figure 2-73. You can see a list of files that match your selection patterns

If you try to recover two or more files with the same name, the program asks you to rename one or more of them so there is no conflict. Type in the new name(s) and press <Enter>. The files reappear in the directory with their original trustee rights.

Do NOT highlight the top two directory listings, the ones marked on the left with "..." and "/". Highlighting either or both of these will cause Salvage to fail or to perform unpredictably. These directory listings look to the parent directory and to the root, and Salvage isn't sure how to handle those. So don't mark them.

You can also use the F6 key to mark files for recovery. Press <F6> and type in a pattern for the files you want. You can use the wildcards "*" and "?". Press <Enter>. The files that match the pattern are marked. You can then press <Enter> to continue with the recovery.

Purging Files

You can also use SALVAGE to purge files. Use the View/Recover Deleted Files or the Salvage From Deleted Directories option to bring up a list of the deleted files you want. Highlight the file or files using the highlighter, the F5 key, or the F6 key, then press <DEL>. You see the "Purge ALL Marked Files window with the Yes option highlighted. Press <Enter> and the marked files are purged from your volume. Highlight NO and press <Enter> and you abort the purge.

As with the recovery procedure, don't highlight the directories marked ".." and "/
". Salvage doesn't know how to handle the purging of these directories and will act
unpredictably if you try to do this.

The DSPACE Utility

The DSPACE utility shows whether or not your supervisor has limited the disk space
that's available on the server. If the supervisor has done so, only the amount of disk space
specified by the supervisor is available for storing all your data. Supervisors can choose
to limit disk space during the NetWare 3.11 installation process, allowing them the
option to limit space when it becomes necessary.

For users, having limited disk space means you may need to keep a close eye on how
much space you have to play with. You need to know when it's time to take old data off
the server. (See "The NBACKUP Utility" in this chapter.) A good way to keep an eye
on how much disk space you have left is through DSPACE.

To access the utility, type DSPACE at the network prompt and press <Enter>. You'll
see the "Available Options" window in the upper-left part of the screen with three
options: Change File Server, User Restrictions, and Directory Restrictions.

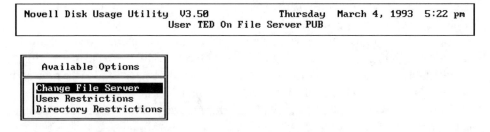

Figure 2-74. The initial screen for the DSPACE utility

Change File Server. This first option is no different from any of the other NetWare
menu utilities. If you want to browse around the servers and see what your disk storage
restrictions are, choose the "Change" option. At the "Available Options" window, select
the "Change File Server" option and press <Enter>. You'll see a list of all the servers
you're currently attached to. To add another server to the list, press <Ins>. You'll see an
"Other File Servers" window listing all available servers on the network. To see the
names of all the servers on the network, press <Ctrl>-<PgDn> to go to the bottom of the
listing, or <Ctrl>-<PgUp> to go to the top. To move a screenful at a time, press <PgDn>
or <PgUp>. Select the name of the other server you want to look at and press <Enter>.

The "Change File Server" option attaches you to the other servers and prompts you for your username and, when appropriate, for your password. Now that you're attached to another server, choose to view that server's space information by highlighting the servername and pressing <Enter>. Notice that the servername has changed at the top of your menu; your username may have changed as well. This change helps you keep track of which server's information you're seeing.

You can also detach from the extra servers in DSPACE by highlighting the servername in the "File Server/User Name" window and pressing <Del>. You'll see a "Logout from server. Yes/No" window with the "Yes" option highlighted. Press <Enter> to log out from that server. If you attach to several servers and you want to log out of them, use <F5> to mark the servers you wish to log out of and then press <Del>. You'll see the "Log out from all marked servers. Yes/No" window with the "Yes" option highlighted. Press <Enter> and you'll log out of those servers. If you accidentally mark the server you're logged in to, you'll see a screen which says, "You cannot log out from your default server. Press ESCAPE to continue."

User Restrictions. This next option in the "Available Options" window allows you to view your restrictions on this server's available volumes. Highlight the "User Restrictions" option and press <Enter>. You'll see a small window that says "Users on Server *servername*" including your login name. Highlight your username and press <Enter>; you'll see a window listing the known volumes on the server. Highlight the name of the volume on which you wish to see disk space restrictions and press <Enter>. You'll see a screen similar to the following one:

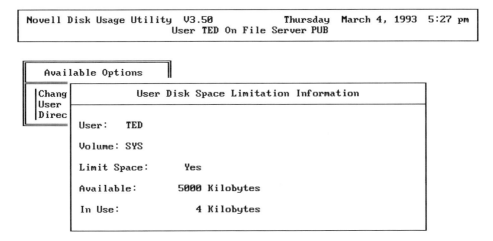

Figure 2-75. Use this screen to see how much space you have available

If the server has only one volume, you won't see the volume options window but will drop directly into the "User Disk Space Limitation Information" window. This window contains the following entries: User, Volume, Limit Space, Available, and In Use. The "User" entry displays your login name. The "Volume" entry shows you the name of the volume you chose to look at if your server has more than one volume.

The "Limit Space" entry simply shows you if you're one of the lucky ones with disk space restrictions. What you see in the "Available" entry is the amount of disk space, in kilobytes, that you can use before running out of disk space. You can tell how close you are to the amount by subtracting the "In Use" entry from the "Available" entry.

Be warned, however, that when you run out of disk space, you won't be able to save or update the document you're working on to the server and you stand to lose your work in that file. If you're an electronic pack rat, which almost everyone is, you'll need to keep better track of which files you use for reference and need to access on a regular basis.

For example, suppose you're limited to 5MB of disk space and you've already used 4.7MB. If all your data files are under the VOL1:USERS\TED directory, you can use the NDIR utility to take a look at the last time you accessed files. Let's say you want to see all the files you haven't accessed for the last six months. Go to the USERS\TED directory and type NDIR /AC BEF 6-5-92 /SUB <Enter>, which essentially tells NetWare to "show me all files that were last accessed before June 5, 1992, and show me files from all subdirectories under directory TED as well."

Once you see the list of files, you'll see at the bottom the total number of bytes those files are taking up (shown in the block line). If the files presented are enough for your purposes, print out this information by typing:

```
NDIR /AC BEF 6-5-92 /SUB >LPT1 <Enter>
```

If this directory dump doesn't print out, type NDIR /AC BEF 6-5-92 /SUB >FILES <Enter>. This command creates a file called FILES and copies the information usually displayed on the screen to FILES. You can then type NPRINT FILES Q=*queuename* and print the file.

You now have a listing of all the files you haven't accessed for the last six months. You can then ask the supervisor to take them off the network (after backing them up, of course), or you can make a copy of the files to floppy disks and then delete the files from your directory. This will free up the space you need. For more information on NDIR, see the heading "Directory and File Management Utilities" in Chapter 3, for more information on NPRINT, see the "Using the NPRINT Command" heading in Chapter 4, and for more information on NBACKUP, see "The NBACKUP Utility" heading later in this chapter.

To get out of the "User Restriction" option, press <Esc>. To exit the DSPACE utility, press <Esc> until you reach the "Exit DSPACE Yes/No" window with the "Yes" option highlighted; then press <Enter>.

The last option you see in the Available Options" window in DSPACE is "Directory Restrictions." NetWare 3.1x allows the supervisor or anyone with the Supervisor trustee assignment to place disk space restrictions on directories.

Please note that these directory limitations affect everyone who has access to directories along the directory path, and the amount of disk space allotted is for all directories combined, not for each directory individually. For example, if the supervisor places a 140MB limit at the NTS3/VOL1:USERS directory level, then all directories beneath USERS have to share that disk space. This limitation can be quite a pain if the amount specified is too low for the number of users saving data to their personal directories. But the capability to limit directory space is there, nonetheless, and as a user you need to be aware of it.

When you select the "Directory Restrictions" option, you first see the "Directory for Space Restriction Information:" window that allows you to type in a directory path to specify which directory you wish to look at. Do this by typing in the directory path and pressing <Enter>, or by pressing <Ins> and selecting the server/volume/directory options displayed in menu on the far left part of the screen until you reach the directory you want. Then press <Esc> to return to the "Directory Information" window and press <Enter>.

The "Directory Disk Space Limitation Information" window shows you the "Path Space Limit," "Limit Space," "Directory Space Limit," and "Currently Available" entries. The "Path Space Limit" entry shows you that either in the directory you've chosen, or in a previous directory, the supervisor has defined space restrictions. This limit is for all directories beneath the directory where the space restriction was set up. Depending on your security, you might be able to creep up the path to where the restrictions began. But in any case, if the "Limit Space" entry shows "Yes," look at the "Directory Space Limit" to see what everyone was allotted, then keep an eye on how much disk space you have left in the "Currently Available" entry. You must then barter with anyone else who is affected for more disk space.

To get out of the "Directory Restrictions" option, press <Esc>. To exit the DSPACE utility, press <Esc> until you reach the "Exit DSPACE Yes/No" window with the "Yes" option highlighted, then press <Enter>.

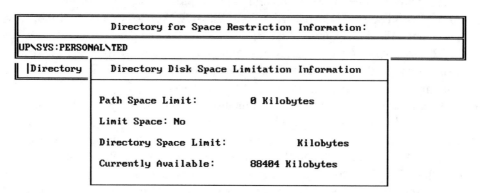

Figure 2-76. Use this screen to keep an eye on how your disk space is limted

The NBACKUP Utility

NetWare 3.11 and 3.12 include a new backup and restore utility called SBACKUP. This utility is designed for use by supervisors, so I won't cover it here. The NBACKUP utility (which I *will* cover here) ships with version 3.1x, and includes a set of warnings to alert you that NBACKUP does not provide comprehensive backup for OS/2 or Macintosh files. You can still use the utility by pressing <Enter> to step through the warning notices. You should use NBACKUP for backing up your personal files, rather than for full server backups or when backing up OS/2 or Macintosh files.

You need Read and File Scan rights in the directory from which you're running NBACKUP, and if you're copying files to a directory on this or another server, you'll need Read, Write, Create, Erase, File Scan, and Modify rights. You'll also need Read, Write, Create, Erase, File Scan, and Modify rights for the directory you set up as your "working directory," which NetWare uses to create backup and error logs.

As some background information, NBACKUP will back up and restore Macintosh files, including the resource and data forks the Mac files use. However, you can't use wild cards to help designate Macintosh files in NBACKUP; you'll also need to place a colon (:) in front of Macintosh file and directory names.

NBACKUP comes with two types of backup devices: *DOS devices*, such as floppy disk drives, hard disk drives, or tape units using DOS device drivers, and *tape backup units*, of which Wangtek comes as the default. However, supervisors can add their own

202

tape backup drivers and devices so they appear in the "Select the Desired Device" window. But since this is a user's guide, we'll keep our focus on DOS devices.

Going Through the NBACKUP Options

Getting around in NBACKUP is a little different from using the familiar NetWare menus created from the C-Worthy library. For example, you can't press <Alt>-<F10> to leave the NBACKUP menu, and for error or warning messages, you press <Enter> instead of <Esc> to leave the message and return to the previous screen. We'll cover any other changes as I go through the utility.

To get into the utility, type NBACKUP <Enter> at the network prompt. You'll see the "Select The Desired Device" window with two options displayed: "DOS Devices" and "Wangtek Tape Drive." Again, since this is a user's guide and since most users won't have access to tape backup devices, we'll focus on the "DOS Devices" option. Highlight "DOS Devices" and press <Enter>. After a moment, you'll see the "Main Menu" window with three options: "Change Current Server," "Backup Options," and "Restore Options."

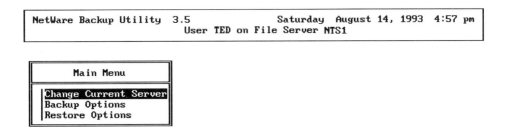

Figure 2-77. With NBACKUP, you can choose to back up or restore files

Changing Servers

The first option, "Change Current Server," is no different from any other NetWare menu utility. Let's suppose you want to store files on server IGOR, to which you're not currently attached. At the "Main Menu" window, select the "Change Current Server" option and press <Enter>.

You'll see a list of all the servers you're currently attached to in the "File Server/User Name" window. To add another server such as IGOR to the list, press <Ins>. You'll see an "Other File Servers" window listing all available servers on the network. To see the names of all the servers on the network, press <Ctrl>-<PgDn> to go to the bottom of the listing, or <Ctrl>-<PgUp> to go to the top. To move a screenful at a time, press <PgDn> or <PgUp>. Or you can use the up/down arrow keys to highlight a server name. In any case, select the name of the server you want to add and press <Enter>. For this example, we'll highlight IGOR <Enter>.

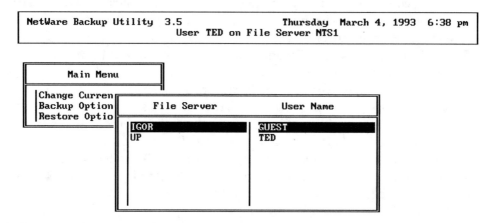

Figure 2-78. You can add or remove servers through the "Change Servers" window

The "Change File Server" option attaches you to the other servers and prompts you for your username and, when appropriate, for your password. Pressing <Enter> places the server into the "File Server/User Name" window. Now that you're attached to another server, press <Esc> to return to the "Main Menu" window without selecting the server you've just added. If you do select the newly attached server, you'll be backing up files on that server instead of the server you're currently logged in to. If that's what you want to do, press <Enter> instead of <Esc> and you'll return to the "Main Menu" window as well. You'll also notice that the second line in the menu screen will change to reflect the server you're currently viewing.

Using the Backup Option

"Backup Options" allows you to back up data from a selected server to floppy disks, local hard disks, other network servers, or backup units using DOS device drivers. The backup options seem more geared to global directory and server backup methods than individual files. For example, you can include and exclude entire directories and their files much more easily than you can back up selected files throughout directories.

Highlight the "Backup Options" selection by pressing the Down arrow key once and then pressing <Enter>. Or type the letter B, which will also highlight the "Backup

204

Options" selection, then press <Enter>. The "Backup Menu" window has four options: "Select Working Directory," "Backup By Directory," "View Backup Log," and "View Error Log." (If you're a supervisor or equivalent, you'll see an additional option— "Backup File Server.")

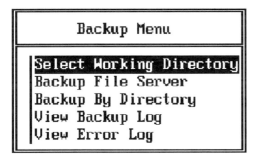

```
Backup Menu

Select Working Directory
Backup File Server
Backup By Directory
View Backup Log
View Error Log
```

Figure 2-79. When you choose the Backup option, you then select which function you wish to perform

Suppose your supervisor says you're using too much disk space in the ADMIN/ SYS:USERS\TED directory path. Let's further suppose you have 8MB of disk space on server ADMIN and your supervisor wants it down to 5MB. A good place to begin your cutting-down process is by looking at all the files you haven't accessed for the last six months. Do this by going to the USERS\TED directory and type NDIR /AC BEF 6-5-92 /SUB <Enter>, which essentially tells NetWare to "show all files that were last accessed before June 5, 1992, and show files from all subdirectories under directory TED."

Once you see the list of files, you'll see at the bottom the total number of bytes those files are taking up on the server (shown in the block line). If you don't need to keep these aged files on the server any more, you may want to print out this information by typing in the NDIR command this way:

```
NDIR /AC BEF 6-5-92 /SUB >LPT1 <Enter>
```

If this directory/file dump doesn't print out, type NDIR /AC BEF 6-5-92 /SUB >NOGOTIN <Enter>. This command creates a file called NOGOTIN and copies the information that is usually displayed on the screen to NOGOTIN. You can then use the NPRINT command to print out the file by typing NPRINT NOGOTIN Q=*queuename* <Enter>.

You now have a listing of all the files you haven't accessed for the last six months. Ask the supervisor to take them off the network (after backing them up, of course), or make a copy of the files to floppy disks and then delete the files from your directories. But for this example, we'll use NBACKUP to take the files off the server.

By running NDIR, you've discovered that you haven't accessed the files in the DATA or GARDNER directories for over six months. These two directories constitute over two megabytes of data you can get rid of. The other nonaccessed files are scattered across six directories and don't add up to even one megabyte. For our first example, let's copy the files in DATA and GARDNER directories to floppy disks. We'll then back up the other files to another file server for a second example. These examples are only to demonstrate NBACKUP's functionality, as you may find much better uses for the utility.

First, choose the "Select Working Directory" option. Through this option, you designate a directory where you'll store the BACK$LOG.*xxx* and BACK$ERR.*xxx* files. Be aware that NBACKUP's "Restore" option relies heavily upon these files; if they're deleted or corrupted, you won't be able to access that backup session for restoring purposes.

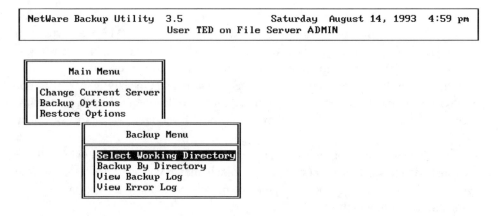

Figure 2-80. You must select a working directory that you have read and write rights in

Select a directory that you can use for all your NetWare backup sessions so you have only one working directory to designate. For the working directory, you need Write, Create, Erase, File Scan, and Modify rights. If you need to look at files in the directory, you need Read rights as well.

When you press <Enter> on the "Select" option, you'll see the "Select Working Directory" window. If you know which directory you want to store the files in—for example, ADMIN/SYS:USERS\TED—type in the directory path. You can also press <Ins> to create the directory path from the menu format. Pressing <Ins> lists all servers, volumes on the selected server, directories, and subdirectories beneath the directory displayed in the "Current Directory Path" window.

Selecting one of the directories in the "Network Directories" window makes the selected directory a part of the "Current Directory Path" window. The subdirectories under the selected directory appear in the "Network Directories" window. Continue selecting until you reach the desired directory, press <Esc>, then press <Enter>.

If you select a local drive, such as Drive A, B, C, or D; NBACKUP will ask you if this drive is removable. The default is Yes. Choosing this tells the program to ask for a new disk or tape if the current one fills to capacity during the backup. Choose No if you are storing your backup on a local hard disk.

The "Insert" option also lets you choose other servers if you need to. Pressing <Ins> at the "File Servers/Local Drives" window brings up the "Other File Servers" window. Suppose, for example, you're attached to server ADMIN, but you want to place the working files in a directory on server NTS3. Choose the "Select Working Directory" option and erase the entire directory path in the "Current Directory Path" window. Press <Ins> and you'll see a "File Servers/Local Drives" window.

If server NTS3 appears in the window, you can select that server directly. Then you can follow the above instructions to get to the designated directory. If server NTS3 doesn't appear in the "File Servers/Local Drives" window, press <Ins> again to see a list of all the servers on the network. Select server NTS3, then enter your login name for that server and your password. Server NTS3 will appear in the "File Servers/Local Drives" window. Highlight and select that server; then you can get to your designated directory path by following the above instructions. Once you reach the desired directory, press <Esc>, then press <Enter>, and you'll return to the "Backup Menu" window.

Next, choose the "Backup By Directory" option. The "Backup Options" window looks similar to the one in Figure 2-81 on the next page.

If you haven't chosen a working directory in the first option, you'll be prompted to select a working directory here. Because of this, you can ignore the "Select Working Directory" option, choose the "Backup By Directory" option, and there type in the working directory. But make no mistake: you must designate a working directory or you'll never reach the "Backup Options" window. But with the working directory in place, you'll see the "Backup Options" window with the following entries:

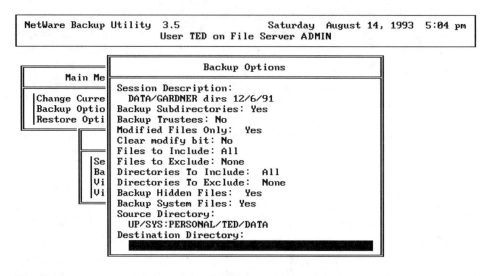

```
NetWare Backup Utility  3.5                Saturday  August 14, 1993  5:04 pm
                        User TED on File Server ADMIN
```

```
┌──────────────────┐┌─────────────────────────────────────────────┐
│          Main Me ││              Backup Options                   │
├──────────────────┤│  Session Description:                         │
│ Change Curre     ││     DATA/GARDNER dirs 12/6/91                 │
│ Backup Optio     ││  Backup Subdirectories: Yes                   │
│ Restore Opti     ││  Backup Trustees: No                          │
├──────────────────┘│  Modified Files Only:  Yes                    │
│                   │  Clear modify bit: No                         │
├──────────────────┤  Files to Include: All                        │
│  Se               │  Files to Exclude: None                       │
│  Ba               │  Directories To Include:  All                 │
│  Vi               │  Directories To Exclude:  None                │
│  Vi               │  Backup Hidden Files:  Yes                    │
├──────────────────┘  Backup System Files: Yes                     │
│                    Source Directory:                              │
│                       UP/SYS:PERSONAL/TED/DATA                    │
│                    Destination Directory:                         │
│                    ██████████████████████████                    │
└───────────────────────────────────────────────────────────────────┘
```

Figure 2-81. You can fill in your own conditions, or use the default conditions

Session Description. This is the first entry in the "Backup Options" window. You must have a session description for NBACKUP to work. If you fail to place something in this field and then try to run a backup session, you'll see "You must enter a description to continue. Press ENTER to continue." Then, if you press <Enter>, you'll see another screen that says "Continue To Edit Form? Press ENTER to Continue/Press <Esc> to Abort." If you press <Enter>, it brings you back to the session form, and if you press <Esc>, it brings you to the "Backup Menu" window.

Use this entry to give this session a unique name for reference, such as the "DATA/ GARDNER Dirs 12/6/92" to follow our example. You have 29 characters to use, including blank spaces. You do need to type in something here, because this description is then used in the status window as you're backing up and in reports you can generate. It's attached to the working files themselves. So be descriptive enough to identify this particular session. When you've accumulated a lot of sessions, it's hard to tell one session from another.

Backup Subdirectories. Choose this entry if you want to back up the subdirectories beneath the directory you designate in the "Source Directory" entry. This entry defaults as "Yes." For our example, if directory GARDNER is one of three subdirectories under DATA, you can answer "Yes" to this entry, then exclude the other two directories (along with their files) at the "Directories to Exclude" entry.

Backup Trustees. This entry is actually for system supervisors and backup managers, for when you answer "Yes," NBACKUP will preserve all the trustee assignments you've given other users to that directory. If you give a lot of users trustee assignments to your directories, type "Y" for "Yes"; otherwise, use the default of No. But if you do use the default, you'll need to again add trustee assignments for those who use your directories. This entry defaults to "No," which is fine for most occasions and most users.

Modified Files Only. This entry allows you to back up only those files that have the DOS Archive bit switched; the entry defaults to "Yes." This means the file has been opened and written to since the last time it was backed up. The Archive bit is handy for regular backup purposes, for you back up only files that have been modified. With this entry, you can make a "working backup copy" of all modified files without changing the Archive bit so files won't miss the normal backup procedures. To do this, however, be sure to set the "Clear Modify Bit" entry to "No." For our example, we'll type "N" for "No," because we want to back up entire directories and take them off the server.

Clear Modify Bit. This entry defaults to "No," but you would change the entry to "Yes" if for some reason you needed to clear the DOS Archive bit after you ran NBACKUP. If you change the entry to "Yes," the files you back up won't be backed up during normal backup procedures (if normal backup procedures only back up files needing to be archived) until you write to them again. But by leaving this entry to "No," you or the normal backup procedure can back up these files again.

Files To Include. This entry allows you to specify which files you want NBACKUP to back up along this directory path. If you type "No" at the "Backup Subdirectories" entry, the files you designate in this Include entry include only the files in the directory you designated as the source directory. If you're including subdirectories, the Include entry affects those subdirectories as well.

For example, pressing <Enter> at the "Files to Include" entry brings up the "Files to Include" window, which indicates any filename. Sometimes you'll see an asterisk (*) wild card in it, which also indicates any filename. If you see the asterisk, you must first delete the asterisk by highlighting it and pressing <Del>. This brings up the "Delete Marked File" window with the "Yes" option highlighted, and pressing <Enter> deletes the include pattern. Then pressing <Ins> brings up another "Files to Include" window that allows you to type in any filename or wild card pattern for NBACKUP to include in its backup procedures.

For example, if you want information on several files that all have the same extension, specify in the "Files to Include" window all the files with that extension, such as *.SCR or *.DAT. The following figure indicates all files with an .SCR extension, regardless of the filename.

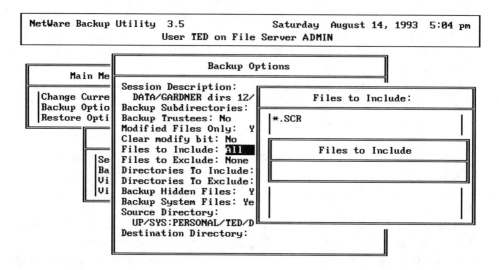

Figure 2-82. You can include and exclude files using wild cards and file extensions

You can designate other file patterns as well. For example, if you want to back up only files that begin with the letter S, put S*.* in the pattern box. You can also use the question mark (?) wild card in NBACKUP. Suppose you want to back up files that start with the letter S, specifically the SL_}SYS.* files. You can enter the file pattern as ????SYS.*, and NBACKUP will back up the SL_}SYS.* files.

You can also type in a string of filenames that you wish to back up. These files will then appear in the "Files To Include" window, and will be the only files backed up. But for our running example, we'll leave this entry blank so we can back up all the files in the directory.

Files to Exclude. This entry allows you to specify a file pattern that you don't want to back up in the source directory or its subdirectories. Suppose you have an abundance of files with an .SCR extension that you don't want to take off the system. Press <Enter> at the "File to Exclude" entry, then press <Ins>. Type in *.SCR to exclude all files with the .SCR extension. Press <Enter> and the .SCR exclude parameter will be added to the "Files to Exclude" window. If you type the file in wrong, you'll see a message that says "Enter a valid DOS filename. Press ENTER to Continue." You can then correct your mistake and type in a proper DOS filename or the proper use of wild cards.

Note that exclude patterns will overwrite include patterns if they conflict. So if you have an include pattern of S* and an exclude pattern of ??SYS*.*, you won't see any files that begin with the S and have SYS two letters into their filename.

Directories To Include. This entry works the same as the "Files to Include" entry except that it allows you to specify which directories you want NBACKUP to back up along this directory path. Be sure to type "Yes" at the "Backup Subdirectories" entry so you can include subdirectories in the NBACKUP procedure.

For example, pressing <Enter> at the "Directories to Include" entry brings up the "Directories to Include" window, which is usually blank, indicating any directory name. Pressing <Ins> brings up another "Directories to Include" window that allows you to type in any directory name or wild card pattern for NBACKUP to include in its backup procedures.

For example, if you want information on only directories that begin with D (such as DATA), you can specify in the "Directories to Include" window D* or, if you use extensions on your directories, D*.*. The following figure shows all directories that begin with D and the GARDNER directory, along with its directory path.

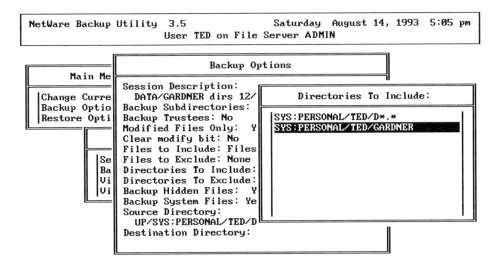

Figure 2-83. You can select which directories you wish to back up files from

You can designate other search patterns as well. For example, if you want to back up only directories that begin with the letter "S", put S*.* in the pattern box. You can also use the question mark (?) wild card in NBACKUP. Suppose you have a number of

211

directories with SYS in the middle, such as JANSYS, AUGSYS, NOVSYS, and JULSYS directories. Also suppose you only want to back up directories that start with the letter J. You can enter the file pattern as J??SYS.*, and NBACKUP will back up only the JANSYS and JULSYS directories.

Directories To Exclude. This entry allows you to specify directory name patterns that you don't want to back up. As a counterexample to the Include entry, suppose you have a number of directories with SYS in the middle, such as JANSYS, AUGSYS, NOVSYS, and JULSYS. Press <Enter> at the "Directories to Exclude" entry, then press <Ins>. Type in ???SYS to exclude all directories with the .SCR extension. Press <Enter> and the ???SYS exclude parameter is added to the "Directories to Exclude" window.

Note that exclude patterns will overwrite include patterns if they conflict. So if you have an include pattern of J??SYS and an exclude pattern of ???SYS*.*, you won't see any directories that begin with the letter J and have SYS two letters into their name.

Backup Hidden Files. This entry defaults to "Yes." Normally, you can't back up files flagged as hidden or system, nor can you copy or delete them. For the purpose of our long-running example, we'll leave the default set to "Yes" even though it doesn't mean anything. However, if we knew there were hidden files in the DATA and GARDNER directories, we'd need to change those files' attributes to something like Normal, then run NBACKUP.

Backup System Files. This entry also defaults to "Yes." Normally, you can't back up files flagged as hidden or system, nor can you copy or delete them. For purposes of our long-running example, we'll leave the default set to "Yes"; however, this entry is normally used for system files and their directories, a category which doesn't include most user files or directories. But if you did happen to have some files flagged with the System attribute in the DATA and GARDNER directories, you'd need to change those files' attributes to something like Normal, then run NBACKUP.

Source Directory. This is where you type in the directory path and directory you wish to back up. If you've marked the "Backup Subdirectories" entry, the source directory is the starting point for backing up files and subdirectories down this directory path. For our example, the source directory is ADMIN/SYS:USERS\TED\DATA.

If you know the directory where you want to begin backing up files (such as ADMIN/SYS:USERS\TED\DATA), press <Enter>. You'll see the "Select Source Directory" window with the server and volume filled in for you, taken from the directory path from which you ran NBACKUP. Type in the rest of the directory path, or press <Ins> to create the directory path from the menu format. Pressing <Ins> lists the directories and subdirectories beneath the volume displayed in the "Select Source Directory" window.

212

Selecting one of the directories in the "Network Directories" window makes the selected directory a part of the "Select Source Directory" window. Highlight the directory you wish and press <Enter>. The subdirectories of your new directory path will appear in the "Network Directories" window. Continue until you reach the desired directory, press <Esc>, then press <Enter>. If you want to back up a directory on a different volume, you can press the Backspace key over the volume, then press <Ins> to see a listing of all volumes on the server.

While supervisors can select the server they wish to back up from within NBACKUP, users can only back up files on the server from which they run NBACKUP. If you use the <Ins> method, you'll only see the server from which you ran NBACKUP in the first place. For example, if drive G: is mapped to NTS3/VOL1:DATA and drive H: is mapped to ADMIN/SYS:USERS\TED\DATA, you'll only be able to back up files on server NTS3 if you run NBACKUP from drive G:, and you'll only be able to back up files on server ADMIN if you run NBACKUP from drive H:. If you try to change servers, you'll see the message "Only directories on file server *servername* are allowed. Press <Esc> to continue."

Destination Directory. This entry is where you want to put the BACK$*xxx*.000 file, into which NBACKUP lumps all the files you're about to back up. The *xxx* matches the number sequence of both the error log file (BACK$ERR.*xxx*) and the log file (BACK$LOG.*xxx*). For example, if this is the first time you're running NBACKUP, the backup file will be called BACK$000.000, the log file BACK$LOG.000, and the error log BACK$ERR.000. Subsequent backups that use the same working directory to store log and error log files will increment, such as BACK$001.000, BACK$LOG.001, and BACK$ERR.001, respectively.

If you're saving to floppy disks and you use more than one, the backup file will increment along with the number of disks it takes to back up the directories, beginning with .000. For example, if your backup session takes three disks, the backup files on each of these disks will be labeled incrementally, such as BACK$001.000, BACK$001.001, and BACK$001.002.

For our example, we want to move the DATA and GARDNER directories off the network and onto floppy disks. So, in the "Destination Directory" entry, we press <Enter>, then type A: in the "Select Destination Path" window and press <Enter> again.

With the entries in the "Backup Options" window filled the way you want them, press <Esc> and you'll see the "Save Changes" window with the "Yes" option highlighted. Pressing <Enter> brings you to the "Start Backup Menu" window with two options: "Start Backup Now" and "Start Backup Later." The "Start Backup Now" option begins the backup procedure immediately, asking you to insert the media disk in the drive you selected, then press <Enter> to begin backing up. The "Start Backup Later" option has you set up for a future backup, then puts the workstation on hold until the actual time of the backup.

If you select the "Later" option, you'll see the "Start Backup Timer" window with the date and time for you to set. Once you set the time and date and press <Esc>, you'll then be prompted to save changes with the "Yes" option highlighted. Pressing <Enter> freezes the workstation and brings up the backup screen with a smaller screen in the middle that shows the date and time the workstation will begin backing up, such as "The backup will begin at 12/05/92 14:15:59." Once the time is reached, the backup process begins. When the backup ends, you'll see a window that shows you the file server with your user name. The next line asks for your password. If you don't type in your password within thirty minutes, you'll be logged out. If you simply press <Enter> without a password, you'll also be logged out and left at the network prompt. If you type in the correct password, you'll return to the network prompt from which you began NBACKUP.

What You See During Backup

When you begin the backup procedure, the backup session screen shows you some useful information.

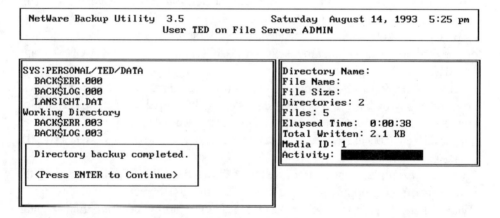

Figure 2-84. NBACKUP keeps you posted on how the backup is progressing

The screen is divided into three windows. One lists the files being backed up, one provides information about the backup session, and one contains messages that pertain to the session. You'll see the files being backed up in the left-hand window, which scrolls the files being backed up along with the directory in which they are stored. You can see

214

pertinent backup information in the right-hand window, and messages (if there are any) appear in the bottom window. These messages are also written to the error log file for your perusal. Below are the entries you can see in the "Backup Information" window as you're running a backup session.

Directory Name. This entry names the directory you're currently backing up. If you're backing up multiple directories, this entry can show you which directory you're currently in.

Filename. This entry shows you which file is currently being backed up. Filenames can fly by pretty quickly.

File Size. This line shows the size of the file currently being backed up. File sizes are shown in bytes, not kilobytes.

Directories. This entry shows you how many directories have been backed up during this session. When NBACKUP finishes a session, you'll see the "Directory backup completed. Press ENTER to Continue" window on the screen. Until you press <Enter> to return to the "Backup Menu" window, you can better see how many directories you have backed up. The number of directories is also listed in the error log file which pertains to this session. You can print out the error log by going into the working directory and typing NPRINT BACK$ERR.extension Q=*queuename* <Enter>.

Files. This shows you how many files have been backed up during this session. Until you press <Enter> to return to the "Backup Menu" window, you can see how many files you have backed up. The number of files is also listed in the error log file which pertains to this session. You can print out the error log by going into the working directory and typing NPRINT BACK$ERR.extension Q=*queuename* <Enter>.

Elapsed Time. This entry shows how much time it took to actually perform the backup session. This information is also recorded in the error log file.

Total Written. This line shows in kilobytes the cumulative amount of copied files and other information written to the destination directory.

Media ID. Here, the number assigned to a tape or cartridge or floppy disk currently being used is shown. For floppy disks, the media ID increments with each disk you use. If your backup session took three disks, the backup files on each disk will be labeled incrementally: for example, BACK$001.000, BACK$001.001, and BACK$001.002.

Activity. This entry lets you know that you're still backing up. You'll see a green bar march from side to side of the Activity entry if you're still backing up data in this session.

If everything was successful, you'll see the "Directory backup completed. Press ENTER to Continue" window and a brief message will flash across the bottom window. The message is stored in the BACK$ERR.*xxx* file that pertains to this backup session. Pressing <Enter> brings you again to the "Backup Menu" window.

It's a good idea to back up the log and error log files from within your working directory. If those files are deleted or damaged, you won't be able to restore the data you just backed up. NBACKUP also makes a copy of those files and stores them on the last media (disk) used for backing up that session. However, another backup won't hurt.

You can also print out these files for your reference. For example, if the log files have a .006 extension, go into the working directory where those files are stored and type NPRINT *.006 Q=*queuename* <Enter>. The printout of the log file can be very helpful when you want to restore only a few files instead of an entire directory. Use the Include feature for this type of restoration.

To follow up on our example, the procedure just described copied all the files from the DATA and GARDNER directories to two high-density disks and one very large file called BACK$007.000 on the first disk and BACK$007.001 on the second disk. (Be sure to label your disks so you can insert the proper disk during restoration procedures.) We have just run NPRINT and have printed out the log and error log files and are poised to delete the files in those two directories. But we also have another 1MB of files to get off the server.

For the second example, let's suppose we have another server where we can store the megabyte of files—NTS3. If you're not attached to the NTS3 server, do so through the "Change Current Server" option in the "Main Menu" window. Choose "Backup Options" <Enter>, then the "Backup By Directory" option from the "Backup Menu." Select a working directory if one hasn't been defined already. Then at the "Backup Options" window for this example, we'll give the session description "1MB transfer to NTS3."

If you know that the files you want to back up are in the TED, REPORTS, INVOICE, and JAN92 directories, make sure the "Backup Subdirectories" entry says "Yes," then place those directories in the "Directories To Include" entry. Then, if you know the names of the files you need to back up, type those names into the "File To Include" entry. For this example, we need to back up all the *.INV files on the INVOICE directory, the RECORD and DRAKE files from the REPORTS directory, the SCAN and ROGER articles from the TED directory, and the OFFICE files in the JAN92 directory. If you can use wild cards, follow the examples described under the "Files to Include" and "Files to Exclude" subhcadings; otherwise, type in the full filenames. There are also other files that haven't been accessed in two other directories, but you get the idea of what to do.

Now at the "Source Directory" entry, type in the directory path to the UP/ SYS:USERS\TED directory, then type in the directory path to the directory where you wish to store the backup file: for example, NTS3/VOL1:PERSONAL\TED. Press <Esc>, then <Enter> to save the changes and <Enter> again to begin the backup procedure. With the BACK$*xxx*.000 file copied over to the TED directory on NTS3, you should also make

216

a quick copy of the BACK$LOG and BACK$ERR files to the last session disk or to the directory storing the backup file for restore purposes. If those files are ever deleted from the working directory, you can always copy them back in from the backup disks.

Viewing Backup and Error Logs

The last two options in the "Backup Menu" window—"View Backup Log" and "View Error Log"—allow you to view the backup log and error log files. Again, these files are stored in the directory you designated as your working directory and can be printed out as described previously. You also see these two options in the "Restore" menu, for NBACKUP uses these two files to restore files and directories previously backed up.

To look at the information found in backup logs, highlight the "View Backup Log" option and press <Enter>. If you've already designated a working directory, you'll see the "Select Session to View Backup Log" window. However, if you left NBACKUP and are just getting back in, you'll need to type in the directory path to the directory that holds the backup log and error log files.

To read the log files from the working directory, you need Read and File Scan rights, but when you create a log file, you need Write, Create, Erase, File Scan, and Modify rights. If you know which directory the files are located in—for example, UP/SYS:USERS\TED—type in the directory path.

```
NetWare Backup Utility  3.5                 Saturday  August 14, 1993  5:26 pm
                        User TED on File Server ADMIN
```

```
                        Select Session to View Backup Log

      Description          Date      Time        Source

   DATA/GARDNER DIRS 12 08/14/93   17:24:46 UP/SYS:PERSONAL/TED/DATA/
   DATA/GARDNER DIRS 12 08/14/93   17:09:36 UP/SYS:PERSONAL/TED/DATA/
   DATA/GARDNER DIRS 12 08/14/93   17:08:16 UP/SYS:PERSONAL/TED/DATA/
   DATA/GARDNER dirs 12 08/14/93   17:07:00 UP/SYS:PERSONAL/TED/DATA/
```

Figure 2-85. You can view historical data on the backups you performed in this directory or disks

You can also press <Ins> to create the directory path from the menu format. Pressing <Ins> lists all servers, volumes on the selected server, directories, and subdirectories under the directory shown in the "Current Directory Path" window.

Selecting one of the directories in the "Network Directories" window makes the selected directory a part of the "Current Directory Path" window. The subdirectories of your new directory path will appear in the "Network Directories" window. Continue until you reach the desired directory, press <Esc>, then press <Enter>, and you'll see the "Select Session to View Backup Log" window.

The "Select Session" window shows all the sessions NBACKUP can find with the BACK$LOG.*xxx* filename. NBACKUP presents backup information in a chronological order with the last backup performed listed at the top. The window has four columns beneath the window's header: "Description," "Date," "Time," and "Source." The description column displays the session description you typed in when you initially named this session. (Here's where you find out how helpful your descriptions are.) The "Date" and "Time" entries tell you when the BACK$LOG file was last written to, which is usually after you have run its backup session. The "Source" column shows you the directory you designated to begin the backup session. From our example's description, let's select DATA/GARDNER Dirs 3/4/93 and press <Enter>. You'll see a screen similar to this one:

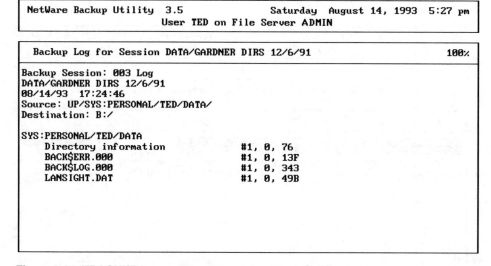

Figure 2-86. NBACKUP keeps a log on your backup activities

The first line below the NBACKUP header says "Backup Log for *title you gave*" along with how much of this backup session is presently displayed on the screen. As you press the up/down arrow keys, you'll see the percentage increment or decrement as you scroll through the log file.

The backup log gives you some storage information about the backup log. For example, the first line, "Backup Session: *xxx* Log," shows you which number this backup session was in relation to the other backup log files that NBACKUP found in your working directory.

The second line displays the session description which you gave this session during the initial backup procedure. The third line shows the date and time when you performed backup. By using the backup's date and time, NBACKUP can then present backup options in a chronological order at the "Select Session" window. The Source line shows you the directory you designated to begin the backup session, and the Destination line shows you where the data was copied to. For our example, this was drive A:.

The rest of the file contains a listing of the directories that were backed up along with the files you backed up. Across from the files, you'll see a listing like #1, 0, 76. The #1, 0, refer to the number assigned to a tape or cartridge or floppy disk which is currently being used. This correlates to the Media ID entry you saw when the utility was backing up the session. For floppy disks, the number increments with each disk you used. If your backup session took three disks, you see #1, 0, until the second disk comes into play, then you see #2, 1, until the third disk, which shows you #3, 2. The letters and numbers that follow the media numbering tell NBACKUP where on the disk it needs to go to begin restoring the corresponding file or directory information.

Don't alter the backup log information, or NBACKUP won't know where to begin restoring information back to the server. Nor should you delete the backup log file, as NBACKUP then won't know this session existed when it looks in your working directory to find BACK$LOG.*xxx* files to restore. To leave the "Backup Log" window, press <Esc>, and to exit the "Select Session" window, press <Esc> again.

The "View Error Log" option is similar to the "View Backup Log" option in its functionality, but contains the messages you saw in the bottom portion of the "Backup Session" window. To view the information contained in the error log files, highlight the "View Error Log" option and press <Enter>. If you've already designated a working directory, you'll see the "Select Session to View Error Log" window. However, if you left NBACKUP and are just getting back in, you'll need to type in the directory path to the directory that holds the backup log and error log files.

The "Select Session" window shows all the sessions NBACKUP can find with the BACK$ERR.*xxx* filename. NBACKUP presents backup information in a chronological order, with the last backup performed listed at the top. The window has four columns beneath the window's header: "Description," "Date," "Time," and "Source." The "Description" column displays the session description you typed in when you initially named this session. (Here's where you find out how helpful your descriptions were.) The "Date" and "Time" entries tell you when the BACK$ERR file was last written to, which is usually after you have run its backup session. The "Source" column shows you the directory you designated to begin the backup session. From our example's description, let's select DATA/GARDNER Dirs 3/4/93 and press <Enter>. You'll see a screen similar to this one:

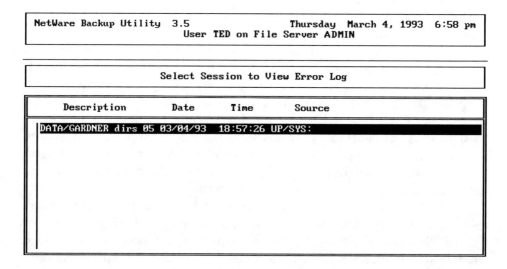

```
NetWare Backup Utility  3.5              Thursday  March 4, 1993  6:58 pm
                    User TED on File Server ADMIN


┌──────────────────────────────────────────────────────────────────────┐
│                  Select Session to View Error Log                      │
└──────────────────────────────────────────────────────────────────────┘

    Description          Date      Time      Source
   ┌────────────────────────────────────────────────────────────────────┐
   │DATA/GARDNER dirs 05 03/04/93  18:57:26 UP/SYS:                       │
   │                                                                      │
   │                                                                      │
   │                                                                      │
   │                                                                      │
   │                                                                      │
   │                                                                      │
   └────────────────────────────────────────────────────────────────────┘
```

Figure 2-87. NBACKUP keeps a log of the errors you received during your backup activities

The first line below the NBACKUP header says "Error Log for *title you gave*" along with how much of this backup session is presently displayed on the screen. As you press the up/down arrow keys, you'll see the percentage increment or decrement as you scroll through the error log file. Error logs usually fit in one screen.

Like the backup log, the error log also gives you some storage information about the backup session. For example, the first line, "Backup Session: *xxx* Errors," shows you which number this backup session was in relation to the other backup log files NBACKUP found in your working directory.

```
NetWare Backup Utility  3.5              Thursday  March 4, 1993  7:00 pm
                        User TED on File Server ADMIN

  Error Log for Session DATA/GARDNER dirs 05/03/93                    100%

Backup Session: 001 Errors
DATA/GARDNER dirs 05/03/93
03/04/93  19:00:06
Source: ADMIN/SYS:USERS/TED
Destination: UP/SYS:PERSONAL/TED/
System Version: NetWare 386 3.0 or 3.1

03/04/93  19:00:09  Successfully backed up 2 directories and 67 files, total
        written:2, 347.3 KB, elapsed time:  0:11:37!
```

Figure 2-88. You can view error data on the backups you have performed

The second line displays the session description that you gave this session during the initial backup procedure. The third line shows the date and time when you performed backup. The "Source" line shows you the directory you designated to begin the backup session, and the "Destination" line shows you where the data was copied to. For our example, this was drive A:.

The "System Version" line shows whether you run NBACKUP on NetWare 3.0 or 3.11. This information is important, for NBACKUP won't let you restore data from a 386 server to a server running NetWare 2.x or vice versa. However, you can restore data from systems that are the same operating system versions. We'll discuss this later.

The next line shows the date and time the backup session took place. Date and time are followed by any messages that you would have seen in the bottom part of the backup window. For our example, you see "Successfully backed up 2 directories and 67 files, total written: 2,347.3 KB, elapsed time: 0:11:37!" This information is similar to what you saw in the right-hand screen while you were backing up files.

You can also see error messages, such as "Backup session terminated" if you abort the backup session. Other error messages include the following:

```
The file filename was not marked after backup.
```

Normally, files that are backed up have their Archived bit cleared until the files are once again written to. In this instance, the Archived bit wasn't removed after it was backed up. While it's no cause for alarm, if the file is very large and you don't want to keep backing it up if it doesn't need to be, go into the file's directory and type FLAG *filename* N <Enter>.

```
The file filename was not backed up because it is in use.
```

Users probably won't see this message, as it normally applies to VAPs and queue files. Because certain system files are always open, system managers may not be able to back up those files.

```
The file filename was not backed up because it is Execute-Only.
```

Any *.COM or *.EXE files that are flagged Execute-Only cannot be copied or backed up. Make sure you have a backup copy of the application before flagging any application Execute-Only. Execute-Only files have to be deleted to change the Execute-Only flag on them; you then have to re-install the application.

You can also see some messages placed in the error log from a restoring procedure. Three of the more damaging error messages include the following:

```
Data must be restored to the same system version as it was
backed up from.
```

This message is probably the most crippling message to users, for it limits your ability to copy files from one server to other servers unless they have matching system versions. Let's suppose you have a NetWare 2.2 server called ADMIN and a NetWare 3.11 server called NTS3. While you can use NBACKUP to store your backup session file from ADMIN to a different system version such as NTS3, you cannot restore files and directories from ADMIN to NTS3. In the first instance, NTS3 is being used as a storage depot, and in the second instance, "NTS3" is the restoration designation.

If you need a lot more flexibility in file movement, use a third-party directory/file manager that lets you use new disks if you run out of space on the disk you are presently using. For example, many file managers or even text editors such as WordPerfect's Program Editor, WordPerfect Office, or WordPerfect itself come with a "List Files" option that allow you to mark directories of files and copy them to a series of disks. These programs are much more versatile and less restrictive than NBACKUP in managing files.

```
Cannot restore directory directoryname, a file by that name al-
ready exists.
```

When you see this message, NBACKUP will have aborted the restore session. At that point, it's probably best to place that file in the "Files to Exclude" entry and rerun the restore session. With the directory in place, you can then restore the file by selecting the "Rename Existing File" or "Rename Restored File" option from Restore's "File Exists" entry.

```
You do not have sufficient rights to create this directory.
```

Again, you must have at least Create, Erase, File Scan, Modify, and Write rights to create a directory and restore files to it.

You'll also see messages like "Restore Session Begin" when the error log records your restore efforts. To exit the error log, press <Esc>; to exit the "Select Session" window, press <Esc> again.

Yes, But Can It Restore?

For cooks, the proof is in the pudding. For Backup, the proof is in the Restore. So before deleting all the files from the DATA and GARDNER directories, let's see if we can restore the files to those directories first. If you have a lot of problems restoring through NBACKUP, you'll have to rely on the supervisor's backup procedure to retrieve your data. Then get a different backup procedure for yourself.

When you use NBACKUP and back up a set of directories to floppy disks, as in our example, a time may come when you wish to restore the entire directory or selected files back to the server. So let's suppose we now desperately need to retrieve the NAMER.JUL, NAMED.JUL, and NAMED.AUG files from our backup disks.

The "Restore" option also has some requirements you need to keep in mind. As mentioned earlier, you can't restore NetWare 2.2 files to a NetWare 3.11 directory structure. You must use as a working directory the directory that contains the proper BACK$LOG.*xxx* and BACK$ERR.*xxx* files. And you must have at least Create, Erase, File Scan, Modify, and Write rights to create a directory and restore files to it.

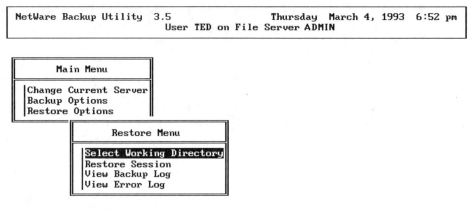

Figure 2-89. When you choose the Restore Options, you then select which function you wish to perform

To use NBACKUP's "Restore" option, type NBACKUP <Enter> at the network prompt if you haven't done so already. Choose the "DOS Devices" option and press <Enter> if you stored the BACK$*xxx.xxx* files on disks, local hard disks, directories on other servers, or backup units using DOS device drivers. Then at the "Main Menu" window, select "Restore Options" and press <Enter>. You'll see the same two warnings about using NBACKUP again. Ignore them and press <Enter> twice until you come to the "Restore Menu" window. The "Restore Menu" window shows you four options: "Select Working Directory", "Restore Session," "View Backup Log," and "View Error Log."

First, choose the "Select Working Directory" option. Through this option you tell NBACKUP on which directory you stored the BACK$LOG.*xxx* and BACK$ERR.*xxx* files. NBACKUP's restore option relies heavily upon these files; if they're deleted or corrupted, you won't be able to access that backup session for restoring purposes.

Select the directory that you used for the NetWare backup sessions. If you've deleted the BACK$LOG.*xxx* and BACK$ERR.*xxx* files, don't despair, for NBACKUP also makes a copy of those files for just such emergencies. (Read on.)

To copy files back to the network as well as for the working directory, you'll need Write, Create, Erase, File Scan, and Modify rights. If you're going to look at files in the directory, add Read rights to the list. When you press <Enter> on the "Select" option, you'll see the "Select Working Directory" window. If you know in which directory you stored the files—for example, ADMIN/SYS:USERS\TED—type in the directory path. You can also press <Ins> to create the directory path from the menu format. Pressing

<Ins> lists all servers, volumes on the selected server, directories, and subdirectories beneath the directory displayed in the "Current Directory Path" window.

Selecting one of the directories in the "Network Directories" window makes the selected directory a part of the "Current Directory Path" window. The subdirectories of your new directory path will appear in the "Network Directories" window. Continue until you reach the desired directory, press <Esc>, then press <Enter>.

The "Insert" option also lets you choose other servers if you've happened to place the BACK$ERR.*xxx* and BACK$LOG.*xxx* files on another server. Pressing <Ins> at the "File Servers/Local Drives" window brings up the "Other File Servers" window if you need to make that server your working place. Suppose, for example, you're logged in to server ADMIN, but you've placed the working files in a directory on server NTS3. Choose the "Select Working Directory" option and erase the entire directory path that appears in the "Current Directory Path" window. Press <Ins> and you'll see a "File Servers/Local Drives" window.

If server NTS3 appears in the window, you can select that server directly. Then you can follow the above instructions to get to your designated directory path. If server NTS3 doesn't appear in the "File Servers/Local Drives" window, press <Ins> again to see a list of all the servers on the network. Select server NTS3, then enter your login name for that server and your password. Server NTS3 will appear in the "File Servers/Local Drives" window. Highlight and select that server; then you can get to your designated directory path by following the above instructions. Once you reach the desired directory, press <Esc>, then press <Enter>, and you'll return to the "Restore Menu" window.

If you select a local drive, such as Drive A, B, C, or D; NBACKUP will ask you if this drive is removable. The default is Yes. Choosing this tells the program to ask for a new disk or tape if it reaches the end of the current one without completing the restoration. Choose No if you are restoring your backup from a local hard disk.

Next, choose the "Restore Session" option. If you haven't typed in a working directory in the first option, you'll be prompted to type it in here. Because of this, you can ignore the "Select Working Directory" option, choose the "Restore Session" option, and there type in the working directory. But make no mistake; you *must* designate a working directory or NBACKUP won't know from which backup file set to restore.

The "Restore Session" option brings you to the "Restore Session" window, which shows all the sessions NBACKUP can find with the BACK$ERR.*xxx* filename from the working directory you designated. NBACKUP presents its backup information in a chronological order with the last backup performed listed at the top. The "Restore Session" window has four columns beneath the window's header: "Description," "Date," "Time," and "Source." The description column displays the session description you typed in when you initially named this session. (Make sure you use helpful descriptions.) The "Date" and "Time" entries tell you when the BACK$LOG file was last written to, usually after you've run its backup session. The "Source" column shows you the directory you designated to begin the backup session.

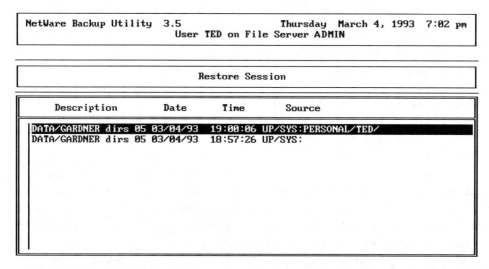

```
NetWare Backup Utility  3.5                    Thursday  March 4, 1993  7:02 pm
                        User TED on File Server ADMIN


┌─────────────────────────────────────────────────────────────────────────┐
│                            Restore Session                                │
└─────────────────────────────────────────────────────────────────────────┘

    Description          Date      Time      Source

 ▌DATA/GARDNER dirs 05 03/04/93   19:00:06 UP/SYS:PERSONAL/TED/▌
  DATA/GARDNER dirs 05 03/04/93   18:57:26 UP/SYS:
```

Figure 2-90. You can choose which data you wish to restore from this directory or from disks

If you don't see the session you're looking for by the description you gave, press <Esc> and choose the "View Backup Log" option to better see what files and directories were backed up. If you've deleted the BACK$LOG and BACK$ERR files, you can press <Ins> to add other sessions from wherever you stored the backup file itself. For example, if you've placed the BACK$*xxx.xxx* file on a disk, type A: in the "Select Destination Path" window. NBACKUP directs you to insert the last media disk of the desired session and press <Enter>; this is where NBACKUP has made a copy of your working directory files for just such an emergency.

You next see the "Insert Session" window, showing you the backup sessions on that disk with four columns: "Description," "Date," "Time," and "Usable." If one of the sessions already appears in the "Restore Session" window, you'll see "No" in the "Usable" column; if the session doesn't appear, you'll see "Yes" in the "Usable" column, meaning you can select that session. NBACKUP then copies the BACK$ERR.*xxx* and BACK$LOG.*xxx* files into your designated working directory, telling you to press <Enter> to return to the "Insert Session" window. Press <Esc> to return to the "Restore Session" window, and you'll now see the added session in the list of session options.

```
NetWare Backup Utility  3.5                Saturday  August 14, 1993  5:29 pm
                         User TED on File Server ADMIN
```

```
                              Restore Session

     Description         Date      Time      Source

   DATA/GARDNER DIRS 12  08/14/93  17:24:46  UP/SYS:PERSONAL/TED/DATA/
   DATA/GARDNER DIRS 12  08/14/93  17:09:36  UP/SYS:PERSONAL/TED/DATA/
   DATA/GARDNER DIRS 12  08/14/93  17:08:16  UP/SYS:PERSONAL/TED/DATA/
   DATA/GARDNER dirs 12  08/14/93  17:07:00  UP/SYS:PERSONAL/TED/DATA/
```

Figure 2-91. NBACKUP keeps a log of your backup activities, which you use for restoration purposes

You can also delete older entries from the "Restore Session" window that you know you'll never call up again. Highlight the entry and press <Del>; you'll see the "Delete Session" window with the "Yes" option highlighted. Press <Enter> to delete the BACK$LOG and BACK$ERR files from the working directory. Again, the restore option relies heavily on these files, so be absolutely sure you want to delete the session.

From our example, let's select DATA/GARDNER Dirs 08/14/93 and press <Enter>. You'll see the "Restore Option" window, with the following entries:

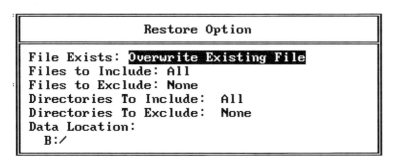

Figure 2-92. You can set restoration options to help you restore files

File Exists. This entry defaults to "Overwrite Existing File," but highlighting the entry and pressing <Enter> brings up the "File Options" window with five options: "Do Not Overwrite," "Interactive," "Overwrite Existing File," "Rename Existing File," and "Rename Restored File." The "Do Not Overwrite" option simply skips restoring any files that already exist with the same name on the destination directory.

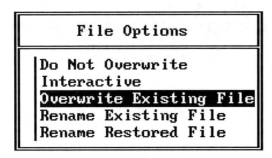

Figure 2-93. You can select how you want to deal with existing files

The "Interactive" option allows you to choose what you want to do if the file does exist on the destination directory. If you choose this entry, you'll have to choose the "Do Not Overwrite," "Overwrite Existing File," "Rename Existing File," and "Rename Restored File" options for each file the restore process presents to you. This can become tedious, but the functionality is there nonetheless. The "Overwrite Existing File" option simply overwrites any files that have the same filename on the destination directory.

The last two options work differently from the "File Exists" entry on a global scale if chosen through the "Interactive" option than they do if chosen on an individual basis. On a global basis, the "Rename Existing File" option renames duplicate files on the destination directory to carry extensions like .B01, .B02, .B03, and so forth. On an individual basis through the "Interactive" option, if you rename the extension or filename, the file carries the new extension or filename. The "Rename Restored File" option works much like the "Existing File option" except that you rename the file you're copying to the destination directory. On a global basis, the "Rename Restored File" option renames the files you're restoring to the destination directory and gives them extensions like .B01, .B02, .B03, and so forth. On an individual basis through the "Interactive" option, if you rename the extension or filename, the file carries the new extension or filename. All file naming procedures are recorded in the error log for your reference.

Files To Include. This entry allows you to specify which files you want NBACKUP to restore along this directory path. If you typed "No" at the "Backup Subdirectories"

228

entry during the backup procedure, the files you designate in this "Include" entry include only the files in the source directory. If you included subdirectories, the "Include" entry affects files for those subdirectories as well.

For example, pressing <Enter> at the "Files to Include" entry brings up the "Files to Include" window, which indicates any filename. Then pressing <Ins> brings up another "Files to Include" window that allows you to type in any filename or wild card pattern for NBACKUP to include in its restore procedures.

For example, to restore a group of files with the same extension, go to the "Files to Include" window and specify all the files that have that extension, such as *.SCR or *.DAT. Figure 2-82 indicates all files with an .SCR extension, regardless of the filenames. You can designate other file patterns as well. For example, if you want to restore only files that begin with the letter "S", put S*.* in the pattern box. You can also use the question mark (?) wild card in NBACKUP. Suppose you want to restore files that start with the letter S, specifically the SL_}SYS.* files. You can enter the file pattern as ????SYS.*, and NBACKUP will restore the SL_}SYS.* files.

You can also type in a string of filenames that you wish to restore. These files will then appear in the "Files To Include" window, and will be the only files restored. But for our running example, we're looking to retrieve files called NAMER.JUL, NAMED.JUL, and NAMED.AUG from our backup disks. You can either simply type in these filenames or use wild cards to specify the filenames. For wild cards, you might type NAME*.JU? and NAME?.AUG. However, if you use wild cards, you'd better make sure there aren't other files that fit the pattern as well. (Here's where a printed copy of the backup log can be helpful.)

Files To Exclude. This entry allows you to specify a file pattern that you don't want to restore in the source directory or its subdirectories. Suppose you have an abundance of files with an .SCR extension that you don't want restored. Press <Enter> at the "Files to Exclude" entry, then press <Ins>. Type in *.SCR to exclude all files with the .SCR extension. Press <Enter>; the .SCR exclude parameter will be added to the "Files to Exclude" window. If you type the filename wrong, you'll see a message that says "Enter a valid DOS filename. Press ENTER to Continue." You can then correct your mistake and type in a proper DOS filename or the proper arrangement of wild cards.

Note that exclude patterns will overwrite include patterns if they conflict. So if you have an include pattern of S* and an exclude pattern of ??SYS*.*, you won't see any files that begin with the S and have SYS two letters into their filename.

Directories To Include. This entry works the same as the "Files to Include" entry, except it allows you to specify the directories you want to restore. For example, pressing <Enter> at the "Directories to Include" entry brings up the "Directories to Include" window, which is usually blank, indicating any directory name. Pressing <Ins> brings up another "Directories to Include" window that allows you to type in any directory name or wild card pattern for NBACKUP to include in its restore procedures.

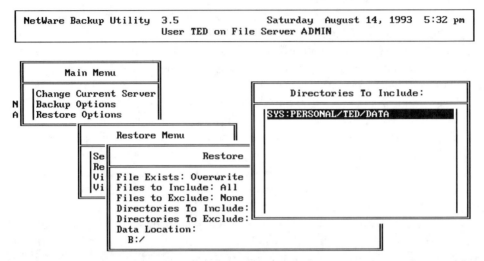

Figure 2-94. You can specify which files and directories you wish to include or exclude when restoring

For example, if you want to restore only directories that begin with the letter D, you can specify in the "Directories to Include" window D* or, if you use extensions on your directories, D*.*. The above figure shows all directories that begin with D, along with its directory path up to that directory. You can designate other search patterns as well. For example, if you want to restore only directories that begin with the letter "S", put S*.* in the pattern box. You can also use the question mark (?) wild card in NBACKUP. Suppose you have a number of directories with SYS in the middle, such as JANSYS, AUGSYS, NOVSYS, and JULSYS directories. Also suppose you want to restore only directories that start with the letter J. You can enter the file pattern as J??SYS.*, and NBACKUP will restore only the JANSYS and JULSYS directories.

Directories To Exclude. This allows you to specify directory name patterns that you *don't* want to restore. As a counter-example to the "Include" entry, suppose you have a number of directories with SYS in the middle, such as JANSYS, AUGSYS, NOVSYS, and JULSYS. Press <Enter> at the "Directories to Exclude" entry, then press <Ins>. Type in ???SYS to exclude all directories with the .SCR extension. Press <Enter> and the ???SYS exclude parameter is added to the "Directories to Exclude" window.

Note that exclude patterns will overwrite include patterns if they conflict. So if you have an include pattern of J??SYS and an exclude pattern of ???SYS*.*, you won't see any directories that begin with J and have SYS two letters into their name.

Data Location. This entry designates where you stored the BACK$*xxx.xxx* file. For our example, the data location is A:.

With the last entry filled in, press <Esc> and you'll see the "Save Changes" window with the "Yes" option highlighted. Press <Enter> and you'll come to the "Start Restore" window with the "Yes" option highlighted. Pressing <Enter> brings you again to the "Restore Session" screen, which matches the "Backup Session" screen.

The screen is divided into three windows: one lists files being restored, one provides information about the restore session, and one displays messages that pertain to the session. You'll see the files being restored in the left-hand window, which scrolls the files being restored along with the directory to which they are being restored. You can see pertinent restore information in the right-hand window; messages (if there are any) appear in the bottom window. These messages are also written to the error log file for your perusal. Below are the entries you can see in the restore information window.

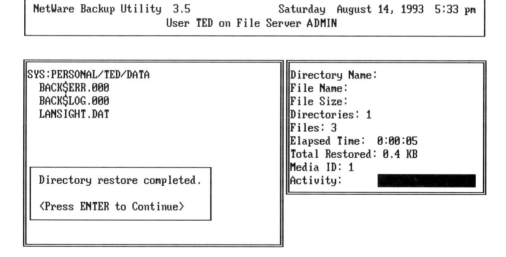

Figure 2-95. The restore process shows you which files are being restored

The "Directory Name" entry names the directory you're currently restoring. If you're restoring multiple directories, this entry shows you which directory you're currently in.

231

The "Filename" entry shows you which file is currently being restored.

The "File Size" entry shows the size of the file currently being restored. File sizes are shown in bytes, not kilobytes.

The "Directories" entry shows you how many directories have been restored during this session. When NBACKUP finishes a session, you'll see the "Directory restore completed. Press ENTER to Continue" window on the screen.

The "Files" entry shows you how many files have been restored during this session. Before pressing <Enter> to return to the "Backup Menu" window, you can see how many files you restored. If you've changed any filenames during the restore process, that information will be listed in the error log file which pertains to this session. You can print out the error log by going into the working directory and typing NPRINT BACK$ERR.extension Q=*queuename* <Enter>.

The "Elapsed Time" shows how much time it took to actually perform the restore session. You can see when the restore session began by looking in the error log file.

The "Total Written" entry shows in kilobytes the cumulative number of copied files and other information written to the destination directory.

"Media ID" shows the number assigned to a tape, cartridge, or floppy disk which is currently being used. For floppy disks, you'll be asked to enter the media ID number. Unfortunately, the media number doesn't match the way the files are labeled on the disks. For example, if your backup session took three disks, the backup files on each disk will be labeled incrementally: for example, BACK$001.000, BACK$001.001, and BACK$001.002. But for media ID purposes, the disks are labeled 1, 2, and 3 respectively, so keep this in mind when you're asked for media by the restore process.

The "Activity" entry lets you know that you're still restoring. You'll see a green bar march from side to side of this entry if you're still restoring data in this session.

If everything is successful, you'll see the "Directory restore completed. Press ENTER to Continue" window and a brief message will flash across the bottom window. The message is stored in the BACK$ERR.*xxx* file that pertains to this restore session. Pressing <Enter> brings you again to the "Restore Menu" window. For our example, the restore session is looking only for NAMER.JUL, NAMED.JUL, and NAMED.AUG files in the DATA directory. Since this directory no longer exists, the restore session creates the directory and places the files in it.

You can also restore files from one server to another if the systems match (NetWare 3.11 to 3.11, etc.). For example, suppose you're moving departments and you want to take your data to a new server that's running the same version of NetWare. You can run your backup procedure as described earlier in this chpater, then log in or attach to the new server. Copy the proper BACK$ERR and BACK$LOG files to your working directory on the other server. My best luck was with a duplicate directory structure on the new

232

server, or at least the same directory name for starting the restore procedure. Since the restore process doesn't designate which directory you should start copying files to, it looks for a matching directory structure to restore to. This may or may not be how your directories are structured.

While such restorations are possible, a good directory/file manager could be the ticket if you have problems with NBACKUP. Another tried and true method is to map a drive to your new server and use the NCOPY utility. For example, if drive F:ADMIN/SYS:USERS\TED is your old home directory, and NTS3/VOL1:PERSONAL\TED is your new home directory, type ATTACH NTS3/TED <Enter> and then type in your password. Next, type MAP N NTS3/VOL1:PERSONAL\TED <Enter>. The N parameter in the MAP command will find the next available drive letter and map it to the TED directory on server NTS3 (in this case, G:).

Next, type RIGHTS G: <Enter> to ensure that you have sufficient rights to copy files to the new directory. For this transfer, you'll need Read, Write, File Scan, Create, Erase, and Modify rights. If you have those rights, go to F: and type NCOPY *.* G: /S/N <Enter>. NCOPY will then copy all your files and subdirectories (/S) to their new home, along with the rights you originally had in those directories (/N). For more information on MAP and NCOPY, see the "Directory and File Management Utilities" heading in Chapter 3.

The last two entries, "View Backup Log" and "View Error Log," are exactly the same as those described in the "Backup Menu" window. Please turn to the "Viewing Backup and Error Logs" subheading earlier in this section for their explanation. To exit the Restore Menu, press <Esc>. To leave this session of NBACKUP, press <Esc> at the "Main Menu" window. You'll see the "Exit NBackup" window with the "Yes" option highlighted. Press <Enter> and you'll return to the network prompt.

Play around with NBACKUP until you feel comfortable trusting the utility with your backup data. Be sure to try both backing up and restoring files.

The HELP Utility

Note: NetWare 3.12 comes with a different Help service that you access through Windows. 3.12's Help is all the manuals that come with NetWare 3.12 and are on-line. To access the on-line manuals in 3.12 go into Windows, select the ET icon in the NetWare group. Installing the DOS Requester makes the NetWare group and icons available to you.

NetWare 3.11 includes an on-line Help database, which you can access simply by typing HELP <Enter>. The HELP feature has an interface based on Folio Corporation's VIEWS product. VIEWS not only provides an easy-to-learn approach to finding information; it's also able, through data compression, to store twice as much of it. Folio has developed what it calls "Underhead Technology," which allows compression of the HELP file to about half its usual size. Since the size of the on-line !NETWARE.NFO help file is 1.1MB, it actually stores 2MB of information.

With VIEWS, you're also able to search for information on a particular command or problem. You can use some common navigational keys to get around in the database, and you can initiate a search using the space bar at any point to find a particular topic. VIEWS also contains a tutorial, which gives you help in addition to the following explanation.

VIEWS at first glance seems difficult because it uses some terms new to the NetWare user. This section will explain these terms and concepts, as well as how to move about in the NetWare HELP infobase. We'll finish up by discussing how to perform a search on a topic. Those wanting to perform searches immediately may wish to skip to the "Using HELP's Search Capabilities" heading in this section.

Concepts of HELP

VIEWS starts with an information database, or infobase. The !NetWare infobase that comes with NetWare contains the HELP text. What you actually see when you type HELP <Enter> is a run-time version of VIEWS called PreVIEWS. It's simply a limited set of functions; PreVIEWS doesn't let you add to the database.

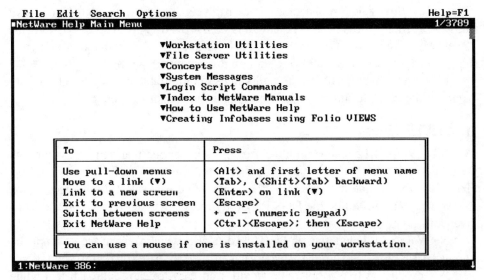

Figure 2-96. NetWare's HELP infobase

The NetWare HELP infobase for version 3.11 has 3,789 folios. These folios are very much like pages in a book, except that each folio covers one topic or idea, depending on how it was initially set up. For you as the user, however, it's simply easier to think of the folios in terms of pages.

The HELP infobase, then, has what we'll call 3,789 pages of text, which you can read through one page at a time. To speed things up, HELP has built-in links that string together one topic, idea, or related information. (This is similar in principle to HyperCard.)

For example, if your topic is "Workstation Utilities," HELP has a link between the pages containing information on workstation utilities already created in HELP. This link is indicated by a down arrow. Folio calls this, appropriately enough, a *link*. By placing your cursor on a link and pressing <Enter>, you can follow the link through page after page of information on workstation utilities.

HELP can have up to 25 windows open. (A window is closed when you press <Esc> to leave it.) Since it's so easy to open windows in HELP, the window counter at the lower left of the screen becomes very important for keeping track of where you are.

Finally, a group in HELP is a set of pages or windows pulled together on a particular topic. For example, if you searched the infobase for references to file server parameters, HELP would bring up a group of pages showing these references. As you page down through the group, the pages appear one at a time on your screen in the order in which they appear in the infobase.

Navigating HELP

To go into HELP, simply type HELP <Enter> at the network prompt.

NetWare HELP uses some familiar keys to move about in the windows. The Up, Down, Left Arrow, and Right Arrow keys move the cursor within the window. <PgUp> and <PgDn> are useful for moving from one window to another if more than one window is available.

The Home key moves the cursor to the start of a line; End moves it to the end of the line. <Ctrl>-Left or Right Arrow moves the cursor one word at a time to the left or right. To move to the first page, press <Ctrl>-<PgUp>. To move to the last page, press <Ctrl>-<PgDn>. To go to a specific page or window, press <Ctrl>-<G>, then type in the page number or window number you want. To call up a menu, you can use the <Alt> key, then the first letter of the menu you want. Pull up the Search menu with <Alt>-<S>, the File menu with <Alt>-<F>, and so forth.

The Tab key moves the cursor to the next link (down arrow) in the window. Pressing the Tab key after you've reached the last link on the current page brings up the next page.

If there are no links on a page, the Tab key works like the <PgDn> key, moving the cursor one page at a time through the remaining pages.

The Shift-Tab key combination moves your cursor to the previous link. If you keep pressing the Shift-Tab combination, your cursor will pop over to the upper left corner of the window. It then will scroll down enough of the previous page to reveal the previous link. If there aren't any links on the previous page, the Shift-Tab combination moves the cursor to the upper left corner of the previous page.

<F1> is the universal help key for HELP. If you pull down a menu and highlight a command, <F1> pops up a window that gives you help with that command. Pressing <F1> anywhere else pulls down the Help menu. (See the following section for more information on the Help menu.)

The Enter key opens a link of related information when your cursor is under the link symbol. As mentioned earlier, if you want to know more about a topic, the links can lead you to it. For example, suppose you're reading a page on how to set up a file server. You come to a section mentioning network printers, and you want to know how to check the network printer. You see that there's a link just before the words "network printers," which means you can find additional pages of material on this subject. Use your Tab key to hop to the link symbol and press <Enter>. A new page of information pops up explaining how to check printers. When you're finished, press <Esc> and you're right back in the section on setting up file servers.

Don't hold down <Enter> after pressing it once; each time you press <Enter>, HELP opens another window. Since these new windows are identical, no change will be apparent on screen. But the multiple open windows will be using up memory.

You can tell how many windows you have open by checking the window counter in the screen's lower left corner. Increments of this counter represent windows. If you do open a few windows, press <Esc> to get back to where you wanted to be.

Occasionally in HELP you'll see a link symbol with no information connected to it. For example, if you put your cursor on the link symbol and press <Enter>, a new window pops open, but it's blank. Just press <Esc> to go back to where you started. The HELP utility is always being updated; these links may be active in the future.

The Plus (+) and Minus (–) keys are also important when working with links. Once you start on a link and move down through several pages of material, you can hop back to the beginning by pressing the Minus key. Pressing the Plus key will bring you back to where you left off before pressing the Minus key. By using the Plus and Minus keys, you can switch between windows without closing them. But if you press <Esc> to back out of your previous location in the link, you close that window.

If you get lost, press <Esc> and you'll eventually come back to the Main Menu, where you can start over. When you're ready to exit HELP, press <Esc> until you return to the network prompt. You can use the shortcut <Ctrl>-<Esc>, which takes you directly to the network prompt.

The HELP Main Menu

The Table of Contents is a list of the most commonly used HELP items; they're actually a shortcut to doing a search.

Note: This Table of Contents varies depending on your NetWare's version's manufacture date. The example is from the 6-08-90 !NETWARE.NFO file. Later versions operate in the same fashion, but offer commands and utilities alphabetically rather than by categories, and a separate Troubleshooting section. Use the following instructions as an example of what you can do with the HELP Table of Contents.

Login Script Commands. This lists the available commands you can place in a login script. Each item has a link to a discussion of the command. The material also appears in the NetWare 3.1x Installing and Maintaining the Network manual.

Index to NetWare Manuals. This is a comprehensive index to all the NetWare manuals. It doesn't, however, take you to the actual pages. Rather, it gives you citations of where you can look up that information in the paperbound volumes.

Creating Infobases using FolioVIEWS. This is actually a brief tutorial on using infobases and FolioVIEWS in general.

So, let's start with what happens when you type HELP <Enter>. After the Folio copyright page pops up, then vanishes, it's replaced by the HELP Main Menu screen:

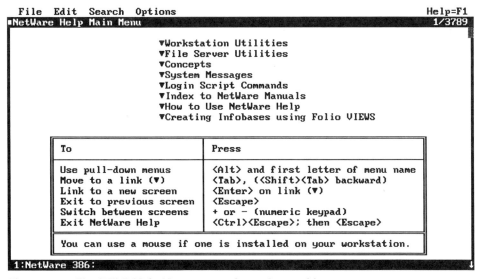

Figure 2-97. The HELP Main Menu screen is made up of four ports

The HELP Main Menu screen is made up of four parts: the *menu bar*, the *window reference line*, the *window* and the *infobase line*. Let's look at each of these parts in detail, starting at the top of the screen.

The Main Menu Bar

The menu bar offers a selection of drop-down menus for performing functions in HELP. You won't often need to use these functions directly from the menus, since the most commonly used function, searching, works from keyboard commands.

At the top of the screen are the names of five drop-down menus: File, Edit, Search, Options, and Help. To access these, press <Alt> and the initial letter of the menu you want to see: <Alt>-<F> drops down the File menu, <Alt>-<E> the Edit menu, and so on. Or with a mouse you can click on the option to bring down the menu.

Once you've dropped down a menu, you can use the Up or Down arrow keys to highlight the individual commands. Some, like those on the Help menu, you activate by pressing the first letter of the command.

Every command has a shortcut; instead of using the menu to select an option, you can type in the function key sequence (such as <Ctrl>-<B> for Block). Most of them use a two-key combination of the <Ctrl> or <Shift> key with an appropriate letter.

Here's a brief description of each of the menus and their options.

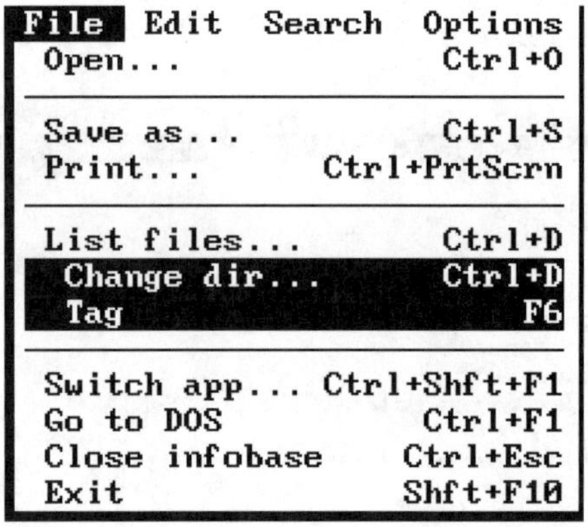

```
File  Edit   Search   Options
Open...                Ctrl+O

Save as...             Ctrl+S
Print...          Ctrl+PrtScrn

List files...          Ctrl+D
 Change dir...         Ctrl+D
 Tag                       F6

Switch app... Ctrl+Shft+F1
Go to DOS             Ctrl+F1
Close infobase       Ctrl+Esc
Exit                 Shft+F10
```

Figure 2-98. The File menu offers nine options

The File Menu

The File menu has nine options: "Open," "Save As," "Print," "List Files," "Change Dir," "Tag," "Switch App," "Go to DOS," "Close Infobase," and "Exit."

Open. This option (<Ctrl>-<O>) opens up an infobase. NetWare 3.11 includes four infobases to open; these are described under "Exploring Other HELP Aspects." You can have all four open at once if your workstation has enough memory. The default infobase is NetWare HELP.

Save As. This option (<Ctrl>-<S>) saves some part of HELP to a text file. For example, to save the results of a search to show your supervisor, press <Ctrl>-<S>, then choose the option "Active View" under "Scope." This saves all the pages that you found containing your search words. The other options, "Active Folio" and "Block," are for saving the current page only, or the text you blocked using the editing keys.

You can save these files into a generic word processor format or to a Folio format. "Generic" means your file will have no hard returns added, so that your word processor will decide line endings. If you want your text to look like it does on screen, use the Folio format. If you're building a file of references, you can save to the same file again. HELP will ask you if you want to append this new material onto the old, or just to replace the old file.

Print. This option uses the quick keys <Ctrl>-<PrtSc>. Don't use the PrtSc key, for HELP doesn't print out a screen dump. Instead, the <Ctrl>-<PrtSc> combination brings up a menu for you to specify what type of printing service you want. A menu offers "Print," "Install Printer," and "Terminate Printing." "Print" brings up another menu for defining the print job. "Install Printer" offers you a list of printers to choose from and a list of ports to print to. "Terminate Printing" asks you whether you want to cancel your current print job sent from HELP, or all the print jobs sent from HELP.

If you *do* want to print out what is on your screen, "Print" also allows you to choose to print the text of the active folio (the page you're looking at), the active view (what's in the window at the moment), or the text you have blocked. You can send this print job to a printer you've defined or you can print the text to a file. HELP even lets you put in a page number at the location of your choice. You can do some limited formatting: page length, margins, and spacing. Use the Tab key to move around to the various options.

The "Print" menu also lets you print to a file. Use the Tab key to move your cursor down to the "Redirect document to:" option. Press the space bar to activate it (the - changes to an X). Then press the right arrow key to type in the path where you want to store the file.

The default options in the "Print" menu show you an IBM ProPrinter and an HP LaserJet as possible printers. You can change the list of printers appearing in this window by pressing <Esc> and selecting "Install Printer." The "Install Printer" menu has a listing of 48 available printer drivers (including most popular brands) and the most common printer ports (LPT1,2; COM1,2). Since the HELP utility is designed for NetWare, installing the printer requires no more than just choosing the correct printer driver for the printer and the port on your workstation that CAPTURE is using.

List Files. This option (<Ctrl>-<D>) shows you a directory tree of your current drive. This isn't particularly useful, since you can only open other infobases, and seeing a directory tree this way is rather clumsy.

Change Dir and Tag. The option "Change Dir" is related to "List Dir" and allows you to change your current directory if you have more than one infobase. The same applies to Tag, which allows you to open two or more infobases every time you enter PreVIEWS.

Switch To Application. You can run another program while in HELP by pressing the <Ctrl>-<Shift>-<F1> key combination to bring up a window where you type in the command you want to run. Use the same commands you would use at the network prompt. The new program then executes. When you exit that program, you return back into HELP. While the other program runs, HELP takes up only 10KB of memory. Most DOS programs—for example, WordPerfect—or NetWare utilities such as SYSCON run fine.

The advantage of using the <Ctrl>-<Shift>-<F1> method to execute programs, rather than simply going to the network prompt with <Ctrl>-<F1>, is that it's faster.

Go To DOS. This option allows you to temporarily exit the HELP menu and go to the network prompt while still in HELP. You can then type EXIT to return to HELP.

Exit. This option allows you to exit HELP and return to the DOS prompt.

The Edit Menu

The Edit menu offers you five options: "Copy," "Cut," "Delete," "Block," and "Paste." You can use these options with the Search function to save you from having to type in a long phrase you want to look for.

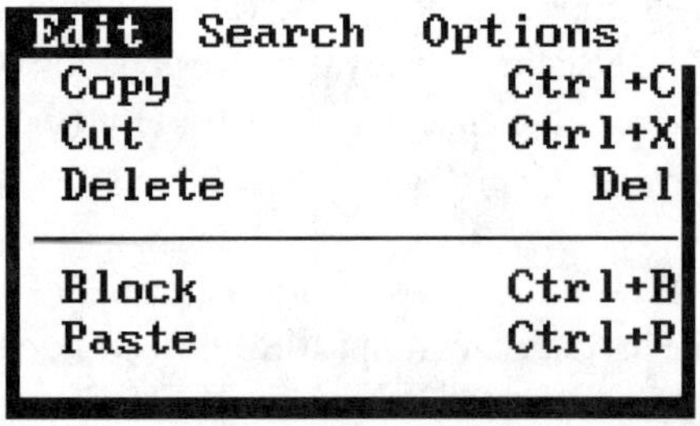

```
┌─────────────────────────────────┐
│ Edit  Search   Options          │
│   Copy            Ctrl+C         │
│   Cut             Ctrl+X         │
│   Delete             Del         │
│                                  │
│   Block           Ctrl+B         │
│   Paste           Ctrl+P         │
└─────────────────────────────────┘
```

Figure 2-99. The Edit menu has five options for you to use

You use the Block function to mark text you want to print. These functions work like similar functions in word processors. In this case, you can Block and Copy while you're viewing text within HELP, but you can't cut and paste text within HELP. However, you can copy text and paste it in the "Query" window of a search. All five work with the "Query" window when you're performing a search. That way you can match a complicated text without retyping it. Obviously, the Cut and Delete functions have limited utility.

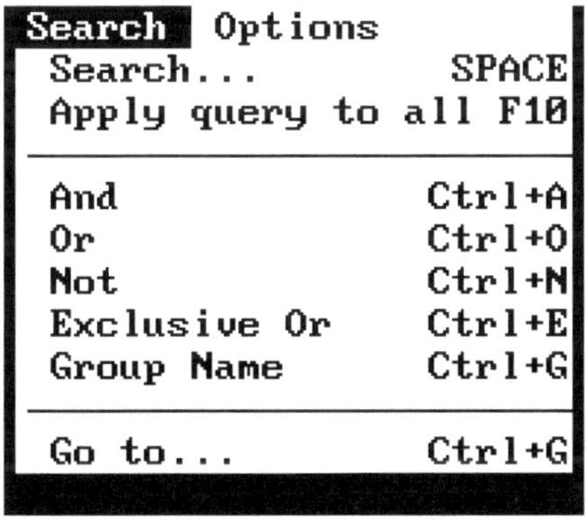

```
Search  Options
 Search...          SPACE
 Apply query to all F10

 And               Ctrl+A
 Or                Ctrl+O
 Not               Ctrl+N
 Exclusive Or      Ctrl+E
 Group Name        Ctrl+G

 Go to...          Ctrl+G
```

Figure 2-100. The Search menu allows for a number of ways to query the infobase

The Search Menu

The Search menu contains options such as "Search," "Apply Query To All," "And," "Or," "Not," "Exclusive Or," "Group Name," and "Go to." You can access most of these options more readily through their quick-key alternatives, which you'll see written to the right of the option. For example, you perform a Search by pressing the space bar. (I described Search earlier in this section.)

Apply Query To All. This category has limited use in HELP. It was designed for systems that use more than one infobase and you need to search through all of them.

And through **Group Name.** "And," "Or," "Not," "Exclusive Or," and "Group Name" are options you can include in the "Query" window when doing a search. For each of these you can use a quick-key alternative, or better yet, use the alphanumeric key that performs that function.

Go To. Go To is useful if you know a particular page number you want to go to. Press <Ctrl>-<G> to see a window where you can type in the page number (Folio #) of the item you want to see. You'll also see a line for View number. If you have two infobases open, or the on-line manual, you could specify which of the two you want to use the option with. But this isn't an option you'll use often.

241

The Options Menu

The Options menu lets you customize your HELP. Unfortunately, most of these changes work only for the current HELP session. Once you leave the session, the default settings are restored unless you select the "User Defaults" option. HELP initially assumes you want to save the file to the SYS:PUBLIC directory where HELP is stored. (For most users, your default rights to SYS:PUBLIC are READ and FILE SCAN only.) When you save your changes using "User Defaults" option, you'll need to save the file to a directory where you have write rights.

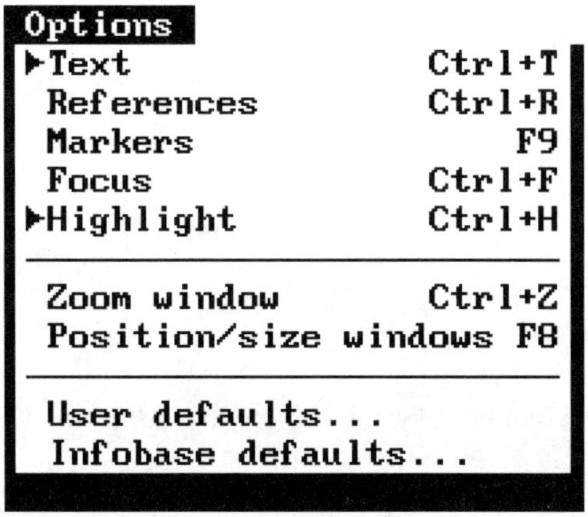

```
┌─────────────────────────────────────┐
│ Options                              │
│ ►Text              Ctrl+T            │
│  References        Ctrl+R            │
│  Markers               F9            │
│  Focus             Ctrl+F            │
│ ►Highlight         Ctrl+H            │
│ ──────────────────────────           │
│  Zoom window       Ctrl+Z            │
│  Position/size windows F8            │
│ ──────────────────────────           │
│  User defaults...                    │
│  Infobase defaults...                │
│                                      │
└─────────────────────────────────────┘
```

Figure 2-101. Use the Options menu to customize your current HELP session

Text through **Focus.** We'll explain the "Text," " References," and "Focus" options under the "Other Search Options" heading. The "Markers" option shows you the break points of each page or folio. This is similar to References, which shows you the name as well as the break point. You can toggle Markers on and off with the F9 key. You can also tell when you've gone to a new page by watching the page counter in the upper right section of the Reference line.

Highlight. This turns the highlight on and off for search words found. The highlight can become distracting if there are many references to the same word on each page.

Zoom Window. This option enlarges or shrinks the current window on the screen. It only works if the window that popped up is smaller than the main screen, then you can toggle it larger or smaller. HELP's own Manual (under Help-<F1>) is one such window.

User Defaults. This option lets you choose a color scheme, the background texture of the screens, whether HELP should automatically determine what kind of monitor you have, whether the "Search" windows should show the "WORDS" and "RESULTS" windows, how fast the screen displays text, where to find the infobases or other temporary files, and where to save changes to your HELP configuration file.

As with the NetWare COLORPAL utility, you can alter most of the screen colors. You're warned, however, that some combinations of colors are unreadable. They can be very annoying even on a monochrome monitor, since each such monitor displays colors with varying shades of grey. Should you, however, wish to explore, the color palette is available under User Defaults. You have a choice of White, Red, Blue, Green, Yellow, Cyan and Mauve. Through selecting the "User Defaults" option, you can change colors on the Backplane, Menus, Search, Shadows, Directory, and Dialog entries.

At the "User Defaults" window, you also have a choice of background patterns. Changing this pattern is of little use, since it appears only when you initially enter HELP, or when you alter the size of the main menu screen so as to reveal the background. You can set the display you are using to auto-detect, color, or black and white. For the most part, leave the automatic display option on auto-detect.

The Display speed deals with some monitors which generate snow under certain speed conditions. If you begin to get snow, you'll have to enter here to change the default to SLOW.

At the "User Defaults" window, the "Search window" option should be left alone. You won't need the Groups windows for reasons already explained. You could delete the "WORDS" window, since that's an infrequently needed option. The "RESULTS" window is almost essential, since it lets you know how successful your search was. Too many results, however, and you're wasting your time looking through extraneous items. Too few, and you may need to expand your search.

The infobase path tells HELP where to find itself. You won't need to alter this, or the temporary file path, since you won't be opening up any temporary HELP files. You may want to change the path for saving settings, since in this way you can change the defaults for your particular HELP without disturbing anyone else's view of the utility. This path can be your home directory. Note that HELP automatically enters the filename for you. Press <Enter> to save your settings, or <ESC> to cancel your changes. You'll then return to the screen where you called up the Options menu.

Infobase Defaults. This last selection in the Options menu covers the whole infobase. This option comes with two entries—Set defaults in the infobase, and Set defaults in the configuration file. If you change these defaults, you change the HELP utility defaults for all users. For most users, the "Set Defaults in the Infobase" entry won't work because they don't have sufficient rights to the HELP directory. However, the "Set Defaults in the Configuration File" entry will work. Be careful, since this changes the network HELP.

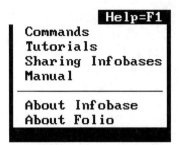

Figure 2-102. Press <F1> to view HELP's own Help options

The Help=F1 Menu

The Help menu provides information on using PreVIEWS, not information on NetWare. You can access the Help menu by pressing either <Alt>-<H> or <F1>. Both drop down the same menu.

The Help=F1 menu has four options, then two information windows. The four options are: "Commands," "Tutorials," "Sharing Infobases," and "Manual." The two information windows are "About Infobase," which currently is empty; and "About Folio," which has a description of the VIEWS product. You can also get help for a specific command in a menu by highlighting the command and pressing <F1>. The relevant section of the on-line manual pops up to explain it.

Commands. The "Commands" option offers you a quick guide to all the hotkeys in HELP. Believe it or not, there are 32 of them.

Tutorials. The "Tutorials" option in the HELP menu brings up a portion of the on-line manual that deals with learning PreVIEWS. Topics include "Infobase and File Management," "Editing Information," "Searching the Infobase," and "Manipulating your Environment." Each of these contains menus of tasks you can perform in HELP, and then explains how to do them through a link.

Sharing Infobases. This option, in the HELP menu, explains the theory behind how you use HELP on a network. Since you're using HELP on the network, you may find this helpful if you use HELP often.

Manual. This contains the on-line PreVIEWS user guide. This is the manual that appears when you highlight a command and press <F1>. The manual is 127 pages long, with sections on each of the drop-down menus.

Window Reference

The window reference line (just beneath the File/Help menu bar) tells you the name of the group this page is part of. It also tells you what page this is and how many total pages there are in the group. This is your table of contents of HELP, and when you first enter HELP, it says "NetWare Help Main Menu."

The numbers on the right of the Reference line are the current page number and the total number of pages. At the Main Menu, this should be 1/3789, since you're at the first page of 3,789 pages of HELP information. When you do a search, this number changes to show you how many pages have the search words on them. For example, when you first access the results of a search on "System Messages," you'll see 1/1083. As you move down through the text, the first number changes to show what page you're currently on.

The Main Menu Window

The initial HELP screen shows you the Table of Contents. Press the Tab key to highlight a link entry or click on the link if you have a mouse. Then press <Enter> to follow the selected link.

The Table of Contents is a list of the most commonly used HELP items; they're actually a shortcut to doing a search.

Note: This Table of Contents varies depending on your NetWare version's manufacture date. The example is from the 6-08-90 !NETWARE.NFO file. Later versions operate in the same fashion, but offer a separate troubleshooting section and lists commands and utilities alphabetically rather than by categories. Use the following instructions as an example of what you can do with the HELP table of contents.

Workstation Utilities. This is a glossary and reference of NetWare Workstation utilities based on the NetWare 3.11 Utilities Reference manual. Each command comes with additional notes which help amplify the explanations. Unfortunately, the HELP explanations lack the logos used in the manual to indicate whether this command is a file server console command, a command-line utility or a menu utility.

File Server Utilities. Like the Workstation Utilities section, these Utilities' reference is a selection of the NetWare 3.11 utilities run on the file server. This section is also based on the NetWare 3.11 Utilities Reference manual and includes explanations for the commands that are similar to those in the Workstation Utilities.

Concepts. This is a glossary of network terms. It's rather extensive, with more than 300 definitions. It follows the material in the paperbound *NetWare 3.11 Concepts* book, but with more specific and shorter explanations. The explanations are also more up-to-date. For example, the UPS monitoring definition explains the UPS Time command, which is undocumented in the version 3.11 Concepts book.

"Concepts" is where you would look for an explanation of general computing terms such as "real mode," "protected mode," or "dynamic memory." It also covers NetWare-specific terms such as "bindery," "effective rights," or "NETX.COM."

System Messages. "System Messages" is a reference to error and system messages with definitions for each message and suggested courses of action when you see a particular message. The section runs to 1,083 pages, so the HELP asks you to use the search feature to locate your particular message. The material is identical to information in the "System Messages" chapter of the NetWare 3.11 *Installing and Maintaining the Network* manual. It also includes the appendix of the manual—the Error Code table—but it isn't labeled as such. This table is located on the last page (1083) of the HELP's system messages section.

Login Script Commands. This lists the available commands you can place in a login script. Each item has a link to a discussion of the command. The material also appears in the NetWare 3.11 Installing and Maintaining the Network manual.

Index to NetWare Manuals. This is a comprehensive index to all the NetWare manuals. It doesn't, however, take you to the actual pages. Rather, it gives you citations of where you can look up that information in the paperbound volumes.

How to Use NetWare HELP. This is a PreVIEWS tutorial. The tutorial is fairly extensive, with explanations for the most often used procedures. The menu covers "Moving Around," "Searches," "Help," "Concepts," "A look at PreVIEWS," and "Creating infobases using FolioVIEWS."

Creating Infobases using FolioVIEWS. This is actually a brief tutorial on using infobases and FolioVIEWS in general. Its explanation is as specific as the How to Use NetWare HELP explanation is of the keys and procedures in using HELP.

The sections you see in the Table of Contents have their own tables of contents, which are made up of links to further information. If you Tab over to "Workstation Utilities" and press <Enter>, you'll see that chapter's own table of contents appear in the window. You can select the topic "Allow" and then a page of text appears giving you an outline of procedures. You find the following chapters in the initial table of contents:

Resizing the Window. For general purposes in the window, you can use <F8> to adjust the size of the window. When you press <F8>, the cursor moves to the center of the screen to let you know that screen resizing is active. Then use your cursor movement keys to place the cursor in one of the four corners of the screen or in the middle of one of the sides. If you put the cursor in one of the corners, pressing the Shift key and an arrow key shrinks or enlarges the screen in that direction. If you put the cursor in the middle of a side, you can only use two of the four arrow keys to enlarge or shrink the screen. Which arrow keys are active depends on which side the cursor is on. The Up and Down arrow keys work when your cursor is in the middle of the top or bottom margin of the screen. The left and right arrow keys work when your cursor is in the middle of the left or right side.

Once you resize a window, you can always undo what you've done by pressing <F8> and moving the cursor appropriately. You can also make the window full-size — that is, filling the screen—by pressing <Ctrl>-<Z>. Press <Ctrl>-<Z> again and the window shrinks back to the previous size if it started out smaller than a full screen.

The Infobase Line

The infobase line is at the bottom of the screen and tells you how many windows you have open, the name of the infobase—NetWare 386 On-line Help, for example—or other details about where you are. Normally it shows you what infobase you're in and the number of open windows. It's also is a context-sensitive help line, giving a brief explanation of the command you're about to execute. The infobase line can also show brief help messages when you're performing certain functions.

When you first enter HELP from NetWare 3.11, the infobase line displays "1:NetWare 386." The first number indicates how many windows you have open in HELP. Each time you follow a link or press <Enter>, you open another window. This number is useful in backing out of some long link path by pressing the Escape key. When you reach 1, you're back at the "real" Table of Contents. I say "real" because you can do a search for a word that happens to appear in the Table of Contents itself. Just by looking at the two screens you couldn't tell which one you were in, but the "real" or base Table of Contents has the number 1 listed at the lower left.

The name "NetWare 386" indicates the name of the infobase you're currently in. Often additional text follows the infobase name, reflecting the name of the window that you're in. So if the infobase line reads "2:NetWare 386: system messages," it indicates that this is the second window you've opened, that you're in the NetWare 386 Help infobase, and that you're looking at the "system messages" page. If you then search for an error message on this page, the name of the next page is added to the infobase line, such as "NetWare 386: system messages abort." In practice you'll find that this page name reference is of limited utility, since the name of the page isn't as important as the contents.

Using HELP's Search Capabilities

When you're in HELP, you can bring up the FOLIO search mode by pressing the Space Bar. This mode shows three windows on screen: "WORDS," "RESULTS," and "QUERY," as you can see in the screen shown in Figure 2-103.

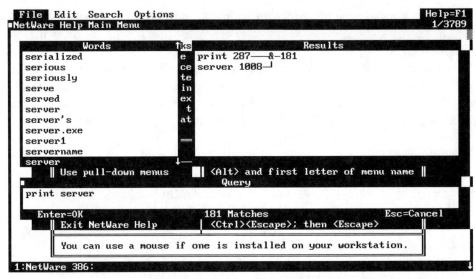

Figure 2-103. You can perform a search at any time by simply pressing the Space Bar

You can perform a search immediately by pressing the Space Bar, then typing in the word or words you want to search for and pressing <Enter>. Pages containing the words appear, with the search words highlighted. You can then use the navigational keys to go through the pages to find out about your topic. Let's first look at each of the three SEARCH windows.

"WORDS" is an alphabetical list of every word in the HELP database. The "RESULTS" window shows you the number of times a word or words appears in the infobase. The "QUERY" window shows you what you typed in for the search. You can press the Down arrow key to scroll up and down through the "WORDS" list to locate a word, or you can use <PgUp> and <PgDn> to move faster through it. If the word appears in the list, press <Ctrl>-<Enter> to insert the word into the search window.

The "RESULTS" window shows you how many pages have occurrences of the search word or words in the infobase. You press <Enter> to see these occurrences. If the number is zero, and you press <Enter>, a blank page will appear. Press <Esc> to get out of it, then the Space Bar to return to the search window.

If there are no occurrences of a word, try a different spelling. The search is dynamic, which means HELP does a search as soon as you type in a word or change one you already entered. To change what you have written in the "QUERY" window you press the backspace key (or Ctrl-Home to erase the whole window), type in the new spelling and see if that makes a difference in the "RESULTS" window.

HELP is very specific. The difference in spelling between "Print Servers" and "Print Server" is 136 occurrences in the "RESULTS" window. HELP only finds exactly what you write in the "Query" window. This makes HELP somewhat tedious to use, since guessing just what spelling brings up a particular reference is frustrating. Still, it is faster than depending on the indexes in the NetWare manuals.

The "QUERY" window is where you type in the search words. You can use the wildcard characters * and ?, but not with quotation marks. Quotation marks allow you to search for a specific string, "PRINT SERVER". You can also use &, ~, /, ^, or | | in the search string.

You don't need to use the WORDS list to perform a search. Just start typing the word or words you're looking for in the "QUERY" window, and you'll see the highlighter bar in the WORDS list move through its contents to find the word or words that most nearly match your typing.

If you want to search the entire HELP infobase, you'll need a "QUERY" window that's empty. If it's not, use the backspace key or <Ctrl>-<Home> to erase the chapter, group, or reference name that appears in the window. This name will be marked with vertical bars | |. A chapter name will appear if you go through a link, then perform a search.

When you're searching for a phrase or combination of words, such as "Print Server," you can avoid getting spurious occurrences by using quotation marks before and after the search words: "PRINT SERVER". Without the quotation marks, HELP thinks you're looking for the two words, PRINT and SERVER and shows all references when a page has both words on it. This means that any references to a file server and print services are also displayed. For example, you see 181 pages with the words PRINT and SERVER on them, but when you use the quotation marks, the number cuts to 147. The other 34 pages have occurrences relating to print services or to file servers.

You can increase this search pattern by searching for two words within a certain number of words of each other. This is called a proximity search. For example, if you want to see those pages with PRINT and SERVER on them within four words of each other, you type "PRINT SERVER"4 <Enter>. You then press the Down Arrow key to look at the references. This is better than typing PRINT SERVER <Enter> because it eliminates those pages which just have PRINT or just have SERVER on them.

You can make this wider search even more comprehensive by using the @ operator. For example, "PRINT SERVER"@4 shows you occurrences of the words PRINT and SERVER on the same page, within four words of each other, just like the previous instruction. But it also shows you occurrences when they are within four words of each other in either order: that is, including as well when SERVER comes before PRINT, but within four words.

You can use the wildcard characters * and ?, but they produce an erratic list of occurrences when used with two or more words. The search string PRINT SERVE*, which might produce occurrences of "Print Server" and "Print Servers," actually produces occurrences of "Print." The wildcards work best with single search words, such as serv*. The * can stand for up to 40 characters in place of the wildcard. The ? stands for only a single character, or none, in a word. These two wildcards can't be used with the quotation marks, either for the phrase search or for the proximity search.

You can also use various operators. These operators are available under the SEARCH menu, or through hotkeys. But since they're also regular keyboard items, it's just as fast to type the real thing as it is to type the hotkey.

The AND operator (&), <Ctrl>-<A>, frequently isn't needed. To do a search for print server, for example, you can type PRINT SERVER. This is the same as PRINT & SERVER. HELP interprets the blank space as an AND operator, and shows you all the pages on which the words PRINT and SERVER appear. (If you only wanted the phrase PRINT SERVER, use the earlier instructions on quotation marks.)

The OR operator (/), <Ctrl>-<O>, shows you occurrences of either of the two words on a page. If you type PRINT/SERVER, you now get 1114 pages, not just 181 for PRINT SERVER or 147 for "PRINT SERVER". Now the occurrences include all those for SERVER, PRINT, and PRINT SERVER.

The NOT operator (^), <Ctrl>-<N>, shows you occurrences of the two words when either one or the other, or both, appears on a page. So PRINT^SERVER will show you pages with just PRINT and pages with just SERVER, as well as pages with both PRINT and SERVER. (It will also show you every page with PRINT SERVERS, the plural, on it.)

The EXCLUSIVE OR operator (~), <Ctrl>-<E>, shows you occurrences of either of the two words on a page, but not both. So PRINT~SERVER shows you pages with the word PRINT on them, pages with the word SERVER on them, but no pages with both PRINT and SERVER on them. (This too, however, will bring up occurrences of PRINT SERVERS, since that is plural.)

A fifth operator, GROUP NAME, isn't useful since HELP uses only a few GROUPS. This operator would be useful if you had a large number of pages in a group and wanted to restrict the search to just those pages.

Search Options

HELP includes the "References" option, which is located under the Options menu. Normally when you perform a search, HELP displays it in text form. The option, "References," when used with the "Focus" option below, displays just the title of each page (folio) instead. Unfortunately, the titles don't often tell much about the contents of the page, but if you need to reduce search time, References may be a start.

To run References, press <Ctrl>-<R>, then <Ctrl>-<T>. The <Ctrl>-<T> tells HELP to remove the text and leave only the references. When you find the page you want, press <Enter>. Once you've read that material, press <Esc> and you pop back to the References list. You can then choose another page, or press <Esc> again to end the search. When you want to go back to the regular text of the search results, press <Ctrl>-<T>, <Ctrl>-<R>. Now the full text of each of the occurrences will be displayed on screen.

HELP also has a potentially useful tool for searches with the "Focus" option. Focus is accessed by <Ctrl>-<F> and produces a list of pages that have your search words. Focus shows just a few words (including the word or words you were looking for) that occur before and after the search word(s) for each page. This lets you quickly scan down the list to find just the right occurrence. Unfortunately, in HELP, the default for the occurrences with Focus on is to show just the search words.

You can change the number of words that Focus shows for each occurrence, but when you see this list, the occurrences are jumbled all together. Each new listing of a page of information is only separated by a bracket from the next page. That makes seeing the separate items difficult. It may not save much time to have to decipher what each of those occurrences is. If you choose to define Focus with enough words before and after the search words, you may see as much as if you turned Focus off and read through the pages normally.

If you want to experiment with the number of words Focus displays, first press <Alt>-<O> to see the OPTIONS menu. Select "Infobase Defaults" by pressing the letter I, select "Set Defaults" in the configuration file, and press <Enter>, then use the Tab key to move down to where the "Focus options" window is displayed on the right side of the screen. Change the number for "words before search term" and "words after search term" to an appropriate number. Then press the Tab key to move down to the option labeled "Override infobase settings." Press the space bar to change the - to an X and press <Enter>.

When you change Focus's default parameters, you're making changes to HELP's configuration file. If an error message appears saying that HELP couldn't create PUBLIC\VIEWS.CFG, it means you don't have write rights to SYS:PUBLIC. Either your supervisor must grant you the proper rights, or you can change the location of the VIEWS.CFG file. Press <Escape> to leave the error message, then use the TAB key to move your cursor down to the Save settings to: line at the bottom of the window. Type in the path to a directory where you do have write rights, such as your personal directory.

Then press <Enter> to save this change. Now you can save changes to the "Focus" option.

Your choices are now saved. Perform a search, then press <Ctrl>-<F> to activate the "Focus" option. All the occurrences of the search word(s) are now displayed as brief bits of text. If this display doesn't agree with you, you can press <Ctrl>-<F> again. The normal page view pops back up.

Exploring Other HELP Aspects

If you want to explore a bit more of the Folio technology beyond the HELP infobase, you can easily do so. Try pressing <Ctrl>-<D>. This brings up a directory tree of your current directory. The .NFO files, the infobases, are stored under SYS:PUBLIC. Move the highlight bar to "Parent," which is the parent directory of your subdirectory, if you happen to be in one. Press <Enter> until you see the directory listing of the root. The root has the LOGIN and PUBLIC directories.

Move the highlight bar to PUBLIC and press <Enter>. PreVIEWS shows you a list, under the indicator .NFO, of the four infobases that come with NetWare. These are "!NetWare," which is the HELP infobase; "CONST," a copy of the U.S. Constitution; "FOLIO," a demonstration of Folio Views; and "PVMANUAL," an on-line users manual. By highlighting the name of each of the infobases, PreVIEWS shows you its title page. Press <Enter> to open the highlighted infobase, then you can proceed to explore the contents.

You can actually have all four of the infobases active if you have enough memory. (You'll need 640KB of conventional memory, but you can have IPX and the NetWare shell loaded and still have enough memory.) If you open up two or more of the infobases, use the + and - keys to move back and forth between them. Once at a particular infobase, you can use all the function keys of the HELP utility to access the information there.

Other Information

HELP also includes the program VIEWER. VIEWER displays .PCX graphics images on your screen and you'll need to have a VGA monitor to do this. To see a particular image, type VIEWER <name>.pcx <Enter>. You must run the program where the .PCX file is stored. This means you'll need to set up a search drive to your .PCX file if you haven't done so already. NetWare 3.11 comes with a variety of .PCX files. They are found in the SYS:PUBLIC directory. You can also get .PCX files from many on-line services.

CHAPTER 3

NetWare Services: The Command-Line Utilities

NetWare has 35 utilities that you can run from the network prompt. These utilities range from network extensions of DOS utilities (such as NCOPY, NDIR, and NPRINT) to utilities specific to NetWare (such as LOGIN, WHOAMI, and SETPASS). Command-line utilities are called both "utilities" and "commands," for they often function much like DOS commands. Each command-line utility listed in this chapter comes with a brief explanation, instructions on typing the command and the command's additional parameters, and a listing of related commands.

Command-Line Utilities

After much thought, I decided to discuss the command-line utilities according to the particular tasks they perform instead of in alphabetical order. This approach makes good sense when you're trying to perform certain tasks. For convenience, I have listed them both alphabetically and by task. If you need a quick reference of parameter syntax without explanations, turn to Appendix C.

ALLOW	LOGIN	RIGHTS
ATTACH	LOGOUT	SEND
CAPTURE	MAP	SETPASS
CASTOFF	NCOPY	SETTTS
CASTON	NDIR	SLIST
CHKDIR	NPRINT	SMODE
CHKVOL	NVER	SYSTIME
ENDCAP	PSTAT	TLIST
FLAG	PURGE	USERLIST
FLAGDIR	REMOVE	VERSION
GRANT	RENDIR	WHOAMI
LISTDIR	REVOKE	

Because many of these utilities have related functions, you can group them by the tasks you need to perform. These groupings include Server Access Utilities, User Identification Utilities, Message Utilities, Directory and File Management Utilities, Directory and File Security Utilities, Working Environment Utilities, and General NetWare Utilities. NetWare also provides various Printing Utilities (as explained in Chapter 4). The utilities by category are:

Server Access Utilities
LOGIN
ATTACH
SETPASS
LOGOUT
SLIST

User Identification Utilities
USERLIST
WHOAMI

Directory and File Management Utilities
CHKDIR
CHKVOL
LISTDIR
NCOPY
NDIR
PURGE
RENDIR

Directory and File Security Utilities
ALLOW
FLAG
FLAGDIR
GRANT
REVOKE
REMOVE
TLIST
RIGHTS

Working Environment Utilities
MAP
SYSTIME

Message Utilities
SEND
CASTOFF
CASTON

General NetWare Utilities
NVER
SETTTS
SMODE
VERSION

Printing Utilities
CAPTURE
ENDCAP
NPRINT
PSC
PSTAT
RPRINTER

The Server Access Utilities assist you in logging in or attaching to servers on your network; such utilities include ATTACH, LOGIN, and LOGOUT. To see which servers you have available, use the SLIST command; to change your password at the command line, use the SETPASS utility.

The User Identification Utilities show you information about yourself and about the other users on the network; these utilities include USERLIST and WHOAMI.

The Directory and File Management Utilities assist you in working with your network files and directories. CHKVOL shows you information about network volumes. CHKDIR shows your disk space limitation if you have been given such. LISTDIR and RENDIR allow you to list and rename directories. NCOPY and NDIR let you copy files and display directory listings. Use PURGE when you're permanently deleting files from the network.

The Directory and File Security Utilities help you assign security to files and directories from the network prompt. The FLAG utility assists you in flagging file attributes, while FLAGDIR assists you in flagging directory attributes. GRANT, REVOKE, and REMOVE allow you to give and revoke trustee assignments for your directories, while ALLOW allows you to modify the directories' Inherited Rights Mask (IRM) at the network prompt. TLIST shows who presently has trustee assignments in your directories, and RIGHTS shows you your effective rights in a given directory.

The Message Utilities (SEND, CASTON and CASTOFF) let you send and receive messages on the network, as well as prevent messages from displaying at your workstation.

The Working Environment Utilities work with your workstation's network environment setup. These utilities include MAP and SYSTIME.

The General NetWare Utilities group includes those utilities that don't lend themselves well to grouping and are often used alone. These include NVER, SETTTS, SMODE, and VERSION.

The Printing Utilities group contains those command-line utilities that you use mostly for printing, including CAPTURE, ENDCAP, NPRINT, PSC, PSTAT and RPRINTER. Chapter 4 covers the Printing Utilities group along with the menu printing utilities.

Getting Around in the Command-Line Utilities

You perform the command-line utilities at the network prompt—that is, the prompt you see after you log in to the network and can access the directories defined by the drive mappings in your login script. The network prompt is the alphabetic designation of one of the drive mappings, and from it you can enter NetWare commands—typing MAP <Enter> or NCOPY <Enter>, for example.

You can often perform the same functions with the command-line utilities that you can perform with the menu utilities. For example, you can map drives through the SESSION menu utility or through the MAP command-line utility. You can view files and give people trustee assignments to your directories through the FILER utility; you can also view files through the NDIR command and give others trustee assignments to your directories through the GRANT command.

The command-line utilities usually come with options, or parameters, that extend the functionality of the command name. Here's a command format example:

```
NCOPY directory path/filename(s) TO directory path/filename(s)
[/options]
```

Suppose you want to run NCOPY to copy some files from one directory to another. Type the command, NCOPY, followed by the directory path you want to copy the files from and the names of the files you want to copy. The TO part of the command is optional, as is frequently the case with command syntax and parameters; it just makes the command syntax seem more logical. You can type the TO command to tell NCOPY "copy these files from this directory TO another destination," or you can replace TO with a blank space and get the same results. After the TO command, put in the destination directory path and, if you wish to change the filenames, put in the new names of the files. For example, to copy *.DAT files from drive G: to drive H:, you can type NCOPY G:*.DAT H: <Enter>.

The /Options addition allows you to then extend NCOPY's functionality. For example, with the /Sub option, you can copy subdirectories and files in those subdirectories to the stated directory path.

Because NetWare utilities are so versatile, they usually offer several ways to execute a NetWare command. For example, execute the SEND command by typing:

```
SEND "Here is a message" TO (user or group) <Enter>
```

Or you can designate the actual connection number instead of a user or group name; or you can change the syntax around and type:

```
SEND TO (user or connection number or group name) "Here comes a
message" <Enter>
```

Or you can use the message-sending capabilities of the SESSION menu utility.

Because of this versatility, you ought to try a couple of methods, then choose the one you like best and stick with it for the sake of familiarity. Otherwise, you may get confused trying to remember the proper syntax when you most need to use the utility. As it is, NetWare 3.1x changes the syntax enough to keep you on your toes without your contributing to the learning curve!

Using Wild Cards

You can use wild cards in filenames with commands such as NCOPY. Through wild cards, you can copy or mark a number of files at the same time.

For example, if you have a number of files with an RPT extension (NEW.RPT, TIMES.RPT, and so forth) and you want to copy all of them from your J: drive to your K: drive, you can type NCOPY J:*.RPT K: <Enter>. The * stands for any number of characters in a filename. All files with an RPT extension in the K: directory path, regardless of what characters are to the left of the period, will be copied to the K: directory path.

The same applies for the question mark (?) wild card. Each question-mark wild card takes the place of one character in a filename. For example, if you have several files, but you want to copy only three—GLSYS.FDM, DRSYS.FED, and SLSYS.FDM—you can type NCOPY J:??SYS*.* K: <Enter>, and NCOPY will copy only those files with that pattern to their filename.

The Versatility of Directory Paths

For another example of the use of directory paths in a command, let's look at the TLIST utility. TLIST shows who has trustee assignments to your directories. (You must have Access Control effective rights in your directories to use TLIST).

To use TLIST, enter the entire directory path, use a drive letter, or simply type TLIST to specify the directory you're currently in. For example, if you're in the NTS3/VOL1:USERS/TED/REPORTS directory, for which you have Access Control rights, and you want to see who has trustee assignments in your NTS3/VOL1: USERS/TED/TEAM directory, type:

```
TLIST NTS3/VOL1:USERS/TED/TEAM <Enter>
```

If NTS3/VOL1 is your default server and volume, type

```
TLIST /USERS/TED/TEAM <Enter>
```

or

```
TLIST :USERS/TED/TEAM <Enter>
```

If the NTS3/VOL1:USERS/TED/TEAM directory is mapped to drive G:, type

```
TLIST G: <Enter>
```

Or if you're in the G: directory, just type TLIST <Enter>.

Suppose you want to see who has trustee assignments in the subdirectories beneath the directory you're in. You have a subdirectory named GOODS beneath the NTS3/VOL1:USERS/TED/TEAM directory that you're in, so type TLIST GOODS <Enter>. At your drive G: directory path (NTS3/VOL1:USERS/TED/TEAM), to see who has trustee assignments in the TED directory above TEAM, type TLIST .. <Enter> at the G: prompt. You'll see NTS3/VOL1:USERS/TED in the directory path entry above the "User Trustees:" line. To see who has trustee assignments in the USERS directory above

TED, type TLIST ... <Enter> at your G: prompt; if you have sufficient rights, you'll see those trustee assignments as well.

Using Options and Their Abbreviations

Command options usually follow the directory path and file specifications. For example, the WHOAMI utility comes with eight options: the groups you belong to (/Group), security equivalences (/Security), if you're an object supervisor (/Object), if you're a workgroup manager (/WorkGroups), your effective rights (/Rights), which servers you're attached to (/System), or specify all of the above (/All), as well as continuous scrolling (/Continuous). For most utilities, you need to use the forward slash before designating an option or parameter, so for consistency's sake, it's easiest to use the forward slash all the time.

You can type out the entire parameter (such as "/Group" or "/Security"), or simply abbreviate the parameter with its first letter (such as "/g" or "/s"—upper or lower case). You'll see these abbreviations throughout Chapters 3 and 4. For example, if you just want to see which groups you belong to on your present server (such as ADMIN), type:

```
WHOAMI ADMIN/GROUP <Enter>
```
or
```
WHOAMI ADMIN/G <Enter>
```

Other Information

Suppose you're attached to two servers and have drive mappings to directories on both servers. When you choose a drive mapping that comes from the server other than your default, you'll have all the rights and privileges that you have on that other server. For example, suppose you're user TED on server ADMIN with regular privileges, and user TED on server NTS3 with supervisory privileges. When you go to the drive letter that connects you to server NTS3 and type SYSCON, you'll have supervisory privileges in SYSCON while you're working on that server. However, when you change your current server in SYSCON to server ADMIN, you'll only have the user privileges that you've been given on server ADMIN.

Some commands, such as NDIR and SLIST, have a pause sequence built in. Other commands don't have a pause sequence; these commands will scroll information across the screen until the command is completed. If you're fast enough, you can hit <Ctrl-S> (depress the Control and the S keys at the same time) to pause the scrolling action. Then press <Ctrl-S> again to continue scrolling. You can also hold down the control key and press the S key if you want to toggle between the scrolling and pause action. However, most commands in NetWare 3.1x have the pause sequence. So with that as an introduction, let's take a look at NetWare's command-line utilities.

Server Access Utilities

The first group of command-line utilities includes those that assist you in logging in or attaching to servers on the network. This book will refer to these utilities as the Server Access Utilities. The utilities include LOGIN, ATTACH, SETPASS, LOGOUT, and SLIST. Use the LOGIN utility to log in to a server and have your login script execute. The ATTACH utility attaches you to other servers. To give yourself a new password from the command line, use the SETPASS utility. To log out from your login or attached servers, use the LOGOUT utility. To see a list of the other servers on the network, use the SLIST (Server LIST) utility.

LOGIN

The LOGIN utility allows you to establish a connection with the server you designate, and then runs your login script to set up your working environment. The easiest place to use the LOGIN command is in your AUTOEXEC.BAT file, which automatically runs your login procedure on the designated server and sets you at a network prompt.

The complete login procedure includes loading DOS at your workstation; loading IPX (used in communicating with the network) or LSL, network board driver, and IPXODI; loading NETX or the DOS Requester (loading the NetWare shell so you can effectively communicate with your server); and running LOGIN, which establishes a connection to a specific server and runs the system login script, then your personal login script. For an explanation of how to create an AUTOEXEC.BAT file, see the "Creating an AUTOEXEC.BAT File" heading in Chapter 5.

After loading the IPX drivers and NETX or (VLM.EXE) files, your AUTO-EXEC.BAT will go to the directory containing the LOGIN.EXE file, which is usually SYS:\LOGIN. If you've set up your prompt so it shows your directory path (PROMPT PG), the network prompt will show that you're at the LOGIN directory. If you're not at the LOGIN directory and you type LOGIN NTS3/TED, you'll receive a "Bad command or filename" message, which means you're not at the LOGIN directory. NetWare defaults the LOGIN directory to C: (for DOS 2.0 and computers without hard drives) or F: (for DOS 3.x and above).

If neither of these drive letters yields the LOGIN directory, press the <Ctrl>-<Alt>-<Del> keys and reboot your computer. (If that doesn't work, turn to the "Troubleshooting Your Workstation" heading in Chapter 5.) The rest of this discussion assumes you're at the LOGIN directory.

Using the LOGIN Command

Here's a list of LOGIN's parameters and their functions, and an explanation of how to use them. If you don't know the correct syntax for typing in the LOGIN command, type LOGIN /H <Enter> at the LOGIN directory and you'll see:

```
F:\LOGIN> login /h
Usage: Login [/Options] [Server/] [Username] [ScriptParameters]
Options :   Clear screen
     No attach
     Script <path spec>
```

LOGIN */Options servername/username.* The only reason for looking at these options is so you won't get confused by seeing available options that aren't discussed in this book. Two of the three options, "Script" and "No Attach," are mostly used for troubleshooting purposes, while "Clear Screen" is a commodity to clear off the descriptions of the login procedure after you type in your password. For example, to clear off the screen as you log in to server NTS3 as user Ted, type LOGIN /C NTS3/TED <Enter>for the login command. Then after you type in your password, the screen will clear. If you or the supervisor haven't used the MAP DISPLAY OFF command in the login script, you'll see your drive mappings display.

The "Script" and "No Attach" options allow you to run a locally stored login script. These options are mainly for the purpose of helping someone who has messed up the login script so badly that it's impossible to log in.

For example, if for some unknown reason you can't log in to the server and you've determined that the problem lies in the login script itself, you can create a small "fix-it" login script and store it on a local drive. In this case, the /S option works the same as the INCLUDE command in the login script, and as long as you follow the rules to create login scripts using the INCLUDE command, you'll be fine. (See the subheading "Setting Up Your Login Script" under "The SYSCON Utility" section in Chapter 2.) The main items to remember are that you need to save the file as an ASCII text file, use login script commands, and be sure to include drive mappings from the system login script because the /S parameter overrides both system and user login scripts. You must also type in the entire directory path as to where to find the file.

As an example, if you follow the above specifications, create a file called FIX, and store it on drive A:, type LOGIN /SA:FIX NTS3/TED /N <Enter> to invoke the FIX file. Note that there's no space between the /S option and the directory path. Note also that you must run the /N option at the end of the LOGIN command for it to work. The /N option lets you run the FIX login script without logging out of currently attached servers while you're attaching to the designated server. If you put /N before the *servername*, the login procedure may not work for you. You can run the /S option without the /N option and have the LOGIN command work fine; however, if you try to run the /N option without the /S option, you'll probably face drive mapping problems. As a last point, don't use the /S option unless you really need to; simply logging in or attaching to servers is much easier.

LOGIN *servername/username.* At the LOGIN directory prompt, you can designate the server and your user name in the LOGIN command. For example, if you want to log in to server ADMIN as user TED, type LOGIN ADMIN/TED at the login prompt. If you're defined as a user on server ADMIN, you may already have a password established for your name and you'll see an "Enter your password:" prompt.

```
A:> F:
F:\LOGIN> LOGIN ADMIN/TED
Enter your password:
```

Type in your password correctly, press <Enter>, and you'll see a login script scroll down the screen. If, before you press <Enter>, you realize you've mistyped your password, press the backspace key until you hear a beep, then retype your password. If you enter a mistyped password, you'll see a message saying something like "Access to server ADMIN denied and you have been logged out. You are attached to server ADMIN." Retype LOGIN ADMIN/TED <Enter> and try again.

You can also type in a servername without attaching your user name. To do this, type LOGIN ADMIN/ <Enter> at the network prompt. (You have to put in the slash so NetWare won't think the name ADMIN is a person's name and ask for its password.) You'll see the "Enter your login name:" prompt. Type in your name and press <Enter>; if you're required to have a password, you'll see the "Enter your password:" prompt. Enter your password correctly, and you're logged in.

LOGIN *server/username scriptparameters.* The "Script Parameters" option allows you to indicate which of several environments you want to set up in your login script. These parameters are prefaced in the login script with a percent sign (%) and follow your login name, on the same line, when you log in to the server. You can define up to nine different scripts to run; the first parameter (%1) is your login name, and the others can be whatever you choose. For example, suppose you log in to server ADMIN, but occasionally you need to access programs on other servers, such as the PFIX program. When you want to use the PFIX program, you can use PFIX as the second parameter and then designate the PFIX environment in your login script, like this:

```
If "%2" == "PFIX" then begin
    attach nts3/ted
    map ins s3:=nts3/byte:users/ted/pfix20
    map s4:=nts3/sys:public
end
```

Once you set up the script in your login script on server ADMIN, it's a simple matter to call it up: just type in the name of the script after your username when you log in. For example, to create the PFIX environment, type:

```
LOGIN ADMIN/TED PFIX
```

So when you type in your login name (the first parameter) and add the second parameter, PFIX, after your login name, the login script will run according to the information found in your personal login script on server ADMIN. In this case, you'll attach to server NTS3 and map two search drives. (For more information on using more than one parameter in your login script, see the subheading "Setting Up Your Login Script" under "The SYSCON Utility" section in Chapter 2.)

When Passwords Expire

With NetWare 3.1x and above, supervisors can force you to change your password every so often. You'll notice this when you try to log in and you're prompted to change your password. When you do change your password, you'll see a line that says, "Would you like to synchronize your passwords on all attached servers? (Y/N)" with a "Y" for "Yes" highlighted. Pressing <Enter> will synchronize your passwords on all the servers you're currently attached to. Password synchronization works out nicely if you want to place an ATTACH command in your login script, for you can attach to the server without being asked for your password.

If you don't want all your passwords synchronized, type the letter "N" and press <Enter>. In any case, this password synchronization won't change your password on any server where your username is different from your username on the server you're logging in to.

Other Information

When you log in to a server, that server becomes your default server. When you log out of a server and are left at the *driveletter*:LOGIN directory, the directory drive letter coincides with the directory you were in when you logged out of the server. When you log in again, the drive letter will be mapped to its proper directory.

When you log out of your default server and are left at the LOGIN directory, you need only type LOGIN TED <Enter> to log back into that server. You can also relog in without logging out of a server; however, if you relog in to your default server when you're already logged in to it, you'll automatically log out from the other servers you're attached to. If those attached servers aren't in your login script, you'll need to reestablish those connections through the ATTACH command. (See the next heading.)

If you're attaching to more than one server and you have drive letters mapped to directories on those servers, be careful which drive letter you log out from. When you log out of all connections at a drive letter that's mapped to one of your attached servers, that server acts as your default server the next time you log in. If you forget or don't realize that fact and type in your usual LOGIN TED with your usual password, and that password is different on this server, you'll see "NTS3/TED: Access to server denied and you have been logged out. You are attached to server NTS3." To access ADMIN, the server you usually log in to, you'll have to type the full LOGIN ADMIN/TED <Enter> in order to make ADMIN your default server again.

To get around this problem, make it a policy to log out from the same drive letter each time, or include the name of the server whenever you log in.

Related Commands

Other related commands are SLIST and ATTACH. The SLIST utility shows all the servers on the internet. For a full explanation of SLIST, see "SLIST" in this section. The ATTACH utility allows you to attach to other servers.

ATTACH

The ATTACH utility allows you to attach to up to seven servers in addition to the server you're logged in to. ATTACH is similar to the LOGIN utility; however, LOGIN runs your login script and displays the directory information you set up in the login script. ATTACH doesn't display a login script—but by attaching to another server, you gain directory access to files, applications, or resources (if you have rights). And everything depends on how you're defined as a user on those servers. If you forget how to use the ATTACH command, type ATTACH /H <Enter> at the network prompt. The syntax for executing the ATTACH utility is:

```
ATTACH servername/username
```

If your name is Pam and you're a user on server ADMIN with a password, type ATTACH ADMIN/PAM. NetWare will prompt you for a password with an "Enter your password" prompt. After you enter your password (or if you're not required to have a password), you'll see "Your station is attached to server ADMIN." But ATTACH won't execute a login script.

You can use the ATTACH command without entering the *servername* or the user name. Simply type ATTACH <Enter> at the network prompt. You'll see a "Server:" prompt; type in the name of the server you want to attach to, press <Enter>, and you'll see a "Username:" prompt. Type in your user name on that server and you'll see the "Password:" prompt (if you require a password on that server). Type in your password and press <Enter>. You'll see a "You're attached to server ADMIN" prompt.

If you just want to see if you can attach to another server, type SLIST <Enter> at the network prompt to see what servers are available. If you're not set up as a user on any other server, select a server and try typing ATTACH *servername*/GUEST. Some servers have passwords for their guest accounts; in order to log in or attach to those servers, you'll need to know the passwords. A server that has a guest account without a password will allow you to attach; however, getting around on a strange server can be quite difficult if you don't know the server's directory structure.

ATTACH Attachments

The maximum number of servers you can be logged in to at one time is eight. Since you're logged in to your default server, you can attach to no more than seven other servers. If you try to attach to an eighth server, you'll see, "You're attached to the maximum number of servers allowed. You must LOGOUT from a server before attaching to another server." If you want to attach to still another server, you must log out from one of your connections by typing LOGOUT *servername* <Enter>, then ATTACH *servername/username* <Enter> to attach to the new server.

Note that server attachments can affect performance. If you're attached to several servers and your performance gets sluggish, drop the attached servers you need the least. Then set up a batch file to attach to those least-used servers when you need to.

Attaching to Servers through a Batch File

For those server attachments that are too infrequent to justify modifying your login script, you can set up batch files that attach you to other servers as well as map drives for you. Suppose, for example, that your name is Ted and you need to access the SYS:REPORTS/AUG directory on server ADMIN only once a week. Rather than using the ATTACH command in your login script, set up a batch file. To set up the batch file, go to the directory that you need to be in when you attach to server ADMIN. (This is when having your own special search drive comes in very handy; see the "Setting Up Your Personal Drive Mapping" heading in Chapter 5.) At the network prompt, type:

```
COPY CON ADMIN.BAT <Enter>
ATTACH ADMIN/TED <Enter>
MAP G:=ADMIN/SYS:REPORTS/AUG ^Z
```

The first two lines say, "Create a batch file named ADMIN which will attach me to server ADMIN with the username Ted." The third line says "Map the drive letter G: to the SYS:REPORTS/AUG directory." You can put in as many drive mappings as you need to that server. But watch which drive letters you designate in your batch file, as you may overwrite other directory mappings. The ^Z is the "End of File" mark, which says "There are no more commands in the batch file." You create the "End of File" mark by pressing the Ctrl and Z keys simultaneously, or by pressing the F6 key. If your batch file creation is successful, you'll see "1 File(s) copied" as you're returned to the network prompt. Remember, unless you've created this file in a search directory (or have copied it to one), you must be in the directory containing the batch file in order to execute it.

Related Commands

As mentioned earlier, you can also attach to servers via your login script. In addition to displaying your drive mappings, the login script can also attach you to other servers as well as allow you to set up drive mappings to those servers. (To modify your login script, see the SYSCON discussion in Chapter 2.)

Use the WHOAMI utility to see how many servers you're attached to. WHOAMI will first list the server you're logged in to, then all the servers you're attached to. (For a full explanation of WHOAMI, turn to the "User Identification Utilities" section in this chapter.)

Other related commands are SLIST and LOGIN. The SLIST utility shows all the servers on the internet. For a full explanation of SLIST, see the last command in this section. The LOGIN utility allows you to log in to a server and have your drive mappings displayed from the login script. (For a full explanation of LOGIN, see the first command in this section.)

SETPASS

SYSCON allows you to change your password from a menu utility; SETPASS allows you to change your password from the command line. Passwords can be as long as 127 characters, or as short as your particular security scheme allows. (In fact, you may not even need a password. But passwords are a very good idea.) NetWare 3.1x also allows you to synchronize your password to all the servers you're currently attached to. However, you can't give passwords to the GUEST login name.

How To Use SETPASS

SETPASS *servername.* To change your password on your default server, type SETPASS at the network prompt and press <Enter>. You'll see a prompt that says, "Enter Old Password for NTS3/TED:". Type in your old password and press <Enter>. You'll see another prompt that says "Enter New Password for NTS3/TED:". Type in your new password and press <Enter>. You'll then be prompted to retype your new password. Re-enter the new password and press <Enter>, and you'll see a line that says, "The password for NTS3/TED has been changed," and you'll return to the network prompt. If you type in the password incorrectly the second time, you'll see "Access denied to NTS3/TED, password not changed." Simply retype SETPASS <Enter> at the network prompt to start again.

In NetWare 3.11, you'll see a line that says, "Would you like to synchronize your passwords on all attached servers? (Y/N)" with a "Y" for "Yes" highlighted. If you wish to have your passwords synchronized on all the servers you're currently attached to, press <Enter>. If you don't wish to have all your passwords synchronized, type the letter "N" and press <Enter>. If you select "Yes", your screen will look similar to this one:

```
D:\USERS\TED\TEAM >setpass
Enter old password for NTS3/TED:
Enter new password for NTS3/TED:
Retype new password for NTS3/TED:
The password for NTS3/TED has been changed:
ADMIN/TED
PUB/TED
[Synchronize passwords on these file servers with NTS3/TED? (Y/N) Y]
The password for PUB has been changed.
The password for ADMIN has been changed.
The password for NTS3-PRINT was not changed.
```

In the above example, the password on server NTS3-PRINT isn't changed because the attachment to NTS3-PRINT is done through the GUEST account; you won't be allowed to change the password on any server on which your user name is different.

When you're on server NTS3 and attached to another server (such as server ADMIN), you can type SETPASS ADMIN and follow the above procedure. When you have a drive mapped on the attached server, you can go to that mapped drive and type SETPASS. For example, if you're logged in to server NTS3 and you have drive G: mapped to server ADMIN, you can go to drive G:, type SETPASS, change your password on server ADMIN, and ignore the synchronization entry. This won't affect your password on server NTS3.

Other Information

As stated before, you can have passwords up to 127 characters long. Remember that you can't use control characters (^Z, ^N, and so forth) in your password—NetWare ignores them. Because of your particular security scheme, your password may need to be a certain length (NetWare's default is five characters long). Otherwise, you may be told your password is too short and you'll have to type in a new one.

Since you can't see the password you're typing, you sometimes type it incorrectly. When you're typing in your password and you know you've made a mistake, press the backspace key until SETPASS beeps, then type in the password again. If you happen to type in your old password incorrectly, but the new password correctly, you'll see the message "Access denied to NTS3/TED, password not changed," and you'll return to the network prompt. When you type or retype your new password incorrectly, you'll see "New password not correctly retyped," and you'll return to the network prompt to try again.

Related Commands

You can also set your password in SYSCON. (See "The SYSCON Utility" heading in Chapter 2.) You may also wish to check your "Accounts Restriction" option in the "User Information" window of SYSCON in order to see your "Minimum Password Length" entry.

Of course, if you're in SYSCON anyway, you might as well change your password there. Remember, however, that your passwords won't be synchronized if you change your password in SYSCON. Run the WHOAMI utility to see which servers you're attached to before deciding to synchronize your passwords.

LOGOUT

The LOGOUT utility ends your working session with the server or servers you're attached to. Since NetWare doesn't want to leave you stranded after you log out, it retains a connection with the server that corresponds to the drive letter you logged out from. For example, if drive G: is mapped to a directory on server ADMIN, and drive H: is mapped to a directory on server PUB, you'll end up with a connection and a drive mapping to the LOGIN directory on whichever server you type LOGOUT from. If you log out from drive G:, you'll have a connection with server ADMIN, and if you log out from drive H:, you'll have a connection with server PUB.

Using the LOGOUT Command

LOGOUT. You can log out of every server you're logged in or attached to by typing LOGOUT <Enter> at the network prompt. Depending on how many server attachments you have, you'll see something like this:

```
TED logged out from server ADMIN connection 11
Login Time: Thursday September 26, 1992 9:05 am
Logout Time: Thursday September 26, 1992 5:05 pm

TED logged out from server NTS3 connection 87
Login Time: Thursday September 26, 1992 9:05 am
Logout Time: Thursday September 26, 1992 5:05 am
```

In the preceding example, if your name is Ted, you've logged out from both ADMIN and NTS3 servers. After each servername in the above example, you see the connection number. This number corresponds to the connection number you see if you type USERLIST <Enter> at the network prompt. (See the "User Identification Utilities" section in this chapter.) The rest of the information shows your login and logout time.

LOGOUT *servername.* You can also designate which servers you wish to log out from. For example, if you want to log out of server NTS3 only, you can type LOGOUT NTS3 <Enter> at the prompt, and NetWare will drop your attachment to server NTS3 along with any drive mappings you have to that server. If you happen to be on a drive mapped to NTS3 when you issue the LOGOUT command, you'll be moved to an active drive, and sometimes to a local drive such as A:. Then if you type MAP, you'll no longer see any drive mappings to the logged-out server.

While you can log out from your default server and retain your attachments and drive mappings to your attached servers, you may find yourself without the necessary search drive mappings to utilities and applications. While it's an interesting experiment, logging out from your default server is a hard way to get around on the network. However, if your default server is for some reason behaving unreliably, you might wish to map a search drive to the SYS:PUBLIC directory on one of your attached servers. Then if you lose your connection to your default server, you'll at least have the attached server's SYS:PUBLIC utilities to fall back on.

Other Information

When you type LOGOUT <Enter>, NetWare normally retains an attachment to the server whose drive you were in when you logged out and remaps that drive as a LOGIN drive. The next time you wish to log in (and if you haven't turned off your machine in the interim), simply type LOGIN *servername/username* <Enter> at the drive prompt, and you'll be asked for your password. And, of course, once you log in, NetWare will present you with your login script.

Other Related Commands

Use LOGOUT in conjunction with the LOGIN and ATTACH utilities.

SLIST

Once a minute, each server on an internetwork lets every other server know that it's still on the internet. This information is stored in each server's bindery (a small database that keeps track of such things). The SLIST utility takes advantage of the server bindery, for SLIST allows you to see all the servers on the network. When you want to see which servers are available for you to attach to, or if you're merely curious as to how many servers there are on your internet, use SLIST.

Using the SLIST Command

SLIST *servername/C.* When you're at the network prompt, or when you log out and you're at the LOGIN prompt, you can type SLIST <Enter> to see which servers are available. You'll initially see a line that says, "Reading servernames...please wait...," and then a list of servers similar to the following:

```
H:\USERS\TED >slist
```

270

```
Reading servernames . . . please wait . . .
File Servers      Network      Node Address      Status
---------------------------------------------------------
AA               [FADE0005]   [  1B022342]
ADAM             [50000006]   [        1]
ADMIN            [     FB]    [ 2608C234732]    Default
ALEX             [   7979]    [        1]
ALICE            [FADE0005]   [       C4]
AMADEUS          [   7979]    [        3]

Press any key to continue ... ('C' for continuous). . .
VORTEX           [FADE0005]   [ 4E]
VOYAGE           [FEED0036]   [ D80007D3]
WATERGATE        [50000006]   [ 42]
XANADU           [FEED0036]   [ 1]

Total of 10 file servers found
```

The information for each server on the internet includes its given name (under the "Known NetWare File Servers" heading), the server's network address (which appears in the "Network" column), and its node address (in the column of the same name). Network addresses are the same for all servers on the same network. However, SLIST doesn't show which servers are attached to the internetwork (if there is one) or the internetwork address. Under the "Status" column you'll see "Default" written to the right of the server that you're logged in to; you'll also see "Attached" written to the right of those servers that you're attached to.

As SLIST fills a screenful of information, you'll see the "Press any key to continue ... ('C' for continuous)" line. You can either press a key such as the space bar and pause at each screenful, or you can press the letter C and SLIST will scroll through the names of all the servers. If you just want to see how many servers are on your internetwork, type SLIST/C <Enter>, and SLIST will automatically scroll through all the servers, then tell you "Total of xxx file servers found" at the end of the server list.

To find out whether a certain server is available for you to log in to or attach to, type SLIST *servername* <Enter>. For example, to make sure server NTS3 is still out there, type SLIST NTS3 <Enter>. If server NTS3 is still talking to your attached server, you'll see a screen similar to this one:

```
H:\USERS\ED >slist nts3
File Servers Network        Node Address      Status
```

```
- - - - - - - - - - - - - - - - - - - - - - - - - - - - - - - - - - - - - - - - - -
NTS3              [    FB]     [ 2608C234732]
Total of 1 file servers found
```

You can also use wild cards in the *servername* part of SLIST. For example, if you know that the name of the server you want to attach to begins with the letter P, type SLIST P* <Enter> at the network prompt and you'll see a list of all servers whose names begin with the letter P.

Related Commands

You usually use SLIST along with the LOGIN and ATTACH utilities. The LOGIN utility allows you to execute your login script. (See the discussion of the LOGIN utility under the "LOGIN" heading earlier in this section.) You can also attach to up to seven servers other than the one you're logged in to. (See the "ATTACH" subheading earlier in this section.)

User Identification Utilities

The second group of command-line utilities help identify you as well as other users who are logged in. In this book, we'll refer to this group as the User Identification Utilities. The User Identification Utilities are USERLIST and WHOAMI. Use the USERLIST utility to display information about all users attached to a server. The WHOAMI utility shows you information about yourself on all servers you're attached to.

USERLIST

The USERLIST utility lists all users currently logged in to your server. It can also list all users on all the servers you're attached to. With USERLIST, you can see each user's connection number, user name, network and node address, the object type as you are known by the server, and the time the user logged in.

Using the USERLIST Utility

If you can't remember the proper syntax for USERLIST, type USERLIST /H <Enter> and you'll see the syntax help screen:

```
Usage: USERLIST [fileserver/][name] [/Address|/Object][/Continuous]
```

USERLIST *fileserver/name.* In order to see the list of users on a server, you must first be attached to that server. Otherwise, you'll see the "You are not attached to *servername*" message. When you specify a servername, you must accompany that name with a forward slash (/); otherwise, the USERLIST command will misinterpret the servername as a user name and you'll see the "No users named *servername*" message.

You must include the servername if that server is not the one your current drive is mapped to, for USERLIST defaults to the server that your present directory path is mapped to. And unlike other NetWare commands, you need to go to the drive letter to run USERLIST on that directory path. For example, if drive G: is mapped to NTS3/ BYTE:USERS/TED and drive H: is mapped to ADMIN/SYS:REPORTS, you'll see server NTS3's user listing when you type USERLIST at the G: prompt and server ADMIN's user listing when you type USERLIST at the H: prompt. If you type USERLIST G: <Enter> from the H: prompt, you'll see "No users named G:" for the effort. So in order to see server NTS3's user listing, you must either to go the G: prompt or type USERLIST NTS3/ <Enter>. You'll see something similar to this:

```
User Information for Server NTS3
Connection     User Name      Login Time
-------        ----------     ------------
1              JOHN           9-16-1993 2:50 pm
2              ADAM           9-16-1993 2:51 pm
8              PAM            9-16-1993 2:50 pm
18             THOM           9-19-1993 2:26 pm
20             * TED          9-20-1993 8:49 am
21             MDAY           9-19-1993 1:48 pm
```

The information you see is similar to what you see about yourself when you run the WHOAMI utility, such as connection number, user name, and login time. But with the USERLIST command, you can see the names of all users presently attached to that server. USERLIST's default information includes users' connection numbers, login names, and the time they last logged in. An asterisk (*) appears by your name, showing you which connection number you're using to run the USERLIST command.

You can also see a listing of all the servers you're attached to by using the asterisk wildcard (*) in the servername parameter. For example, to see who is presently attached to any servers you're attached to, type USERLIST */ <Enter> at the network prompt. You'll see a list of all users on all the servers you're presently attached to. When a screen fills with user listings, you'll see the "Press any key to continue ... ('C' for continuous)" prompt at the bottom of your screen. Pressing any key other than the letter "C" will continue the USERLIST display one screenful at a time.

If you don't want the display to stop at every screen, you can add a /C parameter (for "Continuous") and USERLIST will scroll until all the information is shown. The only time you're likely to use the /C parameter is when you want to save the USERLIST information to a file. Otherwise, using the /C parameter means you might miss the user information displayed first and only see the end of the display.

If you're attached to servers NTS3, ADMIN, and PUB, and you only want to see the currently attached users on ADMIN and PUB, you can type USERLIST A*/P*/<Enter> and you'll see a list of users for only those servers whose names begin with the letters "A" and "P." You can also use the question mark wildcard (?) to designate part of the servername (or user name). For example, if you know that the name of one of your attached servers is three characters long and starts with the letter "P," you can type USERLIST P??/ <Enter>. Of course, it would be easier to type WHOAMI and find out the real servername, but you can use question marks if you want to.

USERLIST *[servername/] username.* You can also see if specific users are logged in with USERLIST. For example, suppose you want to send a message to Tim. To see if Tim is attached to any servers you're attached to, type USERLIST */TIM <Enter> at your network prompt. For the servers that Tim has no connection number on, you'll see a "No users named TIM." If you aren't sure of Tim's login name, you can type USERLIST */T* <Enter> at your network prompt, and you'll see if anyone with a login name that begins with the letter "T" is on your servers.

To designate more than one person, type in their names or use the wildcard approach as described above. For example, to see Tim's and Kelly's connection numbers on server NTS3 in order to send them a message, type USERLIST NTS3/TIM NTS3/KELLY <Enter>, and you'll see a listing similar to this one:

```
User Information for Server NTS3
Connection    User Name    Login Time
-------       ----------   ------------
14            TIM          9-16-1993 2:50 pm
21            KELLY        9-16-1993 2:51 pm
```

If you don't designate a server, USERLIST defaults to the server that your present directory path is mapped to. So if you're on drive G: which maps to server NTS3, you can type USERLIST TIM KELLY <Enter>.

USERLIST *[servername/] username* **/A.** The /Address parameter shows the network and node address of the users listed. For example, if you want to see the network and node addresses for Tim and Kelly on default server NTS3, type USERLIST TIM KELLY /A <Enter> and you'll see a listing similar to this one:

```
User Information for Server NTS3
Connection   User Name Network      Node Address   Login Time
-----------  -------- --------      -------        -------
14           TIM       [ BABE88]    [    4C]       9-16-1993 2:50 pm
21           KELLY     [ BABE88]    [ 1B0B02DD]    9-16-1993 2:51 pm
```

Make sure you include a space between the user name and the option /A. For example, USERLIST<space>TIM<space>Kelly<space>/A.

NetWare knows where to send your requests and answers to your requests by using network, node, and socket addresses. With this method, NetWare is able to narrow down your requests to a specific server, and then to send the reply back to the specific workstation. One example that has long been used likens the network/node/socket addressing to someone receiving a package in a business complex.

In the example, the network address is similar to the street where the complex is located. If you're on the wrong street, you won't find the complex's address; similarly, if you're on the wrong network, you won't be able to find the correct workstation or server. The node address serves the same purpose as the complex's address in that it distinguishes the particular complex the package must reach. Also, the node address tells NetWare which server needs to service the request or which workstation the request must return to.

The socket address is similar to the rows of mail slots at the complex—every business in the complex finds correspondence specifically for them. If the package is routed to your mail slot or desk, you handle the correspondence. NetWare is designed so that socket addresses handle specific types of requests, and only those processes handling that type of request pay attention to the correspondence sent to that socket address. Fortunately, NetWare takes care of this for you, so you don't have to know all the particulars of addressing.

So the network address is a number that differentiates a particular network from the other networks on an internetwork. In the example above, both Tim and Kelly are on the network identified as address BABE88. The node address is the station address set on the network interface board to which the network cable connects on the back of each workstation. On some types of boards, the node addresses are preset by the manufacturer. In the above example, the board in Tim's workstation is set as station address 4C, while Kelly's is set as station address 1B0B02DD.

The cable attached to your workstation is your connection to the network. You'll see the network address assigned to your network and the node address set on your network interface board when you run USERLIST /A. When you send a request to the server, the packet information includes your network and node address so the server will know which workstation asked for the information. The server then uses your network and node address to send a reply back to your workstation.

USERLIST *[servername/] username* **/O.** The /Object parameter shows the object type the server has assigned in order to keep better track of users in the bindery. The bindery is a list or database of objects with five fields of information that identify who you are and what you can do on this server. The object type is one of those fields. Along with the object name (your username) and object ID (a number/letter combination), the object type helps to uniquely identify you.

There's quite a list for different object types in the bindery. For example, you're known as a "User" in the "Object Type" field, while print servers are known as "Print Servers" in the "Object Type" field. Other object types include "User Group," "File Server," and "Print Queue." This knowledge won't help you balance the budget or write a better memo, but if you're curious as to the object types you have on the servers you're currently attached to, type USERLIST */* /O <Enter> and you'll see an object type listing of how every connection is known.

Other Information

When supervisors set the network and node addresses during installation, they must first ensure that everyone on the same network has the same network address. Otherwise, workstations won't receive answers to their server requests. Supervisors must also make certain that no two workstations on the same network have the same node address. In most cases, duplicate node addresses prevent all of the workstations from accessing the server.

Related Commands

Be sure to first ATTACH to the servers whose user listings you want to see. (See the "ATTACH" subheading under the "Server Access Utilities" section.) You can see a list of the users defined on your network through the "User Information" option in SYSCON (see "The SYSCON Utility" heading in Chapter 2), but that doesn't tell you if they're currently logged in to the server. And if you like menus more than command-line utilities, SESSION's "User List" option will also show you what you can see using USERLIST.

WHOAMI

The WHOAMI utility offers you a quick picture of the servers you're attached to, the directories you have rights in, your effective rights in those directories, and the groups you belong to. Some of this information is covered in the SYSCON, RIGHTS, and LOGOUT utilities, but seeing this information all laid out at once can give you a good idea of what you can and can't do on a particular server.

Using the WHOAMI Utility

Here's a list of WHOAMI's parameters, their functions, and an explanation of how to use them. If you can't remember the proper syntax for WHOAMI, type WHOAMI /H <Enter> and you'll see the syntax help screen:

```
USAGE: WHOAMI [Server] [/Security] [/Groups] [/WorkGroups]
[/Rights] [/SYstem] [/Object] [/All] [/Continuous]
```

WHOAMI *Server.* When you want to see your login name, the servers you're attached to, and the time you logged in, you can run WHOAMI. When you want to see that information for only one server you're attached to, such as server ADMIN, type WHOAMI ADMIN <Enter> and you'll see something similar to this:

```
G:\USERS\TED > whoami admin

You are user TED attached to server ADMIN connection 20.
Server ADMIN is running NetWare 3.11(250 user).
Login Time: Thursday September 16, 1993 1:48 pm
```

The first line tells you that you're user TED connected to server ADMIN using connection number 20. The second line tells you which version of NetWare the server is running. The last line shows the time you logged in or attached to the server.

WHOAMI is similar to LOGOUT in that they both display the same type of information. About the only difference is that LOGOUT also shows your logout times beneath the login times.

When you're attached to more than one server and you type WHOAMI, you'll see who you are on all those servers. The screen can hold up to six sets of server attachment information (depending on your NetWare version) and will scroll past the initial attachment information if you have more than six attachments. However, you can specify servers in the WHOAMI utility by servername.

277

WHOAMI *Server /Options.* To specify a particular server, simply type WHOAMI *servername* <Enter> and you'll see that information. For example, if you know you're attached to server CORP and you want to see your connection number, type WHOAMI CORP <Enter> and you'll see the connection number for that server. When you want to see the options for all the servers you're attached to, don't specify any server in the WHOAMI command.

With NetWare 3.1x, WHOAMI comes with eight options that allow you to view: your security equivalences (/Security), the groups you belong to (/Group), whether you are a workgroup manager (/Workgroup) or an object supervisor (/Object), your effective rights (/Rights), general system information (/SYstem), or all of the above (/All). You can also use /Continuous to have NetWare scroll through the screen information. You can type out the entire parameter name, or you can abbreviate it by just typing the capitalized letters shown in the parameters. For example, if you just want to see which groups you belong to on a particular server (such as PUB), you can type WHOAMI PUB /G <Enter> and see information similar to this:

```
G:\USERS\TED > whoami pub /g

You are user TED attached to server PUB connection 20.
Server PUB is running NetWare 3.11(250 user).
Login Time: Thursday September 16, 1993 1:48 pm
You are a member of the following Groups:
    EVERYONE
    TEST1
    NTJ
```

If you're curious as to which users and groups you are security equivalent to on a server (such as PUB), type WHOAMI PUB /S <Enter> and see information similar to this:

```
G:\USERS\TED > whoami pub /s

You are user TED attached to server PUB connection 20.
Server PUB is running NetWare 3.11(250 user).
Login Time: Thursday September 16, 1993 1:49 pm
You are security equivalent to the following:
    EVERYONE (group)
    TEST1 (group)
    NTJ (group)
```

278

FRANK (user)

If you recall, NetWare 3.11 offers two added "helps" to the manager and operator list: *workgroup manager* and *object manager* or *supervisor*. Workgroup managers can create new users and groups, as well as manage users and groups assigned to them. Object managers can't create users or groups, but they can manage users and groups assigned to them. To see whether you're a workgroup manager and who you manage as an object supervisor on a server (such as PUB), type WHOAMI PUB /W /O <Enter> and see information similar to this:

```
G:\USERS\TED > whoami pub /w /o

You are user TED attached to server PUB connection 20.
Server PUB is running NetWare 3.12(250 user).
You are a workgroup manager.
You are Object Supervisor over Frank
Login Time: Thursday September 16, 1993 1:49 pm
```

If you're not a workgroup manager or an object supervisor, you'll just see what you normally see when you type WHOAMI.

When you want to see what your effective rights are in the directories on a server (such as PUB), you can type WHOAMI PUB /R <Enter> and see information similar to this:

```
G:\USERS\TED > whoami pub /r

You are user TED attached to server PUB connection 20.
Server PUB is running NetWare 3.11(250 user).
Login Time: Thursday September 16, 1993 1:49 pm
You have the following effective rights:
[        ] SYS:
[ WC     ] SYS:MAIL
[RWCEMF  ] SYS:MAIL/12005D
[R F     ] SYS:PUBLIC
[RWCEMF  ] SYS:PUBLIC/UTIL
[R F     ] SYS:APPS/WP51
[RWCEMF  ] SYS:APPS/DATA
[RWCEMF  ] SYS:APPS/WIZ
[RWCEMF  ] SYS:APPS/MHS/SW
```

```
[ RWC F   ] SYS:APPS/MHS/MAIL
[ RW  F   ] SYS:APPS/MHS/MAIL/PUBLIC
[ RWCEMF  ] SYS:GAMES
[ RWCEMFA ] SYS:PERSONAL/TED
[ RWCEMF  ] SYS:PERSONAL/RACHEL
[ F       ] SYS:POSTMARK/POSTMARK
[ WC F    ] SYS:POSTMARK/MAIL/USERS/TBEARA
[ R F     ] SYS:POSTMARK/POSTMARK/EXE
[ WC F    ] SYS:POSTMARK/POSTMARK/BOX
```

Your trustee rights are inherited down the directory structure until they are explicitly redefined at some lower directory level. When you run WHOAMI/R, you see your rights assigned only for those directories that have different explicit rights. For example, the USERS/TED/ELSIE directory has different rights than the USERS/TED directory, so you see both directories listed.

The /SYstem option gives you the same general information that you see when you type WHOAMI without any options, so there's little need to use the /SY option. But if you want to see all of these options together on one screen, you can use the WHOAMI /A option. You'll see something similar to the following:

```
You are user TED attached to server PUB connection 20.
Server PUB is running NetWare 3.11(250 user).
You are a workgroup manager.
You are Object Supervisor over Frank
Login Time: Thursday September 16, 1993 1:49 pm
You are security equivalent to the following:
     EVERYONE (Group)
     WP51 (Group)
     GAMES (Group)
     COMM (Group)
You are a member of the following groups:
     EVERYONE
     WP51
     GAMES
     COMM
[         ] SYS:
[ WC      ] SYS:MAIL
[ RWCEMF  ] SYS:MAIL/12005D
[ R F     ] SYS:PUBLIC
```

```
[ RWCEMF  ] SYS:PUBLIC/UTIL
[ R  F    ] SYS:APPS/WP51
[ RWCEMF  ] SYS:APPS/DATA
[ RWCEMF  ] SYS:APPS/WIZ
[ RWCEMF  ] SYS:APPS/MHS/SW
[ RWC F   ] SYS:APPS/MHS/MAIL
[ RW  F   ] SYS:APPS/MHS/MAIL/PUBLIC
[ RWCEMF  ] SYS:GAMES
[ RWCEMFA ] SYS:PERSONAL/TED
[ RWCEMF  ] SYS:PERSONAL/RACHEL
[ F       ] SYS:POSTMARK/POSTMARK
[ WC F    ] SYS:POSTMARK/POSTMARK/MAIL/USERS/TBEARA
[ R  F    ] SYS:POSTMARK/POSTMARK/EXE
[ WC F    ] SYS:POSTMARK/POSTMARK/BOX
Server PUB is not in a Domain.
```

If the information fills more than one screen, you'll need to press a key to see the next screenful, or you can press C for continuous scrolling without pressing a key after every screenful. Or you can simply use the /C option to continually scroll the information. If you want to make a record of your capabilities, you can save the information you see in WHOAMI /A by redirecting what normally scrolls on the monitor screen to a file. To do this, type WHOAMI /A >*filename* <Enter> in a directory in which you have sufficient rights to create a file. You can then print the file. For example, if the file is called EVRYTHNG, you can type NPRINT EVRYTHNG Q=*queuename* <Enter> and you'll have a running record of what you can and can't do on all the servers you're currently attached to. This information can be very handy when you try to do something but can't seem to make it happen.

Other Information

Depending on your NetWare version, you may see [ALL] instead of [SRWCEMFA] when WHOAMI designates your effective rights in a given directory. You may also be surprised by the rights you have in certain directories. This is most likely due to inherited rights and security equivalences. For example, if you were made security equivalent to a supervisor, you would see that you have [ALL] or [SRWCEMFA] rights to the volumes:

```
You have the following effective rights: [ALL] PUB/SYS: [ALL]
PUB/BYTE:
```

Related Commands

You can see your effective rights in a directory through the SESSION utility (see "The SESSION Utility" heading in Chapter 2) or through the RIGHTS and NDIR command-line utilities. (See the next section.) You can see your trustee assignments and security equivalences through the SYSCON utility, and you can also see which groups you belong to in SYSCON (see "The SYSCON Utility" heading in Chapter 2). The LOGOUT command gives you information similar to the initial information you see when you just type WHOAMI <Enter>, but, of course, it logs you out of all servers.

Directory and File Management Utilities

NetWare has a number of utilities to help you get around in its directory structure. This book will refer to them as the Directory and File Management Utilities. These utilities include CHKDIR, CHKVOL, LISTDIR, NCOPY, NDIR, RENDIR, PURGE, and SALVAGE.

CHKDIR displays information on your directory space limitations. CHKVOL displays information about network volumes. LISTDIR and RENDIR allow you to list and rename directories. NCOPY is a network file copy command, and NDIR is a network directory and file-listing utility. PURGE deletes discarded files that you'll never need to recover.

CHKDIR

CHKDIR shows you the number of bytes remaining for this directory's use. These statistics include the maximum size of your volume in kilobytes, the number of kilobytes taken up by files, the number of kilobytes available on the volume; information you can also see in CHKVOL. CHKDIR also shows the maximum space in kilobytes you have available if your supervisor has placed a limit on the amount of space you can use. It shows you how much of that space you have used for files, and how much remains. It then lists the space in use by your current directory.

You'll most likely use the CHKDIR utility when you know you have a limit on your disk space and you're getting error messages saying you can't create a file or that there's no available space on the volume.

Using the CHKDIR Parameter

CHKDIR has one parameter, Path, that lets you specify a different directory to look at. For example, if you want to see the limits on PERSONAL\BILL\TEST, you can type

CHKDIR UP\SYS:PERSONAL\BILL\TEST <Enter>. You can type CHKDIR TEST if you are already at the PERSONAL\BILL directory. You can't use wildcards to specify all the subdirectories, you must give a specific path for each directory or change to that directory and then type CHKDIR <Enter>.

CHKDIR [path]. Since supervisors can limit the amount of disk space you can have on a given volume, you can use CHKDIR to see how much of that disk space you're using. In your present directory, type CHKDIR <Enter>. You'll see information like this:

```
Directory Space Limitation Information for:
UP/SYS:PERSONAL\BILL

Maximum        In Use       Available
71,300 K       66,536 K     4,764 K      Volume Size
 5,000 K        3,573 K     1,427 K      User Volume Limit
                3,573 K     1,427 K      \PERSONAL\BILL
```

The first line tells you which directory you are looking at. The second line gives the actual size of the volume in kilobytes, how much is in use by files, and what is available for new files. The third line shows you any limits set by the supervisor for you as a user, and how much of that space remains. The bottom line shows you how much space your current directory takes, and how much space remains available of your user limit or for the directory limit. If your supervisor has redefined that amount of space you're allowed to access, either as a user or for that directory, you'll see a difference between the number of kilobytes available on the volume and the number of kilobytes available to you.

Related Commands

You can use CHKVOL to see any limit placed on your user account by the supervisor for this volume. However, CHKVOL only shows you that limit, not any for specific directories.

The supervisor uses DSPACE to set limits on how much space any of your directories can take. You can also check your directory limits using DSPACE (see "The DSPACE Utility" heading in Chapter 2). Type DSPACE <Enter>, then select the Directory Restrictions option. Type in the path you want to check, such as UP/SYS:PERSONAL/BILL <Enter>, or you can use the backspace key to erase the current path and use the INS key to select a new one.

CHKVOL

While DOS's CHKDSK shows the number of bytes left on local drives, the CHKVOL utility displays the statistics of a designated NetWare volume. These statistics include the volume space displayed in kilobytes, the number of kilobytes taken up by files, the number of kilobytes available on the volume, the disk space that's available to you, and the number of directory entries left. CHKVOL also lets you look at the volume statistics for all the servers you're attached to.

You're most likely to use the CHKVOL utility when you're getting error messages saying you can't create a file or that there's no available space on the volume. CHKVOL is also a quick way to see how much volume space is left on SYS: (where all printing jobs are stored) if you're having problems printing because volume SYS: is out of space.

Using CHKVOL's Parameters

CHKVOL [path]. If you can't remember the proper syntax for CHVOL, type CHKVOL /H <Enter> and you'll see the syntax help screen:

```
USAGE:  CHKVOL [path] [/Continuous]
```

CHKVOL. Since supervisors can limit the amount of disk space you can have on a given volume, you can use CHKVOL to see how much of that disk space you're using. In your present directory, type CHKVOL <Enter>. You'll see information that looks like this:

```
Statistics for fixed volume GHOST/SYS:

Total volume space:                     58,092 K Bytes
Space used by files:                    42,680 K Bytes
Space in use by deleted files:          13,616 K Bytes
Space available from deleted files:     13,616 K Bytes
Space remaining on volume:              15,412 K Bytes
Space available to ED:                  15,412 K Bytes
```

The first line tells you which server and volume you're looking at. The second line gives the actual size of the volume in kilobytes. The third line shows how much space files collectively take of the volume in kilobytes. The fourth line shows how many kilobytes are taken up by deleted files. (NetWare 3.1x does not record over deleted files until it runs out of unrecorded space on the volume. This allows you to recover files much later after the deletion.) The fifth line shows you the space you can recover from the deleted files, which should usually be the same amount as in the line above. It could be different, however, if your supervisor has used the SET utility to hold deleted files for a period of time so users can recover them without the server deleting them if it needs the space. The sixth line shows how many kilobytes are still available on the volume. The last line shows you how many of those kilobytes are available to you as a user. If your supervisor has redefined the amount of disk space you're allowed to access, you'll see a difference between the number of kilobytes available on the volume and the number of kilobytes available to you.

CHKVOL has two parameters to designate which volumes you wish to look at: volume and drive path. CHKVOL also has a /C parameter you can use to scroll continuously through the volume listings. (This /C parameter works in some versions of CHKVOL and not in others.)

CHKVOL *volume.* If you know which volume you wish to look at, type CHKVOL *servername/*, followed by the volume name (for example, CHKVOL ADMIN/SYS) and press <Enter>. You can also use the asterisk wildcard to designate all volumes; to view all the volumes on server ADMIN, type CHKVOL ADMIN/* <Enter>.

CHKVOL *drive path.* You can look at the volumes that are a part of your drive mappings by designating the drive letter: for example, CHKVOL G. You can also see multiple volume listings by typing in multiple drive letters. For example, if you map drive G: to ADMIN/SYS:REPORTS/AUG and drive J: to PUB/BYTE:USERS/TED, type CHKVOL J <Enter> to see the statistics for server PUB's BYTE volume. Or you can type CHKVOL G J <Enter> to see PUB's BYTE volume and ADMIN's SYS volume. You can also use the question mark (?) wildcard to replace a single character. For example, if you want to see the statistics of all defined volumes that you have drive mappings to, you can type CHKVOL ? <Enter>.

CHKVOL is not limited by security, so you can see information on any volume to any server you're attached or logged in to. You can also use wildcards such as the asterisk (*) to designate the servername or volume. Suppose you're attached to three different servers—PUB, ADMIN, and R&D—and you want to see all the volumes on all three servers. Use the asterisk (*) to designate both the servers and the volumes by typing CHKVOL */* <Enter> at the network prompt.

If you use just one asterisk—for example, CHKVOL * <Enter>— you'll see all the volumes on the server where the directory you're in is located. So if you're attached to more than one server and you have at least one drive mapped on each of the servers, you can use the drive path parameter to see the volumes on each server.

You can also use the question mark wildcard to mark one character in volume or servernames, but since you can run the MAP command to see which servers and volumes you have drives mapped to, the usefulness of the question mark wildcard is limited.

If you're attached to three servers that have more than one volume per server and you type CHKVOL */*, you'll find that the volume information will scroll past on the screen, displaying only the last three statistic groups. You can get around this in two ways. You can look at each server one at a time by typing CHKVOL PUB/* <Enter> at the network prompt, and then do the same for the other servers. Or you can use DOS's redirection character (>) to save to a file the information shown on the screen.

For example, to save all the volume statistics on those three servers to a file named VOLUME, type CHKVOL */* > VOLUME <Enter> at the network prompt. The volume information will be saved to the VOLUME file instead of displaying on the screen. Then you can go into that file from any ASCII editor or word processor to look at the information.

You can also print the file by first defining which printer you want to print it out for you and then sending the job to that printer's print queue. For example, to have the VOLUME file printed by printer 0, serviced by the queue ADMIN-LJII, type NPRINT VOLUME Q=ADMIN-LJII <Enter>; your job will print at that printer. (For a full explanation of NPRINT, see "Using the NPRINT Command" heading in Chapter 4.)

As you can see, this is where the Raymond J. Johnson, Jr., syndrome begins to play a big role. ("You can call me Ray, or you can call me Jay, or you can call me R.J., or you can call me J.J. ...", ad nauseam.) So tinker a bit and you will find other combinations as well.

CHKVOL *Drive path* **/C.** As I explained earlier, the /C parameter allows the volume information to continuously scroll on the screen without pausing when the screen is full. (The /C parameter works in some releases of CHKVOL while not in others.) If you want to have the volume information scroll across the screen, type CHKVOL */* /C <Enter>. If you want to ensure that all the information is saved to a file, as I explained in the above example, type CHKVOL */* /C > VOLUME <Enter>. You can then use NPRINT to print out the file.

Related Commands

You can use the MAP command to see which servers and volumes you have drives mapped to. You can also use the WHOAMI command to see all the servers you're presently attached to. You can see similar information about a volume in the FILER utility. From the FILER "Available Topics" window, press <PgDn> to select the "Volume Information" option and press <Enter>. However, FILER's volume information shows only your present volume; you have to type in a different directory path to see other volumes.

LISTDIR

The LISTDIR utility does exactly what its name implies: it lists the subdirectories under the directory you're presently in. LISTDIR also displays the inherited rights mask for the listed subdirectories as well as your effective rights to those subdirectories. This way, you can see if your effective rights are what they are because of the inherited rights mask or because of a trustee assignment. You can also see the subdirectory's creation date and time. This information is very similar to the information you see in the "Directory Contents" window of the FILER utility in Chapter 2.

Using the LISTDIR Command

Here's a list of LISTDIR's parameters, their functions, and how to use them. If you can't remember the proper syntax for LISTDIR, type LISTDIR /H <Enter> and you'll see the syntax help screen:

```
USAGE: LISTDIR [DirectoryPath [/Option ... Option]]
     Option: Rights, Effective rights, Date/Time, Subdirectory or All
```

LISTDIR DirectoryPath /Options.

If you're at the volume level (SYS:, for example) and you have Read and File Scan rights, you'll see a listing of all the directories under that volume's root directory. Or if you run LISTDIR in your own personal directory, you'll see all your subdirectories, like this:

```
F:\USERS\TED>listdir

The Subdirectories of PUB/BYTE:USERS/TED/
Directory
-----------------------------------------------
->UTIL
->ST
->COLUMNS
->CAD
->TURBOC
5 subdirectories found
```

287

When you use the LISTDIR command, you can write out the entire directory path, use the drive letter, or simply type LISTDIR <Enter> in the directory you're currently in. For example, if you're in the NTS3\VOL1:USERS\TED\TEAM directory and you want to see the subdirectories beneath that directory, type LISTDIR NTS3\VOL1:USERS\TED\TEAM <Enter>. If NTS3\VOL1: is your default server and volume, you can type LISTDIR \USERS\TED\TEAM <Enter>. If the NTS3\VOL1:USERS\TED\TEAM directory is mapped to drive G:, you can type LISTDIR G: <Enter>. If you're in the G: directory, simply type LISTDIR <Enter>. When you want to see the subdirectories in one of the subdirectories beneath the directory you're presently in, you can type LISTDIR *subdirectory name* <Enter>.

LISTDIR comes with five listed options, "/Rights," "/Effective rights," "/Date and Time," "/Subdirectory," "/All," and one standard option, "/C," for continuous scrolling. The capitalized letters on the parameter are the abbreviated letters you can use instead of typing out the entire parameter. If you prefer, of course, you can type out the entire parameter. For NetWare 2.2 and above, some of you may recognize the addition of the forward slash (/) to invoke the options; LISTDIR is one of the commands that needs the forward slash to invoke options. Here's what each option means.

LISTDIR /Rights. You can use the /Rights option when you want to see what rights you have in a directory (your directory rights, or inherited rights mask). If you recall from the discussion of security rights in the Introduction, you must pass through three levels of security to access files and applications in NetWare: permission to access the server through passwords, permission to access a directory through the basic security rights (trustee assignments and directory rights), and permission to access a file through file flags.

What you see with the /R option is your directory and subdirectories' inherited rights mask. For example, to see your directory and subdirectory rights, type LISTDIR /S /R at the network prompt, and you'll see something like this:

```
Inherited        Directory
-------------------------------
[ RWCEMFA ]  -   ELSIE
[ RWCEMFA ]  -   NEWT
[ RWCEMFA ]  -   MAY
[ RWCEMFA ]  -   JUNE
[ RWCEMFA ]  -   NEWT2
[ RWCEMFA ]  -   TIM
6 subdirectories found
```

LISTDIR /Effective rights. You can use the /Effective rights option when you want to see what you can effectively perform in a directory. If you recall from the discussion of security rights in the Introduction, the combination of your trustee assignments being filtered through rights given at the directory level (inherited rights mask) determine what you can effectively perform in a directory—your effective rights. (For a more in-depth look at security, see "Basic Security Rights" in the Introduction.)

What you see with the /E option is your directory and subdirectories' effective rights. For example, to see your directory and subdirectory rights, type LISTDIR /S /E at the network prompt, and you'll see something like this:

```
C:\USERS\TED >listdir /e /s

The subdirectory structure of PUB/BYTE:USERS/TED/
Effective        Directory
--------------------------------
[ RWCEMFA ]  -   ELSIE
[ RWCEMFA ]  -   NEWT
[ RWCEMFA ]  -   MAY
[ RWCEMFA ]  -   JUNE
[ RWCEMFA ]  -   NEWT2
[ RWCEMFA ]  -   TIM
6 subdirectories found
```

One of the best ways to use LISTDIR is to run it using both the /R and /E options. That way, you can see if the rights you have in a directory are from your trustee assignments or from the inherited rights mask. This can help diagnose printing or copying problems you may be having.

LISTDIR /Date and Time. Either of the Date and Time parameters prints on your screen the date and time that your directories and subdirectories were created, or whatever date and time your supervisor has set for your directories. To use this parameter, type LISTDIR /D <Enter> or LISTDIR /T <Enter> at the network prompt. You'll see something similar to this:

```
Subdirectories of PUB/BYTE:USERS/TED/
Date     Time     Directory
--------------------------------
```

```
5-08-92  4:07p    -> ELSIE
2-19-92  5:27p    -> NEWT
3-13-92  12:05p   -> MAY
3-13-92  12:05p   -> JUNE
9-19-91  7:49a    -> NEWT2
4-30-92  6:00p    -> TIM
6 directories found
```

LISTDIR /Subdirectory. The /Subdirectory option allows you to see not only the subdirectories under your current directory, but the subdirectories under those directories as well. For example, if you're in your USERS\TED directory and you want to see the entire subdirectory tree, type LISTDIR /S <Enter> at the network prompt. You'll see a screen similar to this one:

```
The Subdirectory structure of PUB/BYTE:USERS/TED/ Directory
--------------------------------
-> ELSIE
-> NEWT
-> MAY
-> JUNE
-> NEWT2
-> TIM
6 subdirectories found
```

LISTDIR /All. If you want to see all the parameters that LISTDIR offers, use /A. For example, to see all your subdirectories' inherited rights masks and their creation date and time, type LISTDIR /A <Enter> and you'll see something like this:

```
C:\USERS\TED >listdir /a
The subdirectory structure of PUB/BYTE:USERS/TED/
Date      Time      Inherited    Effective    Directory
-----------------------------------------------------
5-08-92  4:07p    [ RWCEMFA]   [ RWCEMFA]   ->ELSIE
2-19-92  5:27p    [ RWCEMFA]   [ RWCEMFA]   ->NEWT
3-13-92  12:05p   [ RWCEMFA]   [ RWCEMFA]   ->MAY
3-13-92  12:05p   [ RWCEMFA]   [ RWCEMFA]   ->JUNE
9-19-91  7:49a    [ RWCEMFA]   [ RWCEMFA]   ->NEWT2
4-30-92  6:00p    [ RWCEMFA]   [ RWCEMFA]   ->TIM
6 subdirectories found
```

LISTDIR /C. The /C parameter allows the information to continuously scroll by on the screen without pausing when the screen is full. If directory information you want to see is at the bottom of the screen and you want to have the directory information scroll across the screen, type LISTDIR /A /C <Enter>.

NCOPY

The NCOPY utility is a network version of the DOS COPY command that allows you to copy files. NCOPY works like the DOS COPY command; however, NCOPY performs a volume-to-volume copy on the server itself, without sending the data to the workstation and then back to the server.

For example, if you're copying a 100KB file using DOS, DOS reads the 100KB file from the server and then writes the file back to the server over the network. NCOPY sends a command that says, "Copy this file from this directory to that directory," and the server copies the file without further involving the workstation. This method can be faster than using COPY and doesn't tie up your network as much. Of course, server-to-server copies will use the network, but the procedure still doesn't involve the workstation.

NCOPY also has a verification flag (/V) that you can use to verify the file copy. NCOPY preserves file attribute flags as you copy files from one directory to another on the same server. However, if you copy files from a NetWare 2.2 server to a NetWare 3.1x server, file attributes will go through an adjustment. For example, suppose you copy the OVER.ALL file with Indexed, Transactional, Read Audit, and Write Audit attribute flags from a NetWare 2.2 directory to a NetWare 3.11 directory. Once the file is copied, the Indexed flag is dropped and the Read and Write Audit flags change to Delete Inhibit and Rename Inhibit. When using NCOPY with NetWare 3.1x, the Purge file attribute won't be preserved on files copied to their destination. You may have other results with your copy endeavors.

You must be logged in or attached to a server in order to copy a file to or from that server's directory. To copy a file from a directory, you must have at least Read and File Scan rights in the directory you're copying from, and you must have at least Create, Write, Erase, File Scan, and Modify rights in the directory you're copying to, even if the file already exists in the directory you're copying to.

Using the NCOPY Utility

NCOPY *directory path/filename(s)* **TO** *directory path/filename(s).* When you copy a file, you can specify the filename if you're in the directory containing the file. For example, if you're in directory G: containing the REPORTS.DAT file, and you want to copy the file to the SYS:REPORTS\AUG directory, type NCOPY REPORTS.DAT SYS:REPORTS\AUG <Enter>. If the SYS:REPORTS\AUG directory is mapped to H:, type NCOPY REPORTS.DAT H: <Enter>. You'll see the source and destination of the file as well as the name(s) of the file(s) being copied:

```
From PUB/BYTE:USERS/TED/REPORTS
To PUB/SYS:REPORTS/AUG
    REPORTS.DAT to REPORTS.DAT
1 file copied.
```

When you're attached to two servers, you can copy files between the servers by mapping drives to the two directories. For example, if you're attached to server PUB and you want to copy the REP.DAT file from the PUB\BYTE:USERS \TED\REPORTS directory to the NTS3\SYS:REPORT92 directory, type NCOPY PUB\BYTE:USERS\TED\REPORTS\REP.DAT NTS3\SYS:REPORT92 <Enter>. If the PUB\BYTE:USERS\TED\REPORTS directory is mapped to drive G: and the NTS3\SYS:REPORT92 directory is mapped to H:, type NCOPY G:REP.DAT H: <Enter>.

If you're in the USERS\TED\REPORTS directory (mapped to G:) and you want to copy the TEST.FIL file from the NTS3\SYS:REPORT92 directory (mapped to H:), type NCOPY H:TEST.FIL <Enter>. NCOPY will copy the file to your present directory, G:. If you're in the G: directory and you want to copy the TEST.FIL file from the NTS3\SYS:REPORT92 directory (mapped to H:) to the USERS\TED\REPORTS\ST directory (mapped to K:), type NCOPY H:TEST.FIL K: <Enter>.

You can also copy files from part of a directory path to other parts of the directory path. For example, if you're in the G: directory that is mapped to PUB\BYTE:USERS \TED\REPORTS and you want to copy the *.DAT files from directory TED to the REPORTS directory, type NCOPY ..*.DAT <Enter>. This says "Copy files with .DAT extension from the directory above the REPORTS directory (..) to the REPORTS directory." You can copy the *.DAT files from the TED directory to the REPORTS\AUG directory by going to the TED directory and typing NCOPY *.DAT REPORTS\AUG <Enter>.

Copying to subdirectories can be a source of confusion if not performed correctly. Suppose you're in directory G: that is mapped to PUB\BYTE:USERS \TED\REPORTS containing the REP.DAT file. Suppose also that you want to copy the file to the JAN directory beneath the SYS:REPORTS directory on drive H:. To do this, you can go to the H: directory (H: <Enter>) and type CD JAN <Enter>. Or, from the G: directory, you can type CD H:JAN <Enter>. Then type MAP H: <Enter> to make sure that drive H: is at the JAN directory. Either way, make sure you're in the G: directory and type NCOPY REP.DAT H: <Enter>.

That's the long way to copy things. Let's further suppose that the SYS:REPORTS directory on drive H: has FEB and MARCH directories directly beneath it. To copy the REP.DAT file into those subdirectories without going through this kind of gyration, you can instead use some copy shortcuts. for example, if you're still in G: and H: is still mapped to SYS:REPORTS\JAN, from the G: directory, type CD H:.. <Enter>, and drive H: will be at the SYS:REPORTS directory. You can then type NCOPY REP.DAT H:FEB <Enter>, followed by NCOPY REP.DAT H:MARCH <Enter>.

If you want to rename the REP.DAT file to REP.FEB for the FEB directory, you can type NCOPY REP.DAT H:FEB\REP.FEB <Enter>. This says "Copy the REP.DAT file to the FEB subdirectory beneath the H: directory path and call the file REP.FEB."

The subdirectory name you specify must be placed directly against the drive letter: for example, NCOPY *.DAT H:JAN <Enter>. NetWare first looks for a directory by the name you specify. If it can't find a directory by that name, NetWare will create a file by that name and copy the contents of REPORTS.DAT into it. Working from the above example, if you misspell MARCH and type NCOPY REPORTS.DAT H:MRACH <Enter>, you'll find a MRACH file in the SYS:REPORTS directory. If the subdirectory isn't directly beneath the directory you specified, you'll end up with a file by that name.

You can also copy files up the directory tree and to other subdirectories. For example, if you're in the PUB\BYTE:USERS\TED\REPORTS\AUG directory and you want to copy the *.DAT files to the PUB\BYTE:USERS\TED\REPORT92 directory, you can type NCOPY *.DAT ...\REPORT92 <Enter>. This says "Copy files with .DAT extension from the REPORTS\AUG directory up two directories to TED (...) and then to the REPORT92 directory (\REPORT92) beneath the TED directory."

This may sound confusing, but with a little practice you, too, can perform all sorts of copy shortcuts. If the shortcuts are confusing, map a drive to the directory you wish to copy from (such as G:) and copy to (such as H:) and perform NCOPY G:*.DAT H: <Enter>.

NCOPY *directory path\filename(s)* **TO** *directory path\filename* **/Options.** NetWare 3.1x comes with a number of new options for NCOPY. Many of these options bring NCOPY up to the functionality of DOS's XCOPY. If you can't remember the proper syntax for NCOPY, type NCOPY /H <Enter> and you'll see the syntax help screen:

```
Usage: NCOPY [path] [[TO] path] [option]
```

```
Options /s    copy subdirectories
        /s/e  copy subdirectories, including empty directories.
        /f    copy sparse files.
        /i    inform when non-DOS file information will be lost.
        /c    copy only DOS information.
        /a    copy files with archive bit set.
        /m    copy files with archive bit set clear the bit.
        /v    verify with a read after every write.
        /h (/?) display this usage message.
```

Here's a list of NCOPY's options and a description of what you can do with each of them.

/Subdirectories. Use the /S option when you want to copy all the subdirectories beneath the directory you're in. Or if you want to copy files with the same extension to directories and accompanying subdirectories, use the /S option. For example, if you're in the USERS\TED directory and want to copy all the *.BAT files in that directory and all your subdirectories to a floppy disk, you can type NCOPY *.BAT A: /S <Enter>. Note that when you use the /S option, NCOPY transfers the subdirectory structure to where you are copying the files.

/Empty subdirectories (/S/E). To preserve your entire structure, including empty directories, use the /S/E option. For example, if you move to another server and you want to keep your entire directory structure intact, you can create a matching home directory, such as NTS3/VOL1:PERSONAL\TED, on drive H:, then go to your home directory (ADMIN\SYS:USERS\TED on drive G:) and type NCOPY *.* H: /S/E/V <Enter>. NCOPY then copies over the files and their respective subdirectories to directory TED on drive H:.

/Force sparse files. Sparse files are files that may have some text, but for the most part are filled with empty blocks. Sparse files create the appearance of being large and are used mainly for testing purposes. Since NetWare ignores such files because it doesn't want to waste disk space, you can use the /F option to force NetWare to copy sparse files from one location to another.

/Copy. NetWare works to preserve file attributes and name space information when it copies files. Name space information applies mainly to an OS/2's and Macintosh's ability to have filenames longer than DOS convention (8 characters .(dot) 3 characters). If you're copying files to another NetWare 3.1x server or to an OS/2 or Macintosh workstation that can handle extended naming conventions and file attributes, don't add this option. Add the /C option only when you want to copy files without preserving naming conventions or extended file attributes.

294

/Inform. The /Inform option warns you that extended attributes and name space information were not copied to the specified server or hard disk. Use this option when you're copying files with OS/2's or Macintosh's extended attributes and name spacing scheme and you want to be warned if the extras are not copied as well.

/Archive and /Modify. You can use NCOPY to only copy those files that have their Archived bit set, and these two options will either leave the Archived bit set or clear the bit. Using the /A option ensures that only files with their Archived bit set are copied to the destination directory, and that the Archived bit on the source file remains intact.

For example, if you want to perform a quick-and-dirty backup of *.DAT files you've been working on lately in your present directory and subdirectories, but you also want the *.DAT files to be backed up by the network's regular backup procedure, go to the directory containing the *.DAT files and type NCOPY *.DAT A: /A/S <Enter>. Be sure to put a space between the destination directory and the options. This way, you get a copy of the last files you've been working on while still letting the network's backup set the Archived bit after the procedure has made a copy of the file.

With the /Modify option, the Archived bit on the source file will be cleared. This means the network's regular backup procedure won't make a copy of the file if that procedure only backs up files with the Archived bit set. For this reason, I strongly suggest that you stay away from the /M option, using the /A option instead when making individual backups of recent files.

/Verify. The verify command ensures that the file you're creating or modifying is identical to the file you copied from. NCOPY performs a read-after-write to verify that the files are the same. For example, if you want to verify that you copied the *.DAT files from G: to H:, type NCOPY G:*.DAT H: /V <Enter>. You will see nothing different on the screen, but if the file did not copy exactly, you'll receive an error message (which I couldn't reproduce).

Using Wildcards

You can use wildcards in filenames when using the NCOPY command. Through wildcards, you can copy a number of files at the same time. For example, if you have a number of files with an RPT extension (NEW.RPT, TIMES.RPT, and so forth) and you want to copy all of them from your J: drive to your K: drive, type NCOPY J:*.RPT K: <Enter>. All files with the RPT extension from the J: directory path will be copied to the K: directory path.

The above also applies to the question mark (?) wildcard. Each question mark wildcard takes the place of one character in a filename. For example, if you have several files but want to copy only three—GLSYS.FDM, DLSYS.FED, and SLSYS.FDM—type NCOPY J:??SYS*.* K: <Enter>. NCOPY will copy only the files with that pattern.

NCOPY Quirks

You need to remember two things or you'll end up copying to places you never dreamed of. The first thing is that a backslash (\) can often mean "copy this file at the root." For example, if you're in G: directory and you want to copy the REP.DAT file to the JAN subdirectory under SYS:REPORTS directory path on H:, don't use a backslash to designate the subdirectory, such as NCOPY REP.DAT H:\JAN <Enter>. In DOS, this is perfectly fine; however, in NetWare, this says "Copy the REP.DAT file to the root directory named JAN, and if there isn't a root directory by that name, rename the REP.DAT file to JAN and place it at the root." So if you have rights at the root directory, you end up with a JAN file; if you don't have enough rights, you'll see "You do not have rights to copy files to the destination directory."

The correct way to perform the above copy is to type NCOPY REP.DAT H:JAN <Enter>. This will copy the file to the JAN subdirectory down the H: directory path. Then if you want to rename the file to REP.JAN, you can then use the backslash to designate this operation as a rename by typing NCOPY REP.DAT H:JAN\REP.JAN <Enter>. But this will work only if you don't have a directory by that name. For example, if you have a REP.JAN subdirectory beneath the JAN directory, NCOPY will simply copy the REP.DAT file to the REP.JAN subdirectory instead of to a file by that name. So the second key is not to give files the same names as directories. NetWare first looks for a directory by that name, and if there isn't a directory by that name, NetWare then copies to a file by that name.

Other Information

If you're copying multiple files and NCOPY can't copy one of them for some reason, NCOPY will continue to copy the rest of the files, then present you with a message similar to this one:

```
From NTS3/VOL1:USERS\TED\NET
To PUB/BYTE:USERS\TED\BOOK
    CHAP3B  to CHAP3B   : DOS - Access denied.
                        : Failed to create file
    CHAP3C  to CHAP3C
    CHAP3A  to CHAP3A
2 files copied.
```

```
1 file NOT copied.
```

The new files you create will have the same update and times as the original files; however, this date and time will change as you access and modify the files.

Related Commands

You can use NDIR to see which files are in a given directory (discussed below). You can use NDIR, LISTDIR, or the RIGHTS command to make sure you have enough rights to copy files from a given directory and to a given directory. (See the "Directory and File Security Utilities" section for the RIGHTS command.)

NDIR

The NDIR command is very different from DOS's DIR command. In DOS, you see filenames, file sizes, the last time (and date) the file was written to, and the subdirectories of the directory you're looking at.

Like DIR, NDIR also gives you filenames, file sizes, and the last time (and date) the file was written to. In addition, NDIR tells you when the files were last accessed or written to, when the files were created, how the files are flagged, and who owns the files. For subdirectories, NDIR lists the name, the inherited rights mask for NetWare 3.1x, the effective rights, the owner, your effective rights, and when the subdirectories were created or copied.

Some Basic Information on NDIR

To list NDIR's options, type NDIR /HELP at the command line. The help message will display (albeit cryptically) how to use NDIR's parameters:

```
usage:      NDIR [path][/option...]
path:       [path][filename][,filename,...] (up to 16 in chain)
options:    [format], [flag], [sortspec], [restriction], [FO]
            (files only), [DO] (directories only),
            [SUBdirectories], [Continuous], [Help]

format:     DATES, RIGHTS, MACintosh, LONGnames

flag:       [NOT] RO, S, A, X, H, SY, T, I, P, RA, WA, CI,
            DI, RI
```

297

```
sortspec:    [REVerse] SORT [OWner], [SIze], [UPdate], [CReate],
                           [ACcess], [ARchive], [UNsorted]

restriction: OWner    <operator> <name>
             SIze     <operator> <number>
             Update   <operator> <date>
             CReate   <operator> <date>
             ACcess   <operator> <date>
             ARchive  <operator> <date>

             operator:    [NOT] LEss than, GReater than,
                          EQual to, BEFore, AFTer
```

To search filenames equivalent to any of the capitalized KEYWORD
options shown above, the filename must be preceded by a drive
letter or path.

To see what you have in your present directory, simply type NDIR <Enter> and
you'll see something similar to this:

```
NTS3/VOL1:USERS\TED
Files:         Size    Last Updated    Flags            Owner
----------     -------  -----------    -------          -------
DOODLE DOC     1,152   3-26-89 12:00p  [Rw-A——————]     TED
FILE               0   7-26-91 9:43a   [Rw————————]     TED
INSTALWP JUN  22,508   4-17-90 8:14a   [RoS———————]     TED
INTRO DOC      4,864   3-26-88 12:01p  [Rw————————]     TED
LL DOC        26,368   4-01-87 9:00a   [Rw————————]     TED
M MNU          4,067   6-28-91 4:27p   [Rw-A——————]     TED
NEW DOC          640   3-26-88 12:26p  [Rw————————]     TED
RESTART 000       29   6-28-91 3:36p   [Rw-A——————]     TED
RESTART 003       25   11-26-90 3:20p  [Rw-A——————]     TED
STUFF          1,339   7-12-93 8:12p   [Rw-A——————]     TED
T BAT             25   6-28-93 4:44p   [Rw-A——————]     TED
TEST1          1,575   6-05-93 2:15p   [Rw-A——————]     TED
WP MNU           266   1-21-93 3:08p   [Rw————————]     TED
WP2 MNU          306   7-08-93 9:13a   [Rw-A——————]     TED


              Inherited    Effective
Directories:  Rights       Rights      Owner      Created/Copied
```

```
----------      ----------      --------      --------      ----------
LETTERS         [-RWCEMFA]      [-------]     TED           5-15-92 11:57a
MEMOS           [-RWCEMFA]      [-------]     TED           5-15-92 11:57a
REPORTS         [-RWCEMFA]      [-------]     TED           4-17-92 8:10p

        63,577 bytes in 14 files
        118,784 bytes in 29 blocks
```

NDIR first lists the directory path, showing which directory's information you're looking at. You then see columns listing Files, Size, Last Updated, Flags, and Owner. Beneath the columns you see the names of the files themselves, with the appropriate information about each file in the proper column. For example, the first line beneath the columns in the above figure shows information on the file DOODLE.DOC, such as the file size (1152 bytes), and the last time (and date) the file was written to (3-26-89 at 12:00pm). In addition, DOODLE.DOC has Write and Archived file flags (is flagged Nonshareable Read/Write) and is owned by Ted.

For subdirectories, NDIR has columns headed Directory Name, Inherited Rights, Effective Rights, Owner, and the time the subdirectories were Created/Copied. In these columns, NDIR lists the subdirectories themselves, with the appropriate information about the subdirectories beneath the headings.

For example, you can see the LETTERS subdirectory, the subdirectory's inherited rights mask (-RWCEMFA), your effective rights in the subdirectory, the owner of the subdirectory (Ted), and the date and time it was created or copied (5-15-90 at 11:57am). You can see your effective rights in directories as well as the inherited rights mask through the LISTDIR utility.

If the information fills more than one screen, a line at the bottom of your screen says "Press any key to continue....('C' for continuous)." Press a key to see the next screenful, or press the letter "C" to scroll through the rest of the display. You can also press <Ctrl>-<C> or <Ctrl>- <Break> to discontinue the display and return to the network prompt.

Using the NDIR Command

NDIR [Path]. NDIR's command format starts with the NDIR command, followed by the file path and the options that you wish to explore. When you use the NDIR command, you can write out the entire directory path, use a drive letter, or simply type NDIR to specify the directory you're currently in (as in the example above).

For example, if you're in the USERS\TED\REPORTS directory and you want to see a file in the NTS3\VOL1:USERS\TED\TEAM directory, type NDIR NTS3\VOL1:USERS\TED\TEAM <Enter>. If NTS3\VOL1 is your default server and volume, type NDIR \USERS\TED\TEAM <Enter>. If drive H: is mapped to NTS3\VOL1:USERS\TED\TEAM, type NDIR H: <Enter>.

You can also work from your current directory level and move up or down from there. For example, if you're currently in the NTS3\VOL1:USERS\TED\TEAM directory and it has a subdirectory named GOODS beneath it, type NDIR GOODS <Enter> to see the files and subdirectories of the GOODS directory. If your drive G: is mapped to NTS3\VOL1:USERS\TED\TEAM and you want to see the files in the TED directory above TEAM, change to drive G: and type NDIR .. <Enter> at the G: prompt. To see if you have any files in the USERS directory above TED, type NDIR ... <Enter> at the G: prompt. If you want to see your files in the NTS3\VOL1: USERS\TED\REPORT92 directory and you are in the directory named NTS3\VOL1:USERS\TED\TEAM, type NDIR ..\REPORT92 <Enter>.

If you have no rights in a given directory, or if no files are found that match the criteria you specify, you will see a list of the subdirectories beneath that directory (depending on security) but no files. Sometimes NDIR displays "Incomplete/erroneous path or unmapped drive. Type 'ndir /help' on the command line for usage information" when you've mistyped the command.

Another important message is "A forward slash (/) must precede the first element of the option list," a reminder you see if you didn't use the forward slash before signifying the first option. Watch closely right after you enter the NDIR command. If you see the message "Searching directorypath" with a spinning line, you'll know that NDIR recognized your command.

To see the files in your current directory and in all subdirectories directly beneath the current directory, you can type NDIR /FO SUB <Enter> to list the subdirectories. In this command, "/FO (Files Only)" means "list only files" and "SUB" means "do the same for all subdirectories under the current directory."

To see only the subdirectories beneath your present directory (and no files), type NDIR /DO SUB <Enter>. In this command, DO tells NDIR to list Directories Only and SUB tells it to do the same for all subdirectories. (The /FO, /DO, and /SUB options will be explained more fully later.)

NDIR's Options

A word of warning: every version on NDIR seems to work a little differently from the one before. So you have to experiment. The options discussed here are from using NDIR.EXE version 3.42. You can check your version by using the VERSION utility (see the "General NetWare Utilties" section in this chapter).

NDIR path, filename /Options. NDIR is so versatile it's almost impossible to figure out all the ways to use it, let alone explain them. NDIR has quite a list of options that you can mix and match in innumerable combinations. For the most part, the options only qualify or shuffle the information you see with the simple NDIR <Enter> command. But if you're interested in how NDIR works, follow along.

NDIR includes major "interactive" categories that allow you work one or more options together. An interactive category is one for which a user can then choose an option to use for that category. For each category, the user can choose from several options that can mix with the other interactive categories. NDIR also has quite a few regular options, and the best way to see how the categories work together is to play around with them.

Let's look again at NDIR's help screen and try to decipher the interactive options first. (To display this help screen, type NDIR /HELP <Enter>.)

```
usage:        NDIR [path][/option...]
path:         [path][filename][,filename,...] (up to 16 in
              chain)
options:      [format], [flag], [sortspec], [restriction],
              [FO] (files only), [DO] (directories only),
              [SUBdirectories], [Continuous], [Help]

format:       DATES, RIGHTS, MACintosh, LONGnames

flag:         [NOT] RO, S, A, X, H, SY, T, I, P, RA, WA, CI,
DI, RI

sortspec:     [REVerse] SORT [OWner], [SIze], [UPdate],
                           [CReate], [ACcess], [ARchive],
                           [UNsorted]

restriction:  OWner    <operator> <name>
              SIze     <operator> <number>
              Update   <operator> <date>
              CReate   <operator> <date>
              ACcess   <operator> <date>
              ARchive  <operator> <date>

              operator:    [NOT] LEss than, GReater than,
                           EQual to, BEFore, AFTer
```

The four major interactive categories are Format, Flag, Sort specifications, and Restrictions. We'll call anything you can substitute for these major categories an option (for lack of a better term). NDIR also has some standard options, such as FO for Files Only, DO for Directories Only, SUBdirectories, Continuous, and HELP. You only have to use the forward slash to signify the first option in a list of options, but you can use the slash on every option if you wish.

In terms of substitution, the second line shows that the Format category can be replaced by three options: DATES, RIGHTS, MACintosh and LONGfiles. You can replace the Flag category with the following file attributes (flag) options: SYstem (SY), Hidden (H), Archived (A), Execute Only (X), Shareable (S), ReadOnly (RO), ReadWrite (RW), Indexed (I), and Transactional (T), ReadAudit (RA), WriteAudit (WA), Purge (P), CreateInhibit (CI), DeleteInhibit (DI), and ReadInhibit (RI). The Sort specifications category has options like SORT (and REVerse SORT) OWner, ACcess, ARchived date, CReate, Update, SIze, and UNsorted. The last category is Restrictions, which include OWner, SIze, UPdate, CReate, ACcess, and ARchive options like the Sort specifications; however, with Restrictions, you can add some operator parameters, such as (NOT) LEss than, GReater than, EQual to, BEFore, and AFTer.

Again, all these categories and options are ways to restrict what you see in NDIR. You can use the categories and their options to then create reports so you have something on hand for a quick reference.

How the Categories and Options Work Together

Let's start with how the categories and options work together. To show basic file information, you can mix filenames and paths with the options. For example, NDIR G:*.BAT,*.DAT <Enter> says "Show the files with .BAT and .DAT extensions in the G: directory path." Be sure there is no space between the directory path designation and filenames.

The operator parameter comes after either the Sortspec or Restriction options. For example, typing NDIR /SI GR 5000 <Enter> requests a list of all files in the current directory that are larger than 5KB. In this example, /SI is used as a restriction option, GR (GReater than) signifies an operator value, and 5000 is the number of bytes from which to measure. So this command is saying, "Show me all files in this directory that are greater than 5000 bytes."

There are many possible combinations you can choose from for the option categories. The capitalized letters in the parameter names indicate the abbreviated form that you can use instead of typing out the entire parameter (although you can sometimes type out the entire parameter if you want). While the NOT option is one of the regular NDIR options, you use it to display the opposite of a regular option. (Although NOT is always shown preceding the Option, in the actual NDIR command you can type it either before or after the selected Option.)

Path\filename,filename,...up to 16 in a chain. As you designate a directory path, be sure you leave no space between the path and the filename. If you know the filenames, such as APRIL.DAT and MAY.RPT, that you want to see in your present directory, you can type NDIR APRIL.DAT,MAY.RPT <Enter>. IF the files are located in drive G:, type NDIR G:APRIL.DAT,MAY.RPT <Enter> to see those two files. You can have up to sixteen filenames in a chain; to see all *.BAT, *.COM, and *.EXE files in a directory path including subdirectories, type NDIR *.BAT,*.COM,*.EXE /SUB <Enter>.

The above discussion applies to the question mark (?) wildcard as well. Each question mark wildcard takes the place of one character in a filename. For example, if you have several files but you want to see only three—GLSYS.FDM, DLSYS.FED, and SLSYS.FDM—type NDIR J:??SYS*.* <Enter>. NDIR will display only those filenames that fit the pattern.

NDIR and the Format Category

NDIR contains four methods of presenting information to the screen. When you type NDIR <Enter>, you see one of four ways to present file and directory information. Through the Format category, you can see three other ways to view file and directory information: through dates (DATES), through rights (RIGHTS), and for Macintosh users looking around on PCs, through the Macintosh option (MAC). All other categories and options which can apply (mainly FO, DO, and SUB) can also be used in presenting the following information to these screen formats.

NDIR /DATES. The Dates option shows you a lot of information about your files, which can be invaluable when trying to decide which files to remove from the network. When you type NDIR /DATES <Enter>, you see a list of files similar to what follows next.

```
NTS3/VOL1:USERS\TED
Files:    Last Updated     Last Archived     * Accessed     Created/Copied
          -------          -----------       -----------    ----------

50K              7-26-92  1:40p 0-00-00  0:00    A 7-26-92   7-26-91 N/A
DOODLE DOC  3-26-92 12:00p 0-00-00  0:00    - 7-25-92   7-25-91 N/A
FILE             7-26-92  5:20p 0-00-00  0:00    - 7-26-92   7-26-91 N/A
INSTALWP JUN 4-17-93  8:14a 10-19-90 12:03p      6-12-93   5-04-90 N/A
```

```
INTRO DOC   5-26-93  12:01p 0-00-00 0:00    A 7-26-93   7-25-91 N/A
* Files marked A are flagged for subsequent archiving.
```

Directories:	Maximum Rights	Effective Rights	Owner	Created/Copied
	-------	-------	-------	----------
LETTERS	[-RWCEMFA]	[——]	TED	5-15-90 11:57a
MEMOS	[-RWCEMFA]	[——]	TED	5-15-90 11:57a

The /DATES option shows you the filenames, the date and time the files were last updated, the date and time the files were last archived, and whether or not the Archive bit has been set, meaning that the file will be backed up during the next backup procedure. You also see when the files were last accessed and when they were created or copied. Most of this information is used by an archive server that understands NetWare's archiving calls.

The Last Updated column is different from the Last Archived column and the Accessed column. These columns are for use by an archive server program that understands NetWare's archiving calls, so you may not ever use this option. An archive server considers a file "updated" if either the DOS Archive bit is set or the NetWare archive date and time is before the modified date and time. Both of these indicate that the file has been modified since the last archive. For the Last Updated column, the archive server considers a file that has been updated since the last archive or has never been Archived.

To see which files in your present directory have been changed since the last archive, type NDIR /DATES and look at the Last Archived column. The Last Archived column allows you to compare your Last Updated date with the Last Archived date. If you see zeroes displayed under the Last Archived column, as in the example display above, this simply means that your files haven't been archived by an archive server. The Asterisk column means the DOS Archive bit is set and the file is ready for subsequent archiving.

The Accessed column refers to the last time the file was opened or accessed, but then closed without being modified. This column can help you see which files you are accessing but not modifying if you need to take files off the server. The Created/Copied column shows you when the file was initially created or copied to this directory. However, the Copied column usually shows N/A, which means that it's not presently supported in NetWare. However, files copied from one directory to another usually have the Archived bit set so they'll be backed up at your next backup session.

NDIR /RIGHTS. The /RIGHTS options shows you a screen displaying the directory's files, file attributes (flags), the Inherited Rights Mask, and Effective Rights, as well as the name of the files' owner. To see the NDIR screen containing all your rights and file flags, type NDIR /RIGHTS <Enter> and you'll see a screen similar to this one:

```
NTS1/VOL1:USERS\TED
                                 Inherited    Effective
    Files:          Flags        Rights       Rights       Owner
                    -------      ----------   ------       ------
    50K             [Rw-A——————]  [-RWCEMFA]   [-RWCEMFA]   TED
    DOODLE DOC      [Rw-A——————]  [-RWCEMFA]   [-RWCEMFA]   TED
    FILE            [Rw————————]  [-RWCEMFA]   [-RWCEMFA]   TED
    INSTALWP DOC    [RoS———————]  [-RWCEMFA]   [-RWCEMFA]   TED
    INTRO DAT       [RoSA——T———]  [-RWCEMFA]   [-RWCEMFA]   TED


                    Inherited    Effective
    Directories:    Rights       Rights       Owner    Created/Copied
                    ----------   ----------   ------   --------
    LETTERS         [-RWCEMFA]   [-RWCEMFA]   TED      5-15-90 11:57a
    MEMOS           [-RWCEMFA]   [-RWCEMFA]   TED      5-15-90 11:57
```

NDIR /MACintosh. You need the Macintosh option only when you have the Macintosh Name Space installed. This option restricts NDIR to show you only Macintosh files and Macintosh subdirectories within a given directory path. If you're a Mac user and you're at a PC workstation, you can go to a Macintosh directory and type NDIR /MAC <Enter> to see something similar to this:

```
SYS:MDAY
Long Name        Size      Date       Time      Owner
----------       -----     -----      -----     ------
AFMISSIO.txt     14994     5-11-92    10:16p    MDAY
beep.bat.bak     1112      5-11-92    10:16p    MDAY
beep.bat         1112      5-11-92    10:16p    MDAY
lunch.bat        294       5-11-92    10:16p    MDAY
text macros      529       5-01-92    6:56p     MDAY

Directory Name   Max Rights   Eff Rights   Owner   Created/Copied
--------------   ----------   ----------   -----   ------------
DBXL             [-RWCEMFA]   [——————]     MDAY    3-07-91 3:48p
Quotes, Text     [-RWCEMFA]   [——————]     MDAY    12-27-91 8:33a
SQL              [-RWCEMFA]   [——————]     MDAY    3-15-91 12:56a
```

```
Transfer          [-RWCEMFA]   [————]      MDAY   1-20-91 10:41a
    4 subdirectories found
Total: 5 files using 18041 bytes
Total disk space in use: 32768 bytes (8 blocks)
```

The Macintosh option shows files and directories using the Macintosh's long name structure. For files, you see Long Name, Size, Date, Time, and Owner columns, which is more like what DOS's DIR command displays than what NDIR normally shows you. However, for directories you'll see the same directory information as other network users.

Using the File Flag Options

The second category of NDIR options deals with file attributes, which NDIR also displays with each file. The file flags appear in the Flags column, as in this example:

```
NTS3/VOL1:USERS\TED
Files:        Size   Last Updated   Flags         Owner
-------       -----  ----------     -----         -----
DOODLE DOC    1,152  3-26-92 12:00p [Rw-A————]    TED
FILE          0      7-26-92 9:43a  [Rw————]      TED
INSTALWPBIN   22,508 4-17-92 8:14a  [RoS————]     TED
INTRO DOC     4,864  3-26-90 12:01p [Rw————]      TED
```

Here are some of the possible combinations you can choose from for the Flag option. The capitalized letters in the parameter names indicate the abbreviated form that you can use instead of typing out the entire parameter. Each combination must be preceded with the NDIR command and a forward slash if the flag option is the first option typed. The NOT option is one of the regular NDIR options, but is shown in these examples so you can see how you can use it.

[NOT] /Read Only. The first two letters displayed in the Flags column are either Ro for Read/Only or Rw for Read/Write. Most files will be Read/Write unless you have flagged a file Read/Only. Suppose you want to look at all Read/Only files larger than 50KB in your current directory. To do this, type NDIR /RO SI GR 50000 <Enter>. Notice that Read Only can be abbreviated RO. Since there isn't a flag for Read/Write, to look at all Read/Write files, type NDIR /NOT RO <Enter>.

[NOT] /Shareable. The letter S in the second position in the Flags column stands for Shareable. If no S appears, then the file is nonshareable (the default attribute). To see all filenames in your current directory that have been flagged Shareable, type NDIR /S

306

<Enter>. You can use the NOT option to look at all files except those flagged Shareable: for example, NDIR /NOT S <Enter>.

[NOT] /Archived. The third letter in the Flags column is A for Archived, and displays an A whenever the DOS Archive bit is set on files. To look at all files in your current directory that are flagged with the Archive file attribute, type NDIR /A <Enter>. You can use the NOT option to look at all files except those flagged Modified: for example, NDIR /NOT A <Enter>.

[NOT] /eXecute only. The letter X in the fifth position in the Flags column stands for Execute Only. When an .EXE or .COM program is flagged Execute Only, it can't be copied—only run. Supervisor rights are necessary to flag files Execute Only, but you can use NDIR to list any Execute Only files. To do this, type NDIR /X <Enter>. You can use the NOT option to look at all files except those flagged Execute Only.

[NOT] /Hidden. The letter H in the Flags column indicates a hidden file. Hidden files, like system files, don't appear in a normal DIR directory listing. To look at all files in your current directory that are flagged Hidden, type NDIR /H <Enter>. You can use the NOT option to look at all files except those flagged Hidden: for example, NDIR /NOT H <Enter>.

[NOT] /SYstem. The next symbol in NDIR's Flags column is Sy for System. System is a DOS file attribute reserved for certain files used exclusively by the operating system. System files are not displayed in a normal DIR directory listing. To see all files in your current directory that are flagged as system files, type NDIR /SY <Enter>. You can use the NOT option to look at all files except those flagged System.

[NOT] /Indexed. The next position in NDIR's Flags columns displays the letter I if a file is flagged Indexed. Normally, only files that are over 10MB in size are Indexed, so the chances that you'll need to use this parameter are pretty slim. To see all files in your current directory that are flagged Indexed, type NDIR /I <Enter>. You can use the NOT option to look at all files except those flagged Indexed, which would be a more common use of this option.

[NOT] /Transactional. The next position in NDIR's Flags column will show the letter T for a file flagged Transactional. A transactional file is usually a database file or some other data file protected by NetWare's transaction tracking system (TTS). To see all files in your current directory that are flagged Transactional, type NDIR /T <Enter>. You can use the NOT option to look at all files except those flagged Transactional.

[NOT] /Read audit /Write audit. Since NetWare 3.11 presently doesn't support the Read audit and Write audit flags, you need not worry about these flag options. But if you want to see files with these flags set, type NDIR /RA WA <Enter>.

[NOT] /Purge. NetWare 3.1x has four other flags that files may possess, and the Purge flag is one of them. If you're running on NetWare 3.1x and you want to see if files have the Purge flag, type NDIR /P <Enter>.

[NOT] /CopyInhibit /DeleteInhibit /RenameInhibit. NetWare 3.1x and Macintosh users can use this flag for Macintosh files for which supervisors wish to restrict copy rights. So if you want to see if your Macintosh files have the CopyInhibit invoked, type NDIR /CI MAC <Enter>. To see if DOS files have the Delete or RenameInhibit set (meaning you can't delete a file or rename it), type NDIR /DI RI <Enter>.

Sorting the NDIR Listings

The Sortspec Category on the NDIR command lets you sort NDIR's output. The SORT and REVerse SORT options are shown across from the Sortspec option in the NDIR help screen. You use the restriction parameters as the criteria to sort on.

For example, when you want to sort your files by size, type NDIR /SORT SIZE <Enter>. NDIR will sort the files in ascending order according to their size. You can reverse the Sort option so you sort files in descending size order by typing NDIR /REV SORT SIZE <Enter>.

As another example, this time using the UPdate option, you can type NDIR J:*.RPT /SORT UPDATE <Enter> to see all the .RPT files in directory J: in the order in which they were last updated. Or you can type NDIR J:*.RPT /REV SORT UP <Enter> to see them in reverse update order (starting with the most recently updated .RPT files).

You can do this type of sorting for all the options in the Sortspec category, including OWner, SIze, UPdate, CReate, ACcess, ARchive, and UNsorted. Experiment to see what you can do with them. One last note: NDIR, by default, lists files and subdirectories in alphabetical order, so specifying SORT ON FILENAME would be unnecessary.

Sortings are mainly used with the Restrictions category, which combines the Sortspec options with two other parameters: the operator and the name, number, or date parameters. These parameters help you zero in on the types of information you'd like to see or save to a file and then put in a report. Let's look at how these elements work together.

How Restrictions and Operator Options Work Together

/OWner [NOT] *<operator> username*. To see only those files in your current directory that you, Ted, are the owner of, type NDIR /OW = TED <Enter>. If you're Ted and you want to see all files in your current directory that you're not the owner of, type NDIR / OW NOT = TED <Enter>.

/ACcess [NOT] BEFore | = | AFTer *<date>*. Suppose you want to see all the .DAT and .RPT files in your present directory that were accessed after January 30, 1992. Type NDIR *.DAT,*.RPT /AC AFTER 1-30-92 <Enter>. You can substitute GR (GReater Than) for AFT if you prefer. Dates must follow the MM-DD-YY format in order for them to work.

This variation becomes particularly useful when your server is running out of disk space. You can use NDIR to determine which files haven't been accessed in the last six months. Then you can copy those files onto floppies and take them off the server. Enter the command by going to your root directory and typing NDIR /FO AC BEF 3-15-92 SUB <Enter>. As with most NDIR commands where you include a date as the Value parameter, it's easiest to use the BEFore and AFTer operators and leave NOT out of it.

You can also include a second combination of parameters to see only files that were accessed between two dates. For example, typing NDIR *.RPT, *.DAT /AC AFT 1-30-92 AC BEF 3-15-93 <Enter> would show you only the .RPT and .DAT files accessed between January 30 and March 15, 1993.

When you include dates, put the month first, then the day, then the year (*mm–dd–yy*). If you reverse the month and day (and the day specified is above 12), you may see a message like "The specified month does not exist. Type "ndir /help" on the command line for usage information." If you don't use the exact format, you may get different dates than the dates you meant. For example, if the day is 12 or below, you could inverse the days and the months and not get what you expected. Be sure to also include the full date, or NDIR may not yield the results you intended. NDIR will display the message, "Date is missing or mistyped, *mm–dd–yy* expected" if you leave the year off or don't type the date in the specified manner.

/Update [NOT] BEFore | = | AFTer *<date>*. Suppose you're working on a project and you want to see all .RPT files in your default directory that were updated after January 30, 1993. Type NDIR *.RPT /UP AFT 1-30-93 <Enter>. You can substitute GR (GReater Than) for AFT, if you prefer. Files with the same update time are sorted by filename. (Use the BEFore and AFTer operators instead of NOT when you deal with dates. Type the date as described for the ACcess option above.)

/CReate [NOT] BEFore | = | AFTer *<date>*. Suppose you're working on a project and you want to see all .RPT files in your default directory that were created after January 30, 1992. Type NDIR *.RPT /CR AFT 1-30-92 <Enter>. (Use the BEFore and AFTer operators instead of NOT when you deal with dates. Type the date as described for the ACcess parameter above.)

/SIze [NOT] GReater than | = | LEss than *<number>*. Suppose you want to look at all files in your present directory that are larger than 50KB. Type NDIR /SI GR 50000

309

<Enter>. Or if you want to see all the files that are less than 50000 bytes, type NDIR / SI NOT GR 50000 <Enter>. The number you specify is in bytes. If you want to see all files in your current directory that are flagged Read/Only and that are smaller than 50KB, use the LEss than parameter instead of the NOT option. Type NDIR /RO SI LE 50000 <Enter>.

/ARchive [NOT] BEFore | = | AFTer <*date*>. This archived date parameter is for those backup and archiving programs out there; it doesn't apply to you as a user.

The Rest of the NDIR Options

So far, we've talked about NDIR's interactive categories, mentioning some of the regular NDIR options (such as NOT and Files Only) in passing. The regular NDIR options include Files Only, Directories Only, SUBdirectory, Continuous, and HELP. You can include these options with most of NDIR's interactive options, as well as with other options that don't conflict with a given command. For example, you can't have Files Only and Directories Only in the same command.

Here's a list of the regular NDIR options and some examples of how to use them. The capitalized letters in the option names indicate the abbreviated form that you can use instead of typing out the entire option (although you can sometimes type out the entire option and have it work). Experiment with these options, for you can use them in more ways than just those covered here.

NDIR /Files Only (/FO). When you want to see only the files in a given directory and not any of the subdirectory information, you can designate Files Only in the command. For example, to see only the files in the directory drive G: is mapped to, type NDIR G: /FO <Enter>; to see only the files in your present directory, type NDIR /FO <Enter>.

NDIR /Directories Only (/DO). When you want to look at only the subdirectories under the directory you're in, type NDIR /DO <Enter>. If you want to see the subdirectories under a different directory, you can specify the directory path in the command. For example, to see the subdirectories of the directory drive G: is mapped to, you can type NDIR G: /DO <Enter>.

NDIR /SUBdirectory (/SUB). When you want to see not only the files and subdirectories in your current directory, but the also the files and subdirectories in all subdirectories beneath your present directory, type NDIR /SUB <Enter>. To see the listing for a different directory path, specify the path. For example, type NDIR G: /SUB <Enter> to see the information for drive G:. When you just want to see all the subdirectories under your present directory without having to wade through the files, type NDIR /DO SUB <Enter>.

NDIR /Continuous (/C). Most command-line utilities stop after the screen is full of information. If some of the information you seek is at the bottom of information flow, type NDIR with the /C option to watch the information continually scroll until it reaches the end of the information. You don't need to use /C when saving information to a file.

NDIR /HELP. To display the NDIR help screen, type NDIR /HELP at the command line. (You can't use this option with any other NDIR option.) The help screen displays the command syntax and all of NDIR's options and their parameters.

NDIR at a Glance

Now that you know about all of NDIR's categories and options and parameters, you can start experimenting and coming up with your own combinations and variations. With NDIR, you can tailor your directory listing to see exactly what you want to see—no more, no less. The possibilities are endless, especially when you start combining the category options with one another and a few regular options all in the same command. For example, NDIR /UP AFT 10-1-92 RO SORT SI FO SUB <Enter> is a valid NDIR command!

As you play with NDIR, keep in mind that some variations require that you adhere to a strict command format in order for them to work properly. This is especially true when you're using the NOT option. The following chart summarizes NDIR's command format, options, and parameters. Once you become familiar with how NDIR works, you can refer to this chart for a quick review of the possibilities.

When You Can, Abbreviate

Typically, you can type just the first two letters of an option, such as RO for Read/Only and FN for Filename. A list of NDIR's option and parameter abbreviations for quick reference follows.

NDIR Options

NOT	= NOT	FLag	= FL
SOrt ON	= SO	REVerse SORT	= REV SORT
Files Only	= FO	Directories Only	= DO
SUBdirectory	= SUB	Continuous	= C
MACintosh	= MAC	RIGHTS	= RIGHTS
DATES	= DATES	HELP	= HELP

Sortspec Options

OWner	= OW	ACcess	= AC

ARchived	= AR	UNsorted	= UN
UPdated	= UP	CReate	= CR
SIze	= SI		

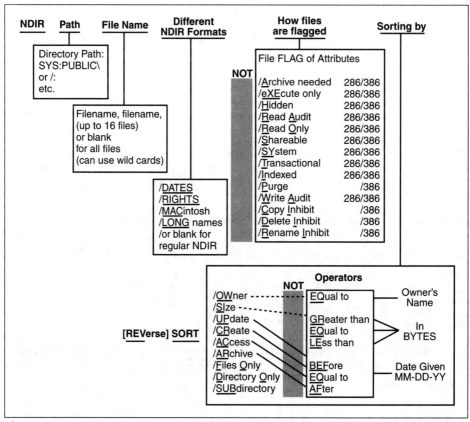

Figure 3-1. The NDIR options at a glance

Operators Parameters

EQual	= EQ or =	GReater than	= GR
LEss than	= LE	BEFore	= BEF
AFTer	= AFT		

Flag Options

Read/Only	= RO	Shareable	= S
Archived	= A	eXecute only	= X
SYstem	= SY	Hidden	= H
Indexed	= I	Transactional	= T
Read Audit	= RA	Write Audit	= WA
Purge	= P	Copy Inhibit	= CI
Delete Inhibit	= DI	Rename Inhibit	= RI

Other Information

NDIR uses NetWare pattern matching, which is slightly different from DOS pattern matching. For instance, DOS lets you type DIR *.DAT to view all files with a .DAT extension. NetWare is more flexible. For example, if you can't remember the full filename, but know the filename has TEL in it, you can type *TEL* as the filespec in NDIR. You'll see a list of all files that contain TEL in their filename, such as ATELBC.DAT, TEL or ABC.TEL.

On the other hand, DOS interprets *TEL* to mean "display a directory of all files matching *", stops reading after the first *, and throws away the TEL* part of the pattern. You get the same listing you get when you type DIR *.

In addition, NetWare considers a dot or period character before an extension (as in *.DAT) as a regular character. So if you type *TEL* for a file spec in an NDIR command, NDIR will list those files with the three characters together, but not a file such as ABCT.EL.

Putting NDIR Information Into Files

From time to time, you may want to print out a copy of what NDIR displays on the screen. For example, it would be helpful to have a list of the files you haven't accessed in a long time when you're ready to back up these files to floppy disks so you can delete them from the server.

NDIR recognizes the DOS redirection symbol (>) and will send the requested information to a file rather than to the screen. For example, if you type NDIR > TEST <Enter>, NDIR will send the requested data to the file TEST and tell you that it's writing to that output file. When you redirect data to a DOS text file in this way, no pagination occurs.

You can also redirect the output directly to a printer by using the CAPTURE command. To do this, type CAPTURE LPT1: S=*servername* Q=*queuename* <Enter>. Then type either NDIR > LPT1 <Enter> or NDIR > PRN: <Enter> (PRN: is the DOS name for the printer device). NDIR will treat the LPT1 port or the PRN: device as a file and send the data to wherever CAPTURE specifies. (See "Using the CAPTURE Command" in Chapter 4 for more information on CAPTURE). However, depending on your printer, you may end up with entire columns written out beyond your paper carriage. When this happens, send the data to a file and print the file through NPRINT or PCONSOLE instead. (See "Using the NPRINT Command" heading in Chapter 4, and "The PCONSOLE Utility" heading for PCONSOLE.)

PURGE

You can use the PURGE utility when you want to irrevocably delete files that are only sort-of deleted. When you use DOS's DEL or ERASE commands or when you delete files through the FILER utility, those files are marked as deleted, and you can't access them (except through the SALVAGE utility—see "The Salvage Utility" heading in Chapter 2). However, those files still remain on the disk, and they still retain their directory entry as deleted files. If you're getting low on directory entries and you've deleted a lot of files, running PURGE will free up those remaining directory entries. But once you run PURGE, those files are really gone.

The PURGE command affects only the files you delete under your login name. If others know your password, they can go in and irrevocably delete your files—one more reason to keep your login passwords a secret and to back up your files regularly. To run the PURGE command, type PURGE <Enter>. You'll see a message that says "User's salvageable files on *servername* have been purged."

You can also specify the files you wish to purge or use wildcards to specify a number of files at once. This way you don't have to purge all files in all your directories.

NetWare 3.1x users will see "Only specified files on *servername* have been purged from current directory." Since NetWare 3.11 has a different internal file structure that can store many deleted versions of files, the PURGE utility limits you to purging files that you own in the directory from which you run the command. However, if you wish to delete all files in your current directory and its subdirectories, type PURGE /All <Enter>, and you'll see "Only specified on *servername* have been purged from current directory and its subdirectories." You can also set directory and file attributes that will immediately purge all files in a directory, or immediately purge deleted files with the

Purge attribute set on them. See "The FILER Utility" heading in Chapter 2 or the FLAG or FLAGDIR utilities in the next section.

Related Commands

You can still salvage deleted files as long as you haven't done any file copying or deleting since the time you deleted the files. In those cases, you can run the SALVAGE command. (See "The SALVAGE Utility" in Chapter 2.) But SALVAGE won't do any good after you've run PURGE.

RENDIR

The RENDIR utility allows you to rename a directory. To rename a directory, you need both Create and Modify rights in the directory you wish to rename. If you're renaming a subdirectory beneath the directory you're in, you'll need Create and Modify rights in your present directory. When you rename a directory, you affect only the directory's name and not the trustee assignments connected to that directory. So when you change the directory's name, the new name will appear in those users' trustee assignments found in SYSCON along with the rights they had under the old directory name. And when you type MAP, you'll see that MAP reflects the changes as well. However, you'll need to change your login script to reflect the change or you'll receive a "directory path not locatable" message the next time you log in.

How To Use RENDIR

RENDIR *directory path* **TO** *directory name.* If you can't remember the proper syntax for the RENDIR command, type RENDIR /H <Enter> and you'll see:

```
Usage: RENDIR Path [TO] DirectoryName
    OldDirectoryPath must be an existing subdirectory path.
    NewDirectoryName must be a valid DOS directory name.
```

If you don't have enough rights in the directory you wish to change, you'll see the message "There are insufficient rights to rename directory." If you receive such a message, type RIGHTS (*directory path*) to see if you have Create and Modify rights in the directory.

When you use the RENDIR command, you can write out the entire directory path, use the drive letter, or use a period (.) to specify the directory you're currently in. For example, if you have Create and Modify rights in your NTS3\VOL1:USERS\TED\TEAM directory and you want to rename the TEAM directory to TWORK, type RENDIR

NTS3\VOL1:USERS\TED\TEAM TO TWORK <Enter>. If NTS3\VOL1 is your default server and volume, type RENDIR \USERS\TED\TEAM TO TWORK <Enter>. If the NTS3\VOL1:USERS\TED \TEAM directory is mapped to drive G:, type RENDIR G: TO TWORK <Enter>, or simply RENDIR G: TWORK <Enter>. If you're in the G: directory, you can use the period and type RENDIR . TWORK <Enter>. You'll see:

```
Directory renamed to TWORK
```

If you're in NTS3\VOL1:USERS\TED\TEAM directory and you want to rename the RECORDS subdirectory to RECEIVE, type RENDIR RECORDS RECEIVE <Enter> and you'll see:

```
Directory renamed to RECEIVE
```

You must be attached to a server in order to rename a directory on that server. If you have drive mappings to directories on different servers, use the drive letter in your RENDIR command. If you write out the directory path, you'll have to include the server and volume name in the command.

Related Commands

Be sure you have enough rights (at least Create and Modify rights) to perform the directory renaming. To check, go to the directory you wish to rename and type RIGHTS. (For a fuller explanation of the RIGHTS command, see the "Rights" subheading in the next section.) If you need to attach to other servers, turn to the "Attach" subheading in the "Server Access Utilities" section of this chapter for an explanation of the ATTACH command.

Directory and File Security Utilities

NetWare comes with a number of command-line utilities that allow you to view and (with proper rights) manipulate network security on files and directories in your area of the directory structure. These utilities perform the same or similar functions to those found in the SYSCON, FILER, and SESSION menu utilities. These command-line utilities include FLAG, FLAGDIR, GRANT, REVOKE, REMOVE, ALLOW, TLIST, and RIGHTS.

The FLAG command allows you to view and set attributes on files, much as you can in FILER. The FLAGDIR command allows you to hide a directory (System and Hidden) as well as a number of other attribute settings, which you can also do in FILER.

Like FILER, the GRANT utility allows you to grant others trustee assignments to your directories. The REVOKE command allows you to take back those rights granted through the GRANT command. The REMOVE utility drops that person or group from the trustee list in your directory. (See the "REMOVE" subheading later in this section for the distinction between REMOVE and REVOKE.) ALLOW lets you set the directory inherited rights mask from the command line instead of using FILER. The TLIST utility lists those who have trustee assignments to your directories. Finally, the RIGHTS utility shows your effective rights in a specified directory.

ALLOW

The ALLOW utility allows you to change the Inherited Rights Mask for a directory or file. The Inherited Rights Mask controls users' abilities to see and access files or utilities in a directory or the same rights to a specific file. This is the same capability that you have in FILER. (See "The FILER Utility" heading in Chapter 2.) You must have Access Control rights in a directory before you can change the Inherited Rights Mask. (You can give yourself that right if you have the supervisory right.) If you don't have Access Control rights and you try to use the ALLOW command, you'll see a message showing the Inherited Rights Mask of the directory you tried to modify and saying "Not Changed."

If you recall the Introduction's discussion of security rights, you need four permissions to access files and applications in NetWare: to access the server through *passwords*, to access a directory through the *basic security rights (trustee assignments, group assignments, and security equivalences)*, to access directories or files through the *inherited rights mask* and the flags.

The Inherited Rights Mask helps control which files and applications you or other users can access in a given directory. When you set the Inherited Rights Mask in one of your directories or for one of your files, that Inherited Rights Mask extends to all the subdirectories under that directory until you set a new Inherited Rights Mask at that lower level. When you set the Inherited Rights Mask for a given file, it only applies to that file. When you set the Inherited Rights Mask, other users and groups will see that they have gained or lost rights to that directory and its subdirectories or for that file the next time they look at the Inherited Rights Mask in FILER or with ALLOW. The Inherited Rights Mask overrides any rights given to users with their trustee assignments. It also modifies your rights to that directory and subdirectories, or to the file.

Using the ALLOW Utility

What follows is a list of ALLOW's parameters and their functions, along with an explanation of how to use them. The capitalized letters on the parameters indicate the abbreviations you can use instead of typing out the entire parameter. Of course, if you prefer you can type out the entire parameter. If you can't remember the proper syntax for ALLOW, type ALLOW /H <Enter> and you'll see the syntax help screen:

```
Usage: ALLOW [PATH [TO INHERIT] [rightslist*]

386 Rights:
- - - - - - - - - - - - - -
All = All
N   = No Rights
S   = Supervisor
R   = Read
W   = Write
C   = Create
E   = Erase
M   = Modify
F   = File Scan
A   = Access Control
* Use abbreviations listed above, separated by spaces.
```

ALLOW [PATH [TO INHERIT] [rightslist]]. The rights list includes Read, Write, Create, Erase, Modify, File Scan, Access Control, No Rights, All Rights and Supervisor. The ALLOW utility allows you to designate the directory path or directory path and filename, the rights you wish to give. You must specify the complete path (and filename if you are defining the mask for the file); otherwise you'll see the syntax help screen appear. You must also place a space between each right you specify; otherwise, you'll see the ALLOW help appear.

For example, if you have a small database in one of your directories that you want yourself and others to only Read, you can type ALLOW SYS:USERS\TED\DATA R F <Enter>. If you want to be able to drop files into the database as well as to read files, you can type ALLOW SYS:USERS\TED\DATA W R C E M F <Enter>. If the NTS3/VOL1:USERS/TED/DATA directory is mapped to drive G:, type ALLOW G: R F <Enter>.

Remember that when you change the Inherited Rights Mask, you change it for all users, including yourself. If you remove the Access Control right, you won't be able to modify the mask. You'll need to have your supervisor change the mask then if you made a mistake in removing the Access Control right.

ALLOW. Type ALLOW <Enter> to see any inherited rights masks set for this or subsequent subdirectories and for any files in this or in the subdirectories. You'll only see the masks for the first set of subdirectories. To see the masks for any sub-subdirectories, you'll have to change to the level just above them, then type ALLOW <Enter>. For example, if you type this command at F:\PERSONAL\TED\DATA, you'll see a screen similar to this:

```
Files:
    TEST.PRG    [ RWCEMFA]
    TEST.DAT    [ R     F ]
Directories:
    SUB1        [ R     F ]
    SUB2        [ RWCEMFA]
```

The two subdirectories of DATA that have masks are SUB1 and SUB2. There could be many other subdirectories of DATA, but these are the only two with masks. The same applies to the files. There are many more files in these directories, but only TEST.PRG and TEST.DAT have masks set for them. Note that ALLOW will show you masks for files one level up from where you are. In this example, TEST.PRG could be in F:\PERSONAL\TED\DATA, or it could be in F:\PERSONAL\TED.

The seven rights you can set (users can't set the Supervisor right) in the Inherited Rights Mask are:

Read. This right allows you to read information already contained in a file and is usually given along with File Scan rights for files. For example, if you want users to be able to look at files in your database directory, type ALLOW F:\PERSONAL\TED\DATA R F <Enter>. On your screen, you'll see:

```
Directories:
DATA    [ R     F ]
```

Write. This right allows you to place information in a file (write to a file); you need Write, Create, File Scan, and usually Modify (WCFM) rights in your directory to actually write to a file or to copy a file into the directory. If you want users to be able to copy files into your data directory, type ALLOW SYS:USERS\TED\DATA W C F M <Enter>. (You'll need the Read right if you want to read the file.) You'll see:

319

```
Directories:
DATA    [ WC FM ]
```

Create. This right allows you to create and write to new files as well as create directories. You usually need to set Read rights along with Create; if you don't, users can't re-open the file once it's closed.

Erase. This allows you to delete existing files and directories. You often use this right in conjunction when granting RWCEMF rights.

File Scan. This lets you to search a directory for files and directories if the Private directory flag has been invoked. If you don't have this right in a directory, you'll see the "File not found" message when you type DIR in that directory. Depending on your security, you also need this right to copy files from and to directories. File Scan is often used in conjunction with the Read right to open and read in applications for use.

Modify. This right allows you to change file and directory attributes, or flags. If you want someone to be able to change a file's flags in your directory, you can set this right. If you're trying to control how others use your files, don't grant this right. However, certain applications and utilities often need Modify rights in order to work properly, so you'll need to experiment with files or utilities in your directory. (For a discussion of file flags [attributes], see the "FLAG" subheading later in this section.)

Access Control. This right allows you to grant and revoke trustee rights to users and groups. With the Access Control right, you can also modify the directory rights mask. Since you may need Access Control rights to modify the Inherited Rights Mask, it's not a good idea to revoke this right unless you don't plan on changing the mask.

The ALLOW utility also has two options covering a broad spectrum of rights: No rights and ALL.

No rights. Use this option to set the mask to allow no rights to any user to this specific directory or file. If you don't want to access this file or directory anymore, type ALLOW F:\PERSONAL\TED\DATA\SUB1 N <Enter> and you'll see:

```
Directories
SUB1        [      ]
```

Once you revoke all rights in the mask, you won't be able to reset them, since you need the Access Control right to do that. You'll need to see your supervisor to restore these rights.

ALL. Use this option to set all eight trustee rights in your inherited rights mask. For example, if you're sharing a project with other users and you want them to have total rights to your G: directory, which is SUB1, type ALLOW G: ALL <Enter> and you'll see:

```
Directories
SUB1            [ RWCEMFA]
```

Supervisor. This right is the exception to the Inherited Rights Mask. You cannot use ALLOW to modify the mask to remove the Supervisor right.

Other Information

If you want to copy a file, you need at least RF rights in the directory you're copying from, and at least Write, Create, and File Scan (WCF) rights and sometimes Modify in the directory you wish to copy to. The file you're copying must not be flagged Hidden or System, or you won't be able to copy the file. Set the file flags (attributes) to Normal before copying files. (See "FLAG DIR" and "FLAG" subheadings next in this section.)

Also, if the supervisor gives you the supervisor trustee right using SYSCON for a directory or file, and you have Supervisory rights in the inherited rights mask, you can always restore any rights taken away by an Inherited Rights Mask at that or any subsequent directory level.

Related Commands

The ALLOW utility offers the same capability that you have in FILER, but at the network prompt. Use the Current Directory Information option. (System supervisors can set the inherited rights mask in SYSCON or in FILER.

FLAG

File attributes are the fourth level of security NetWare offers. Use the FLAG command to see which attributes (or flags) a file has been given and to flag files with different attributes. You need at least Modify rights to change a file's attributes. While there isn't much need for users to change a file's attributes, the ability to do so comes in handy from time to time.

Suppose you're letting a number of users read and write to files in one of your directories, but you want to make sure they don't delete or copy the files. Or suppose you want to make sure a particular file is backed up again, but its Archive bit hasn't been set. You can use FLAG to perform these types of tasks. Here's the list of attributes you can place on a file:

```
USAGE: FLAG [path [option | [+|-] attribute(s)] [SUB]]
386 Attributes:

----------------
RO Read Only
RW Read Write
S Shareable
H Hidden
SY System
T Transactional
P Purge
A Archive Needed
RA Read Audit
WA Write Audit
CI Copy Inhibit
X Execute Only
DI Delete Inhibit
RI Rename Inhibit


ALL ALL
N Normal
SUB
```

NetWare 3.1x also comes with the /C option, which allows for continuous scrolling if you're changing the attributes on a number of files. You now can add or delete attributes by using the plus and minus sign (+ or -), similar to DOS's ATTRIB method, so if you know ATTRIB, you won't have too many problems here.

To see how your files are presently flagged in your present directory, type FLAG *.* <Enter> or FLAG <Enter>. You'll see the files and their attributes in the directory, similar to the following:

```
BARBARA.LET          [ Rw - A - - -- - - -- -- ]
TOVA.LET             [ Rw - A - - -- - - -- -- ]
KEN.LTR              [ Rw - A     -- - - -- -- ]
BANQUET.LET          [ Rw - A - - -- - - -- -- ]
CVR-SHT.FAX          [ Rw - A - - -- - - -- -- ]
ROGER2.ART           [ Rw - A - - -- - - -- -- ]
REGISTER.TST         [ Ro S A - H -- I - -- -- ]
```

With earlier versions of NetWare, you could change only four attributes from the FLAG command: Shareable or Nonshareable, Read-Only or Read-Write, Indexed, and Transactional. To set the other file attributes, you had to be in FILER. (See "The FILER Utility" in Chapter 2.) However, in NetWare 3.1x, you can set all attributes from the command line. (Remember that flagging files Execute Only means the files can't be backed up or copied. Furthermore, you must delete them in order to get rid of the Execute Only flag.) Another difference in NetWare 3.11 is that you needn't flag files nonshareable. Files flagged without the Shareable attribute are considered nonshareable.

Using the FLAG Utility

Here's some information on the attributes you can use in the FLAG command and an example of how to set them.

FLAG *directorypath\filename*(s) **/Option.** To see how a file or set of files is flagged, type FLAG filename <Enter>. For you to flag a set of files all at once, you need to work with files that have some similar wild card potentials, such as the *.DAT extension. Then you can type FLAG *.DAT <Enter>, and you'll see a screen similar to this one:

```
VOL.DAT              [ Rw  - A - - -- - - -- -- ]
CAP.DAT              [ Rw  - - - - -- - - -- -- ]
PAL.DAT              [ Rw  - A - - -- - - -- -- ]
VOLIN.DAT            [ Rw  - A - - -- - - -- -- ]
DEFAULT.DAT          [ Rw  - - - - -- - - -- -- ]
```

You can view file attributes in other directories by typing the drive letter, followed by the filename: for example, FLAG G:*.RPT <Enter>. Or you can type in the entire directory path: for example, FLAG VOL1:USERS/TED/REPORTS/*.RPT <Enter>. To flag a file in another directory, type the drive letter, followed by the filename and the desired flags: for example, FLAG G:JUNE.RPT RW <Enter>. Or you can type in the entire directory path: FLAG VOL1:USERS/TED/REPORTS/JUNE.RPT RW <Enter>, for instance.

The /C option allows the files to continuously scroll across the screen until all files in the directory are displayed. Otherwise, if you change more than one screenful of files with the FLAG command, you'll be asked to "Press any key to continue ('C' for continuous)" when one screenful of files is reached. Most users won't use the /C option often, if ever.

FLAG *directorypath\filename*(s) **+ - attributes.** You can use the plus and minus signs (+ -) to add or delete any of the file attributes except Normal, ALL, and SUB. If

323

you have a list of attributes you wish to add or delete with one command, you'll need to group the commands together behind the sign you're using.

For example, suppose you accidentally flag the file RIGOR.DAT with all attributes, but you didn't want Transactional and Read-Audit attributes. You can type FLAG RIGOR.DAT -T RA <Enter> to get rid of the unnecessary flags. To flag the file RIGOR.DAT with Read-Write and Archive attributes at the same time, type FLAG RIGOR.DAT +RW A -T RA H Sy CI DI RI P <Enter>.

File Flag Attributes

Flagging files can be fun, but have a purpose for your choices. File flags affect everyone who tries to access the files, including you. Here's a list of what each attribute means.

Shareable. Flag a file with this only if that file is never written to; when you do flag a file as Shareable, you should also flag it Read-Only. Files flagged with Shareable and Read-Only attributes are usually executable files, such as applications and utilities.

For example, if you have a little utility such as CED.COM in the TED\UTIL directory, you can go to that directory and type FLAG CED.COM S RO <Enter> at the network prompt. When you flag other files (such as help files or overlays) as Shareable, you're telling the application using the file that it's all right for many users to read the file's information. The main thing to watch out for is applications and utilities that write to themselves instead of to overlay files. If you have a small utility that won't run after you flag it Shareable and Read-Only, chances are the utility writes to itself and you'll need to flag it Read-Write. Normally files flagged Read-Write are not shared, for one person may overwrite your activities in the file.

Files you flag Shareable can be accessed by more than one user at a time. This is fine for programs and utilities, but not for personal files and data. If you've placed your favorite utilities in your all-purpose search directory, or if you have other files in the directory that you share with your cohorts, you can flag those utilities and files as Shareable.

Read-Only. Files flagged with this attribute can be read, but not written to. Many application files are flagged Shareable and Read-Only; most *.COM and *.EXE files, for example, have such file attributes.

To mark your application and utility executables (executed when you type their prefix, such as 123 or WORD), type FLAG *filename.extension* SRO <Enter>. On your screen, you'll see:

```
VOLIN.EXE [ Ro S - - - -- - - - -- -- ]
```

One last tip: A file flagged Read-Only cannot have its name changed until you flag the file Read-Write.

Read-Write. Usually files flagged Read-Write don't have the Shareable attribute invoked, which gives the files a nonshareable status. Files flagged Read-Write can be read and modified.

This flag is good for any files that need to be modified, including *.BAT, *.DAT, and any other files you're adding data to or deleting data from. For example, you can flag your batch files Read-Write, allowing only one person to access them at one time, yet making it possible to modify them.

Hidden or SYstem. You can flag the file with either of these if you want to hide a file in the directory. If you flag a file with the Hidden or System attribute, you won't be able to delete or copy that file until you change the file's attribute back to Normal. You also won't see that file listed when you type DIR at the system prompt. But if you know it's there and you know the filename, you'll be able to access the file.

Indexed. Files given this flag are usually larger than 10MB (megabytes) in size. (The payoffs for flagging a file Indexed usually don't show until the file is 10MB or greater.) These files get a special File Allocation Table (FAT) to speed up data access.

For the most part, you won't have to do much with this flag. Anyway, data files of less than 10MB don't benefit much from being Indexed. If the need arises for flagging larger files, such as a 15MB REPORT.DAT file, mark the file FLAG REPORT.DAT RW I (Read-Write, Indexed) <Enter> at the network prompt. On your screen, you'll see:

```
REPORT.DAT[ Rw - - - - -- I - -- -- ]
```

Transactional. Files given this flag are sent to the server as a transaction, which means that all the data in the transaction is completely written to disk, or none of the transaction is written to disk. This prevents data you've already saved on the disk from being corrupted by a partial write of new data, followed by some kind of power or hardware failure.

For the most part, files are flagged Transactional by your supervisor; while you can also flag files as Transactional, it's good to talk it over with your supervisor before you do. To flag a data file Transactional, type FLAG *filename.extension* T <Enter>.

Read Audit and **Write Audit.** Since these two options are not presently used by NetWare, setting their flag won't mean anything. However, if you want to see if the Read and Write Audit attributes are set, type FLAG *filename* <Enter>; if you want to set the attributes, type FLAG *filename* RA WA <Enter>.

Purge. This attribute allows you to purge files as soon as you delete them. This is useful when you have temporary files that you won't need to salvage but want to recover the space from.

With NetWare 3.11, deleted files are still salvageable through the SALVAGE utility (see "The SALVAGE Utility" in Chapter 2). Once you delete a file, the file is still kept track of by NetWare and is protected to not be written over for 1 minute and 59 seconds.

NetWare keeps writing new files past the deleted files until the entire volume is filled with deleted and present files. Once the volume is full, and you need create or delete another version of your data files, NetWare will take the least recently accessed file(s) and purge them so it can use their disk space. This means that at any given time, you may have a lot of deleted files that you can look at. However, if everyone is doing this, NetWare volumes can remain full of deleted files, which can degrade performance.

To get around this situation, you can set the Purge attribute on files. To set this attribute, add P to your FLAG command, such as FLAG *filename* P N <Enter>, which flags a file as Normal, Purge.

RenameInhibit. This option prevents you or others from accidentally renaming the file. To set this attribute, add RI to your FLAG command, such as FLAG *filename* RI N <Enter>, which flags a file as Normal, RenameInhibit. In order to rename the file, you'll need to reset the file attribute without the RenameInhibit option by typing FLAG *filename* N <Enter>.

DeleteInhibit. This option prevents you or others from accidentally deleting the file. If you then want to delete the file, you'll need to reset the file attribute without the DeleteInhibit option.

CopyInhibit. The CopyInhibit option prevents you or others from copying the file. In order to copy the file, you'll need to reset the file attribute without the CopyInhibit option.

ALL. If you want to set a file with all the attributes (except Execute Only) available to you, type FLAG *filename* ALL <Enter>. Such files will have the Hidden and SYstem attributes on, so you won't be able to see them by typing DIR *filename* <Enter>. But if you know the filename, you can access the file. Files with attributes set by the ALL option do show up when you type FLAG *.* in the directory. You can then reflag the file if you need to.

Normal. This option flags files Nonshareable and Read-Write. Instead of typing FLAG *filename* +RW -S <Enter>, simply type FLAG *filename* N <Enter> at the network prompt. Sometimes the Archive bit does stay set, but often it doesn't. If you want the file's Archive bit set, you'll need to type FLAG *filename* A N <Enter>. If you reverse the order, the Archive bit attribute won't be set.

SUBdirectory. This option flags files in your present directory, affecting all subdirectories under that directory as well. These files will have to be flagged through a global command, such as FLAG *.DAT RW SUB <Enter> at the network prompt. On your screen, you'll see:

```
Files in PUB/BYTE:USERS/TED
    VOLIN.DAT    [ Rw - - - - -- - - -- -- ]
    PAL.DAT      [ Rw - - - - -- - - -- -- ]
Files in PUB/BYTE:USERS/TED/REPORTS
    PUBLIC.DAT   [ Rw - - - - -- - - -- -- ]
    ADD.DAT      [ Rw - - - - -- - - -- -- ]
Files in PUB/BYTE:USERS/TED/JOURNAL
    OFFSET.DAT   [ Rw - - - - -- - - -- -- ]
```

FLAGDIR

The FLAGDIR utility allows you to hide a directory (System and Hidden). This way you can hide directories and directory names from prying eyes. You can also set the Purge flag on the directory, as well as set the Delete and RenameInhibit attributes. You need only Modify rights to use the FLAGDIR utility.

How To Use FLAGDIR

FLAGDIR [*directory path*]/[*options*]. FLAGDIR's options are Normal, System, Hidden, and Private. If you can't remember the proper syntax to use the FLAGDIR command, type FLAGDIR /H <Enter>, you'll see:

```
386 Usage: FlagDir [path [option...]]

Options: Normal
         System
         Hidden
         DeleteInhibit
         Purge
         RenameInhibit
```

When you're in a directory where you don't have Modify rights and you try to flag a directory, you'll see the "Unable to change attributes" message. If you receive such a message, type RIGHTS *directory path* <Enter> and see if you have Modify rights.

Directory path. When you use the FLAGDIR command, you can write out the entire path, use the drive letter, or use a period (.) to specify the directory you're currently in. For example, if you have Modify rights in your NTS3/VOL1:USERS/TED/TEAM directory, and you want to flag the TEAM directory as HIDDEN (H), type FLAGDIR NTS3/VOL1:USERS/TED/TEAM H <Enter>. If NTS3/VOL1 is your default server, type FLAGDIR :USERS/TED/TEAM HIDDEN <Enter>. If the NTS3/VOL1:USERS/TED/TEAM directory is mapped to drive G:, type FLAGDIR G: HIDDEN <Enter>, or simply FLAGDIR G: H <Enter>. If you're in the G: directory, use the period and type FLAGDIR . H <Enter>. You'll see:

```
NTS3/VOL1:USERS/TED/TEAM
     TEAM HIDDEN
```

Normal. Use this option to take off the directory attributes you have set. For instance, if you flagged your G: NTS3/VOL1:USERS/TED/TEAM/RECORDS directory from Purge to Normal, type FLAGDIR G: N <Enter>.

System and **Hidden.** Both the System and Hidden options hide your directory so that only those who know the directory exists can map a path to the directory. If you type DIR in the directory above the one you flagged Hidden or System, the name of the flagged directory won't appear on the screen. For example, to flag the RECORDS directory (mapped to drive G:) as Hidden, type FLAGDIR G: H <Enter> at your network prompt.

DeleteInhibit. This prevents you or others from accidentally deleting the directory. To set this attribute for G: mapped to NTS3:VOL1/USERS/TED/RECORDS, type FLAG G: D <Enter>. If you then want to delete the directory, you'll need to reset the directory flags without the DeleteInhibit option by typing FLAG G: N <Enter>, for example.

Purge. This option allows you to purge directory contents as soon as you delete them. This is useful when you have an application that performs backups every five or ten minutes.

With NetWare 3.11, deleted files are still salvageable through the SALVAGE utility (see "The SALVAGE Utility" heading in Chapter 2). Once you delete a file, the file is still kept track of by NetWare and is protected to not be written over for 1 minute and 59 seconds.

NetWare keeps writing new files past the deleted files until the entire volume is filled with deleted and present files. Once the volume is full, and you need create or delete another version of your data files, NetWare will take the least recently accessed file(s) and purge them so it can use their disk space. This means that at any given time, you may have several deleted files that you can look at. However, if everyone is doing this, NetWare volumes can remain full of deleted files, which can degrade performance.

To get around this situation, you can set the Purge Directory attribute on the directories where you save your backup files. This way, you will still have your backup file saved as a real file if the server goes down, but you won't be needlessly filling the disk with every five minute version of the backup file. To set this attribute for your G: drive mapped to NTS3/VOL1:USERS/TED/RECORDS directory, type FLAGDIR G: P <Enter>, for example.

RenameInhibit. This option prevents you or others from accidentally renaming the directory. To set this attribute for G: which is mapped to NTS3:VOL1/USERS/TED/ RECORDS, type FLAG G: R <Enter>. In order to rename the directory, you'll need to reset the directory flags without the RenameInhibit option by typing FLAGDIR G: N <Enter>, for example.

GRANT

The GRANT utility allows you to grant trustee assignments (the ability to see and access files or utilities) in your directories to other users and groups. This is the same capability that you have in FILER. (See "The FILER Utility" heading in Chapter 2.) You must have Access Control or Supervisory rights in a directory before you can give other users trustee assignments to that directory. If you don't have one of these rights and you try to use the GRANT command, you'll see, "You have no rights to grant trustee assignments for that directory."

If you recall from the discussion of security rights in the Introduction, you need three permissions to access files and applications in NetWare: permission to access the server through *passwords*, permission to access a directory and file through *directory and file attributes,* and permission to access a directory and file through the *basic security rights.* The permission to access a directory entails trustee and directory rights, which are controlled by the basic security rights. Trustee rights help control which files and applications you can access in a given directory. When you give another person a trustee assignment in one of your directories, that trustee assignment extends to all the subdirectories under that directory, depending on the directory and file inherited rights mask. This setup changes only when you redefine the trustee assignments on a subdirectory level or change directory or file IRMs. When you define trustee rights for other users or groups, they will see that they have gained a trustee assignment the next time they look at their assignments in SYSCON, FILER (both in Chapter 2), or TLIST (later in this section).

Using the GRANT Utility

What follows is a list of GRANT's parameters and their functions, along with an explanation of how to use them. The capitalized letters on the parameters indicate the abbreviations you can use instead of typing out the entire parameter. Of course, if you prefer you can type out the entire parameter. If you can't remember the proper syntax for GRANT, type GRANT <Enter> and you'll see the syntax help screen shown next.

```
Command line arguments violate grammar defined for GRANT.

Usage: GRANT rightslist* [FOR path] TO [USER|GROUP] [options]
Options: /SubDirectories | /Files

386 Rights:
----------
All =    All
N   =    No Rights
S   =    Supervisor
R   =    Read
W   =    Write
C   =    Create
E   =    Erase
M   =    Modify
F   =    File Scan
A   =    Access Control
```

GRANT *rightslist* **FOR** *directory path* **TO** *username/group.* The rights list includes Supervisor, Read, Write, Create, Erase, Modify, File Scan, Access Control, No Rights, and All Rights. You can include ONLY and ALL BUT before specifying the options; that way, if a user has rights other than ones you wish to specify, those rights will be replaced with the rights you specify. The GRANT utility allows you to designate the rights you wish to give, the directory path (if it isn't your present directory), and who you want to give rights to. You need to place a space between each right you specify; otherwise, you'll see "Specified rights unreadable or invalid. Spaces required between each right."

For example, if you have a small database in one of your directories that you want others in group RAW to only Read, you can go to that directory path and type GRANT R F TO RAW <Enter>. If you want that group to be able to drop files into the database as well as to read files, you can type GRANT W R C E M F TO RAW <Enter>. If you want to give BILL Read and File Scan rights to your NTS3/VOL1:USERS/TED/TEAM directory, type GRANT R F FOR NTS3/VOL1: USERS/TED/TEAM TO BILL <Enter>. If the NTS3/VOL1:USERS/TED/TEAM directory is mapped to drive G:, type GRANT R F FOR G: TO BILL <Enter>.

A discussion of the seven rights you can give a user or group follows.

Supervisory. The Supervisory right allows you to have all rights to the assigned directory, its subdirectories, and files within the directory. This right overrides all other restrictions placed on subdirectories as well as files.

You cannot use GRANT to assign the Supervisory right. You can only do this if you are a supervisor or supervisor-equivalent using SYSCON.

Read. This right allows you to read information already contained in a file and is usually given along with File Scan rights for files. For example, if you want Roy to be able to look at files in your present directory, type GRANT R F TO ROY <Enter>. On your screen, you'll see:

```
VOL1:USERS/TED
ROY Rights set to [R F ]
```

Write. This right lets you place information in a file (write to a file); you need Write, Create, Erase, File Scan, and usually Modify (WCEFM) rights in your directory to actually write to a file or to copy a file into the directory. If you want Roy to be able to copy files into your default directory, type GRANT W C E F M TO ROY <Enter>. You'll see:

```
VOL1:USERS/TED
ROY Rights set to [ WCEFM ]
```

Create. This option allows you to create and write to new files as well as create directories. You usually need to grant Read rights along with Create; if you don't, users can't re-open the file once it's closed.

Erase. This gives you the power to delete existing files and directories. You often use this right in conjunction when granting WCEMF rights.

File Scan. This right allows you to search a directory for files and directories if the Private directory flag has been invoked. If you don't have this right in a directory, you'll see the "File not found" message when you type DIR in that directory. Depending on your security, you also need this right to copy files from and to directories. File Scan is often used in conjunction with the Read right to open and read in applications for use.

Modify. This option lets you change file and directory attributes, or flags. If you want someone to be able to change a file's flags in your directory, you can give that user this right. If you're trying to control how others use your files, don't grant this right. However, certain applications and utilities often need Modify rights in order to work properly, so you'll need to experiment with files or utilities in your directory. (For a discussion of file flags, see the "FLAG" subheading earlier in this section.)

Access Control. With this, you can grant and revoke trustee rights to users and groups. You can also modify the directory rights mask. Since you may have only Access Control rights to your own home directory, it's not a good idea to give someone else your Access Control rights.

The GRANT utility also has two options covering a broad spectrum of rights: NO RIGHTS and ALL.

No Rights. Use this option to revoke rights that you granted through the GRANT or FILER utilities to this specific directory. If you don't want Bill in your G: directory any more, and Bill's only access to this directory is by means of the rights you gave him through GRANT or FILER, type GRANT NO RIGHTS FOR G: TO BILL <Enter> and you'll see:

```
VOL1:USERS/TED
BILLRights set to [ ]
```

But if you've granted rights to Bill on a different directory level, such as USERS/ TED/REPORTS, you won't revoke any rights on the TED directory level unless you specify that level in the command.

Another factor that affects Bill is inherited rights. You may be able to revoke the rights you gave Bill in this directory, but if he has rights through being part of a group or through a security equivalence, he will still have rights in that directory. GRANT only affects the specified directory and those rights granted at that directory level.

ALL. Use this option to grant someone all eight trustee rights to your directory. For example, if you're sharing a project with Kelly and you want her to have total trustee rights to your G: directory, type GRANT ALL FOR G: TO KELLY <Enter> and you'll see:

```
VOL1:USERS/TED
KELLY    Rights set to [ RWCEMFA]
```

GRANT..../SubDirectories /Files. GRANT also comes with two options: / Subdirectories and /Files. However, neither of them yet works at this writing.

Other Information

If you want to copy a file, you need at least RF rights in the directory you're copying from, and at least Write, Create, Erase, and File Scan (WCEF) rights and sometimes Modify in the directory you wish to copy to. The file you're copying must not be flagged Hidden or System, or you won't be able to copy the file.

Related Commands

The GRANT utility offers the same capability that you have in FILER (see "The FILER Utility" in Chapter 2), but at the network prompt. (System supervisors can give users trustee assignments in SYSCON or in FILER.) Another related command is REVOKE, which allows you to take away rights you've given users in FILER or in GRANT. If you give a user or group a trustee assignment and later revoke those rights, the user or group is still a trustee of your directory. The REMOVE utility removes that user or group from the directory's trustee list.

If you want to see who has trustee assignments to your directory, go into that directory and type TLIST <Enter>. (See the "TLIST" subheading later in this section.) The TLIST (Trustee LIST) utility will list the users and groups, the trustee assignments, and the full names of the trustees (if assigned). Use SYSCON to see all of your trustee assignments as a user (see the "The SYSCON Utility" in Chapter 2) and as a group. Or type WHOAMI /A <Enter> at the command line. You can type USERLIST <Enter> to get a list of users on your server. (See the "User Identification Utilities" section in this chapter.) To get a list of known groups and users, you'll need to go into SYSCON.

REVOKE

The REVOKE utility takes away the trustee rights that some person or group has in one of your directories. (You can also do the same through the GRANT utility by using the ONLY and ALL BUT parameters.) You must have Access Control or Supervisory rights in that directory to revoke another person's or group's trustee rights. If you don't have one of these rights and you try to use the REVOKE command, you'll see, "You have no rights to alter trustee assignments for the specified directory," or "Error scanning trustee list." Use REVOKE to take away trustee rights given through the GRANT, SYSCON, or FILER utilities.

How to Use the REVOKE Utility

Here's a list of REVOKE's parameters and their functions, along with an explanation of how to use them. The capitalized letters on the parameters indicate the abbreviations you can use instead of typing out the entire parameter. If you prefer, of course, you can type out the entire parameter. If you can't remember the proper syntax for REVOKE when you're at the network prompt, type REVOKE <Enter> and you'll see the syntax help screen. It may not look exactly like this, but you'll get the idea:

```
Usage: REVOKE rightslist* [FOR path] FROM [USER|GROUP] name [options]
Options: /SubDirectories | /Files

286 Rights:                    386 Rights
- - - - - - - - - - - - - -    - - - - - - - - - - - - - - - - -
ALL =   All                    ALL =   All
R   =   Read                   S   =   Supervisor
W   =   Write                  R   =   Read
O   =   Open                   W   =   Write
C   =   Create                 C   =   Create
D   =   Delete                 E   =   Erase
P   =   Parental               M   =   Modify
S   =   Search                 F   =   File Scan
M   =   Modify                 A   =   Access Control

* Use abbreviations listed above, separated by spaces.
```

Although what you see here doesn't exactly match what you see on the screen, a later revision of the REVOKE help screen may drop the NetWare 286 reference.

With NetWare 3.1x, you need to place a space between each right you specify; otherwise, you'll see "Invalid right specified."

REVOKE *rightslist* **FOR** *directory path* **FROM** *username/group.* The rights list includes Supervisory, Read, Write, Create, Erase, Modify, File Scan, Access Control, and All rights. The REVOKE utility allows you to designate the rights you wish to take away, the directory path (if it isn't your present directory), and who you want to take the rights from. For example, suppose that members of a group called RASPY have been dumping files into your directory. You decide to set up your directory so the group can only read the files (Read and File Scan). Let's also say that group RASPY has Read, Erase, Write, File Scan, Modify, and Create rights. Go to that directory path and type REVOKE E W C M FROM RASPY <Enter> and you'll see:

334

```
G:\USERS\TED\JAN > revoke e w c m from raspy
BYTE:USERS/TED/JAN
Trustee's access rights set to [R F ]
```

If you have Access Control rights to the NTS3/VOL1:USERS/TED/TEAM directory, and you want to revoke Bill's Read and File Scan rights, type REVOKE R F FOR NTS3/VOL1:USERS/TED/TEAM FROM BILL <Enter>. If the NTS3/VOL1:USERS/TED/TEAM directory is mapped to drive G:, you can type REVOKE R F FOR G: FROM BILL <Enter>.

A discussion of the rights that you can revoke from another user or group follows.

Supervisory. This right allows you to have all rights to the assigned directory, its subdirectories, and files within the directory. It overrides all other restrictions placed on subdirectories as well as files.

You cannot use REVOKE to remove the Supervisory right. You can only do this if you are a supervisor or supervisor-equivalent using SYSCON.

Read. Revoking this option takes away a person's ability to open and read information in a file. The Read option is usually used in conjunction with File Scan rights (RF). For example, if you want Roy to stop reading files in your default directory, you can type REVOKE R F FROM ROY <Enter>.

Write. Removing this option revokes a person's ability to open and write to files. You usually need Write, Create, Erase, Modify, and File Scan rights to actually write to a file or to copy a file into a directory. Deleting any one of those rights will prevent a user or group from copying files into this directory. To prevent Roy from copying files into your default directory, type REVOKE W C E M F FROM ROY <Enter>.

Create. Revoking this option prevents users and groups from creating and writing to new files. You often use this right in conjunction with revoking WCEMF rights.

Erase. Without this right, users and groups can't delete existing files, directories, and subdirectories. You often use this right in conjunction with revoking WCEMF rights.

File Scan. Removing this right prevents users and groups from searching the directory for files. Users and groups will see a "File not found" message when they type DIR in a directory in which they don't have this right.

Modify. You revoke this right to prevent others from changing file and directory attributes, or flags. You can also use Modify to rename files, directories, and subdirectories. This is a good flag to revoke if you're trying to control other users' access to your files. However, certain applications and utilities often need Modify rights in order to work properly, so you'll need to experiment with files or utilities in your directory.

335

Access Control. Without this right, users and groups can't grant and revoke trustee rights. Since you may have Access Control rights only to your own home directory, you'll want to revoke Access Control rights from those who use your directories. To revoke Access Control and Modify rights from Bill (who has all rights) in your G: drive, type REVOKE M A G: FROM BILL and you'll see:

```
VOL1:USERS/TED
Trustee's access rights set to [RWCE F ]
```

The REVOKE utility has one other option that includes every right—the ALL option.

ALL. Use this option to revoke rights that you granted through either the GRANT or FILER utilities to this specific directory. If you don't want Bill in your G: directory any more, and Bill's only access to this directory is by means of the rights you gave him through GRANT or FILER, type REVOKE ALL G: FROM BILL <Enter> and you'll see:

```
VOL1:USERS/TED
Trustee's access rights set to [ ]
```

But if you've granted rights to Bill on a different directory level, such as USERS/TED/REPORTS, you won't revoke any rights on the TED directory level unless you specify that level in the command.

Another factor that affects Bill is inherited rights. You may be able to revoke the rights you gave Bill in this directory, but if he has rights through being part of a group or through a security equivalence, he'll still have rights in that directory. Unless you use the /S option, REVOKE only affects the specified directory and those rights granted at that directory level.

REVOKE..../SubDirectories /Files. REVOKE also comes with two options: /Subdirectories and /Files. The /S option for REVOKE does work (which it doesn't for the GRANT utility); it revokes the rights you specified from all subdirectories, but not from the current directory specified in the directory path. However, the /File option revokes trustee assignments at the file level.

Suppose you've granted Bill RWCEFM rights to the \USERS\TED, \USERS\TED\DATA, and \USERS\TED\DATA\JAN directories. Let's also suppose you want to let Bill have rights only in the \USERS\TED directory, but not in any of the subdirectories. If you're in the \USERS\TED directory, you can type REVOKE ALL

FROM BILL /S <Enter>, and all of Bill's trustee assignments in the subdirectories beneath \USERS\TED are revoked.

Related Commands

You can use the REVOKE utility to revoke trustee rights you set up in FILER and GRANT. (System supervisors give users trustee assignments in SYSCON and in FILER.) When you give a user or group a trustee assignment and you later revoke those rights, the user or group is still a trustee of your directory. Using the REMOVE utility removes that user or group from the directory's trustee list.

If you want to see who has trustee assignments in your directory, go into that directory and type TLIST <Enter> (covered later in this section). The TLIST (Trustee LIST) utility will display a list of the users and groups, their trustee assignments, and their full names (when defined). If you like, run TLIST before revoking a person's trustee rights and then afterwards as a doublecheck.

REMOVE

Through the GRANT and FILER utilities you can give users and groups trustee assignments to any directory that you have Access Control rights to. When you revoke all trustee rights from a person or group with the REVOKE utility, that person or group is still enrolled as a trustee in your directory. The REMOVE utility drops that person or group from the trustee list in your directory. So if you want to remove people—and not just their rights—from your directory, run REMOVE instead of REVOKE. You must have Access Control rights in a directory in order to use the REMOVE utility in that directory. If you don't have Access Control rights and you try to use the REMOVE command, you'll see, "You have no rights to remove trustees" or "Error scanning trustee list."

How to Use the REMOVE Utility

REMOVE *username/groupname* **FROM** *directory path*. If you can't remember the proper syntax for REMOVE when you're at the network prompt, type REMOVE and you'll see the syntax help screen:

```
Usage: REMOVE [USER|GROUP] Name [FROM path] [option]
Options: /Subdirs /Files
```

To illustrate, suppose you have in one of your directories a small database you've been sharing with others in group RASPY, and now you want to remove them from your directory. Go to that directory path and type REMOVE RASPY <Enter>. In another scenario, if you have Access Control rights to the NTS3/VOL1:USERS/TED/TEAM directory, and you want to remove Bill, type REMOVE BILL FROM NTS3/ VOL1:USERS/TED/TEAM <Enter>. If the NTS3/VOL1:USERS/TED/TEAM directory is mapped to drive G:, type REMOVE BILL FROM G: <Enter> and get the same results. To remove Bill's rights from the JUNE subdirectory beneath the NTS3/ VOL1:USERS/TED/TEAM directory, type REMOVE BILL FROM G:JUNE <Enter>. You'll see a screen similar to this one:

```
NTS3/VOL1:USERS/TED/TEAM/JUNE
User "BILL" is no longer a trustee to the specified directory.

Trustee "BILL" removed from 1 directories.
```

REMOVE */Subdirectories /Files.* REMOVE also comes with two options: / Subdirectories and /Files. Unlike the GRANT utility, the /S option for REMOVE does work and deletes the trustee from all subdirectories, but not from the current directory specified in the directory path. The /File option removes trustees who had assignments at the file level.

Let's follow up on the /S example presented in the discussion of the REVOKE utility. Suppose you've revoked Bill's trustee rights to the subdirectories beneath \USERS\TED, and now you wish to remove Bill as a trustee from those subdirectories. If you're in the \USERS\TED directory, you can type REMOVE BILL /S <Enter>; all of Bill's trustee assignments in the subdirectories beneath \USERS\TED are removed.

Related Commands

Use the REMOVE utility to remove users and groups from the trustee list for your directory that you set up in FILER and GRANT. (System supervisors give users trustee assignments in SYSCON and in FILER.) You can also use REMOVE in conjunction with the REVOKE command. (See the "REVOKE" subheading in this section.) If you want to see who has trustee assignments in your directory, go into that directory and type TLIST.

TLIST

The TLIST utility shows which users and groups have trustee rights to a particular directory. These rights correspond directly to the trustee assignments that your supervisor set up in SYSCON or FILER, or that you set up from either the FILER or GRANT utilities. Trustee assignments are neither the inherited rights mask nor a person's effective rights; trustee rights are the rights you give users and groups. Trustee rights also apply to all subdirectories that lie beneath those defined directories. As a result, when you give someone else trustee rights to a directory, that trustee assignment extends to all subdirectories under that directory. This setup changes only when you redefine that person's trustee assignment on a subdirectory level.

Since you're looking at the rights that others have to your directory, you must have Access Control rights in that directory and all other directories in which you want to look at trustee assignments. If you want to see trustee assignments on a different server, you must first attach to that server and have Access Control rights in the directory that you wish to look at.

How to Use the TLIST Utility

If you can't remember the proper syntax for TLIST when you're at the network prompt, type TLIST /H <Enter> and you'll see the syntax help screen:

```
TLIST displays a list of trustees (users or groups)
for a directory, along with their trustee rights.
You MUST have Access Control rights in that directory.
Usage: TLIST [path [USERS | GROUPS]].
```

TLIST. To see who has trustee assignments in your present directory, type TLIST <Enter>, and you'll see a listing similar to this one:

```
G:\USERS\TED\REPORTS >tlist

BYTE:USERS\TED\REPORTS
User trustees:
    TED                         [RWCEMFA] Ted E. Beara
Group trustees:
    WORKGRP1                    [RWCEMF ]
    BUYERS                      [RWCEMF ]
```

Notice that in the case of the user trustee list, you see the full name (if defined) of the person who has this particular directory as part of his or her trustee assignments. This does not correspond to the directory's owner, unless the owner also has that directory as part of his or her trustee assignments.

After the user's name, you'll see a box listing the basic security rights a user has when given a trustee assignment to a directory. These rights may include any of the following: Supervisory, Read, Write, Create, Erase, Modify, File Scan, and Access Control.

TLIST *directory path*. When you use the TLIST command, you can write out the entire directory path, use the drive letter, or simply type TLIST to specify the directory you're currently in. For example, if you're in your NTS3/VOL1:USERS/TED/REPORTS directory and you want to see who has trustee assignments in your NTS3/VOL1:USERS/TED/TEAM directory, type TLIST NTS3/VOL1:USERS/TED/TEAM <Enter>. If NTS3/VOL1 is your default server, type TLIST :USERS/TED/TEAM <Enter>. If the NTS3/VOL1:USERS/TED/TEAM directory is mapped to drive G:, type TLIST G: <Enter>. If you're in the G: directory, type TLIST <Enter>.

To see who has trustee assignments in the subdirectories beneath the directory you're in, type LISTDIR <Enter> to see a list of the subdirectories you have in this directory. (Remember, you must have Access Control effective rights in the directory you want to look at.) You can also type DIR *. and list only those directories and files that aren't using DOS extensions. (You won't see files or directories such as TEAM.92.) For example, if you have a subdirectory named GOODS beneath the NTS3/VOL1:USERS/TED/TEAM directory, you can type TLIST GOODS <Enter> and see something similar to the following:

```
VOL1:USERS/TED/TEAM/GOODS
User trustees:
    BARBARA              [R  F ] Barbara Hume
    TED                  [RWCEMFA] Ted E. Beara
    DAVE                 [RWCEMF ] Dave Doering
No group trustees.
```

At your drive G: directory path (NTS3/VOL1:USERS/TED/TEAM), to see who has trustee assignments in the TED directory above TEAM, type TLIST .. <Enter> at your G: prompt. You'll see NTS3/VOL1:USERS/TED in the directory path entry above the "User trustees:" line. To see who has trustee assignments in the USERS directory above TED, type TLIST ... <Enter> at your G: prompt. (If you don't have rights in a directory, you'll see this message:

```
You only have rights to see trustee assignments that relate to you.

NTS3\SYS:PERSONAL
No trustees found.
```

TLIST *directory path* **Users | Groups.** If you wish to see only the users in your current directory, type TLIST . USERS <Enter>, or TLIST . U <Enter> at your network prompt. (You'll need to use a period [.] to designate your present directory.) If you're in drive G:, and you wish to see the trustee assignments in drive H:, type TLIST H: U <Enter>. You'll see something similar to this:

```
H:\USERS\TED\TEAM >tlist . users
BYTE:USERS\TED\TEAM
User trustees:
    TED                        [RWCEMFA] Ted E. Beara
    DAVE                       [RWCEMF ] Dave Doering
```

To see a list of only the groups that have trustee assignments in your present directory, type TLIST . GROUPS <Enter> or TLIST . G <Enter>. (You'll need to use the period [.] to designate your present directory.) If you're in drive G: and you wish to see the trustee assignments for groups in drive H:, type TLIST H: G <Enter>. You'll see something similar to this:

```
G:\USERS\TED\REPORTS >tlist h: g
BYTE:USERS\TED\TEAM
Group trustees:
    WORKGRP1                   [RWCEMF ]
    BUYERS                     [RWCEMF ]
```

If you have an incredible number of trustee assignments in a given directory, you can use the /C option to allow continuous scrolling. Otherwise, you have to press a key to continue scrolling the information.

Related Commands

You usually use TLIST with the GRANT, REVOKE, and REMOVE commands. The GRANT command allows you to give trustee assignments in your directories to fellow workers, and you can run TLIST to see who presently has rights and which rights they presently have. You can also use TLIST before running REVOKE or REMOVE.

RIGHTS

The RIGHTS utility shows what kind of final rights (effective rights) you have in a directory. If you recall from the discussion of security rights in the Introduction, you need three permissions to access files and applications in NetWare: permission to access the server through *passwords*, permission to access a directory and file through the *basic security rights*, and permission to access a directory and file through directory and file *attributes*. The permission to access a directory entails your trustee assignments and directory rights, which are controlled by basic security rights.

Your effective rights means that NetWare has looked at your trustee assignments in a given directory and has looked to see if you also have any trustee assignments in that directory path from other users or groups to whom you're security equivalent. If you do have other security equivalences, NetWare first adds your user trustee rights to the rights of those groups or users. Then NetWare compares your combined group and user rights to the rights the directory itself contains (directory inherited rights mask). At this point, NetWare takes away from your user and group rights anything you haven't been granted on the directory level. This gives you your effective rights, or the rights that you can effectively use in the directory.

Despite all the above, RIGHTS does not take into account how file or directory attributes are flagged. For example, if you have all the rights you need to copy a file to another directory (Read, Create, Erase, Write, and File Scan rights), but that file's personal flags are Shareable and Read-Only, you still won't be able to copy the file. (You need Modify rights to change file flags as well as rename files and directories.) See the "FLAG" command earlier in this chapter for flagging a file.

Using the RIGHTS Command

If you can't remember the proper syntax for RIGHTS, type RIGHTS /H and you'll see the syntax help screen:

```
Usage: RIGHTS [path]

Rights = All | Supervisor | Read | Write | Create | Erase |
              Modify | Filescan | Access Control
```

RIGHTS. Use RIGHTS to see what you can effectively do in a directory. To see your effective rights in the directory you're presently in, type RIGHTS <Enter> and you'll see something similar to this:

```
F:\USERS\TED>rights
ADMIN/VOL1:USERS/TED
Your Effective Rights are [ RWCEMFA]:
  * May Read from File                    (R)
```

```
  * May Write to File                    (W)
    May Create Subdirectories and Files  (C)
    May Erase Subdirectories and Files   (E)
    May Modify File Status Flags.        (M)
    May Scan for Files                   (F)
    May Change Access Control            (A)
  * Has no effect on directory.
  Entries in Directory May Inherit [ RWCEMFA ] Rights.
```

When you use the RIGHTS command, you can write out the entire directory path, use the drive letter, or simply type RIGHTS <Enter> to specify the directory you're currently in. For example, if you're in your NTS3/VOL1:USERS/TED/TEAM directory, type RIGHTS NTS3/VOL1:USERS/TED/TEAM <Enter> to see your effective rights. If NTS3/VOL1 is your default server, type RIGHTS :USERS/TED/TEAM <Enter>. If the NTS3/VOL1:USERS/TED/TEAM directory is mapped to drive G:, type RIGHTS G: <Enter>. Finally, if you're in the G: directory, and you want to see your rights in the H: directory, type RIGHTS H: <Enter>.

If you want to check your rights in subdirectories beneath the directory you're in, type LISTDIR for a list of the subdirectories you have in this directory. You can also type DIR *. <Enter> to list only those directories and files that aren't using DOS extensions (you won't see files or directories such as TEAM.92). For example, if you have a subdirectory named GOODS beneath the NTS3/VOL1:USERS/TED/TEAM directory, you can type RIGHTS GOODS <Enter> and, depending on your rights, you'll see something similar to this:

```
F:\USERS\TED\TEAM>rights goods
NTS3/VOL1:USERS/TED/TEAM/GOODS
Your Effective Rights are [R F ]:
  * May Read from Files.         (R)
  * May Scan for Files           (F)
* Has no effect on directory.
Entries in Directory May Inherit [ RWCEMFA ] Rights.
```

At your drive G: directory path (NTS3/VOL1:USERS/TED/TEAM), to see your effective rights in the TED directory above TEAM, type RIGHTS .. <Enter> at your G: prompt. You'll see NTS3/VOL1:USERS/TED in the directory path entry above the "Your Effective Rights are [ ]" line. If you want to see your effective rights in the USERS directory above TED, type RIGHTS ... <Enter> at the G: prompt. To see your effective rights in the root directory (in this example, the USERS directory), type RIGHTS \ <Enter> at the G: prompt.

Related Commands

You can also see your effective rights through the NDIR utility. In NDIR, you can see the file flags, the directory's inherited rights mask, and the directory's effective rights mask. To see the subdirectories under a directory, use the LISTDIR command. (See the "NDIR" and "LISTDIR" subheadings in the "Directory and File Management Utilities" section.)

Working Environment Utilities

Another group of command-line utilities helps you access files and utilities as well as protect your working environment when using very old non- NetWare utilities. In this book, we'll refer to this set of command-line utilities as the Working Environment Utilities. The utilities that affect your workstation's network environment are MAP and SYSTIME.

MAP

The basic purpose of the MAP utility is to map drive letters to directories for quick access. You establish drive mappings by using the MAP command in your login script or by using the MAP utility at the network prompt. However, any map commands and changes not recorded in the login script are not permanent; you'll have to set them up again when you log back in to the server. (See "The SYSCON Utility" heading in Chapter 2 for information on using MAP in the login script.)

In NetWare, you can have up to twenty-six drive mappings, assigned to letters A through Z. You can use sixteen of those drive mappings as search drives. You have two other features in the MAP command—MAP ROOT and MAP NEXT. Here are MAP's parameters and how to use them.

If you are having problems with losing local drive designations from the PATH statement, see "Search Drive Mappings and the PATH Statement" in Appendix A.

Using the MAP Command

MAP. Use this command to see how your current directories are mapped. For example, at the network prompt, type MAP <Enter>, and you'll see which directories are presently mapped to which drive letters. If you're logged in to server PUB with the current drive mappings as shown in this example, you'll see:

```
H:\USERS\TED >map
Drive   A:  maps to a local disk.
```

```
Drive    B:   maps to a local disk.
Drive    C:   maps to a local disk.
Drive    D:   maps to a local disk.
Drive    E:   maps to a local disk.
Drive    F:   = PUB\BYTE: \USERS\TED\ELSIE\AUG
Drive    G:   = PUB\SYS:   \NEWWORK\JULY
Drive    J:   = PUB\BYTE: \USERS\TED
Drive    L:   = PUB\BYTE: \USERS\TED\REPORTS
Drive    M:   = NTS3\VOL1: \USERS\TED\CODE
- - -
SEARCH1:= Z:.    [PUB\SYS: \PUBLIC]
SEARCH2:= Y:.    [PUB\SYS: \PUBLIC\MSDOS\V5.00]
SEARCH3:= X:.    [PUB\BYTE: \APPS\WP52]
SEARCH4:= W:.    [PUB\SYS: \PUBLIC\UTIL]
SEARCH5:= V:.    [PUB\BYTE: \USERS\TED\ST]
```

When working with NetWare drive mappings from the network prompt, designate a drive letter by using the letter itself, followed by the directory path to the directory you want to access. For example, to access information in the TED directory, type MAP H:=PUB\BYTE:USERS\TED <Enter>. Then every time you type H: at the network prompt you'll be mapped to the TED directory.

MAP *drive letter.* When you want to see which directory is at the end of a particular drive letter, type MAP followed by the drive letter. For example, if you want to see which directory is mapped to F: (as in the above example), type MAP F: <Enter>, and you'll see:

```
Drive F: = PUB\SYS:NETWORK\JULY
```

If you happen to type in a drive letter that's not mapped to any directory, you'll see, "Drive E: is not defined."

MAP *directory path.* You can use the directory path parameter either to put in an entirely different directory path or to extend the present directory path. Use the directory path parameter when you're in the directory path that you want the drive letter to change to. For example, if you're in a drive mapped to SYS:NEWWORK\JULY, and you want to map F: to BYTE:USERS\TED\REPORTS\JULY on server PUB, type MAP BYTE:USERS\TED\REPORTS\JULY <Enter>. You'll see "Drive F: = PUB\BYTE:USERS\TED\REPORTS\JULY" on your screen.

You can also get the same effect by typing MAP J: JULY <Enter> while in the F: directory. This says, "Make F: equivalent to J:, but extend the directory path to include JULY."

Or, if you simply want to extend the J: directory path (J: = PUB\BYTE:USERS \TED\REPORTS) to include the JULY directory, first go to the J: directory path by typing J: <Enter> at the network prompt, then type MAP JULY <Enter>. You'll see "Drive J: = PUB\BYTE:USERS\TED\REPORTS\JULY" on your screen. To extend the J: directory path to include the JULY\OUT directories, go to the J: directory path, type MAP JULY\OUT <Enter> and you'll see "Drive J: = PUB\BYTE:USERS \TED\REPORTS\JULY\OUT" on your screen.

If the server you normally log in to has only one volume defined on it (such as SYS:), you don't need to put the servername or volume in the MAP command. For example, if server ADMIN has only volume SYS: and you want to map to SYS:DATA\AUG directory, type MAP J:=\DATA\AUG <Enter> and NetWare will map the drive for you. To be sure that the server you log in to has only one volume, type CHKVOL <Enter> at the network prompt. If you're attached to a server with only one volume, you'll need to write out the servername and volume name.

MAP *drive letter*: = *drive letter* or *directory path*. When you remap drives to directories that aren't on your default server, be sure to include the full directory path, including the servername. For example, if you want to map E: to directory ADMIN\VOL1:USERS\TED\ELSIE on file server ADMIN, type MAP E: = ADMIN\VOL1:USERS\TED\ELSIE <Enter>. If you're already attached to server ADMIN, the drive will be mapped for you. However, if you're not attached to server ADMIN, you'll be prompted to enter your user name and your password (if needed). You'll then have your drive mapping, as the following illustrates:

```
H:\USERS\TED >MAP E: = ADMIN\VOL1:USERS\TED\ELSIE
Enter user name for server ADMIN: TED
Enter your password for user TED on server ADMIN:
Drive E: = ADMIN\VOL1:USERS\TED\ELSIE
```

If you want to map drive L: to PUB\BYTE:USERS\TED\REPORTS\OUT and you know that drive J: is already mapped to PUB\BYTE:USERS\TED\REPORTS, type MAP L: = H:OUT <Enter>. On your screen, you will then see "Drive L: = PUB\BYTE:USERS\TED\REPORTS\OUT". If you simply want to make two drive mappings have the same directory, type something like MAP L: = J: <Enter>. To map L: to PUB\BYTE:USERS\TED instead, type MAP L: = J:.. <Enter> and you'll see

"Drive L: = PUB\BYTE:USERS\TED" on your screen. This example says, "Map L: to the same directory as J:, but move up one directory (..) when you do." To map to the TIMES directory under directory TED, type MAP L: = J:..\TIMES <Enter> and you'll see "Drive L: = PUB\BYTE:USERS\TED\TIMES" on your screen.

From here you're just going to have to experiment, because the combinations can get pretty complex.

If you try to map a directory to a drive designated as a local drive, you'll see a message like:

```
Drive B is in use by a local disk
Do you want to assign it as a network drive? (Y\N)Y
```

Press <Enter> and the drive will be mapped as you designated it. Then when you type MAP, you'll see something like:

```
Drive B: = PUB\BYTE:USERS\TED\TIMES
```

MAP [INSert] *search drive***: =** *drive letter* **or** *directory path***.** The Insert parameter is generally used for search drive mappings. When you type a command at your network prompt, DOS looks through the directory you're in so it can execute the command. If DOS can't find the command in your current directory, it looks through the drives you've designated as "search drives" until it finds and executes the command. If DOS can't find the command in your search drives, you'll see, "Bad command or filename."

A search drive is a directory where the operating system will look for a command that you specified at the network prompt, and which the operating system couldn't find in your current directory. Search drives start at the letter Z: (usually designated as SYS:PUBLIC) and work backwards through the alphabet. Here are Ted's search drive mappings on server PUB:

```
SEARCH1:=    Z:. [PUB\SYS:PUBLIC]
SEARCH2:=    Y:. [PUB\SYS:PUBLIC\MSDOS\V5.00]
SEARCH3:=    X:. [PUB\BYTE:APPS\WP51]
SEARCH4:=    W:. [PUB\SYS:PUBLIC\UTIL]
SEARCH5:=    V:. [PUB\BYTE:USERS\TED\ST]
```

For example, let's say you want to have one search drive mapped to a directory (such as ST) which contains all your terminate-and-stay resident (TSR) programs, batch files, and utilities. By making this directory a search drive, you have your most useful functions in an area where you can call them up from any directory you're in.

At the network prompt, type MAP S16:=PUB\BYTE:USERS\TED\ST <Enter>. S16 is the maximum number of search drives you can have; when you designate an S16 drive, NetWare will automatically place the search drive at the next available search drive number, which in this example is search drive S5.

Since DOS searches through search drives from Z: backwards (type PATH <Enter> at your network prompt to verify), you may want to change the order of your search drives. Suppose that the SYS:PUBLIC\UTIL directory in the fourth search drive slot has a utility with the same name as one of yours, but it behaves very differently and you want to use your program instead. You can either type MAP S4:=PUB\BYTE:USERS\TED\ST or MAP INS S4:=PUB\BYTE:USERS\TED\ST <Enter>.

The MAP S4: option overwrites the SYS:PUBLIC\UTIL mapping with your directory; the MAP INS S4: option inserts your directory path and bumps the SYS:PUBLIC\UTIL mapping down to search drive S5. Whichever you choose, your utility will be run first—but by using the Insert method, you'll also be able to access any other utilities in the SYS:PUBLIC\UTIL directory.

Remember, you'll have to put this MAP command in your login script if you want this setup to be in effect the next time you log in.

MAP DEL *drive letter***: or MAP REM** *drive letter***.** Use MAP REM or MAP DEL to remove a drive mapping. Choose a directory and type MAP REM D: or MAP DEL D: <Enter>, and you will see a "The mapping for drive D: has been deleted" message. When you type MAP <Enter>, you won't see the drive mapping; however, if the drive mapping is part of your login script, that drive mapping will reappear the next time you log in.

Depending on your version of NetWare, you may see a prompt when you delete a search drive. For example, if you type MAP DEL S3: <Enter>, you may see:

```
Drive X: is used by the following search mapping:
SEARCH3:
Do you still want to change it? (Y/N)Y
```

When you press <Enter> to designate "Yes," you'll see:

```
Mapping for drive X: has been deleted.
```

MAP ROOT. While this command can be executed from the command line or login script, you can only run the MAP NEXT command from the command line.

When system supervisors or workgroup managers add an application, they create a directory and then install the application in that directory. This application directory may be underneath other directories: for example, PUB\BYTE:APPS\LOTUS. However, some applications need to be at the root directory in order to create their directories during installation, as well as to read and write to files within the directory. And because you usually won't have any rights in the root directory, you won't be able to use the application. The MAP ROOT command tricks applications into believing they're at a root directory when they're actually in a subdirectory.

If you need to access and use such applications, or if your directory paths are getting too long for other applications or simply for aesthetics, use the MAP ROOT command. Your supervisor will take care of applications that need the MAP ROOT command, but you can also make good use of the command.

For example, if the PUB\BYTE:USERS\TED\REPORTS\OUT directory mapped to drive G: is too long for your application, or if you simply wish to shorten it, type MAP ROOT G: <Enter> and the OUT directory will equal G:. Or type MAP ROOT G:=PUB\BYTE:USERS\TED\REPORTS\OUT <Enter>. When you type MAP <Enter>, you'll see that the backslash has moved from between the volume marker (colon) and USERS directory to just past the OUT directory, as in this example:

```
Drive G: = PUB\BYTE:USERS\TED\REPORTS\OUT \
```

Then as you type G: <Enter>, you'll see no directory path extended beyond the drive letter, for the OUT directory has essentially become the root directory. This is very similar to what you see if you use DOS's SUBST(itute) command. If you type DIR, you'll see all the same files and subdirectories beneath the OUT directory. Then as you type CD AUG <Enter>, the drive letter will now carry G:\AUG> as the network prompt. Experiment with it and see which way you like the best.

Again, you'll have to put this MAP command in your login script if you want this setup to be in effect the next time you log in.

MAP NEXT. The MAP NEXT command finds the next available drive letter for you and maps your next drive specification to that letter. For example, suppose you want to map a drive to the PUB\BYTE:USERS\TED\DATA directory and don't care what the drive letter will be. Type MAP N BYTE:USERS\TED\DATA <Enter> and NetWare will map the DATA directory to the next available drive letter. The NEXT command doesn't work with search drives; for search drives, use the MAP S16:= specification, and MAP will find the next available search drive mapping for you.

Related Commands

When you want to permanently change your mappings, you must make the changes in your login script in SYSCON. (See "The SYSCON Utility" heading in Chapter 2.) You can attach to other file servers through the ATTACH command. (See the "Server Access Utilities" section in this chapter.) To make a subdirectory, use the MD (Make Directory) command at the directory path from which you want the subdirectory to branch.

When you use the command CD, you also temporarily change that drive mapping. For example, if you have drive F: mapped to PERSONAL\TED, and you type CD\APPS while at F:\PERSONAL\TED, you change the mapping for drive F: to F:\APPS. This lasts as long as you are logged in or until you use CD to change drive F: back to PERSONAL\TED.

SYSTIME

Many of you are already familiar with the SYSTIME utility. Through SYSTIME, you can view the current date and time of your login server or any other server you're attached to. Running SYSTIME also resets your workstation's internal clock to the date and time of the server you call up, so if you want to synchronize your workstation to your file server's time, run SYSTIME.

How to Use the SYSTIME Utility

If you can't remember the proper syntax for SYSTIME when you're at the network prompt, type SYSTIME HELP ME <Enter> and you'll see the syntax help screen:

```
G:\USERS\TED >systime help me
Usage: SysTime [Server]
```

SYSTIME. When you want to synchronize your workstation with the server you're currently logged in to, type SYSTIME <Enter> at the network prompt. You'll see something similar to this:

```
G:\USERS\TED >systime
Current System Time: Wednesday, September 15, 1992 3:32 pm
```

SYSTIME *servername.* To see the system time on other servers you're attached to, include the servername in the command. For example, if you're attached to server NTS3 and you wish to see that server's date and time, type SYSTIME NTS3 <Enter>. This also means that your workstation will synchronize its date and time to match server NTS3. If you aren't logged in or attached to the server you specify, you'll see "You are not attached to server NTS3" on your screen.

Sometimes you'll notice that no two servers show the same time when you type LOGOUT <Enter>. This means they haven't been set to the same time, or that one server's internal clock may run a bit faster than the other's.

Related Commands

If you want to see the server time on another server, first attach to that server through the ATTACH command. To see a list of available servers, type SLIST <Enter> at the network prompt. (See the "Server Access Utilities" section in this chapter for these two commands.)

Message Utilities

NetWare has three command-line utilities that allow you to send messages to others as well as prevent messages from being sent. The message utilities include CASTON, CASTOFF, and SEND. The SEND utility is similar to the message-sending capability in SESSION, except that you perform SEND at the network prompt. Use the CASTON command to prevent others from sending you messages, and the CASTOFF command to cancel the effects of CASTON.

SEND

Use the SEND command when you want to send a message to a person or a group. With NETX, the message appears on the bottom of the screen; with the DOS Requester, the message appears on the top of the screen. You can also send the same message to more than one user or group. The message can be up to 45 characters long, but that total includes the characters in your login name and your connection number (which appear with your message) as well as the message itself. The total does not include the characters in the name of the user you're sending the message to. Because SEND is a command-line utility, you won't be able to see when you run out of characters—your message is just cut off.

You might want to do two things before sending a message. If you're sending a message to someone on your server, you can type USERLIST <Enter> to see who you'd like to send a message to. If you want to send a message to someone on a different server, such as server CORP, you can type USERLIST CORP/ <Enter> to see which users are available on that server. (You must be attached to that server in order to use the

USERLIST command on it.) To send a message to someone on that server, you must also be attached to that server.

Using the SEND command

Like most command-line utilities, SEND comes with a small help screen. To see SEND's help screen, type SEND /H <Enter> and you'll see a screen similar to this one:

```
Usage:
SEND "message" [TO] [[USER|GROUP] [server/] name [,server/] name ...]
                [server/] CONSOLE
                [server/] EVERYBODY
                [STATION] [server/] n[,n...]
```

SEND "message" TO [USER | GROUP]. To send a message to Pam and Kim on your server, you can type SEND "Hail hail, the gang's all here!" TO PAM KIM <Enter>. If the message doesn't fit along with your name and connection number, or if your message is longer than 45 characters, your message will lose letters at the end of your message.

Here's a trick to help you find out how many characters your name and number take up so your messages won't get scrunched. Write a message of just numbers—0 through 9—until you fill the message screen. Then send your message to yourself. Count how many numbers appear in your message screen. The message will include your login name and connection number, so any numbers left on the screen will tell you how many characters long your messages can be. Once you eyeball this length a couple times, you'll have your message lengths down to a science.

SEND Shorthand

You can use just connection numbers instead of user names. If Kim and Pam are on your default server, type USERLIST and jot down their connection numbers. Let's say Kim's connection number is 14 and Pam's number is 17. You can then type SEND "Hail hail, the gang's all here!" 14 17 <Enter>. You'll see a message like:

```
Message sent to NTS3/KIM (station 14).
Message sent to NTS3/PAM (station 17).
```

Kim and Pam will receive the message on one line at the bottom of their screens, looking something like this:

```
>> From TED[7]: Hail hail, the gang's all here! (CTRL-ENTER to clear)
```

To clear the message, Kim and Pam will press the <Ctrl>-<Enter>. The message buffer can hold one message (an additional 45 characters) other than the one on the screen. All other messages are lost.

If you want to send a message to the CARPOOL group, type SEND "Times a-wastin', traffic ain't!" CARPOOL <Enter>. If your group has the same name as a person, type GROUP in front of the group name when you use the SEND command.

SEND "message" TO [*server/user server/group*]. To send a message to users or groups on a different server (such as server NTS3), you first need to attach to that server. Then you can type SEND "Hail hail, the gang's gone!" TO NTS3/THOMAS <Enter>. If you want to write the message in connection shorthand, you can type USERLIST CORP/ <Enter> at the network prompt. Then jot down the connection number for Thomas (let's say it's 32); then you can type SEND "Hail hail, the gang's gone!" TO CORP/32 <Enter>. If you want to get really sneaky, use a wildcard to denote all the servers you're attached to, and if you know that no one else has Thomas as a login name, you can type SEND "Hail hail, the gang's gone!" TO */32 <Enter>.

When you want to send a message to the group TIMES on server ADMIN, you can type SEND "Need some serious talking!" ADMIN/TIMES <Enter>. If you want to send to a group and also to a person—for example, Frank—who isn't a member of that group, on the same server, you can type SEND "Need some serious talking!" ADMIN/TIMES ADMIN/FRANK <Enter>. Or if you know Frank's connection number is 2, you can type SEND "Need some serious talking!" ADMIN/TIMES ADMIN/2 <Enter>. When you want to send messages to different groups on different servers, such as group TIMES on server ADMIN and group STAFF on server NTS3, you can type SEND "Come to Meeting!" ADMIN/TIMES NTS3/STAFF <Enter>. You can do the same with individuals as well.

SEND "message" TO EVERYBODY, CONSOLE. When you want to send a message to everybody who is logged in to a server like ADMIN, you can type SEND "Who munched the last Nachos???" ADMIN/EVERYBODY <Enter>. If you're on a directory path whose directory is on server, you can simply type SEND "Who munched the last Nachos???" EVERYBODY <Enter> to get the same effect. You can use the group EVERYONE to get similar results.

You can also send messages to the server console screen. For example, if you know Dave is in the server room, working on or near server ADMIN's console screen, you can type SEND "Dave, call me when you have a minute, OK?" ADMIN/CONSOLE <Enter>. Then when Dave sees the message, he can give you a call.

353

SEND TO [USER] [GROUP] "Message". You can also reverse the order of the SEND command. For example, to send a message to Jill and to group TEST, who are both on the same server, type SEND JILL TEST "We need to meet at 4 pm today! OK?" <Enter>. Try both methods, then stick with the one you like the best.

Error Messages You May Receive

If your SEND message doesn't reach its destination, you'll see an error message such as "User NTS3/TOM has not logged in." or "User/Group NTS3/TOM does not exist." If you see this message, run USERLIST to make sure the group is still logged in (see the "User Identification Utilities" section in this chapter) or check to see if you spelled the login name right. Another message you might see is "Your station is not attached to server PUB." When you receive this message, run the ATTACH command and attach to that server. (See the "Server Access Utilities" section in this chapter.) Another message is "Message NOT sent to NTS3/TED (station 3)." This message can mean that Ted has run the CASTOFF utility so he won't receive any messages, or that Ted has a message on his screen and another in the message buffer and can't receive any more messages.

Additional Information

If you receive a message from a user on a different server, you don't have to attach to that server to send a message back to that person. Written into the message you received is the connection number that the person used to send you the message. Suppose you receive a message "From GUEST [45]: Come see me as soon as you can." Instead of trying to figure out who GUEST [45] is, you can send a message like SEND 45 "Can you give me your name?" <Enter>. Since GUEST already has a connection to your server, you can send a message using that connection number.

Related Commands

If you plan to send messages to people on servers other than your default server, you'll need to attach to those servers first. You can also use the USERLIST command to find a user's connection number, allowing you to send messages using connection shorthand.

Sometimes when you're in the middle of a project, receiving SEND messages can be irritating. You can use the CASTOFF command to prevent SEND messages from reaching you. Then when you're feeling sociable again, use the CASTON command to reenable receiving SEND messages.

CASTOFF

The CASTOFF utility prevents any messages from being sent to your screen. CASTOFF keeps the screen clear from any intruding messages; however, you can still use the SEND command to send messages to others. The CASTOFF utility stays in effect until you log out or until you type CASTON at the network prompt. To use this utility, type CASTOFF (STation, All, or Console) <Enter>.

CASTOFF Flags

CASTOFF comes with three flags, each flag preventing a different kind of message from appearing on the screen. These flags include:

CASTOFF STations. The Stations flag prevents you from receiving messages from other workstations. While you can write out the entire stations flag, you can also use the abbreviated version by typing CASTOFF ST <Enter>. You'll receive the message "Broadcasts from other stations will now be rejected."

CASTOFF Console. The Console flag stops all messages from workstations as well as supervisor messages that you may receive from the server's console. However, you'll still receive broadcast messages that are time-related, such as a message telling you that you need to log off from the server because your time is up. While you can write out the entire console flag, you can also use the abbreviated version by typing CASTOFF C <Enter>. You'll receive the message "Broadcast messages from the console and other stations will now be rejected."

CASTOFF All. The All flag stops all messages, whether they're from other workstations or supervisors at the console. You can write out the entire All flag, or use the abbreviated version by typing CASTOFF A <Enter> at the network prompt. You'll receive the message "Broadcast messages from the console and other stations will now be rejected."

Related Commands

If friends or supervisors send you messages, you'll see those messages appear at the bottom of your screen. Pressing <Ctrl>-<Enter> simultaneously gets rid of the message. However, some screens (and applications) don't recognize the LINE 25 signal (where SEND or MESSAGE appear) and when someone sends a message, your screen seems to hang for no reason. Since the message never reaches the screen, pressing the <Ctrl>-<Enter> keys doesn't necessarily come to mind.

About the only command that CASTOFF relates to is the CASTON command, which allows you to receive SEND and BROADCAST messages from the network. The

SEND command is a means of sending messages to other people or groups on servers across the network. (For a full explanation of SEND, see the "SEND" subheading in this section.) The BROADCAST command is similar to the SEND command, except that supervisors use it from either the server console or from the FCONSOLE utility.

CASTON

CASTON cancels the effects of CASTOFF, allowing a workstation to receive messages again. These messages come from other workstations, other servers, other forms of servers, or NLMS. The CASTON utility has no flags or parameters. At your network prompt, type CASTON <Enter>. You'll see the message "Broadcast messages from the console and other stations will now be accepted."

Related Commands

The CASTON command is used in conjunction with the CASTOFF utility, which prevents you from receiving SEND and BROADCAST messages from the network. The SEND command is a means of sending messages to other people or groups on servers across the network. (For a full explanation of SEND, see the "SEND" subheading in this section.) The BROADCAST command is similar to the SEND command, except that supervisors use it to send messages from either the server console or from the FCONSOLE utility.

General NetWare Utilities

These last command-line utilities don't fit into any of the other utility categories, so we've lumped them together under the category of General NetWare utilities. General NetWare utilities include NVER, SETTTS, SMODE, and VERSION.

NVER shows version information about network software. The SETTTS utility, involving those files that have been marked as "transactional," is used with those systems that have transaction tracking. SMODE gives an application the ability to find its auxiliary files so the application can perform its tasks. The VERSION utility is useful when you call a NetWare support person about a certain utility and the support person asks you for the utility's version number.

NVER

The NVER utility displays version information about seven kinds of network software. NVER displays all the version information about a particular workstation's NetBIOS, IPX, SPX, NetWare shell, and DOS versions. NVER also displays version information about the workstation's LAN driver and the server software for servers that the workstation is attached to.

How To Use NVER

To use the utility, type NVER <Enter> at the network prompt. You'll see a screen similar to this one:

```
E:\USERS\TED\REPORTS >nver
NetWare Version Utility, Version 3.75

IPX Version:3.30
SPX Version:3.30

LAN Driver: NetWare Ethernet NE-2000 V1.05EC (900718) V1.00
            IRQ = 3, Port = 300h, no DMA or ROM

Shell: V3.27 Rev. A
DOS: MSDOS V5.00 on IBM_PC

FileServer: PUB
Novell NetWare V3.11(250 user) (02/20/91)

FileServer: NTS3
Novell NetWare v3.12 (250 user) (4/16/93)
```

Workstations running IPXODI drivers and the NetWare DOS Requester will see a screen similar to the following:

```
NETWARE VERSION UTILITY, VERSION 3.75

IPX Version: 3.30
SPX Version: 3.30

LAN Driver:  Novell NE1000 Ethernet V1.00
             IRQ 5, Port 0300

Shell:       V4.00 Rev. A
DOS:         MSDOS V5.00 on IBM_PC

FileServer: PUB
```

357

```
Novell NetWare v3.11 (250 user) (2/20/91)

FileServer: NTS3
Novell NetWare v3.12 (250 user) (4/16/93)
```

NetBIOS, IPX, and **SPX.** NVER sends a packet requesting the version information for each piece of software that can be loaded in a workstation. If you don't have the particular software loaded, such as NetBIOS, you won't see anything about the software. Otherwise, you'll see the version numbers for NetBIOS, IPX, and SPX, as in the above example.

LAN Driver. The LAN driver information displayed by NVER identifies the LAN driver and the configuration option used during WSGEN to generate the workstation shell. This is the same shell description information that you see when you load IPX and the NetWare shell after you initially boot up your computer. NVER first displays the name and version number of the LAN driver your shell was linked with, then the hardware settings (interrupt, I/O base address, and so forth) that were selected in WSGEN. The LAN driver should correspond to the type of network interface board installed in your workstation.

The settings selected in WSGEN must match your actual board settings, or your workstation won't work at all. For this reason, be careful borrowing another person's boot disk. That person may have settings that don't work with your board.

The LAN driver information in the previous example indicates that the workstation has a NetWare Ethernet NE-1000 board installed that is using interrupt 3 and is sending its input/output (I/O) to the base address of 300h (hexadecimal). If you're ever asked what your board settings are, run NVER to get the answer.

If you are running IPX ODI communications drivers, you'll find the LAN driver entry to be a little different. Instead of running WSGEN, IPX ODI drivers set the board setting through the NET.CFG file. (See Chapter 5 for more information on IPX ODI and NET.CFG.)

Shell, DOS, and **File Server.** NVER displays which NetWare shell (v4.00 is the DOS Requester) and DOS version are running on your workstation. The servername and operating system version displayed are the same information as you see when you choose the "File Server Information" option from SYSCON's "Available Topics" window. (See "The SYSCON Utility" heading in Chapter 2.) The servername and OS (operating system) version are read directly from the operating system itself. NVER will show you information about all of the servers you're attached to. (NetWare allows you to be attached to as many as eight servers.)

Other Information

NVER is written for NetWare 2.15 or greater. If your shell isn't acting properly, NVER may display a message like "The NetWare shell is not loaded. Unable to provide version information." More likely, though, if your shell is messed up, NVER will display a bunch of gibberish instead of the shell version because NVER goes to a specific place in the NetWare shell to retrieve the shell information. And more often than not, you can't boot up to even run NVER if your shell is corrupted enough to receive an error message.

SETTTS

The SETTTS utility helps applications that send files marked as transactional to NetWare systems running the Transaction Tracking System (TTS). If your NetWare has TTS installed, you may need to learn about SETTTS. SETTTS is a supervisor utility, so you should consult your supervisor before using this utility.

In order to use SETTTS, you need three things:

1. You need to have NetWare running the Transaction Tracking System.

2. You must be running an application whose data files are flagged Transactional. You can flag files Transactional in FILER or with the FLAG command.

3. The application must be using file locks for something else, requiring you to set the file locking parameters at new beginning points, which is what you use SETTTS for.

Here's a brief explanation of transaction tracking and how SETTTS fits into this picture.

A Little on Transaction Tracking and SETTTS

Transaction tracking helps prevent your databases from being corrupted if there is a power failure or if your system fails as your database is being updated. Data corruption occurs when the power goes out while information you're sending to the server is being written to the server's hard disk, and only part of the information you sent gets written to disk.

To prevent this from happening, NetWare has a software feature known as the Transaction Tracking System, or TTS. This system looks at a block of data as a transaction to be entirely written to the disk, or in case of failure, to be completely aborted, in which case nothing is written to the disk. That way, you'll either get all the data within the transaction updated, or none of the corrupted transaction data is saved, thus preserving your database.

The TTS works from file locks, which can be either logical or physical locks. When you mark a file as transactional, you tell the TTS that this file needs TTS protection. Then when you run an application that opens that file, TTS looks at the file lock to "implicitly" begin a transaction, and waits until the file is unlocked. TTS then takes the information and sends it as a transaction to the disk.

But some applications use file locking for other purposes. The SETTTS command allows supervisors and users to set the logical and physical lock threshold on any given application, allowing TTS to ignore any logical or physical record locks that occur before the number you specify. For example, the dBASE III PLUS 1.0 version of dBASE III used a logical record lock for copy protection, which was not released until you exited the program. You can get around this problem by upgrading your dBASE package or by typing SETTTS 1 <Enter>. TTS will skip the initial logical file lock and you're on your way. (Subsequent dBASE versions have rectified the problem and can be used without SETTTS.)

Using the SETTTS Command

SETTTS logical locks physical locks. SETTTS comes with two parameters: the first parameter sets logical locks, and the second parameter sets the physical locks. For example, to set up a two logical and one physical threshold, type SETTTS 2 1 <Enter>. To set up a one physical lock, type SETTTS 0 1 <Enter>; and to set up a one logical lock, type SETTTS 1 <Enter>.

You have to run SETTTS each time you enter the application. Once you set up SETTTS, you can change the settings only by using the SETTTS command again, by logging out, or by rebooting your workstation. So if you have more than one application that needs to use SETTTS (a situation that's highly unlikely), have your supervisor set up batch files that take care of the SETTTS command as they call up the application. As a user, the chances that you will need to use SETTTS are very slim.

Other Information

Other applications that may need SETTTS set to 1 (logical lock) are some versions of MicroFocus Cobol and Revelation version G2B. Some versions of Revelation also use a logical record lock (always open when you enter the program) to mark how many users are in the program. However, consult the documentation for the application in question to make sure this is still the case, for application versions do change (another corollary to Murphy's Law).

Your supervisor can set up the SETTTS command in a batch file that also calls up your application. That way, you won't have to fuss with remembering to run SETTTS before such applications.

SMODE

SMODE helps make sure applications can find the auxiliary files they need in order to perform their tasks. Many applications, when started, also open a number of other files (such as overlay files and data files) that are used as a resource to the application. The SMODE (Search Mode) command determines when applications can look in your NetWare search drives to find these auxiliary files.

To understand how SMODE works, you need to understand a little about the way DOS handles searching for auxiliary files. Most often, when an application's executable file (a file with either an .EXE or a .COM extension) requires an auxiliary file, it will specify a path to that file as part of its setup menu or routine. These paths are often specified in the DOS SET command: for example, SET TEMP=C:\WIN30 \TEMP. DOS will always look in this path whenever a path is specified. If a path isn't specified in the application, DOS will search the default directory (the directory you start the application from). In a stand-alone environment, if DOS doesn't find the files, you may not be able to successfully start the application.

This is where SMODE comes in. If you have search drives set up for your workstation in your login script, NetWare will take over where DOS leaves off, continuing to look in the search drives for the necessary files. Some applications only open their auxiliary files and read their contents; other applications need to both read and write to the files.

You may not have the rights necessary to write to or modify files in your search drive directories, so you might have to restrict the searches to those open requests that are read-only requests. You'll have to check with your network supervisor or consult the documentation for each application to determine if the application just reads its auxiliary files or reads and writes to them.

Although this doesn't affect many users (SMODE is actually a supervisor utility for a small number of applications, such as programming applications), you may have an application that needs to open a different set of auxiliary files in another directory: for example, if an application usually opens the RPT.DAT file in the PUBLIC/REPORTS search drive directory, but you want the application to look for the RPT.DAT file in your USERS/TED/REPORTS directory. SMODE can prevent the application from looking on any search drives for files with the same filenames.

Using the SMODE Command

The SMODE command comes with a number of modes, all of which limit some aspect of how the application can use the search paths to find its files. If you can't remember the proper syntax for SMODE, type SMODE ? <Enter> to see the syntax help screen:

```
USAGE: Smode [filespec [/MODE=mode [SUB]]
SMODE operates on executable files and ignores non-executable files

Modes:
    0 - shell default search mode
    1 - search on all opens with no path
    2 - do not search
    3 - search on read-only opens with no path
    4 - (reserved, do not use)
    5 - search on all opens
    6 - (reserved, do not use)
    7 - search on all read-only opens
```

The SUB option causes SMODE to affect the specified directory and all subdirectories of that directory.

SMODE *directory path/drive letter*: *filename.* To see how an application's search modes are currently set up, type SMODE and designate a directory path by writing out the directory path or by using the drive mapping letter. Then designate the name of the application. For example, if you want to see what the modes are on the USER2.EXE file in drive G: USERS/TED/REPORTS, type SMODE USERS/TED/REPORTS USER2.EXE <Enter>, or type SMODE G:USER2.EXE <Enter>.

If you want to see the modes of all executable files in the TED directory above the REPORTS directory, type SMODE G:.. <Enter>. To see the modes of all the executable files in the JULY directory below the REPORTS directory, type SMODE G:REPORTS <Enter>. And to see all the executable files in the REPORTS directory and all of its subdirectories, type SMODE G: SUB <Enter>.

To see the modes of all *.COM and *.EXE files in your present directory, simply type SMODE <Enter>. To see only the *.EXE files in your present directory, type SMODE *.EXE <Enter>. When there aren't any files that match your filename specification (*.EXE), you'll see the "No Executable files could be found with pattern "*.EXE" message along with the directory path used. If there aren't any executables in a given directory, you'll see a "No Executable files could be found with pattern *.*" message.

SMODE *directory path/drive letter*: *filename* **/MODE = x.** SMODE comes with a number of mode options to choose from. Each mode specifies a different way of using search drives. A brief explanation of each mode is given below. Remember that DOS will always look in a specific path (if specified in the application) and then in the default directory, regardless of which search mode you specify.

Here's a list of available modes that a program can use to find a file on the search drives:

Table 3-1. How SMODE settings relate to search drives

Mode	NO PATH Read-Only	Read-Write	PATH Read-Only	Read-Write
1	Yes	Yes	No	No
2	No	No	No	No
3	Yes	No	No	No
5	Yes	Yes	Yes	Yes
7	Yes	No	Yes	No

Here's an explanation of the different modes and what they mean:

SMODE *directory path/drive letter*: *filename* **/MODE = 0.** Mode 0 is the default setting for all executable files, and it means there are no search instructions. The application first looks in the default directory, and then follows whatever mode the shell has set. You can change this command to another mode setting at the command line or in your NET.CFG file. (See Chapter 5.)

SMODE *directory path/drive letter*: *filename* **/MODE = 1.** This is the "shell default search mode" for SMODE. When you use this setting, the shell will look in the search drives only when no path is specified in the application (and after DOS has searched the default directory). The search is allowed for both Read-Only and Read-Write requests. NetWare displays this mode on the screen as "Search on all opens with no path."

For example, to set the USER2.EXE file in the G: drive mapping to Mode 1, type SMODE G: USER2.EXE /M=1 <Enter>, or SMODE G: USER2.EXE 1 <Enter>. You'll then see, "USER2.EXE mode = 1, search on all opens with no path." To set all the executable files within a directory, type SMODE G: . M=1 <Enter>. To set all the executable files in the directory above the directory specified in the path, type SMODE G: .. M=1 <Enter>. (This will work only if you have rights in that directory.)

SMODE *directory path/drive letter*: *filename* **/MODE = 2.** When you use this search mode, the shell won't look in any search drives to find auxiliary files. The application will behave as if you were running it on a stand-alone machine with DOS only. When the application has no defined path to search for the files, it will search only in the directory the application is in. NetWare refers to this mode as "Do not search." To set the USER2.EXE file in the G: drive mapping to Mode 2, type SMODE G: USER2.EXE M=2 <Enter>; you'll see "USER2.EXE mode = 2, do not search."

SMODE *directory path/drive letter*: *filename* **/MODE = 3.** This search mode is exactly like Mode 1, except that the shell will look in the search drives only if the open request is a read-only request. NetWare calls this "Search on read-only opens with no path." To set the USER2.EXE file in the G: drive mapping to Mode 3, type SMODE G: USER2.EXE 3 <Enter>; you'll see "USER2.EXE mode = 3, search on read-only opens with no path."

SMODE *directory path/drive letter*: *filename* **/MODE = 5.** When you use this search mode, the shell will always be able to look in the search drives, even if the application specifies a path. NetWare refers to this mode as "Search on all opens." To set the USER2.EXE file in the G: drive mapping to Mode 5, type SMODE G: USER2.EXE 5 <Enter>; you'll see "USER2.EXE mode = 5, search all opens."

SMODE *directory path/drive letter*: *filename* **/MODE = 7.** This search mode is exactly like Mode 5, except that the shell will look in the search drives only if the open request is a read-only request. No requests to read and write to the file will be allowed to use the search drives. To set the USER2.EXE file in the G: drive mapping to Mode 7, type SMODE G: USER2.EXE 7 <Enter>; you'll see "USER2.EXE mode = 7, search on all read-only opens."

Other Information

Applications are becoming more and more network-aware: 90% of you will never install applications that will need to use SMODE. An application's SETUP utility will often take care of any extra directory paths that an application may need, so allowing the application to look through search drives may be unnecessary. It all depends on the type of application you're running and the amount of information it needs from outside its default directory. If installing an application gets too complicated, ask your supervisor to help you.

VERSION

The VERSION utility shows your NetWare utility's version. This information can be useful when you must contact Technical Support with a question about a NetWare utility. If Technical Support asks which version your utility is, you can run VERSION and tell them.

VERSION is specific to NetWare. It looks in a certain place in the utility for the version number as well as its checksum. Most other utilities won't have version information in the same place.

Using the VERSION Utility

VERSION *directory path filename.* To use the VERSION utility, simply type VERSION and the filename. Since all the NetWare utilities for users are stored in the SYS:PUBLIC directory—a search drive directory—you can use VERSION in just about any directory you wish. For example, if you want to see which version of the SYSCON utility you have, type VERSION SYSCON <Enter>. You'll see something similar to this:

```
H:USERS\TED > version syscon
SYSCON.EXE: .....
    Version 3.69
    Requires Overlay Version 1.02
    (c) Copyright 1983-1993, Novell, Inc. All rights reserved
    Checksum is 44F76.
```

You can see some of the same version information in the screen headers of the menued utilities: for example, the top-left part of the screen shows the version number of the menued utility. Some of the NetWare menu utilities have an overlay (a set of extra files, such as help files), which also has versions. The overlay version doesn't appear on the utility's screen header. If you need that information, you'll need to run VERSION.

To see the version number of a command-line utility, type VERSION and the title name. For example, to see the SEND utility's version number, type VERSION SEND <Enter>. You'll see something similar to this:

```
H:USERS\TED > version send
SEND.EXE:
    Version 3.50
    (c) Copyright 1983-1993, Novell, Inc. All rights reserved
```

```
    Checksum is FFFFE71F.
```

If you happen to try VERSION on other utilities that are not NetWare-specific, you may see something similar to this:

```
H:USERS\TED > version ced
CED.EXE: .
Version number not found.
    Checksum is 2C14.
```

Summary

Chapter 3 covered the command line utilities that can assist you in getting around in NetWare. Each section covered different utilities for different tasks. Take time to acquaint yourself with the many utilities and what they perform. You will find some you will use often, while others you may never use.

The next chapter, Chapter 4, looks at the command line and menu utilities that apply to printing with NetWare.

Printing Up a Storm

From a user's perspective, printing has never been intuitive. It's a struggle to print on a stand-alone, and it's even more of a struggle on a network. Many of you will struggle with reading this chapter. Fortunately, most of the material in this chapter covers features that you won't need unless you want to print to a printer other than the one you normally use. For 99% of your printing needs, your supervisor has set up NetWare to send your application printing jobs to the proper printer.

Let's take a look at a printing theory of operation, then we'll look at the utilities NetWare offers to assist you in printing on the network.

Printing Theory

NetWare uses a print server approach. LAN workstations can access printers connected directly to the server or to workstations on the network. Supervisors install printing services on the file server or bridge (router) by using PSERVER.NLM. By using this approach, the file server also becomes the print server. Supervisors or print server managers can move printing services off the file server by installing printing services on a dedicated workstation through PSERVER.EXE. This way the workstation becomes the print server, thereby freeing up the file server to take care of other duties.

NetWare's print server utility allows users to take advantage of even those printers scattered throughout the network. For example, you can access printers that are attached to workstations by running a TSR called RPRINTER on those workstations. Before the implementation of NetWare print servers, you needed third-party printing utilities, such as Brightwork's PS-Print or Intel's LANSpool (and others). These third-party products still offer features not implemented in NetWare's printing services.

Supervisors or queue managers set up print queues that are stored on the file server where they are created. By having the print services run on a dedicated workstation, the print server can service queues on as many as eight different file servers. The same is true if the administrator is running the print server software (.NLM) on the file server itself.

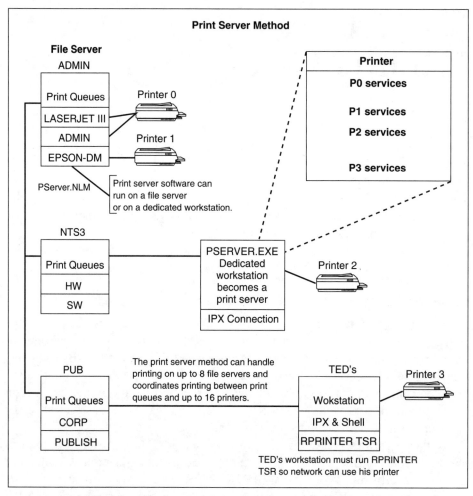

Figure 4-1. The different techniques of printing on a NetWare network

Print services also extend the number of printers you can access. Whether you're running print services on the file server or on a dedicated print server (workstation), you can access up to sixteen printers per print server. These printers can be attached to the file servers, to print servers, or to workstations This allows better placement of printers along the network, rather than forcing the strategic placement of file servers on the network or requiring third-party software to allow remote printer access.

368

When you send a print job, that job is usually stored in the print queue of the file server you log in to. The print server polls the print queues for the next job and, if it finds a job, the service sends the print job to one of as many as sixteen printers assigned to service that queue. If more than one printer is assigned to a print queue, the print server hands the next available print job to the next idle printer. If a printer is assigned to more than one queue on any of the file servers, supervisors can prioritize one queue over others for greater printer access.

Applications and NetWare

Applications generally come with printing features, allowing you to print data or files you create within those applications. Most applications are not particularly aware of the network they run on, but they are aware of which printer port (designated as LPT1, LPT2, LPT3, COM1, or COM2) they're using. (Think of a "printer port" simply as an area of your workstation where the application sends the data on its way to the printer. In computer jargon, this is called "printing to" the port.)

To enable you to print on the network, your supervisor usually sets up your software to print jobs to a particular printer port (usually LPT1) and tells NetWare which printer port that is. Depending on the application, your supervisor may have to set up NetWare's CAPTURE utility to "capture" print jobs being sent to LPT1 and redirect those jobs to a print queue on a specified server.

This chapter will help you understand how to use NetWare's printing utilities when you want to print somewhere other than on your usual printer. There are three aspects to successful printing on the network: knowing which printer port your applications are using to print, telling NetWare where to pick up the print job, and telling NetWare where you want to print the job (you do this through the CAPTURE utility). These are the three most important things you need to understand if you want to control the printing process yourself.

Your supervisor should have already set up your NetWare printing functions to make sure your data goes from your workstation to the correct printer. But there may be times when you'll want to print to a different printer. Or you might want to print a lengthy file at midnight so your colleagues won't scowl and mutter while your job hogs the printer for an hour and a half. This chapter will explain the functions of the printing utilities so you'll know what NetWare offers when you need printing assistance.

When you choose to go outside the comfort zone provided by your applications and your system supervisor, NetWare includes three menu and six command-line utilities to help you print your work.

The menu utilities are PCONSOLE, PRINTCON, and PRINTDEF. PCONSOLE allows you to monitor your network printing, place DOS-type print jobs in a queue for printing (we'll explain that process later), and change parameters in your print jobs. PRINTCON is a convenience utility for setting up print job configurations for use by the actual printing utilities—PCONSOLE, CAPTURE, and NPRINT. Your supervisor uses the PRINTDEF utility to fix some printing problems.

The command-line print utilities are CAPTURE and ENDCAP, NPRINT, RPRINTER, and PSC. Use the CAPTURE utility to direct printing jobs from applications to wherever you want them to go—to the proper servers, print queues, and printers. Most applications don't know about networks and network printing, so you use CAPTURE to perform those functions. ENDCAP simply ends the effects of the CAPTURE command.

NPRINT is the network version of DOS's PRINT command, but with some extra features. NPRINT prints out DOS text or graphics files. (DOS text files consist of straight data without word processing codes. You can instruct your application to save files as DOS text files.) You may be running an RPRINTER TSR (terminate-and-stay-resident program) that allows printers attached to your workstation to be shared with other users as network printers. To watch the status of print servers and printers, you can use the PSC utility.

Your supervisor has set up most of the large applications you use (for example, WordPerfect or Lotus 1-2-3) to send their print jobs to the proper printer. You see some of these applications when you type MAP and look at your search drives. If you occasionally want to send a print job to a different printer, you can use CAPTURE (see the "Using the CAPTURE Command" heading later in this chapter). However, if you've put a small program (for example, PCCALC) in one of your personal directories and you want to print the data from that program to a network printer, you might find the following information helpful.

What Applications Can Do

We've already mentioned the importance of knowing which printer port—LPT1, LPT2, LPT3, COM1, or COM2—your application is printing to. In terms of printing, there are basically three kinds of applications: *dumb* applications, *smart* applications, and *network* applications. Each kind of application has some method for printing to a printer port.

A dumb application prints only to LPT1. Depending on your keyboard, pressing <Shift>-<PrtSc> or just the Print Screen key is all you have to do to print to LPT1. A smart application, on the other hand, has a SETUP program that allows you to designate which LPT or COM port you want to send your print jobs to. Any application that allows you to designate a printer port can be called a smart application. (The network version of Lotus 1-2-3 is one example.) If an application does print to a port other than LPT1, you must be sure to tell NetWare's CAPTURE command which port the data went to so NetWare can pick it up there to send it on to the printer.

The third kind of application is the network application—that is, an application that takes advantage of the networking environment. Network applications can send print jobs to print queues without your having to use NetWare printing utilities such as CAPTURE. An example of such an application is WordPerfect 4.2, which allows you to designate both a server and a printer. From within WordPerfect 5.1 and 5.2, you can designate a server and a printer queue. This means you don't have to tell NetWare how to print those jobs; you tell WordPerfect instead. This also alleviates double queuing, which occurs when both the application and NetWare queue the job.

Printing Aspects of Queue Management

In versions of NetWare before 2.1x, your print jobs "spool" at the server, where they wait their turn to print at a specific printer. But NetWare 2.1x and above have what's known as a queue management service. Queue management is a method of first storing jobs at a directory (queue) and then forwarding those jobs to some service device, such as a printer.

At some time during installation, your supervisor also defined and assigned print queues to these printers to service your print jobs. A printer may service one print queue or many print queues, depending on your network needs. For printing services running from an NLM, or dedicated workstation, printers and print queues are defined later through the PCONSOLE utility. In the print queue, your job waits its turn to be printed. While your job is in the print queue, you may change different parameters through PCONSOLE. For example, you might request the printing of more than one copy.

Printing Application Files and DOS Text Files

Most users live inside their applications, not realizing that it's the application that formats their files for good-looking output. Files that you create while in the application are saved in that application's format, and must be printed from the application itself if you want to use the application's formatting capabilities. (I will discuss the exception to this.)

Once you know where your application is sending your print jobs, you need to tell NetWare where to pick up that print job and which print queue to send the print job to if the application itself doesn't know how to do this. When setting up your system, your supervisor probably included a CAPTURE command to send your print jobs to a print queue serviced by a printer. With the CAPTURE command in place, you can print files to the designated printer while you're in the application. The application formats the print job; NetWare CAPTURE sends it to the right place.

The other two utilities, PCONSOLE and NPRINT, are network versions of DOS's PRINT command, and are used only to print DOS text files. Don't use PCONSOLE or NPRINT to print a file saved in an application format. Each application puts in its own fonts and features which, without the application interpreting the parameters, may print out as so much guacamole from PCONSOLE and NPRINT. When you save a file in an application, print it from the application; when you save a file just as text (without the application's format), you can print that file from PCONSOLE and NPRINT.

Sending Print Jobs to a File

On the other hand, you might want to set application files aside to print later when you're not in that application. For example, suppose you need to print a lengthy file with plenty of nice graphics, but you don't want to enrage your coworkers by tying up the printer for a couple of hours. Instead of sending that print job directly to a printer, you can print it to a file on a network directory. All the formatting codes will go along as well. Later, you can print your file, nicely formatted, through PCONSOLE or NPRINT without having to go back into the application to do it.

Using the CAPTURE Command

Applications are becoming more powerful in their printing features and capabilities. But there are still many applications that don't directly take advantage of NetWare's printing capabilities. So when you want to send a file to a network printer using the features and setups your application offers, you may also need to run the CAPTURE command to designate which server, queue, or printer you want the file to go to. CAPTURE lets you redirect a workstation's LPT ports to network printer devices, queues, and files.

CAPTURE also comes in handy when you want to print on a server other than the one you initially log in to. With CAPTURE, you can redirect all print jobs to the server and printer most convenient for you or your workgroup. You can also have more than one CAPTURE running at the same time; CAPTURE allows you to redirect up to three LPT ports to various printers or files, and since these are logical connections, your workstation doesn't need three physical LPT ports.

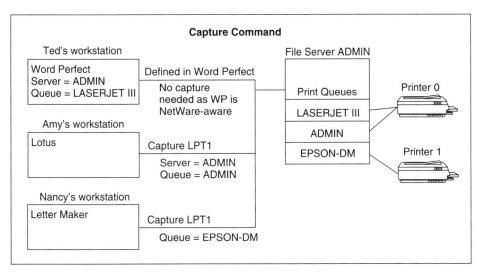

Figure 4-2. Unless applications are NetWare-Aware, workstations use CAPTURE to route print jobs to respective print queues

Your supervisor may already have a CAPTURE command designated in the system login script to enable you to print to a specific queue and printer. Or you may have a CAPTURE command designated in your personal login script to let you print to a specific printer. (Remember, personal login script commands override matching system login script commands.)

Either way, you can use CAPTURE to specify jobs, servers, queues, printers, and filenames. You can also set printing specifics, such as number of copies, time-outs, tabs, banners, text names, formfeeds, autocaps, and endcaps. (We'll explain all of these parameters in the course of discussing CAPTURE.) With a few exceptions, parameters defined in CAPTURE are also defined in PRINTCON. See Table 4-1 later in this chapter for a chart showing the similar parameters.

CAPTURE's Parameters

If you want to see a listing of CAPTURE's parameters at the network prompt, type CAPTURE /H <Enter>, and you'll see the following:

```
USAGE: CAPTURE /SHow /Job=jobname /Server=fileserver
/Queue=queuename /Local=n /Form=form or n /CReate=path
/Copies=n (1-255) /TImeout=n /Keep /Tabs=n (1-18) /No Tabs
```

```
/Banner=bannername /NAMe=name /No Banner /FormFeed /No FormFeed
/AUtoendcap /No Autoend /NOTIfy /No NOTIfy /DOmain=domain
/EndCapture /CAncel /All
```

What you'll see is a list of CAPTURE's parameters and their functions. The capitalized letters on the parameters are the abbreviated letters you can use instead of typing out the entire parameter. (Of course, if you prefer, you can type out the entire parameter.) Three parameters—servers, queues, and LPT port specifications—are the stable settings that become the basis for printing. You can add or modify the other parameters simply by typing CAPTURE and the parameter setting you wish, such as CAPTURE /NB <Enter> for "no banner." This makes the CAPTURE command a little easier to work with, because you don't have to type in a big hairy string of CAPTURE commands every time you want to modify a parameter.

However, in order for this trick to work, the CAPTURE you are using must match the default CAPTURE you set up through PRINTCON. If you haven't set up a default print job in PRINTCON, CAPTURE will build on your present CAPTURE statement. If you have a default print job in PRINTCON, CAPTURE uses that default definition to modify the parameter. Keep this in mind if you end up printing to a different printer than the one you're used to.

Here's the list of CAPTURE parameters and how to use them. (The Domain parameter isn't used).

/Server = *servername*. Use this command to print to a server other than the server you logged in to. For example, suppose you're logged in to server PUB, and you want to send a print job to printer 0 on server NTS3. At the network prompt, type CAPTURE S=NTS3 and press <Enter> before entering your application; your file will go to whatever print queue is set up as a default on server NTS3. If you're not attached to server NTS3, CAPTURE will supply you with an attachment as user GUEST (as long as user GUEST has no password on that server). With the print server concept, this idea can be expanded to include queues on as many as eight file servers that have their print jobs taken care of by up to sixteen printers across the network.

Sometimes the supervisor attaches you to servers as user GUEST for printing purposes. This attachment can be a source of frustration when you need to be attached under your own user name so you can access applications or utilities on that server. This means that when you attach to that server using your user name, you lose the GUEST connection and therefore the printing capabilities you once had as user GUEST.

About the only way around this dilemma is to place the command to attach to this server in your personal login script (or in a batch file if you don't need the attachment very often.) Then be sure to include the same CAPTURE statement in the login script or batch file as the supervisor uses for the user GUEST. This way, when you attach, you won't lose your ability to print.

/Queue = *queuename*. With 2.1x NetWare began using a queue management procedure to keep better track of job-related services such as printing. For printing, queue management means you send your print jobs to a particular directory called a queue; the printers assigned to that queue will service those print jobs.

For example, suppose you're logged in to server PUB, but you want to print to printer 2 on server NTS3, which services print queue REPORTS. At the network prompt, type CAPTURE S=NTS3 Q=REPORTS <Enter> and your print jobs will print at printer 2 on server COMM. Ask your supervisor which print queues have been defined on your server and which printers service those queues.

/Local = *1, 2, or 3*. CAPTURE allows you to have up to three captures going on at the same time. CAPTURE does this by logically allocating the maximum number of LPT ports your workstation can have; since these are logical connections of the NetWare shell, you don't need any physical LPT ports at all. You would use the different LPT ports only if you were using LPT1 for something other than printing. Or, if you'd like to have a particular application print to someplace other than your default printer, you can set up a CAPTURE for LPT2.

But keep in mind that if you use CAPTURE to designate LPT2 for printing, your application also has to send its print jobs to LPT2. Therefore, you need to set up your application to print to that LPT port. For example, suppose you want to print your Turbo PASCAL program to a dot-matrix printer, but you want to keep printing your WordPerfect files to a laser printer. Your supervisor has already set up a CAPTURE on LPT1 to collect your WordPerfect files and send them to the laser printer. To print from Turbo PASCAL to the dot matrix, set up Turbo PASCAL to print to LPT2. Then run another CAPTURE command: CAPTURE LPT2 S=servername Q=queuename <Enter>. Now your WordPerfect print jobs will go to the laser printer, and your Turbo PASCAL print jobs will go to the dot matrix printer.

/Copies = *1–255*. With the copy flag, you can print anywhere from 1 to 255 copies of your print job. (Of course, copiers are more economical for creating large quantities of a report and won't tie up the printer.) If you're on server PUB and want to make two copies of a small document that's being sent to print queue FILES2GO on server NTS3, type CAPTURE S=NTS3 Q=FILES2GO C=2 <Enter> at the network prompt.

/Job = *job configuration name*. Use this parameter if you've created print job configurations in the PRINTCON utility (explained later in this chapter). If you or your supervisor has defined your printers and queues in PRINTCON, and you want to print using that particular job configuration (such as REPORTS), type CAPTURE J=REPORTS <Enter> at the network prompt. The Job parameter designates the name of that print job. NetWare uses PRINTCON's defaults to begin with, and then modifies the defaults with the parameters you specify in CAPTURE.

/Form = *form name* **or** *number.* "Form" means the kinds of paper you're printing on. Your supervisor defines these forms in PRINTDEF, and you can see which forms you have available through that utility (explained later in this chapter). The forms you use can be designated by numbers between 0 and 255, or they can have actual names, depending on how your supervisor defined them.

If your form description doesn't match your printer's form description, you'll be asked to change the form description, and you won't be able to print. Forms can be rather messy, for most supervisors haven't defined any forms and only use the default Form 0. Many users assume that form numbers begin with Form 1; this isn't the case, and if Form 1 isn't defined, printing may stop. You don't need to change forms unless they've been defined for your use. My mentioning forms in the first edition of this book has caused many supervisors to reach for the Maalox.

Use forms only when necessary. When you whimsically change print jobs to another form, the server stops printing while it waits for another form to be mounted. (Supervisors or print server operators can go into the "Printer Status" option under the "Print Server Status and Control" window and dynamically mount the specified form. The PSC utility can also do this.) So don't go changing forms unless you know there are other form numbers you can use.

/Banner = *ASCII string.* The banner identifies the print job by sending an identifying sheet of paper through first. (See the "About Printer Banners" subheading for a figure of the banner.) In CAPTURE, you can designate up to twelve characters or letters, such as CAPTURE B=REPORTING9-2 <Enter>, to appear on the banner. Spaces are not allowed in the banner name, so if you wish to designate a space, use the underline: for example, TITLES_93. (In PRINTCON, you designate this name through the "Banner File" entry.) If you have a slow printer, or if the printers are used only moderately, you may not need a banner to designate your print job. In such cases, type NB in the CAPTURE command.

/NAMe = *text.* This is the name that will appear on the banner page. The default name is your login name. However, if you want to see a different name—for instance, Phil—type CAPTURE B=REPORTING9-2 NAM=PHIL <Enter>. Spaces are not allowed in the name, so if you wish to designate a space, use the underline: for example, TITLES_93.

376

/No Banner. Include this parameter if you want to omit the banner page when you print—for example, CAPTURE S=PUB Q=PONS NB <Enter>.

/Tabs = 1–18. When printing a simple DOS (ASCII text) file that contains no special application formatting codes, you may need to designate how wide your tab space is. The Tabs parameter lets you designate the number of spaces in your tabs while you're in the application; eight characters is the default. Most applications do this for you through their printer format, but if they don't, use this parameter.

/No Tabs. If you're printing out some DOS files and their tabs are messing up, you can specify No Tabs in the CAPTURE command to cancel all the tab specifications CAPTURE may have put in. Making this change doesn't affect how an application will print the file through its own printer format; it only affects the way CAPTURE handles tabs.

If you're using a printer that accepts loadable fonts or graphics, you'll want to use the "/NT" option. NetWare defaults to /No Tabs, which is the preferred printing method for most situations.

/Autoendcap. This parameter allows you to print your captured data when you exit your application, or when you physically type ENDCAP. When you set this entry to "Yes" (the default), any captured data will be sent to the printer as you exit the application.

/No Autoendcap. This parameter allows you to exit an application without printing captured data to a file or printer. However, you can print your data to a file or a printer by executing ENDCAP, by using the TImeout flag, or by logging out. You won't have many occasions to use this command. But if you want to go into a number of applications and send one big print job to the printer down the hall, you can designate NA in the CAPTURE command and then type ENDCAP <Enter> when you want to print the job.

/TImeout = 0–1000 seconds. While Autoendcap sends data when you exit an application, the Timeout parameter allows you to print while you're still in the application. As the application sends data to the queue for printing, it may pause periodically to do calculations. Since the print queues are very fast and NetWare prints the job as soon as data stops being sent to the print job, NetWare may interpret the pause to mean the job is over. If this happens, you end up with portions of your file being printed separately.

By placing some seconds in the Timeout parameter, you'll be able to have the print queue wait until the entire print job is finished. Some applications have trouble with the default of 0, so you may wish to set your parameter to 5 seconds by typing CAPTURE /TI=5 <Enter> in your CAPTURE command.

/Form Feed and **/No Form Feed.** These options allow you to choose whether or not you want the next print job to start at the top of the next page. The default option for Form Feed is "Yes." However, some printers also send a form feed, so you end up with a blank sheet of paper between print jobs. If you don't want to waste paper, type /No Form Feed (or /NFF) in your CAPTURE command.

/CReate = *(drive:/directory)filename.* This parameter is useful for capturing screen dumps and saving them into a file, or for saving your print jobs to a file instead of printing them. CAPTURE uses LPT1 for this option, particularly if you use <Shift>-<PrtSc> to capture data. These files are like an ASCII text file format with all blank spaces saved as hard spaces. In other words, it saves the entire screen as a block of data—2,052 bytes per screen dump. Depending on what you call it, the file will end up in the directory you're in if you type CAPTURE /CR=filename <Enter>. The filename must conform to DOS's naming scheme: eight characters . (dot) three characters.

If you're in your J: directory, however, and you want to put the file in your G: directory under the file named GLIP, type CAPTURE /CR=G:GLIP <Enter>. Or if you want to do it the hard way, replace the directory letter with the directory path. For example, if G: is the drive letter designated for NTS3/SYS:SALES/JAN, type CAP-TURE /CR=NTS3/SYS:SALES/JAN/GLIP <Enter> for the same results.

If you want to print your data to a file while you're in an application, specify the file before going into the application. (Some applications will let you specify the file after you enter the application.) Suppose, for example, that you want to print your word processing data into a file called REPT10-6. Type CAPTURE /CR=REPT10-6 <Enter> at the network prompt and then go into your application (which must be set up to send data to LPT1). Then, as you print your data, that data is sent to the file instead of to the printer. When you leave the application, type ENDCAP <Enter>, and your data will be saved into the file REPT10-6. Then you can print the file through PCONSOLE or NPRINT and all of your application's printing features will appear as well. That's the only way you can print an application file without being in the file while you print it.

/Keep. If your workstation blows up and interrupts your sending data to the proper print queue, the Keep flag will print out your print jobs, even though you may not have a workstation to go back to. If you're using the /CR= parameter, your captured data will be saved to a file. (The data saved includes only the data that has been placed in CAPTURE but hasn't yet been printed or saved to a file.) To use this parameter when you're saving data to a file, type CAPTURE /CR=filename /K <Enter>. If you don't use this command and your workstation hangs, the server discards the print job or file.

/NOTIfy. Suppose it's a long walk to the printer and you want to be notified when your print job's completed. When you want to be notified, add the Notify parameter by

378

typing CAPTURE /NOTI <Enter>. Then, as the printer finishes printing your job, you'll receive a message at the bottom of your screen saying something like "LPT1 Catch printed on LaserJet IIIP." When you type CAPTURE SH <Enter>, the second line displays a notice that you'll be notified when files are printed.

/No NOTIfy. If you've set up to be notified when print jobs print but you don't want to be notified anymore, you can type CAPTURE /NO NOTI <Enter> to reset the notify parameter only. The Notify parameter is then taken from CAPTURE while the rest of the CAPTURE command stays intact.

/SHow. You can type CAPTURE SH(ow) <Enter> to see statistics on the current parameters of CAPTURE. For example, if your LPT1 port is saving to the CAP.SCR file on server NTS3 and your LPT2 port is sending your print jobs to printer 2 on server PUB, you'll see:

```
LPT1: Capturing data to server NTS3 in a file. User will not be
notified after the files are printed.
Capture Defaults: Enabled    Automatic Endcap: Enabled
Banner   : (None)       Form Feed:      No
Copies   : 1            Tabs:           converted 8 spaces
Form     : 0            Timeout Count:  5 seconds

LPT2: Capturing data to server PUB queue ADMIN. User will be
notified after the files are printed.
Capture Defaults :Enabled    Automatic Endcap: Enabled
Banner   : LST:         Form Feed:      Yes
Copies   : 1            Tabs:           No conversion
Form     : 0            Timeout Count:  3 seconds

LPT3: Capturing Is Not Currently Active.
```

In this example, the first LPT port is capturing its data to a file on server NTS3. All print jobs routed through LPT1 go to that file. (You can specify ENDCAP LPT1 <Enter> to close just that CAPTURE parameter.) LPT2 is sending any print jobs it receives to ADMIN on server PUB. With this setup, only applications sending their print jobs to LPT2 will print to this second CAPTURE parameter; those applications sending to LPT1 will print to the file.

The second line of a port designation shows whether the user will be notified when the job has been printed. The third line shows that the Capture Defaults and Automatic Endcap are both enabled, which means that no parameters other than the defaults are being used for printing this job. The Banner listing on the LPT2 CAPTURE identifies the print job by sending a sheet of paper through first. If you don't designate a description, you'll see LST: displayed on the banner. ("LST:" is an old term for printers; it has no real significance.)

The Form Feed has been set to "No" on LPT1 and "Yes" on LPT2. This doesn't apply to the file specified on LPT1; however, the printer servicing ADMIN doesn't receive a form feed. It could also mean that the people printing on LPT2 want to get a paper separator after a print job. On LPT2, copies are set to 1, and the tabs are set to No Conversion. No Conversion means you're printing from an application that will interpret tab sizes for you. The "Form" entry shows that this print job is using 0, and forms can be set up in PRINTDEF by the supervisor. The Timeout Count shows how many seconds you've instructed the NetWare shell to wait before sending the print job to a print queue.

/DOmain=domain. Certain versions of NetWare contained domains, which were an interim step toward NetWare 4.0's Directory Services. Domains are a way to lump servers together by sharing the information you place on one server with the other servers in the domain. Suppose you are a part of the NTS domain; to ensure you are sending to printers on that domain, you would include /DO=NTS as part of your CAPTURE statement.

/EndCapture. The /EndCapture parameter allows you to automatically terminate your LPT1 printing session through the CAPTURE statement instead of through the ENDCAP command. To initiate the process, type CAPTURE /EC <Enter> at the network prompt. You can do the same from the command line using the ENDCAP command.

/CAncel. The /CAncel parameter is used in conjunction with the /EndCapture statement. The /CAncel parameter not only allows you to end the LPT1 port capture, but it also stops you from printing jobs that haven't yet reached the print queue. To use this parameter, type CAPTURE /EC /CA <Enter> at the network prompt. You can do the same from the command line using the ENDCAP command.

/All. The /All parameter is used in conjunction with the /EndCapture statement. The /All parameter ends capture on all LPT port designations, and stops printing jobs that haven't yet reached the print queue or haven't been released to be printed. To use this parameter, type CAPTURE /EC /A at the network prompt. You can do the same from the command line using the ENDCAP command.

About Printer Banners

Printer banners are a means of indicating where one print job ends and another begins. The banner itself identifies the print job by first sending through a sheet of paper that looks something like the following.

```
..........................................................................................
:
:   User Name: TED                          Queue: REPORTS
:   File Name: RPTJUL.DAT                    Server: PUB
:   Directory: PUB/BYTE:USERS/TED
:   Description: RPTJUL.DAT
:   Date:11/22/91                            Time: 16:37:16
:.........................................................................................
:
:       TTTTT  EEEEE  DDDD
:         T    E      D   D
:         T    E      D    D
:         T    EEE    D    D
:         T    E      D    D
:         T    E      D   D
:         T    EEEEE  DDDD
:.........................................................................................
:
:       L      SSSSS  TTTTT
:       L      S        T
:       L      S        T
:       L      SSSSS    T
:       L          S    T
:       L          S    T
:       LLLLL  SSSSS    T
:.........................................................................................
```

Figure 4-3. Sample print banner sheet

Here's what the entries on the banner mean:

User Name. This is the name you specify in the Banner Name entry by highlighting the Banner Name description field and typing in the name you want to appear on the banner. The default name is your login name, followed by your connection number.

Filename. This is the name of the DOS file you wish to print. You'll see the actual filename when using PCONSOLE and NPRINT. Leaving the Banner File blank will give you LST in CAPTURE as well. In PRINTCON, you designate this name through the Banner Name entry (up to twelve characters long).

Directory. This option tells you which directory your file is printing from. You'll see the directory path when using PCONSOLE and NPRINT, but not with CAPTURE.

Description. This option, which gives a brief description of the file, can be set up in PCONSOLE. If you don't designate a description, you may see the letters LST: displayed on the banner. (LST:, an old term for printers, is a holdover from earlier days and has no real significance.) Some programs can insert their own descriptions.

Date and **Time.** These options show the date and time the file was queued.

Queue. This option shows which file server and print queue this file was routed to and printed from.

Server. This entry designates the print server you're printing this job on. If you're using core printing services, you'll see the name of the file server in this position.

User name and **banner name.** Below the banner header is the user name you designate in the Name entry, which defaults to your login name if you don't put in anything else. Beneath your user name is the banner name entry. Printers with proportional fonts give you a convoluted banner—one that's hard to read. However, your supervisor can define nonproportional fonts (depending on the printer) in a printer definition to make the banner look good.

Most Commonly Used CAPTURE Parameters

Some of the most commonly used parameters are Server, Queue, No Banner, No Tabs, No Form Feed, and TImeout = x. For example, suppose you want to print to queue CAP that is serviced by printer 1 (next to your desk) on server NTS3, you don't want any banners or extra papers coming through, and you want to print while you're in the application. Set up your CAPTURE command with CAPTURE S=COMM Q=CAP NB NT NFF TI=5.

For more information on when you would change your supervisor's default CAPTURE, turn to the "When You Would Change Your CAPTURE" heading at the end of this chapter.

ENDCAP

ENDCAP allows you to terminate any one or all three of these printing sessions. Use the ENDCAP utility to cancel the effects of the CAPTURE utility. The CAPTURE utility is normally used for printing and capturing screen images; it also allows you to have up to three different printing sessions running at the same time.

The ENDCAP command comes with five parameters: Local=n, ALL, Cancel, CancelLocal=n, and Cancel ALL. If you can't remember the syntax at the network prompt, type ENDCAP /H <Enter> and you'll see:

```
Usage: ENDCAP [/CANCEL]
    or  ENDCAP [/CANCEL] [/LOCAL=N]
    or  ENDCAP [/CANCEL] [/ALL]
```

Here are the parameters and how to use them.

/Local=*n*. You can replace the n parameter with one of the LPT port numbers—1, 2, or 3. For example, if you want to drop your CAPTURE on LPT2, type ENDCAP /L=2 <Enter> or ENDCAP LPT2 <Enter> at the network prompt. You can do the same for the other ports as well.

/ALL. When you want to end all your LPT port captures, type ENDCAP /ALL <Enter> at the network prompt.

/Cancel. This parameter not only allows you to end the LPT1 port capture, but it also stops you from printing jobs that haven't yet reached the print queue. The Cancel parameter will also cancel your file if you're capturing the LPT1 port to a file (if you're doing CR=). To use it, type ENDCAP /C <Enter> at the network prompt. You'll see "Device LPT1: set to local mode. Spooled data has been discarded."

/CancelLocal=*n* (CL=*n*). This parameter works similarly to the "Local" and "Cancel" parameter options. To use this parameter, replace the n parameter with one of the LPT port numbers—1, 2, or 3. The CancelLocal=n parameter also ends any data that hasn't already been queued and released to the printer; to use it on your LPT2 CAPTURE, type ENDCAP /CL=2 <Enter> at the network prompt.

/Cancel ALL. If you want to end the capture of all your LPT ports as well as end any data that hasn't already been queued and released to be printed, type ENDCAP /C ALL <Enter> at the network prompt. You'll see "LPT1:, LPT2:, and LPT3: set to local mode. Spooled data has been discarded."

Other Related Commands

The ENDCAP command is used exclusively with the CAPTURE command. If you want to see what LPT ports you're using through the CAPTURE command, type CAPTURE /SH <Enter> at the network prompt.

Using the NPRINT Command

The NPRINT command allows you to print any files you've saved as text files, graphics files, or files that are prepared for a specific printer, usually by printing to a file instead of to a printer. NPRINT contains a whole list of parameters to help you in your printing process, much like those you saw in CAPTURE. You can use NPRINT's parameters to specify jobs, filenames, servers, queues, and printers. You can also set printing specifics, such as number of copies, tabs, banners, and formfeeds. If you can't remember the syntax at the network prompt, type NPRINT /HELP ME <Enter>, and you'll see:

```
Unknown flag ME in the flag list.
Usage: NRPINT path flaglist
```

```
flaglist: /Banner=bannername /NAme=name /No Banner
          /[No] FormFeed /[No] NOTIfy
          /Tab=n (1-18) /No Tabs
          /Copies=n (1-999) /Delete /Form=form or n
          /Job=jobconfiguration /PrintServer=printserver
          /Queue=queuename/Server=fileserver /DOmain=domain
```

Here's a list of the parameters, their functions, and how to use them. The capitalized letters on the parameters are the abbreviated letters you can use to designate the parameters. (Of course, if you prefer, you can type out the entire parameter.) You can use NPRINT parameters without the forward slash (/), but if you want to be consistent with the other command-line utilities, go ahead and use the forward slash.

NPRINT's Parameters

NPRINT directory path filename. When you're not printing a file from the directory you're presently in, you can specify the directory path, all the way up to the server. For example, if you're in the directory path PUB/BYTE:USERS/TED and you want to print the NEW.RPT file from NTS3/VOL1:USERS/TED/REPORTS, type NPRINT NTS3/ VOL1:USERS/TED/REPORTS/NEW.RPT S=*servername* Q=*queuename* <Enter>. Be sure to attach to server NTS3; otherwise, you'll see a "You're not attached to the source server NTS3" message. If you're attached and if NTS3/VOL1:USERS/TED/ REPORTS is mapped to drive K:, type NPRINT K:NEW.RPT S=*servername* Q=*queuename* <Enter>.

If the file isn't in the directory path you specified, you'll see a "The file NEW.RPT not found" message. If you type in the wrong directory path, you'll see an "Illegal path specification or path specified relative to local drive" message. When you see this message, check to make sure you've typed the directory path correctly. Don't put a space between the drive mapping and the filename (NPRINT K: NEW.RPT), or a space instead of a slash between the directory and the filename (USERS\TED\REPORTS NEW.RPT). If you do, you'll see an "Unknown flag in the flag list," or, "The specified form could not be found" message. Be sure your file is connected to your directory path with a backslash (\), and be sure there are no spaces between your drive map letter and filename.

Through wild cards, you can print a number of files at the same time. For example, if you have a number of DOS text or graphics files (also known as ASCII text files) with an RPT extension (NEW.RPT, TIMES.RPT, etc.) and you want to print all of them, you can type NPRINT K:*.RPT S=*servername* Q=*queuename* <Enter> and all files with the

384

RPT extension will print. Using commas, you can combine more than one directory path for files you want to print. For example, if you want to print the *.RPT files from the K: directory and from the G: directory, type NPRINT K:*.RPT, G:*.RPT S=*servername* Q=*queuename* <Enter>, and all files with the RPT extension from either of those directories will print. You can also write out the directory path, such as NPRINT K:*.RPT, G:*.RPT, SYS:REPORTS*.RPT S=*servername* Q=*queuename* <Enter>, and all files with the RPT extension in those directory paths will print.

You can also use the question mark (?) wild card. For example, if you have many files but you only want to print three files—GLSYS.FDM, DLSYS.FED, and SLSYS.FDM—you can type NPRINT ??SYS*.* S=*servername* Q=*queuename* <Enter>, and NPRINT will print only those files with that pattern.

Server = *servername*. Use this command when you want to print to a server other than the server you log in to. For example, if you're logged in to server PUB and you want to print the file NEW.RPT on printer 0, which is on server NTS3, type NPRINT NEW.RPT S=NTS3 <Enter>. If you're not attached to server NTS3, NPRINT will supply you with an attachment to print the file. If you don't designate a printer on server NTS3, you'll print to whichever printer is servicing the default queue on that server. You'll see a message like this one:

```
Queuing data to Server NTS3, Queue ADMIN
NTS3/VOL1:USERS/TED
    Queuing file NEW.RPT
```

The first line tells you where the print job is being sent. The second line tells you the directory path and directory where the file you designated for printing resides. The third line tells you which file or files you designated for printing.

/Queue = *queuename*. With the advent of 2.1x, NetWare began using a queue management procedure to keep better track of job-related services, of which printing is one. For printing, queue management means you send your print job to a particular queue; printers assigned to that queue will service those print jobs.

For example, if you log in to server PUB, but you know that the printer next to your desk services print queue REPORTS on server NTS3, type NPRINT NEW.RPT S=NTS3 Q=REPORTS <Enter> and you'll print to printer 2 on server NTS3. (If the queue is on your default server, you won't need to specify the server in your command.) A wrong queue name will receive a "The print queue REPORTS cannot be found" message. You can use the PCONSOLE utility to see which print queues are available to you.

385

/PrinterServer = *printserver*. If you have more than one print server accessing queues on the file servers you deal with, you can type NPRINT PS=*printserver* S=*fileserver* Q=*queue* <Enter> to designate which print server you want to access the print queue. For the most part, you won't have to worry about this command.

/Copies = *1–999*. With the copy flag, you can print from 1 to 999 copies of your print job. If you're on server PUB and you want to make two copies of a document (NEW.RPT) that's being sent to queue ADMIN on server NTS3, type NPRINT NEW.RPT S=NTS3 Q=AMDIN C=2 <Enter> at the network prompt.

/Delete. Use this parameter when you want to delete a file after you print it. If you're capturing your print jobs to a file called GLIP, for example, and you want to print as well as delete file GLIP after you print it, type NPRINT GLIP Q=ADMIN D <Enter>. After the file is printed, it will disappear from your directory.

/Job = *job configuration name*. Use this parameter if you've created print job configurations in the PRINTCON utility. (See "The PRINTCON Utility" heading in this chapter.) Suppose, for instance, you've defined your printers and queues in PRINTCON and you want to print to a particular job configuration, such as REPORTS. Type NPRINT NEW.RPT J=REPORTS <Enter> at the network prompt. The job configuration will contain all the server and queue parameters necessary to print to the necessary place. It's a convenient tool when you repeatedly print to the same printers.

/Form = *form name* or *number*. "Form" refers to the different kinds of paper you can print on. Your supervisor defines these forms in PRINTDEF, and you can see which forms you have available through that utility. (See "The PRINTDEF Utility" heading in this chapter.) The forms you use can be designated by numbers from 0 to 255, or they can have actual names, depending on how your supervisor defined them. Be sure your form description matches your printer's form description, or you'll be asked to change the form description and sometimes you won't be able to print until the file server is told that it has a new form mounted.

Forms can be rather messy because most supervisors haven't defined any forms other than the default form 0. When you do change to another form, the printer will stop printing while it waits for another form to be loaded. (Supervisors or print server operators can go into the "Printer Status" option under the "Print Server Status and Control" window and then dynamically mount the specified form. The PSC utility can also fix this.) So don't change forms unless you know there are other form numbers you can use. Even if there are, they may or may not print immediately, depending on how the form service mode is set up.

/Banner = *ASCII string*. The banner identifies the print job by sending a sheet of paper through first. In NPRINT, you can designate up to twelve characters or letters in the banner name; in PRINTCON, you can also designate this name through the Banner File entry (up to twelve characters long). Spaces aren't allowed in the banner name; to designate a space, use the underline, such as NPRINT Q=ADMIN B=TITLES_90 <Enter>. If you have a slow printer, or if the printers in your work area are used only moderately, you may not need a banner to designate your print job.

/Name = *your name* **(default).** This is the name that will appear on the banner page. The defaulted name is your login name. However, if you want to see a different name—Paul, for instance—type NPRINT NEW.RPT J=REPORTS B=NEWREPORTS N=PAUL <Enter>. Spaces are not allowed in the banner name; to designate a space, use the underline. For example, NPRINT NEW.RPT J=REPORTS B=NEWREPORTS N=TITLES_90 <Enter>.

/No Banner (NB). If you want to omit the banner page, type NB in NPRINT's command. For example, type NPRINT NEW.RPT Q=PRINT_0 NB <Enter>. If you've designated NB (no banner) in one of PRINTCON's job configurations, you can also run that job configuration (provided it matches where and how you want to print).

/Tabs = *1–18.* When printing a simple DOS text file (ASCII text file) that contains no special application formatting codes, you may need to indicate how many spaces long you want the tab to be; the default is eight characters long. The Tabs parameter lets you indicate how many spaces you want in your tabs while you're in the application. Most applications do this for you through their own printer format, but if they don't, you can indicate your preference here. Try printing something. If the tabs look good, leave them; if they don't, try changing them to something like 5 by typing NPRINT NEW.RPT Q=ADMIN NB T=5 <Enter>. Normally, tabs are useful only if you're printing program source code; most of the time, you'll use the No Tabs parameter.

/No Tabs. If you're printing out DOS files, and you see that the tabs are messing up, you can specify No Tabs in the NPRINT command to cancel all tab specifications. If the previous tab example doesn't work, try taking out NPRINT's tabs. For example, type NPRINT NEW.RPT Q=PRINT_0 NB NT <Enter>.

If you're printing a file that has embedded printer commands, such as a print job you printed to a file using the CAPTURE CR= command, you'll want to specify the NT parameter in both CAPTURE and NPRINT.

/No Form Feed. These options allow you to choose whether you want the next print job to start at the top of the next page. The default option for Form Feed is Yes. However, some printers also send a form feed, so you end up with a blank sheet of paper between print jobs. If you don't want to waste paper, type No Form Feed (or NFF) in your NPRINT command. For example, NPRINT NEW.RPT Q=PRINT_0 NFF <Enter>.

/NOTIfy. Suppose it's a long walk to the printer and you want to be notified when your print job has been completed. When you want to be notified, add the Notify parameter by typing NPRINT GLIP Q=ADMIN /NOTI <Enter>, and you'll be notified when the print job begins printing. Then as the printer finishes printing your job, you'll receive a message at the bottom of the screen saying something like "LPT1 Catch printed on LaserJet IIIP." You'll need to use the Notify parameter even if you designate the Notify parameter in your CAPTURE command.

/No NOTIfy. If you're set up to be notified when print jobs print but you don't want to be notified on this print job, you can type NPRINT GLIP Q=ADMIN /NO NOTI <Enter> at the network prompt.

The PCONSOLE Utility

For network personnel, the Printer CONSOLE (PCONSOLE) utility displays information about what's happening in print queues and print servers. Through PCONSOLE, you can look at the defined queues on the servers, view information on print jobs, and create, delete, or send print jobs. You can also view information on queue status, identification, operators, servers, and users. For Print Queue and Print Server operators, PCONSOLE offers much more. Let's first look at PCONSOLE from a user perspective.

To get into this utility, type PCONSOLE <Enter> at the network prompt. You'll see the "Available Options" window with three selections: "Change Current File Server," "Print Queue Information," and "Print Server Information."

```
NetWare Print Console  V1.65              Thursday  March 4, 1993  7:04 pm
                    User TED On File Server NTS3 Connection 7
```

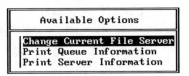

```
      Available Options
Change Current File Server
Print Queue Information
Print Server Information
```

Figure 4-4. The PCONSOLE Utility's initial screen

As you get around in PCONSOLE, pressing <Enter> on a highlighted option brings you to the next screen available under that option, and pressing <Esc> brings you to the previous screen. For example, from the "Available Options" window, select the "Print Server Information" option by pressing <PgDn> on the numeric keypad. Once an option is highlighted, press <Enter>. <PgDn> brings you to the bottom of the list of options and <PgUp> brings you to the top of the list. You can also use the Up (8) and Down (2) arrow keys to highlight and select an option, or you can type the first letters of the option you wish to select and the selector bar will move to that option.

Never feel tangled up in the menus—pressing <F1> at any time will provide an explanation of the menu options currently on the screen. Each help screen gives you information specific to the option choice currently displayed. Once you've chosen another menu option by pressing <Enter>, pressing <F1> will bring you a different set of help screens relating to the newly selected option. However, some of the help screens for PCONSOLE offer scant information.

You'll also notice that the second line on the screen header contains information not only on the user and server, but also on the station (connection) number. This information can be handy if you're logged in to a server at more than one workstation; it will help you keep track of where you're printing from.

Selecting Different Servers and Queues

The first option listed in the "Available Options" window is "Change Current File Server." This option allows you to change servers so you can view and print to different queues and servers within PCONSOLE. When you're actually ready to create and print a job from within PCONSOLE, PCONSOLE doesn't let you change printers or queues at that point—you do that here.

Select the "Change Current File Server" option. The "File Server/User Name" window will appear in the center of your screen, listing all the servers you're currently attached to. The selector bar will highlight the name of the server from which you entered PCONSOLE. To change to a different server, use the up/down arrow keys to highlight the server name and press <Enter>. When you return to the "Available Options" window, the second line on the screen header will reflect the change.

When you want to print a job on a server not listed in the "File Server/User Name" window, press <Ins> to display the "Other File Servers" window. You'll see a list of servers currently on the internetwork (if you have more than one server). Choose another server by typing in the server name and pressing <Enter>. Or, if you prefer, select the name from the list presented in the "Other File Servers" window.

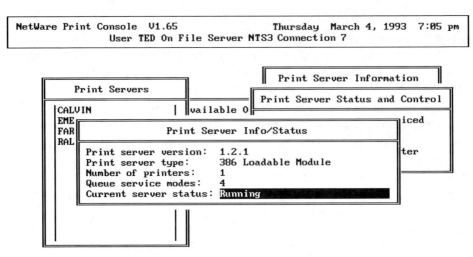

Figure 4-5. You select different servers to see the print queues on them

If you happen to type the servername or your password incorrectly, you'll see a screen that says, "Access to file server denied. Press Escape to continue." Try again, or press <Esc> again to return to the "Other File Servers" window, where you can press <Esc> once more to return to the "File Server/User Name" window. You can also log out of a server at the "File Server/User Name" window by highlighting the name of that server with the selector bar and pressing <Del>. You'll see the "Logout From Server" window with the "Yes" option highlighted. Press <Enter> to log out from the designated server. (However, you can't log out from the server on which you're logged in to the network; you'll get a warning message to that effect if you try.)

After you've found the correct server, enter your login name and password (if necessary) for that server and the servername will be added to the "File Server/User Name" window. You can then select that server by highlighting the servername through the up/down arrow keys and by pressing <Enter>. You'll return to the "Available Options" window and the second line on the screen header will reflect the change.

Looking At Your Print Queue Information

The second option listed in the "Available Options" window is "Print Queue Information," which shows you which print queues are available on that server. To select "Print Queue Information," highlight the selection and press <Enter>. You'll see a list of defined print queues.

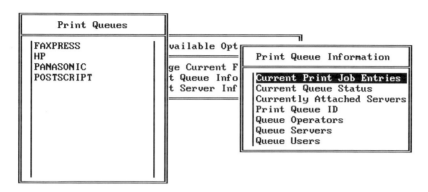

```
┌─────────────────────────────────────────────────────────────────────────┐
│ NetWare Print Console   V1.65              Thursday  March 4, 1993  7:06 pm │
│                  User TED On File Server NTS3 Connection 7                  │
└─────────────────────────────────────────────────────────────────────────┘
```

Figure 4-6. Selecting a print queue brings up the "Print Queue Information" window

The "Print Queue" window lists the queues you can use on this server. The previous figure lists four print queues: FAXPRESS, HP, PANASONIC, and POSTSCRIPT. Supervisors and print queue operators can add, delete, or rename print queues at this point. As a user, you can select the name of a print queue to see the "Print Queue Information" window with seven available options: "Current Print Job Entries," "Current Queue Status," "Currently Attached Servers," "Print Queue ID," "Queue Operators," "Queue Servers," and "Queue Users."

Each print queue defined comes with the group EVERYONE as a member; however, queue operators can specify the individuals they'll allow to use a print queue. If you're not defined as a queue user, you'll see only the "Print Queue ID," "Queue Operators," "Queue Servers," and "Queue Users" options. This means you won't be able to add print jobs to the queue or see its status. So you'll see whichever list of options you have rights to see for the print queue you select.

Looking at Queue Information in PCONSOLE

To see which print jobs are in a queue, highlight the name of the queue you want to examine and press <Enter>. At the "Print Queue Information" window, select the "Current Print Job Entries" option and press <Enter>. Depending on the jobs that are in the queue, you'll see a screen similar to this one:

391

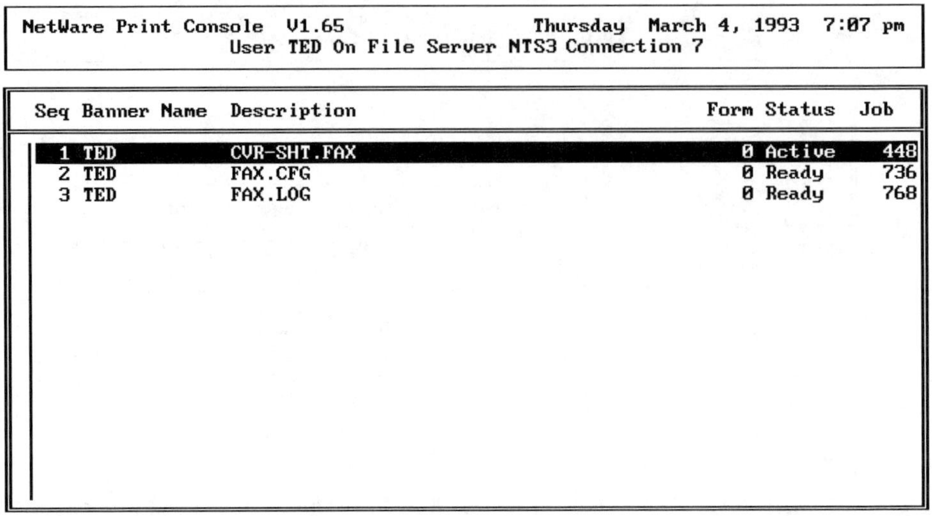

```
NetWare Print Console  V1.65                Thursday  March 4, 1993  7:07 pm
                 User TED On File Server NTS3 Connection 7
```

```
Seq Banner Name  Description                          Form Status   Job

  1 TED          CVR-SHT.FAX                             0 Active    448
  2 TED          FAX.CFG                                 0 Ready     736
  3 TED          FAX.LOG                                 0 Ready     768
```

Figure 4-7. You can view the print jobs that are in the print queue

The information in the print queue is updated every five seconds. The figure above shows the following headings across the top: Seq, Banner Name, Description, Form, Status, and Job. Here's what they mean:

Seq(uence). This header shows the number of jobs currently in the queue (within the five-second update) and which order they're in. Queue operators can change the order in which jobs are printed by pressing <Enter> on a job entry, thereby bringing up the "Print Queue Entry Information" window. The operator can then select the Service Sequence entry and change that number to indicate the job's new position in the queue.

Banner Name. The Banner header displays the name that will show up on the top portion of the banner itself. The banner header will be your login name unless you designate a different name in PRINTCON. You can also choose not to print out any banner, but this action doesn't affect what you see here.

Description. This header shows what the bottom portion of the banner is going to look like; its appearance varies, depending on what the application or utility you're printing from puts in the description field. For example, CAPTURE puts in the LST designation you see in Figure 4-3. NPRINT defaults to the filename. In PCONSOLE, you can type in your own description. Applications that aren't using CAPTURE need to designate a description or you won't see one, as with Ted's print job in the previous figure.

Form. This header shows which form number was specified when the job was submitted to the queue. If you see a lot of forms other than 0 in the queue, the supervisor or print-server operator may have set up the queue to hold the other form types until jobs with the present form are printed.

Status. Five descriptions can appear under this header: Adding, Ready, Active, Held, and Waiting. Adding means the application or utility initiates a print job file in the queue but the file hasn't been closed yet. This occurs when you submit a job in CAPTURE that doesn't print until you either leave the application or type ENDCAP. Or you'll see this when adding any print job to the queue. You can also submit jobs through NPRINT and PCONSOLE.

The application finishes sending the print job and, if the CAPTURE command uses the "timeout" option, sends an "end of job" signal. The shell interprets the "end of job" signal into a "this print job is ready to be printed" signal from the queue. In the status entry, you see the job flagged as Ready. Active means the job is being printed; if multiple printers are servicing the queue, multiple jobs can be marked Active. Held means the queue operator or the user who submitted the job has put the job on hold. Waiting signifies that a job has been submitted to print at a later date and/or time.

Job. This header shows the job number of the printer job in the queue. Job numbers, assigned by the server, are between 0 and 999.

If you watch the queue screen for a while, you'll see that it moves along quickly, depending on your printer and the type of text it's printing. While your print jobs are in the queue, you can use three options from the queue screen: "Insert," "Delete," and "Select." For more information on the Insert method, go to the next section, "Printing through PCONSOLE."

You can delete your queue entries at the queue screen. If you're not a queue operator, you can delete only your own print job; queue operators can delete any job within their assigned print queues. If you decide you don't want to print a copy of something, or if you've put a job on Hold to print later but have now decided to cancel that job, highlight the job entry and press <Del>. You'll see the "Delete Queue Entry Yes/No" window with the "Yes" option highlighted. Press <Enter> to delete the entry. If you want to delete more than one job in the queue, highlight each of those job entries and press the F5 (Mark) key. Then when you press <Del>, you'll see the "Delete All Marked Queue Entries Yes/ No" window with the "Yes" option highlighted. Press <Enter> to delete the entries.

To see how a print job is set up, select a print job from the queue and press <Enter>. You'll see a "Print Queue Entry Information" window listing all the parameters you can select when you submit a job. If it's your own job, you'll be able to edit the print job on the fly. Suppose, for example, you've submitted a print job that's been "captured" and you want to change the number of printed copies from one to three. Get out of your application, type PCONSOLE, select the proper server (hope it's your default server—

it takes time to add another server, and in that time your job may have printed) and print queue, then select the "Current Print Job Entries" option. See if your print job is still in the print queue. If your print job's still there, press <Enter>, go down to the Number of Copies entry, and type 3. Press <Esc> and your job entry will print three copies.

However, if you're making several changes to a print job, go down to the User Hold entry and type "Y." Make your changes, then go back to the User Hold entry and type "N." Otherwise, the print job you wish to modify may already be printed before you finish the changes.

As you look at a print job from the "Print Queue Entry Information" window, you'll see the Status entry change to reflect your job's present status, such as "Being serviced by servername" or "Ready to be serviced, waiting for Print Server." When the job prints, you'll see "Job has been removed from the queue." Status entry changes happen quickly. If you want to modify a print job, put the job on hold as soon as you can; otherwise, you'll miss your chance to modify the screen.

Printing through PCONSOLE

You can also submit jobs to the print queue. For example, suppose you know that the HP LaserJet IIIP printer is servicing queue ADMIN on your present server, and you want to print a file there. Highlight ADMIN and press <Enter>, bringing up the "Print Queue Information" window. Then select the "Current Print Job Entries" option and press <Enter>. You'll see the queue screen with print jobs popping in and out. To add a print job, press <Ins>; you'll see the "Select Directory to Print From" window appear just beneath the screen header information, containing the directory path of the directory you're currently in.

You can enter your chosen directory in two ways. If the directory is below the directory path you're currently in, you can type a backslash (or a frontslash) and the name of the new directory. For example, if you want to get to the files in a directory named REPORTS that's beneath the one you're currently in, type \REPORTS <Enter> to see the available files. If you want to go to the REPORTS\APRIL directory, type \REPORTS\APRIL <Enter>. If you're attached to another server and you want to print from a directory path on that server, press the backspace key over the present path in the "Select Directory to Print From" window and type in the new directory path.

Presenting the wrong directory path will get a "The specified directory does not exist" window, which means you may have typed in the wrong path or that you don't have enough rights to print from that directory. Once you type in the proper directory path, press <Enter> and you'll see the "Available Files" window, listing the files in that directory. This directory path becomes your new default path if you press <Ins> key at the queue screen again to add another file.

You can also put in the directory path by pressing <Ins>. For example, if you want to go to the REPORTS directory beneath your present directory, press <Ins>; you'll see the "Network Directories" window, listing all the subdirectories directly beneath your present directory. Highlight the "REPORTS" option and press <Enter>. Press <Esc> to return to the directory path; then press <Enter> to display the "Available Files" window, listing the files in that directory.

The Insert key will list all the servers you're currently attached to. If you're attached to another server and you want to print from a directory path on that server, press the Backspace key over the entire directory path in the "Select Directory to Print From" window and press <Ins>. For example, suppose you're attached to server ADMIN, but you want to print a file to the print queue you're presently in. By deleting the directory path and pressing <Ins>, you'll see the "File Servers/Local Drives" window, listing all the servers you're presently attached to.

To choose the server that begins your directory path, highlight the servername and press <Enter>. For example, suppose you want to print a file from the PUB/BYTE:USERS/ TED/REPORTS/APRIL directory. First, choose server PUB by highlighting the option and pressing <Enter>. The selected servername becomes a part of the "Select Directory to Print From" window. Next, you'll see the names of the volumes you can choose from; select volume BYTE and press <Enter>. Follow the same process down the proposed directory path name; press <Enter> at each step. Once you reach the desired directory, press <Esc> to return to the directory path. Then press <Enter> to display the "Available Files" window, listing the files in that directory. This directory path becomes your new default path if you press <Ins> at the queue screen.

If the directory you want is in a server that doesn't appear in the "File Servers/Local Drives" window, press <Ins> to see the "Other File Servers" window listing the current servers on the internetwork. Choose another server by typing in the servername and pressing <Enter>. At the "User Name" window, type in your name (and password when necessary); the server will be added to the "File Servers/Local Drives" window.

If the NetWare version you're using has the "Macintosh" option installed, your supervisor can flag all the directories on a volume as Private, which means if you don't have at least File Scan rights in a directory, you won't see that directory. Suppose, for example, you want to print a file from the directory path ADMIN/VOL1:DEPT/GUIDE/ REPORTS. Let's suppose also that you don't have any rights in the DEPT directory. You can choose server ADMIN and then VOL1: through the Insert method, but since you have no rights to the directory DEPT, that directory won't appear in the "Network Directories" window. You'll have to press <Esc> to return to the "Destination Directory" window and type in the directory name on the keyboard. Then if you have rights to the GUIDE directory below DEPT, you can press <Ins> again and add the GUIDE/ REPORTS directory specification, or you can complete the directory path by typing it in at the keyboard.

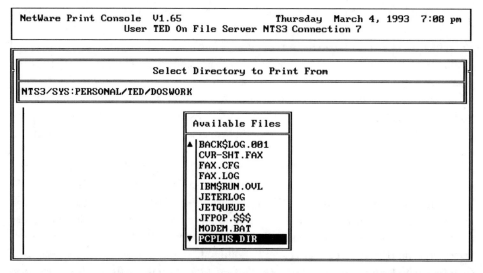

```
NetWare Print Console   V1.65              Thursday  March 4, 1993   7:08 pm
                       User TED On File Server NTS3 Connection 7


                          Select Directory to Print From

NTS3/SYS:PERSONAL/TED/DOSWORK


                                Available Files

                            ▲ BACK$LOG.001
                              CVR-SHT.FAX
                              FAX.CFG
                              FAX.LOG
                              IBM$RUN.OVL
                              JETERLOG
                              JETQUEUE
                              JFPOP.$$$
                              MODEM.BAT
                            ▼ PCPLUS.DIR
```

Figure 4-8. Once you've designated a directory path, press <Enter> to see the files

Once you've typed in the proper directory path, press <Enter>. You'll see the "Available Files" window, listing the files in that directory. Choose the file you want to print and press <Enter>. You'll see the "Print Job Configurations" window listing the configurations you can choose from. If you've created print job configurations in PRINTCON, those configurations will also be listed. (See the "Setting up Print Job Configurations" subheading under "The PRINTCON Utility" heading in this chapter.)

Choose a job configuration name by highlighting the one you wish to print from and pressing <Enter>. Choosing a predefined job configuration means that ten of the entries in the "New Print Job to be Submitted" window will reflect those settings. These entries include: "Number of Copies," "File Contents," "Tab Size," "Suppress Form Feed," "Notify When Done," "Form," "Print Banner," "Name," "Banner Name," and "Target Server." (See the figure on he next page) The rest are options you control in PCONSOLE.

If you want to see the defaults PCONSOLE offers, highlight the "PConsole Defaults" option and press <Enter>. You'll see the "New Print Job to be Submitted" window, displaying PCONSOLE's default printing parameters. This screen allows you to set up the way the print job will be received by the printer.

396

```
┌─────────────────────────────────────────────────────────────────────────┐
│ NetWare Print Console  V1.65              Thursday  March 4, 1993  7:08 pm │
│                User TED On File Server NTS3 Connection 7                    │
└─────────────────────────────────────────────────────────────────────────┘

╔═════════════════════════════════════════════════════════════════════════╗
║                     New Print Job to be Submitted                         ║
╠═══════════════════════════════════════════════════════════════════════════╣
║Print job:                         File size:                              ║
║Client:              TED[5]                                                ║
║Description:         ▓B1O.ED▓▓▓▓▓▓▓▓▓▓▓▓▓▓▓▓▓▓▓▓▓▓▓                        ║
║Status:                                                                    ║
║                                                                           ║
║User Hold:           No            Job Entry Date:                         ║
║Operator Hold:       No            Job Entry Time:                         ║
║Service Sequence:                                                          ║
║                                                                           ║
║Number of copies:    1             Form:              standard             ║
║File contents:       Byte stream   Print banner:      Yes                  ║
║Tab size:                          Name:              TED                  ║
║Suppress form feed:  No            Banner name:       PCPLUS.DIR           ║
║Notify when done:    No                                                    ║
║                                   Defer printing:    No                   ║
║Target server:       (Any Server)  Target date:                           ║
║                                   Target time:                           ║
╚═══════════════════════════════════════════════════════════════════════════╝
```

Figure 4-9. When you add a print job, you can hold the job or defer it to be printed later

Don't confuse this screen with the "Print Queue Entry Information" screen. (Both are essentially the same screen.) The "New Print Job to be Submitted" window appears only when you're adding a print job to the queue through PCONSOLE. This allows you to modify the print job you're submitting to look the way you want it. You can see the "Print Queue Entry Information" window by highlighting a print job already in the queue and pressing <Enter>. You can modify entries in this window as well, but you usually need to place the job on "Hold" to do it. Here are the entries you see within either window.

Print Job and **File Size.** As shown in the preceding figure, the top of the "New Print Job to be Submitted" window has two entries: "Print Job" and "File Size." The "Print Job" entry is the job number on the queue screen when you see a file queued for printing. Since PCONSOLE starts with 0 to keep track of its print jobs, the print job numbers may not match the job numbers you see at the print queue screen. Jobs are assigned by the server and number anywhere from 1 to 999. The only time you'll see anything in the "Print Job" entry is when you press <Enter> on the name of a job waiting to be printed. At that time you can also see how big the file size is. The "File Size" entry shows the size of the file in bytes.

Client and **Description.** The "Client" entry shows your user name, followed by your connection number. This is how NetWare keeps track of who you are on a given server (especially if you're logged in more than once on a server). Beneath the "Client" entry is the "Description" entry. PCONSOLE is the only place where you can put a brief description of the file's contents. Your description can be up to forty-nine characters long (including blank spaces); characters beyond forty-nine will be cut off. If you choose to print a banner, you'll see the "Description" entry just below the Banner's "Directory" entry. You'll see the filename defaulted in this entry.

To change the description, highlight the description field and start writing. If you activate the field by pressing <Enter>, you'll have to press the Backspace key to erase the filename and then type in a brief description if you wish.

Status. PCONSOLE uses this entry to let you know where this print job stands in relation to getting printed. The only time you'll see anything in the "Status" entry is when you press the <Enter> key on the name of a job waiting to be printed. Then you'll see messages like, "Being serviced by file server NTS3," or "Being serviced by Print Server NTS-PE," or, "Job has been removed from the queue," if the job printed while you were looking at the "Print Queue Entry Information" window.

User Hold and **Operator Hold.** These entries allow you or the queue operator to put a hold on the print job. When you put a job on hold and exit the "New Print Job to be Submitted" window, you'll see that your printing status has changed to "Held" as you return to the queue screen. If you highlight the queue entry and press <Enter>, you'll see "User Hold On Job" on the Status entry line. If a queue operator has put the job on Hold, you'll see, "Operator Hold On Job." Queue operators can shut off a user's hold parameter, but a user can't shut off a queue operator's hold parameter (unless that user is also a queue operator). About the only time you might want to put a job on hold while defining a new print job is when you want to send several files to the printer at once.

Server Sequence. Queue operators use this entry to change the sequence number on the print job and, thus, change when the job gets printed. For example, a queue operator can prioritize a print job by changing its sequence to 1. Then the print job will be placed at the beginning of the print queue, even if the queue is full of other jobs. This function is usually performed after this screen is filled out. The print job is then selected at the queue screen, bringing up the "Print Queue Entry Information" window.

Job Entry Date and **Time.** PCONSOLE uses these entries to show when you put a job on Hold or when the print job was placed in the queue. You view these entries, with their respective fields, filled in from the "Print Queue Entry Information" window. When you exit the "New Print Job to be Submitted" window, highlight the job entry in the queue screen and press <Enter>; you'll see the date and time you submitted that print job.

The next nine entries include "Number of Copies," "File Contents," "Tab Size," "Suppress Form Feed," "Notify When Done," "Form," "Print Banner," "Banner Name," and "Banner File." When you choose a predefined job configuration that you created in PRINTCON, you won't have to set these entries, for PCONSOLE will use those defaults. If you like those defaults or PCONSOLE's defaults, use them. But if you want to change any of those settings, change them here.

Number of Copies. This entry defaults to 1, but can go as high as 65,000. If you want to change the number to 4, position the highlight bar on the number field of the "Number of Copies" entry and type the number 4. Or press <Enter> and then type the number 4. If you want to print 41 copies, type the number 41, which will appear in the field. You must have at least one copy selected; if you select 0, you'll see the "Value must be between 1 and 65000 inclusive. Press Escape to continue" message.

File Contents. This entry lets you choose how the file will print. Pressing <Enter> brings up the "File Contents" window with two options—"Byte Stream" and "Text," with the "Byte Stream" option highlighted as the default. When you print a simple DOS (ASCII text) file that contains no special application formatting codes, choose the "Byte Stream" option unless you want to convert the tabs to spaces. If you choose the "Text" option, you can also choose how many spaces you want in the tab size, which can be from 1 to 18 characters and defaults to eight characters long. Since you're not presently in an application, you won't be able to take advantage of the application's formatting commands: Printing a file that contains an application's printing codes is not a good idea while you're in PCONSOLE. However, if you've saved a print job to a file, you can print that file from PCONSOLE; then it's a good idea to choose "Byte Stream."

Tab Size. This marks the number of spaces in your tabs. If you chose the "Text" option and you want to set the "Tab" option to something other than eight characters (for example, five), make sure the "Tab Size" number field is highlighted, and then type the number 5. Then press <Enter> or <Esc>. You can specify from 1 to 18 spaces for each tab entry; all entries above or below those numbers will receive the "Value must be between 1 and 18 inclusive. Press Escape to continue" window.

Suppress Form Feed. This option allows you to choose whether or not you want the next print job to start at the top of the next page. It defaults to "No," but, some printers and applications automatically send a form feed, so you end up with a blank sheet of paper between print jobs. If you don't want the blank sheet, make sure the selection field is highlighted and type the letter Y. The "No" parameter will toggle to "Yes"; you can toggle back to "No" by typing the letter N.

Notify When Done. This option defaults to "No." Type the letter Y for "Yes" when you want the NetWare printing services to notify you when this print job is at the printer. For those who work in companies that have printers scattered across multiple floors or in some obscure corner, this option can be very handy. Type "N" to set the entry back to "No."

Form. To the right of the "Number of Copies" entry is the "Form" entry. Pressing <Enter> will display the "Valid Forms" window, which lists the actual names (instead of the numbers) of all the forms your supervisor has set up in the PRINTDEF utility. (Utilities like CAPTURE and NPRINT use the form number instead of the form name.) These forms tell the printer which type of paper you'll be using for a particular job, including length and width.

For example, suppose you want to print some mailing labels. Your supervisor can define the form to be thirty characters wide and thirty-five lines long, and give the form the name "Labels." You then choose the "Labels" option from the "Valid Forms" window. If no forms are defined in PRINTDEF, you'll only be allowed to select the form numbers.

Print Banner. This entry defaults to "Yes" and toggles between "Yes" and "No." The banner identifies the print job by first sending through a sheet of paper listing the user name, filename, directory, description, time and date, queue, and server. (For a detailed explanation and figure of a banner, see Figure 4-3.) If you choose "No" in the "Print Banner" entry, no banner will be printed with the print job and the "Banner Name" and "Banner File" entries on this screen will be left blank.

Name and **Banner Name.** The "Name" entry defaults to your login name unless you change it. Specify a name by highlighting the "Banner Name" description field and typing in the name you want to appear on the banner. The field will support up to 12 characters. The "Banner Name" entry defaults to the DOS filename you wish to print. You can specify a different name by highlighting the "Banner Name" description field and typing in the filename you wish to see on the banner. This field also supports up to 12 characters.

Defer Printing. This is one thing you can do in PCONSOLE that you can't do anywhere else. When you set the "Defer Printing" entry to "Yes," you'll jump over to the "Target Date" entry, which will give you a 2:00 am default for the next day. To change the "Target Date" entry, press <Enter> and use the Backspace key to type over the default date, then type in the date when you want to print the file and press <Enter>. You'll then jump to the "Target Time" entry. To change the "Target Time" entry, press <Enter> and use the Backspace key to type over the default date, then type in the time you wish to print the file and press <Enter>. Or you can highlight the entry and start typing in the time. Be sure to designate the AM or PM aspect (the entry defaults to AM).

Target Server. Pressing <Enter> jumps you to this entry. When you've deferred a print job and the time has come for that job to print, the print job goes into this queue; any printer servicing the queue can service the job. When you press <Enter> on the "Target Server" entry, you'll see the "Valid Target Servers" window, which defaults to any server that is servicing the queue. You can specify a particular server (and therefore a particular printer) by highlighting the server option you want and pressing <Enter>. If you're running the NetWare print services from an NLM or on a dedicated print server station, the "Valid Target Servers" window shows the print servers that are available to you.

When you press <Esc> to exit the "New Print Job to be Submitted" window, you'll see the "Save Changes Yes/No" window with the "Yes" option highlighted. Press <Enter> to save the job entry and return to the print queue screen, where you'll see your job filed into the queue and then printed (providing you didn't put it on Hold or defer printing until later). If you don't want to print the job, answer "No," press <Enter>, and you'll return to print queue screen without the print job. At the queue screen, press <Esc> to return to the "Print Queue Information" window.

If you want to submit a print job to a different print queue, press <Esc> again and return to the "Print Queues" window, where you can select another print queue and go through the process all over again. If you want to choose a different server and print to its queues, go back to the "Available Options" window and select the "Change Current File Server" option.

Printing Multiple Files

PCONSOLE also allows you to print several files at the same time. After choosing a print queue from the "Print Queues" window, select "Current Print Job Entries" from the "Print Queue Information" window. Then at the queue screen, press <Ins> to get the directory path from which you wish to print the file. Once you've typed in the proper directory path, press <Enter>; you'll see the "Available Files" window, listing the files in that directory. Choose multiple files by highlighting the names of the files you want to print and marking each with the F5 (Mark) key. Then press <Enter>. If you've created print job configurations in PRINTCON, you'll see the "Print Job Configurations" window along with PCONSOLE's default printer configuration option.

The only difference in preparing multiple files for print is that, at the "New Print Job to be Submitted" window, you'll see "(filename)" in the Description field and at the Banner File entry. This means that each file selected will have its filename inserted into those fields, but if you change the Description entry, every file will reflect the change. Everything else stays the same; however, any changes you make to the "New Print Job to be Submitted" window affects all the files you have marked.

When you've finished modifying the configuration, press <Esc>; you'll see the "Save Changes" window with the "Yes" option highlighted. Press <Enter> and these files hop into the print queue in the order they were in when you selected them from the "Available Files" window. To return to the "Current Print Job Entries" option, press <Esc>.

Other Options You See in the "Print Queue Information" Window

That pretty well covers the "Current Print Job Entries" option in the "Print Queue Information" window. Other options in the window include "Current Queue Status," "Currently Attached Servers," "Print Queue ID," "Queue Operators," "Queue Servers," and "Queue Users."

Current Queue Status. This option lets you look at the queue status and the operator flags. Highlight it, press <Enter>, and you'll see the "Current Queue Status" window appear in the middle of your screen.

```
NetWare Print Console  V1.65              Thursday  March 4, 1993  7:08 pm
                     User TED On File Server NTS3 Connection 7
```

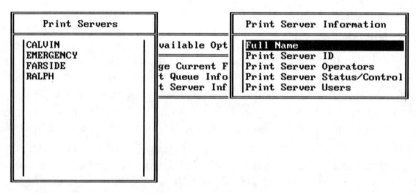

Figure 4-10. This screen shows information such as how many entries are in the queue and how many print servers are servicing the queue

Number of Entries in Queue and **Number of Servers Attached.** These entries are updated every five seconds. The previous example shows that three entries are queued for printing and one server is servicing that queue. If only one server is attached to this queue, it's the server you see in the "Currently Attached Servers" option under the "Print Queue Information" window. (Depending on how your printing services are set up, the servers can also be print servers.)

Operator Flags. The queue operator uses the next three entries to regulate this queue. Suppose a supervisor or queue operator wants to fix a printer and needs to shut down the queues serviced by that printer. The "Users can place entries in queue" entry allows queue operators to toggle the entry between "Yes" and "No." (To change a flag, type "Y" or "N" and press <Enter>.)

When the flag is set to "No," users won't be able to place print jobs into the queue until the flag is reset to "Yes." The supervisor or queue operator can set the "Servers can service entries in queue" entry to "No," meaning that print servers won't be allowed to service jobs in the queue until the flag is reset once again to "Yes." Supervisors or queue operators wanting to prevent other print servers from servicing a special queue can set the "New servers can attach to queue" entry to "No," thereby preventing print servers from attaching to the queue until the flag is again toggled to "Yes."

To exit the "Current Queue Status" window, press <Esc>.

```
┌─────────────────────────────────┐
│ Currently Attached Servers      │
├─────────────────────────────────┤
│ │FARSIDE          │    042       │
└─────────────────────────────────┘
```

Figure 4-11. The "Currently Attached Servers" window

Currently Attached Servers. This next option shows you which servers have printers servicing that queue. Highlight the option and press <Enter>. You'll see a list of the servers that are servicing that queue, along with the connection number they have to the server possessing the queues. If print servers are accessing the queues, you'll see the name of the print server in this window.

```
┌─────────────────────────────────┐
│ Object ID:  000C004F            │
│ On File Server: NTS3            │
└─────────────────────────────────┘
```

Figure 4-12. The "Print Queue ID" window

Print Queue ID. This shows the identification number of the print queue as it's known in the bindery. The NetWare operating system uses this object number to distinguish the queue from servers, printers, other print queues, or other devices on the network. If you ever get the chance to look, you'll see directories with matching names under the SYS:SYSTEM directory, where the print queue directories are stored. To look

403

at this identification number, highlight the "Print Queue ID" option and press <Enter>. You'll see a small screen in the lower-right part of your screen, similar to this one:

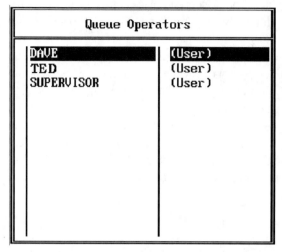

Figure 4-13. The "Queue Operators" window

To exit the option, press <Esc>.

Queue Operators. This option allows a system supervisor to add users and groups as queue operators. Supervisors are automatically made queue operators, and the group EVERYONE is automatically made a queue user. To see who has been assigned a queue operator or this queue, highlight the option and press <Enter>. Queue operators can add and delete other people's print jobs in a queue and prioritize those jobs if they wish. Queue operators can also place on hold any job in the print queue. Only supervisors and equivalents can add or delete queue operators.

To exit the option, press <Esc>.

Queue Servers. This option shows you which servers or print servers can print jobs from this print queue. To see a list of those servers, highlight the "Queue Servers" option and press <Enter>. The designation on the left tells you if the server is a print server or a file server. To exit the option, press <Esc>.

Queue Users. This option shows who has been assigned to use this queue. To see who has been assigned to this queue, highlight the "Queue Users" option and press <Enter>. You'll see a screen similar to the on the next page.

NetWare 3.11 automatically adds the group EVERYONE as members of queues. However, supervisors or queue operators can delete that group and add in whomever they want to let access the queue. If you're not a member of one of the designated groups,

404

or if you're not designated as a user here, your print jobs won't be captured to this queue. However, if you need to print to this queue, your supervisor or queue operator can add you to the "Queue Users" option. To exit the option, press <Esc>.

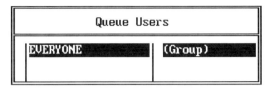

Figure 4-14. The "Queue Users" window

That's it for options in the "Print Queue Information" window. To look at the "Print Server Information" option in the "Available Options" window, press <Esc> until you reach that window.

Looking at Print Server Information

The last option on PCONSOLE's "Available Options" window is "Print Server Information." While this section will have some relevance to users, it's mostly useful for those of you who have been designated print server operators.

As discussed earlier in the chapter, the print server method makes using NetWare's print services easier. A print server approach means that LAN workstations can access up to sixteen printers connected directly to the server or to workstations on the network.

The print server sends files from designated queues on as many as eight file servers to the printer. A print server can be a file server, or it can be software running within the server itself to take care of this process. The idea behind the additional server software is that it can run on a dedicated workstation to act as a print server, thus freeing up the file server to perform other functions. Or, the additional software can run on the file server itself.

To see the print server's information, select the "Print Server Information" option at the "Available Options" window and press <Enter>. You'll see the "Print Servers" window listing the available print servers defined on this server. To see the available print server on other file servers, you'll first need to change your current server, then go into "Print Server Information" option. Since one print server can service the print queues on multiple servers, you'll see the same print servername on those servers in order for multiple file servers to share printers.

Supervisors need to have three steps in place for a print server to service multiple file server. First, they need the same print servername defined on all the file servers. Second, they need the same printer "numbers" defined on all the file servers. Third, they

405

need the file server (from where they run PSERVER.NLM or PSERVER.EXE) to have all the file servers listed in the "File Servers To Be Serviced" option of the "File Server Configuration Menu" window.

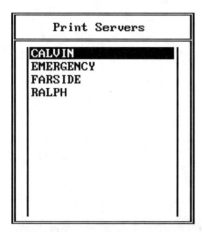

Figure 4-15. Selecting the "Print Server Information" option, you can see a list of available print servers on this server

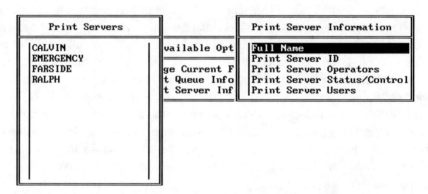

Figure 4-16. Once you select a print server, you can see information about it

Select one of the servers in the "Print Servernames" window and press <Enter>. Users and print server operators will see five options: "Full Name," "Print Server ID," "Print Server Operators," "Print Server Users," and "Print Server Status/Control." Supervisors or those with equivalent status can see two additional options: "Change Password" and "Print Server Configuration."

You'll see the "Print Server Status/Control" option only if the print server you select is actively running; for nonactive print servers, the option is unavailable. Here's how these different options work:

Full Name. This option shows you the full name of the print server you selected from the "Print Servernames" window. To look at the server's full name, highlight this option and press <Enter>. You'll see a small screen in the lower part of your screen, similar to this one:

```
Full Name: Network Technical Services LaserJetIIIP
```

Figure 4-17. The Full Name window

If you select a server that doesn't have a full name, you'll see the "No full name specified" message in the "Full Name" window. To exit the option, press <Esc>.

Print Server ID. This ID is the identification number the NetWare operating system uses to distinguish the print server from other servers, printers, print queues, and other devices on the network. To look at this identification number, highlight the "Print Server ID" option and press <Enter>. In the window, you see the Object ID as it pertains to the file server from which you are running PCONSOLE. The second line shows you the file server's name, which matches the server you see in the PCONSOLE screen header. When you change to another file server and choose the same print servername (if there is one defined), you'll see a different Object ID and On File Server designation.

Print Server Operators. This option allows a system supervisor to add users and groups as print server operators. Supervisors are automatically made print server operators, and the group EVERYONE is automatically made a print server user. To see who has been assigned a print server operator for this print server designation, highlight the option and press <Enter>. You'll see a screen similar to the one on the next page.

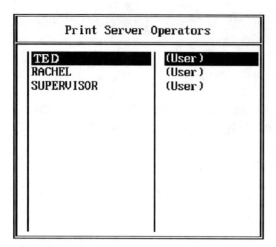

Figure 4-18. Use this option if you need to know who is a print server operator

While print server operators can't create or configure new print servers, (they're assigned to a print server after it's created), or assign other users as a print server operator, they can do almost everything else to maintain printers, print queues, and print servers. Some of their duties include adding printers to printer queues on a temporary basis, changing queue priorities or adding/deleting queues from a server, changing printer forms, controlling printers, attaching to file servers for queue access, and bringing down the print server. Because print server operators must also manipulate print queues from time to time, they should be print queue operators as well.

Only supervisors and equivalents can add or delete print server operators. To exit the option, press <Esc>.

Looking at the Status of Print Servers

Print Server Status/Control. While as a user you can use this option to view the print server's status, the print server operator can use this option to manage the print servers he/she is assigned to. To view the "Print Server Status/Control," highlight the option and press <Enter>. You'll see the "Print Server Status and Control" window with the following options: "File Servers Being Serviced," "Notify List for Printer," "Printer Status," "Queues Services by Printer," and "Server Info." Let's look at these options from a user's and then a print server operator's perspective.

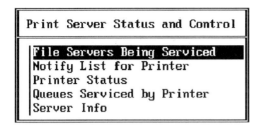

Figure 4-19. Print server operators use this screen to manage a print server

The "File Servers Being Serviced" option shows the file servers that have been assigned to this print server. The print server polls the print queues of the file servers on this list to see if any print jobs are ready for printing. The print server polls the print queues about every fifteen seconds for print jobs, then coordinates the jobs ready for printing to their assigned printer or printer group.

Figure 4-20. This screen shows you which file server the print server is servicing

Print-server operators can add or delete file servers from this list. To delete a file server form the list, highlight the server and press <Del>. You'll see a "Delete File Server from Service List" window with the "Yes" option highlighted. Pressing <Enter> deletes the server, unless the server is the default server from which the print server is running. If it's the default server, you'll see an error message telling you this. To add a file server, press <Ins> and you'll see the "Available File Servers" window. Highlight the server you wish to add and press <Enter>. If that server has a password associated with it, you'll need to type in the password. Passwords for file servers are added by supervisors or equivalents, so if you need a password, ask the supervisor for it. (You'll also see the password window if there are no print queues on the file server.) Once you give the password, the file server is added to this window.

However, additions and deletions made by the print server operator are not permanent and must be made again if the print server is brought down and back up again. To make permanent additions and deletions to this window, you must have supervisor or equivalent status and must make the changes to the "File Servers To Be Serviced" option in the "Print Server Configuration" window.

The "Notify List For Printer" option shows you who will be notified when a printer needs attention. When you highlight this option and press <Enter>, you'll see a list of those printers that have been configured for network use. (Supervisors or equivalents configure printers and the notification list from the "Print Server Configuration" window). To see who will be notified, highlight a printer and press <Enter>. You'll see a screen similar to this one:

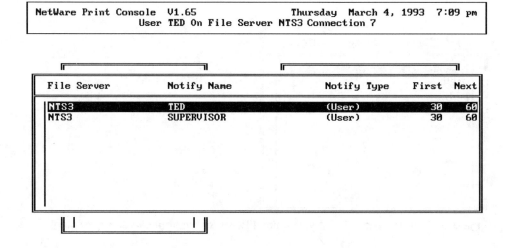

Figure 4-21. You can see who will get notified if a printer has problems

The "Notify List" window shows you the file server (which matches the server you see on the header screen), the name of the user or group who will be notified, whether the notify names are users or groups, and the First and Next columns. The First column shows how many seconds (defaults to 30) after the printer has problems that users are notified. Number of seconds can be between 1 and 3600 (60 minutes). The Next column shows how many seconds (defaults to 60) PCONSOLE waits before sending another notification message to the list of users.

Print server operators can add or delete users and groups from the list on a temporary basis. First, highlight the printer you wish to have maintained and press <Enter>. Then by pressing <Ins>, you'll see a list of Notify Candidates from which to choose (those defined users and groups on this file server). Highlighting a name and pressing <Enter> brings up the "Notify Intervals" window with "First" entry showing 30 seconds and "Next" entry showing 60. To modify the entries, highlight them and type from 1 to 3600 (60 minutes) into the entry field. Press <Esc> when you're finished and save the changes. The name is added to the "Notify List" window.

To delete someone temporarily from the "Notify List" window, highlight the person or group and press <Del>. You'll see the "Delete Object From Notify List" window with the "Yes" option highlighted. Press <Enter> to remove the name from the list.

However, additions and deletions made by the print server operator are not permanent. They must be made again if the print server is brought down and back up again. To make permanent additions and deletions to this window, you must have supervisor or equivalent status and must make the changes to the "Notify List For Printer" option in the "Print Server Configuration" window.

The "Printer Status" option shows you what a selected printer is currently doing. To view the printer's status, highlight the "Printer Status" option and press <Enter>, then highlight a printer from the "Active Printers" window and press <Enter>. You'll see a screen similar to this one:

```
NetWare Print Console  V1.65              Thursday  March 4, 1993  7:10 pm
                   User TED On File Server NTS3 Connection 7
```

```
                            Status of iiip

 Status:              Printing job                      Printer Control

 Service mode:        Change forms as needed
 Mounted form:        0

 File server:         NTS3
 Queue:               ADMIN
 Job number:          448
 Description:         CVR-SHT.FAX
 Form:                0

 Copies requested:            1        Finished:        0
 Size of 1 copy:           7428        Finished:        0
 Percent completed:        0.00
```

Figure 4-22 The Status option shows the present state of the printer you select

411

Here's what the entries on the "Status" window mean:

The "Status" entry can display a number of messages which describe the status of the printer. The messages you see in the "Status" entry include:

A "Waiting for job" message means that there are currently no print jobs in the queue(s) the printer services that need to be printed.

You see a "Mount form n" message when you print a job using a form other than the one currently printing. The supervisor or print server operator can set up the print queue to place print jobs needing other forms mounted on hold. (See the "Service Mode" entry.) A print server operator can then change the "Mounted Form" entry to match the form number designated at the "n" entry and get the printer going again.

You see the "Printing Job" message when the printer is currently in the process of printing a print job.

When the printer has been paused by the supervisor or print server operator in PCONSOLE or PSC, you'll see "Paused" or "Stopped." When the printer is taken off "Paused" you'll see only the "Printing Job" entry or "Waiting For Job," unless something else happens to warrant another message.

You'll see the "Ready to go down" message when the supervisor or print server operator has issued the command to "down" or take the print server out of service. NetWare 3.1x supervisors and print server operators can bring down the print server from within PCONSOLE's "Current Server Status" entry in the "Print Server Info/ Status" window, or a supervisor can unload the PSERVER.NLM from the server console.

The "Stopped" message means the supervisor or print server operator has issued the STOP printer command from PCONSOLE or PSC. When the START command is issued, you'll see "Waiting for Job" or "Printing Job" messages in the "Status" entry.

A "Not Connected" message will show up when a remote printer configuration has been defined for the print server, but the workstation with the remote printer attached isn't running the RPRINTER TSR utility. When a workstation runs the RPRINTER utility, the utility tells the print server which printer number the attached printer will use and asks for its configuration. The print server then takes the information stored in the printer's configuration file and sends it to RPRINTER. If the configuration file's printer settings match the actual printer settings, you'll see the "Waiting for Job" message. If the settings don't match, the printer will remain "Not Connected."

You'll see the "In Private Mode" message when the designated printer has been used for network services and is now being run as a local printer. The supervisor or print server operator can do this by issuing the PRIvate command from PSC.

You can see either the "Off Line" or "Out of Paper" message in conjunction with two other messages: "Printing Job" and "Mark/Eject." So under the "Printing Job" message, you might see either "Off Line" or "Out of Paper" messages (among other messages). The same is true with "Mark/Eject."

These are most of the messages you can see, but you may come across a few other obscure messages as well.

The "Service Mode" and "Mounted Form" entries allow supervisors and print server operators to set up how a printer should handle form changes. Users can see four messages in the "Service Mode" entry: "Change forms as needed," "Minimize form changes across queues," "Minimize from changes within queues," and "Service only currently mounted form."

The "Change Forms as Needed" option means the supervisor or print server operator will be changing forms whenever users send a print job requesting a different form. If they want to store other form jobs until there's bunch of them, they can choose the "Service Only Currently Mounted Form" option. Then they can change forms at designated times of the day or evening and post those times for those users needing different forms printed. Whatever forms specified in the "Mounted Form" entry will then be the mounted form of choice.

Supervisors or print server operators can also print out all the print jobs of the present forms in one queue or in all queues the printer is servicing by using the "Across Queues" and "Within Queues" options. They can then change the form and print out those print jobs. If they have more than one printer servicing queues, they can designate one form per printer through the "Mounted Form" entry, then use the "Service Only Currently Mounted Form" option to make the printer use only the designated form. They can set this up for one queue or for all the queues the printers may service.

To be permanent, changes in the "Service Mode" and "Mounted Form" entries must be performed in the "Configuration" option. To make permanent additions and deletions to this window, you must have supervisor or equivalent status and must make the changes to the "Printer Configuration" option in the "Print Server Configuration" window.

The entries from "File Server" through "Form" give you information on what you are currently printing. This information includes the file server, the print queue on the file server, the job number of the print job and its description, and the form number. This is the same information you can see about a print job if you highlight a job in a print queue and press <Enter>.

The "Copies Requested" entry shows you how many copies are being printed within the print job you are looking at. The "Finished" entry across from the "Copies

Requested" then shows you how many copies have been completed so far. The "Size Of 1 Copy" entry shows you how big the file is in bytes; the "Finished" entry shows you how much of the copy has been completed.

The "Percent Completed" entry shows you how much of the total print job is completed. This is a funny and often inaccurate entry, for if you are printing more than one copy, the "Percent" entry often gets confused and doesn't reflect where it actually is in the printing process.

Print server operators and supervisors will see one more entry in this "Status" window—"Printer Control." It comes with seven options: "Abort Print Job," "Form Feed," "Mark Top of Form," "Pause Printer," "Rewind Printer," "Start Printer," and "Stop Printer." Let's look at these options next.

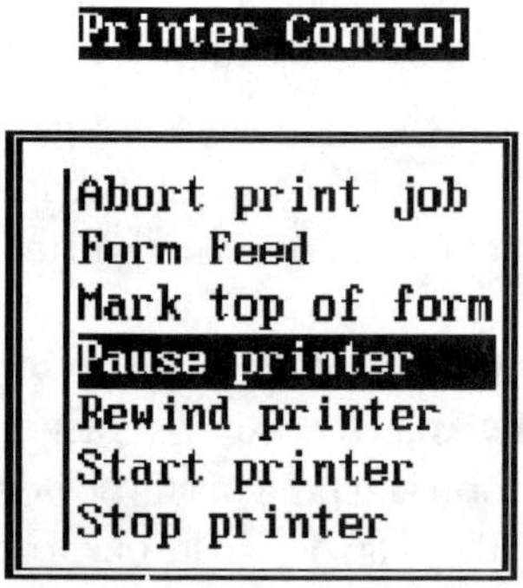

Printer Control

```
Abort print job
Form Feed
Mark top of form
Pause printer
Rewind printer
Start printer
Stop printer
```

Figure 4-23. You use the "Printer Control" window to restart, pause, and rewind the printer

Use the "Abort Print Job" option when you want to trash the current print job out of the queue and into the proverbial bit bucket. Once that print job is deleted, the rest of the jobs in the print queue will begin printing.

Choose the "Form Feed" option when you want the printer to advance to the top of the next page. You can also use this parameter to print out a print job that didn't include a "Form Feed" at the end of its print job.

Suppose you want to make sure the printer is functioning properly by sending a sheet of paper with asterisks marked across the page. Sometimes you need to send this option with another print job. The "Mark Top of Form" option can be useful to show you that the printer can print from the network; if you know the printer can print a line of asterisks, you can troubleshoot whatever problem you are having somewhere else. Or you can use this option to align a page of paper on the printer.

414

The "Pause Printer" option allows you to temporarily stop the printer so you can perform maintenance duties (such as clearing paper jams) or place commands to the printer, such as the Form Feed and Mark commands. You'll then need to choose the "Start Printer" option to have printing continue.

Use the "Rewind Printer" option when you've paused the printer for servicing and you now want to continue printing from the page where you left off, not print the whole job again. When you select this option, you'll see a small screen allowing you to rewind the print job a certain number of bytes, or you can specify a number of bytes in a single copy or the copy number (if you have multiple copies).

After stopping or pausing a printer, you can start the print back up by selecting the "Start Printer" option.

When you wish to stop a printer, select the "Stop Printer" option. If you happen to stop the printer while it's printing a job, that job will be placed back into the print queue for printing. You must choose the "Start Printer" option to have printing continue.

Press <Esc> until you return to the "Print Server Status and Control" window.

To find out which print queues are being serviced by which printers on a given print server, highlight the "Queues Serviced By Printer" option and press <Enter>. You'll see the "Active Printers" window with those printers that have been configured for this print server. To see which queues each printer accesses, highlight one of the printer configurations and press <Enter>. You'll see a screen similar to this one:

File Server	Queue	Priority
NTS1	ADMIN	1
NTS1	LANSPOOL_SI_QUEUE	1
NTS1	PRINTQ_0	1
NTS1	SPSHEET	1
NTS3	ADMIN	1

Figure 4-24. Select the "Queues Serviced by Printer" option to see which print queues are being serviced by this print server

In the screen you see three columns: File Server, Queue, and Priority. Printers can access more than one queue on more than one file server, so what you see here is a listing of the queues and which servers those queues reside on. The Priority column shows you which priority the print queue is set to. Priorities are useful for those managers who think their work is more important than those of us who get the work gone. They can set their queues to a higher priority (1 to 10—1 being the highest) and have their queues serviced more often than queues with a lower setting.

Print server operators and supervisors can add and delete print queues to this window. To add a print queue, press <Ins> and you'll see the "Available Queues" window; highlight the queue and press <Enter>. You'll see a "Priority" window which defaults to 1 and through which you can change to a different number (1 to 10). One method is to set all print queues at a lower priority, such as 5, leaving priority room for those rush jobs that inevitably come through. This way, all print queues are accessed at the same priority level until you establish the rush queue, and you won't have to delete all the other queues and add them again at a lower priority if you do need to add a high priority queue.

To add a queue on a different file server, press <Esc> until you reach the main "Available Options" window, then choose the "Change Current File Server" option. Select the server through the method explained earlier, then choose the "Print Server Information" option. Choose the matching print servername from the "Print Servers" window, press <Enter>, and choose the "Print Server Status/Control" option and press <Enter>. Choose the "Queues Serviced By Printer" option, select the matching printer number, and press <Enter>. (The printer name may be different to reflect where the printer is actually located.) When you press <Ins>, you can now include the queues on that file server.

To delete a queue from the "Queue" screen, highlight the queue and press <Del>. You'll see the "Delete Queue From Service List" window with the "Yes" option highlighted. Press <Enter> and the queue is removed. However, additions and deletions made by the print server operator are not permanent and will have to be made again if the print server is brought down and brought back up again. To make permanent additions and deletions to this window, you must have supervisor or equivalent status and must make the changes to the "Printer Configuration" option in the "Print Server Configuration Menu" window.

The last option on the "Print Server Status and Control" window is "Server Info." This option shows you the print server version, server type, number of printers, service modes, and the current server status. To view the information in this option, highlight the "Server Info" option and press <Enter>. You'll see a screen similar to this one:

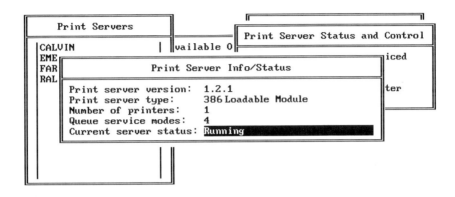

```
NetWare Print Console   V1.65              Thursday  March 4, 1993  7:10 pm
                     User TED On File Server NTS3 Connection 7
```

```
   Print Servers                   ┌─────────────────────────────────────┐
                                    │  Print Server Status and Control    │
CALVIN              │ vailable 0├──┴─────────────────────────────────────┤
EME┌──────────────────────────────────────────────┐           iced
FAR│            Print Server Info/Status           │
RAL│                                               │           ter
   │  Print server version:  1.2.1                 │
   │  Print server type:     386 Loadable Module   │
   │  Number of printers:    1                     │
   │  Queue service modes:   4                     │
   │  Current server status: Running               │
   │                                               │
   │                                               │
   └───────────────────────────────────────────────┘
```

Figure 4-25. Current print server status

The "Print server version" entry shows the version of the print server software. If you're running print server software on the file server, you'll see "386 Loadable Module" across from the "Print server type" entry. And if the print server software is running on a dedicated workstation, you'll see "Dedicated DOS" across from the entry.

The "Number Of Printers" entry shows you how many printer configurations have been defined (not how many printers are actually running). "Queue Service Modes" reflects how many service modes supervisors and print server operators have to choose from—not very useful information. The last entry, "Current Server Status," shows whether the print server is currently Running, Going down after it services the current print jobs, or simply Down without servicing the current print jobs.

Print server operators can use this entry to select one of the three options. For example, you can select the "Down" option and press <Enter> to bring down the print server. For dedicated workstations running PSERVER.EXE, about the only way to bring down the printer server running on dedicated workstations is through the "Down" option. While you can bring down print servers running as NLMs from this option, you can also bring down NLMs from the file server console. (For NetWare 3.1x, the proper command is LOAD PSERVER *servername* and UNLOAD PSERVER.) Press <Esc> to exit the "Server Info" option, and press <Esc> again to return to the "Print Server Information" window.

The last option on the "Print Server Information" window is "Print Server Users." This option shows who has been assigned to use this print server. To see who's been assigned to this print server, highlight the "Print Server Users" option and press <Enter>. You'll see a screen similar to this one:

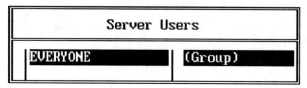

Figure 4-26. The default print server user is group EVERYONE

NetWare 3.1x automatically adds the group EVERYONE as members who can use the print server. However, supervisor or print server operators can delete that group and add in whoever they want to access the print server. If you're not a member of one of the designated groups, or if you're not designated as a user here, you probably aren't using this print server designation when you print. However, if you need to print to this queue, your supervisor or print server operator can add you to the "Print Server Users" option.

To exit the option, press <Esc>.

To exit PCONSOLE, press the <Alt>-<F10> keys simultaneously and you'll see the "Exit PConsole Yes/No" window with the "Yes" option highlighted. Press <Enter> and you'll return to the network prompt.

PSC

Here's another utility that's handy for print server operators, but that offers regular users only limited information. PSC (Print Server Command) allows print server operators to control print servers and network printers. PSC offers a command-line equivalent of PCONSOLE to many of the printer tasks print server operators need to perform. Regular users can use PSC to view the status of print servers and their network printers.

Looking at PSC's Parameters

PSC comes with a number of parameters you can use to view operational statistics on print servers as well as manipulate printers. If you can't remember how to use PSC's syntax, type PSC /H <Enter> at the network prompt. You'll see a screen similar to this one:

```
Usage: PSC PS[=]print_server P[=]printer_number Flaglist ...
     Flaglist:    CancelDown, FormFeed, PAUse,
                  PRIvate, SHared, STARt, STATus,
                  ABort,
                  STOp [Keep],
                  MArk [character], and
                  MOunt Form=n.
```

Let's first look at the only parameter that users have access to—STATus.

/STATus. Use this option if you want to see how printers are doing on a particular print server. For example, if you have a print server named FARSIDE and you wanted to see the status on all its printers, type PSC PS=FARSIDE STAT <Enter>. You'll see a screen similar to the following one.

```
Printer 0: HPLaserJet at Bill's WS
Printing Job
Paused

Printer 1: Epson on NTS3 server
Waiting for job

Printer 3: Laserjet II server ADMIN
Not connected
```

If you have a particular printer you wish to see the status of—printer 0, for example—type PSC PS=FARSIDE P=0 STAT <Enter>. You can see information similar to this:

```
Printer 0: HPLaserJet at Bill's WS
Printing Job
Paused
```

In this example, Printer 0, which is attached to Bill's workstation, was in the process of printing a job but was placed on Pause while the job was printing. The description following Printer 0 is the printer description given instead of Printer 0 in PCONSOLE's "Printer Configuration" option. This description can be used to help define where printers are located as well as the printer type. The "Printing Job" and "Paused" status are two of a number of messages you can see under the printer heading. Other messages include those described in the following paragraphs.

You see a "Waiting for job" message when no print jobs are ready for printing in the print queue(s) the designated printer looks after.

You see the message "Mount form n:" when you print a job using a form other than the one currently printing. The supervisor or print server operator can set up the print queue to place on hold any print jobs needing other forms mounted. A print server operator can run PSC, mount the form number designated at the "n" entry, and get the printer going again.

The "Printing Job" message comes up when the printer is currently in the process of printing a print job.

The message "Paused" shows up when the printer has been paused by the supervisor or print server operator in PCONSOLE or PSC. At this point, you'll see two messages: "Printing Job" and "Paused." When the printer is taken off "Paused" you'll see only the "Printing Job" entry unless something happens to warrant another message.

You'll see the "Ready to go down" message when the supervisor or print server operator has issued the command to stop the print server. NetWare 3.11 supervisors and print server operators can bring down the print server from within PCONSOLE's "Current Server Status" entry in the "Print Server Info/Status" window, or supervisors can unload PSERVER.NLM at the server console.

The "Stopped" message means the supervisor or print server operator has issued the STOP printer command from PCONSOLE or PSC. When the START command is issued, you'll see "Waiting for Job" or "Printing Job" messages.

You'll see the "Mark/Form Feed" message if the supervisor or print server operator has placed a Mark or Form Feed flag on the print job. The Mark character gives the print server operator a chance to see where the next print job is starting, and the Form Feed flag ensures that the next print job will begin at the top of the next page.

A "Not Connected" message will be displayed when a remote printer configuration has been defined for the print server, but the workstation with the remote printer attached isn't running the RPRINTER TSR utility. When a workstation runs the RPRINTER utility, the utility tells the print server which printer number the attached printer will use and asks for its configuration. The print server then takes the information stored in the printer's configuration file and sends it down to RPRINTER. If the configuration file's printer settings match the actual printer settings, you'll see the "Waiting for Job" message. If the settings don't match, the printer will remain "Not Connected."

A print server can coordinate up to sixteen printers all over the network. These printer numbers are 0–15 inclusive, so if you type PSC PS=FARSIDE P=4 <Enter> and no printer has been defined as printer 4, you'll see the "Not Installed" message. Type PSC PS=FARSIDE STAT <Enter> to see a listing of available printers.

You'll see the "In Private Mode" message when the designated printer has been used for network services and is now being run as a local printer. The supervisor or print server operator can do this by issuing the PRIvate command from PSC.

You can see either the "Off Line" or "Out of Paper" message in conjunction with two other messages: "Printing Job" and "Mark/Form Feed." So, under the "Printing Job" message, you might see either "Off Line" or "Out of Paper" messages (among other messages). The same is true with "Mark/Form Feed" commands.

As mentioned earlier, the rest of PSC's parameters are for supervisors or equivalents and print server operators. If you try to run the other commands and you don't have the equivalence, you'll see "You must be an operator on print server NTS-PE to issue this command." Here's a list of the other parameters as they're listed in the PSC help menu:

/CancelDown. In the "Print Server Information" option of PCONSOLE, you can select the "Server Info" option under the "Print Server Status and Control" window. Once you select the "Server Info" option, one of the entries in its window is "Current Server Status," which can show "Running," "Down," and "Going Down After Current Jobs." If the "Going Down" option is selected, the print server will still be running until the last print job is sent to the printer. Before that time, you can type PSC PS=FARSIDE CD <Enter> to effectively cancel the DOWN command. You'll see "The DOWN command to the print server was canceled successfully" on the screen.

/FormFeed. When you want to send a form feed to spit out the print job that is currently in the printer or a blank sheet of paper, type PSC PS=FARSIDE P=0 FF <Enter> to send the form feed through. You can also use this parameter to print out a print job that didn't include a Form Feed at the end of its print job.

/PAUse. The Pause parameter allows you to temporarily stop the printer so you can perform maintenance duties or send commands to the printer, such as the Form Feed and Mark commands. To use the pause parameter, type PSC PS=FARSIDE P=0 PAU <Enter>, and you'll see "The PAUSE command to printer 0 was successful."

/PRIvate. Use this parameter when you want a printer currently used for network services to run as a local printer on a workstation. You can't use this command on any printers attached to print servers or file servers. To remove the remote printer from the list of network resources, type PSC PS=FARSIDE P=0 PRI <Enter> and you'll see "Remote printer 0 has become private." On that workstation, you'll also need to run ENDCAP to get rid of any CAPTURE commands. Also, be sure that you don't have any conflicting local printer permissions in the NET.CFG file. You must also make sure that the application you wish to use can print to the port where the printer resides.

/SHared. Use the Share parameter when you want to remove the Private mode set on a remote printer so it can again become a network printer resource. To make a printer once again available at a remote workstation, type PSC PS=FARSIDE P=0 SH <Enter>, and the print server can then pick up the printer resource. You'll see the message "Remote printer 0 has become shared." Be sure you have the RPRINTER TSR running at the workstation.

/ABort. To stop a print job from continuing to print, type PSC PS=FARSIDE P=0 AB <Enter> and the print job will be flushed to the proverbial bit bucket in the sky. Once that print job is deleted, the rest of the jobs in the print queue will begin printing.

/STOp [Keep]. When you wish to stop a printer, type PSC PS=FARSIDE P=0 STOP <Enter>. If you happen to stop the printer while it's printing a job, that job will be lost unless you also include the Keep parameter: for example, PSC PS=FARSIDE P=0 STOP K <Enter>.

/STARt. After stopping or pausing a printer, you can start the printer back up by typing PSC PS=FARSIDE P=0 START <Enter>.

/MArk [character]. Suppose you wanted to make sure the printer is functioning properly. First, Pause or Stop the printer (PSC PS=FARSIDE P=0 STOP <Enter>), then type PSC PS=FARSIDE P=0 MA <Enter> followed by PS=FARSIDE P=0 FF <Enter> to send a form feed through. You then follow the command with a Start parameter to get things going again (PSC PS=FARSIDE P=0 START <Enter>). (The MA command defaults to a row of asterisks.) Then if you know the printer can print a line of asterisks, you can troubleshoot whatever problem you are having somewhere else.

/MOunt Form=_n_. Suppose the printer won't print, so you type PSC PS=FARSIDE P=0 STATUS <Enter> and you see the message "Mount Form 1." You can use this Mount parameter when someone has sent a print job to the printer using a form other than the one that is currently printing. You can then type PSC PS=FARSIDE P=0 MO F=1 <Enter> and you'll see "Form 1 was mounted on printer 0 successfully." But be aware, for the print queue services print jobs as they come into the queue, and if the next job needs form 0, you'll see the "Mount Form 0 message."

To get out of this form-mounting teeter-totter, have your supervisor (if you aren't supervisor-equivalent) go into PCONSOLE, choose the print server coordinating this printer, and then choose the "Print Server Configuration" option from the "Print Server Information" window. Next choose the "Printer Configuration" option, then choose the printer designated in the "Configured Printers" window. Highlight the "Queue Service Mode" entry and press <Enter>. You'll see four service modes you can choose from: "Change Forms As Needed" (which you're probably in), "Minimize Form Changes Across Queues," "Minimize Form Changes Within Queues," and "Service Only Currently Mounted Form."

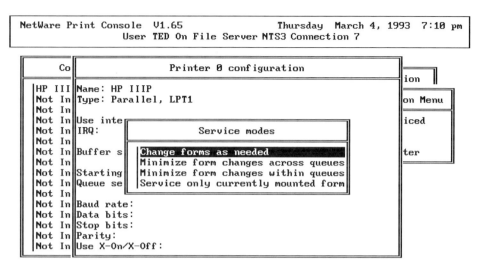

```
NetWare Print Console   V1.65                 Thursday  March 4, 1993  7:10 pm
                      User TED On File Server NTS3 Connection 7
```

```
        Co              Printer 0 configuration                        ion
 HP III Name: HP IIIP                                                  on Menu
 Not In Type: Parallel, LPT1
 Not In
 Not In Use inte                                                       iced
 Not In IRQ:                    Service modes
 Not In
 Not In Buffer s    Change forms as needed                             ter
 Not In             Minimize form changes across queues
 Not In Starting    Minimize form changes within queues
 Not In Queue se    Service only currently mounted form
 Not In
 Not In Baud rate:
 Not In Data bits:
 Not In Stop bits:
 Not In Parity:
 Not In Use X-On/X-Off:
```

Figure 4-27. Set the "Service Modes" option to the "Service only currently mounted form" option to store the other forms for later printing

The "Change Forms as Needed" option means you'll be changing forms whenever users send a print job requesting a different form. If you want to store other form jobs until you get a bunch of them, choose the "Service Only Currently Mounted Form" option. Then change forms at designated times of the day or evening and post those times for those needing different forms. Whatever form you specify through PCONSOLE or PSC will then be the mounted form of choice.

You can also print out all the print jobs of your present forms in one queue or in all queues the printer is servicing. You can then change the form and print out those print jobs. If you have more than one printer servicing queues, you can designate one form per printer through the "Starting Form" entry, then use the "Service Only Currently Mounted Form" option to make the printers print only the designated forms. You can set this up for one queue or for all the queues the printers may service.

Changing these parameters in the configuration file makes permanent changes, but to perform the same feat on a temporary basis, go to the "Print Server Status/Control" option in the "Print Server Information" window, then choose the "Printer Status" option and the printer you're addressing. You can now set the "Service Mode" and "Mounted Form" the same way I explained under the "Print Server Configuration" option.

423

PSC and the DOS SET Command

Suppose you have only one print server and you don't want to type in the print servername every time you run PSC. Or suppose that you have only one printer or you maintain one printer more than the others. You can use the DOS SET command to set up PSC defaults so all you would have to do is add the PSC commands. To do this, type SET PSC=PSprintserver Pprinternumber <Enter> at the network prompt. An example would be SET PSC=PSFARSIDE P0 <Enter>. Then type PSC parameter <Enter> to initiate any commands on print server FARSIDE and printer 0.

If you need to look at printer 1, simply type out the print server and printer names: for example, PSC PS=FARSIDE P1 STAT <Enter>. If you want to change the defaults to printer 1, add the SET command: for example, SET PSC=PSFARSIDE P1 <Enter>. To place this in your system login script so you don't have to type it in every time you log in, type SET PSC="PSprintserver Pprinternumber" in the login script.

Printing Remotely through the RPRINTER Utility

Through the RPRINTER utility, workstations with attached printers can have their local printers designated as network resources. Users run the RPRINTER TSR (terminate-and-stay-resident program) which defaults to 4KB and which sets up communication with the print server. Many workstations will be loading RPRINTER from the AUTOEXEC.BAT file, saving you the bother of typing in the command.

Depending on how the supervisor or print server operator has things set up, here's a checklist of what you must have for RPRINTER to run successfully at your workstation.

> ➤ If the printer is attached, find out which port type as well as which interrupt it's using.

> ➤ Make sure the printer is using a different interrupt than the network interface board. For LPT ports (7 and 5), this is easy; for COM ports (4 and 3), this may not be so easy.

> ➤ The workstation needs to be attached to the same network as the print server that is using the printer.

> ➤ If the supervisor has assigned you a printer number to use (RPRINTER *printserver printernumber*), the printer configuration will probably match the way the printer is set up.

➤ If the supervisor has created some generic printer configurations, you may need to know which port and interrupt the printer is using. You can get this information from the supervisor or the print server operator.

From a DOS point of view, the workstation's serial and parallel ports are assigned names with interrupts for sending data to attached devices, one of which can be a printer. For example, DOS 4.01 and 5.0 can have four serial (COM) ports, with the four ports using interrupts (IRQs) 4 and 3. The four serial devices share two interrupts, with COM1 and COM3 sharing IRQ 4 and COM2 and COM4 sharing IRQ 3. Parallel ports LPT1 and LPT2 are also interrupt-driven and use IRQ 7 and IRQ 5. LPT3 is generally a polled port, which RPRINTER doesn't support in NetWare 3.11, but does in NetWare 3.12.

In this context, "polled" means that the BIOS (Basic InPut/OutPut System) is responsible to see if the printer is ready to receive more data. And interrupts used by serial and parallel ports can be summed up as signals that "interrupt" the computer from its present activities to perform another activity. When that activity is finished, the interrupt then hands back control to the program that's running. A peripheral device (such as a printer) uses interrupts to get the main CPU's attention, and interrupts 3, 4, 5, and 7 are designated interrupts for printers and other devices to use.

Looking at RPRINTER's Parameters

If you can't remember how to use RPRINTER's syntax, type RPRINTER /H <Enter> at the network prompt. You'll see a screen similar to this one:

```
Usage: [RPrinter] to use menu, or
       [RPrinter PrintServer PrinterNumber] to install, or
       [RPrinter PrintServer PrinterNumber -R] to remove, or
       [RPrinter -S] to show status.
```

NetWare 3.12 users will see a different screen that looks like the following:

```
***********************   RPRINTER V3.12 USAGE   ***********************

To install:     RPRINTER [PrintServer PrinterNumber] [-P]
        menus are used if PrintServer and PrinterNumber are omitted
        -P forces use of polled mode, ignoring any interrupt settings

To remove:      RPRINTER -R
        The last installed RPrinter will be removed
```

```
To show status:  RPRINTER -S
        Installed RPrinters are displayed in the order they were loaded

Examples:
    RPRINTER              install using menus
    RPRINTER -P           install using menus; force Polled mode
    RPRINTER MYSERVER 2   install as printer #2 on running PServer
                              'MYSERVER'
    RPRINTER MYSERVER 2 -P install as printer #2 on MYSERVER; use
                              Polled mode
```

****

NetWare 3.12 also adds the -P parameter to force the RPRINTER to work in polled mode. While the rest of the screen looks different, it covers basically the same material as is covered in NetWare 3.11.

RPRINTER *PrintServer PrinterNumber.* If you know the name of the print server you use (such as FARSIDE) and the printer number of the print configuration file your attached printer is to use (0), type RPRINTER FARSIDE 0 <Enter> and you'll see a message like "Remote Printer `Epson at Ted's Desk' (printer 0) installed." If that printer definition has been taken, you'll see the message "Printer 0 on print server FARSIDE is already in use."

You can either type in the name of the print server and its printer number, or you can simply type RPRINTER, which brings you to a menu screen, similar to this one:

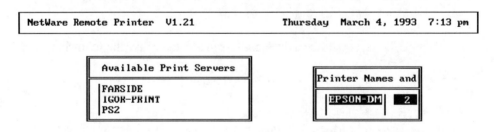

Figure 4-28. By typing RPRINTER, you'll see a menu screen that lets you choose which printer you wish to activate

The Remote Printer screen shows you the available print servers under the "Available Print Servers" window. Most users will see only one print server selection, simply because only one print server will be active on the network. If you do have more than one selection, ask your supervisor or print server operator which one to select (if you're not already loading RPRINTER from your AUTOEXEC.BAT file). Highlight the print server of choice and press <Enter>.

After selecting a print server, you'll see the "Printer Names and Numbers" window, showing you the printers you can choose from. You may not see all the printer configurations that have been defined; you'll see only those printer configurations that are currently available. Highlight the printer selection you were told to use and press <Enter>. You'll then return to the network prompt with a message like "Remote Printer 'Epson at Ted's Desk' (printer 0) installed."

The supervisor often sets up a printer configuration for your printer to use. The printer configuration file contains the proper port and interrupt settings for your printer to work. All you need to know is the printer number. You then simply use the printer number as part of the command you type in to load RPRINTER.

The supervisor may have left the port settings undefined, allowing for more workstations to use a printer number. These printers are set up under the "Remote Other/ Unknown" option in the printer configuration part of the PCONSOLE utility. If this is the case, you'll need to supply the printer configuration information when you load the RPRINTER TSR at your workstation. For example, suppose you type RPRINTER <Enter>, choose the proper print server, then choose the proper printer name/number; you will see a screen that allows you to define your printer ports and interrupts.

When you see this screen, chances are that the port settings are undefined. When you run RPRINTER, the remote printer TSR asks the print server you designated for printer configuration information about the printer you designated. The print server sends all the information found in the printer configuration file to RPRINTER— mostly which printer port and interrupt to use.

If you're using a COM port, you'll also need to put in the printer's baud rate, data bits, stop bits, and parity, and indicate whether it's using Xon/Xoff handshaking. This can get very confusing, so you may just need to tell the supervisor or print server operator to set up a printer number for your COM port specifications. This is especially true since all COM port specifications default to interrupt 4, Baud rate of 9600, 8 data bits, 1 stop bit, no parity, and no Xon/Xoff. So let the supervisor do all the work, then all you have to do is choose the printer number and you're off and running.

It's a little easier to set up parallel ports remotely. All you need to know is which LPT port the printer's attached to; the LPT ports default to an interrupt. For your information, however, all interrupts for LPT ports in RPRINTER default to 7, with LPT1 using interrupt 7 and LPT2 using interrupt 5 (polled interrupts which LPT3 uses are not supported by RPRINTER). However, NetWare 3.12 allows you to choose pulled printing instead of fussing with LPT ports. Be sure you have the proper interrupt for the LPT port the printer is attached to.

With the proper LPT port designated, press <Esc> and you'll return to the network prompt with a message like "Remote Printer 'Epson at Ted's Desk' (printer 0) installed." But you'll see this even if no printer is attached, or if you've designated the wrong interrupt for the printer port. The proof is in the printing—if you can print, the printer configuration matches the printer port and the printer can be used as a resource by the network.

You need to run RPRINTER for each remote printer attached to your workstation. Simply go through the same steps as explained above for each attached printer.

You can also run RPRINTER on a local floppy drive or hard disk. Simply copy the RPRINTER.EXE and SYS$ERR.DAT files to the floppy disk or local disk. If you have the room and want RPRINTER's help information, also copy the following files: IBM$RUN.OVL, RPRINTER.HLP, RPRINT$$.EXE, SYS$HELP.DAT and SYS$MSG.DAT. These files are all found in the SYS:PUBLIC directory. You can also load RPRINTER from the AUTOEXEC.BAT file so RPRINTER will install every time you turn the workstation on.

RPRINTER *PrintServer PrinterNumber* **-R.** Use the -R parameter to remove the RPRINTER TSR from the workstation's memory. The RPRINTER TSR can take from 4KB to 11KB of workstation memory per RPRINTER session. A 6KB buffer size gives you the best performance for the workstation memory it uses. To get rid of printer 1's definition, type RPRINTER FARSIDE 1 -R <Enter>. With NetWare 3.12, you simply type RPRINTER -R, without print server and printer number designations. If the workstation is using the extended or expanded memory shell, you can't use the -R parameter to remove RPRINTER from memory. For these cases, you'll need to reboot the workstation to remove the RPRINTER TSR. However, it will work with the DOS requester.

RPRINTER -S. When you want to see the status of the RPRINTER program running on your workstation, type RPRINTER -S <Enter>. You'll see a screen like this one:

```
Print Server:  FARSIDE
Printer:       0
Printer name:  HPLaserJet at Bill's WS
Printer type:  LPT1
```

```
Using IRQ:      7
Status:         Waiting for job
```

You can see this information even if you simply load the RPRINTER TSR, but it does give you the basic information on the way the printer configuration you've selected is set up. What you're seeing is the name of the print server that you've selected to type in, the printer number, and the name as it's defined on the file server used to invoke the print server. Then you see the printer type, which shows you the port the printer is using to communicate with the workstation. This information is followed by the interrupt the printer port is using to communicate with the workstation.

The last line you see in the example is Status. This shows you what the printer is currently doing. The messages you can see here are described in the following paragraphs.

A "Waiting for job: (xxxOUT-OF-PAPERxxx)" message means that there are no print jobs in the queue(s) the printer services that are ready to be printed. With NetWare 3.12, you'll also see the xxxOUT-OF-PAPERxxx message if it can't find a printer (or the printer is actually out of paper).

You see the message "Mount form n:" when you print a job using a form other than the one currently printing. The supervisor or print server operator can set up the print queue to place on hold all print jobs needing other forms mounted. (See the information below Figure 4-27 for more detail.)

When the printer has been paused by the supervisor or print server operator in PCONSOLE or PSC, you'll see "Paused" or "Stopped." When the printer is taken off Paused you'll see only the "Printing Job" entry, unless something happens to warrant another message.

You'll see the "Ready to go down" message when the supervisor or print server operator has issued the command to stop the print server. NetWare 3.1x supervisors and print server operators can bring down the print server from within PCONSOLE's "Current Server Status" entry in the "Print Server Info/Status" window, or supervisors can unload the PSERVER.NLM at the server console.

The "Stopped" message means the supervisor or print server operator has issued the STOP printer command from PCONSOLE or PSC. When the START command is issued, you'll see "Waiting for Job" or "Printing Job" messages.

You'll see the "In Private Mode" message when the designated printer has been used for network services and is now being run as a local printer. The supervisor or print server operator can do this by issuing the PRIvate command from PSC.

The "Off Line" and "Out of Paper" messages result from just about anything going wrong at the printer.

RPRINTER -P (NetWare 3.12). NetWare 3.12 allows you to set printers to polled mode rather than to an LPT designation. This action can speed up printing performance in many instances. To use the polled mode designation, type RPRINTER *servername printer number* -P <Enter> at the network prompt.

Other Information

Sometimes when a workstation running RPRINTER hangs, and you press <Ctrl>-<Alt>-<Del> to reboot, you can no longer access that printer configuration. Because RPRINTER uses SPX to establish its connection with the print server, you need to wait at least twenty seconds after the workstation goes down to be sure the SPX connection has gone away before running RPRINTER again. However, there are times when, even if you wait, you can no longer access the printer number. When this happens, the supervisor must delete the printer configuration and create a new one in order for you to be able to access it.

For the Sake of Convenience—The PRINTCON Utility

PRINTCON is the PRINTer job CONfiguration utility that lets users and supervisors establish an easy method of putting in all those parameters you hated reading about in NPRINT, CAPTURE, and PCONSOLE. Once you've defined those parameters and placed them into a job description, you'll never have to define the parameters in those other utilities again if you use that description. The changes you make in PRINTCON are reflected in the other printer utilities as the basic parameters they'll work from if the parameters aren't modified in those utilities. You can also create a number of these definitions so you can print differently, depending on the print job.

When you use PRINTCON in conjunction with the printer definition utility (PRINTDEF), you set up all of your printer jobs for use in PCONSOLE, CAPTURE, and NPRINT. For example, CAPTURE's own defaults consist of Auto Endcap enabled, Banner displaying LST, Form Feed enabled, No tabs, 1 copies, For 0, and Timeout Count disabled. These defaults often need customization. You can customize them by using the utilities themselves or by setting up new defaults through PRINTCON. Then CAPTURE will use those defaults every time you modify a parameter without typing out the whole CAPTURE string.

Here's a list of all the printing parameters that you can set up in all of the utilities that affect printing. The list shows the general parameters that two or more utilities may possess. (These parameters are explained in the various utilities.)

You can see that by setting up job configurations in PRINTCON, you can take care of almost every parameter necessary for printing jobs through the printing utilities. And while you can't specify printers in PRINTCON, you can specify the print queues that the printers service. You can set up your system to let you print to different servers, printers, and queues, as well as to handle specific tasks, such as printing in compressed printing from applications that don't understand a printer's functionality.

Table 4-1. Features supported by various utilities

Utilities:	PRINTCON	CAPTURE	PCONSOLE	NPRINT
General Parameters				
Server = n	Yes	Yes	Yes	Yes
Print Server = n			Yes	Yes
Queue = n	Yes	Yes	Yes	Yes
Printer = n	Yes		Yes	
Local = n	Yes	Yes	Yes	
Copies = n	Yes	Yes	Yes	Yes
Job = n	Yes	Yes	Yes	Yes
Form = n	Yes	Yes	Yes	Yes
Banner (NB)	Yes	Yes	Yes	Yes
Filename	Yes	Yes	Yes	Yes
Text or Byte	Yes		Yes	
Tabs = n	Yes	Yes	Yes	Yes
Form Feed	Yes	Yes	Yes	Yes
Notify	Yes	Yes	Yes	Yes
Timeout = n	Yes	Yes		
Autoendcap	Yes	Yes		

Setting Up Print Job Configurations

To get into the utility, type PRINTCON <Enter> at the network prompt. You'll see the "Available Options" window with two options: "Edit Print Job Configuration" and "Select Default Print Job Configuration."

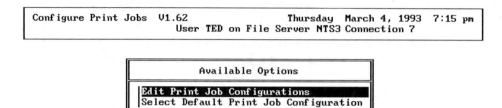

Figure 4-29. The PRINTCON Utility's initial screen

To get around in PRINTCON, pressing <Enter> on a highlighted option brings you to the next screen available under that option, and pressing <Esc> brings you to the previous screen. <PgDn> brings you to the bottom of the list of selections, and <PgUp> brings you to the top of the list. You can also use the Up (8) and Down (2) arrow keys to highlight and select an option, or you can type the first letters of the option you wish to select and the selector bar will move to that option.

Never feel stranded in the menus—pressing <F1> at any time will provide at least a rudimentary explanation of the menu options currently on the screen. Each help screen gives you information specific to the option choice currently on the screen. Once you've chosen another menu option by pressing <Enter>, pressing <F1> will bring you a different set of help screens relating to the newly selected option. When you have a field selected, you can also press <F1> to see a help screen specific to the field you've highlighted.

To set up a print job configuration, highlight the "Edit Print Job Configurations" option and press <Enter>. You'll see the "Print Job Configurations" window listing all the jobs you have presently defined. To add a new job configuration, press <Ins>. You'll see a small window asking you to enter the new name of the job configuration. Type in a name—preferably one that is memorable and pertinent to the job under consideration. For example, if you want to print a job relating to your customers in Great Britain, you can name this print job ENGLISH. Then press <Enter> and you'll see a screen similar to this one:

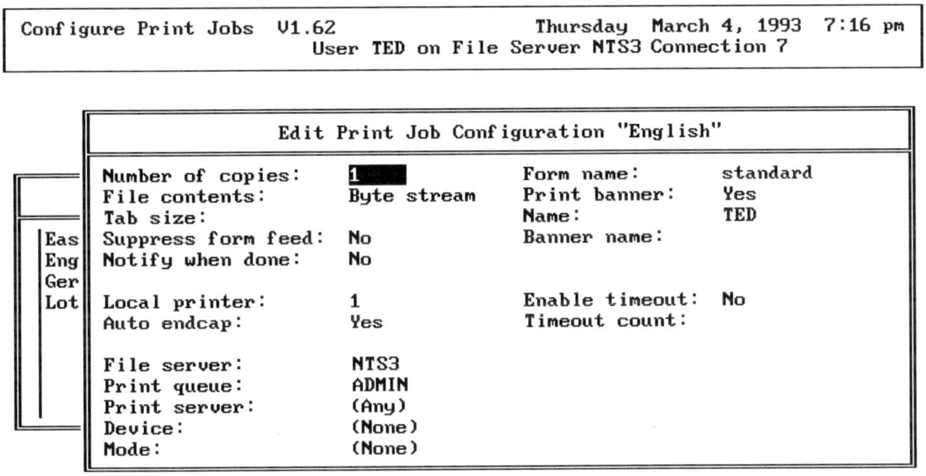

```
┌─────────────────────────────────────────────────────────────────┐
│ Configure Print Jobs  V1.62         Thursday  March 4, 1993  7:16 pm │
│                 User TED on File Server NTS3 Connection 7          │
└─────────────────────────────────────────────────────────────────┘
```

```
        ┌─────────────────────────────────────────────────────────┐
        │         Edit Print Job Configuration "English"          │
        │                                                         │
        │ Number of copies:    1        Form name:      standard  │
        │ File contents:    Byte stream  Print banner:   Yes      │
        │ Tab size:                      Name:           TED      │
┌───┐   │ Suppress form feed:  No        Banner name:             │
│Eas│   │ Notify when done:    No                                 │
│Eng│   │                                                         │
│Ger│   │                                                         │
│Lot│   │ Local printer:       1         Enable timeout:  No      │
└───┘   │ Auto endcap:       Yes         Timeout count:           │
        │                                                         │
        │ File server:       NTS3                                 │
        │ Print queue:       ADMIN                                │
        │ Print server:      (Any)                                │
        │ Device:            (None)                               │
        │ Mode:              (None)                               │
        └─────────────────────────────────────────────────────────┘
```

Figure 4-30. Us this screen to edit a print job configuration

The "Edit Print Job Configurations" window already comes with its own default parameters that are all you need to print a job using CAPTURE, PCONSOLE, or NPRINT utilities. You can take these default parameters and modify them into a specific job configuration, as you see in the previous figure.

Print Job Name. The top of the "Edit Print Job Configurations 'English'" window shows you the name of the print job. In this example, the print job is named English.

Number of Copies. This is the first entry in the window. It defaults to 1 and can go as high as 65,000. If you want to change the number to 4, position the highlighter bar on the number field of the "Number of Copies" entry and type the number 4. Or press <Enter> and then type the number 4. If you want to print 41 copies, type the number 41, which will appear in the field. You must have at least one copy selected; if you select 0, you'll see the "Value must be between 1 and 65000 inclusive. Press Escape to continue" message.

After you type a number, the cursor will blink on that field, meaning you'll have to press <Esc> or <Enter> to proceed to the next option field. If you press <Esc> and you're brought to the "Save Changes" window before you've made all your changes, press <Esc> again to return to the job configuration window.

File Contents. This entry lets you choose how the file will print. Pressing <Enter> brings up the "File Contents" window with two options—"Byte Stream" and "Text," with the "Byte Stream" option highlighted as the default. When printing a simple DOS

433

file (ASCII text) that contains no special application formatting codes, choose the "Text" option. When you're printing from within an application and you want to use the application's formatting commands, choose the "Byte Stream" option (the option most commonly used).

Tab Size. This marks how many spaces are in your tab. If you chose the "Text" option and you want to set the "Tab" option to 5, make sure the "Tab Size" number field is highlighted and then type the number 5, which changes the number field. Then press <Enter> or <Esc>. You can specify from one to eighteen spaces for each tab entry; all entries above or below those numbers will receive the "Value must be between 1 and 18 inclusive. Press Escape to continue" window.

Suppress Form Feed. This option allows you to choose whether or not you want the next print job to start at the top of the next page. This option defaults to "No," meaning "send a Top Of Page parameter." However, some printers also send a form feed, so you end up with a blank sheet of paper between print jobs. If you don't want the blank sheet, make sure the selection field is highlighted and type the letter Y. The "No" parameter will toggle to "Yes," which you can toggle back to "No" by typing the letter N. Press <Enter> to jump to the next entry.

Notify When Done. Suppose it's a long walk to the printer and you want to be notified when your print job has been completed. When you want to be notified, highlight this entry and type the letter Y. The "No" parameter will toggle to "Yes," which you can toggle back to "No" by typing the letter N. Then, as the printer finishes printing your job, you'll receive a message at the bottom of the screen saying something like "LPT1 Catch printed on LaserJet IIIP."

Form Name. After you press <Enter>, you'll jump over to this entry. Pressing <Enter> will display the "Forms" window, which lists all the forms that your supervisor has set up in the PRINTDEF utility (if any are created). These forms tell the printer which type of paper you'll use for a particular job, including length and width. (See "The PRINTDEF Utility" heading later in this chapter.)

For example, suppose you want to print some mailing labels. Your supervisor can define a form to be thirty characters wide and thirty-five lines long and give the form the name "Labels." (Form definitions are performed in PRINTDEF.) You then choose the "Labels" option from the "Form Name" entry; whenever you want to print to the labels, you can use this print job configuration. In PRINTCON and PCONSOLE, you use the form name; in CAPTURE and NPRINT, you use the form number equivalent.

Don't change this option unless you're sure you need the different form. Print jobs requiring another form can cause the printer to stop as it waits for the new form name (or number) to be loaded. However, supervisors or print server operators can set up print queues so all jobs with other print forms are held until they set up the printer to take care of the jobs. Talk to your supervisor or print server operator about setting up a system by which print jobs with other forms will be printed. If the demand is heavy enough, you may end up sending those print jobs to another print queue.

Print Banners. This entry defaults to "Yes" and toggles between "Yes" and "No." If the "Print Banner" entry is set to "Yes," you'll be able to define the "Name" and "Banner Name" entries. The banner itself identifies the print job by first sending through a sheet of paper which looks something like the one illustrated in Figure 4-3.

Name and **Banner Name.** The "Name" entry defaults to your login name unless you change it. Specify a name by highlighting the "Banner Name" description field and typing in the name you want to appear on the banner. The field will support up to 12 characters. The "Banner Name" entry defaults to the DOS filename you wish to print. You can specify a different name by highlighting the "Banner Name" description field and typing in the filename you wish to see on the banner. This field also supports up to 12 characters.

Since you're setting this up for yourself, I suggest you leave your name as the description in the "Name" entry and leave the "Banner Name" entry blank. That way, each file you print will have its filename placed in the "Banner Name" entry for your reference. Otherwise, it's pretty hard to give a generic name to cover all the files you might print out under this job description. However, you could name the banner ENGLISH to designate all the print jobs under this job description.

Parameters You Set Up for the CAPTURE Utility

In PRINTCON, you designate all the parameters you need in order to print by means of the PCONSOLE, NPRINT, and CAPTURE utilities. Four of these parameters are used only by CAPTURE: "Local Printer," "Auto Endcap," "Enable Timeout," and "Timeout Count." When you designate these parameters within a job configuration, you won't have to redefine them when you run CAPTURE—you simply use the job name and all the parameters are taken care of.

Local Printer. In DOS, various print devices are assigned names, such as LPT1, LPT2, or LPT3 for parallel connections, and COM1, COM2, COM3, and COM4 for serial connections. For NetWare printing, these are logical rather than physical selections (you don't even need a parallel or serial port), and NetWare uses the LPT ports to designate where print jobs need to go. The "Local Printer" entry shows which LPT option you plan to use when sending a file to the printer. You can set the "Local Printer" entry to 1, 2, or 3 (default is 1).

To change the entry, highlight the number field and type either 1, 2, or 3. Then press <Enter> and you'll go to the "Auto Endcap" entry. But keep in mind that if you use PRINTCON, (and, therefore, CAPTURE), to designate LPT2 for printing, your application also has to send its print jobs to LPT2. So, you need to set up your application to print to the designated LPT port.

Auto Endcap. This entry allows you to print your captured data when you exit your application, or when you physically type ENDCAP <Enter>. When you set this entry to "Yes" (the default), your captured data will be sent to the printer as you exit the application. When you set this entry to "No," you'll need to specify a timeout for you to print, or you'll need to type ENDCAP or logout in order to print.

Enable Timeout and **Timeout Count.** These options, which are usually found below the "Banner File" entry, send data once you exit an application, but "Enable Timeout" allows you to print while you're still in the application. As the application sends data to the queue for printing, it may pause periodically to do calculations; this is especially true with graphics. Since the print queues are very fast and NetWare prints the job as soon as data stops being sent to the print job, NetWare may interpret the pause as meaning the job is over. This means you end up with portions of your file being printed separately.

By typing the letter Y, you'll be able to have the print queue wait until the entire print job is finished. Then at the "Timeout Count" entry (which defaults to 5), you can specify how many seconds you want the NetWare shell to wait before the print job is queued. You can have from 1 to 1,000 seconds in the "Timeout Count" entry. Some applications have trouble with the default of five, so for applications that do extensive calculations, you may wish to set your parameter to a higher number, such as fifteen seconds. For graphics, set the number to twenty or higher, or use a third-party package designed to handle graphics printing by achieving better characters-per-second (CPS) throughput.

File Server. This option allows you to choose any active server on the network. To select a different server than your present file server, press <Enter> and you'll see a "Servers" window listing all active servers.

To select a server, begin typing in the server's name, and the selector bar will go to that server. Then press <Enter>. Some supervisors haven't defined printers or forms in the PRINTDEF utility that correspond to your "Forms" entry definition. If this is the case and you go to a server that has no forms defined, you'll see a message like "There are no forms defined on server *servername*, therefore you'll not be able to change the form, unless you change the server first. Press Escape to continue," on your screen. Or you'll see a message like "There was no form for this definition. Press Escape to continue." So if you want to print to different servers, stick with Form 0 (standard).

436

Print Queue. When you press <Enter> on this option, you'll see a "Queues" window listing the queues available on the server you specified in the "File Server" entry. You can always send print jobs to printer 0 on any server, so what you see in the "Print Queue" entry are those queues servicing printers on the selected server. Since queues don't tell you which printer they're serviced by, if you have a number of queues to choose from you'll need to ask your supervisor which queues are being serviced by which print server and to which printers.

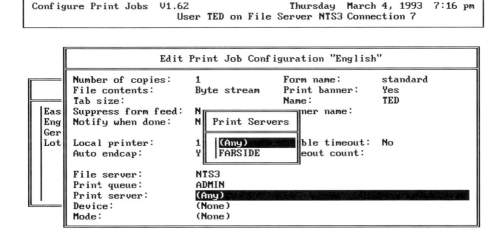

Figure 4-31. You can select the print server you wish to service your print jobs, or use the default of "Any."

Print Server. Press <Enter> to see a list of available print servers. You'll be able to specify which print server you want to service the job configuration. The print servers you see listed are only those designated to service the file server and print queues you specify. Note that CAPTURE presently doesn't support print servernames in its parameters. Highlight the choice you want, then press <Enter> to return to the main menu.

Device and **Mode.** These entries both pertain to what your supervisor has set up in the PRINTDEF utility. For applications that have poor or no print drivers for a printer you're using, supervisors can define the printer's functionality through a series of escape sequences. By defining the functionality of the printer "device" itself, supervisors can then break up the functionality into specific "modes" of operations. Once having defined the printer's functions, the supervisor can also define the mode of operation that tells the printer how to print a particular job.

The "Device" entry lists the defined printer devices you can choose from. For example, suppose your supervisor has defined a C.Itoh as a printer device. As you choose the C.Itoh option, you'll see the "Mode" option obtain one of the modes defined for the printer device (usually the Reinitialize mode). When you press <Enter>, you'll see the "Modes" window listing the modes that have been defined; for our example, we chose English 17cpi. (This refers to a mode choice you make in PRINTDEF.) The "Reinitialize" option resets the printer so your job configuration won't affect everyone else who is printing after you. This option is incorporated in the other modes as well, so it's not a good choice on its own. The device you choose must be mapped to the print queue you choose in the "Print Queue" entry, or you won't be able to print to those mode specifications.

After you've finished selecting various options in the "Edit Print Job Configuration *jobname*" window, press <Esc> and you'll see the "Save Changes" window with the "Yes" option highlighted. Press <Enter> and this configuration will be added to the "Print Job Configurations" window. If it's the first job configuration, it will become your default configuration. Your default configuration is what CAPTURE, NPRINT, and PCONSOLE will use unless you specify other parameters in them or unless you select a different configuration.

Deleting, Renaming, and Modifying Your Print Job Configuration

With your print job configurations in place, you may find that you can't remember a particular job name, or that one of the configurations simply doesn't work. You can delete a job configuration by highlighting the option in the "Print Job Configurations" window through the up/down arrow keys and pressing the Delete key. You'll see the "Delete Current Print Job Configuration Yes/No" window with the "Yes" option highlighted. Press <Enter> and that job configuration is gone. (However, you can't delete the default job configuration here.)

You can also modify a print job configuration name by highlighting that name through the up/down arrow keys and pressing the F3 (Modify) key. You'll see a small "Change Name To:" window in the center of the screen along with the job name. Press the Backspace key to erase the job's name, then type in a new name—one that you'll remember. Then press <Enter> and the new name will appear in the "Print Job Configurations" window.

You can modify any of the entries you've made to a job configuration by highlighting that job name and pressing <Enter>. You'll again return to the "Edit Print Job Configuration *jobname*" window, where you can edit any of your changes. When

438

you press <Esc> to exit the job, you'll see the "Save Changes" window with the "Yes" option highlighted. Press <Enter> and this modified configuration will be sent back to the "Print Job Configurations" window. To return to the "Available Options" window, press <Esc>.

Choosing Your Default

The second option on the "Available Options" window is "Select Default Print Job Configuration." When you have a number of job configurations that are very specific to particular jobs, you don't want one of them to become your default—that is, the configuration that PCONSOLE, CAPTURE, and NPRINT automatically use whenever you don't specify something else.

A way around this problem is to create one generic job configuration. And a good configuration for this job—let's call it "Easy"—is basically comprised of the default parameters you receive when you first create a job configuration. (However, you may want to change a few parameters to suit your own printing environment.)

With a generic job configuration defined, you now need to make that configuration your default. To do so, choose the "Select Default Print Job Configuration" from the "Available Options" window and press <Enter>. You'll see all of the job configurations listed in alphabetical order.

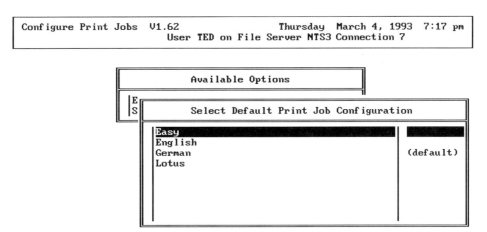

Figure 4-32. You can change which configuration you want as a default

439

To choose the "Easy" option, highlight the option by using the up/down arrow keys, then press <Enter>. The "(default)" label in the right column will move to face the option you've selected, making that option your printing default. Then when you want to use a different job configuration when you print something, simply designate the configuration name before you open the application (for example, by typing CAPTURE J=ENGLISH <Enter>), and those parameters will be used instead.

Supervisors and workgroup managers will see one more option: "Copy Print Job Configurations." This option allows them to designate a source user whose PRINTCON defaults and special configurations are exemplary and needed by other users. After the supervisor or workgroup manager designates the source user, he or she then designates the target user who will receive a new PRINTCON.DAT file with its configurations. All defined print job configurations are stored in the PRINTCON.DAT file in the user's personal MAIL directory under SYS:MAIL.

If you decide you don't ever use the PRINTCON defaults, you can get rid of the PRINTCON.DAT file. The name of the MAIL directory corresponds to your user ID, which you can see in SYSCON (see "The SYSCON Utility" heading in Chapter 2), and the corresponding directory is located under the SYS:MAIL directory. Since you probably won't have the rights to delete the PRINTCON.DAT file, have your supervisor or workgroup manager (if he or she has Erase rights in that directory) delete the PRINTCON.DAT file.

To exit PRINTCON, press <Esc> until you see the "Exit Printcon Yes/No" window with the "Yes" option highlighted. Press <Enter> and you'll see the "Save Print Job Configurations" window with the "Yes" option highlighted. Press <Enter> to save the configurations and return to the network prompt.

If the only change you've made is to your default configuration, don't use the <Alt>-<F10> keys to exit PRINTCON. You will, however, see the "Save Print Job Configurations" window if you've added or changed the job configurations themselves. Press <Enter> to save the configurations and return to the network prompt.

The PRINTDEF Utility

PRINTDEF is actually a supervisor's utility. Users can only look around to see how things are set up; you can't actually do anything in the utility. The fact is that most users will never use PRINTDEF or even look in it, but the explanation is here for the adventurous and curious souls out there who want to see how everything works.

PRINTDEF allows supervisors to define how a printer will print by defining the functionality of the printer (device) itself. Having once defined the printer's functions, the supervisor can also define the "mode" of operation that tells the printer how to print a particular job. The functionality the supervisor defines can't be compared to an application's printer driver, which allows you to print bold, italic, portrait, landscape, and so on at any moment in the document. You don't have that flexibility here; you'll be limited to only a select few commands per mode, such as bold and landscape. The entire document will be bold and landscape, not just selected parts of the document.

There are four reasons for using the PRINTDEF utility: your print jobs are adversely affected by previous print jobs; your application can't take advantage of your printer and you want it to; you've pulled a document from a mini or mainframe environment and you have no application on the file server to print the document from; or you need specific paper forms defined for certain print jobs.

One of the main purposes of PRINTDEF is to make sure the printer is in a working state for the next job that comes through. Use PRINTDEF's parameters when your print jobs look strange because the previous print job didn't put the printer back into a nice state. For example, suppose someone sent a print job through in landscape printing mode (this turns the job so it prints the long way on the paper). But you're using a word processor and you need portrait mode, normal for printing out word processing documents.

In this case, your supervisor can go into PRINTDEF and define the Re-initialize mode to make sure print jobs set the printer back to portrait printing after printing a job. But note here that PRINTDEF resets the printer only for jobs submitted through the PCONSOLE, CAPTURE, and NPRINT utilities, and you can only set up sending jobs with modes through the PRINTCON utility. The supervisor can then choose a print job configuration which uses the reinitialization mode and choose that job configuration when sending a small print job to the printer through PCONSOLE or NPRINT. The printer would be reset back to portrait printing.

An application's printer driver capability is only one aspect of printing. Your printers may have many capabilities that your applications don't know how to take advantage of. In such instances, PRINTDEF can come in handy by defining a specific way or mode to print something out, creating a very basic print driver.

For example, suppose you're in a text editor, such as Brief, and you want to print a job in compressed print. Brief knows nothing about compressed printing, but your printer does. Your supervisor can go into PRINTDEF and define all the printer's capabilities through the "Device" option, defining compressed printing as one of the modes of printing. When you want to print a document from Brief in compressed mode, designate COMPRESS mode in one of PRINTCON's job configurations and then designate that job configuration in your CAPTURE before you enter Brief. The supervisor can also place the proper sequence in the Re-initialize mode for setting the

441

printer back to normal after the print job. The Re-initialize mode is part of whatever mode setup the supervisor selects and any printer sequences for reinitialization are then run at the end of the print job.

Another reason for using PRINTDEF is to define which forms of paper you may use, such as NORMAL for $8^1/_2$" x 11" letters and reports, and GREENBAR for spreadsheets. Supervisors often handle these paper differentiations by having one printer handle one kind of paper and another printer handle a different kind of paper. When the server finds a print job in the queue with a form other than Normal (0), the server stops printing in the queue and notifies the supervisor or print server operator that printing has stopped. The supervisor or print server operator can then take this time to change paper types in the printer and tell the server the new form is mounted. The server will then print out this form until it experiences another form change.

The process of telling the server another form has been mounted can quickly become quite tedious. With NetWare 3.1x, supervisors can designate the server to print only one form type, or to print all jobs of one form in the print queue before it stops printing, then have the supervisor change the form type and print all the jobs of that form. Supervisors and print server operators can use PCONSOLE and PSC utilities to work with printer forms instead of typing in all commands at the file server.

What a User Can Do in PRINTDEF—Just Look Around

About all you as a user can do in PRINTDEF is to see if your supervisor has set up any devices, modes, or forms. You can use the devices, modes, and forms your supervisor created in PRINTDEF to fill out certain print job configurations in PRINTCON. If your supervisor hasn't used PRINTDEF, you can still use PRINTCON; you simply won't include devices, modes, or forms in your print job configurations. But if your supervisor has set up printer definitions, you can use PRINTCON to take advantage of this added functionality when you need to. Once your print jobs are configured through PRINTCON, you can jump between printers and printing styles with a single command. But again, you can use only one printing style and printer per print job.

To see whether your printers have been defined, type PRINTDEF <Enter> at the network prompt. You'll see the "PrintDef Options" window with two options: "Print Devices" and "Forms." Select the "Print Devices" option by pressing <PgUp> and then pressing <Enter>. If you don't have any printer devices defined and you're printing with no problems, don't worry. However, if you do have defined devices, you may see device names similar to those in the following figure.

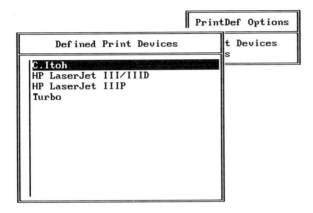

```
Printer Definition Utility  V1.61        Thursday  March 4, 1993  7:18 pm
                      User TED On File Server NTS3 Connection 7
```

```
                               PrintDef Options
        Defined Print Devices      t Devices
                                   s
   C.Itoh
   HP LaserJet III/IIID
   HP LaserJet IIIP
   Turbo
```

Figure 4-33. The "Print Devices" option shows which devices you can presently use

In the figure, three defined devices are named in the "Defined Print Devices" window: C.Itoh, HP LaserJet IIIP, and Turbo. These names may or may not be the names of your printers. However, it's helpful to have these names indicate the kinds of printers you are using. Unless your supervisor has a list explaining where the printers are located and what they're called on the network, using obvious names may be the only way to know which printer is servicing which queue. Ask your supervisor which network printers are servicing which queues. Then when you specify in PRINTCON the queue you want the print job to go to, you'll know which queues are being serviced by which device.

Looking at the Modes a Device Has

A mode is a specific set of functions that can print a job a certain way. To see the modes a particular device has, highlight one of the device names listed in the "Defined Print Devices" window and press <Enter>. You'll see the "Print Device Options" window with two options: "Device Modes" and "Device Functions." For our example, let's choose the C.Itoh option from the "Defined Print Devices" window, then the "Device Modes" option.

443

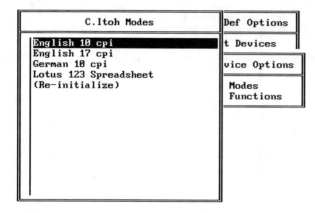

```
Printer Definition Utility  V1.61           Thursday  March 4, 1993  7:22 pm
                         User TED On File Server NTS3 Connection 7
```

```
              C.Itoh Modes              Def Options

        English 10 cpi                  t Devices
        English 17 cpi
        German 10 cpi                   vice Options
        Lotus 123 Spreadsheet
        (Re-initialize)                   Modes
                                          Functions
```

Figure 4-34. Defined devices have different modes so you can print differently

In the figure, five modes have been defined. (The Reinitialize mode is always included.) Suppose you're in an application that doesn't know anything about the particular typeface labeled English 17cpi (characters per inch), but you want to print in English 17cpi. In one of your job configurations (let's call it ENGLISH) in PRINTCON, choose the C.Itoh device and the English 17cpi mode. Then type CAPTURE Job=ENGLISH before going into your application, and as your application prints, you'll see English 17cpi characters printed. (Just make sure the C.Itoh printer is servicing your designated queue.)

If you're curious to see which functions make up the English 17cpi Mode, highlight the option and press <Enter>. After you finish, press <Esc> to return to the "C.Itoh Modes" window, and <Esc> again to return to the "Print Device Options" window. If you're curious as to which functions have been defined for a device, choose the "Device Functions" option from the "Print Device Options" window and press <Enter>. Depending on how your device is defined, you'll see a screen similar to this one:

444

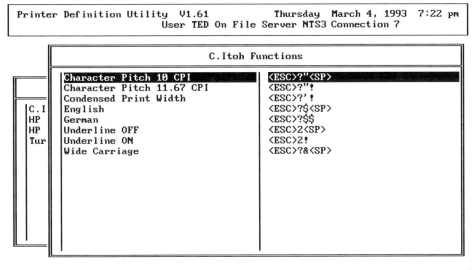

```
Printer Definition Utility  V1.61          Thursday  March 4, 1993  7:22 pm
                     User TED On File Server NTS3 Connection 7
```

```
                            C.Itoh Functions

              ┌───────────────────────────────┬──────────────────┐
              │Character Pitch 10 CPI          │<ESC>?"<SP>       │
              │Character Pitch 11.67 CPI       │<ESC>?"!          │
              │Condensed Print Width           │<ESC>?'!          │
     C.I      │English                         │<ESC>?$<SP>       │
     HP       │German                          │<ESC>?$$          │
     HP       │Underline OFF                   │<ESC>2<SP>        │
     Tur      │Underline ON                    │<ESC>2!           │
              │Wide Carriage                   │<ESC>?&<SP>       │
              │                                │                  │
```

Figure 4-35. Device modes are broken into functions—a series of escape sequences used to tell the printer how to print something

A function is an Escape sequence that your printer interprets to mean something that you want to see, like italics, bold, or underline. From these general functions, your supervisor then chooses the functions specific to the single mode that you can use for printing, such as the "Character Pitch 11.67cpi," and the "English" options from the functions described in the preceding figure. You then end up with the functionality for the English 12cpi Mode.

Since most applications have their own printing drivers and do this for you already, your supervisor has to go into this kind of printer detail only when the need arises (if ever). Your supervisor doesn't have to define every functional aspect of the printer, either— you can only use a couple functions per print job, anyway. So it's best to focus on just those functions that you'll use in your everyday printing.

To get out of the "Device Functions" option, press <Esc>. To look at the defined modes of the other devices, return to the "Defined Printer Devices" window, highlight another selection, and press <Enter>. Then follow the above procedures to see their modes and functions.

445

Seeing What Forms Are Defined

To see what forms have been defined, press <Esc> until you return to the "PrintDef Options" window. Then press <PgDn> to highlight the "Forms" option and press <Enter>. You'll see a "Forms" window, listing all the defined forms. If you have forms defined, the "Forms" option in PRINTDEF is the only place to see those definitions.

To see how a form is defined, highlight one of the options and press <Enter>. Depending on your definition, you will see a screen similar to this one:

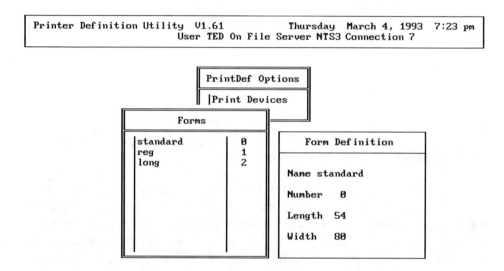

Figure 4-36. Use the default form unless informed otherwise

This figure shows you the "Forms Definition Form" window, listing the form's name, the number your supervisor has assigned to it, and the form's length and width. Each form can be defined differently, and you can then designate the forms in PRINTCON, PCONSOLE, CAPTURE, and NPRINT by either the form's name or number, depending on the utility you're in. For PRINTCON and PCONSOLE, you use the form names; for CAPTURE and NPRINT, you use the form numbers.

As stated before, forms can be rather messy, for most supervisors haven't defined any forms and use only the default Form 0. Many users believe that forms begin with Form 1; this isn't the case, and if Form 1 isn't defined, printing may stop. You don't need to change forms unless they've been defined for your use.

Use forms only when needed and necessary. When you change print jobs to another form, the server stops printing while it waits for another form to be mounted.

446

(Supervisors or print server operators can go into the "Printer Status" option under the "Print Server Status and Control" window and dynamically mount the specified form. The PSC utility can also do this.) So don't change forms unless you know there are other form numbers you can use.

To exit the "Forms" option, press <Esc>. To exit PRINTDEF, press <Esc> again, or press the <Alt>-<F10> keys simultaneously. You'll see the "Exit PrintDef Yes/No" window with the "Yes" option highlighted. Press <Enter> and you'll return to the network prompt.

Putting It All Together

When you want to print a DOS file but not from an application, use the NPRINT or PCONSOLE utility. When you want to print a file from within an application, use the CAPTURE utility. (You can also use a job description from PRINTCON.)

When you want to send information to a file that you normally receive on the screen, use the DOS redirection parameter >. For example, if you want to send your directory structure from the NDIR utility, type NDIR /DO SUB > DIRSTRUC <Enter>, and your screen data will be placed in the DIRSTRUC file. You can then print the DIRSTRUC file through NPRINT by typing NPRINT directory path\DIRSTRUC / PS=*printservername* /Q=*queuename* <Enter>.

When you want to print in a certain style, but your application doesn't understand what you want, have your supervisor designate a special mode through PRINTDEF, then use that mode in PRINTCON. (Be sure the supervisor fills out the Re-initialization mode, too.) Next, use the job description from PRINTCON in your CAPTURE when you want to print something reflecting that special mode.

When You Would Change Your CAPTURE

For the most part, your supervisor probably has set up your CAPTURE in the network login script, so every time you log in, you can print to a network printer. To see how your CAPTURE is set up, type CAPTURE SH <Enter> at the network prompt; you'll see how your print jobs have been set up to go to a printer.

There are three basic reasons to change your printing from the supervisor's default: to send print jobs to a different printer, to use LPT1 to print to a different printer, and to use a local printer.

In CAPTURE's "LPT" option, I talked about how to avoid CAPTURE's LPT1 setting by having a small application print using CAPTURE's "LPT2" option. If your supervisor hasn't put anything at CAPTURE's "LPT2" option, you can place a CAPTURE command, such as #CAPTURE LPT2 S=PUB Q=ADMIN NT NB TI=5,

447

in your personal login script. Then when you log in and type CAPTURE SH <Enter>, you'll see something like this:

```
LPT1: Capturing data to server PUB queue REPORTS.
    User will not be notified after the files are printed.
    Capture Defaults:Enabled    Automatic Endcap:Enabled
    Banner:LST:                 Form Feed:    No
    Copies:1                    Tabs:         No conversion
    Form:  0                    Timeout Count:5 seconds

LPT2: Capturing data to server PUB queue ADMIN.
    User will not be notified after the files are printed
    Capture Defaults:Enabled    Automatic Endcap:Enabled
    Banner:LST:                 Form Feed:    No
    Copies:1                    Tabs:         No conversion
    Form  :0                    Timeout Count:5 seconds

LPT3: Capturing Is Not Currently Active.
```

In this example, the first LPT port is capturing its data to queue REPORTS on server PUB. The next line shows that you won't be notified when the files are finished printing. The third line shows there is a banner but no form feeds or tabs, and the timeout count is set to 5. LPT2 is sending any print jobs it receives to ADMIN on server PUB. With this setup, only applications sending their print jobs to their LPT2 port will print to this second CAPTURE parameter.

But what if your application only uses LPT1, and you need to overwrite your supervisor's parameter in order to print to a different printer? You can set up two batch files in your personal search drive directory to enable you to jump between one printer and the other. Taking information from the CAPTURE SH display, in your personal search directory, type:

```
COPY CON DEFAULT.BAT
CAPTURE S=PUB Q-REPORTS NFF NT TI=5
^Z (Ctrl-Z)
```

This batch file sets up a default CAPTURE command, which is like your supervisor's CAPTURE command.

Next, create a batch file for your personal application that will enable it to print to a different printer. Let's suppose that instead of being able to send the previous example to CAPTURE's LPT2 designation, you have to send it to LPT1. You type:

```
COPY CON MINE.BAT
CAPTURE S=PUB Q=ADMIN NFF NT TI=5
^Z (Ctrl-Z)
```

This batch file says, "Send my captured print jobs to print queue ADMIN, with no form feeds and no tabs, and send the print jobs five seconds after the queue receives them." (If you don't specify an LPT designation, CAPTURE defaults to LPT1.) Then when you want to go into your own application, type MINE <Enter> (before entering the application) to designate printing from ADMIN, and when you get out of the application, type DEFAULT <Enter> to have your CAPTURE return to your supervisor's parameters. You can also set up print job configurations called MINE and DEFAULT, so you then type CAPTURE J=MINE <Enter> or CAPTURE J=DEFAULT <Enter> to achieve the same results.

When you want to print to a local printer, you must first run the ENDCAP command, which ends your capture to a network printer. Then you can set up a batch file in your personal search drive directory to enable you to regain the CAPTURE your supervisor has set up. Taking information from the CAPTURE SH display, in your personal search directory, type:

```
COPY CON DEFAULT.BAT
CAPTURE S=PUB Q=REPORTS NFF NT TI=5
^Z (Ctrl-Z)
```

This batch file sets up a default CAPTURE command, which is like your supervisor's CAPTURE command. When you need to print to your local printer, type ENDCAP <Enter> and print locally; then when you need to print to the network again, type DEFAULT <Enter>, and your CAPTURE command will set you up. Be careful, too, that you don't have the "PRINTERS = 0" option set in your NET.CFG file if you're printing to a local printer, or you won't be able to print locally.

Experiment. There are many ways to perform most tasks in NetWare, but you won't become skilled at these functions until you use them and find out what you can and can't do.

449

Summary

Chapter 4 covered the various menu and command line utilities used to help you print on a NetWare network. The chapter is ordered by showing those utilities you may use the most down to the utilities you may use the least. For example, to print to a network printer with most applications, you'll need to use the CAPTURE command. This is normally placed in the system login script or in your user login script.

Chapter 5 is for the more-advanced user and goes into some of the particulars on how to set up and maintain your workstation on a NetWare network.

Workstation Maintenance

Those of you who have worked with NetWare for some time will probably understand the basic troubleshooting procedures covered in this chapter. But if you're new to NetWare, here's some information about what you can do to keep your workstation running. This chapter presents some basics to help you better understand the workstation environment.

This chapter tells you what you need to know to keep your workstation running smoothly. In particular, it shows you how to set up a search drive mapped to a directory containing your own batch files and utilities (including terminate-and-stay-resident programs), and how to create a workstation boot disk, which includes creating CONFIG.SYS, AUTOEXEC.BAT, and NET.CFG files. We'll look at setting up workstations so they can load the NetWare shell in high memory; we'll also look at Windows setup. This chapter also covers the basics of installing and setting up the DOS Requester.

Setting Up Your Personal Drive Mapping

If you have batch files, utilities, and terminate-and-stay-resident (TSR) programs that only you use, it's a good idea to have your own personal search drive mapping to a directory containing these files. You should have Access Control rights in this directory or all the other rights except Access Control rights—Read, Write, Create, Erase, Modify, and File Scan rights.

Suppose you've created the directory UTILS, where you want to store a memory-resident calculator program and some batch files. In your personal login script, you can type the following:

```
MAP S16:=NTS3/VOL1:USERS/TED/UTILS
```

MAP S16 means, "Map this search drive after all other search drives have been mapped." Use the S16 designation to prevent your drive mapping from overwriting any other system search drive mappings the supervisor has set up in the system login script.

A potential problem exists with the S16 mapping. NetWare searches the search drives in order, from S1 to S16. You can have problems if the program or utility you want has the same filename as another program in one of the previous search drives and you need to use your setup defaults to run the program. In this case, NetWare will run the first program it finds with that filename as it goes through the search drive mappings. If your personal search drive is last on the list, NetWare will never reach the program you want.

One way to prevent this is to type in your login script:

```
MAP INS S1:=CORP/VOL1:USERS/TED/UTILS
```

MAP INS S1 means "Insert this search drive mapping before all other search drives, and bump the other search drives down to the next available search drive slot." So the SYS:PUBLIC mapping, which is usually S1, becomes S2, and your other search drive mappings follow suit.

However, talk to your supervisor before using this procedure. Some applications may be set up to find files in a certain search drive identified by drive letter or number (such as Y: or S2). Bumping all your search drive mappings down one would create a problem in this situation. Other commands, such as COMSPEC, wouldn't be able to find the files they need.

If you're having problems with conflicting utility names, the best solution is to use the first example for your search drive mapping. Put your programs in your utilities directory (UTIL or whatever), and when you need to access a program, simply precede the command with the drive letter your search drive is mapped to (for example, W:CALC). This approach works fine for utilities in personal directories, but can tie up utilities in shared (designated search drive) directories and shouldn't be used. Alternately, you can set up access to the program through a batch file that places you in your utilities directory and then invokes the program. You can store this batch file in your search drive directory.

Another solution would be to rename your program with the DOS REName command. For example, if you have your own CAPTURE.EXE utility, you can rename it to CAPT.EXE to distinguish it from the NetWare CAPTURE utility. (This method only works for one-file utilities that don't call supplement files that look for the original name or themselves.)

Also important to note is that DOS runs .COM files before .EXE files, so if you have a CAPTURE.COM and a CAPTURE.EXE file in the same directory, CAPTURE.COM will always run when you type CAPTURE <Enter>. Keep this in mind when you're determining whether any of your utilities have conflicting filenames.

About TSRs

If you want to use TSR programs on your workstation, you should either load them from your AUTOEXEC.BAT file or load them after you leave your login script and before you enter the MENU utility. To load TSRs from an AUTOEXEC.BAT file, be sure to put the program files either on your boot disk or in a directory on your hard disk where the AUTOEXEC can find them. If you want to load TSRs after you've logged in to the network, place the program files in your personal search drive directory.

You should never invoke TSR programs from your login script or from NetWare's MENU utility. Both the login script and MENU begin by creating a working copy of COMMAND.COM and then loading themselves into memory. If you run a TSR program from either of these utilities, the TSR will load into memory above these other programs. When you leave the login script or MENU, you end up with a memory hole that can't be accessed or used because of the TSR's memory location. Instead of your TSR taking 12KB of memory, it now takes 40KB or 70KB; you won't be able to access larger applications that require lots of memory.

You can use your TSRs (after they've been loaded into memory) while in a utility like MENU. Simply press the proper keys to activate the program. But remember, the TSR may conflict with your applications as well as with the NetWare shell or DOS Requester. So be careful with TSRs; some work fine, but others simply don't work at all. Sometimes it's the order in which you load TSRs that causes conflicts with other programs; experiment with the order in which you load the TSRs.

Another aspect of TSRs is their loading order. Some TSRs can be unloaded while others cannot. For example, all the latest NetWare communications drivers, the NetWare Shell or DOS Requester can be unloaded from memory by using the -U or /U parameter following the program's name. For example to unload the DOS Requester, type VLM /U < Enter > in the C:\NWCLIENT directory. However, you can't do this if you have loaded other TSRs after loading the DOS Requester if those TSRs can't be unloaded as well. If you wish to be able to unload the NetWare TSRs at any time, be sure to load them last or be sure the TSRs you load after the NetWare TSRs can be unloaded.

Creating Your Workstation Boot Disk

It's good to know the steps involved in creating a boot disk in case you ever have to make a new one for your workstation or you can't boot from your hard disk. These steps include formatting a boot disk, creating the CONFIG.SYS and AUTOEXEC.BAT files, creating a NET.CFG file, and placing on your disk the NetWare files necessary to access the server, such as IPX.COM (or LSL, network board driver and IPXODI), NETX.COM, (or VLM.EXE) and, if applicable NETBIOS.EXE and INT2F.COM. We'll cover how to set up workstations using ODI drivers, and we'll show you how to place the NetWare shell into high memory on workstations that have memory managers, including workstations with DOS 5.0 and 6.0. Finally, we'll look at how to set up your NetWare and Windows workstation environment.

In order for you to create a boot disk, your workstation must have at least one floppy disk drive, and you need a blank floppy disk and a version of DOS. You can use the DOS on the network to format a disk, but for this example, we'll work from the DOS system disk on a workstation with two disk drives and a hard disk drive. If you don't have a DOS manual, get one. The copyright laws require each workstation running DOS to have a manual. Besides, it can be an invaluable reference for maintaining your workstation environment.

To format a new boot disk, place the DOS system disk in drive A: and an unformatted blank disk in drive B:. Then go to drive A: and type FORMAT B: /S <Enter>. The /S parameter places the COMMAND.COM file as well as the hidden IBMBIO.COM and IBMDOS.COM files onto the blank disk. At the prompt, you'll see a message that says, "Insert new disk for drive B: and strike ENTER when ready." Press <Enter> and the disk in drive B will be formatted. If you need greater assistance in formatting a disk, see your DOS manual. If you're using DOS 5.0 or 6.0 and you want to create a new boot disk from an laready formatted one, insert the DOS System disk in drive A: and type FORMAT B:/Q/U/S <Enter>.

If you have a hard disk drive, you might want to make a boot disk in case you can't access your local hard disk. You can set up this boot disk in two ways—to load everything from the boot disk or to call the programs from the local hard disk. For this example, we will create a boot disk from which all programs will load.

To format the boot disk, place a blank disk in drive A: or B:. Then go to the directory containing the DOS programs (such as C:\DOS) if you don't have the DOS directory as part of your PATH statement. If the disk is in drive A:, type FORMAT A:/S < Enter> to format the new boot disk with the system files.

Creating the CONFIG.SYS File

Use the CONFIG.SYS file to help set up the DOS environment for your workstation. Whereas the NET.CFG file helps set up the network environment on your workstation, the CONFIG.SYS and AUTOEXEC.BAT files help you set up your workstation environment. These two files allow you to create your DOS environment the way you like. We'll cover how to use these files in each of the DOS setups I describe. Let's first look at setting up a regular boot disk using CONFIG.SYS and AUTOEXEC.BAT.

The DOS 3.3 manual has 44 pages and the DOS 5.0 manual has more than 30 pages to assist you in creating a CONFIG.SYS file, although most commands won't be covered here. However, there are a few commands you can put in the CONFIG.SYS to help your network environment function better.

To create a CONFIG.SYS file on your newly formatted disk, go to drive B: and type COPY CON CONFIG.SYS <Enter>. Then type in the options you want, each on a separate line. When you've typed in the options you desire, type ^Z (which you create by pressing the F6 key, or by pressing the <Ctrl> and Z keys simultaneously).

Here's a typical example of a CONFIG.SYS file for network use:

```
COPY CON CONFIG.SYS  <Enter>
FILES = 30   <Enter>
DEVICE=ANSI.SYS  <Enter>(optional)
LASTDRIVE=E  <Enter>
^Z   <Enter>
```

In this example, the FILES = 30 entry shows the number of files the workstation can have open at once. Programs that extend DOS's functionality, such as DESQview 386 and Microsoft Windows, may need add more open files (50, for example) to cover the extra DOS sessions you're running.

The number of open files is an issue with the DOS Requester. Previously, you set FILES=xx in the CONFIG.SYS for the number of open files needed for the workstation local drives. You then set FILE HANDLES=xx in the NET.CFG file for the number of open files needed for network drives. Now, you set the total number of open files through the CONFIG.SYS file with the FILES=xx statement. (Include enough for Windows, if used, such as 90.)

If you have an older NET.CFG file with a FILE HANDLES=xx statement in it and you are using VLMs, remove the File Hanldes statement and increase the number of files in the FILES=xx line in the workstation's CONFIG.SYS file. Otherwise, you may see "Insufficient file" or "Insufficient file handles" error messages or the programs simply refuse to load.

The "Device = ANSI.SYS" option tells DOS to replace the standard I/O support with an enhanced standard I/O device driver. For DOS version 3.3 and above, this device driver supports color monitors and enhanced keyboards. You'll need to put the ANSI.SYS file on your floppy disk so CONFIG.SYS can find it. The ANSI.SYS file comes on the DOS system disk. If you have a hard drive with a directory area created for DOS, you can call the ANSI.SYS file from that directory. (See the next CONFIG.SYS example.) However, if you don't use color in your screen prompt, or if you don't rearrange keyboard functionality, don't load ANSI.SYS.

The "Lastdrive" option allows you to set the number of drives you can access in the DOS environment. The choice you make here affects where the NetWare environment begins (at drive E:). The last drive default in CONFIG.SYS for DOS version 3.x and above is drive E:, which gives you the capability of having two floppy disk drives, two hard disk drives, and a virtual disk drive (for IBM ATs and compatibles). Then your NetWare environment begins at drive F:.

You can expand the NetWare environment by changing the "Lastdrive" option to reflect the number of local devices you really have. For example, if you have only two floppy disk drives (A: and B:), and you use C: as a virtual disk drive, you can type LASTDRIVE = C <Enter>. This would allow NetWare to use drives D: and E: for network drive mappings, such as D:=BYTE:USERS/TED. As long as you set up your drive mappings using the MAP *1= variation of the MAP command, NetWare will start its network drive mappings at the next drive after the one you specify with the "Lastdrive" option. If you don't specify a particular drive letter in your MAP command (such as MAP D:=SYS:REPORTS), NetWare will fill that drive letter, such as D:=SYS:LOGIN, which you may not have any rights in.

If you use a lot of local drive mappings in your local environment (which you can do using the DOS SUBSTitute command), you can expand the "Lastdrive" option to, say, drive L: or M:. However, by doing this you will limit your NetWare environment, for your NetWare drive mappings always begin after the drive specified in the "Lastdrive" option.

Because the DOS Requester uses DOS's network drive capability to take care of drive mapping, you need to set the Lastdrive entry to Z, such as LASTDRIVE=Z <Enter>. If you do not, you will not have search drive mapping capability.

Here's an example of another CONFIG.SYS file that can expand your DOS environment. (The Device = Fconsole should appear on your screen with all of its parameters on one line.)

```
COPY CON CONFIG.SYS
DEVICE=C:\DOS\ANSI.SYS
BREAK=ON
BUFFERS=18
FILES=50
SHELL=C:\COMMAND.COM /P /E:512
DEVICE=C:\UTIL\FCONSOLE.DEV /G=512 /H=0 /L=1 /M=0 /P=2 /R=100 /
  S=10920 /W=1 /Y=0
```

456

```
DEVICE=C:HIMEM.SYS
DEVICE=C:\WIN31\EMM386.EXE /NOEMS
DEVICEHIGH=C:\WIN31\SMARTDRV.SYS 2048 512
DEVICEHIGH=C:\UTIL\MSMOUSE.SYS
LASTDRIVE=C
```

In this example, the ANSI.SYS file is called from the DOS directory on hard drive C:. The device files shown in the above example (FCONSOLE.DEV, HIMEM.SYS, SMARTDRV.SYS and MSMOUSE.SYS) are scattered in a number of directories on the C: drive. (If you don't have a hard drive, these files must be copied to your boot disk.) Setting the "BREAK" option to "on" lets you press <Ctrl>-<Break> to break out of a program when it refreshes the screen.

The Buffers entry is a block of memory that holds disk reads and writes from the workstation's hard disk drive. This entry can be adjusted according to the amount of memory your workstation has to work from and the size of your hard disk. (See your DOS manual for details.) Setting the "Buffers" option between 10 and 25 speeds up local directory and subdirectory access; however, unless you use your local hard disk a lot, you won't need to use this entry. Each buffer is 528 bytes in size; so, if you're constantly running large applications, you may hurt their performance by using this additional memory for buffers.

The Files entry shows the maximum number of files you can concurrently have open on your workstation. This number can be between 8 and 255 files. If you're running programs that extend DOS's functionality, such as Windows 386 or DESQview 386, thirty files may not be enough to handle your extended environment. (Fifty to sixty would be better). The easiest way to allocate files to these environments is to figure on twenty open files per session. This option doesn't affect network files running IPX and NETX; that's done in NET.CFG. However, the DOS Requester uses only the FILES = entry in CONFIG.SYS. Also, certain applications, like WordPerfect, still use files in the DOS environment, even though you're running the applications from the network. For WordPerfect, set the entry to FILES = 35 at least.

The "Shell" option tells DOS which command processor file (usually COMMAND.COM) to use and where to find it. (This option defaults to COMMAND.COM; it doesn't affect the COMSPEC command or BASIC's SHELL command.) In MS DOS 6.0, setting the COMAND.COM in the SHELL entry also sets COMSPEC so you don't need the redundant SET COMSPEC command. In this example, the COMMAND.COM file is in the root directory on drive C:. The /P parameter causes COMMAND.COM to run the AUTOEXEC.BAT file when it first loads. (This is the default.) The /E parameter allows you to set aside more space in memory for the DOS environment.

Depending on your DOS version, the environment defaults to 160 bytes, and can go up to 32KB; our example shows the DOS environment set up to 1024 bytes. You need to expand this environment when you use a lot of the ANSI.SYS capabilities. You may also need extra environment space for the more experimental parameters in the MENU utility.

If you are using the DOS Requester, be sure the environment parameter is set high enough to allow room for search drive mappings (the NetWare drive mappings also use this environment space). If the environment parameter is set too low, you won't be able to map search drives. If you see environment errors and can't add search drive mappings, make sure your LASTDRIVE = is set to Z. If the LASTDRIVE parameter is already set to Z, increase the environment size in the SHELL = parameter until you no longer experience the error. For example, if you are receiving error messages and your environment parameter is set to /E:300 in the SHELL = entry, you would want to increase the parameter to /E:600, or a higher number until the problem disappears.

The four Device options load a Fancy Console utility, a high memory driver, a "smart" driver, and a mouse driver along with their parameters. For MS DOS, HIMEM.SYS and EMM386.EXE help set up the high memory environment. The SMARTDRV.SYS program sets up file caching for Windows. Through CONFIG.SYS, you can set up a very powerful working environment. These examples only scratch the surface of what you can do. For more information on setting up your CONFIG.SYS file, see your DOS manual.

Setting Up Your AUTOEXEC.BAT File

When you boot DOS, DOS looks first for the CONFIG.SYS file. Then it looks for the AUTOEXEC.BAT file and executes any commands stored in that file. The AUTOEXEC.BAT file must be in the directory you start DOS from, whether it's on your boot disk or in the root directory of your hard drive.

Before you can access the applications and data on the network, your workstation must load certain software programs that enable your network interface board to communicate with the server. To make logging in easier, you can place these files on your boot disk or hard disk, where they can be called from your AUTOEXEC.BAT file. You can also load TSRs from your AUTOEXEC file, or you can call them after your login script completes and before you go into the MENU utility.

The files your boot disk needs in order to access and communicate with the network interface board and NetWare include:

```
IPX.COM  (or LSL.COM, a network board driver, and IPXODI.COM)
NETX  (or VLM.EXE)
NETBIOS.EXE  (optional)
INT2F.COM  (optional)
TCPIP  (optional)
TELAPI  (optional)
```

You can use IPX.COM with the NetWare shell or with the DOS Requester, and you can use ODI communication drivers with the NetWare shell or with the DOS Requester. However, certain NetWare utilities that come with NetWare 3.12 expect users to be using the DOS Requester instead of the NetWare shell. For example, it has been my experience that the RPRINTER menu utility won't be able to load its Help if you are using the NetWare shell instead of VLM.EXE. However, the utility worked fine.

(The NETBIOS.EXE and the INT2F.COM files are necessary only if you're running application software that requires NetBIOS to communicate. The same is true if you need TCP/IP connectivity.)

To create an AUTOEXEC.BAT file, go to the drive containing your new boot disk and type COPY CON AUTOEXEC.BAT <Enter>. Then type in the commands you want to execute, each on a separate line. When you've finished, type ^Z (by pressing the F6 key or by pressing the <Ctrl> and Z keys simultaneously).

Here's an example of a basic AUTOEXEC.BAT file for network use:

```
COPY CON AUTOEXEC.BAT <Enter>
PROMPT $P$G <Enter>
IPX <Enter>
NETX <Enter>
F: <Enter> (depends on CONFIG.SYS)
LOGIN ADMIN/TED <Enter>
^Z <Enter>
```

The first line modifies the DOS PROMPT command to display the directory path you're currently in. This PROMPT command isn't mandatory, but it helps you to know which directory you're in at all times. Next, the AUTOEXEC loads the IPX driver, establishing your communications with the network interface board and to the network. Once a connection to the network is established, the AUTOEXEC executes the NETX file, which loads the NetWare workstation shell. The shell attaches you to the first server that answers the "Is there a file server out there I can talk to?" broadcast.

AUTOEXEC then changes to the first network drive, which is shown here as F:. (Normally, with DOS 3.x and above, the first network drive is F:, but you can set this to another drive letter in the CONFIG.SYS.) Next comes the login command, including the name of the server and the user name of the person logging in. In this example, Ted is logging in to server ADMIN. (If you're running programs that require TCP/IP, you'll also need to put TCP/IP and TELAPI in your AUTOEXEC.BAT file and put their program files on the disk.)

Here's an example of a basic AUTOEXEC.BAT file using the DOS Requester for connecting to the network:

```
COPY CON AUTOEXEC.BAT <Enter>
PROMPT $p$g <Enter>
LSL <Enter>
NE2000 <Enter> (or a different network driver)
IPXODI <Enter>
VLM.EXE <Enter>
F: <Enter> (depends on First Network Drive = entry in the NET.CFG)
LOGIN ADMIN/ED ^Z <Enter>
```

In this example LSL, NE2000, and IPXODI take the place of IPX.COM, and the DOS Requester (VLM.EXE) is loaded instead of the NetWare shell. Since the DOS Requester has you set the Lastdrive entry to Z in the CONFIG.SYS file, the drive F: entry depends on how you have set the First Network Drive = entry in the NET.CFG file. However, F: is the default. This is discussed in detail under the "Using the NET.CFG File with the DOS Requester" heading later in this chapter.

You can also load any other programs you think you might need to make your DOS environment more accessible to you. Following is an example of another AUTOEXEC.BAT file that contains a few more parameters and programs.

```
cls
echo off
verify on
prompt $p $t$h$h$h$h$h$h $d$_$g
PATH=C:\UTIL;C:\DOS
SET COMSPEC=C:\COMMAND.COM
quickkey
ced -b2048,218,512,256,128,128 -fc:\util\initced
cls
LOADHIGH IPX
```

```
LOADHIGH NETX
D:
login nts3/ted
```

In this example, the AUTOEXEC.BAT file first clears the screen. Then the "echoing" of commands is turned off so that you only see the answers to the commands on the screen, not the commands themselves. (You can set this up so you don't see any answers to the commands—place a >NUL after each command and the command answers are sent to the NUL "black hole," not to the screen. This is fine for cleaning up the screen, but makes it hard to know which line to start troubleshooting in the CONFIG.SYS and AUTOEXEC.BAT files if a problem arises.)

The DOS verify command is turned on so that DOS will check files after you copy them to ensure an accurate copy. The PROMPT command changes the DOS prompt to show the path, the time (without the seconds), and the date. The $_ drops the command to the next line, and $G gives you the > prompt sign. (Consult your DOS manual for more information on the PROMPT command.)

If you have a hard disk, you (or your supervisor) probably created a DOS subdirectory containing the files from the DOS disks, along with a UTIL subdirectory containing various utilities. You can put a PATH command, such as PATH=C:\UTIL;C:\DOS <Enter>, in your AUTOEXEC so you can access DOS commands and the utilities no matter what directory you're currently in. To further assist you in your local environment, you can include a COMSPEC command in your AUTOEXEC.BAT as shown, so that DOS knows where to find the COMMAND.COM file when it needs to reload it.

Your supervisor may have set up a search drive to a DOS directory in the system login script, along with a COMSPEC designation to that directory. This setup allows you to load COMMAND.COM from the network without having to access your A: drive or your hard drive. The SET COMSPEC designation in the login script will override your AUTOEXEC's COMSPEC designation, and DOS will follow its COMSPEC path. This will speed up your workstation because network access is faster than floppy disk access, and is often just as fast as or faster than accessing a local hard disk.

If you're faced with a situation (for example, the server going down) in which you can't get on the network and must run as a stand-alone workstation, you can either rerun your AUTOEXEC.BAT file to reset your local COMPSEC designation, or you can type the SET COMSPEC command at the DOS prompt (for example, SET COMSPEC=C:\DOS\COMMAND.COM <Enter>). This way, your local applications or utilities can still find the COMMAND.COM file when they need to, and you won't be prompted to insert the DOS system disk whenever you exit an application.

The sample AUTOEXEC.BAT file next loads two TSR utilities, QUICKKEY and CED, along with appropriate parameters. With the workstation environment in place, the AUTOEXEC.BAT file then loads IPX and NETX into high memory, and then executes the LOGIN command.

The AUTOEXEC.BAT file provides a great deal of flexibility and convenience in setting up your working environment. Use your DOS manual to explore more of what you can and can't do with your AUTOEXEC file.

Finishing Your Boot Disk

With the CONFIG.SYS and AUTOEXEC.BAT files in place, you now need to add your IPX.COM and NETX.COM files to the boot disk. (You may also need to set up a NET.CFG file for additional shell parameters. See the "Setting Up Your NET.CFG File" heading later in this chapter. Ask your supervisor if you also need NETBIOS or ICP/IP programs.) If you're using extended or expanded memory, you must add the corresponding NetWare shell files to the boot disk. For ODI and the DOS Requester, you'll need the corresponding IPX and shell files that are found in the C:\NWCLIENT directory on your hard disk or on the "NetWare Workstation for DOS" disk in the "Setting Up ODI" heading later in this chapter.

For NetWare 3.11, you can copy all these files (except IPX.COM) directly from the original NetWare WSGEN disk. NetWare uses NETX.COM to cover all versions of DOS. Ask your supervisor for the latest NetWare Shell versions (they can be found on NetWire or from local dealers). The IPX.COM file is created through the WSGEN utility and must be configured specifically for the type of network interface board (and board settings) you're using.

Running WSGEN is normally part of the installation procedure, so it won't be covered in much detail here. The two main purposes of WSGEN are to generate an IPX.COM network communication file to match your network interface board and to make sure the settings you select don't conflict with your present hardware, such as attached printers, modem boards, and other adapter boards.

Most computers with the basic communications ports and monitors will run fine with the default settings on any network interface board. The main point in running WSGEN is to make sure the IPX.COM file will work with the IRQ (interrupt), I/O base address, DMA, and memory buffer settings actually set on your board. If they don't match, you'll see many different error messages, such as the ones explained in the Workstation Error Message chapter.

Ask your supervisor for a copy of the NETX.COM file, the NETBIOS.EXE and INT2F.COM files (if necessary), and the IPX.COM file that was generated for your workstation. If you need ODI drivers, expanded, or extended shell files, get those from the supervisor as well. Copy them to your new boot disk. If you're interested in learning how to run WSGEN, ask your supervisor to show you how. You can find a description of the procedure for running WSGEN in Chapter 4 of the *NetWare Version 3.11 Installation* manual. You can find the board settings in the supplement manuals supplied by Novell or the board manufacturer.

To install the network interface board, refer to the operations manual that came with your workstation. This manual usually has loads of pictures and explanations for taking out and installing a board.

To give you further information on creating boot disks, the next sections of this chapter cover some added NETX and IPX parameters you find with version 3.x and greater shell versions. I'll also cover using expanded and extended NetWare shells, setting up ODI and the DOS Requester, and three examples of Windows workstation environments.

Additional NETX and IPX Parameters

NetWare 3.11 and above come with additional parameters to help provide information about the network files you're using. There are also parameters to help you with resetting configuration parameters or unloading the NetWare shell. To see which parameters are available to you for the NETX file, go to the directory or floppy disk containing the NETX file and type NETX/? <Enter>. You'll see a screen similar to this:

```
NetWare V3.26 - Workstation Shell (910731)
(C) Copyright 1991 Novell, Inc. All Rights Reserved.

Usage : NETX [<option>]
Valid <options> :

/? Display shell usage
/I Display shell version and type
/U Unload the NetWare shell from memory
/F Forcibly unload the NetWare shell, in spite of TSRs loaded
   after the shell
      (CAUTION: The /F option could hang your workstation)
/PS=<server> Specify a preferred server
```

/C=[path\]<filename.ext> Name your NetWare shell configuration
    file
Note: For use with DOS V3.0 through V5.0.

Parameters for the NETX file are as follows:

NETX /Information. When you want to check which shell versions you're running, you can go to the directory (or floppy disk) where the shell is stored and use the "/I" option. For example, if you wanted to see information about the shell version you're running and you load the NetWare shell from C: drive, you can go to C: and type NET3 /I <Enter> if you're running the shell on DOS 3.x, or NETX /I <Enter> for all versions of DOS. You'll see information similar to this:

    NetWare V3.26 - Workstation Shell (910731)
    (C) Copyright 1991 Novell, Inc. All Rights Reserved.

You can also get the same information (and much more) without having to go to the directory containing NETX by typing NVER <Enter> at the network prompt. (See the "General NetWare Utilities" heading in Chapter 3.)

NETX/Unload. The /U parameter unloads the NetWare shell from the workstation's memory. By unloading the shell, you effectively log out of every server you're attached to. You'll need to reload the shell to receive a LOGIN prompt. But if you want to unload the NetWare shell you're running and you load the NetWare shell from C: drive, you can go to C: and type NETX /U <Enter>. When the /U command is successful, you'll see information similar to this:

    NetWare V3.26 - Workstation Shell (910731)
    (C) Copyright 1991 Novell, Inc. All Rights Reserved.

    You're being logged out of all servers....
    Memory for resident shell is being released.
    The NetWare shell has been unloaded.

You can receive a number of messages when the unload isn't successful. For example, if the NetWare shell isn't loaded and you try to use the /U parameter, you'll see:

    Error unloading NetWare shell -
    NetWare shell not loaded

If you're unloading the NetWare shell from expanded or extended memory, you may see:

```
Error unloading NetWare shell -
Different NetWare shell or a NetWare shell interrupt has been
hooked
```

In this case, the NetWare shell hooks an interrupt into the extended (high) memory shell area and can't be unloaded through the /U parameter. If you have a TSR loaded above the NetWare shell, you may see:

```
Error unloading NetWare shell -
There is a TSR loaded above the loaded shell
```

In this case, you'll probably end up rebooting the workstation to unload the shell and the TSR (as well as everything else). As a special note, you can unload both the expanded and extended memory shells (EMSNET*x* and XMSNET*x*) through the /U parameter. But again, you lose all connections to file servers when you unload the shell.

NETX /F. The /F command is a forced unload of the NetWare shell. With this command you can unload the shell even though you have loaded other TSRs above it in memory. However, if another utility has hooked one of the shell's interrupts while it has been running, you may hang the workstation when you unload NETX.

If you're unloading the NetWare shell from expanded or extended memory, or from upper memory through MS DOS 5.0 or 6.0's LOADHIGH command (HILOAD in DRDOS 6.0), you may see the following message:

```
Error unloading NetWare shell -
Different NetWare shell or a NetWare shell interrupt has been
hooked
```

In this case, you'll need to reboot the workstation to unload the shell. But if you're lucky, you can unload the NetWare shell without hanging the workstation or the TSR loaded above it.

NETX PS=*servername*. The PS (Preferred Server) parameter allows you to establish a connection to the specified server rather than to the first server that answers the "Is there any server I can talk to?" broadcast. (The name of the server that answers is what you see on the "Attached to server *servername*" line as the shell loads.) If for some reason you've unloaded the NetWare shell and you want to reload it and attach to NTS3, type NETX PS=NTS3 <Enter>. You'll see something similar to this:

```
NetWare V3.26 - Workstation Shell (910731)
(C) Copyright 1991 Novell, Inc. All Rights Reserved.

Established Preferred Server connection.
Attached to server NTS3
Tuesday, November 22, 1992 4:58:42 pm
```

You can also include this parameter in the NET.CFG file and attach to a specific file server every time you log in, providing the server is available. (See the heading "Setting Up Your NET.CFG" later in this chapter).

NETX /C=[*path*]<*filename.ext*>. You can designate different shell configuration files, such as typing in C:\UTIL\NET.CFG instead of using the NET.CFG file found in the C:\ directory root. The configuration file can also have a different name as long as the configuration parameters match how IPX and NETX can recognize them.

To see which parameters are available to you for the IPX file, go to the directory or floppy disk containing the IPX file and type IPX /? <Enter>. You'll see a screen similar to this:

```
Invalid parameter. Use "I" option to query ipx-spx type,
or "D" to display hardware options,
or "0#" to load with an alternate hardware option.
```

Parameters for the IPX file are as follows:

IPX /I. Use this option when you wish to see the IPX revision number, plus the hardware settings of the network interface board. For example, if you want to see information about IPX and you load IPX from the C: drive, you can go to C: and type IPX /I <Enter>. You'll see information similar to what follows.

```
Novell IPX/SPX V3.02 Rev B (901218)
(C) Copyright 1985, 1990 Novell Inc. All Rights Reserved.

LAN Option: NetWare Ethernet NE1000 V3.02EC (900813)
Hardware Configuration: IRQ = 3, I/O Base = 300h, no DMA or RAM
```

You can also get the same information (and much more) without having to go to the directory containing IPX by typing NVER <Enter> at the network prompt.

IPX /D. If you want to see which options are available for your network interface board, you can type IPX /D <Enter> and you'll see a screen similar to this:

466

```
Novell IPX/SPX V3.02 Rev B (901218) (C)
Copyright 1985, 1990 Novell, Inc. All Rights Reserved.

LAN Option: NetWare Ethernet NE1000 V3.02EC (900813)
Hardware options available:
*  # 0. IRQ = 3, I/O Base = 300h, no DMA or RAM
   # 1. IRQ = 2, I/O Base = 320h, no DMA or RAM
   # 2. IRQ = 4, I/O Base = 340h, no DMA or RAM
   # 3. IRQ = 5, I/O Base = 360h, no DMA or RAM
   # 4. IRQ = 2, I/O Base = 300h, no DMA or RAM
   # 5. IRQ = 3, I/O Base = 320h, no DMA or RAM
   # 6. IRQ = 5, I/O Base = 340h, no DMA or RAM
   # 7. IRQ = 4, I/O Base = 360h, no DMA or RAM
   # 8. IRQ = 4, I/O Base = 300h, no DMA or RAM
   # 9. IRQ = 5, I/O Base = 320h, no DMA or RAM
   #10. IRQ = 2, I/O Base = 340h, no DMA or RAM
   #11. IRQ = 3, I/O Base = 360h, no DMA or RAM
```

When the system supervisors or network installers create the IPX file for your workstation, they run WSGEN and choose one of these settings to match the way the network interface board is set. For example, the first line has an asterisk in front of it, showing you which option IPX is currently using. The interrupt and the base memory address are used by the network interface board when communicating with the network.

No other component in the workstation can use a matching interrupt or base memory setting; otherwise, two devices may vie for CPU time on the same channel; to prevent further problems under those circumstances, the CPU would stop working. For example, interrupt 3 is also used by the COM2 on most workstations. If you had a mouse or modem actively using the COM2 port and you tried to set the network interface board to IRQ 3, you'd have interrupt conflicts and the workstation would likely not work. But if your workstation didn't have a COM2 port, or did have the port but never used it, you could disable the port and use this option. Interrupt 4 is used by COM1, and Interrupt 5 is used by parallel port 2 (LPT2). IRQ 2 can be used for network interface boards because no parallel or serial ports use the interrupt. Other likely candidates are Interrupts 3 and 5.

The I/O base memory address is the address in memory used to hold or transfer data from one point to another. Other types of network interface boards will use DMA (direct memory access) to hold and transfer information. Arcnet network interface boards use C:0000 or D:0000 RAM memory buffer areas for data transfer. Because of the way this slice of memory is used, it's important that nothing else use the memory as well. For example, certain video drivers can take a lot of this C:0000 and D:0000 memory address space, which can overlap with a network interface board's use of this memory.

All of this means that you have to be very careful when configuring the workstation so there are no interrupt, base I/O address, DMA, or RAM buffer area conflicts. This is why I haven't gone into much detail as to how to set up network interface boards or running WSGEN, for all this moves quickly into the realm of the network supervisor.

IPX /O#. This option is good for emergencies, for it allows you to select a different board setting option on the fly without running WSGEN and making a permanent copy of the IPX settings for the network interface board. Suppose something goes wrong with your floppy boot disk and you borrow someone else's boot disk. But this person's disk has an IPX file with a different hardware option than yours (same network interface board, different settings).

If you know how your network interface board was set to option 1 (another good reason for saving NVER statistics), you can type IPX /D <Enter> to make sure the option matches, then type IPX /O1 <Enter>. IPX will then load using option 1. If this matches your network interface board, you'll then need to load the NETX.COM file so you can log in. (Be sure the NETX file matches your version of DOS or you'll receive an error message; NETX.COM matches all DOS versions from 3x to 5x. You can also use it with DOS 6.0, but you'll need to include the SETVER command in your CONFIG.SYS.) Once you're back on the network, contact your supervisor and tell the supervisor the board type and option settings for the IPX file you need, or simply move to ODI drivers.

Additional DOS Requester Settings

Note: NetWare 3.12 comes with both the DOS Requester and the NetWare Shell, including XMSNETX.EXE, EMSNETX.EXE and NETX.COM. However, if you want to use the Packet Burst (PBurst) capabilities or if you want to use the Windows client software (User Tools and ElectroText), you will need to use the DOS Requester. Otherwise, you can migrate to VLMs from the NetWare Shell at your leisure.

The DOS Requester comes with a number of options that you can use when it's loading or running. To see all of the options that are available, type VLM ? <Enter> at the network prompt. You'll see a screen similar to the following:

```
VLM.EXE     - NetWare virtual loadable module manager v1.0 (930210)
(C) Copyright 1993 Novell, Inc. All Rights Reserved. Patent pending.

Available command line options:
/?     Display this help screen.
/U     Unload the VLM.EXE file from memory.
/C=[path\]filename.ext
```

```
          Specify a configuration file to use (Default is NET.CFG).
   /Mx    The memory type the VLM.EXE file uses where x is one of the
following:
          C = Conventional memory.
          X = Extended memory (XMS).
          E = Expanded memory (EMS).
   /D     Display the VLM.EXE file diagnostics.
   /PS=<servername>
          Preferred servername to attach to during load.
   /PT=<tree name>
          Preferred tree name to attach to during load.
   /Vx    The detail level of message display where x is one of the
following:
          0 = Display copyright and critical errors only.
          1 = Also display warning messages.
          2 = Also display VLM module names.
          3 = Also display configuration file parameters.
          4 = Also display diagnostics messages.
```

Here's a brief description of each of the VLM options.

VLM /?. This option shows the help screen you are looking at. If you can't remember a DOS Requester parameter, type VLM /? in the directory where you load VLM.EXE.

VLM /U. Use this option when you want to unload VLM.EXE from memory. Be sure the DOS Requester is the last TSR loaded when you do this, or only load other TSRs that you can unload like the DOS Requester. The /U parameter makes it easy to try new configurations without having to reboot the workstation. You can modify the NET.CFG file to use other options, type VLM /U to unload the DOS Requester, and then retype VLM to try out the new settings.

VLM /C=<path\filename>. Use this option to specify the path to a NET.CFG file other than the one found in the directory where you normally load VLM.EXE. For example, if you wanted to use the NET.CFG found in the C:\UTIL directory, you would type VLM /C=C:\UTIL\NET.CFG <Enter>.

VLM /Mx. The DOS Requester is unique in how it loads into the workstation's memory. The DOS Requester uses extended (XMS) or expanded (EMS) memory that is allocated by the XMS or EMS Memory Managers (according to the LIM XMS 2.0 or LIM EMS 4.0 specification). This loads the majority of VLM modules into extended or expanded memory. You can also use memory managers to load TSRs into the upper memory block (UMB) area between 640KB and 1,024KB, and to load DOS or a different TSR into the high memory (HMA) area between 1,024KB and 1,088KB. Without this designation, DOS and TSRs load into conventional memory.

The DOS Requester automatically detects if an XMS Memory Manager is installed and then asks the manager to allocate extended memory for VLM.EXE and its modules. Since this is an automatic process, only use the VLM /MX option to ensure that extended memory is the first place the DOS Requester tries to load into. Once this memory is allocated, VLM.EXE and its modules load much of their code into the extended memory area. For more information about workstation memory management, see the heading "The NetWare Workstation and Memory Management," later in this chapter.

VLM /ME. If your workstation is using expanded memory (EMS) instead of extended memory, the DOS Requester can detect this and load VLM.EXE and its modules into expanded memory. To ensure that the first place the DOS Requester tries to load is into expanded memory, type VLM /ME <Enter>. If you don't specify the expanded memory manager over the extended memory manager, XMS takes precedence over EMS.

Using extended or expanded memory managers, VLM.EXE can take up as little as 4KB in conventional memory if you have enough upper memory blocks (UMBs) available for loading VLM modules high. The DOS Requester allocates two blocks of memory in these areas: the transient swap block, and the global block. VLM.EXE uses the transient swap block (about 8.5KB) to swap modules and data between conventional memory and extended or expanded memory. The global block is about 22KB in size and will also load into the upper memory area as space permits.

If there are enough upper memory blocks to hold these two memory blocks, you will see about a 3.5KB VLM footprint in conventional memory. If there isn't, you'll see more of the DOS Requester in conventional memory.

VLM /MC. The VLM /MC option loads the DOS Requester into conventional memory. Some network boards and slower computers may not see good performance loading the DOS Requester into expanded or extended memory. The tradeoff in using conventional memory is the memory required by VLM.EXE and its modules. For example, if you load VLM with just Bindery Services, you stand to lose about 58KB of conventional memory; with printing services added, it's about 63.5KB (depending on the version of the DOS Requester you have).

VLM /PS=servername. Use the /PS= option when you want to specify which server you want to attach to when you initially log in. You can do the same thing, however, by using the PREFERRED SERVER = <servername> parameter in the

470

NET.CFG file. (See the heading "NET.CFG Parameters for the DOS Requester" later in this chapter.)

VLM /PT=treename. The /PT option is for NetWare 4.0 users and doesn't apply to NetWare 3.11 or 3.12.

VLM /Vn. The /Vn option tells the DOS Requester how much information to display when it initially comes up. Each setting increments the information displayed. For example, the /V0 setting only shows you the copyright sign-on message and any critical errors that occur as the modules load. The /V1 (default) setting adds any warning type messages as the modules load. The /V2 setting adds the module names as they load. The /V3 setting adds configuration information along with the module names. This includes the load order of the modules along with version date and code number, followed by the NET.CFG parameters you have set that are different than the parameter defaults. The /V4 setting displays diagnostic messages, which are different from the diagnostic information you see by typing VLM /D <Enter> at the command line.

VLM /D. The VLM /D option presents diagnostic information about the VLM's present running state. You type VLM /D in the directory where you initially loaded VLM.EXE. You can read about this option under the heading "The DOS Requester Diagnostics" in the troubleshooting section of Chapter 6.

Setting Up ODI and the DOS Requester

With NetWare 3.11 and 3.12, you can carry connections to NetWare networks using IPX as well as to UNIX systems using a different method of communications, such as TCP/IP. The method is called ODI, or Open Data-Link Interface, and allows you to communicate with different systems through one network interface board. ODI does this by creating a link support layer (LSL) that allows you to include more than one communications protocol stack. The LSL then sorts through which stack the communications request is using and sends the request to the proper network platform.

This approach's usefulness has grown as more network interface boards support more than one protocol at one time and your workstation needs to connect to more than one network system. For example, you can have IPX and TCP/IP running on the same workstation.

For setting up ODI in your CONFIG.SYS file, be sure your settings read are at least FILES=50 and BUFFERS=30. For setting up ODI in the AUTOEXEC.BAT, you need these files in this order:

LSL   (link support layer program so you can run multiple protocols)

NE2000   (or whatever the LAN driver file you're installing)

IPXODI   (the protocol stack for IPX)

NETX   (or the DOS Requester—VLM.EXE)

For NetWare 3.11, all the files listed are on the NetWare WSGEN disk under the ODI directory except NETX.COM. You may also need to create a NET.CFG file for protocols that can't use the default settings for IPXODI, or if the other protocol stack needs some extra tweaking. Since NET.CFG can be complicated, refer to the "Customize ODI workstation configurations with NET.CFG" section in the *Using the Network* manual from Novell.

Running the DOS Requester Installation Program

For NetWare 3.12, you install the DOS Requester from four disks. The actual INSTALL program is located on the NetWare Workstation for DOS WSDOS_1 disk. The other needed disks include two ODI driver disks—WSDRV_1 and WSDRV_2, and WSWIN_1, a disk containing Windows drivers (if you are using Windows).

To begin installation, insert the WSDOS_1 disk in a local drive such as A: and type A:INSTALL <Enter>. You'll see the main menu screen shown in Figure 5-1. This single screen provides access to all five steps for installing the client software.

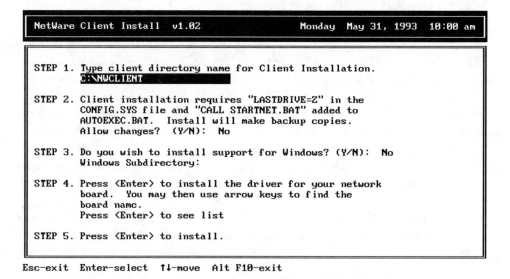

Figure 5-1. The DOS Requester INSTALL program's main menu

The first step shows you the directory path where the installation program intends to install the VLM files, as well as the latest ODI drivers. By default, this is C:\NWCLIENT. You can change the path by highlighting it and typing in the desired directory path name. For consistency's sake and supervisor maintenance, it's best to use the same directory name on all the workstations.

The second step discusses the changes that the installation process will make to the workstation's CONFIG.SYS and AUTOEXEC.BAT files. These changes consist of changing the LASTDRIVE entry in the CONFIG.SYS file to Z. If you use a different drive letter other than Z, you won't have any search drive mappings. For the AUTOEXEC.BAT file, the Install program adds a CALL STARTNET.BAT entry.

You can choose to make these changes yourself by accepting the default of No, or you can have the Install program do them for you by highlighting the No entry, typing Y, and pressing <Enter>.

The third step is to choose whether you want Windows support. If you would like Windows support, highlight the entry, type Y, and press <Enter>. You'll need to modify the Windows directory path if your path is not C:\WINDOWS.

The fourth step allows you to update your network drivers to support ODI, which allows a single network board to support multiple protocols. For example, you can have both IPX and TCP/IP protocols actively using an Ethernet network board, thus giving you access to NetWare through IPX and to UNIX through TCP/IP. When you choose Step 4, insert one of the driver disks, and you'll see a list of the different ODI drivers plus an option for Dedicated (Non-ODI) IPX.

Select the driver that matches the workstation's network board. If none of the drivers match your board on this disk, press <Escape>, then <Enter>, and then insert the second driver disk and see if the driver is on that disk. You can also use the ODI drivers that come from the network board manufacturer. Simply press <Escape>, highlight Step 4, press <Enter>, and insert that disk when Install asks for the driver disk. If another driver's disk is already inserted in the drive, remove that disk and insert the proper disk before pressing <Enter>.

If you are running on the network when you run the INSTALL program, the DOS Requester will detect which board and driver you have running and match the board settings and driver with the latest driver version from the WSDRV_ disks. When you press <Enter>, you'll be asked to place one of the driver disks into drive A:. If you are using drive B:, type in that path and press <Enter>. If the driver is on the disk you put in, you'll see a message telling you the driver was installed successfully. If the DOS Requester could not find the driver on that disk, insert the WSDRV_2 disk or the disk containing ODI drivers that came with the network board and try again.

Once you select the correct network board driver, you can edit the settings by highlighting the driver name and pressing <Enter>. You'll see a screen like the one shown in Figure 5-2. This allows you to match the interrupt, base I/O port, and memory I/O address to the network board settings. If you don't know what these settings are, you can press Alt-F10 to leave the Install program, and type either IPX -i <Enter> or IPXODI -I <Enter> in the directory where you load your NetWare drivers. The -i parameter will display your present network board's configuration. (For ODI drivers, you can look in the NET.CFG file to see the board's settings.)

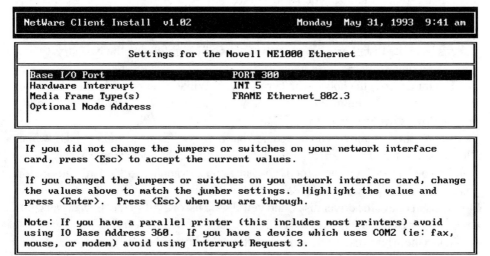

Figure 5-2. You can match the interrupt, base I/O port, and memory I/O address to the network board settings

The third entry in the board setting window shows the "Media Frame Type(s)" that a protocol can use. For Ethernet users, the frame type defaults to 802.2 unless you are already running on Ethernet 802.3. In this case, the Install program picks up the protocol type and places it in the Media Frame Type(s) entry.

Running Ethernet 802.2 can cause problems if your network is using 802.3, which NetWare 3.11 and earlier versions automatically use. If you are running Ethernet, ask your supervisor which frame type you are using on the network. The supervisor can check this out by going to the server console and typing CONFIG <Enter>.

On NetWare 2.2 and earlier, you can't specify a frame type, and Ethernet defaults to 802.3. Be sure to highlight the Media Frame Type(s) entry, press <Enter>, and select

474

the proper frame type for your network. If you can't find out what your Ethernet frame type is, chances are it's 802.3, so change the Frame Type entry accordingly. This also applies to Token-Ring, which defaults to Token-Ring MSB.

When you finish selecting the driver information, press <Escape>. For the last step, press <Enter> to install your selections. Put in the disks when they are asked for. The Install program copies the appropriate files into the directory specified in Step 1 (C:\NWCLIENT by default). If you chose to install Windows support, the Install program adds files to your Windows directory and makes some changes to the PROGMAN.INI and SYSTEM.INI files. As you leave the Install program, it tells you to remove any lines used to load IPX or NETX from your AUTOEXEC.BAT file.

Example AUTOEXEC.BAT Files

As an example of ODI, here are two AUTOEXEC.BAT files. One works with ODI in conventional memory, while the other AUTOEXEC file places the communications drivers in high memory.

```
echo off
PATH=C:\util;C:\DOS;c:\win31;c:\
set temp=c:\win31\temp
set wpc=/nt-1/u-bil
prompt $p$g
dosedit
C:\DOS\SHARE
c:\lsl
c:\ne1000
c:\ipxodi a
VLM
h:
login nts3/bill
```

In this example, Bill is setting up a temporary path to his local TEMP directory, as well as setting up his network parameters for running WordPerfect. Bill next loads DOS's SHARE utility, which allows him to run a minor database he has set up on one of his network drives.

Bill also loads LSL, the NE1000 network driver, and IPXODI with the A parameter. The A parameter cuts down on the size of IPXODI by stripping out the network management capabilities of IPX, as well as SPX capabilities. Check with your supervisor to see if you can use this IPXODI function; otherwise, you may not be able to load applications that use SPX for guaranteed communications.

The next example shows how to place NetWare into high memory using DR-DOS 6.0.

```
@ECHO OFF
:DRDOSBEG
PATH C:\DRDOS;C:\UTIL;C:\
set comspec=c:\command.com
VERIFY OFF
SHARE /L:20
PROMPT  $P$G
SET TEMP=C:\TEMP
IF NOT "%TEMP%"=="" MD %TEMP% >NUL
set os=DRDOS
set VER=6.0
set WPC=/nt-1/u-teb
MEMMAX +U
hiload C:NWCLIENT\LSL
hiload C:NWCLIENT\NE2000
hiload C:NWCLIENT\IPXODI
c:NWCLIENT\VLM
MEMMAX -U
F:
login admin/ted
```

In this example, user Ted is running DRDOS 6.0 as the workstation operating system. Much of the first part are the defaults that DRDOS builds, such as the @ECHO OFF, :DRDOSBEG, PATH, VERIFY OFF, SHARE, TEMP, and MEMMAX lines.

In particular, the MEMMAX +U line allows you to load the LSL, NE2000, IPXODI, and NETX files into upper memory. By loading NetWare files into upper memory (DRDOS uses HILOAD and MSDOS uses LOADHIGH), you can have as much as 630KB for running DOS applications. In order to do this, however, you must have a memory manager loaded through the CONFIG.SYS file. (See the "NetWare Workstation and Memory Management" heading later in this Chapter.)

However, certain programs expect DOS to occupy the first 40 KB of conventional memory and give you an error message when you have too much memory. A simple way around the error is to load one of the files in conventional memory. Once you get below somewhere like 600KB of conventional memory, this problem goes away.

Other lines worth noting include SET OS=DRDOS and SET VER=6.0. These SET parameters can then be used in your login script to ensure you map to the correct DOS version on the network. The network SET COMSPEC will then overwrite the local setting you see in this example.

To use ODI, you must include to which interrupt settings the network interface board is set. For example, Novell's NE2000 board set to the board's interrupt 5 and Port 320h will contain the following statements in the NET.CFG file:

```
# Setup the NE2000 card
Link driver NE2000

    INT 5
    PORT 320
```

Be sure to keep a space between the Link line and the Interrupt line (INT 5). Also be sure to indent the statements below the Link drive line, and be sure the NET.CFG file is in the same directory as the ODI files.

In many ways, ODI boards are easier to set up than regular IPX, for you don't have to run WSGEN to configure the network board driver. For example, if you have an NE1000 Ethernet network board that is set to the default settings of Int 3 and Port 300h, you would put the following in the NET.CFG file:

```
# Setup the NE1000 card
Link driver NE1000

    INT 3
    PORT 300
```

With ODI drivers in place, you can load more than one communications protocol at the same time. The next example is a batch file that shows TCP/IP running along with the NE2000 driver.

```
CD NWCLIENT
LSL
NE2000
IPXODI
TCPIP
TELAPI
```

477

```
VLM
CD ..
F:
LOGIN NTS3/PAM
```

In this example, Pam runs a batch file from her C: local NWCLIENT directory, where she first loads her NetWare communications software, then the TCPIP and TELAPI drivers to set up her communications environment on TCP/IP. She then loads the DOS Requester and logs in to file server NTS3. You can also load TELAPI into high memory through MS DOS's LOADHIGH or DR-DOS's HILOAD commands if you load EMM386 in the CONFIG.SYS file. See the next section in workstation memory management.

How you set up your NET.CFG file for multiple communication protocols is also important. Here's an example of Pam's NET.CFG file for IPX and TCP/IP.

```
LOCAL PRINTERS = 0
IPX RETRY COUNT = 120
SPX ABORT TIMEOUT = 2040
SPX LISTEN TIMEOUT = 200
MODE = 5
Preferred Server = NTS3
First Network Drive = F

Link Support

     Max Stacks 8
     Buffers 8 1500
     MemPool 4096

;**Modify for the appropriate driver**
Link Driver NE2000

     INT 340
     PORT 300
     Frame Ethernet_802.3
     Frame Ethernet_II
     Frame Ethernet_SNAP
     Protocol IPX 0 Ethernet_802.3
     Protocol TCPIP 8137 Ethernet_II
```

478

```
;TCPIP ip_address and ip_router
;**Modify the last digit on ip_address**
Protocol TCPIP
    ip_address      137.65.6.25
    ip_router       137.65.6.254
    ip_netmask      255.255.255.0
    tcp_sockets     8
    udp_sockets     8
    raw_sockets     1
    nb_sessions     4
    nb_commands 8
    nb_adapter      0
    nb_domain       PROVO.MKTG.NTS.COM
```

The top part of the NET.CFG file shows configuration settings for your workstation and these settings are covered in the "Setting Up Your NET.CFG File for the DOS Requester" heading later in this chapter. The second grouping, "Link Support," is used to ensure that two protocols can share the same network interface board.

The third group, "Link Driver NE2000," links both IPXODI and TCP/IP to the board. In the case of Ethernet, this is done by defining the Ethernet frame type, then which protocol (IPX or TCP/IP) will use which Ethernet frame type, the Protocol IPX O Ethernet_802.3. The fourth group, "Protocol TCPIP," shows the settings for TCP/IP communications. Most of this information is what your system supervisor will have to go through to establish a TCP/IP connection.

NET.CFG Parameters for NetWare

The NET.CFG file is a specialized text file you can create with any ASCII text editor. The NET.CFG file contains configuration values that your workstation reads and interprets when it connects to the network. The values specified in NET.CFG adjust some of the operating parameters of the NetWare shell, IPX, or NetBIOS. I'll cover those NET.CFG parameters for the DOS Requester in the next section, "NET.CFG Parameters for the DOS Requester".

Since you really have to know what you're doing when tweaking the IPX.COM and NETBIOS.EXE parameters, we'll leave those for your supervisor (except for one) and focus on what you can do with the NETX.COM parameters. Even then, there are some NETX.COM options that ought to be set by your supervisor and won't be discussed here.

You may need to be aware of one parameter for the EMSNETX.COM file, which will be discussed here as well.

You don't have to do anything to use the default parameters. However, if you have a need to change one of the parameters from the default, you can do this by creating a NET.CFG file. If you want to create a NET.CFG file at the command line, go to the boot directory or floppy disk where you want to save the NET.CFG file. To create the file, begin by typing COPY CON NET.CFG <Enter>, and then type in the options you want to change. When you've finished, type ^Z by pressing the F6 key, or by pressing the <Ctrl> and Z keys simultaneously.

If your workstation has expanded memory and you're using the EMSNETX.COM file for your NetWare shell, you may need to set the ENTRY STACK SIZE=number parameter. Use this parameter in conjunction with the Expanded Memory Specification (EMS) shell, which is the EMS version of the NETX file (EMSNETX.EXE). The EMS version allows workstations to load the NetWare shell (except for 7KB) into expanded memory, thus giving the workstation 32KB more of DOS's 640KB available for application use. You'll need to load an EMS 4.0 driver through the CONFIG.SYS file.

When the shell receives another shell request while it's busy doing something else, the shell must save the memory page mappings it's busy with. The "Entry Stack" option allows the workstation to configure the internal page mapping stack size that the shell will use. The stack can be 5 to 40 in size, and defaults to 10. If you see the message "Entry stack size too small," increment the default value by five and try it again. If the EMSNETX file isn't working right, you can place a command in the NET.CFG file to look like this:

```
ENTRY STACK SIZE=15
```

The parameters you can change in the NETX.COM shell file fall into three groups: those you can easily affect, those that deal with a multitasking environment, and those you should leave alone. The parameters you can easily affect include the following (shown here with their default settings):

```
CACHE BUFFERS = 5
PRINT HEADER = 64
PRINT TAIL = 16
PREFERRED SERVER = servername
FIRST NETWORK DRIVE = (none) or F
LOCAL PRINTERS = (no default)
LONG MACHINE TYPE = IBM_PC
SHORT MACHINE = IBM
```

480

```
SEARCH MODE = 1
SET STATION TIME = ON
```

The parameters that deal with a multitasking environment include:

```
FILE HANDLES = 40
MAXIMUM TASKS = 31
SHOW DOTS = OFF
TASK MODE = 1
ENVIRONMENT PAD = NBYTES
SEARCH DIR FIRST = OFF
```

The parameters you should leave alone include:

```
ALL SERVERS=OFF
EOJ = ON
HOLD = OFF
SHARE = ON
LOCK RETRIES = 3
LOCK DELAY = 1
READ ONLY COMPATIBILITY = OFF
MAX CUR DIR = 64
MAX PATH LENGTH = 255
SPECIAL UPPERCASE = OFF
PATCH = <byte offset> <value>
```

Parameters That Affect the NetWare Environment

An explanation of the shell parameters that you can easily affect follows.

CACHE BUFFERS = 5. Workstation cache buffers show the number of files that may be cached at one time. Workstation cache buffers are 512 bytes in size and the default is 5 (2.5KB). Memory is rare and precious when you're working under DOS's 640KB limitation. Still, if you work in Windows or DESQView 386, and have a lot of applications open, increase the number of cache buffers to 10. If you are using word processors or spreadsheets only, use the default. You can have from 0 to 64 cache buffers.

PRINT HEADER = <number>. Use this option in conjunction with PRINTDEF and PRINTCON. PRINTDEF is a supervisor's utility that allows a supervisor to define the functionality of the network printers (devices). These functions control such things as the font, size, spacing, pitch, and orientation of the printed output. Having defined the printer's functions, the supervisor then groups the functions into several modes of operation, which tell the printer how to print a particular job (for example, letter quality or draft quality). Some print modes are small, containing only two or three functions, while others are large.

The "Print Header" option allows you to change the size of the print header buffer if you need more space to accommodate the larger mode functions. The times you would change this are for printers that emulate another printer, or have many modes that require a lengthy setup, such as laser printers.

Unfortunately, there isn't an easy way to find out how big your buffer needs to be. Because the size depends on how many functions the largest print mode contains, you have to go into PRINTDEF, determine which mode has the most functions, and count every character in each of the functions of that mode. Then resize your buffer accordingly, allowing for one byte per character. When counting a function's characters, treat all characters within a pair of delimiter brackets (<>) as one character, and each character outside the delimiters as one character. For example, <Esc>2!<SP> is four characters long— one character for <Esc>, two characters for 2!, and one character for <SP>.

If you don't use PRINTDEF or PRINTCON, use the default print header buffer size, which is 64 bytes (characters). If you use these printing utilities a lot, adjust your print header to handle the largest defined mode.

PRINT TAIL = *<number>*. The print tail always contains the Reinitialize mode functions from PRINTDEF. Most Reinitialize modes are short. For example, Hewlett-Packard's reinitialization sequence consists of <Esc>E, a two-character count. However, the IBM Proprinter reinitialization sequence systematically turns off every function you defined in the Proprinter mode, so its Reinitialized mode is large.

Go into PRINTDEF and look at the Reinitialize modes for all your defined devices and determine which one contains the most characters. Then set your Print Tail size to accommodate the largest Reinitialize mode. If you don't use PRINTDEF, use the default Print Tail size, which is 16 bytes.

PREFERRED SERVER = *servername*. The IPX driver establishes an avenue for communication with the network interface board and attached cable, allowing access to attached workstations and servers. Then as the NetWare shell loads, it first establishes a connection to a network server by using IPX to broadcast "Get Nearest Server." The first server to respond to the request establishes a connection with that workstation. When you initially load the NetWare shell, you'll see "Attached to server *<servername>*" after the shell parameters. The server named in this message may or may not be the server you wish to log in to.

The "Preferred Server" option allows you to specify the server you wish to attach to; the shell then attempts to connect the workstation to the specified server rather than to the first server that responds to the "Get Nearest Server" broadcast. Be sure to use a valid servername when you use this option.

The NetWare shell will also attempt up to five other server connections in case it can't establish a connection with the specified server. That way, you'll receive a server connection even though it won't be with the server you specified.

FIRST NETWORK DRIVE = <NONE> or F. This parameter applies to all the network services you may tie into. If you run the DOS Requester's installation program, you will have the first network drive equal to F as the default. However, the default may change to be the first available drive letter. If you don't have this parameter, the NetWare shell or the DOS Requester's GENERAL module will look at your local drive table and map the first available drive letter as the first network drive. If you are used to having F or G as your first network drive, you can place this entry in the NET.CFG file to ensure the drive mapping will always be what you select.

LOCAL PRINTERS = <*number*>. Use this parameter to set the number of local printers attached to your workstation. If your workstation doesn't have a local printer, set this parameter to 0 (0 is the default for NetWare 3.12); then your workstation won't hang if you accidentally press <Shift>-<Print Screen> and you don't have CAPTURE running. (Actually, your workstation doesn't always hang; it just takes a very long time in its attempt to write to the printer.) Pressing <Shift>-<Print Screen> erroneously is a common mistake made by people using the older IBM PC keyboards on which the Shift and Print Screen keys are close to each other.

If you ever add a local printer to your workstation or run RPRINTER to use the printer as a network resource, that printer won't work with the Local Printers parameter set to 0. You can spend a lot of unnecessary time checking ports and cables before you realize that the problem is actually with the local printer setting. When you attach a printer to your workstation, don't include the Local Printers parameter in the NET.CFG file; the NetWare shell will determine how many local printers you have from your workstation's BIOS.

LONG MACHINE TYPE = IBM_PC. The long machine type is used with the %MACHINE variable in the login script. The example in the *NetWare Supervisor Reference* manual is that the %MACHINE variable can be used in a "generic" DOS directory mapping, as follows.

```
MAP S2:=SYS:PUBLIC\%MACHINE\%OS\ %OS_VERSION
```

483

If you have a non-IBM workstation that runs its manufacturer's own version of DOS (such as a COMPAQ machine running MS DOS as published by Compaq Computers), and your supervisor has loaded this version of DOS onto a network directory, you can use the long machine type to indicate what you want the login script to replace the %MACHINE variable with. For example, suppose your supervisor has created two DOS directories:

```
SYS:PUBLIC\IBM_PC\MSDOS\V3.30
SYS:PUBLIC\COMPAQ\MSDOS\V3.30.
```

If you type LONG MACHINE TYPE = COMPAQ <Enter> in your NET.CFG file, your workstation will access the Compaq DOS directory instead of the IBM PC DOS directory. (IBM_PC is the default long machine type.)

SHORT MACHINE TYPE = IBM. Some monitors emulate color monitors by using gray scales instead of actual colors. These monitors, particularly some of those from AT&T and Compaq, need to use the CMPQ$RUN.OVL file found in the SYS:PUBLIC directory, instead of the default IBM$RUN.OVL file. The CMPQ$RUN.OVL file has a black-and-white default palette for the menu utilities. Without it, you may not be able to see the gray scales differentiated from the background, and your display will be unreadable.

To make your workstation call the CMPQ$RUN.OVL file when you access a NetWare menu utility, type SHORT MACHINE TYPE = CMPQ as the short machine name parameter in your NET.CFG file. The short machine type can't be more than four characters long; the default is IBM.

SEARCH MODE = *<number>*. The "Search Mode" option helps determine when an application can use the search drives when searching for auxiliary files. Many applications, when started, also open a number of other files (such as overlay files and data files) that are used as a resource to the application. This option determines when applications can look in your NetWare search drives to find these auxiliary files.

To understand how the "Search Mode" option works, you need to understand a little about the way DOS searches for auxiliary files. Usually, when an application's executable file (a file with either an .EXE or a .COM extension) requires an auxiliary file, the application will specify a path to that file as part of its setup menu or routine. DOS will always look in this path whenever it is specified. If no path is specified in the application, DOS will search the default directory (the directory you start the application from). In a stand-alone environment, if DOS doesn't find the files, you can't start the application.

484

This is where Search Mode comes in. If you have search drives set up for your workstation in your login script, the NetWare shell will take over where DOS leaves off and continue looking in the search drives for the necessary files. With the "Search Mode" option in the NET.CFG file, you can tell the shell exactly how and when to use the search drives.

One other factor comes into play with the "Search Mode" option. Some applications only open their auxiliary files and read their contents; other applications need to both read and write to the files. You may not have the necessary rights to write to or modify files in your search drive directories, so you may have to restrict the searches to those open requests that are read-only requests. You'll have to check with your network supervisor or consult the documentation for each application to determine if the application just reads its auxiliary files, or reads and writes to them.

Search Mode has five possible settings: Mode 1, Mode 2, Mode 3, Mode 5, and Mode 7. (Modes 4 and 6 are reserved for future use.) Each mode specifies a different way of using search drives. A brief explanation of each mode appears below. Remember that DOS will always look in a specific path (if specified in the application), and then in the default directory, regardless of which search mode you specify.

Mode 1 is the "shell default search mode" for the NET.CFG file. When you use this setting, the shell will look in the search drives only when no path is specified in the application (and after DOS has searched the default directory). The search is allowed for both read-only and read-write requests. NetWare displays this mode on the screen as "Search on all opens with no path."

When you use the search mode, Mode 2, the shell won't look in any search drives to find auxiliary files. The application will behave as if you were running it on a stand-alone machine with DOS only. If the application has a defined directory path that allows it to search and open files, the application will search for the files in that defined path. NetWare refers to this mode as "Do not search." Mode 2 provides the best performance, so if you're not using any applications that look for auxiliary files, choose this mode.

This search mode, Mode 3, is exactly like Mode 1, except that if the application has no defined directory path to search and open files, the shell will look in the search drives only if the open request is a read-only request. NetWare calls this "Search on Read-Only opens with no path."

When you use the Mode 5 search mode, the shell will always be able to look in the search drives, even if the application specifies a path. NetWare refers to this mode as "Search on all opens."

The Mode 7 search mode is exactly like Mode 5, except that the shell will look in the search drives only if the open request is a read-only request. NetWare calls this mode "Search on all Read-Only opens."

The search mode you set in your NET.CFG file will apply to all applications, so you should choose the mode that works for the majority of your programs. (The default search mode works fine in most situations.) If certain applications don't work correctly with the shell's search mode, you can set the search mode for individual applications with the SMODE command-line utility. This will override the NET.CFG search mode setting just for those applications.

The table below shows when the "Search Mode" option allows the shell to use the search drives, according to whether a path is specified in the application and whether the open request is a read-only request or a read-write request.

	NO PATH		PATH	
Mode	Read-Only	Read-Write	Read-Only	Read-Write
1	Yes	Yes	No	No
2	No	No	No	No
3	Yes	No	No	No
5	Yes	Yes	Yes	Yes
7	Yes	No	Yes	No

SET STATION TIME = ON. When you log on to the network, the NetWare shell will synchronize the internal clock in the workstation to the time on the file server you log in to. This parameter defaults to ON so the synchronization is done automatically. If for some reason you don't want your workstation's time to synchronize to the file server (such as logging in to servers across time zones), place SET STATION TIME = OFF <Enter> in the NET.CFG file.

Parameters That Affect the Multitasking Environments

Here's an explanation of the NET.CFG options that deal with a multitasking environment.

FILE HANDLES = <number>. In your DOS CONFIG.SYS file, you can set the "FILES =" option anywhere between eight and 255 files. DOS uses these open file handles when running applications and utilities in the local environment. Within that open file range, each program or application can have twenty files open at any time because DOS's file handle table has room for twenty entries. Of those twenty entries, however, five are already taken for standard input, output, error, auxiliary, and printer functions. This leaves a limit of fifteen file handles per application. DOS's file handles affect local devices and applications in a stand-alone environment.

The NetWare Shell uses its own file handle tables; these are different from the ones DOS uses. In fact, the two operating systems don't often share open files between them (depending on the network application). So the NetWare shell has its own default of 40 file handles—ample for most network applications. Each file handle is 32 bytes in size, so the shell default of 40 handles takes up 1.2KB of memory space. You need to increase the number of file handles if you get an error message saying you don't have enough file handles. Applications often use file handles to access peripheral information not contained in their .EXE files. And as applications become more sophisticated, they'll open more and more files. The File Handles parameter in the NET.CFG file can be extended to 255.

In determining how many file handles to specify, you also need to consider operating systems that can have multiple applications open. These operating systems (Windows 386, DESQview 386, and so on) can have 20 file handles open per application, but they can also have more than one application open at the same time. When their collective number of open files reaches the NetWare shell's 40-handle default, the next application trying to open an additional file will fail. When you start getting error messages like "No file handles" or "Unable to open file," check the file handles setting in both the CONFIG.SYS (for local drive access only) and NET.CFG (for network access) files. You may need to increase the number of file handles in both. Also if you are running RPRINTER with Windows, up your file handles to 60 or better.

In NetWare 3.12 and the DOS Requester, you set the total number of open files through the CONFIG.SYS file with the FILES=xx statement. (Include enough for Windows, if used.) If you are running the DOS Requester and have an older NET.CFG file with a FILE HANDLES=xx statement in it, remove the statement and increase the number of files in the FILES=xx line in the workstation's CONFIG.SYS file. Otherwise, you may see "Insufficient file" or "Insufficient file handles" error messages.

MAXIMUM TASKS = *<number>*. This parameter sets the maximum number of tasks a workstation can have active at one time. For the most part, you have only a few tasks running at the same time, so the default of 31 is a generous number. However, with multiwindowing, multitasking environments running on top of DOS (such as Windows 386 and DESQview 386), you may need to increase this number. The minimum number you can set this parameter to is 8; the maximum is 128.

SHOW DOTS = OFF. Programs like Windows allow you to move up directories in the directory path by highlighting "." and ".." entries and pressing <Enter> or by clicking on these path entries. With shell versions prior to the release of version 3.01, however, the NetWare file server doesn't have such directory entries to let you do this. The Show Dots option allows these programs to use the "." and ".." options to change directories. If you're using Microsoft Windows, set SHOW DOTS = ON <Enter> in the NET.CFG file.

TASK MODE = *<number>* (defaults to 2). Microsoft's Windows 3.0 operating system creates a "virtual machine mode" with each 640KB of memory it can grab. Each 640KB chunk (virtual machine) expects certain DOS environment parameters to exist. When you create another virtual machine mode, the shell copies the environment parameters from the default virtual machine (VM1) to the next mode.

Sometimes the VM1 environment isn't a good environment to copy to the other virtual machine modes, and inconsistencies from the first environment get transferred to the other environments. If you experience this difficulty when running an earlier version of Windows than 3.0 or running another multitasking program, set the Task Mode parameter to 1. The NetWare shell will then create a new environment for each new mode you add. If you're not using any such programs, you can set the Task Mode parameter to 0 for a bit of performance gain. However, this setting is more for Windows 3.0, not Windows 3.1.

ENVIRONMENT PAD = *n*bytes. The Environment Pad allows you to extend additional environment space for applications using the set environment variables when they are running. This means you can allocate more than the minimum required space for an application, thus improving its performance. When you load DOS-based applications, Windows creates a virtual DOS session in which the application runs and which carries the environment space created by DOS before you entered Windows.

However, some applications need different environmental SET parameters in order to work. You can set this entry to force Windows to add the bytes you type in to the DOS environment. There is no default, and adding 512 bytes will be ample for most all DOS-based applications. But if you need more, add them.

SEARCH DIR FIRST = OFF. This entry tells certain Windows programs that you want to search files before directories. The entry defaults to OFF, meaning the shell searches for files instead of directories first. If you want Windows to search for directories first, set this parameter to ON.

NET.CFG Parameters for the DOS Requester

Below is a list of NET.CFG parameters for NetWare 3.12's DOS Requester. There are other NET.CFG parameters for ODI and the protocol stacks that are not covered here. When setting these parameters, place them under the heading NETWARE DOS

REQUESTER in the NET.CFG file and indent them three to five spaces. While not all of them need to be indented, it is easier to indent them all than to decide which ones need to be indented.

A number of the parameters affect the performance of the DOS Requester. These are to be attended to carefully if you find the DOS Requester's performance to be sluggish.

```
CACHE BUFFER SIZE = <protocol frame size minus 64 bytes>
CACHE WRITES = ON
CHECKSUM = 1
LARGE INTERNET PACKETS = ON
LOAD LOW CONN = ON
LOAD LOW IPXNCP = ON
PB BUFFERS = 3
PRINT BUFFER SIZE = 64
SIGNATURE LEVEL = 1
TRUE COMMIT = OFF
```

Those parameters that don't affect performance but flesh out the NET.CFG parameters specific to the DOS Requester include:

```
AUTO RETRY = 5
AVERAGE NAME LENGTH = 48
BIND RECONNECT = ON
CONNECTIONS = 8
LOAD CONN TABLE LOW = OFF
MESSAGE LEVEL = 1
NETWORK PRINTERS = 3
SET STATION TIME = ON
USE DEFAULTS = ON
VLM = <path><vlm>
```

There is a group of generic NET.CFG parameters that apply to both NetWare 3.11 and 3.12. Refer to the parameter explanations found under the "NET.CFG Parameters for NetWare 3.11" heading in this chapter. The generic NET.CFG parameters include:

```
CACHE BUFFERS = 5
PRINT HEADER = 64
PRINT TAIL = 16
```

```
PREFERRED SERVER = servername
FIRST NETWORK DRIVE = <none> or F
LOCAL PRINTERS = 0
LONG MACHINE TYPE = IBM_PC
SHORT MACHINE TYPE = IBM
SEARCH MODE = 1
MAXIMUM TASKS = 31
READ ONLY COMPATIBILITY = OFF
```

Parameters That Affect the DOS Requester's Performance

CACHE BUFFER SIZE = <protocol frame size minus 64 bytes>. The DOS Requester's FIO module automatically determines the physical packet size of the protocol you are using (such as Ethernet, Arcnet, Token-Ring, and so on) and then subtracts 64 bytes from the packet size. The FIO module uses this number for the amount of data that can be cached by the DOS Requester. Since this is done automatically for you, leave it as it is.

CACHE WRITES = ON. Cache writes fills the local cache buffers before writing the data to the network, as opposed to writing it immediately to the network. This allows you to return a write success to be returned to the application more quickly, so you can get on with other work. An important note is that your workstation's data can be affected if the server goes down or runs out of disk space. Either way, you'll lose the data in the cache. There are a number of client caches, such as Norton Cache or Super PC-Kwik, that have the same restriction.

CHECKSUM = 1. This parameter is an IPX checksum, which you can have in addition to other error checking your network board and driver may already be doing. If you are running Ethernet 802.3, this checksum does not apply and will be ignored, no matter what you set it to. The settings are 0 for disabled; 1 for enabled but not preferred (default); 2 for enabled and checksum preferred; and 3 for required.

Running extra IPX checksums can degrade your performance because it is an extra step that communications has to go through. If you are running on Ethernet 802.3 or if you simply don't want this capability, type CHECKSUM = 0 in the NET.CFG.

LARGE INTERNET PACKETS = ON. The DOS Requester uses this setting to allow internetwork packets that are larger than 512 bytes to pass through a bridge or a router that can handle larger packets. Leaving this parameter set to ON offers the best performance, especially for larger networks.

LOAD LOW CONN = ON. The connection table manager, CONN.VLM, keeps track of the workstation's connections to the servers you log in to or attach to, as well

490

as the tasks that are currently executing. Because the CONN.VLM supports all layers of the VLM architecture, loading it low makes it more accessible than having VLM.EXE swap the CONN module in and out of extended or expanded memory all the time. This helps improve performance.

The module takes about 3KB when it is loaded low. If there is any upper memory available, VLM.EXE will use these UMBs rather than conventional memory. This helps keep the VLM footprint in conventional memory to a minimum.

LOAD LOW IPXNCP = ON. The IPX transport module, IPXNCP.VLM, implements the transport layer for IPX. IPXNCP.VLM takes about 4KB when it is loaded low and helps improve performance. However, like the CONN.VLM, if there are any upper memory blocks available, VLM.EXE will use these UMBs rather than conventional memory.

PB BUFFERS = 3. The Packet Burst (PB) entry works as either Off when set to 0, or On when set on any number from 1 to 10 (including the default of 3). Since the ODI driver set is fast enough, the DOS Requester currently allocates three ECBs (Event Control Blocks) and packet burst headers (without the full packet size buffers). Three should be enough to cover your needs. If you're running Packet Burst at the server, set this parameter to a nonzero value (or leave it at the default); if you're not, set it to 0 to save some memory.

PRINT BUFFER SIZE = 64. What you set this parameter to depends a lot on the applications you are running. The print buffer is a character catch for Interrupt 17h requests, which are single-character print requests. Once the 64-byte (default) print buffer is filled, it will call the FIO module to go through a file write request instead of calling FIO for each character.

Applications that use the Interrupt 17h routine to print will need this parameter set higher (the setting can be from 0 to 256 bytes). However, most newer applications open a printer port (such as LPT1) and write to a printable file rather than go through Interrupt 17h.

SIGNATURE LEVEL = 1. This parameter is really for NetWare 4.0 and its added security features. Therefore leave it set to 1 or turn it Off by setting it to 0.

TRUE COMMIT = OFF. The True Commit parameter increases data integrity by waiting until the data is written to the server's disk rather than to the server's cache. Databases perform this when they are not using NetWare's transaction tracking features, but still require guaranteed data storage. The workstation will wait until data is written to disk and the FAT tables are updated, which can mean an 80 to 90 millisecond delay. If you need this kind of data integrity, set this parameter to On; otherwise, leave it Off.

Other NET.CFG Parameters Specific to the DOS Requester

AUTO RETRY = 5. You use this parameter in conjunction with automatic reconnection features found with the AUTO.VLM module and the Bind Reconnect = ON parameter. Since the AUTO.VLM module isn't loaded automatically, you'll need to add the line VLM = AUTO.VLM <Enter> under the NETWARE DOS REQUESTER heading in the NET.CFG file. (Be sure to indent the line under the heading.) This way, VLM.EXE will load its automatic modules and add the AUTO module as well.

When you see an "Abort, Retry" error message because of a connection loss, the AUTO.VLM automatically does the retrying for so you don't have to keep pressing Retry. The Auto Retry parameter sets how long AUTO.VLM waits before retrying to reestablish its connection to the file server once a connection is lost. You can set the Retry parameter from 0 to 3,640 seconds (about an hour).

AVERAGE NAME LENGTH = 48. The NetWare shell was configured to hold eight 48-byte servernames—one for each connection allowed. Most servernames are relatively short (from 6 to 12 characters), so you can set the name length to the longest name and save a bit of memory. You can set servername lengths anywhere from 2 to 48 characters. Since this number is an average, if a servername is longer than what you have set up, the name will wrap to take care of the extended name set. If you run out of space and try to add another server, however, you can lose all your connections.

BIND RECONNECT = ON. You use this parameter in conjunction with automatic reconnection features found with the AUTO.VLM module and the Auto Retry = 5 parameter. The Bind Reconnect = On parameter is only in force if the AUTO.VLM is loaded. Since the AUTO.VLM module isn't loaded automatically, you'll need to add the line VLM = AUTO.VLM <Enter> under the NETWARE DOS REQUESTER heading in the NET.CFG file. (Be sure to indent the line under the heading.) This way, VLM.EXE will load its automatic modules and add the AUTO module as well.

If you don't want automatic reconnection capabilities, simply don't load the AUTO.VLM, or set the Bind Reconnect to Off. However, automatic reconnection capabilities can be very useful. As downed servers become available again, the AUTO.VLM module reconnects to the server and then rebuilds the user's environment, including connection status, drive mappings, and printer connections. Open files are restored, which means your recovery from the connection loss depends on how the application you were running recovers from a connection loss and reestablishment.

Automatic reconnection is also very handy when running Windows locally and accessing applications or data files on the network. You may lose your connection to an application, but Windows doesn't hang as often in the process.

CONNECTIONS = 8. For compatibility with the utilities in NetWare versions 3.x and earlier, as well as applications written to the older NetWare shell API set, the default is set to 8. While you can have more than eight connections active on NetWare 3.x and earlier, you will see only eight server attachments when you type WHOAMI. In the end, this confusion to the utilities can be too much for your connection to function properly. For NetWare 3.x and below, use the default of 8.

LOAD CONN TABLE LOW = OFF. This parameter was added because of a programming anomaly; NetWare 4.0 utilities were looking for the CONN.VLM's connection table to be in conventional memory instead of extended or expanded memory. Setting this parameter to On helped 4.0 utilities find the connection table. Since this is a NetWare 4.0 problem and not a NetWare 3.1x problem, keep the default setting of Off.

MESSAGE LEVEL = 1. The Message Level parameter tells the DOS Requester how much information to display when it initially comes up. Each setting increments the information displayed. For example, the 0 setting only shows you the copyright sign-on message and any critical errors that occur as the modules load. The 1 (default) setting adds any warning-type messages as the modules load. The 2 setting adds the module names as they load. The 3 setting adds configuration information along with the module names. This includes the load order of the modules along with version date and code number, followed by the NET.CFG parameters you have set that are different from the parameter defaults. The 4 setting displays diagnostic messages, which are different from the diagnostic information you see by typing VLM /D <Enter> at the command line.

NETWORK PRINTERS = 3. The default for network printers is 3, but with the DOS Requester you can have 9 if needed. If you set this parameter to 0, the PRINT module won't load. If you set Network Printers to 1 or 2 and you have more CAPTURE statements than you allow printers through this parameter, CAPTURE will think it has set up connections to the printer. However, the PRINT.VLM module won't allocate connections to those statements.

USE DEFAULTS = ON. You use this parameter to control how you want VLM modules loaded. You can leave this entry set to On and VLM.EXE will use its default list to load VLM modules. You can leave this entry set to On and add other modules, such as AUTO.VLM, under the NetWare DOS Requester heading in the NET.CFG file. VLM.EXE will load its default list, then add other specified VLM modules.

When you set this parameter to OFF, you are telling VLM.EXE to only load the VLM modules designated in the NET.CFG file. When you do this, you must type in all the VLM modules you wish to load (in the correct loading order). Otherwise, VLM.EXE won't work. For NetWare 3.12 or earlier, the bare minimum list should include the following:

```
USE DEFAULT = OFF
   VLM = CONN.VLM
   VLM = IPXNCP.VLM
   VLM = TRAN.VLM
   VLM = BIND.VLM
   VLM = NWP.VLM
   VLM = FIO.VLM
   VLM = GENERAL.VLM
   VLM = REDIR.VLM
   VLM = NETX.VLM
   VLM = PRINT.VLM
```

If you don't want printing, remove the PRINT.VLM from the list. Don't forget the Preferred Server and First Network Drive parameters if you need them. You can sometimes get by without the NETX.VLM module, but you stand to lose application or utility compatibility if you do.

VLM=<path>\<VLM>. You can use all relevant DOS path names to load specific VLM modules from local directories. For example, I tried the following different options, and they all worked.

```
VLM = C:\NWCLIENT\CONN.VLM
VLM = C:\NWCLIENT\TEMP\IPXNCP.VLM
VLM = ..\NWCLIENT\TEMP..\TEMP\TRAN.VLM
```

According to VLM specifications, you can have up to 50 VLMs loaded at one time, which leaves a lot of room for future expansion. Each loaded VLM, however, is another link the VLM manager must go through when passing information along the DOS Requester. You may see better performance by only loading the VLM modules you actually need and use.

Sample NET.CFG Files for the DOS Requester

Following are a couple of sample NET.CFG files to help you better see how to use the NET.CFG parameters with the DOS Requester. Example 1 shows some performance tuning to the DOS Requester, while Example 2 takes a minimum configuration approach.

Example 1
```
LINK DRIVER NE2000
     INT 2
     PORT 320
     FRAME ETHERNET_802.3
NETWARE DOS REQUESTER
     SHOW DOTS=ON

     NETWORK PRINTERS=2
     FIRST NETWORK DRIVE=F
     PREFERRED SERVER = NTS3
;MEMORY OPTIMIZATIONS
     SIGNATURE LEVEL=0
     CONNECTIONS=5
     AVERAGE NAME LENGTH=10
     CACHE BUFFERS=3
;PERFORMANCE OPTIMIZATIONS
     CACHE WRITES=ON
     LOAD LOW CONN=ON
     LOAD LOW IPXNCP=ON
     CHECKSUM=0
```

In this first example, Dave has set the workstation's network interface board to interrupt 2 and port 320 using Ethernet 802.3 protocol for network communication. Then under the NetWare DOS Requester heading, Dave has placed his Network Printer setting to 2, which means he won't be able to run CAPTURE using the LPT3 option. Because he is running the DOS Requester, Dave designates his first network drive and his preferred server. (Notice the use of the semicolon for designating comments. You can also use the semicolon to remark out parameters if you wish to see how your workstation runs under certain parameters.)

Under the Memory Optimizations heading, Dave has turned off the signature level, dropped his number of connections to 5, dropped the average servername length to 10 characters, and dropped the number of cache buffers to 3. Then, under the Performance Optimizations heading, Dave keeps the cache writes On (the default) and turns the checksum Off.

Example 2
```
Link Support
     Max Stacks 8
```

495

```
        Buffers 8 1500
        MemPool 4096

    Link Driver NE2000
        INT 3
        PORT 300
        Frame Ethernet_802.3
        Frame Ethernet_802.2

    ;Modify if you have a different setting or card
        Protocol IPX 0 Ethernet_802.3

    SHOW DOTS ON
    NETWARE DOS REQUESTER
        CACHE BUFFERS = 10
        BUFFER SIZE = 1024
        USE DEFAULTS = OFF
        VLM = CONN.VLM
        VLM = IPXNCP.VLM
        VLM = TRAN.VLM
        VLM = BIND.VLM
        VLM = NWP.VLM
        VLM = FIO.VLM
        VLM = GENERAL.VLM
        VLM = REDIR.VLM
        VLM = PRINT.VLM
        VLM = NETX.VLM
        VLM = AUTO.VLM
        PREFERRED SERVER = ADMIN
        CHECKSUM = 0
        LARGE INTERNET PACKETS = OFF
        FIRST NETWORK DRIVE = F
        BIND RECONNECTION = ON
        AUTO RETRY = 10
        MESSAGE LEVEL = 3
        SIGNATURE LEVEL = 0
```

In this second example, user Ted is loading two protocol frame types, Ethernet_802.3 and Ethernet_802.2. Because of this, Ted needs to designate which protocol he wants

IPX to bind to, which in this case is Ethernet_802.3. If your network is only running one protocol frame type, don't load both frame types, for it adds to the size of the ODI driver.

The next significant change is that Ted turned Off the DOS Requester default loading list, so Ted needed to type in all the VLM modules he wanted to load. Ted then set the Auto Retry parameter to 10 second checking for network reconnection. He then set the Message Level to 3 so he can see how the NET.CFG parameters are loading with the DOS Requester.

Some versions of the DOS Requester will give you a warning that the AUTO.VLM is loading without the NDS.VLM module. However, this is just a warning message and can be ignored.

You can experiment loading the DOS Requester and the NET.CFG parameters by running the DOS Requester for a time, and then tweaking the NET.CFG parameters for performance or memory optimization, typing VLM /U <Enter> from the DOS Requester directory. Once the DOS Requester unloads, type VLM <Enter> and the new NET.CFG parameters will load with the DOS Requester.

If you still can't get the performance you are looking for, type VLM /MC <Enter> and load the DOS Requester into conventional memory. In conventional memory, the DOS Requester is as fast as or faster than the NetWare shell. However, you take about a 70KB memory hit when you load all of the DOS Requester into conventional memory. At that point, you'll have to weigh memory considerations versus performance considerations.

Other Performance Elements to Think About

386- and 486-based workstations can drastically improve performance over 286-based workstations by as much as 100% or more. Also, DX-based microprocessor chips can greatly improve performance over SX-based microprocessor chips.

Another performance element is the type of network interface board your workstation is running. Tests done by Compaq and others have shown that 286-based computers with 16-bit network interface boards can perform just as fast or faster than 386-based computers with 8-bit network interface boards. Network board drivers that support larger packet sizes can also show improved throughput.

Windows 3.1 runs much better with 4MB to 6MB of RAM, especially when running Windows-based applications. This also depends on how many applications you have open at one time. Also, caching programs such as Windows SMARTDRV or VDISK can help improve workstation performance.

As a final tip, store application overlay files at the workstation instead of on the server. This can improve application performance and cut down on network traffic.

Locally storing the temporary or backup files that the applications create can also cut down on network traffic. This is also true with Windows.

The NetWare Workstation and Memory Management

Workstations running DOS applications have five types of available memory. The first is conventional memory, or the first 640KB of available memory. The second type is Upper Memory Blocks (UMBs), or the memory between 640KB and 1024KB (1MB). The third type is the High Memory Area (HMA), an anomaly in programming that allows DOS to access the first 64KB of extended memory above the 1MB mark. Workstations may also have extended and expanded memory that lies above 1MB. Here's a brief explanation of each type of memory.

Conventional Memory. DOS-based workstations have 640KB of conventional memory for applications and TSRs. One example of a TSR is DOSEDIT.COM, which saves the commands you type in at the DOS prompt, so you can then use the up/down arrow keys to reselect and/or modify the commands. This can save you a lot of retyping when performing tedious tasks.

Other examples of TSRs are NetWare communication drivers (IPX.COM, or LSL.COM, network board driver, and IPXODI.COM) and the NetWare shell NETX.COM or the DOS Requester. Unless you use a memory manager, each program takes an amount of conventional memory to keep it resident. Sometimes when you have too many TSRs loaded, you won't have enough memory left to load certain applications.

Upper Memory Blocks (UMB). The upper memory block area is used to store BIOS information for video cards, network interface board adapters, and system ROM BIOS (Basic Input/Output). Upper memory blocks are broken into hexadecimal memory addresses, with each block segment containing 64KB of memory, as follows:

```
A000 - AFFF 640KB -  704KB
B000 - BFFF 704KB -  768KB
C000 - CFFF 768KB -  832KB
D000 - DFFF 832KB -  896KB
E000 - EFFF 896KB -  960KB
F000 - FFFF 960KB - 1024KB
```

However, each memory segment can be doled out in 4KB chunks. For example, B000 to B0FF is 4KB of memory, and B000 to B1FF is 8KB. (How small of a memory segment piece you can access depends on the memory manager you use.) Regardless of the system you have, chances are there are many holes in the upper memory area that can be made available to memory managers and to you. This added memory can amount to additional memory for placing TSRs out of conventional memory.

High Memory Area. The high memory area (HMA) is the first 64KB of extended memory, which is located above the 1MB address boundary (1024KB to 1088KB). The high memory area is unique because, through an XMM (extended memory manager), the area can be used by DOS applications in real mode rather than in extended mode.

HMA was discovered when adding the highest amount of memory (FFFF) in the register offset register and to the regular register. The end result is 64KB (minus 16 bytes) of extended memory that DOS can address. Those memory managers written to the Extended Memory Specification (XMS) make this area available to DOS programs. An example of a high memory manager is MS DOS's HIMEM.SYS.

Only one program can control A20 at a time, so programs and utilities placed in HMA must use it as much as possible. A good candidate for HMA is the DOS program itself, along with hard disk buffers.

Expanded Memory. Expanded memory is another means of working with upper memory blocks that lie between 640KB and 1MB. Back when 8086/8088 computers were lucky to have 640KB of memory, spreadsheets began to stretch their memory limits and were quickly running out of memory to work in. To provide additional memory to spreadsheets, Lotus, Intel, and Microsoft collaborated to define the LIM EMS (Expanded Memory Specification) board. The LIM 3.2 specification creates a window or a page frame in 64KB of upper memory in order to access memory on the LIM board. The 64KB page frame is broken into four 16KB pages of memory that must be contiguous within the upper memory. The LIM 3.2 specification meant that LIM boards could access up to 8MB of expanded memory.

With growing support from spreadsheets and CAD programs, LIM 3.2 became a standard. However, the 64KB of contiguous upper memory had been a problem for many machines, so the group created a new specification—LIM 4.0. The LIM 4.0 specification removes the 64KB contiguous page frame requirement and allows you to instead use 1 to 64 pages in 16KB page blocks. LIM 4.0 also allows for backfilling, which starts at 640KB and can use down to 256KB of conventional memory.

The Expanded memory manager (EMM) creates a 64KB area (also known as a page frame) in upper memory, which maps to the LIM board's memory. There the workstation can access up to 8MB (LIM 3.2) or 32MB (LIM 4.0) of expanded memory. The LIM board uses 16KB of physical page frames in upper memory to access its expanded memory banks. Each page frame can access multiple physical pages by first mapping the address of the frame to its expanded memory location and then swapping in the pages (in 16KB pages) as needed. LIM 4.0 also allows you to have more than one application running at the same time and also offers multitasking capabilities.

With 8086/8088 and most 80286 computers, you need both a LIM board and an Expanded Memory Manager to use expanded memory applications. With 80386 and 80486 computers, memory managers such as EMM386.EXE can convert the computer's extended memory into expanded memory. EMM386 allows you to run expanded memory programs without the need of a LIM board.

Since other devices such as video cards and LAN boards also use this area in high memory, you need to keep track of which boards you have installed and the memory address areas they occupy. If you have an addressing conflict with any of your installed boards, those boards will not work and will often hang the computer when two programs access the same memory address at the same time.

A simple example of setting up the expanded memory manager for MS DOS 5.0 and above includes the following in the CONFIG.SYS file:

```
DEVICE=C:\DOS\HIMEM.SYS
DEVICE=C:\DOS\EMM386.EXE RAM I=D000-EFFF
DOS=HIGH,UMB
```

In this example, the RAM parameter activates expanded memory and UMBs. The Include (I=) statement tells EMS to include the D000 to EFFF range for the EMS driver or RAM.

An example for DR-DOS 6.0 looks similar to the following:

```
DEVICE=C:\DRDOS\EMM386.SYS /F=D000 /B=FFFF /R=AUTO
HIBUFFERS=20
HIDOS=ON
```

Setting the /F(rame) parameter to AUTO allows the expanded memory manager to find and designate a 64KB window for EMS, and the D000 forces EMS to use allocate 64KB at that memory segment. (For more information about the different settings for EMM386.SYS, consult your DR-DOS manual.)

Extended Memory. Extended memory is what most 80286, 80386, and 80486 computers come with. Extended memory must be contiguous—there can be no holes in the memory extension. This memory begins at the 1024KB address and extends up to 16MB for 80286 computers, and 4GB for 80386 computers. Most computers come with

640KB of conventional memory and 384KB or 1408 extended memory, giving them 1MB or 2MB of RAM. Many computers now come with 4MB standard.

While DOS applications can only address 640KB, other programs extend DOS itself to take advantage of a workstation's extended memory, such as Windows 3.x and DESQview 286 and 386. These programs use an eXtended Memory Manager (XMM) which conforms to the Lotus/Intel/Microsoft AST extended memory specification (XMS) version 2.0. EMM386.EXE also conforms to XMS specifications, which allows you to select extended memory, expanded memory, or both, when calling on a memory manager program.

When you install an XMS driver, applications can allocate extended memory by making calls through the XMS driver. Extended memory becomes a large memory pool and use a dynamic allocation scheme for data. This allows the extended memory manager to release and reallocate memory as applications warrant.

An example of setting up the XMS memory manager for MS DOS 5.0 and above includes the following in the CONFIG.SYS:

```
DEVICE=C:\DOS\HIMEM.SYS
DEVICE=C:\DOS\EMM386.EXE NOEMS
DOS=HIGH,UMB
```

Briefly, the HIMEM.SYS file loads the extended memory manager, and the EMM386.EXE file allows you to use Upper Memory Blocks (UMBs) for loading TSRs between 640KB and 1,024KB. The NOEMS parameter prevents the expanded memory manager from loading. The DOS=HIGH command places the DOS kernel into the High Memory Area (HMA) above 1,024KB, and the DOS=UMB command activates UMBs for TSR placement, thereby making UMBs available for the DOS Requester.

For DR-DOS 6.0, your settings will look similar to the following:

```
DEVICE=C:\DRDOS\EMM386.SYS /F=NONE /K=3072 /B=FFFF /R=AUTO
HIDOS=ON
HIBUFFERS=20
```

Loading EMM386.SYS can set up the LIM memory manager for XMS (or EMS), but the /F(rame)=NONE parameter deactivates the expanded (EMS) memory manager. The EMM386.SYS file and the HIDOS=ON command allow you to load DOS into HMA, and the HIBUFFERS command loads buffers into HMA as well. Through the

EMM386.SYS command, the UMB area is activated for the DOS Requester. (For more information about the different settings for EMM386.SYS, consult your DR-DOS manual.)

Novell has written two NetWare shells that can run in expanded or extended memory. With the LIM board (if needed) and EMS driver in place, you simply copy the EMSNETX.EXE file, then add the line EMSNETX <Enter> instead of NETX <Enter> in the AUTOEXEC.BAT file:

```
COPY CON AUTOEXEC.BAT      <Enter>
PROMPT $P$G <Enter>
IPX <Enter>
EMSNET   <Enter>
F:  <Enter>
LOGIN ADMIN/TED ^Z   <Enter>
```

(The EMSNETX.EXE file is located on the WSGEN disk—you'll need to ask the supervisor for a copy of the file.) The only "gotchas" include your need to use DOS 3.x and above, to make sure the EMS driver is version 4.0 or greater, and the driver is in place before loading the shell. The EMSNETX shell can also use whatever parameters you designate in the NET.CFG file. Loading the NetWare shell into expanded memory gives you 33KB more memory for applications in conventional 640KB memory used by DOS. The EMSNETX file leaves about 7KB of the shell in conventional memory.

For those workstations that have extended memory, NetWare 3.11 comes with an extended memory shell. For those workstations that have extended memory, NetWare 3.11 comes with an extended memory shell. You'll need to copy the HIMEM.SYS and EMM386.EXE files. (You only use the EMM386.EXE file if you have a 386-based workstation.) Then, in your AUTOEXEC.BAT, type XMSNETX <Enter> in place of the NETX <Enter> command.

The XMSNETX.EXE file is located on the WSGEN disk; you'll need to ask the supervisor for a copy of the file. To avoid a frequently made error, use DOS 3.x and above and place the XMS memory manager in CONFIG.SYS before loading the shell. The XMSNETX shell can also use whatever parameters you designate in the NET.CFG file. Loading the NetWare shell into extended memory gives you 34KB more memory for applications in conventional 640KB memory used by DOS. The XMSNETX file leaves about 6KB of the shell in conventional memory.

The DOS Requester and Memory Management

The DOS Requester is unique in how it loads into the workstation's memory. The DOS Requester uses extended or expanded memory that is allocated by the XMS or EMS memory managers. You can use memory managers to load TSRs into the upper memory block (UMB) area between 640KB and 1,024KB, and to load DOS or a different TSR into the high memory (HMA) area between 1,024KB and 1,088KB. Without this designation, DOS and TSRs load into conventional memory.

The DOS Requester automatically detects if an XMS Memory Manager is installed and then asks the manager to allocate extended memory for VLM.EXE and its modules. The VLM footprint that stays in conventional memory can be as small as 4KB if you have XMS or EMS memory managers active and if you have enough UMBs available for loading VLM modules high. The DOS Requester allocates two blocks of memory in the UMB area: the transient swap block, and the global block.

VLM.EXE uses the transient swap block (about 8.5KB) to swap modules and data between conventional memory and extended or expanded memory. The global block is about 22KB in size and will also load into the upper memory area as space permits. If there are enough upper memory blocks to hold these two memory blocks, you will see about a 3.5KB VLM footprint in conventional memory. If there isn't, you'll see more of the DOS Requester in conventional memory.

The Windows Addition

Microsoft's Windows program adds another wrinkle to setting up workstations on the network. The main points to keep in mind are how much memory your workstation has, the workstation's CPU (80286, 80386, or 80486), and whether Windows is set up on the local C: or D: drive or run from a network drive. The gamut of issues involved in setting up Windows on NetWare could almost be a book unto itself. The subject has been covered in detail in Novell's *NetWare Application Notes*, January 1991, under the title "NetWare and Microsoft Windows Integration." For Windows 3.1, the subject is explained in Novell's Research Report called "Integrating NetWare and Windows 3.1." Those wishing to obtain a copy can call 1 (800) 377-4136.

With that said, here are four examples of Windows workstation environments set up using expanded and extended shells and ODI. The first example uses DOS 4.0 and Windows for the workstation environment. The second example uses DOS 5.0, ODI, and Windows. The third uses DOS 5.0, QEMM's memory manager, and Windows, for greater kilobyte size for its virtual windows. The fourth example uses MS DOS 6.0, ODI, the DOS Requester, and Windows. Here are the CONFIG.SYS and AUTOEXEC.BAT files for those examples:

Example 1
CONFIG.SYS:

```
BREAK=ON
BUFFERS=30
FILES=60
SHELL=C:\DOS\COMMAND.COM /P /E:1024
DEVICE=C:\DOS\ANSI.SYS
DEVICE=C:\WIN3\HIMEM.SYS
DEVICEHIGH=C:\WIN3\SMARTDRV.SYS 2048 512
LASTDRIVE=E
```

AUTOEXEC.BAT:

```
PROMPT $P$G
PATH=C:\DOS;C:\WIN3;C:\TOOLBOOK;C:\
SET TEMP=C:WIN3\TEMP
IPX
XMSNETX
F:
LOGIN
```

In the CONFIG.SYS: file of this first example, Windows is running locally on a Compaq 386. The "Buffers," and "Files" entries all reflect DOS environment settings with a few added for Windows. I discussed the Shell, ANSI.SYS., and LASTDRIVE earlier. The HIMEM.SYS and SMARTDRV.SYS devices were added by Windows 3.1's SETUP program. The HIMEM.SYS program allows you to make use of high memory for loading the XMSNETX file. The SMARTDRV.SYS file is a caching program, is Windows aware, and is used because Windows is running locally (the example shows its default settings). You don't need this file when Windows is running on a network drive, as the file can't cache network drives.

In the AUTOEXEC.BAT file, you see a local path to the C: drive and a temporary setting to the C:\WIN3\TEMP directory. The TEMP directory stores any temporary files that Windows needs to as it runs. Next, the AUTOEXEC file loads IPX, then the

XMSNETX file, into high memory. The user then goes to F: and receives a LOGIN prompt to log in to the network.

Example 2
CONFIG.SYS:

```
SHELL=C:DOS5\COMMAND.COM /E:2048
BUFFERS=32
FILES=60
STACKS=32,128
BREAK=ON
DEVICE=C:\DOS5\HIMEM.SYS
DEVICE=C:\DOS5\EMM386.EXE /NOEMS
DEVICEHIGH=C:\DOS5\SMARTDRV.SYS 2048 512
DOS=UMB, HIGH
LASTDRIVE=E
```

AUTOEXEC.BAT:

```
LOADHIGH C:\LSL.COM
LOADHIGH C:\NE2000.COM
LOADHIGH C:\IPXODI COM D
LOADHIGH C:\NETX.COM
F:
LOGIN LANLORD/VINCE IBM V20
```

In this second example, user Vince adds a STACKS entry to support data stacks in Windows. The first number in the entry shows the number of stacks and the second number shows the size of stacks. Vince next uses DOS 5.0's HIMEM, EMM386, and SMARTDRV files instead of similar Windows files, but both can do the same job. The /NOEMS parameter on the EMM386.EXE file has EMM386 manage the workstation's high memory area as extended memory. If you're running programs that need expanded memory instead of extended memory, you would use the /RAM parameter. The /RAM parameter also handles high memory and provides expanded memory simulation in extended memory.

Through using the DOS=UMB, HIGH command, DOS 5.0's COMMAND.COM is loaded into the high memory area (HMA). The UMB parameter (Upper Memory Blocks) activates the upper memory area between 640V and 1024KB.

In the AUTOEXEC.BAT file and through DOS 5.0's LOADHIGH utility, Vince places all his ODI files into high memory as well. The D parameter on the ODI.COM file gets rid of the diagnostic responder code inherent in IPXODI. While this move saves you 4KB of memory, on the other hand, diagnostic programs won't recognize the workstation as a node. If your workstation won't ever use SPX connections, you can use the A parameter on the IPXODI.COM file. The A parameter prevents SPX and the diagnostic responder from loading, giving you about an 8KB smaller IXP footprint. But if you use the A parameter, don't run RPRINTER on your workstation.

Example 3
CONFIG.SYS:

```
BUFFERS=30
FILES=60
DEVICE=QEMM386.SYS RAM /R:2 ST:M
DEVICE=LOADHI.SYS /R:2 ANSI.SYS
DOS=UMB, HIGH
```

AUTOEXEC.BAT:

```
LOADHI /R:2 MOUSE.COM
LOADHI /R:1 IPX
LOADHI /R:3 NETX
F:
LOGIN
```

This third example is interesting, for it uses Quarterdeck's Expanded Memory Manager 386 instead of Windows' or DOS's EMM386.SYS and HIMEM.SYS files. Since this particular example is an expanded memory setup, the /RAM parameter on the QEMM386.SYS file provides expanded memory simulation in high memory.

QEMM's LOADHI commands have added a /R:# parameter, representing the region of memory where a driver will best fit. QEMM's MANIFEST or DOS 5.0's MEM utilities can supply this placement information. Then after IPX and NET5 are loaded into high memory, you can have as much as 630KB for Windows.

Windows-Specific NET.CFG Parameters

When running Windows, set the following parameters in your NET.CFG for best performance:

```
SHOW DOTS=ON
FILE HANDLES = 60
ENVIRONMENT PAD = 512
SEARCH DIR FIRST = OFF
```

The Show Dots parameter defaults to OFF, but should be set to ON when running Windows. The option will return directory entries for current (.) and parent (..) directories. The File Handles parameter defaults to 40, but if you receive the message that no files are available or if you are having problems printing on the network from Windows, try a value of 60.

The Environment Pad allows you to extend additional environment space for applications using the set environment variables. There is no default, and 512 bytes is ample for most all DOS-based applications. The "Search Dir First" entry defaults to OFF, meaning the shell searches for files instead of directories first. If you want Windows to search for directories first, set this parameter to ON.

Example 4:
CONFIG.SYS

```
DEVICE=C:\DOS\SETVER.EXE
DEVICE=C:\DOS\HIMEM.SYS
DEVICE=C:\DOS\EMM386.EXE NOEMS HIGHSCAN WIN=F500-F7FF WIN=F200-F4FF
BUFFERS=30,0
FILES=80
DOS=UMB
LASTDRIVE=Z
FCBS=4,0
SHELL=C:\DOS\COMMAND.COM C:\DOS\ /E:800 /P
BREAK   = ON
STACKS=9,128
DEVICEHIGH=C:\DOS\ANSI.SYS
DOS=HIGH
DEVICEHIGH /L:1,44240 =C:\DOS\DBLSPACE.SYS
```

AUTOEXEC.BAT

```
LH /L:0;1,42384 /S C:\DOS\SMARTDRV C 1024
PATH C:\DOS;C:\WIN31;C:\UTIL;C:\;C:\NU
SET TEMP=C:\WIN31\TEMP
```

```
PROMPT $P$G
SET WPC=/NT-1/U-EAL/PS-Y:\APPS\WP51\SETUP
LH /L:1,56928 C:\DOS\MOUSE
LH /L:1,22688 C:\NWCLIENT\LSL
LH /L:1,21568 C:\NWCLIENT\NE2000
LH /L:1,30576 C:\NWCLIENT\IPXODI
LH DOSEDIT
C:\NWCLIENT\VLM
F:
LOGIN NTS/TED
```

In this example, user Ted is running MS DOS 6.0 and Windows 3.1. Ted used MS DOS's MEMMAKER program to place NetWare and other TSRs into upper memory. This included the DOUBLESPACE disk compressor. The /L: positions the different programs into areas where MEMMAKER had tested them to fit. This particular configuration gave Ted 592KB of conventional memory for Windows and DOS applications.

By running MEM /C in MS DOS 6.0, you can see how applications fit into all areas of workstation memory.

Modules using memory below 1 MB:

Name	Total		=	Conventional		+	Upper Memory	
MSDOS	19245	(19K)		19245	(19K)		0	(0K)
SETVER	832	(1K)		832	(1K)		0	(0K)
HIMEM	1168	(1K)		1168	(1K)		0	(0K)
EMM386	4144	(4K)		4144	(4K)		0	(0K)
COMMAND	2960	(3K)		2960	(3K)		0	(0K)
NE2000	5152	(5K)		5152	(5K)		0	(0K)
VLM	47728	(47K)		13184	(13K)		34544	(34K)
DOSEDIT	2176	(2K)		1984	(2K)		192	(0K)
ANSI	4240	(4K)		0	(0K)		4240	(4K)
DBLSPACE	44288	(43K)		0	(0K)		44288	(43K)
SMARTDRV	27280	(27K)		0	(0K)		27280	(27K)
MOUSE	17088	(17K)		0	(0K)		17088	(17K)
LSL	22448	(22K)		0	(0K)		22448	(22K)
IPXODI	16304	(16K)		0	(0K)		16304	(16K)
Free	607056	(593K)		606400	(592K)		656	(1K)

Memory Summary:

```
Type of Memory      Total       =      Used      +      Free
----------------    ------------------  ------------------  ------------------
Conventional        655360   (640K)     48960    (48K)   606400   (592K)
Upper               167040   (163K)    166384   (162K)      656     (1K)
Adapter RAM/ROM     131072   (128K)    131072   (128K)        0     (0K)
Extended (XMS)    20018048 (19549K)   1342336  (1311K) 18675712 (18238K)
----------------    ------------------  ------------------  ------------------
Total memory      20971520 (20480K)   1688752  (1649K) 19282768 (18831K)

Total under 1 MB    822400   (803K)    215344   (210K)   607056   (593K)

Largest executable program size        606112   (592K)
Largest free upper memory block           608     (1K)
MS DOS is resident in the high memory area.
```

Notice that VLM.EXE didn't all make it into UMBs, as well as the transient swap block.

Tips When Using Memory Managers

The following are a few pointers when dealing with memory managers, each of which is expanded upon next.

1. Create a working boot disk of your present workstation environment.

2. Use a batch file organizer.

3. Work for a number your applications can live with.

4. Load by order, and then experiment.

5. Understand that programs can expand when you change their settings.

6. Learn how to prevent the "Corrupt Packet" error message.

Create a bootable disk. Before making any changes to any settings, be sure to finish that boot disk we started earlier in this chapter. The boot disk should contain your present DOS environment settings so you can always boot your computer and fix any missteps. Once you format a disk with the /S parameter, perform an XCOPY of all files in your

C:\ root directory. If you are calling programs from other directories, include those directories and programs as well.

Use a batch file organizer. Such organizers include BOOT.EXE from Stephen C. Kick. BOOT is a shareware program that allows you to have multiple CONFIG.SYS and AUTOEXEC.BAT files in a BOOT.CFG file. You label each type of configuration, such as Local, NetWare Lite, NetWare 3.x, and so forth.

You then launch the program by typing BOOT in the directory where you store the program, or from the command line if you place the program's files in a PATH-specified directory. Once you type BOOT, the program displays a list of your configurations. Highlight the configuration you wish and press <Enter>.

BOOT now goes out and overwrites your current CONFIG.SYS and AUTOEXEC.BAT files with the ones for your chosen configuration. You then press the Ctrl+Alt+Del keys to start the program again with the new configuration, and you're on your way.

This procedure eliminates having numerous REMed out commands in your CONFIG.SYS or AUTOEXEC.BAT files as well as having a growing number of .BAK, .OLD, .NEW, etc., versions of these files.

Work for a number your applications can live with. When working with memory managers that come with DOS, you can fiddle with the order of loading TSRs for quite some time. A better approach is to get a conventional memory number your applications can live with. For example, some programs need up to 525KB to run their basic offerings, and the more memory you have above that number means the more program options you can use. If you are running Windows, you also have that overhead to figure into the equation (about 12-15KB). You'll also want the DOS windows to be as large as you can get them.

Once you choose a number, such as 560KB, set up a generic CONFIG.SYS and AUTOEXEC.BAT that will reach that number and live with that number. But remember, not all memory managers and workstation BIOS allocations are created equal when it comes to how many UMBs you have to work with. You can have as much as 186KB of UMB space to play with, and as little as 74KB.

Also, the workstation's type of hardware becomes important when figuring the amount of UMBs you have to work with. For example, CD-ROM drivers can take a chunk of UMBs for their configuration. IOMEGA's Bernoulli box also uses conventional memory or UMBs for its configuration. The type of video boards also take away from UMBs. But don't let this discourage you, for memory managers such as Quarterdeck's QEMM386 or Qualitas's 386MAX can handle these hardware differences quite well, giving you plenty of UMB support.

510

Load by order, and then experiment. Ordering how to best place TSRs into UMBs can get tricky and you can spend a lot of time fussing with the loading order. Here are a few rules to work from. For the CONFIG.SYS file using MS DOS 5.0 or 6.0, load HIMEM.SYS before EMM386.EXE, use DEVICEHIGH= after loading EMM386.EXE, use DOS=HIGH to load DOS into HMA, and use DOS=UMB to link UMBs to conventional memory. For AUTOEXEC.BAT files, load TSRs that can't unload before those that can, and load NetWare TSRs in proper order (IPX then NETX or ODI then VLM.EXE).

You can sometimes place smaller TSRs in conventional memory in order to load a larger TSR into UMBs. The amount of memory the two smaller TSRs take should be less than the larger TSR. This is where you can spend most of your time, and while it often becomes a challenge to get the most you can, don't lose sleep over a couple of kilobytes!

Understand that programs can expand when you change their settings. You can change settings in DOS, IPX or ODI, NETX, the DOS Requester, and others, and therefore change the size of these programs. You change DOS's size through Buffers, Files, Stacks, environment variables, and so on. IPX and ODI, TCP/IP, NETX, and the DOS Requester are all affected by the settings placed in the NET.CFG file, and can ultimately expand the size of each of these files. Also, each version of IPX or NETX is a little larger or smaller than its predecessors.

DOS's SMARTDRV, RAMDRIVE, and so forth, are affected by the size you set them up to be upon installation. And their memory sizes reflect those settings. Because of the dynamic nature of file configurations, you'll need to work with the numbers you see when you type MEM /C <Enter> at the network prompt. Your workstations may show very different numbers.

Learn how to prevent the "Corrupt Packet" error message. Sometimes you'll get a "Corrupt Packet" error message if you have more than 609KB or conventional memory. Certain programs use a compiler that looks for a program to be loaded in the first 40KB of conventional memory. When they don't find one there, they return a "Packet was Corrupted" message and won't load.

You can easily alleviate this problem by not loading one of the workstation's programs that is larger than 20KB, such as NETX. Loading NETX in conventional memory drops the memory to around 590KB. I have personally found the problem goes away at about 607KB, but you may wish to experiment to see where your workstations work best. If you are using MS DOS, you can also type the prefix LOADFIX before the program name. For example, to load WordPerfect's Personal Editor into 617KB of memory, you can type LOADFIX PE <Enter> at the network prompt. You can also place the LOADFIX prefix in the command line statement when Windows calls DOS applications.

Troubleshooting Your Workstation

Few things are more disheartening than to have a workstation hang in the middle of a big project. When this happens, you want to get your workstation back up and running as quickly as possible. With this in mind, here's a quick checklist to help you see where to start:

➤ How many workstations are affected?

➤ Are you using anything different, such as a new shell version or memory manager, a new workstation, a new application, or a new server?

➤ Are there any error messages displayed on your monitor?

➤ Can your workstation boot DOS?

➤ Can your workstation load the NetWare shell?

➤ Are the people between you and the server still working? The people after you?

➤ How is your workstation cabled to the server?

➤ Is your workstation using a bridge to get to the server and, if so, can the server communicate with the bridge?

When your workstation hangs, first determine if yours is the only one having trouble or if other workstations are hung, too. (The simplest way to find out is to yell, "Is anyone else having workstation problems?") When more than one workstation stops communicating with the server, the problem is most likely with either the cabling system or the server. So, if several workstations go down at once, catch up on your paperwork and let your supervisor tackle the problem because there's not much you can do at a workstation level.

Error messages can also give you a starting point to work from. (The error messages that your workstation shell and IPX can issue are listed at the end of this chapter.) For example, an error message like, "Network Error on Server PUB: Error writing to network. Abort or Retry?" tells you that the NetWare shell was unable to complete your last request to the server.

But error messages don't always clarify the source of the problem. The problem could lie in the physical cable connection; if you're given the choice to abort or retry, press <R> a couple of times to retry sending the last request. If processing doesn't resume after several retries, the communications channel and your data have been lost, and all you can do is reboot.

With NetWare 3.12 you can use the automatic reconnection capabilities of the DOS Requester to reconnect for you. As downed servers become available again, the AUTO.VLM module reconnects to the server and then rebuilds the user's environment, including connection status, drive mappings, and printer connections. But if it can't reconnect after a fashion, you can then try rebooting.

There are many different reasons for a workstation to hang. Sometimes a program gets confused—one program pointer says you should be here in the document, while another pointer says you should be somewhere else. Whenever your own workstation is the only one affected and no error message appears on your screen, try rebooting. Rebooting flushes out your workstation's memory and rebuilds your workstation environment. You may also try turning your computer off, waiting a few seconds, and then turning it back on again. If, after rebooting, you can reestablish your connection with the server, go to the same application and see if your workstation hangs again at the same point. There may be a glitch in the software that you need to report to your supervisor.

Some word processing and desktop publishing programs don't handle excessively large files very well, especially when the files contain a lot of graphics. So, if your particular application keeps hanging or bringing you to one part of the file when you want to be in another part of the file, try splitting the data files in half and see if things work any better. (Of course, splitting data files in half is not a feasible option when you're working with large imaging files.)

Checking Cabling

If rebooting doesn't help, the next step is to check your cabling. Make sure you haven't accidentally pulled out the power plug or network cable. Disconnect your cable from the network interface board and then reconnect the cable. When your workstation cable connects to a network connector such as an active hub, passive hub, transceiver, or bridge, be sure to check your connection to such devices. If you connect to the server through a bridge, check the cabling from your workstation to the bridge and from the bridge to the server. Also, make sure the bridge is still running. (Bridges can hang occasionally, just like workstations.)

Another problem to look for is damage to the cable connection to your network interface board caused by shoving your workstation against the wall. Be careful with your network cables. If your cables are located where you or your fellow employees can walk or trip over them, get those cables out of the traffic path. Finally, make sure your network interface board is firmly seated in your workstation (you have to open the computer to do this). Then try rebooting.

Loading DOS and the NetWare Programs

If you can't reestablish your network connection, try loading just DOS at your workstation. This will let you know whether or not the workstation can boot up and load DOS as a stand-alone station. Place a DOS disk that contains the system files (COMMAND.COM and two hidden files) in drive A: and turn your workstation off. Wait a few seconds, then turn your workstation back on.

Your workstation will run a self-test of the hardware the ROM BIOS says is present. Sometimes computers beep when the self-test completes. One beep means everything is okay; two beeps means the BIOS is having problems communicating with one of the components. The IBM PC/AT, PS/2, and most compatibles will display an error message indicating the configuration error. If your workstation has a hardware problem or can't load DOS, inform your supervisor and explain what you've done so far. But here are some hardware points you can look at:

➤ Make sure you're plugged in. Don't laugh; it's a common mistake. Check the power cord connection between the back of the workstation and the wall socket, as well as the monitor power cable and/or connection cable.

➤ Don't push your workstation tightly against the wall, as this can damage connection cords or the network interface cables.

➤ Listen for the fan. If the fan doesn't work, you may have a power problem within the workstation, a faulty power cable, or a faulty socket.

➤ If the monitor light is on but you have no picture, be sure the monitor's brightness and contrast knobs are not simply turned down.

➤ See if the computer goes through its internal RAM and ROM testing procedures. You'll often see a memory check in the upper left-hand corner of the screen (if the screen is working) as the workstation is booting up. Most computers display an error message when there's a configuration error.

➤ Faulty power can knock out the CMOS RAM storage area that contains workstation setup parameters. If messages (such as memory, CMOS, or drive errors) appear on the screen when you first turn on the workstation, you may need to run SETUP or contact your supervisor.

514

➤ Check the keyboard connection for possible problems. Type a few characters to see if they appear on the screen. (Be sure the screen is working first.) Be sure the keyboard isn't locked through a hardware key or loaded software. If nothing happens when you type on the keyboard, connect a different keyboard and try typing on that keyboard. Some AT-type keyboards don't have extended or expanded keyboard BIOS capabilities and therefore don't work with the newer 286- and 386-based computers.

➤ Be sure the hard drive or drive A: light comes on when the workstation performs its internal testing. If it doesn't, place a disk in drive A: and type DIR <Enter> to see if the drive light comes on, or transfer to the hard disk drive (usually by typing C:) and type DIR <Enter>. Bad controller boards often leave the disk light on all the time.

If your workstation can load DOS, see if you can load IPX or ODI and the NetWare shell or the DOS Requester by typing IPX <Enter> or LSL, network board driver, IPXODI, then NETX <Enter> or VLM. If IPX doesn't load successfully, it may mean that IPX can't communicate with your network interface board. This often happens when the IPX file has been configured to different hardware interrupt settings than the settings currently on the network interface board. You'll often see an accompanying error message. You may need to replace your NetWare files or the network interface board.

With ODI, make sure the network board settings in the NET.CFG file match the board's actual settings. You will usually see an error message if they don't.

Before replacing the board, however, try using the new boot disk you've been building to see if it works, or try your boot disk in someone else's machine. You can also borrow a boot disk from someone who's using the same network interface board. However, make sure the IPX file matches the same board type and interrupt settings as your network interface board; otherwise, it won't work. But if the workstation comes up, you simply need a new boot disk.

You may receive the error message, "A File Server could not be found" when you reboot. This error message means that IPX and the shell have successfully loaded, but the shell is having problems communicating with the server. If everyone is running but you, this error message means you probably have a cabling or local hardware problem.

If your workstation still can't load IPX or the shell, try replacing your network interface board. Be sure to set the replacement board to the same configuration settings as the board you pull out. You'll only compound the problem if you don't use the same configuration settings, because your old IPX.COM file won't work with different hardware settings. Using different settings only makes the task of pinpointing the problem more difficult. Here's where ODI becomes easier, for changing the board settings is a matter of changing the board's configuration lines in the NET.CFG file. Place the NET.CFG file in the directory where you store your ODI files to make sure NetWare can find that file when it brings up ODI.

By replacing the board at this point, you'll either fix the problem, or at least narrow the field a bit. If a new board and new shell files don't help, try relocating the network interface board in a different slot. If that doesn't help, try replacing the cable (if possible) from your workstation connection to the next network connector, such as an active or passive hub, or a bridge.

Sometimes you'll find that a combination of things will lead to the final solution. So be thorough and go step by step until the problem is solved.

By now, if you still can't get your workstation running again, and you've checked 90% of your potential workstation problems, then it's safe to conclude you're in the realm of the system supervisor. Explain to your supervisor what you've done so far and go do some paperwork. You've done all you can.

Other Helpful Troubleshooting Hints

Here are some helpful hints to assist you in solving workstation problems.

Create a backup boot disk that contains at least the DOS system files (COMMAND.COM and the hidden files), IPX.COM (or ODI) and NETX.COM (or VLM.EXE). (An AUTOEXEC.BAT file is optional.) This backup disk can save you time when troubleshooting your workstation.

While your workstation is running, create a list of the DOS version, network board type, network board configuration settings, and station (node) address for your workstation. You can most easily do this by typing NVER >LPT1 <Enter> for all but the station address information. For that, you'll need to type USERLIST /A <Enter>. These handy references can be real time-savers when you need to replace the network board.

Write the board type and station address on a removable label on the outside of each network board's mounting bracket. This way you won't have to open your machine unnecessarily if you lose your workstation list.

Create a boot disk that has only DOS on it. This disk can have a very generic CONFIG.SYS file that doesn't load any device drivers or other batch files on it (especially an AUTOEXEC.BAT file). This disk will come in handy when you need to load DOS without any other programs.

Workstation Theory of Operations

I'm including this brief theory of operations to help you better understand and interpret the error messages listed in the next chapter. It explains how your workstation communicates with the network and with the DOS and NetWare environments.

Your workstation communicates with the server through two memory-resident programs: IPX.COM (or ODI) and NETX.COM (or VLM.EXE). These two files are often collectively referred to as the NetWare shell, although technically only the DOS Requester or NETX.COM contains the workstation shell program. IPX or ODI loads a communication language, called the Internetwork Packet eXchange (IPX) protocol, which NetWare uses to communicate with the network.

The NETX.COM or VLM.EXE file contains the software necessary to establish a packet sending-and-receiving relationship between your workstation and the server via IPX. The WSGEN program links a driver that is written specifically for your type of network board with the IPX.COM file. In WSGEN, you match the actual interrupt settings on the network interface board to the driver option that matches those settings. The board driver uses these interrupts to communicate with the workstation's CPU when it needs some CPU time to send and receive information through the network board.

The driver builds the network packet using IPX to send and receive its requests and replies. With IPX, requests are broadcast over the network cabling to the network.

ODI works the same way, only you load the communications files in three pieces— LSL, the network board driver such as NE1000 or NE2000, and IPXODI. Instead of "hard coding" the network board interrupt settings into IPX, ODI lets you set the board's interrupt settings through the NET.CFG file.

Once this communication relationship is established, your workstation can make requests to, and receive replies from, the server. The first task the NetWare shell or the DOS Requester performs after IPX is loaded is to issue a "Get Nearest Server" broadcast request. The first server to answer the broadcast with a "Give Nearest Server" reply will be the server the shell talks to as it initially loads.

If the server you want to log in to doesn't answer the initial "Get Nearest Server" broadcast, you'll see on the screen that you're attached to a different server than the one you wanted. This is perfectly normal. Because the attachment depends on which server answers the shell's request first, you might get attached to a different server each time you cold boot (turn off your workstation) or warm boot (press <Ctrl>-<Alt>-<Del> simultaneously). However, you can place a "Preferred Server" request in the NET.CFG file to ensure that you will always attach to the server you initially log in to. (See the "NET.CFG Parameters for NetWare 3.11" heading earlier in this chapter.)

By not using the preferred server method, once the NetWare shell is attached to a server, you can log in to any server that the attached server can talk to. You can see a list of these servers by typing SLIST <Enter> at the network prompt. When you type a login command, such as LOGIN NTS3/TED <Enter>, the shell first looks into the bindery of the attached server to see if the requested server exists. The shell then issues a "Get Local Target" call to establish a connection with the targeted server.

If you're physically connected to the server you want to log in to, the shell connection will be immediately passed back to that server and every subsequent NetWare request will be answered directly. You have not only a physical (cabling) connection, but a logical (shell) connection as well. If the server you're logging in to isn't on the same network as the one you're physically attached to, the shell sends a broadcast via IPX which says, in effect, "I'm trying to talk to this network; can you help me get there?" The server or bridge that has the best route to the requested server will become the designated path that the workstation uses during this connection. In this case, the NetWare shell has only a logical (shell) connection to the desired server.

The NetWare shell acts as a request sorter. When a workstation makes a request, the shell determines whether DOS or NetWare should respond to the request. For instance, the NetWare shell looks at the requests coming in to it to see if the request belongs to a network drive or a local drive. If it's a server request, the shell translates the request into a NetWare Core Protocol (NCP) request packet and sends it to the designated server. The targeted server processes the request and sends the reply back to the workstation.

If the request the shell receives belongs to a local drive, the shell hands the request to DOS's command processor for processing. In this way, DOS takes care of DOS calls, and NetWare takes care of NetWare cas.

CHAPTER 6

Workstation Error Messages

When you receive an error message on your screen, it's possible the message has come from IPX or the NetWare shell. This chapter lists error messages you can receive from IPX and the NetWare shell that apply directly to your workstation environment. These messages are listed in alphabetical order, followed by the page number of this book where you can find the message itself and its explanation. These messages are followed by those that appear in the ODI files under the "IPXODI Additions" and "LSL Additions" headings. The last messages show what you see when using the DOS Requester's diagnostics capabilities.

Error during MAP MULTIPLE PAGES
    **EMM Error: <number> during EMM function <number> — page 526

Error during MOVE MEMORY REGION
    **EMM Error: <number> during EMM function <number> — page 526

Error unloading NetWare shell —<error> — page 527

Expanded Memory Manager is not v4.0 or better. Cannot continue initialization — page 528

Expanded memory used has been released — page 528

Extended Memory Manager is not v2.0 or better. Cannot continue initialization — page 528

File Server has no free connection slots — page 529

Hardware Configuration: IPX/SPX already loaded — page 529

High Memory Area (HMA) does not exist. Cannot continue initialization — page 529

High Memory Area (HMA) has been released — page 530

Invalid Parameter. Use "I" option to query shell type, or use the "U" option to unload the shell from memory — page 531

IPX has not been loaded. Please load and then run the shell — page 531

Memory for resident shell has been released — page 532

Net Driver Crash: <driver error message> — page 532

NetWare Workstation Shell has already been loaded — page 533

Network Error: <error> during <operation>.
File<drive>:<filename> — page 533

Network Error on Server <*servername*>:<*error*> — page 538

Network Spooler Error: (probably out of space on SYS: volume) — page 541

No Expanded Memory Manager present. Cannot continue initialization — page 541

No Extended Memory Manager present. Cannot continue initialization — page 542

Not enough pages of expanded memory for installation — page 542

Not running on top of DOS version 2.x — page 542

Not running on top of DOS version 3.x — page 543

Not running on top of DOS version 4.x — page 543

PIPE not found in resident portion of COMMAND.COM — page 543

Program Aborted — page 544

Shell error: No active File Server attachments — page 544

The Network is inactive or you are not connected properly — page 544

Too many devices defined in DOS (over approx 32). Device Table Overflow — page 545

Warning: disk write error in file <*filename*> — page 545

Warning: Byte value greater than 255 was truncated — page 546

XMS Error during Free High Memory Area — page 546

**XMS Shell Error:<*cause*> — page 546

You are being logged out of all servers — page 547

You are not connected to any file servers. The shell will try to connect to a file server whenever the current default drive is changed to an invalid drive — page 547

Now we'll examine each of these error messages in more detail. You'll receive a brief explanation under each message of why you received this message and possible solutions. Sometimes a message is actually several messages in one; look carefully at each part of the message to better understand what's causing the error.

A File Server could not be found.

Problem.

You've loaded IPX and the NetWare shell or DOS Requester, but the shell can't find a server to attach to. This might mean you have a poor cable connection to the server. Or the hardware settings on your network interface board don't match the configuration used in WSGEN to generate the LAN driver. In this case, the shell can't even communicate with your network board and concludes there aren't any servers out there to connect to.

Solution.

Make sure your IPX.COM file or the NET.CFG for ODI are properly configured to the hardware configuration settings on your network interface board. Also make sure that IPX was linked with the correct LAN driver in WSGEN. Check your cabling to make sure you have a firm connection between the cable and the board. Check your connection to any active or passive hub, terminator, or bridge. See if anyone else is having the same problem. If so, the problem is most likely not something in your workstation.

(CTRL-ENTER to clear)

Problem.

You've received a message from another person through the SEND command, from the supervisor through the BROADCAST command, or from NetWare itself through the BROADCAST command. This message appears at the bottom of your screen (line 25).

Solution.

To get rid of the message, press the <Ctrl> and <Enter> keys simultaneously. If you want to prevent your workstation from receiving any further messages, run the CASTOFF utility. (See the "CASTOFF" subheading in Chapter 3.)

Could not route to File Server.

Problem.

The workstation is trying to connect to a file server, but the connection request can't be routed properly to the specified server. In this instance, the file server may not be running. Or, as the request is passed through a router, the router's routing table may be too corrupted to properly send the request.

Solution.

First see if the file server is up and running by typing SLIST *servername* <Enter> at the network prompt to see if the file server is listed. This is more a server or bridge problem, and the supervisor can run RESET ROUTER on the bridge to rebuild the routing tables once the file server is up and running. Or through the natural course of router updates, the routing tables will add the file server again and you can log in.

EMM Error during DEALLOCATE PAGES.

Problem.

This error message is specific to the expanded memory manager (EMM) you're running. You get this error when the file handle used to deallocate the EMS becomes corrupt or is already corrupt, or if for some reason the EMM driver can't properly give back the memory used to create the memory pages. You can also get this error if you've unloaded and reloaded a new copy of the NetWare shell.

Solution.

The first two problems are vendor-specific; you'll need to check the vendor's documentation for possible solutions. For the last cause, just be sure to use the same copy of the NetWare shell to load and unload the shell itself. (This includes version, revision, and file size.)

523

`**EMM Shell Error: <number> during EMM function <number>`

Problem.

When you use the EMSNETX file and load most of the NetWare shell into expanded memory, the shell relies on the expanded memory driver for swapping memory pages in and out of expanded memory. The message tells you the NetWare shell received an error from the EMM driver when the shell tried to do something.

Solution.

The error messages are vendor-specific; you'll need to check the vendor's documentation for possible solutions. You may wish to first reinstall the memory manager, then the EMSNETX file. If the problem persists, write down the numbers you see, then get your supervisor to call the vendor, or Novell, or both.

`Entry Stack Size too small.`

Problem.

When the expanded memory shell receives another shell request while it's busy doing something else, the shell must save the memory page mappings it's busy with. If the entry stack size is too small, the shell runs out of room while saving the page mappings and you see this message.

Solution.

Use the Entry Stack parameter in the NET.CFG file, which allows the workstation to configure the internal page mapping stack size that the shell will use. The stack size can be 5 to 40, and defaults to 10. If you see the message "Entry stack size too small," increment the default value by five or ten and try it again until the error goes away.

`Error allocating Hi Memory Area (HMA): <cause>.`

You see this message when the extended memory shell has problems allocating some high memory space for its use. The cause part of the message shows what the shell was trying to do but couldn't. Each cause in the list has a probable solution to follow.

Cause 1—"HMA already in use." You'll see this message when another program is already using your computer's 64KB of high memory area, such as DOS if you have DOS = High in the CONFIG.SYS file. If you want to use the high memory for running the XMSNETX shell, you'll first need to unload whichever program is presently there.

Cause 2—"unknown error code." This isn't a good message to get, because it means that the extended memory driver didn't return an error code that the XMS shell could interpret. About the best thing you can do is reinstall the XMS driver and try again. If the problem persists, call the XMS driver vendor.

Cause 3—"VDisk detected." You'll see this message when the XMS driver (usually Microsoft's version 2.0 HIMEM.SYS file) finds that VDISK.SYS or RAMDISK.SYS is currently taking up the high memory area space. There have been problems with using IBM's VDISK.SYS with Microsoft's 2.0 XMS driver, so you'll either have to use different XMS drivers or different virtual disk drivers if you want to use both of them. Otherwise, don't use the virtual disk option.

Cause 4—"XMS driver /HMAMIN=parameter too high." If the minimum usage parameter overshoots the high memory area, you'll see this message. You should not see this message, but if you do, you'll need to reduce the parameter so it functions within the high memory region.

```
Error during ALLOCATE PAGES
**EMM Error: <number> during EMM function <number>.
```

Problem.

You see this error when the expanded memory shell has problems allocating expanded memory pages for its use. Instead of allocating pages to the shell's memory page request, the EMM gave the error numbers you're looking at.

Solution.

The error messages are vendor-specific; you'll need to check the vendor's documentation for possible solutions. You may wish to first reinstall the memory manager, then the EMSNETX file, and see if the problem goes away. But if the problem persists, write down the numbers you see in the error message, then get your supervisor to call the vendor, or Novell, or both.

525

```
Error during GET SIZE OF PARTIAL PAGE
**EMM Error: <number> during EMM function <number>.
```

Problem.

The expanded memory manager gave this error message when the expanded memory shell tried to allocate memory for the page-swapping array.

Solution.

The error messages are vendor-specific; check the vendor's documentation for possible solutions. You may wish to first reinstall the memory manager, then the EMSNETX file, and see if the problem goes away. But if the problem persists, write down the numbers you see in the error message, then get your supervisor to call the vendor, or Novell, or both.

```
Error during MAP MULTIPLE PAGES
**EMM Error: <number> during EMM function <number>.
```

Problem.

The expanded memory manager can't allocate the necessary memory pages into the expanded memory page frame when the expanded memory shell initializes.

Solution.

The error messages are vendor-specific; check the vendor's documentation for possible solutions. You may wish to first reinstall the memory manager, then the EMSNETX file, and see if the problem goes away. But if the problem persists, write down the numbers you see in the error message, then get your supervisor to call the vendor, or Novell, or both.

```
Error during MOVE MEMORY REGION
**EMM Error: <number> during EMM function <number>
```

Problem.

The expanded memory manager can't move the NetWare shell's data request to expanded memory. The NetWare shell moves to expanded memory so you have more conventional memory to work.

Solution.

The error messages are vendor-specific; check the vendor's documentation for possible solutions. You may wish to first reinstall the memory manager, then the EMSNETX file, and see if the problem goes away. But if the problem persists, write down the numbers you see in the error message, then get your supervisor to call the vendor, or Novell, or both.

```
Error unloading NetWare shell —<error>.
```

Problem.

With NetWare 3.11, you can use the /U or /F parameter to unload the NetWare shell from the workstation's memory (the /F parameter forces unloading to occur). While this isn't a common practice (since you lose your connection to the file servers you're attached to), it's an available option that you should use only when you have to. The error part of the message shows what stopped the shell from unloading. Each error in the list has a probable solution to follow.

Error 1—"CRITICAL—error freeing shell memory." You see this message when DOS flakes out and can't free the memory where the shell used to reside. When this happens, you'll need to reboot the workstation.

Error 2—"Different NetWare shell or a NetWare shell interrupt has been hooked." When you go to a directory other than the one that stored the shell you initially loaded, you'll see the different shell message. This can happen if you boot from a floppy disk, but go to a directory containing a different shell copy (either version, revision, or size difference) and use the "/U" option. Simply make sure you unload the shell with the same shell you used when you initially booted.

The shell interrupt problem occurs when a TSR is loaded after the NetWare shell and also uses an interrupt the shell uses. This causes the interrupt to be hooked. You'll have to unload the TSR through a TSR load/unload program before unloading the NetWare shell. Or simply reboot the workstation.

Error 3—"NetWare shell not loaded." You can't unload the shell simply because the shell hasn't yet been loaded (is not found in memory).

Error 4—"The shell indicates it can't be unloaded." When a program uses the same interrupts as the NetWare shell and hooks into the shell itself, you'll need to reboot the workstation to untangle the two. Be sure to save any data work you can before rebooting.

Error 5—"There's a problem with DOS's management of the Memory Control Blocks for the shell." All you can do is reboot the workstation.

Error 6—"A TSR is loaded above the load shell." With a TSR program in place above the shell, you'll need to unload the TSR before unloading the shell TSR. Otherwise, you'll create an unstable environment as well as memory hole. If you can't unload the TSR, reboot the workstation.

```
Expanded Memory Manager is not v4.0 or better. Cannot continue
initialization.
```

Problem.

You see this when LIM/EMM (Lotus/Intel/Microsoft expanded memory manager) doesn't support this version of the EMS driver, or you're not using version LIM/EMS 4.0 or greater.

Solution.

Make sure that you're using LIM/EMS 4.0 or greater, or make sure that the EMM driver supports this driver.

```
Expanded memory used has been released.
```

Problem.

This is simply a message you see if the expanded memory used by the resident expanded memory shell is successful when it unloads from memory. Since this is a message, there is no solution.

```
Extended Memory Manager is not v2.0 or better. Cannot continue
initialization.
```

Problem.

You see this when the extended memory manager doesn't support the specifications for version 2.0 or above.

528

Solution.

Make sure you're using an XMS driver that does support 2.0 or greater.

`File Server has no free connection slots.`

Problem.

The connection table to the server you want to attach to is full. Servers can handle up to 100 simultaneous connections from users and other servers and bridges. When all of these connections are in use, you won't be allowed to establish a connection with this server.

Solution.

Wait until someone logs out from the server or until the server dispenses with an old connection that hasn't responded to the server's queries for fifteen minutes. Then, as a connection becomes available, you'll be able to attach to the designated server.

`Hardware Configuration: IPX/SPX already loaded.`

Problem.

If you've already loaded IPX (which loads SPX at the same time) and then try to reload IPX, you'll see this message. IPX prevents itself from being loaded more than once on a workstation.

Solution.

With IPX loaded, you can load the NetWare shell and log in to a designated server. If you want to load a different IPX.COM file, you'll have to reboot your workstation.

`Hi Memory Area (HMA) does not exist. Cannot continue`
`initialization.`

Problem.

You see this message when the XMS driver can't find any extended memory starting at the 1MB boundary. Extended memory goes from the address where memory ends in the workstation and extends into fields above DOS's 1MB (1024KB) limit. Another 64KB of memory, beginning directly at

529

1024KB, is known as the high memory area; this memory is addressable from real mode as well. This is what the XMS drive is using.

DOS's 1MB memory addressing limit is broken into two types: 640KB (known as main or RAM memory), which applications and utilities use, and 384KB (known as reserved memory or upper memory blocks), which the DOS operating system uses to store the addresses for its hardware drivers, monitor cards, LAN boards, and other devices.

Since applications can address only 640KB in DOS, most PC and XT computers have a 640KB maximum; many have only 512KB of memory. (DOS reserved memory will work within the workstation's RAM constraints.) But with the advent of the 80286-based AT computers, hardware technology expanded beyond the 640KB limit to 16MB. And with 80386-based computers, users can (theoretically) access up to 4GB (gigabytes) of physical memory.

When adding memory to a workstation, be sure the memory board begins its addressing at the point where the workstation ends its memory (not including DOS's reserved memory). For example, If a workstation has 512KB you would have to make sure the memory board began at 513K.

Solution.

Make sure that you have extended memory and that it has no memory holes. When getting additional memory, determine where the computer begins extended memory addressing and make sure the memory board you wish to purchase can begin at that address. Or place the memory on the workstation's system board. Be sure to match the speed and size of memory chips to what the workstation presently has. Otherwise, change out all workstation's memory to one size and speed.

Many memory boards, however, have configurable memory that you can set through hardware jumpers or software. These boards allow more flexibility.

```
High Memory Area (HMA) has been released.
```

Problem.

This is simply a message you see if the extended memory used by the resident extended memory shell is successful when it unloads from memory.

Solution.

Since this is a message, there is no solution.

```
Invalid Parameter. Use "I" option to query shell type, or use
the "U" option to unload the shell from memory.
```

Problem.

You have typed in the NETX command with extra characters after the command. Or you have queried the NetWare shell for its version type and added a parameter other than "I" or "U."

Solution.

When you type the NetWare shell name to load the shell, don't add any parameters in the syntax other than the parameters supported by NETX. To query the shell for its version, type NETX I <Enter> in the directory where NETX.COM is located. Use the U or F to unload the shell from memory. Use ? to see what options are available to you.

Use PS=*servername* to signify an attachment to a preferred server. You can also use the C=[path\]*<filename.ext>* to type in where your NET.CFG or SHELL.CFG or whatever name you gave the configuration file. Be sure you use conventions and parameters that the shell will understand. (The C= parameter is primarily for MSDOS 3.x to 5.0.)

```
IPX has not been loaded. Please load and then run the shell.
```

Problem.

You tried to load the NetWare shell (NETX.COM) without first loading IPX.

Solution.

Load IPX first, then load the NetWare shell.

```
Memory for resident shell has been released.
```

Problem.

This is simply a message you see if the normal NetWare shell has been successful when unloading from the workstation's memory. Since this is a message, there is no solution.

```
Net Driver Crash: <driver error message>
```

Problem.

The LAN driver linked to the NetWare shell has a critical problem that produces an ABEND (ABnormal END) condition. This condition occurs whenever further problems to the system would develop if the driver were to keep going in its present condition. These error messages are always "fatal," and will always prevent you from accessing the server. You receive this error message only if you're having a hardware problem with the network interface board or cabling, or if you're having workstation memory problems.

Solution.

Look at the driver error message to see if it gives any indication of the cause of the problem. Write down the exact text of the message and always report it to your supervisor, even if it only happens once or if you fix it yourself.

Each driver will have different error messages, and they vary with each type of network interface board. Since there are over seventeen different brands of boards (and over 115 types of boards), listing them all would be arduous. As an example, though, here are the driver error messages that you can receive for the NE/2000 Ethernet board:

```
NE/2 is hung
```

```
NE/2 Failed Reset
```

Try to reboot your workstation. If the problem repeats, make sure that your IPX file is properly configured for the configuration settings you have on your network interface board, and that it was linked with the appropriate LAN driver in WSGEN. If you are running ODI, make sure the settings in the NET.CFG file match the network board settings. Also, make sure the NET.CFG file is in the same directory as the ODI files. You might also check to see if someone else left a boot disk in your machine; if another user has different board settings or a different board type (Ethernet vs. Arcnet), that person's boot disk won't work in your machine.

`NetWare Workstation Shell has already been loaded.`

Problem.

You've already loaded the NetWare shell (NETX.COM file) and then you've tried to reload NETX. The NetWare shell prevents itself from being loaded more than once on a workstation.

Solution.

Once the NetWare shell is loaded, you can log in to a designated server. If you want to load a different NETX.COM file, you'll have to reboot your workstation.

`Network Error: <error> during <operation>. File =`
`<drive>:<filename> Abort, Retry? or Abort, Retry, Fail?`

Problem.

Your workstation shell is trying to perform an operation, but can't because of an error received during the operation. Since many DOS function calls can create this error message, the message can mean anything from problems in your server setup and operation to problems with the applications you're running.

The *<drive>*:< > tells you which file on which drive is causing the error. When you see the PUBLIC: drive specified, that means the file is located on a search drive.

Solution.

Try pressing the R key to see if the retry will work. If it doesn't, write down the information displayed in the error message and pass that information on to your network supervisor. Most likely, you will have to abort or reboot to get out of your present predicament.

With NetWare 3.12 you can use the automatic reconnection capabilities of the DOS Requester to reconnect for you. As downed servers become available again, the AUTO.VLM module reconnects to the server and then rebuilds the user's environment, including connection status, drive mappings, and printer connections. But if it can't reconnect after a fashion, you can then try rebooting.

<error>: The following messages could appear in the *<error>* portion of the message.

A "Bad Directory Handle" error message usually means you have an internal error problem, probably a memory error.

You see the "Bad Local Network Address" message when the network address in the request packet is invalid or no longer valid because the server or bridge is down. If the server or bridge is up, the supervisor can type RESET ROUTERS on the server or bridge console to help them build more up-to-date router tables.

An application locks, uses, and unlocks a file; sometimes it tries to use the file again without going through the same locking and unlocking procedure. When this happens, you might get a "File Detached" message. This could mean that you simply need to exit and re-enter the program to get rid of the message. But a more likely cause of the error message is that your application has a file-locking bug.

The "File in Use" message comes up when another process or application is using the file specified in the *<filename>* parameter. This usually means the application you're using is a stand-alone application incapable of network sharing, and someone else is updating the file. Wait until that person releases the file before you enter it.

You'll see the "File Server Went Down" message when the server goes down during the specified operation that generated this error message.

The internal consistency check error message, "Illegal Completion Code," means the operation received an invalid completion code. You should rarely get this error message. If you do, your NetWare files may be corrupted, or you may have intermixed different versions of the NetWare operating system, shells, and utilities. Your supervisor may need to reinstall the

NetWare operating system and utilities, and you may need an updated workstation shell.

The "Invalid File Handle" error message usually means you have an internal error problem, probably a memory error.

An "IO Attempted to Physically Locked Area" message means the application you're running tried to read or write to a part of a file that is physically locked with a physical record or file lock. This usually means you're using a stand-alone application that's trying to access data currently in use by a network-aware application. This message usually indicates that someone else is using that physical area of the file; you'll have to wait your turn to access this disk location.

If the message is "IO Error in Directory Area," the application received an error while trying to read or write to the directory entry that appears in the *<filename>* portion of this message. This message usually means the server is having a hardware failure at the disk drive, the disk controller, or the associated cables. Inform your supervisor as soon as possible.

The "IO Error Network Disk" message indicates that the application received an error while trying to read or write to the network drive that appears in the *<drive>* portion of this message. This message usually means the server is having a hardware failure at the disk drive, the disk controller, or the associated cables. Inform your supervisor as soon as possible.

A "No Read Privilege" message means you're trying to read the file that appears in the *<filename>* portion of the message, and you don't have Read rights in that file's directory. Your effective rights in that directory must include the Read right for you to read the file.

If a "No Write Privilege" or "File Read Only" message comes up, you're trying to write to the file that appears in the *<filename>* portion of the message, but you don't have Write rights in that directory, or the file itself has been flagged read-only. You'll need to flag the file read-write, and you'll need to have write-effective rights in this directory to write to the file. Type RIGHTS in that directory to see what rights you do have. You can also type FLAG *filename* <Enter> to see how the file is flagged.

"Out of Directory Handles" signals that the server has run out of directory handles. To get rid of this error, you and your colleagues will have to reduce the number of drive mappings you have in your login scripts. After reducing your drive mappings, you may need to change directories through the DOS CD command or SESSION.

"Out of Disk Space" means, obviously, that the directory shown in the *<drive>* slot is out of space. When you see this message, back up on floppies the files you don't use often and delete them from the server. This will free up some disk space. Then if you need to access one of your archived files, restore only that file.

The "Out of Dynamic Work Space" message isn't a good sign. It means your NetWare operating system has run out of memory. To get rid of this error, you and your colleagues will have to reduce the number of drive mappings in your login scripts as well as the number of open files. Write down the error message and inform your supervisor of the situation.

The message, "Out of File Handles" signals that the server has run out of file handles. When you get this message, your supervisor will need to go into NETGEN or ELSGEN and increase the maximum number of open files on the server.

<operation>: The following messages could appear in the *<operation>* portion of the message. The DOS function calls listed can help you when you see those function calls listed in other messages and you're curious as to how they apply in NetWare. You'll need to consult the *DOS Technical Reference Manual* for the DOS function call explanations.

CHANGE FILE MODE. This is the Change File Mode (CHMOD) call; it corresponds to the DOS function call 43h.

CHANGE THE CURRENT DIRECTORY. This is the Change the Current Directory (CHDIR) call; it corresponds to the DOS function call 3Bh.

CLOSE. Used to close a file, this corresponds to the DOS Function Call 10h.

CLOSE A FILE. Used to close a file handle, this corresponds to the DOS function call 3Eh.

CREATE. This is used to create a file; it corresponds to the DOS function call 16h.

536

CREATE A FILE. This is used to create a file handle; it corresponds to the DOS function call 3Ch.

CREATE A SUBDIRECTORY. This is the Create a Subdirectory (MKDIR) call; it corresponds to the DOS function call 39h.

CREATE NEW FILE. This is used to create a new file; it corresponds to the DOS function call 5Bh.

CREATE TEMP FILE. This is used to create a unique file; it corresponds to the DOS function call 5Ah.

CURRENT DIRECTORY. This is the Get Current Directory call; it corresponds to the DOS function call 47h.

DELETE. Used to delete a file, this corresponds to the DOS function call 13h.

DELETE A FILE. This is used to delete a file from a specified directory; it corresponds to the DOS function call 41h.

FIND FIRST MATCHING FILE. This is the Find the First Matching File (FIND FIRST) call; it corresponds to the DOS function call 4Eh.

FIND NEXT MATCHING FILE. This is the Find the Next Matching File (FIND NEXT) call; it corresponds to the DOS function call 4Fh.

GET CURRENT DIRECTORY. This call corresponds to the DOS function call 47h.

GET SET A FILE DATE AND TIME. This call is used to Get/Set a file's date and time. It corresponds to the DOS function call 57h.

IO CONTROL FOR DEVICES. This is the I/O Control for Devices (IOCTL) call. It corresponds to the DOS function call 44h.

MOVE FILE POINTER. This is the Move File, Read Write Pointer (LSEEK) call. It corresponds to the DOS function call 42h.

OPEN. This call is used to open a file; it corresponds to the DOS function call 0Fh.

OPEN A FILE. This call is used to open a file handle; it corresponds to the DOS function call 3Dh.

READ FROM A FILE. Used to read from a file or device, this call corresponds to the DOS function call 3Fh.

REMOVE A SUBDIRECTORY. This is the Remove a Subdirectory (RMDIR) call; it corresponds to the DOS function call 3Ah.

RENAME A FILE. Used to rename a file, this call corresponds to the DOS function call 56h.

SEARCH FIRST. Used to search for the first matching filename in the current directory, this call corresponds to the DOS function call 11h.

SEARCH NEXT. This call is used to search for the next matching filename in the current directory. It corresponds to the DOS Function Call 12h.

SET ATTRIBUTES. This is the Network Environment Function 228_Set File Attributes_call. It corresponds to the NetWare function call 228 (E4h).

UPDATE FILE SIZE. This is the Network Environment Function 229_Update File Size (FCB)_call. It corresponds to the NetWare function call 229 (E5h).

WRITE TO A FILE. Used to write to a file or device, this call corresponds to the DOS function call 40h.

```
Network Error on Server <servername>:<error> Abort or Retry?
```

Problem.

These messages are usually caused by hardware problems such as improper bus termination, exceeding the maximum cable distance, and broken or bad cables and connectors. The message usually interrupts normal communication between your workstation and the specified server. This message may (on rare occasions) indicate problems with internal consistency checking of NetWare packets.

Solution.

Try pressing the R key to see if the retry will work. If it doesn't, write down the information in the error message and pass that information on to your network supervisor. Most likely, you'll have to abort or reboot to get out of your present predicament.

With NetWare 3.12 you can use the automatic reconnection capabilities of the DOS Requester to reconnect for you. As downed servers become available again, the AUTO.VLM module reconnects to the server and then rebuilds the user's environment, including connection status, drive mappings, and printer connections. But if it can't reconnect after a fashion, you can then try rebooting.

<error>: The following messages could appear in the *<error>* portion of the message.

An "Attempted Access to Illegal or Down Server" message means your workstation has attempted to communicate with the specified server, but the server is down or the server's internal tables are corrupt and you can no longer communicate with the server. It could also mean that bad information was passed to a NetWare-specific function call, causing this error.

A network packet's header contains three types of numbers (addresses): a network number, a node number, and a socket number. The "Bad Local Network Address" message means the node address you're sending to is invalid, which means either the packet was bad or your workstation's shell driver is having a problem.

A "Connection No Longer Valid" message means that your workstation sent a packet to a server to which you no longer have a valid connection. Whenever your workstation is unable to communicate with the server for fifteen minutes, the server will invalidate the connection. This loss of connection can mean that you have some bad cable, or that your route to the server, or even the server itself, has gone down.

A network packet's header contains three types of numbers (addresses): a network number, a node number, and a socket number. The "Could Not Route to File Server" message indicates the shell couldn't find a route to the network your server is on, which means you may have a bad piece of cable or a bad terminator or that your bridge has gone down.

Sometimes one of your data packets can't find the desired destination; you press Retry, which causes the shell to look for alternate routes to the designated server. The "Error Locating Router" message says that the shell couldn't find an alternate route to the specified server. It may mean the

539

server or bridge went down. It could also mean something happened to your cabling. When you reboot, type SLIST <Enter> to see if the server is listed.

"Error Receiving from Network" means the shell didn't receive a reply to a request within its specified time and timed out, giving you this error. Your workstation is having problems receiving and decoding NetWare packets. This error message could indicate a hardware problem, so check bus terminators, cables and cable connections, and the network interface board. It could also mean that your server or bridge went down or that your network is very busy. Retry a couple of times to see if you can regain the connection.

"Error Sending to Network" means your workstation is having problems formatting and sending NetWare packets. This is usually a hardware problem, so check bus terminators, broken or bad cables and cable connections, and the network interface board. Also see if your bridge or server went down.

A "Reply Invalid Header" message means the server sent a reply packet with an invalid IPX packet header to your workstation. You may have received a bad packet, or your workstation's memory might be corrupted. Try shutting your workstation off and then restarting it. If the problem persists, have your workstation's memory checked.

"Reply Invalid Sequence Number" means that the server sent a reply packet with an invalid packet sequence number to your workstation. You may have received a bad packet, or perhaps your workstation's memory is corrupted. Try shutting your workstation off and then restarting it. If the problem persists, have your workstation's memory checked.

The "Reply Invalid Slot" message signifies that the server sent a reply packet with an invalid slot number to your workstation. You may have received a bad packet, or your workstation's memory could be corrupted. Try shutting your workstation off and then restarting it. If the problem persists, have your workstation's memory checked.

If you got a "Reply Packet Lengths Don't Match" message, the server sent a reply packet to your workstation, but the actual length of the packet didn't match the expected length. You get this error only from a failed internal consistency check; the failed check could mean your workstation's memory has been corrupted. Try shutting your workstation off and then restarting it. If the problem persists, have your workstation's memory checked.

"Unknown Communications Error Code" tells you that the completion code that your workstation returns in an ECB (Event Control Block) indicates an unknown communications error code. Try shutting your workstation off and then restarting it. You could have a bad network interface board, or one of the network problems mentioned earlier: terminators, cables, bridges, or servers.

```
Network Spooler Error: (probably out of space on SYS: volume).
```

Problem.

The network spooler can no longer operate. The most common cause for network spooler failure is that the SYS volume has run out of space. The SYS volume is where the spooler stores the data that needs to be printed.

Solution.

Your supervisor will need to delete or move files from volume SYS to other volumes so the network spooler can work. For your part, back up your data on floppies and delete the files you don't often use from volume SYS. Then, if you need to access one of your archived files, you can restore that file.

```
No Expanded Memory Manager present. Cannot continue
initialization.
```

Problem.

You need to load the EMM driver before you load the EMSNETX file. The EMSNETX file couldn't find the EMM driver in memory and assumed it wasn't installed.

Solution.

Install the EMM driver through CONFIG.SYS, as well as any other parameters at the time. Be sure you typed in the driver name and directory path correctly in the CONFIG.SYS file. Check the vendor's documentation for the correct method of installing the driver.

```
No Extended Memory Manager present. Cannot continue
initialization.
```

Problem.

> You need to load the XMS driver before you load the XMSNETX file. The XMSNETX file couldn't find the XMS driver in memory and assumed it wasn't installed.

Solution.

> Install the XMS driver through CONFIG.SYS, as well as any other parameters at the time. Be sure you typed in the driver name and directory path correctly in the CONFIG.SYS file. Check the vendor's documentation for the correct method of installing the driver.

```
Not enough pages of expanded memory for installation.
```

Problem.

> As the expanded memory shell is loading into memory, the shell finds there are too few memory pages available to load properly. Either the EMM driver hasn't allocated enough pages, or another program is hogging the pages.

Solution.

> If another program is already using the expanded memory pages, you may need to unload the program before loading the EMSNETX shell. If not, check the EMM driver specifications and ensure that it's loaded or working correctly. A good place to start is the vendor's documentation that comes with the software.

```
Not running on top of DOS version 2.x.
```

Problem.

> Your version of DOS doesn't match your NetWare shell (NET2.COM) file. In this instance, you're running either DOS 3.x or 4.x, but you're running the NET2.COM version of the NetWare shell.

Solution.

Make sure you're running the correct version of DOS with the correct NetWare shell file. NET2.COM requires DOS 2.x in order to run properly. Better yet, upgrade to NETX.COM, which is DOS-version independent.

```
Not running on top of DOS version 3.x.
```

Problem.

Your version of DOS doesn't match your NetWare shell (NET3.COM) file. In this instance, you're running either DOS 2.x or 4.x, but you're running the NET3.COM version of the NetWare shell.

Solution.

Make sure you're running the correct version of DOS with the correct NetWare shell. NET3.COM requires DOS 3.x in order to run properly. Better yet, upgrade to NETX.COM, which is DOS-version independent.

```
Not running on top of DOS version 4.x.
```

Problem.

Your version of DOS doesn't match your NetWare shell (NET4.COM) file. In this instance, you're running either DOS 2.x or 3.x, but you're running the NET4.COM version of the NetWare shell.

Solution.

Make sure you're running the correct version of DOS with the correct NetWare shell. NET4.COM requires DOS 4.x in order to run properly. Better yet, upgrade to NETX.COM, which is DOS-version independent.

```
PIPE not found in transient portion of COMMAND.COM.
```

Problem.

The NetWare shell can't locate the filename it uses for DOS PIPE functions. Your NetWare shell needs to change this filename in order for piping to work properly with the server. This message usually means you have a corrupt COMMAND.COM file or a corrupt NetWare shell.

Solution.

Try recopying the COMMAND.COM file onto your boot disk. If your workstation reboots with no problem but receives the error message when accessing the COMMAND.COM file on a network search drive (used with the COMSPEC command), have your supervisor recopy the COMMAND.COM file onto the network. If this doesn't work, replace your NetWare shell file.

Program Aborted

You see this message when you choose the "Abort" option from error messages that display "Abort, Retry, Fail?" or "Abort, Retry?" Selecting the "Abort" option terminates the program you're executing and returns you to DOS.

Shell Error: No active File Server attachments.

Problem.

This message means your workstation is no longer logged in or attached to any servers. You'll see this message when the servers you're logged in or attached to have gone down.

Solution.

Reboot your workstation when the server you log in to is back up and running.

The Network is inactive or you are not connected properly.

Problem.

Your NetWare shell established communications with the server, but for some reason the shell can no longer communicate with the server.

Solution.

Check your cable connections to ensure that they're properly fastened. You may have a bad or improper cable, terminator, or network interface board. Make sure your network interface board is securely fastened and that you're using the correct shell and driver for the board you're running. Then reboot.

544

```
Too many devices defined in DOS (over approximately 32)...
Device Table Overflow
```

Problem.

You'll see this message when you fill DOS's device table and NetWare can't insert its device name into the table. If you fill the device table (through CONFIG.SYS) with too many devices (about thirty-two entries), the NetWare shell aborts.

Solution.

Remove your least-used device drivers from your CONFIG.SYS file and reboot your workstation.

```
Warning: disk write error in file <filename>.
```

Problem.

This is a NetWare operating system message that displays at your workstation instead of at the server console. You see this message when NetWare tries to verify a disk write and that verification fails. The server console will also display part of the error message: "Write Error: dir = sss file = FILENAME.EXT vol = VOLUMENAME."

You'll see this error if part of the network disk you're writing to has gone bad and Hot Fix isn't functioning properly. Hot Fix performs an automatic read-after-write verification on all disk writes and redirects the data written from the bad sector to a good sector. You can also see this error if the server's Disk Coprocessor Board (DCB), disk controller, or disk drive is beginning to fail.

Solution.

If you're in an application when you see this error message, save the file under a different filename; the original file will be corrupt. Then leave the original file on that bad part of the disk. Don't erase the file, for that will free up the bad disk space and someone else might try to write to the bad disk block and end up with a corrupt file as well. Rename the file to something like FILE.BAD so you'll know the file is bad and won't use it any more. If you do have to retrieve the information from the file, try copying the file to

another filename with a command like COPY FILE.BAD REPORTS.DAT.
Be sure to inform your supervisor of the problem as soon as possible.

Warning: Byte value greater than 255 was truncated.

Problem.

You'll see this message when you enter a number in your NET.CFG file
that's greater than 255. For example, let's say you're changing your "Cache
Buffers" option to 100 and you accidentally type 1000. The next time you
boot your workstation, you'll see this warning message immediately followed by "Cache Buffers" option set (truncated) to 255 bytes. NetWare
brings the number back to the maximum value permitted.

Solution.

Go into the NET.CFG file from any text editor and change the option within
the proper values. You must save the NET.CFG file as a DOS text file (not
a word processor file) for it to work.

XMS Error during Free High Memory Area.

Problem.

You see this error when the XMS goes into an "unpredictable state" as it tries
to free up memory used by the NetWare shell.

Solution.

Check the vendor's documentation to see if the XMS driver was installed or
configured correctly. You may have to reboot the workstation. If the
problem persists, call the vendor.

**XMS Shell Error: <cause>

You see these messages when the extended memory shell has problems
having the XMS driver handle its requests. The cause part of the message
shows the shell's request that couldn't be completed. Each cause in the list
has a probable solution to follow.

Cause 1—"A20 Error Occurred." The XMS driver couldn't enable or
disable the A20 line from the workstation's CPU. This could be an XMS

driver problem or the workstation CPU's problem and there may be some incompatibility issues between the workstation and the XMS driver. Also check the workstation's memory.

Cause 2—"Function Not Implemented." The XNS driver doesn't support enabling or disabling the A20 line from the workstation's CPU. If this is the case, you'll either have to get an XNS driver that does support the Local Enable A20 or Local Disable A20 calls, or you simply won't be able to use the extended memory shell.

Cause 3—"VDisk detected." You'll see this message when the XMS driver (usually Microsoft's version 2.0 HIMEM.SYS file) finds that VDISK.SYS or RAMDISK.SYS is currently taking up the high memory space. There have been problems using IBM's VDISK.SYS with Microsoft's version 2.0 XMS driver, so you'll either have to use different XMS drivers or different virtual disk drivers if you want to use both of them. Otherwise, don't use the virtual disk option.

`You are being logged out of all servers.`

Problem.

This is simply a message you see if the normal NetWare shell is successful when it unloads from the workstation's memory. The NetWare shell must first log you out of all servers before it can unload. Since this is simply a message, there is no solution.

`You are not connected to any file servers. The shell will try to connect to a file server whenever the current default drive is changed to an invalid drive.`

Problem.

For some reason, you've lost all of your server connections and the shell can't find any server to connect to.

Solution.

When you choose a non-DOS drive letter (one of your network drive letters), NetWare will try to connect you to another server. NetWare 3.11 allows you to do this in lieu of rebooting your workstation. If the shell can connect you to another server, you'll have an attached connection and you'll see the LOGIN prompt, similar to what you see when you log out from your server. You can then type SLIST <Enter> to see if your server is on the network. If your server is present, log in. If the shell can't connect you to another server, it will retry for some time (the time can be different for each network interface board/driver and IPX) and you'll see the same message again.

Since you once had a connection, check with your co-workers to see if the problem is widespread. If it isn't, check your cable connections to ensure that they're properly fastened. You may have a bad or improper cable, terminator, or network interface board. Make sure your network interface board is securely fastened, and that you're using the correct shell and driver for the board you're running. Then reboot.

IPXODI Additions

```
FATAL: Board # doesn't provide enough look ahead. IPX needs 18
or more bytes.
```

Problem.

When packets come into the workstation, IPX needs at least the first 18 bytes to check for packet validation. In this case, IPX is not getting enough bytes to create a buffer in order to examine initial packet information.

Solution.

You can add this ability through the NET.CFG file. Under the Link Drive line, type in LOOK AHEAD SIZE 18 <Enter> before listing the interrupt settings. This will fulfill IPX's request.

```
FATAL: Different IPX or an IPX interrupt has been hooked.
```

Problem.

You can unload IPXODI.COM and LSL.COM file from memory by typing IPXODI or /U <Enter> or IPXODI /F <Enter>. The /U parameter looks to see if there are any other TSRs loaded into memory above IPXODI, or if another program has "hooked" an interrupt that IPXODI is also using, thereby preventing its release from memory without hanging the workstation. The /F parameter forces IPXODI to be unloaded even though other TSRs are using the program. This will usually hang the workstation as well.

548

When you see this message, it usually means you have a different version of IPXODI for unloading IPX than you did when you loaded it in the first place. But it usually means another program is sharing one of IPX's interrupts, which prevents the program from being unloaded, or as it unloads, it will hang the workstation.

Solution.

First, ensure you are using the same IPXODI.COM file that you used when you initially installed the file. Next, unload the program that is using one of IPX's interrupts before using the /U or /F parameters to unload the TSR.

`FATAL: Invalid Parameter`

Problem.

When loading IPXODI, you typed in some extra characters on the command line. IPXODI has a number of parameters that you can use when loading and unloading the file. For example, IPXODI A stops loading the built-in reply piece for remote diagnostics, as well as SPX. The D parameter stops loading the built-in reply piece for remote diagnostics only. You can use the ? parameter to see information about the available parameters, and the U parameter to unload IPXODI when nothing is above it, or the F parameter to forcibly unload IPXODI.

Solution.

Use one of the parameters that IPXODI recognizes.

`FATAL: IPX already loaded`

Problem.

Despite what you see, this is only informational. It means that you have already run IPXODI and it can only be loaded once. You don't have to do anything.

`FATAL: IPX is already registered with the LSL.`

Problem.

You see this message when you unload IPXODI through the U or F parameter, but LSL still registers its presence.

Solution.

At this point, you are forced to reboot the workstation.

```
FATAL: IPX is not loaded
```

Problem.

Despite what you see, this is only informational. It means that you need to run IPXODI to load IPX.

```
FATAL: No more room in the LSL for another protocol stack.
```

Problem.

You see this message when you already have eight protocol stacks registered with the LSL. To add another protocol stack, you'll need to release one first.

Solution.

Use the U parameter on one of the network drivers you have presently in place. For example, to release the NE2000 network driver, type NE2000 U <Enter> in the directory where the driver is located.

```
FATAL: There is a TSR above the loaded IPX
```

Problem.

You'll see this message when you use the "IPXODI U" option and there is another TSR that is above IPXODI in memory.

Solution.

Unload the TSR first before unloading IPXODI. If you can't, try the IPXODI F parameter to force IPX to unload from memory. However, this often hangs the workstation. If you can, load the TSR before loading the communications drivers so you won't have this problem in the future.

```
FATAL: This old LSL in not supported.
```

Problem.

For some reason, the IPXODI driver you are running can't work with the version of LSL.COM you are running.

Solution.

Get a newer version of LSL.COM that will support this version of IPXODI.

`IPX protocol bound to <name> MLID Board # <number>.`

Problem.

This is an informational message that you see after you load the IPXODI file. You will see the name of the network driver fill the *<name>* part of the message, and you will the board assignment fill the *<number>* part.

Solution.

This is purely informational, so you don't have to do anything.

`IPX protocol successfully removed.`

Problem.

This is an informational message that you see after you unload the IPXODI file.

Solution.

This is purely informational, so you don't have to do anything.

`Using configuration file NET.CFG/SHELL.CFG`

Problem.

As you are loading NetWare communications files (IPX.COM, LSL.COM, IPXODI.COM, or NETX.COM), these files look for the NET.CFG file for additional or modified parameters that are found in the communications files. If the files can't find a NET.CFG or if it can't recognize the parameters listed in the NET.CFG, the communications files will next look for the SHELL.CFG file.

Solution.

Once a valid NET.CFG or SHELL.CFG file is found, you see the above message. This is purely informational.

```
WARNING: NET.CFG ignored - file length must be less than 4097
bytes.
```

Problem.

You'll see this message if the NET.CFG file is larger than 4097 bytes. Both IPXODI and LSL think the NET.CFG file has been corrupted or won't fit into the place where they look at the file, and therefore ignore the file.

Solution.

If you have a valid NET.CFG file but it's larger than 4096 bytes, see what you can take out of the file and still have it do what you need.

LSL Additions

```
FATAL: Different LSL or an LSL interrupt has been hooked.
```

Problem.

You can unload IPXODI.COM or LSL.COM file from memory by typing LSL or /U <Enter> or LSL /F <Enter>. The /U parameter looks to see if there are any other TSRs loaded into memory above LSL, or if another program has "hooked" an interrupt that LSL is also using, thereby preventing its release from memory without hanging the workstation. The /F parameter forces LSL to be unloaded even though other TSRs are using the program. This will usually hang the workstation as well.

When you see this message, it usually means you have a different version of LSL.COM for unloading LSL than you did when you loaded it in the first place. But it usually means another program is sharing one of LSL's interrupts, which prevents the program from being unloaded, or as it unloads, it will hang the workstation.

Solution.

First ensure you are using the same LSL.COM file that you used when you initially installed the file. Next, unload the program that is using one of LSL's interrupts before using the /U or /F parameters to unload the TSR.

`FATAL: Invalid Parameter`

Problem.

When loading LSL, you typed in some extra characters on the command line. LSL has a number of parameters that you can use when loading and unloading the file. For example, you can use the ? parameter to see information about the available parameters, the U parameter to unload LSL when nothing is above it, or the F parameter to forcibly unload LSL.

Solution.

Use one of the parameters that LSL recognizes.

`FATAL: LSL already loaded`

Problem.

Despite what you see, this is only informational. It means that you have already run LSL and it can only be loaded once. You don't have to do anything.

`FATAL: LSL is not loaded`

Problem.

Despite what you see, this is only informational. It means that you need to run LSL to put in place this support layer link.

`FATAL: Multiplex interrupt 2Fh has no free slots`

Problem.

You see this when you have already loaded an application that has used up the approximately 63 multiplex slots that are available on your workstation.

Solution.

Since LSL is only looking for one slot, load LSL first. Then load your applications.

```
FATAL: There is a TSR above the loaded LSL.
```

Problem.

You'll see this message when you use the "LSL U" option and there is another TSR that is above LSL in memory.

Solution.

Unload the TSR first before unloading LSL. If you can't, try the LSL F parameter to force the link support layer to unload from memory. However, this often hangs the workstation. If you can, load the TSR before loading the communications drivers so you won't have this problem in the future.

```
LSL successfully removed.
```

Problem.

This is an informational message that you see after you unload the LSL TSR.

Solution.

This is purely informational, so you don't have to do anything.

```
Number of buffers <number1>, Buffer size <size> bytes, Memory
pool <number2> bytes
```

Problem.

When you place extra information to assist the protocol stacks in the NET.CFG, you will see these parameters displayed on the screen when they successfully load. For example, if you have placed the following under the Link Support entry:

```
Link Support
     Max Stacks 8
     Buffers 8 1500
     MemPool 4096
```

you'll see the following:

```
Number of buffers 8, Buffer size 1500 bytes, Memory pool
4096 bytes
```

when you boot up. You normally don't need to specify these parameters; however, you may need to add these parameters if you are loading TCP/IP or something else whose documentation instructs you to add them.

The first number entry shows the number of communications buffers that LSL allocates. The size entry should match those specified by your documentation. In the example for TCP/IP, the setting was 1500 bytes. The memory pool entry shows how much memory to allocate into the LSL's free memory pool. Again, only add when the documentation specifies it.

Solution.

This is informational and you don't need to do anything about it.

The DOS Requester's Diagnostics Screen

The DOS Requester comes with diagnostic information that can assist you in unraveling some of the problems you might encounter. The /D option presents diagnostic information about the VLM's present running state. When you type VLM /D <Enter> in the directory where you initially loaded VLM.EXE, you will see a screen similar to the one shown below.

```
VLM.EXE      - NetWare virtual loadable module manager v1.02
(930422)
(C) Copyright 1993 Novell, Inc.  All Rights Reserved. Patent
pending.

The VLM.EXE file v1.2  is currently loaded
VLM transient switch count : 3589
VLM call count             : 45098
VLM current ID             : 0040h
VLM memory type            : XMS
VLM modules loaded count    : 12
VLM block ID (0 if CON)    : A902h
VLM transient block        : D6A4h
VLM global seg (0 if CON)  : CE67h
VLM async queue (h, t, s)  : 0000:0000, 0A4B:0030, 0
VLM busy queue (h, t, s)   : 0000:0000, 0A4B:003C, 0
```

```
VLM re-entrance level      : 1
VLM full map count         : 3587

VLM Control Block information       Address   TMemSize  GMemSize  SMemSize
ID   Flag Func Maps Call TSeg GSeg Low  High Para K    Para K    Para K
― ― ― ― ― ― ― ― ― ― ― ―
0001 A000 0005 0000 55AA 0A4B 083C FFFF FFFF 00FF 0003 0000 0000 0000 0000
0010 B000 0011 0000 23AC CE67 CF1F FFFF FFFF 00B8 0002 0018 0000 0194 0006
0021 B000 000B 0000 0B99 CF37 D01D FFFF FFFF 00E6 0003 00A2 0002 0067 0001
0020 E000 000B 0001 0617 CF37 D01D FFFF FFFF 00E6 0003 00A2 0002 0067 0001
0061 A000 0005 009A 0099 D6A4 D0BF 0000 0000 0106 0004 0000 0000 00CE 0003
0032 A000 0010 00AF 009E D6A4 D0BF 1060 0000 0171 0005 00B9 0002 003F 0000
0031 A000 0010 00C4 009F D6A4 D178 2770 0000 00B8 0002 001C 0000 002E 0000
0030 A000 0011 00FC 00DD D6A4 D194 32F0 0000 00B1 0002 0071 0001 0048 0001
0041 A000 000B 00E7 019E D6A4 D205 3E00 0000 01A2 0006 0284 0010 0020 0000
0043 A000 000A 015E 0143 D6A4 D489 5820 0000 006B 0001 001E 0000 0051 0001
0040 A000 0009 05F0 0418 D6A4 D4A7 5ED0 0000 0239 0008 005F 0001 004B 0001
0042 A000 000E 00E0 00C8 D6A4 D506 8260 0000 00DA 0003 00AC 0002 0059 0001
0050 A000 0007 01E6 1AAC D6A4 D5B2 9000 0000 0215 0008 00F1 0003 007F 0001
Total                                        0DB2      069E
Maximum                                      0239      0284      0194
```

Most of this information is intended for debugging the VLM modules by programmers, but supervisors and advanced users can glean information from this diagnostic screen as well. The top of the diagnostic screen contains 12 lines of information, beginning with the VLM Transient Switch Count.

VLM Transient Switch Count. This entry shows the number of times VLM.EXE swapped modules into the Transient switch block from expanded or extended memory. The entry correlates with the total from the Maps column under the VLM Control Block Information heading. However, the Maps column shows its numbers in hexadecimal.

VLM Call Count. This count represents the total calls that are going on between the DOS Requester client and a resource. The VLM.EXE manager interacts with every step of a request and keeps track of the calls it makes to the various modules. The number you see in the Call Count entry corresponds to the Call column under the VLM Control Block Information heading. The entries in the Call column show which VLM modules are used the most.

You can tell which number corresponds to which module by looking in the ID column and matching the number to the list presented under the next subhead. For example, VLM ID number 1 (which is the VLM.EXE memory manager) is being called the most often. This is followed by the CONN.VLM (ID number 10) and the NETX.VLM (ID number 50). The call number should roll over frequently under heavy usage. Again, all numbers in the VLM Control Block Information are in hexadecimal.

VLM Current ID. This entry shows which ID number from the ID column under the "VLM Control Block Information Heading" is currently mapped into the Transient Swap block area. When I took this snapshot of VLM activity, the Current ID was 0040h (the REDIR.VLM module). Here's a listing of the Identification numbers given to VLM.EXE and the current VLM modules:

```
01 = VLM.EXE          34 = RSA.VLM
10 = CONN.VLM         40 = REDIR.VLM
20 = TRAN.VLM         41 = FIO.VLM
21 = IPXNCP.VLM       42 = PRINT.VLM
22 = TCPNCP.VLM       43 = GENERAL.VLM
30 = NWP.VLM          50 = NETX.VLM
31 = BIND.VLM         60 = AUTO.VLM
32 = NDS.VLM          61 = SECURITY.VLM
33 = PNW.VLM         100 = NMR.VLM
```

VLM Memory Type. This entry tells you the type of memory the VLM.EXE is using—extended, expanded, or conventional. You can use this to ensure you are using the correct memory manager. If you thought you were loading the DOS Requester with a different memory manager than the one displayed, check your CONFIG.SYS file and modify it (if needed). Once you are sure you are loading the memory manager correctly, use the appropriate /Mx parameter when loading VLM.EXE.

If the workstation is using MS DOS 5.0 or higher, your start-up screen shows you if you are installing a memory manager. However, this does not mean you have correctly configured the memory manager to use Upper Memory Blocks (UMBs). To do this, see the section on "NetWare Workstations and Memory Management" earlier in this chapter.

VLM Modules Loaded Count. This line lets you know which VLMs have been loaded successfully. VLM.EXE's default listing loads 12 VLM modules, which are CONN.VLM, IPXNCP.VLM, TRAN.VLM, SECURITY.VLM, NDS.VLM, BIND.VLM, NWP.VLM, FIO.VLM, GENERAL.VLM, REDIR.VLM, PRINT.VLM, and NETX.VLM.

You may not want to use VLM.EXE's defaults to load modules you won't use. You can load extra modules through the NET.CFG file (such as the AUTO.VLM module).

Since you can prevent some of the VLM modules from loading, you can run VLM.EXE and look at the diagnostics screen to determine which modules the workstation is running. Once you know this, you can determine if your problem is caused by an unloaded module.

VLM Block ID (0 if CON). This entry is for debugging purposes. The block ID is the enhanced memory handle allocated for the XMS or EMS memory manager. If you are loading the DOS Requester in conventional memory this number will be 0 (there isn't a handle associated with conventional memory).

VLM Transient Block. This entry points to the beginning of the transient block area, where transient memory is being swapped in and out. You can use the number you see to determine whether the VLM is loading high or not. The above example shows the transient block beginning at the memory address of D6A4h in the UMB area.

VLM Global Seg (0 if CON). This entry is for debugging purposes and points to the beginning of the global memory block area. You can use this number to determine whether it is loading high. If you are loading the DOS Requester in conventional memory, this number will be 0. In the above example, the transient block (VLM Transient Block) is loaded in upper memory beginning at the D6A4h memory address, while the global segment (VLM Global Seg) is loaded in upper memory beginning at CE67h. Numbers between 0000h and 9999h constitute conventional memory. Numbers from A000h to FFFFh constitute UMBs.

The transient block segment and the global memory block segment either load into upper memory or they load into conventional memory. But the block segments won't partially load into upper memory and partially load into conventional memory. The DOS Requester tries to load transient and global high if possible. You can load VLM.EXE high as well (UMB space permitting). But if performance considerations are greater than memory considerations, you may use VLM /MC <Enter> and load all of the DOS Requester into conventional memory. However, it can take as much as 70KB to do so.

VLM Async Queue (H, T, S) and VLM Busy Queue (H, T, S). These two entries are for debugging purposes. The H, T, and S stand for the head, tail, and size. Normally, the tail points to the

beginning of the list, so you should see 0000:0000 for the head, some address for the tail, and 0 for the size. If a request gets orphaned, the size element increments and points to VLM.EXE's dequeuing mechanism, which should not happen.

VLM Re-entrance Level. This entry should be 1 and represents the same thing as the Async and Busy queue. The DOS Requester tries to ensure that when it performs a request that drops multiple levels deep, it comes out to the same level as when it began to perform the request. If this is not the case, something is misbehaving and you may be having problems with the DOS Requester.

VLM Full Map Count. This is the number of VLM map out requests the DOS Requester is counting when it talks to modules stored by the memory manager. Both the number you see here and the number you see in the VLM Transient Switch Count entry should be fairly close. The above example shows the two being two counts off. If you load all your VLMs in conventional memory, this number should be 0.

The next portion of the DOS Requester diagnostic screen shows raw information. Briefly, here's the topic headings and their corresponding column headings.

VLM Control Block Information. This heading applies to the entire bottom portion of the diagnostic screen. Directly beneath this heading, you see seven column headings. These include ID, Flag, Func, Maps, Call, Tseg, and Gseg.

The ID column shows the different module's identification numbers as known internally to VLM.EXE. The present list of numbers is given under the "VLM Current ID" heading earlier in this section. The Flag column shows how a particular VLM module is flagged by the VLM.EXE. For example, A000 entry stands for valid and loaded, while B000 stands for valid, loaded, and loaded low. In our example, the CONn.VLM and IPXNCP.VLM modules are loaded low as per their defaults. The E000 entry stands for valid, loaded, and masqueraded (such as the multiplexor module TRAN.VLM that goes away because there is only one child module).

The Func column shows a count of the functions that are supported by the VLM, and has a direct correlation to the VLM's call-by-number interface for calling the VLM modules. The Maps column shows how often each VLM module is being mapped into the transient block segment memory or global segment memory. The Call column shows how often a particular VLM module is called to perform a task. Use this information to see how often particular VLM modules are used in your present configurations.

If you have been tracking certain modules over a long period of time and they are never used, you may want to remove this if it isn't a multiplexor module (or isn't necessary). For example, the NDS.VLM module is one of the default loading modules, but if you are not tying into NetWare 4.0's Directory Services, you don't need to load this module.

The Tseg column shows the transient segment for the VLM modules, and the GSeg shows the global segment for the VLM modules.

Address Low/High. Near the middle of the screen are the Address heading and the Low/High columns. The Address heading columns show the enhanced memory location of the transient memory for VLM.EXE and loaded modules. Those loaded in FFFF are loaded in conventional memory, while the other modules are loaded in swapped

559

enhanced memory. If you are using EMS, the Low column shows the EMS handle and the High column shows the logical EMS page. If you are using XMS, the Low/High columns show the relative D-Word address.

Next come three headings with two columns beneath each heading. The headings are TMemSize, GMemSize, and SMemSize. The columns include Para(graph) and K(ilobytes). While the K column shows the memory sizes in K, the column is always rounded down to the nearest K rather than up. Therefore, if you have 1.9KB, you will see 1KB rather than 2KB. To get a more accurate number, use the formula in the next paragraph with the numbers in the Para column.

The number you see under the Para column of TMemSize, GMemSize, and SMemSize is the hexadecimal number in paragraphs and there are 16 bytes per paragraph. To see the actual size of the block in bytes, change the number to decimal, and then multiply the decimal number by 16. To get the actual size (in Kilobytes), divide the bytes by 1,024.

TMemSize Para/K. TMemSize stands for the transient memory block size for each of the VLM modules loaded. For this memory block, the single largest VLM module loaded determines the actual size of the transient memory block. In this example, the largest VLM module is REDIR.VLM at 0239h, or 9,104 bytes, or 8.89KB. This number represents the size of the transient block that begins in memory as shown in the VLM Transient Block line (explained earlier). The D6A4h memory location on the VLM Transient Block line is going to be 0239h, or 9,104 bytes (8.89KB) in size. Note that this number won't be exactly right if the transient memory block is loaded into conventional memory. For simple diagnostic purposes, total the numbers you see in the K column.

GMemSize Para/K. The GMemSize heading stands for Global Memory Size. To get the absolute size, you need to add the VLM modules together by looking at the number in the Total entry at the bottom. Then change the hexadecimal value to decimal, multiply by 16 for the byte count, and then divide by 1,024 for the kilobyte count. The Total column should be accurate if no VLMs are loaded low (if the Address column Low/High does not equal FFFF FFFF). For simple diagnostic purposes, total the numbers you see in the K column.

SMemSize Para/K. The SMemSize heading stands for Start Memory Size and shows the number of start paragraphs there are for each of the VLM modules loaded. This is mainly for programmers and developers.

Newer versions of the DOS Requester (such as v1.03) will improve upon the diagnostics you see when you type VLM ID. While the top part of the diagnostics screen stays the same, the bottom screen adds the module names to the lists so you don't have to look up which module is which. The TMemSize, GMemSize, and SMemSize columns are converted to TSize, GSize, and SSize columns and appear under the Memory Statistics column. These columns show the sizes of the modules in actual kilobytes rather than hexadecimal.

Summary

This chapter is intended for the advanced user or supervisor who needs to know how to keep workstations up and running. In this chapter we learned about the error messages you can receive, what they mean, and what to do about them.

This ends the chapter portions of the NetWare User's Guide for 3.11 and 3.12. The Appendices cover aspects of DOS and NetWare, and offers quick references to the menu utilities and command line utilities, as well as some steps for users when they are asked to manage some network tasks.

The last two Appendices are for NetWare 3.12 users, for they discuss how to use the NMENU utility (a new menu utility to NetWare) and the FIRSTMAIL utility, a new electronic mail package that is bundled with NetWare 3.12.

How NetWare and DOS Compare

Those of you who are familiar with DOS may want a quick list showing which DOS utilities have features similar to features in NetWare utilities. Below is a list of the common DOS utilities that you can use in both DOS and NetWare environments. This listing is followed by a list of DOS utilities that have counterparts in the NetWare utilities.

Finally, we'll look at a few DOS commands that work differently in the network environment than in a local drive environment. (DOS commands always work normally in the local drive environment.)

Commonly Used DOS Commands with No NetWare Counterparts

CLS	COMMAND
DISKCOPY	MORE
PROMPT	

DOS Utilities Similar to NetWare Utilities

DOS Utilities	NetWare Utilities
APPEND	SMODE
ASSIGN (A=C B=C)	MAP (*1:= or S1:=)
ATTRIB	FLAG, FLAGDIR
BACKUP	NBACKUP, SBACKUP
BREAK	SET BREAK (system and user login scripts)

DOS Utilities	NetWare Utilities
CHDIR (CD)	SESSION (Current Drive Mappings and <F3>)
CHDIR (CD)	FILER (Select Current Directory)
CHKDSK (workstation)	CHKVOL (server), CHKDIR
COPY, XCOPY	NCOPY, FILER (Copy File option)
DEL, ERASE	FILER (File Info option and <Del>)
DATE (mm-dd-yy, etc.)	SYSTIME
MKDIR (MD)	FILER (Subdirectory option and <Ins>)
MODE	SMODE
PATH	MAP
PRINT	NPRINT, PCONSOLE
RECOVER	NBACKUP, SBACKUP
RENAME (files)	RENDIR (directories)
RESTORE	NBACKUP, SBACKUP
RMDIR (RD)	FILER (Subdirectory option and <Del>)
SET (name=[parameter])	SET (system and user login script)
SORT	NDIR (with SORT option)
SUBST	MAP (*1:= S1:=)
TIME (hh:mm:ss)	SYSTIME (shows date and time)
TREE	LISTDIR
TYPE	FILER (View File option)
UNDELETE	SALVAGE
VER (DOS version)	NVER (NetBIOS, IPX, LAN driver, etc.)
VOL (HD and disk names)	CHKVOL, VOLINFO (server volumes)

DOS Utilities That Work Differently in DOS Than in NetWare

ASSIGN. Use the MAP utility to assign equivalences on the network. Use ASSIGN for local drives only.

BACKUP. DOS BACKUP can't recognize Macintosh files. Use NBACKUP (NetWare 3.11) for backing up Macintosh files. (Use NBACKUP for personal files only.)

CHKDSK. Can't be used on network drives—local drives only. Use CHKVOL for network volumes and CHKDIR for network directories.

COMP. You can specify the server or volume name in the directory path by using two backslashes for the servername and one backslash instead of a volume root colon. For example, DIR \\NTS3\SYS\PERSONAL\TED*.RES gives you all the .RES files found under Ted's personal directory on server NTS3. However, this designation is overly cumbersome and it's easier to use drive mappings. This applies to COMP., COPY, DIR, DEL, MKDIR, RD, and XCOPY.

COPY. You can specify directories from the volume root (:) by using the backslash key (\). If you wish to copy to a different volume, use the drive mappings. You can also use NCOPY. Another difference is that COPY won't copy a Macintosh resource fork, and NCOPY will.

DEL or ERASE. You can specify directories from the volume root (:) by using the backslash key (\). If you wish to copy to a different volume, use the drive mappings. DEL works the same way.

DIR. You can specify directories from the volume root (:) by using the backslash key (\). If you wish to copy to a different volume, use the drive mappings. You can also use NDIR.

DISKCOMP. Won't work on the network. Use only on local disk drives.

DISKCOPY. Won't work on the network. Use only on local disk drives.

FORMAT. Won't work on the network. Use only on local disk drives.

LABEL. Don't use on the network. If you do, you will see a message stating that you cannot label a network drive.

MKDIR. You can specify directories from the volume root (:) by using the backslash key (\). If you wish to copy to a different volume, use the drive mappings.

PATH. While the PATH command works normally, it may be better to use MAP in the network environment. However, you can use the SESSION utility to add local drive mappings to the PATH command.

RECOVER. Won't work on the network. Use only on local disk drives. Use NetWare's SALVAGE for the network.

RENAME. Be sure to conform to standard DOS conventions when you use this command or it won't work.

RESTORE. You must be in the same directory in which you back up files in order to restore them. For NetWare 3.1x, use NBACKUP for personal files. (Supervisors use SBACKUP for system backups.)

RMDIR (RD). You can specify directories from the volume root (:) by using the backslash key (\). If you have Modify, Create, Erase and File Scan rights, you can use this command.

SUBST. This command works only on your local disk drives. Use MAP for mapping network drives. Both use the 26 letter limitation for their commands.

UNDELETE. This command works only on local drives. Use SALVAGE for undeleting files on network drives.

XCOPY. You can specify directories from the volume root (:) by using the backslash key (\). If you use XCOPY, you'll have to be in the directory that you're copying from or use mapped drive letters. You can also use NCOPY. Another difference is that XCOPY won't copy a Macintosh resource fork, and NCOPY will.

Search Drive Mappings and the PATH Statement

Have you ever wondered why you lose local drive mappings when you log in to a NetWare network? It doesn't usually occur all at once, but one or two are lost every time you log in.

Search drive mappings are added to the PATH statement. Where network drive mappings are placed in the PATH statement depends on the method by which you add search drives. For example, you can add search drive mappings using the following methods:

```
MAP INS S1:=SYS:\PUBLIC        (Z:. in PATH statement)
MAP S2:=VOL1:\APPS\WP60        (Y:. in PATH statement)
MAP S16:=SYS:\PUBLIC\UTILS     (X:. in PATH statement)
```

NetWare assigns the drive letters regardless of any sequence in which they may appear when you type MAP <Enter>. However, each method places the network search drive mappings in different areas in the PATH statement.

Suppose you have C:\DOS;C:\UTILS;C:\WINDOWS;C:\XTREE in your PATH statement before logging in to NetWare. Also suppose that as you log in, you have the above MAP statements in the system login script. The MAP INS method inserts Z:. to the beginning of the PATH statement and the MAP S16 method appends X:. to the end of PATH statement.

However, when you use the MAP S2: method, NetWare overwrites the second drive designation in the PATH statement (C:\DOS) and makes it Y:. (This is C:\DOS instead of C:\UTILS because the MAP INS S1: command prepends to the beginning of the PATH statement, which makes C:\DOS the second drive designation.) Then as you log out, the LOGOUT utility simply pulls out the Z:., Y:., and X:. designations out of the PATH statement, which makes C:\DOS the second drive designation.) Then as you log out, the LOGOUT utility simply pulls out the Z:., Y:., and X:. designations out of the PATH statement, leaving you with just your local drives, minus the one that was overwritten. (The LOGIN utility also cleans the PATH statement from any old NetWare drives—those drive letters with a colon and period, such as Z:.)

Because NetWare overwrites drive designations when you use the MAP Sn: command, you end up overwriting one of your local drive mappings every time you log in to this server. The easiest way around this problem is to use the MAP INS command to insert network drive mappings into the PATH statement, or you can use the MAP S16: command to simply append the more nonessential search drive mappings to the end of the PATH statement.

APPENDIX B

Menu Utilities
Quick Reference

This quick reference gives you just the essential keystrokes for doing what you want in the NetWare menu utilities: COLORPAL, DSPACE, FILER, HELP, NBACKUP, PCONSOLE, PRINTCON, PRINTDEF, SALVAGE, SESSION, SYSCON, and VOLINFO. The tasks are grouped according to the options in each utility's main menu. NetWare 3.12 has two other menu utilities, NMENU and First Mail. These can be found in Appendices E and F respectively.

To exit any menued utility, press <Alt> and <F10> simultaneously, or press <Esc> until you come to the "Exit *Menuname* Yes/No" window with the "Yes" option highlighted. Press <Enter> and you're back at the network prompt.

COLORPAL

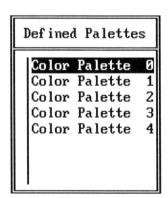

```
┌─────────────────────┐
│ Defined Palettes    │
├─────────────────────┤
│┌───────────────────┐│
││Color Palette   0  ││
││Color Palette   1  ││
││Color Palette   2  ││
││Color Palette   3  ││
││Color Palette   4  ││
││                   ││
││                   ││
│└───────────────────┘│
└─────────────────────┘
```

Use COLORPAL to set the color scheme for all NetWare menu utilities, including menus created with MENU. The default color palettes (palettes 0 through 4) affect the NetWare menu utilities; additional palettes affect the menus you create.

Before you run COLORPAL. Refer to Chapter 2 for the preparatory steps you must take before running COLORPAL.

To change NetWare's default color palettes (0–4). COLORPAL <Enter>, select a palette <Enter>, select an attribute <Enter>, select a color <Enter>, repeat previous two steps until done, <Esc>, <Esc>, <Enter>, <Enter>.

To create a new color palette. COLORPAL <Enter>, <Ins>, <Enter>, select an attribute <Enter>, select a color <Enter>, repeat previous two steps until done, <Esc>, <Esc>, <Enter>, <Enter>.

To assign a new color palette to your menu. Access your menu script file, add the number of the new color palette to the end of the menu name and location command (for example, %My Menu,10,40,5).

To change an existing color palette. COLORPAL <Enter>, select a palette <Enter>, select an attribute <Enter>, select a color <Enter>, repeat previous two steps until done, <Esc>, <Esc>, <Enter>, <Enter>.

To delete a color palette. COLORPAL <Enter>, select a palette <Del>, <Enter>, <Esc>, <Esc>, <Enter>, <Enter>.

DSPACE

Use DSPACE to see your hard disk space information. You can see the file servers you are currently attached to, the limits the supervisor set for your volume disk space, and your directory disk space limits too.

Change File Server

To change to a server you're attached to. DSPACE <Enter>, Change Current File Server <Enter>, select a server <Enter>.

To change to a server you aren't attached to. DSPACE <Enter>, Change Current File Server <Enter>, <Ins>, select a server <Enter>, type your username <Enter>, type your password <Enter>, select that server name <Enter>.

To log out of a server you're attached to. DSPACE <Enter>, Change Current File Server <Enter>, select a file server (or use <F5> to mark more than one) <Del>, <Enter>.

To change to a different user name on another server. DSPACE <Enter>, Change Current File Server <Enter>, select a file server <F3>, type your new user name <Enter>, type your password <Enter>, <Enter>.

User Restrictions

To see the volume restrictions on the current server. DSPACE <Enter>, select User Restrictions <Enter>, <Enter>, choose a volume <Enter>.

To see how much disk space you're currently using. DSPACE <Enter>, select User Restrictions <Enter>, <Enter>, choose a volume <Enter>.

Directory Restrictions

To see directory space restrictions. DSPACE <Enter>, select Directory Restrictions <Enter>, type in the path for the directory you want to check <Enter>.

FILER

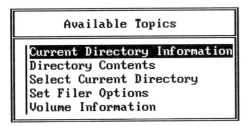

```
┌─────────────────────────────────────┐
│       Available Topics              │
├─────────────────────────────────────┤
│ Current Directory Information       │
│ Directory Contents                  │
│ Select Current Directory            │
│ Set Filer Options                   │
│ Volume Information                  │
└─────────────────────────────────────┘
```

Use FILER to work with volume, directory, and file information. You can also view and modify directory security, trustee rights assignments, and file attributes.

Current Directory Information

(View information about the directory displayed in FILER's screen header.)

To view when the directory was created. FILER <Enter>, Current Directory Information <Enter>.

To view your effective rights in the directory. FILER <Enter>, Current Directory Information <Enter>.

To view the directory's inherited rights mask. FILER <Enter>, Current Directory Information <Enter>.

To add rights to the directory's inherited rights mask. FILER <Enter>, Current Directory Information <Enter>, Inherited Rights Mask <Enter>, <Ins>, select a right (or use <F5> to mark multiple rights) <Enter>.

To delete rights from the directory's inherited rights mask. FILER <Enter>, Current Directory Information <Enter>, Inherited Rights Mask <Enter>, select a right (or use <F5> to mark multiple rights), <Del>, <Enter>.

To view trustee assignments in the directory. FILER <Enter>, Current Directory Information <Enter>, Trustees <Enter>.

To add a user or group as a trustee in the directory (requires Access Control rights). FILER <Enter>, Current Directory Information <Enter>, Trustees <Enter>, <Ins>, select user or group to add (or use <F5> to mark more than one) <Enter>, <Esc>.

To assign a trustee additional rights in the directory (requires Access Control rights). FILER <Enter>, Current Directory Information <Enter>, Trustees <Enter>, select user or group <Enter>, <Ins>, use <F5> to mark rights to add <Enter>, <Esc>.

To delete rights from a trustee in the directory (requires Access Control rights). FILER <Enter>, Current Directory Information <Enter>, Trustees <Enter>, select user or group <Enter>, use <F5> to mark which rights to delete <Del>, <Enter>, <Esc>.

To delete a user or group trustee in the directory (requires Access Control rights). FILER <Enter>, Current Directory Information <Enter>, Trustees <Enter>, select user or group to delete (or use <F5> to mark more than one), <Del>, <Enter>, <Esc>.

To view the owner of the directory. FILER <Enter>, Current Directory Information <Enter>.

Directory Contents

(View and change information about the files in the directory displayed in FILER's screen header.)

To delete a file (requires Erase rights). FILER <Enter>, Directory Contents <Enter>, select a file <Del>, <Enter>.

To delete multiple files (requires Erase rights). FILER <Enter>, Directory Contents <Enter>, use <F5> to mark files, <Del>, <Enter>.

To rename a file (requires Modify and File Scan rights). FILER <Enter>, Directory Contents <Enter>, select a file <F3>, change filename <Enter>.

To rename a group of files (requires Modify and File Scan rights). FILER <Enter>, Directory Contents <Enter>, <F6>, type file pattern <Enter>, <F3>, type pattern to be replaced <Enter>, type the rename pattern <Enter>.

To view a file's attributes. FILER <Enter>, Directory Contents <Enter>, select a file <Enter>, View/Set File Information <Enter>.

To set file attributes for a file (requires Modify and File Scan rights). FILER <Enter>, Directory Contents <Enter>, select a file <Enter>, View/Set File Information <Enter>, <Enter>, <Ins>, select an attribute (or use <F5> to mark multiple attributes) <Enter>, <Esc>.

To remove file attributes from a file (requires Modify and File Scan rights). FILER <Enter>, Directory Contents <Enter>, select a file <Enter>, View/Set File Information <Enter>, select an attribute (or use <F5> to mark multiple attributes), <Del>, <Enter>, <Esc>.

To set file attributes for multiple files (requires Modify and File Scan rights). FILER <Enter>, Directory Contents <Enter>, use <F5> to mark files or <F6> to specify a file pattern <Enter>, Set Attributes <Enter>, <Ins>, select an attribute (or use <F5> to mark multiple attributes) <Enter>, <Esc>, <Enter>, <Esc>.

To copy a file to another directory. (Requires Read and File Scan rights in source directory; Write, Create, and File Scan, and sometimes Modify rights in destination directory.) FILER <Enter>, Directory Contents <Enter>, select a file <Enter>, Copy File <Enter>, specify destination directory path <Enter>, specify destination filename <Enter>.

To see when a file was created. FILER <Enter>, Directory Contents <Enter>, select a file <Enter>, View/Set File Information <Enter>.

To see when a file was last accessed. FILER <Enter>, Directory Contents <Enter>, select a file <Enter>, View/Set File Information <Enter>.

To see when a file was last modified. FILER <Enter>, Directory Contents <Enter>, select a file <Enter>, View/Set File Information <Enter>.

To see who created a file. FILER <Enter>, Directory Contents <Enter>, select a file <Enter>, View/Set File Information <Enter>.

To see the size of a file (in bytes). FILER <Enter>, Directory Contents <Enter>, select a file <Enter>, View/Set File Information <Enter>.

To look at a file's contents. FILER <Enter>, Directory Contents <Enter>, select a file <Enter>, View File <Enter>.

Use the following steps to create, rename, or delete subdirectories of the current directory and view information about them.

To create a subdirectory (requires Modify rights). FILER <Enter>, Directory Contents <Enter>, <Ins>, type new subdirectory name <Enter>.

To rename a subdirectory (requires Modify rights). FILER <Enter>, Directory Contents <Enter>, select a subdirectory <F3>, type new subdirectory name <Enter>.

To rename a group of subdirectories with similar names (requires Modify rights). FILER <Enter>, Directory Contents <Enter>, use <F5> to mark subdirectories or <F6> to specify a marking pattern <F3>, type name pattern to be replaced <Enter>, type the rename pattern <Enter>.

To delete all files in a subdirectory (requires Erase and File Scan rights). FILER <Enter>, Directory Contents <Enter>, select a subdirectory (or use <F5> to mark more than one) <Del>, Delete Subdirectory's Files Only <Enter>, <Enter>.

To delete an entire subdirectory structure (files and all). (Requires Modify, Erase, and File Scan rights.) FILER <Enter>, Directory Contents <Enter>, select a subdirectory (or use <F5> to mark more than one) <Del>, Delete Entire Subdirectory Structure <Enter>, <Enter>.

To view when the subdirectory was created. FILER <Enter>, Directory Contents <Enter>, select a subdirectory <Enter>, View/Set Directory Information <Enter>.

To view the subdirectory's inherited rights mask. FILER <Enter>, Directory Contents <Enter>, select a subdirectory <Enter>, View/Set Directory Information <Enter>.

To add rights to the subdirectory's inherited rights mask (requires Access Control rights). FILER <Enter>, Directory Contents <Enter>, select a subdirectory <Enter>, View/Set Directory Information <Enter>, Inherited Rights Mask <Enter>, <Ins>, select a right (or use <F5> to mark multiple rights) <Enter>.

To delete a right from the subdirectory's inherited rights mask (requires Access Control rights). FILER <Enter>, Directory Contents <Enter>, select a subdirectory <Enter>, select a right (or use <F5> to mark multiple rights) <Del>, <Enter>.

To add rights to the inherited rights masks of multiple subdirectories (requires Access Control rights). FILER <Enter>, Directory Contents <Enter>, use <F5> to mark subdirectories <Enter>, Set Inherited Rights <Enter>, <Ins>, select a right (or use <F5> to mark multiple rights) <Enter>, <Esc>, <Enter>.

To delete rights from the inherited rights masks of multiple subdirectories (requires Access Control rights). FILER <Enter>, Directory Contents <Enter>, use

<F5> to select subdirectories <Enter>, Set Inherited Rights <Enter>, select a right (or use <F5> to mark multiple rights) <Del>, <Enter>.

To view the owner of the subdirectory. FILER <Enter>, Directory Contents <Enter>, select a subdirectory <Enter>, View/Set Directory Information <Enter>.

To view trustee assignments in a subdirectory. FILER <Enter>, Directory Contents <Enter>, select a subdirectory <Enter>, Trustees <Enter>.

To add a user or group as a trustee in a subdirectory (requires Access Control rights). FILER <Enter>, Directory Contents <Enter>, select a subdirectory <Enter>, Trustees <Enter>, <Ins>, select user or group to add (or use <F5> to mark more than one) <Enter>, <Esc>.

To assign a trustee additional rights in a subdirectory (requires Access Control rights). FILER <Enter>, Directory Contents <Enter>, select a subdirectory <Enter>, Trustees <Enter>, select user or group <Enter>, <Ins>, use <F5> to mark rights to add <Enter>, <Esc>.

To delete rights from a trustee in a subdirectory (requires Access Control rights). FILER <Enter>, Directory Contents <Enter>, select a subdirectory <Enter>, Trustees <Enter>, select user or group <Enter>, use <F5> to mark rights to delete <Del>, <Enter>, <Esc>.

To delete a user or group trustee in a subdirectory (requires Access Control rights). FILER <Enter>, Directory Contents <Enter>, select a subdirectory <Enter>, Trustees <Enter>, select user or group to delete (or use <F5> to mark more than one) <Del>, <Enter>, <Esc>.

Select Current Directory

(Change the current directory path displayed in FILER's screen header. You must already be in FILER.)

To change to another directory on the current server (quick method). Select Current Directory <Enter>, specify directory path <Enter>.

To change to a lower directory on the current server (level-by-level method). Select Current Directory <Enter>, <Ins>, select subdirectory (as needed) <Enter>, <Esc>, <Enter>.

To change to a higher directory on the current server (level-by-level method). Select Current Directory <Enter>, <Ins>, select ".." (as needed) <Enter>, <Esc>, <Enter>.

To change to a directory on another server you're attached to. Select Current Directory <Enter>, delete path with <Backspace>, <Ins>, select server <Enter>, select volume <Enter>, select directory <Enter>, select subdirectory (as needed) <Enter>, <Esc>, <Enter>.

To change to a directory on a server you aren't attached to. Select Current Directory <Enter>, delete path with <Backspace>, <Ins>, <Ins>, select file server <Enter>, type your login name <Enter>, type your password <Enter>, select file server name <Enter>, <Ins>, select volume <Enter>, <Ins>, select directory <Enter>, <Ins>, select subdirectory (as needed) <Enter>, <Esc>, <Enter>.

Volume Information

(View information about the volume that contains the current directory.)

To view the volume information. FILER <Enter>, Volume Information <Enter>.

HELP

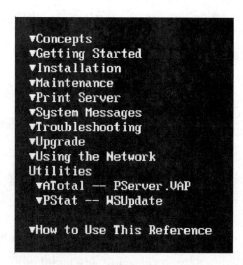

Use HELP to find explanations about NetWare commands.

To search for a particular command. HELP <name of command> <Enter>.

To search while in HELP. HELP <Enter>, Space bar, type in subject or command <Enter>.

NBACKUP

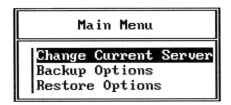

Use NBACKUP to store an archive copy of your files onto a floppy disk or local hard drive. (Use **ONLY** for personal files. Supervisors use SBACKUP for system backup or if using non-DOS file tapes.)

Change Current Server

To change to a server you're attached to. NBACKUP <Enter>, DOS Devices <Enter>, Change Current Server <Enter>, select a server <Enter>.

To change to a server you aren't attached to. NBACKUP <Enter>, DOS Devices <Enter>, Change Current Server <Enter>, <Ins>, select a server <Enter>, type your username <Enter>, type your password <Enter>, select that server name <Enter>.

To log out of a server you're attached to. NBACKUP <Enter>, DOS Devices <Enter>, Change Current Server <Enter>, select a file server (or use <F5> to mark more than one server) <Del>, <Enter>.

Backup Options

To select the directory to back up. NBACKUP <Enter>, DOS Devices <Enter>, Backup Options <Enter>, Select Working Directory <Enter>, type in the directory path <Enter>.

To back up files in a directory. NBACKUP <Enter>, DOS Devices <Enter>, Backup Options <Enter>, Backup by Directory <Enter>, type in path or use <Ins> to see available options <Enter>, type in name of session <Enter>, type in source directory <Enter>, type in destination directory or drive <Esc>, <Enter>, select Backup Now or Backup Later <Enter>, if using a floppy disk press <Enter>.

To see what files have been archived. NBACKUP <Enter>, DOS Devices <Enter>, Backup Options <Enter>, View Backup Log <Enter>, select a session <Enter>.

To see what errors occurred during the backup session. NBACKUP <Enter>, DOS Devices <Enter>, Backup Options <Enter>, View Error Log <Enter>, select a session <Enter>.

Restore Options

To select a directory to restore the files to. NBACKUP <Enter>, DOS Devices <Enter>, Restore Options <Enter>, Select Working Directory <Enter>, type in a path or use <Ins> to choose a path <Enter>.

To restore a file. NBACKUP <Enter>, DOS Devices <Enter>, Restore Options <Enter>, Restore Session <Enter>, <Esc>, <Enter>, <Enter>.

PCONSOLE

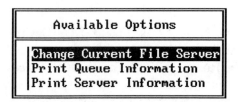

Use PCONSOLE to view print queue and print server information and to control network printing from your workstation.

Change Current File Server

(Change from one server to another to view printing information. You must already be in PCONSOLE.)

To change to a server you're attached to. Change Current File Server <Enter>, select a server <Enter>.

To change to a server you aren't attached to. Change Current File Server <Enter>, <Ins>, select a server <Enter>, type your username <Enter>, type your password <Enter>, select that server name <Enter>.

To log out of a server you're attached to. Change Current File Server <Enter>, select a file server (or use <F5> to mark more than one) <Del>, <Enter>.

To change to a different username on another server. Change Current File Server <Enter>, select a file server <F3>, type your new username <Enter>, type your password <Enter>, <Enter>.

578

Print Queue Information

(View and manipulate jobs in a print queue.)

To see which print queues are defined on the current server. PCONSOLE <Enter>, Print Queue Information <Enter>.

To see the print jobs in a print queue. PCONSOLE <Enter>, Print Queue Information <Enter>, select a print queue <Enter>, Current Print Job Entries <Enter>.

To see information about a print job in a print queue. PCONSOLE <Enter>, Print Queue Information <Enter>, select a print queue <Enter>, Current Print Job Entries <Enter>, select a print job <Enter>.

To put a user hold on a print job in a print queue. PCONSOLE <Enter>, Print Queue Information <Enter>, select a print queue <Enter>, Current Print Job Entries <Enter>, select a print job <Enter>, highlight User Hold, type Y <Enter>, <Esc>.

To remove a user hold from a print job in a print queue. PCONSOLE <Enter>, Print Queue Information <Enter>, select a print queue <Enter>, Current Print Job Entries <Enter>, select a print job <Enter>, highlight User Hold, type N <Enter>, <Esc>.

To change the number of copies while a print job is in a print queue. PCONSOLE <Enter>, Print Queue Information <Enter>, select a print queue <Enter>, Current Print Job Entries <Enter>, select a print job <Enter>, highlight Number of Copies, type new number <Enter>, <Esc>.

To change how a print job will be printed. PCONSOLE <Enter>, Print Queue Information <Enter>, select a print queue <Enter>, Current Print Job Entries <Enter>, select a print job <Enter>, highlight File contents, Tab size, Suppress form feed, Form, Print banner, Banner name <Enter>, <Esc>.

To defer printing a print job until a later time. PCONSOLE <Enter>, Print Queue Information <Enter>, select a print queue <Enter>, Current Print Job Entries <Enter>, select a print job <Enter>, highlight Defer Printing, type Y <Enter>, type target date <Enter>, type target time <Enter>, <Esc>.

To change the print server you want to print a job. PCONSOLE <Enter>, Print Queue Information <Enter>, select a print queue <Enter>, Current Print Job Entries <Enter>, select a print job <Enter>, highlight Target server, select print server <Enter>, <Esc>.

To delete print jobs from a print queue. PCONSOLE <Enter>, Print Queue Information <Enter>, select a print queue <Enter>, Current Print Job Entries <Enter>, select a print job (or use <F5> to mark more than one) <Del>, <Enter>.

To submit print jobs to a print queue. PCONSOLE <Enter>, Print Queue Information <Enter>, select a print queue <Enter>, Current Print Job Entries <Enter>,

<Ins>, type directory path to print from <Enter>, select a file (or use <F5> to mark more than one) <Enter>, select a print job configuration <Enter>, change any of the settings you need to for each file <Esc>, <Enter>.

To see the status of a print queue. PCONSOLE <Enter>, Print Queue Information <Enter>, select a print queue <Enter>, Current Queue Status <Enter>.

To see which print servers are currently attached to a print queue. PCONSOLE <Enter>, Print Queue Information <Enter>, select a print queue <Enter>, Currently Attached Servers <Enter>.

To see a print queue's identification number. PCONSOLE <Enter>, Print Queue Information <Enter>, select a print queue <Enter>, Print Queue ID <Enter>.

To see who is assigned as a queue operator for a print queue. PCONSOLE <Enter>, Print Queue Information <Enter>, select a print queue <Enter>, Queue Operators <Enter>.

To see which print servers are assigned to a print queue. PCONSOLE <Enter>, Print Queue Information <Enter>, select a print queue <Enter>, Queue Servers <Enter>.

To see who is assigned as a queue user for a print queue. PCONSOLE <Enter>, Print Queue Information <Enter>, select a print queue <Enter>, Queue Users <Enter>.

Print Server Information

(See information about the current file server's print servers.)

To see what print servers are available to the current server. PCONSOLE <Enter>, Print Server Information <Enter>.

To see a print server's full name. PCONSOLE <Enter>, Print Server Information <Enter>, select a print server <Enter>, Full Name <Enter>.

To see a print server's identification number. PCONSOLE <Enter>, Print Server Information <Enter>, select a print server <Enter>, Print Server ID <Enter>.

To see who is assigned as a print server operator. PCONSOLE <Enter>, Print Server Information <Enter>, select a print server <Enter>, Print Server Operators <Enter>.

To see which file servers a print server accesses. PCONSOLE <Enter>, Print Server Information <Enter>, Print Server Status/Control <Enter>, File Servers Being Serviced <Enter>.

To see who gets notified when print jobs are completed. PCONSOLE <Enter>, Print Server Information <Enter>, Print Server Status/Control <Enter>, Notify List for Printer <Enter>, select a printer <Enter>.

To see what print job is being serviced by a printer. PCONSOLE <Enter>, Print Server Information <Enter>, Print Server Status/Control <Enter>, Printer Status <Enter>, select a printer <Enter>.

To see what queues a printer services. PCONSOLE <Enter>, Print Server Information <Enter>, Print Server Status/Control <Enter>, Queues Serviced by Printer <Enter>, select a printer <Enter>.

To see the status of the print server. PCONSOLE <Enter>, Print Server Information <Enter>, Print Server Status/Control <Enter>, Server Info <Enter>.

To see who is assigned as a print server user. PCONSOLE <Enter>, Print Server Information <Enter>, select a print server <Enter>, Print Server Users <Enter>.

PRINTCON

```
┌──────────────────────────────────────────────────────────────────┐
│ ║              Edit Print Job Configuration "English"           ║ │
│ ╠══════════════════════════════════════════════════════════════╣ │
│ ║ Number of copies:   1          Form name:       standard      ║ │
│ ║ File contents:      Byte stream Print banner:   Yes           ║ │
│ ║ Tab size:                       Name:           TED           ║ │
│ ║ Suppress form feed: No          Banner name:                  ║ │
│ ║ Notify when done:   No                                        ║ │
│ ║                                                               ║ │
│ ║ Local printer:      1           Enable timeout: No            ║ │
│ ║ Auto endcap:        Yes         Timeout count:                ║ │
│ ║                                                               ║ │
│ ║ File server:        NTS3                                      ║ │
│ ║ Print queue:        ADMIN                                     ║ │
│ ║ Print server:       (Any)                                     ║ │
│ ║ Device:             (None)                                    ║ │
│ ║ Mode:               (None)                                    ║ │
└──────────────────────────────────────────────────────────────────┘
```

Use PRINTCON to set up your print job configurations to use when you print with PCONSOLE, CAPTURE, and NPRINT.

Edit Print Job Configurations

(Create, modify, and delete print job configurations.)

To create a print job configuration. PRINTCON <Enter>, Edit Print Job Configurations <Enter>, <Ins>, type a configuration name <Enter>, set the printing options, <Esc>, <Enter>.

To edit a print job configuration. PRINTCON <Enter>, Edit Print Job Configurations <Enter>, select a configuration <Enter>, change the printing options, <Esc>, <Enter>.

To rename a print job configuration. PRINTCON <Enter>, Edit Print Job Configurations <Enter>, select a configuration <F3>, delete name with <Backspace>, type new name <Enter>.

To delete a print job configuration. PRINTCON <Enter>, Edit Print Job Configurations <Enter>, select a configuration <Del>, <Enter>.

Select Default Print Job Configuration

(Choose which configuration you want to be the default.)

To select the default print job configuration. PRINTCON <Enter>, Select Default Print Job Configuration <Enter>, select a configuration <Enter>.

PRINTDEF

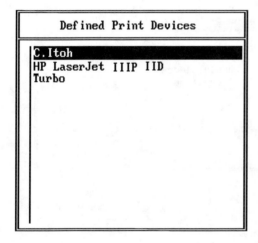

Use PRINTDEF to see how your network printers are defined in terms of functions, modes, and forms.

Print Devices

(View the functions and modes defined for your server.)

To see what print devices are defined. PRINTDEF <Enter>, Print Devices <Enter>.

To see what modes are defined for a print device. PRINTDEF <Enter>, Print Devices <Enter>, Edit Print Devices <Enter>, select a print device <Enter>, Device Modes <Enter>.

To see what functions are defined for a print device. PRINTDEF <Enter>, Print Devices <Enter>, select a print device <Enter>, Device Functions <Enter>.

To see what forms are defined. PRINTDEF <Enter>, Forms <Enter>.

SALVAGE

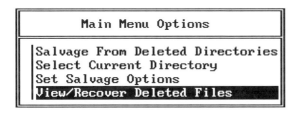

```
┌─────────────────────────────────────────┐
│          Main Menu Options              │
├─────────────────────────────────────────┤
│ Salvage From Deleted Directories        │
│ Select Current Directory                │
│ Set Salvage Options                     │
│ View/Recover Deleted Files              │
└─────────────────────────────────────────┘
```

Use SALVAGE to recover deleted file(s) erased through the FILER utility or through use of the DOS DEL or ERASE commands.

With NetWare 3.1x, your deleted files are stored for possible recovery later on. If you run PURGE, deleted files from the current directory can no longer be recovered.

To recover files from a deleted directory (you need Modify, Create, and File Scan rights to the DELETED.SAV directory). SALVAGE <Enter>, select Salvage from Deleted Directories <Enter>, select a volume <Enter>, type in the filename pattern <Enter>, select directory to recover from <Enter>, select subdirectory as needed <Enter>, select file to recover (or use <F5> to mark files or <F6> to specify a file pattern) <Enter>, <Enter>.

To select the current directory. SALVAGE <Enter>, Select Current Directory <Enter>, type in the directory path <Enter>.

To see a list of salvageable files in the current directory and recover them. SALVAGE <Enter>, select View/Recover Deleted Files <Enter>, type in a filename pattern <Enter>, select a file or use <F5> to mark files or <F6> to specify a file pattern <Enter>, <Enter>.

583

SESSION

```
┌─────────────────────────────────┐
│    Available Topics             │
├─────────────────────────────────┤
│ ▌Change Current Server▐         │
│  Drive Mappings                 │
│  Group List                     │
│  Search Mappings                │
│  Select Default Drive           │
│  User List                      │
└─────────────────────────────────┘
```

Use SESSION to set up your drive mappings, to select your default drive, and to send messages to users and groups.

Change Current Server

To change to a server you're attached to. Session <Enter>, select Change Current Server <Enter>, select a server <Enter>.

To change to a server you aren't attached to. Session <Enter>, select Change Current Server <Enter>, <Ins>, select a server <Enter>, type your username <Enter>, type your password <Enter>, select that server name <Enter>.

To log out of a server you're attached to. Session <Enter>, select Change Current Server <Enter>, select a server (or use <F5> to mark more than one) <Del>, <Enter>.

To change to a different user name on another server. Session <Enter>, select Change Current Server <Enter>, select a file server <F3>, type your new user name <Enter>, type your password <Enter>, <Esc>.

Drive Mappings

(View, add, modify, or delete your drive mappings for the time that you remain logged in.)

To see your drive mappings. SESSION <Enter>, Drive Mappings <Enter>.

To see your effective rights in a drive's directory. SESSION <Enter>, Drive Mappings <Enter>, select a drive mapping <Enter>.

To add a new drive mapping. SESSION <Enter>, Drive Mappings <Enter>, <Ins>, type letter you want to use <Enter>, specify the directory path <Enter>.

To modify an existing drive mapping. SESSION <Enter>, Drive Mappings <Enter>, select a drive mapping <F3>, specify new directory <Enter>.

To use a local drive for a network drive mapping. SESSION <Enter>, Drive Mappings <Enter>, select a local drive <F3>, specify network directory <Enter>, <Enter>.

To delete a drive mapping. SESSION <Enter>, Drive Mappings <Enter>, select a drive mapping (or use <F5> to mark more than one) <Del>, <Enter>.

Group List

(View a list of groups and send a message to a group.)

To see a list of groups on the current server. SESSION <Enter>, Group List <Enter>.

To send a message to a group. SESSION <Enter>, Group List <Enter>, select a group (or use <F5> to mark more than one) <Enter>, type the message <Enter>.

Search Mappings

(Add, modify, or delete search drive mappings for the time that you remain logged in.)

To see your search drive mappings. SESSION <Enter>, Search Mappings <Enter>.

To see your effective rights in a search drive's directory. SESSION <Enter>, Search Mappings <Enter>, select a search drive mapping <Enter>.

To add a new search drive mapping. SESSION <Enter>, Search Mappings <Enter>, <Ins>, type number you want to use <Enter>, specify the directory path <Enter>.

To modify an existing search drive mapping. SESSION <Enter>, Search Mappings <Enter>, select a search drive mapping <F3>, specify new directory <Enter>.

To set up a local drive as a search drive mapping. SESSION <Enter>, Search Mappings <Enter>, <Ins>, type number you want to use <Enter>, specify a local drive/ directory <Enter>.

To delete a search drive mapping. SESSION <Enter>, Search Mappings <Enter>, select a search drive mapping (or use <F5> to mark more than one) <Del>, <Enter>.

Select Default Drive

(Choose the drive you want to be your default drive until you select another one or until you log out.)

To select which drive will be your default drive. SESSION <Enter>, Select Default Drive <Enter>, select a drive <Enter>.

User List

(View a list of users and send a message to a user.)

To see a list of users currently attached to the server. SESSION <Enter>, User List <Enter>.

To see connection information about an attached user. SESSION <Enter>, User List <Enter>, select a user <Enter>, Display User Info <Enter>.

To send a message to a user. SESSION <Enter>, User List <Enter>, select a user <Enter>, Send Message <Enter>, type the message <Enter>.

To send a message to more than one user. SESSION <Enter>, User List <Enter>, use <F5> to mark multiple users <Enter>, type the message <Enter>.

SYSCON

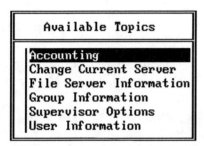

```
┌─────────────────────────────────┐
│      Available Topics           │
├─────────────────────────────────┤
│ Accounting                      │
│ Change Current Server           │
│ File Server Information         │
│ Group Information               │
│ Supervisor Options              │
│ User Information                │
└─────────────────────────────────┘
```

Use SYSCON to see how the server is set up, to see information about the defined users and groups, and to change your password and login script.

Accounting

(See information about NetWare's accounting option if it's installed on the current server.)

To see the names and types of servers that charge for their services. SYSCON <Enter>, Accounting <Enter>.

To see the charge rates for disk reads. SYSCON <Enter>, Accounting <Enter>, Blocks Read Charge Rates <Enter>, <Esc>.

To see the charge rates for disk writes. SYSCON <Enter>, Accounting <Enter>, Blocks Written Charge Rates <Enter>, <Esc>.

To see the charge rates for connection time. SYSCON <Enter>, Accounting <Enter>, Connect Time Charge Rates <Enter>, <Esc>.

To see the charge rates for disk storage. SYSCON <Enter>, Accounting <Enter>, Disk Storage Charge Rates <Enter>, <Esc>.

To see the charge rates for file service requests. SYSCON <Enter>, Accounting <Enter>, Service Requests Charge Rates <Enter>, <Esc>.

Change Current Server

(Change from one server to another. You must already be in SYSCON.)

To change to a server you're attached to. Change Current Server <Enter>, select a server <Enter>.

To change to a server you aren't attached to. Change Current Server <Enter>, <Ins>, select a server <Enter>, type your username <Enter>, type your password <Enter>, select that file server name <Enter>.

To log out of a server you're attached to. Change Current Server <Enter>, select a file server (or use <F5> to mark more than one) <Del>, <Enter>.

To change to a different username on another server. Change Current Server <Enter>, select a file server <F3>, type your new username <Enter>, type your password <Enter>, <Enter>.

File Server Information

(Look at operating system information, network address, and node address for any server on the internetwork.)

To see information about a file server's operating system. SYSCON <Enter>, File Server Information <Enter>, select a file server <Enter>.

Group Information

(See information about the groups defined on the server.)

To see a list of groups on the current file server. SYSCON <Enter>, Group Information <Enter>.

To see the full name assigned to a group. SYSCON <Enter>, Group Information <Enter>, select a group <Enter>, Full Name <Enter>.

To see who the members of a group are. SYSCON <Enter>, Group Information <Enter>, select a group <Enter>, Member List <Enter>.

To see the identification number of a group you're a member of. SYSCON <Enter>, Group Information <Enter>, select a group <Enter>, Other Information <Enter>.

To see the trustee directory assignments of a group you're a member of. SYSCON <Enter>, Group Information <Enter>, select a group <Enter>, Trustee Directory Assignments <Enter>.

Supervisor Options

(For supervisors only. Users see only an error message if they choose this option.)

User Information

(See information about yourself and other users, change your password, work with your login script.)

To see your account balance information (accounting must be installed). SYSCON <Enter>, User Information <Enter>, select your username <Enter>, Account Balance <Enter>.

To see your account, password, and login restrictions. SYSCON <Enter>, User Information <Enter>, select your username <Enter>, Account Restrictions <Enter>.

To change your password. SYSCON <Enter>, User Information <Enter>, select your username <Enter>, Change Password <Enter>, type new password <Enter>, retype new password <Enter>.

To see the full name assigned to your user name. SYSCON <Enter>, User Information <Enter>, select your username <Enter>, Full Name <Enter>.

To see the full name assigned to another user name. SYSCON <Enter>, User Information <Enter>, select a user name <Enter>, Full Name <Enter>.

To see what groups you belong to. SYSCON <Enter>, User Information <Enter>, select your user name <Enter>, Groups Belonged To <Enter>.

To see what groups another user belongs to. SYSCON <Enter>, User Information <Enter>, select a user name <Enter>, Groups Belonged To <Enter>.

To set up your login script. SYSCON <Enter>, User Information <Enter>, select your username <Enter>, Login Script <Enter>, add login script commands <Esc>, <Enter>.

To see what groups or users you manage. SYSCON <Enter>, User Information <Enter>, select your username <Enter>, Managed Users and Groups <Enter>.

To see what group(s) or user(s) is your manager. SYSCON <Enter>, User Information <Enter>, select your username <Enter>, Managers <Enter>.

To see other information about yourself. SYSCON <Enter>, User Information <Enter>, select your username <Enter>, Other Information <Enter>.

To see your security equivalences. SYSCON <Enter>, User Information <Enter>, select your username <Enter>, Security Equivalences <Enter>.

To see what workstations you're allowed to log in from. SYSCON <Enter>, User Information <Enter>, select your username <Enter>, Station Restrictions <Enter>.

To see what days and times you're allowed to log in. SYSCON <Enter>, User Information <Enter>, select your username <Enter>, Time Restrictions <Enter>.

To see all of your trustee directory assignments. SYSCON <Enter>, User Information <Enter>, select your username <Enter>, Trustee Directory Assignments <Enter>.

To see all of your trustee file assignments. SYSCON <Enter>, User Information <Enter>, select your username <Enter>, Trustee File Assignments <Enter>.

To see what restrictions you have on a volume. SYSCON <Enter>, User Information <Enter>, select your username <Enter>, Volume/Disk Restrictions <Enter>, select a volume <Enter>.

VOLINFO

```
Page 1/1          Total      Free      Total      Free      Total      Free

Volume name          SYS                  BEAT
KiloBytes        192,464    88,280    119,088    25,108
Directories       17,792     7,359      8,896     4,782

Volume name
KiloBytes
Directories
```

```
Available Options

Change Servers
Update Interval
```

Use VOLINFO to see information about each volume on your file server.

To see volume information for your current server. VOLINFO <Enter>.

Change Servers

(Change from one server to another to view volume information.)

To see volume information for a server you're attached to. VOLINFO <Enter>, Change Servers <Enter>, select a server <Enter>.

To see volume information for a server you aren't attached to. VOLINFO <Enter>, Change Servers <Enter>, <Ins>, select a server <Enter>, type your username <Enter>, type your password <Enter>, select that file server name <Enter>.

Update Interval

(Change the time interval between volume information updates. You must already be in VOLINFO.)

To increase or decrease the update interval. Update Interval <Enter>, delete interval with <Backspace>, type new interval <Enter>.

APPENDIX C

Command-Line Utilities Quick Reference

Here's a quick list of the command-line utilities available in NetWare 3.11. The listing, in alphabetical order, gives a brief description of each utility, the general format of the command itself, and examples of how to use the command. The examples provided are by no means an exhaustive listing; they are meant only to give you a guideline for typing in the commands. The capitalized letters in the commands indicate the abbreviations you can use.

You run command-line utilities from the network prompt, which means you must be logged in or attached to a server and have access to the SYS:PUBLIC directory. You must also have Read and File Scan rights in the SYS:PUBLIC directory in order to use the command-line utilities. Rights to perform the utilities themselves varies with each utility.

For most utilities in NetWare 3.11 and 3.12, you need to use the forward slash (/) before designating an option or parameter. So, for consistency's sake, it's easiest to use the forward slash as often as possible—even if some of these examples don't show it.

ALLOW lets you see the inherited rights mask of files and directories. If you have Access Control rights to the file or directory, you can also set or modify the mask.

Format

ALLOW *path* TO INHERIT *rights*

Rights = Supervisory (S), Read (R), Write (W), Create (C), Erase (E), Modify (M), File Scan (F), Access Control (A), ALL, No Right (N)

Example

To see what the inherited rights mask is for the current directory, type ALLOW <Enter>. To change the mask to Read and File Scan for a file

MEMO.TXT, type ALLOW MEMO.TXT R F <Enter>. For the directory MEMO, type ALLOW MEMO R F <Enter>.

ATTACH allows you to attach up to seven servers other than the server you are logged in to.

Format

ATTACH *servername/username*

Example

To attach to server ADMIN as user Ted, type ATTACH ADMIN/TED <Enter>. You'll probably see the prompt, "Enter your password." Type in your password, press <Enter>, and you'll attach to the server. If you're not created as a user on server ADMIN, type ATTACH PUB/GUEST <Enter>.

CAPTURE enables you to specify jobs, servers, queues, and filenames. You can also set printing specifics, such as number of copies, timeouts, tabs, banners, text names, formfeeds, autocaps, and endcaps.

Format

CAPTURE *options*

Options = /S=servername; /Q=queuename; /Local=number; /Form=number or form name; /CReate=filename; /Copies=number; /TImeout=number; /Tabs=number, /No Tabs; /Banner=text, /No Banner, /Form Feed, /No Form Feed, /Autoendcap, /No Autoendcap, /Keep, /SHow, /NOTIfy, /No NOTIfy, /DOmain=domain, /End Capture, /CAncel, /ALL

Example

To send a print job to print queue QUE_T on server ADMIN, using LPT1, and sending two copies, no tabs, no banner, no form feed, and using a timeout of five seconds, type CAPTURE LPT1 S=ADMIN Q=QUE_T C=2 NT NB NFF TI=5 <Enter>. To see how you're presently using CAPTURE, type CAPTURE SH <Enter>.

CASTOFF stops any messages from being sent to your screen.

Format

CASTOFF *options*

Options = STations, All, Console

Example

To block messages from other workstations, type CASTOFF ST <Enter>. To block messages from workstations and the server console, type CAST-OFF C <Enter>. To block all messages, type CASTOFF A <Enter>.

CASTON cancels the effect of CASTOFF and allows messages to be received again at the workstation.

Format

CASTON

CHKDIR shows you the size and space limitations for the specified directory. You must have Read and File Scan rights for that directory.

Format

CHKDIR *path*

Example

To see the size and limits for your default directory, type CHKDIR <Enter>. To see the information for a specific directory, PERSONAL\TED, type CHKDIR F:\PERSONAL\TED <Enter>, or CHKDIR F: <Enter>.

CHKVOL shows a volume's disk space, the byte count of files, the number of available bytes, and the number of directory entries that are left.

Format

CHKVOL *servername/volume or drive letter: /Continuous*

Examples

To see statistics on your default volume, type CHKVOL <Enter>. To see statistics on a specific volume (such as SYS), type CHKVOL SYS <Enter>.

To see all volume statistics on an attached server, such as PUB, type CHKVOL PUB/* <Enter>. To see all volume statistics on all attached servers, type CHKVOL */* <Enter>. To see volume statistics from designated drive letters, such as K:, type CHKVOL K: <Enter>.

ENDCAP cancels the effects of the CAPTURE utility.

Format

ENDCAP /*options*

Options = Local=number, ALL, Cancel

Example

To end your CAPTURE on LPT1, type ENDCAP /LPT1 <Enter>. To end all of your present captures, type ENDCAP /ALL <Enter>. To end your captures and cancel your queued print jobs on LPT1, type ENDCAP /C <Enter>; to end and cancel only on a port, such as LPT2, type ENDCAP / C /L=2 <Enter>. To end all your captures and print jobs on all LPT ports, type ENDCAP /C /ALL <Enter>.

FLAG allows you to flag file attributes from the command line instead of going into FILER.

Format

FLAG *path/filename /options*

/options = All, Shareable, Hidden, SYstem, Read-Only (RO), Read-Write (RW), Transactional, Normal, SUBdirectory, HELP, Copy Inhibited, Delete Inhibited, Rename Inhibited, Purge, Archive Needed, Read Audit (RA), Write Audit (WA), and EXecute Only (X).

Example

To flag an executable file, such as ART.COM, as Shareable and Read-Only, type FLAG ART.COM SRO <Enter>. To flag a modifiable file, such as BILLS.DAT, as Nonshareable and Read-Write, type FLAG BILLS.DAT N <Enter>. To flag all the *.DAT files as Nonshareable and Read-Write in your present directory and subdirectories, type FLAG *.DAT N SUB <Enter>.

594

FLAGDIR allows you to hide the directory or the subdirectory structure from those who don't have File Scan rights. You need Access Control effective rights to use this command.

Format

FLAGDIR *directory path options*

Options = Normal, System, Hidden, Deleteinhibit, Renameinhibit, and Purge. Type FLAGDIR /H to see HELP.

Example

To flag the directory you're presently in as Hidden, type FLAGDIR . H <Enter>. To flag the TEAM directory on directory path G:, type FLAGDIR G: H <Enter>. To flag all your subdirectories so that only those with File Scan rights can see the directory structure, type FLAGDIR G: P <Enter>. To unflag a directory, go to the directory and type FLAGDIR . N <Enter>.

GRANT allows you to grant trustee assignments (the ability to see and access files or utilities) in your directories to other users and groups. This is the same capability that you have in FILER. You must have Access Control rights in a directory before you can give other users trustee assignments to that directory.

Format

GRANT [ONLY] *options* for *directory path* to *username/groupname*

Rights Options = Read (R), Write (W), Create (C), Erase (E), Access Control (A), File Scan (F), Modify (M), No Rights (N), ALL, Supervisor (S)

In addition, you can append two options to the command: /SubDirectories and /Files. With these options you can then grant rights to the subdirectories also or to just the files specifically. Be sure to put spaces between letters.

Example

To grant RWCEF rights to group SECS in your present directory, type GRANT R W C E F TO SECS <Enter>. To grant RF rights to Bill, who already has RWCEF rights in your present directory, type GRANT ONLY R F TO BILL <Enter>. To grant all rights to Ted in the H: directory path, type GRANT ALL FOR H: TO TED <Enter>. The other rights work in the same way.

LISTDIR lists the subdirectories under your present directory. Through its options, LISTDIR displays the inherited rights mask and the directory's creation date and time.

Format

LISTDIR *directory path /options*

Options = Subdirectory, Rights, Effective Rights, Date/Time, All

Examples

To list the directories beneath your present directory, type LISTDIR <Enter>. To see the subdirectories, as well as their subdirectories, beneath your present directory, type LISTDIR /S <Enter>. To see the directory rights mask on your subdirectories, type LISTDIR /R <Enter>. To see the directories' creation date and time, type LISTDIR /D <Enter>. To see all the parameters together, type LISTDIR /A <Enter>. You can also designate the full directory path or the drive letter for other directories.

LOGIN allows you to establish a connection with the designated server and runs your login script to set up your working environment.

Format

LOGIN *servername/username*

Example

To log in to server ADMIN as user Ted, type LOGIN ADMIN/TED <Enter>. You'll probably see the prompt, "Enter your password." Type in your password and you'll log in.

LOGOUT ends your working session with the server or servers and retains a connection with the server that corresponds to the drive letter that you logged out from. You can also log out from attached servers and retain a connection with your default server.

Format

LOGOUT *servername*

Example

For blanket logout, type LOGOUT <Enter>. To log out from specific servers (such as PUB), type LOGOUT PUB <Enter>.

MAP maps drive letters to directories for quick access. If you want permanent map changes, put the changes in the login script.

Format

MAP

MAP *drive letter:*

MAP *directory path*

MAP drive letter:=*drive letter or directory path*

MAP [INSert] drive letter:=*drive letter or directory path*

MAP DEL drive letter:

MAP REM drive letter:

MAP ROOT drive letter:=*directory path*

MAP Next *directory path*

Examples

To see your map listings, type MAP <Enter>. To see which directory is mapped to a particular drive letter, such as D:, type MAP D: <Enter>. To change F: from BYTE:USERS/TED to SYS:NETWORK JULY, type MAP SYS:NETWORK JULY <Enter> at the F: prompt. To map a new drive letter (M:) to a directory path (such as BYTE:USERS/TED), type MAP M:=BYTE:USERS/TED <Enter>. To insert a search (S2) so you don't overwrite other search drives, type MAP INS S2:=PUB/BYTE:USERS/TED/BATCH <Enter>. To remove a drive mapping such as J:, type MAP DEL J: <Enter> or MAP REM J: <Enter>. To create a false root for the program GRAPH that needs to be loaded at the root, type MAP ROOT H:APPS/GRAPH <Enter>. To use the next available drive letter, type MAP N SYS:USERS/TED <Enter>.

MENU allows you to run a personal or system menu.

Format

MENU *path/filename*

Examples

To run the MAIN menu, type MENU MAIN <Enter>. You don't need to type the filename extension if it's .MNU. For your own personal menu, substitute MAIN with your menu name.

NCOPY is a network version of COPY that allows you to copy files.

Format

NCOPY *directory path/filename(s)* to *directory path/filenames /options*

Options = Copy, Inform (/I), Subdirectories (/S), Subdirectories and Empty Subdirectories (/S/E), Parse files (/F), Help (/H), Verify (/V), Archive (/A), Modify (M), DOS information (/C)

Examples

To copy *.DAT files from J: to K: directories, type NCOPY J:*.DAT K: <Enter>. To copy the REPORTS file from your current directory to subdirectory JAN, type NCOPY REPORTS JAN <Enter>. You can also write out the directory paths of the source directory and the destination directories: for example, NCOPY SYS:REPORTS*.DAT BYTE:USERS\TED\REPORTS <Enter>. To verify a file transfer to a local disk drive, type NCOPY J:*.DAT K: /V <Enter>. You can also use wild cards in this command. To include all subdirectories, type NCOPY J:*.* K: /S <Enter>. If some of the subdirectories are empty, type NCOPY J:*.* K: /S /E <Enter>.

NDIR gives you filenames, file sizes, the last time and date the file was written to, when files were last accessed, file creation date, file flags, and file owner. In addition, you can see subdirectories, their creation date, their inherited rights mask, your effective rights, and subdirectories owners.

Since the combinations you can perform with NDIR options are almost inexhaustible, the simplest way to use NDIR is to type NDIR <Enter>. Here's a graph to show the different options and their parameters. To get an idea of how to use NDIR, the "NDIR" subheading under the "Directory and file Management Utilities" heading in Chapter 3.

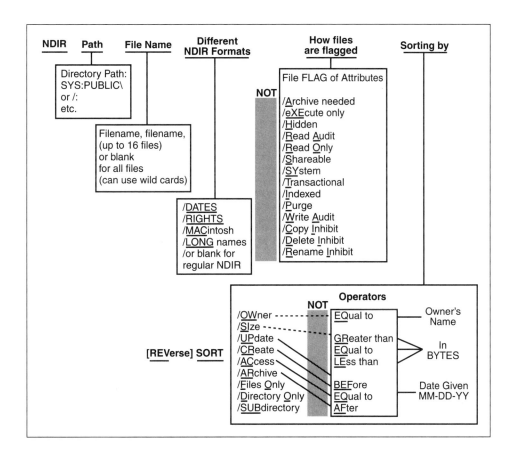

NETBIOS tells you which NetWare version you're running, whether NETBIOS is running and with which interrupts, and allows you to unload the NETBIOS.

Format

NETBIOS *options*

Options = Information, Unload

Examples

To unload the NETBIOS, type NETBIOS U <Enter>. To see the version information, type NETBIOS I <Enter>.

NPRINT allows you to print any files you've saved as text files, graphics files, or files that are prepared for a specific printer, usually by printing to a file instead of a printer. You can use NPRINT's parameters to specify jobs, servers, queues, printer servers, and filenames. You can also set printing specifics, such as number of copies, tabs, banners, and formfeeds.

Format

NPRINT *directory path: filename options*

Options = Server=*servername* (/S); Queue=queuename (/Q); Print Server=name (/PS); Job=job configuration name (/J); Form=number or form name (/F); Copies=number (/C); Tabs=number (/T), No Tabs (/NT); Banner=text (/B); Name=your name (/NA); No Banner (/NB); No Form Feed (/NFF); Delete (/D); NOTIfy (/NOTI); No NOTIfy (/NONOTI), Domain=domain (/DO)

Example

To print the file JAN.RPT to print queue QUE_T on server ADMIN, using LPT1, and sending two copies, no tabs, no banner, no form feed, type NPRINT JAN.RPT S=ADMIN Q=QUE_T C=2 NT NB NFF <Enter>.

NVER displays version information on NetBIOS, IPX, SPX, NetWare shell, DOS, your workstation's LAN driver, server, and server software.

Format and Example

NVER

PSC allows you to see the status of print servers and to control the network printer if you are a print server operator.

Format

PSC PS=*print server* P=*printer number flaglist*

Flaglist = STATus, PAUse, ABort, STOp, Keep, STARt, Mark, FormFeed, MOunt Form=n, PRIvate, SHared, CancelDown

Examples

To see whether the print server NTS is running, type PSC PS=NTS STAT <Enter>. If you're a print server operator and want to abort a print job, type

PSC PS=NTS AB <Enter>.

PURGE irrevocably deletes files on the network hard disks.

Format

PURGE [filename | wildcard [/ALL] | /A]

REMOVE allows you to drop a person or group from the trustee list in your directory. Where REVOKE takes away user or group rights, REMOVE takes those people as objects from the directory trustee list. You must have Access Control rights to use the command.

Format

REMOVE *username groupname* from *directory path /Sub*

Example

To remove group SECS from your present directory, type REMOVE SECS <Enter>. To remove Bill, who already has RWCEF rights in directory J:, type REMOVE BILL FROM J: <Enter>.

RENDIR allows you to rename a directory. You need Access Control and Modify rights in the directory you wish to rename.

Format

RENDIR directory path TO directory name

Example

To rename the TEAM directory which resides at the end of the G: directory path to TWORK, type RENDIR G: TO TWORK <Enter>. To specify the full directory path (such as PUB/BYTE:USERS/TED/TEAM), type PUB/BYTE:USERS/TED/TEAM TO TWORK <Enter>. If you're in the TEAM directory, type RENDIR . TWORK <Enter>.

REVOKE allows you to take away trustee rights in one of your directories. You must have Access Control rights in that directory to revoke another person's or group's trustee rights. Use REVOKE to take away trustee rights given through the GRANT, SYSCON, or FILER utilities.

Format

REVOKE *rights options* for *directory path from username/groupname* /options

Rights options = Read, Write, Create, Erase, Access Control, File Scan, Modify, ALL, Supervisor (S)

Options = SUBdirectories, Files

Examples

To revoke RWCEF rights to group SECS in your present directory, type REVOKE R W C E F FROM SECS <Enter>. To revoke RF rights from Bill, who already has RWCEF rights in your present directory, type REVOKE W C E FROM BILL <Enter>. To revoke all rights from Ted in the H: directory path, type REVOKE ALL FOR H: FROM TED <Enter>. The other rights work in the same way. If you want to include all subdirectories, use the /SUB option.

RIGHTS shows you the effective rights you have in a designated directory.

Format

RIGHTS *directory path*

Example

To see your effective rights in your present directory, type RIGHTS <Enter>. To see your rights in the J: directory, type RIGHTS J: <Enter>.

SEND allows you to send a message to a person or to a group.

Format

SEND *"message"*to *username groupname*

SEND *"message"* to *servername/username servername/groupname*

SEND to *username groupname "message"*

Example

To send a message to user Tom and group CARPOOL on your default server, type SEND "We'll go soon" TO TOM CARPOOL <Enter>. To send a message to Tom on server PUB and group CARPOOL on server ADMIN while you're on server PUB, first attach to the designated servers and then type SEND "We'll go soon" TO PUB/TOM ADMIN/CARPOOL <Enter>. To reverse the order of message and sender, type SEND TO TOM CARPOOL "We'll go soon" <Enter>.

SETPASS lets you change your password from the command line.

Format

SETPASS *servername/username*

Example

At the network prompt, type SETPASS <Enter>. You'll be asked to enter your new password and to retype your new password. If you're attached to more than one server, you'll be asked if you want to synchronize your passwords as well.

SETTTS Use SETTTS with files that have been marked "transactional" within those systems that have transaction tracking system (TTS) installed. Use SETTTS when your program uses file locking for its own purposes and you need to set the locking threshold to compensate.

Format

SETTTS logical locks physical locks

Examples

To set up a 2 logical and 1 physical threshold, type SETTTS 2 1 <Enter>. To set up a 1 physical lock, type SETTTS 0 1 <Enter>, and to set up a 1 logical lock, type SETTTS 1 <Enter>.

SLIST shows you a list of the servers communicating with the server you're logged in to. You can type SLIST from the LOGIN directory to see which servers are available.

Format

SLIST *servername* /Continuous

603

Example

To see a complete list of active servers, type SLIST <Enter>. To see the total number of servers without pausing after a screenful, type SLIST /C <Enter>. To see if a specific server (such as ADMIN) is on the network, type SLIST ADMIN <Enter>.

SMODE ensures that an application can find the necessary auxiliary files so the application can perform its functions.

Format

SMODE directory path | drive letter: filename MODE = x /Sub x = the following: MODE 0 = No search instructions. Use instructions in NET.CFG file. MODE 1 = Search if no path specified. If path specified, search only that path. MODE 2 = Doesn't use search drive to find data files. MODE 3 = Uses search drives only if no path is defined and application request to only read a file (not write to it). MODE 5 = Will always be able to use search drives. MODE 7 = Will use search drive if request to open files is to read the file only.

Example

To specify a directory path, filename, and mode 1, type SMODE G: USER2.EXE M=1 <Enter>. The other modes perform the same. Use the option /Sub with a defined path to search all subdirectories in the path.

SYSTIME resets your workstation's internal clock to the date and time of the server you call up.

Format

SYSTIME *servername*

Example

To see your present server time, type SYSTIME <Enter>. To see the server time on a server you're attached to (such as ADMIN), type SYSTIME ADMIN <Enter>.

TLIST shows you which users and groups have trustee rights to a particular directory. These rights correspond directly to the trustee assignments set up by your supervisor in SYSCON, or by you from either the FILER or GRANT utilities. You must have Access Control rights to use the command.

Format

TLIST *directory path* USERS GROUPS

Example

To see who has trustee assignments in your present directory, type TLIST <Enter>. To see which groups have trustee assignments in drive J:, type TLIST J: G <Enter>. To see a user list, type TLIST J: U <Enter>.

USERLIST lists the users on the server you're currently logged in to, as well as the users on the server you're attached to. You can see the connection number, username, network and node address, and login time.

Format

USERLIST *servername/username /options*

/options = /Address, /Object, /Continuous

Examples

To see a list of the users on your present server, type USERLIST <Enter>. To see a list of the users on server PUB, to which you're already attached, type USERLIST PUB/ <Enter>. To see the connection number, username, network and node address, and login time of users on server PUB, type USERLIST PUB/ /A <Enter>. To select a single person (for instance, Jan) on server PUB, type USERLIST PUB/JAN /A <Enter>. To see what types of objects are connected, type USERLIST PUB/ /O <Enter>.

VERSION shows you the version number of the NetWare utility. You see similar information on the menued utilities.

Format

VERSION *directory path: filename*

Examples

Since this is a NetWare-specific utility, and all the utilities for users are on SYS:PUBLIC, all you have to do is to type the filename from any directory.

To see which version of SYSCON you're using, for example, type VER-SION SYSCON <Enter>. To see which version your NDIR utility is, type VERSION NDIR <Enter>.

WHOAMI lists the servers you're attached to, the directories you have rights in, your effective rights in those directories, and the groups you belong to.

Format

WHOAMI *servername /options*

/options = /Groups, /Security, /Rights, /Object, /SYstem, /Workgroups, /All, /Continuous, /Server

Examples

To see which servers you're currently logged in to and the name(s) you used to log in, type WHOAMI <Enter>. To see your rights on a server you're attached to, such as PUB, type WHOAMI PUB <Enter>. To see the groups you belong to, type WHOAMI /G <Enter>. To see your security equiva-lences, type WHOAMI /S <Enter>. To see your effective rights on the server, type WHOAMI /R <Enter>. To see your groups, security equiva-lences, and effective rights together, type WHOAMI /A <Enter>.

When Users Manage

While this book has been written primarily for NetWare users, many users are taking on more managerial responsibilities. These managerial responsibilities have more than doubled from earlier versions of NetWare. The five areas of managerial responsibilities that users can participate in without becoming a supervisor or equivalent include:

➤ Workgroup manager

➤ User account manager

➤ Console operator

➤ Print queue operator

➤ Print server operator

Here's a look at each of these managers' duties. The duties described here are to show the extent of the manager's authority without supervisor equivalence. If some of the steps seem cumbersome or handled better through supervisor equivalence, your supervisor may opt for a less tight security scheme and grant certain users supervisor equivalence. But if virus control is an issue, the fewer personnel with supervisor equivalence the better the server's security scheme will be.

If you're a system supervisor, in this section you can learn the step-by-step process of giving users the ability to assume these different management responsibilities.

Workgroup Manager

A workgroup manager is the closest thing to being a supervisor or equivalent, for you can create other users or groups as well as manage directories on a selected volume. As a workgroup manager, you can manage your newly created or assigned user accounts. You can make another user who is a part of your responsibility a user account manager, who can then manage the users or groups you assign to him or her. You also have the ability to delete user and group accounts that are under your responsibility.

What Your Supervisor Must Do

In order to make you a workgroup manager, your system supervisor must perform two duties: add you as a workgroup manager and give you sufficient rights to a volume or directory structure. To add you as a workgroup manager, the supervisor goes into SYSCON, selects "Supervisor Options" <Enter>, then selects the "Workgroup Managers" option <Enter>. If your name doesn't appear in the "Workgroup Managers" window, the supervisor presses <Ins>, highlights your name, then presses <Enter>.

The supervisor then selects the "User Information" option from the "Available Topics" window, selects your name, then selects "Trustee Directory Assignments" <Enter>. Here the supervisor must give you sufficient trustee assignments to assist the users and groups you are to manage. These rights are given at the "Restrict Volume" option. In order to modify trustee assignments for the personnel and groups you manage, you'll need trustee assignments that include Access Control rights to the \USER directory (wherever user directories are stored), and to the \APPS directory (wherever applications are stored). Supervisors don't have to assign the Supervisory trustee assignment, only the Access Control assignment. Without Access Control rights, you can't grant other users trustee assignments to their own or to other directories.

If the supervisor assigns other workgroup managers to take care of certain applications, the supervisor can specify the application directory in which you have all rights. For example, if your assignment is to take care of the WordPerfect directory, you may have all rights to the \APPS\WP51 directory instead of all rights to the \APPS directory.

Supervisors can also assign you users and groups by highlighting your name in the "User Names" window, then selecting the "Managed Users And Groups" option from the "User Information" window. By pressing <Ins>, the supervisor can then add users and groups for you to manage. Again, be sure you have sufficient rights to manage those assigned to you.

What the Workgroup Manager Can Do

As a workgroup manager, you can create new users and groups to add to the ones your supervisor may have given you. Instead of a long list of details of your duties, here are the quick steps to get you on your way. You can then read about the particulars from the supervisor manuals supplied by Novell or at bookstores.

Creating Users

Let's suppose you've been assigned as manager over Tim, who isn't set up on the network. To create a new user, such as Tim, go into SYSCON and choose the "User

608

Information" option <Enter>, then press <Ins>. Type in the user's login name (TIM) in the "User Name:" window and press <Enter>. If you don't have management duties over group EVERYONE, you'll see a message explaining this. Your supervisor must then add your newly created users to the group EVERYONE for NetWare utility access (among other things).

You next see the "Path To Create User's Home Directory" window with a default directory path to where the user directories reside—for our example, the directory path is ADMIN\SYS:USERS\TED. Press <Enter>, then verify the creation of the new directory that matches the user's login name by highlighting the "Yes" option and pressing <Enter>. Now highlight TIM, press <Enter>, and you'll see the "User Information" window with the same options you see when you look at your personal user information.

You can modify nearly all options in the "User Information" window to the extent of your authority, and I'll discuss more about this as I go through the options. If the server has accounting in place, you can set up an account balance for Tim by highlighting the "Account Balance" option and pressing <Enter>. You can then assign an account balance, allow unlimited credit, and set up a low account limit by typing in the numbers or selection you wish and pressing <Enter>. Press <Esc> to return to the "User Information" window.

The "Account Restrictions" option allows you to enable or disable the account, set up an expiration date for the account, and limit the number of connections Tim can have to the file server at the same time. You can also set up password restrictions. When you're finished, press <Esc> to return to the "User Information" window. In the "User Information" window, you can also give Tim a password through the "Change Password" option, as well as a full name through the "Full Name" option.

In the "Groups Belonged To" option, you can assign Tim to any groups you're a manager over. When you press <Enter> on this option, then <Ins> for a list of the groups Tim doesn't belong to, you'll see only those groups you're managing. If Tim needs to be a part of other groups, such as group EVERYONE, the supervisor will need to add Tim to those groups. Or the supervisor may place those groups under your loving care. Highlight the groups you wish Tim to belong to and press <Enter>, then press <Esc> until you return to the "User Information" window.

When you select the "Login Script" option, you'll initially see the "Login Script Does Not Exist" window with Tim's name listed after the "Read Login Script From User" entry. You can press <Enter> and create Tim's login script, or you can backspace over Tim's name, type in the name of someone else you manage, press <Enter>, and use that person's login script as a template for Tim. See the "Setting Up Your Login Script"

609

subheading in "The SYSCON Utility" heading in Chapter 2. for tons of explanation about login scripts. When you're finished, press <Esc>, then <Enter> to the "Save Changes" window, and you'll return to the "User Information" window.

Speaking of login scripts: Because you're not a supervisor or equivalent, you can't modify the system login script. But if you need to set up some universal script parameters for the users you manage, here's a way to ensure that those parameters are included. First, create a group that contains all the users you manage—TEDSGROUP, for example. Then have the supervisor place the following line at the bottom of the system login script:

```
IF MEMBER OF "TEDSGROUP"THEN INCLUDE SYS:USERS\TED\SCRIPT
```

The INCLUDE command allows you to place parts of the login script in a file kept outside of the NET$LOG.DAT file, which stores the system login script. This command says "If you belong to the group TEDSGROUP, then include those commands in the SCRIPT file found in the \USERS\TED directory." You can then add the necessary login script commands for your users to access the applications they need to do their job, and the SCRIPT file is in an accessible directory for you to maintain.

The "Managed Users And Groups" option shows who Tim has been set up to manage as a user account manager or workgroup manager. User account managers are discussed later in this appendix. There's a lot of Direct/Indirect management grantings that can get very confusing if you don't pay attention to it. For example, when you select this option, you can see whether Tim manages users or groups directly or indirectly. Direct means by direct assignment—you have given Tim rights to manage users or a group. Indirect means Tim has managerial assignments by being a member of a group that is designated as a manager or by sharing security equivalence with someone who is managing users or groups. So as a workgroup manager or account manager, pay close attention to security schemes, for if Tim is made security equivalent to Ted, Tim has all the rights that Ted has, including being a workgroup manager.

The "Managers" option shows who's been assigned to manage Tim. Presently, only Ted appears, but as a workgroup manager, you can assign Rachel as an account manager over Tim. Suppose Rachel is the Lotus wizard of your department and has agreed to be an account manager over those using the application, including Tim. (Make sure this is a part of her job description so she knows how much time to spend performing this function.)

You can add Tim to Rachel's group three ways. At Tim's "Managers" option, press <Enter>, then <Ins> and add Rachel. You can also go to Rachel in the "User Names" window, select her name, choose the "Managed Users and Groups" option, and add each person individually that Rachel will be over. Or you can create the group LOTUS and simply add the LOTUS group to Rachel's responsibilities. Again, you only see the users and groups you have managerial responsibilities for, and can only add those users and groups. But all in all, groups are the best method for adding this type of managerial responsibilities.

If you as the workgroup manager have Access Control rights over the \APPS\LOTUS directory, you can then grant Rachel Access Control rights over the \LOTUS directory so she can perform Lotus upgrade functions as well as grant read or write rights to other users when the need arises. If you don't want to give her Access Control rights over the \LOTUS directory, be prepared to perform upgrade and trustee assignment functions.

As a workgroup manager, you can't affect the "Other Information" option in Tim's "User Information" window. However, you can modify the "Security Equivalences" option by adding those users and groups within your responsibilities. Select the option, then press <Ins> to bring up the window to add other users or groups. However, take a good look at your security scheme before granting security equivalences, for they can lead to problems when setting up user account managers.

You can also set up station restrictions for Tim through the "Station Restrictions" option in the "User Information" window. Highlight the option and press <Enter> then <Ins> to first designate a network address restriction, then the node number of the workstation you wish to restrict him to. (You get node numbers of presently logged-in workstations through the USERLIST /A command.) If you don't want restrictions, leave this option blank so Tim can log in from any workstation. Press <Esc> to return to the "User Information" window.

The "Time Restrictions" option in the "User Information" window covers the hours when Tim is allowed to log in to the server. The default is all the time, but you can restrict server access if you need to. Highlight the option <Enter>, then use <F5> and the up/down/Side arrow keys to mark a block of time. Press the Delete key to delete the marked block. You can also mark a place that's already been deleted, then press the asterisk key (*) to fill the block again with asterisks. Press <Esc> to return to the "User Information" window.

The last option I'm going to speak about in detail is the "Trustee Directory Assignments" option. Through this option, you can grant Tim ALL rights to his personal directory. Or, if you don't want Tim granting trustee assignments to other users in his directory, you can grant him all rights except Access Control. Highlight the "Trustee Directory Assignments" option and press <Enter>, then highlight one of the trustee assignments and press <Enter>.

Suppose you want to delete Access Control from Tim. Highlight the USERS\TIM entry <Enter>, then highlight the "Access Control" entry and press <Del>. Answer "Yes" to the "Revoke Trustee Right" window and that right is now revoked. To add a right, press <Ins> at the "Trustee Rights Granted" window and select a right from the "Trustee Rights Not Granted" window and press <Enter>. The right is restored. You can also use the F5 key to highlight a number of rights for adding or deleting.

To add another directory assignment to Tim, press <Ins> at the "Trustee Directory Assignments" window. You'll see the "Directory In Which Trustee Should Be Added" window, to which you either type in the directory path or press <Ins> to build a directory path one directory at a time. (This procedure has been covered ad nauseam throughout the book.) With the directory path in place, press <Enter> and that directory path is added to the "Trustee Directory Assignments" window. You can then modify the trustee assignment as you wish— Read and File Scan rights for read-only capabilities, and Write, Create, Erase, Modify, and File Scan rights for write-only capabilities. If you try to create a directory path where you have no rights yourself, you'll see the "You have insufficient rights to alter trustee assignments in directoryname. Press <Esc> to continue" window, and you won't be able to add that directory path as a trustee assignment. To exit the "trustee Directory Assignments" window, press <Esc>.

That's it for adding or modifying a user entry. There's much more to the management aspect, but for help with that, go to Novell's manuals or other books on the subject. Now let's look at creating groups and managing applications.

Managing Groups and Applications

Many users become incredibly proficient in a particular application, to the point where other users use that person for help much more than the supervisor. Because of this, a supervisor may defer questions about that application to the user and allow that user to manage the application and the application's directories as part of being a workgroup manager. So a workgroup manager can also be a person who has been given the rights necessary to access, update or modify a given application directory. These managers may also maintain printing for that application, which may include becoming a print queue or a print server operator.

Since groups are most often used to control user access to applications, let's look at the "Group Information" option in SYSCON's "Available Topic" window. Go into SYSCON and select the "Groups Information" option. You'll see all the groups set up on this server, including the ones you're a member of and those you have managerial responsibilities over. Let's suppose you've been handed a new application, WordPerfect

5.2, to manage. As a designated workgroup manager, select the "Group Information" option at SYSCON's "Available Topics" window. Then at the "Group Names" window, press <Ins> to create a new group, and type in the group name—for example, WP52. Press <Enter> until you see the "Group Information" window, which shows you six options: "Full Name," "Managed Users and Groups," "Managers," "Member List," "Other Information," and "Trustee Directory Assignments." This is the same screen you see when you're a member of a group, but now you can manipulate most of the options.

To modify the group's full name, highlight the entry and press <Enter>, then type in the name you wish to give the group—for example, "WordPerfect 5.2 Group"—and press <Enter>. To modify the name, select it again and retype whatever name you want. The "Managed Users and Groups" option shows which users or groups the group WP52 can manage. If you don't wish group WP52 to manage anything, leave this option blank. If you do wish group WP52 to manage a set of users, then press <Ins> and you'll see those users and groups you have managerial responsibilities over. You can then choose from this list. When you're finished, press <Esc> and return to the "Group Information" window.

While it's only an opinion, I believe that it's better to have one user manage the applications a group can access than allow a whole group to manage the application. The "Managers" option allows you to designate one person to manage the group, and as a workgroup manager, you'll also see your name in the "Managers" window. Press <Ins> to select a manager for the group if you're not going to manage the group yourself. Once you've selected a manager, press <Esc> to return to the "Group Information" window.

The "Member List" option allows you to select who'll be a part of the group and who can therefore access the application. Highlight the "Member List" option <Enter>, then press <Ins> to add those users you manage to become group members. You can use the F5 key to mark a number of users, then press <Enter> to add those users to the "Group Members" window. If there are other users who need access to this group and application, they'll have to be added by the system supervisor. Press <Esc> to return to the "Group Information" window.

You can't change anything in the "Other Information" option. The last option is the "Trustee Directory Assignments" option. Through this option, you can grant members rights to access the application. For many applications and with personal user directories in place, you only need to grant group members Read and File Scan rights to the \APPS\WP52 directory. However, to select different printer drivers from the \APPS\WP52\PRINT directory, users will need read and write rights, which include Read, Write, Create, Erase, Modify, and File Scan rights.

Highlight the "Trustee Directory Assignments" option and press <Enter>, then press <Ins> to see the "Directory In Which Trustee Should Be Added" window. You can either type in the directory path or press <Ins> to build a directory path one directory at a time. With the directory path in place, press <Enter> and that directory path is added to the "Trustee Directory Assignments" window with Read and File Scan rights in place.

For the WP52 directory where the WP.EXE file resides, this is fine. But for the \WP52\PRINT directory, you'll need to create another trustee assignment following the same procedure explained above. Then when you add the PRINT directory to the "Trustee Directory Assignments" window, press <Enter> then <Ins>. From the "Trustee Rights Not Granted" window, add all rights except Access Control. You can experiment. Sometimes you don't need to add the Modify right, but for some applications you do. If you've set up WordPerfect to allow users to save their supplemental dictionaries in the \WP52\SPELL directory, follow the same procedure as described for the PRINT directory. If you try to create a directory path where you have no rights yourself, you'll see "You have insufficient rights to alter trustee assignments in directoryname. Press <Esc> to continue" and you won't be able to add that directory path as a trustee assignment. To exit the "Trustee Directory Assignments" window, press <Esc>.

To manage an application as a workgroup manager, you must be given Access Control rights to the application's directory. Otherwise, you can't give trustee assignments to that directory. If you have these rights, you can then go to the \APPS directory, create a WP52 directory, and run the program's setup to install the application. While you don't need Access Control rights to install an application, you will need Read, Write, Create, Erase, Modify, and File Scan rights. A growing number of applications check the bindery to see if you're a system supervisor or equivalent. If you can't install the application because of this, have your supervisor install the application to your specification. Then all you have to do is maintain the application.

Unless specified by the application's documentation, don't grant Write rights to the directory containing the application's executable program (such as WordPerfect's WP.EXE file, which runs the WordPerfect application). If possible, use file flags to flag *.COM and *.EXE files as Shareable, Read/Only. If you want further protection from copy theft, flag the executable files Execute Only, but only do this if the executable file doesn't write to itself.

You can test an application by first flagging the executable file Shareable, Read/Only, then running the program. The executable file won't run if it needs to write to itself and has such a file flag setting. However, most good network versions write to .DAT or to files other than the executable file. These peripheral files, which need to be flagged

Read/Write, are often temporarily saved to users' personal directories, where the users have sufficient rights to write to files. The Execute Only flag also prevents the application from being backed up, so be sure you have a backup copy of the application disks before using this flag.

User Account Manager

The user account manager has many of the same responsibilities explained under the workgroup manager heading. However, user account managers can't create new users or group accounts; they can only manage existing user and group accounts. That is, they can assign users to groups, as well as delete the user and group accounts they manage.

To follow up on a previous example, you can look at the "Managed Users and Groups" option under Rachel to see the users and groups that have been assigned to her. This makes her either a user account manager or a workgroup manager. If you can see a user or group in Rachel's "Managers" option, chances are Rachel is an account manager. For a workgroup manager or supervisor to make Rachel an account manager, select the "Managed Users and Groups" option, then press <Ins> at the "Managed Users and Groups" window to add those users and groups for Rachel to manage. You can use the F5 key to mark the users and groups, then press <Enter>. Rachel is now an account manager over those users and groups.

In order for Rachel to do her job, she'll need to be given ALL rights to the \USER directory (wherever user directories are stored) if she is to grant and revoke trustee assignments to the users she manages. With NetWare 3.1x, supervisors don't have to assign the Supervisory trustee assignment, only the Access Control assignment for enabling trustee assignments. Rachel will also need at least read and write rights to the \APPS directory or \APPS\LOTUS directory (wherever applications are stored) if she is to manage that application.

For an account manager to add a user to a group, the account manager can choose the "Group Information" option from the "Available Topics" window, select the group the manager manages <Enter>, select the "Member List" option <Enter>, then press <Ins> and select the users to add to the group. To delete a user from the group, highlight the user's name, press the Delete key, and the users won't be a part of the group. The same holds true for the users and groups they manage.

From a management point of view, be careful whom you assign as workgroup and account managers, for it takes planning and preparation to set up a good security scheme on the network using workgroup managers and account managers.

Console Operator

The console operator (also known as the file server console operator) is allowed rights to manage the file server through the FCONSOLE utility. Within FCONSOLE, the console operator can view server and connection statistics, prevent users from logging in, set the server date and time, view LAN driver information, purge salvageable files, and broadcast console messages. However, one function a console operator can't do in FCONSOLE is to bring down the file server.

The supervisor sets up a console operator in SYSCON by choosing the "File Server Console Operators" option under the "Supervisor Options" window. With the "File Server Console Operators" option selected, the supervisor presses <Ins> to add a user or group as a console operator. Being so designated allows the user or group to access server information and perform certain console tasks without being at the file server console.

With NetWare 3.11 and 3.12, FCONSOLE is much more limited than in NetWare 2.x; you'll have to observe most server statistics at the console or through RCONSOLE, the remote console utility. If you've been designated a console operator, type FCONSOLE at the network prompt and press <Enter>.

Since FCONSOLE has enough information to fill a couple of chapters by itself, I won't go into any detail here in this appendix. However, we'll cover the quick steps to look at pertinent information, as well as point out some of the entries you should watch out for as a console operator.

To broadcast a console message. Type FCONSOLE <Enter>, select Broadcast Console Message <Enter>, type in the message, and press <Enter>. Message can be 55 characters long, including spaces.

To change to another file server. If you have console operator or supervisor equivalence on another file server, type FCONSOLE <Enter>, select Change Current File Server <Enter>, highlight the server <Enter>. If the server doesn't appear in the window, press <Ins>, highlight the server, and press <Enter>.

To view connection information on currently attached users. Type FCONSOLE, select Connection Information <Enter>, and select a connection <Enter>. You can then broadcast a message to this specific user. Through the "Other Information" option, you see the object name and type, the user's full name, the user's login time, and the network address.

To view the server's status. Type FCONSOLE <Enter>, select the "Status" option and press <Enter>. Here you can change the server's date and time, enable and disable the login process, and enable or disable transaction tracking if installed.

To view the server's operating system version information. Type FCONSOLE <Enter>, select the "Version Information" option, and press <Enter>.

Print Queue Operator

A print queue operator can make print queues available or unavailable for use, create print queues, and manage print jobs in the print queues by changing print job priorities. You can also delete print jobs from within a print queue. As a print queue operator, you can allow print servers to access a queue. You will either work in conjunction with a print server operator, or you will also have that added responsibility.

The system supervisor adds queue operators by going into PCONSOLE, selecting a print queue, then selecting the "Queue Operators" option from the "Print Queue Information" window. The supervisor then presses <Ins>, highlights the name, and presses <Enter> to add that user to the "Queue Operators" window. This assigns you to that one queue only.

Since the responsibilities of the queue operator have been covered in our discussion of print queues, here's a quick list of what you can perform.

To see information about a print job in a print queue. Type PCONSOLE <Enter>, select Print Queue Information <Enter>, select a print queue <Enter>, select Current Print Job Entries <Enter>, select a print job <Enter>.

To put an operator hold on a print job in a print queue. Type PCONSOLE <Enter>, then select Print Queue Information <Enter>, select a print queue <Enter>, Current Print Job Entries <Enter>, select a print job <Enter>, highlight the Operator Hold entry, and type Y <Enter>.

To remove an operator hold from a print job in a print queue. Type PCONSOLE <Enter>, select Print Queue Information <Enter>, select a print queue <Enter>, Current Print Job Entries <Enter>, select a print job <Enter>, highlight Operator Hold, type N <Enter>, <Esc>.

To change the number of copies while a print job is in a print queue. Type PCONSOLE <Enter>, select Print Queue Information <Enter>, select a print queue <Enter>, Current Print Job Entries <Enter>, select a print job <Enter>, highlight Number of Copies, type new number <Enter>, then press <Esc>.

To change how a print job will be printed. Type PCONSOLE <Enter>, select Print Queue Information <Enter>, select a print queue <Enter>, Current Print Job Entries <Enter>, select a print job <Enter>, highlight File contents, Tab size, Suppress form feed, Form, Print banner, Banner name <Enter>, and after the changes press <Esc>.

617

To defer printing a print job until a later time. Type PCONSOLE <Enter>, select Print Queue Information <Enter>, select a print queue <Enter>, Current Print Job Entries <Enter>, select a print job <Enter>, highlight Defer Printing, type Y <Enter>, type the target date <Enter>, then type the target time <Enter>, <Esc>.

To change the print server you want to print a job. Type PCONSOLE <Enter>, select Print Queue Information <Enter>, select a print queue <Enter>, Current Print Job Entries <Enter>, select a print job <Enter>, highlight Target server <Enter> and select print server <Enter>, then press <Esc>.

To delete print jobs from a print queue. Type PCONSOLE <Enter>, select Print Queue Information <Enter>, select a print queue <Enter>, Current Print Job Entries <Enter>, then select a print job (or use <F5> to mark more than one) and press <Del>, then <Enter>.

To submit print jobs to a print queue. PCONSOLE <Enter>, Print Queue Information <Enter>, select a print queue <Enter>, Current Print Job Entries <Enter>, <Ins>, type directory path to print from <Enter>, select a file (or use <F5> to mark more than one) <Enter>, select a print job configuration <Enter>, change any of the settings you need to for each file and press <Esc>, then <Enter>.

To see the status of a print queue. Type PCONSOLE <Enter>, select Print Queue Information <Enter>, select a print queue <Enter>, then select the "Current Queue Status" option and press <Enter>.

To see what print servers are currently attached to a print queue. Type PCONSOLE <Enter>, select Print Queue Information <Enter>, select a print queue <Enter>, then select the Currently Attached Servers and press <Enter>.

Print Server Operator

While print server operators can't create new print servers or assign other users as print server operators, they can do pretty much everything else in ensuring that printers, print queues, and print servers are doing their jobs. Some of the duties a print server operator must perform include adding printers to printer queues, changing queue priorities, changing printer forms, attaching to file servers for queue access, and bringing down the print server. Because print server operators must also manipulate print queues, they are often print queue operators as well.

The system supervisor adds print server operators by going into PCONSOLE, selecting a print server, then selecting the "Print Server Operators" option from the "Print Server Information" window. The supervisor then presses <Ins>, highlights the name, and presses <Enter> to add that user to the "Print Server Operators" window. This assigns you to that one print server only.

618

Since the responsibilities of the print server operator have been covered in our discussion of print servers, here's a quick list of what you can perform.

To see who is assigned as a print server operator. Type PCONSOLE <Enter>, select Print Server Information <Enter>, select a print server <Enter>, then select Print Server Operators <Enter>.

To see which file servers a print server accesses. Type PCONSOLE <Enter>, select Print Server Information <Enter>, Print Server Status/Control <Enter>, then select the "File Servers Being Serviced" option and press <Enter>. To add another server to the list, press <Ins> <Enter>.

To see who gets notified when print jobs are completed. Type PCONSOLE <Enter>, select Print Server Information <Enter>, Print Server Status/Control <Enter>, select Notify List for Printer <Enter>, then select a printer you wish to look at and press <Enter>. The information includes the file server, the name of the person to be notified, when to first notify the person, and when to next notify the person.

To see what print jobs are being serviced by a printer. Type PCONSOLE <Enter>, select Print Server Information <Enter>, Print Server Status/Control <Enter>, Printer Status <Enter>, then select a printer you wish to look at and press <Enter>. You can also manipulate the "Printer Control" option, including abort print job, form feed, mark top of form, pause printer, rewind printer, stat printer, and stop printer.

To see what queues a printer services. Type PCONSOLE <Enter>, select Print Server Information <Enter>, Print Server Status/Control <Enter>, select Queues Serviced by Printer <Enter>, then select a printer you wish to look at and press <Enter>. You'll see a listing of file servers, their queues, and the queue priority.

To see the status of the print server. Type PCONSOLE <Enter>, select Print Server Information <Enter>, Print Server Status/Control <Enter>, then select Server Info <Enter>. You can see the print server version, type, number of printers, number of queue service modes, and the current server status. Current status includes Down, Going down after current jobs, and Running.

To see who is assigned as a print server user. PCONSOLE <Enter>, Print Server Information <Enter>, select a print server <Enter>, then select the "Print Server Users" option and press <Enter>.

APPENDIX E

NetWare 3.12's NMenu Utility

NetWare 3.12's NMENU utility is different from the MENU utility found in NetWare versions 3.11 and earlier. However, the old version of the MENU utility is also available for NetWare 3.12. If you wish to use that utility, you will find it explained under "The MENU Utility" heading in Chapter 2. In this appendix, we'll cover the new NMENU utility.

NMENU is a derivative of Saber Systems' Saber Menu. Like the older MENU utility, NMENU allows you to set up your own menu program so you can easily access programs and utilities through that menu. If you're adventurous, you can create quite an extensive menu to assist you in your work. Unlike MENU, however, NMENU needs to compile through the MENUMAKE program a working copy of the menu you create.

In this appendix we'll cover two methods of creating menus under the NMENU utility. The first way is to change an existing NetWare *.MNU file to work with NMENU; the second will show you how to create a menu from scratch.

The examples given here are in no way an exhaustive listing of what you can accomplish in NMENU; rather, they only hint at the possibilities. With a little ingenuity you can set up marvelous environments, calling up different menus for each day of the week or for different occasions.

Converting an Older *.MNU File for NMENU

A good place to begin discussing NMENU is to convert a menu that's you've already created. So let's look at converting the sample menu file called MAIN.MNU. This file is located in the SYS:PUBLIC directory; if you type DIR Z:*.MNU <Enter> and that file doesn't appear, go to the heading below called "Creating A *.SRC File for NMENU."

If you do have a MAIN.MNU file, go to a directory where you have read and write rights (RWFCEM rights) and type MENUCNVT Z:MAIN.MNU <Enter>. The system will begin to create your new version.

If you have a personal menu you wish to convert, such as TED.MNU, go to the directory where you have that file stored and type MENUCNVT TED.MNU <Enter>. Again, you need read and write rights for the MENUCNVT program to work.

After you run the MENUCNVT program, you will notice you have a new *.SRC file, such as MAIN.SRC. You can edit this file with a text editor as explained later in this appendix.

Once you have touched up the .SRC file, you need to run MENUMAKE.EXE to compile the *.SRC file so it can run with NMENU. For example, to compile MAIN.SRC, you would go to a directory where you have the MAIN.SRC file stored and type MENUMAKE MAIN.SRC <Enter>. Again, you need read and write rights (RWFCEM rights) in that directory.

The MENUMAKE program compiles a *.DAT file that you then use with the NMENU utility. When in that directory, type NMENU MAIN.DAT <Enter> at the network prompt and you'll see MAIN's "Main Menu" window.

If you follow the above procedure without first editing the *.SRC file, you will see that you have capital letters followed by numbers after each entry in the menu. To get rid of the double marking of each entry, you need to edit the SRC file. Go into any text editor, call up the *.SRC file, and edit out the numeric sequences, as NMENU uses capital letters to mark a series of options. Once edited, you then need to run the MENUMAKE program again and recompile the *.SRC file to become a *.DAT file.

NetWare's main menu lists eight menu options, a logout sequence, and an Exit option to exit from NMENU. The menu options it displays are for NetWare's SESSION, FILER, VOLINFO, SYSCON, FCONSOLE, PCONSOLE, PRINTCON, and PRINTDEF utilities. These utilities work just as they do when you run them from the network prompt, except that as you exit a utility, you return to this menu. The "Logout" option will log you out of all your attached servers and leave you in the LOGIN directory at the network prompt. The "Exit" option allows you to exit from the NMENU utility.

To select an option, use the Up arrow key to move the selector bar up an option; use the Down arrow key to move it down an option. To choose the selected option, press <Enter>. You can also select an option by typing the initial letter of the option. This selects the option without having to press <Enter>. To exit NMENU, move the selector bar to the Exit option and press <Enter> or type the corresponding letter.

622

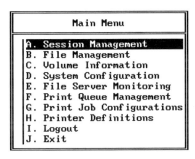

```
Novell Menu System  V3.12              Monday  June  14, 1993  1:53pm
```

```
                  Main Menu
          A. Session Management
          B. File Management
          C. Volume Information
          D. System Configuration
          E. File Server Monitoring
          F. Print Queue Management
          G. Print Job Configurations
          H. Printer Definitions
          I. Logout
          J. Exit
```

Figure E-1. The initial screen to menu MAIN

Creating A *.SRC File for the NMENU Utility

If you don't have a MAIN.MNU file to work from, go into any text editor and type in
the following lines (I'll cover how the syntax works as I go along). You can also use any
word processor that can save files as DOS text.

```
MENU 01,Main Menu { }
    ITEM Session Management { }
        EXEC Session
    ITEM File Management { }
        EXEC Filer
    ITEM Volume Information { }
        EXEC VolInfo
    ITEM System Configuration { }
        EXEC SysCon
    ITEM File Server Monitoring { }
        EXEC FConsole
    ITEM Print Queue Management { }
        EXEC PConsole
    ITEM Print Job Configurations { }
        EXEC PrintCon
```

```
ITEM Printer Definitions { }
    EXEC PrintDef
ITEM Logout { }
    EXEC LOGOUT
ITEM Exit { }
    EXEC EXIT
```

When you have typed the above lines into a file, save it as a DOS text file with a .SRC extension. For example, Ted could save the file as MAIN.SRC in a directory where he has read and write rights. Once saved, Ted then needs to run the MENUMAKE program and compile the *.SRC file to become a *.DAT file. The following discussion works from the above MAIN.SRC and MAIN.DAT files.

Looking at the Guts of the MAIN.DAT File

You've now seen what the MAIN.DAT file looks like when you run it, as well as what the MAIN.SRC file looks like. To use the NMENU utility, you need Read, File Scan, Write, Create, and Erase rights in the directory from which you invoke the program. To rename the file, you'll also need Modify rights. So go either to your home directory (where you probably have all rights) or to your personal search drive directory.

Now let's rename the MAIN.SRC file and use it to make your own menu program. To rename the file for Ted to use, you would type RENAME MAIN.SRC NEWMENU.SRC <Enter>. (Remember that you must have Modify rights to rename an existing file.) If you copied the MAIN.MNU file from the SYS:PUBLIC directory to be converted, the file might be flagged Read Only; you might need to flag the file Read/Write before renaming it. If you try to rename the file but receive an error message such as "Duplicate filename or file not found," type FLAG MAIN.MNU N <Enter>. Then rename the file.

With the file renamed, go into your text editor or word processor and pull up the renamed file. (It will be in DOS text form.) The file structure of the NEWMENU.SRC file looks like this (the same as MAIN.MNU above):

```
MENU 01,Main Menu { }
    ITEM Session Management { }
        EXEC Session
    ITEM File Management { }
        EXEC Filer
    ITEM Volume Information { }
        EXEC VolInfo
```

624

```
ITEM System Configuration { }
    EXEC SysCon
ITEM File Server Monitoring { }
    EXEC FConsole
ITEM Print Queue Management { }
    EXEC PConsole
ITEM Print Job Configurations { }
    EXEC PrintCon
ITEM Printer Definitions { }
    EXEC PrintDef
ITEM Logout { }
    EXEC LOGOUT
ITEM Exit { }
    EXEC EXIT
```

The first line—MENU 01,Main Menu { }—begins with the number of this menu, contains the menu's name, and ends with two curly brackets. The MENU command designates which menu will come up first; menus are layered side by side and you can have up to ten submenus per menu. The menu name or title can be up to 40 characters long. In this case, the title is Main Menu, and for the other menu utilities you see in NetWare, this title is usually "Available Options."

Beneath the Menu line are the available options, preceded by the ITEM command. Options execute submenus, commands, or programs. The second line—ITEM Session Management { }—begins one of the options that you can select from the menu itself. The commands to invoke the option do not need to be indented beneath the option itself as the third line of our example shows, but it does help you keep track of what is a command and what is an item.

In the Session Management example, you use the EXEC command to invoke the option, followed by the name of the utility itself—in this instance, SESSION. You see this structure throughout the NEWMENU.SRC file. (Options can have many more commands than you see in this example. The following examples deal with other commands to set up the environment the way you want it.) The last option in this example, ITEM Exit { }, exits you out of the NMENU utility and back to the network prompt.

NMENU's Command Set

The NMENU utility comes with a number of commands that aren't in the original MENU utility. These commands fall into two categories: organizational and control. The organizational commands are MENU, which is used to identify menu titles, and ITEM, which is used to identify options under the menu. Control commands include EXEC, LOAD, SHOW, GETO, GETR, and GETP. None of these commands needs to be capitalized. Each command and its syntax is explored next.

MENU number,menuname. You use the MENU command to identify a menu screen through a menu number and menu name. Our example shows MENU 01,Main Menu { } as the first menu on the screen, with Main Menu as the main title. There is no space between the number, the comma, and the menu name. Menu names can be up to 40 characters long.

The first menu will always be the first menu displayed, regardless of the number given to it; however, all submenus are affected by the numbering system. While you don't need to have all the numbers in sequential order (such as 1, 2, 3, and so forth), it helps to use sequential numbering for clarity of writing the menu program. Numbers can go from 1 to 255.

ITEM name {option}. You use the ITEM command to display the options you wish to have in a menu screen. The NMENU utility automatically assigns a letter to each option and assigns letters to the items in alphabetical order (from A to Z). To change the order items appear in the menu, type them in the order you wish them to appear.

To give an item a different letter, type a carat (^) followed by the letter you wish that item to appear with (such as ^XEXIT). Note, however, that this does not change the order in which the option item appears in the menu, and it may change the letters used for the other items. If such letter changing becomes a nuisance, give all ITEMs a carat and letter.

{OPTIONS}. The ITEM command comes with four options that you place within the squiggly brackets { }. You can have more than one option within the brackets if you place a space between the options. The options you can have are BATCH, CHDIR, SHOW, and PAUSE.

You can use the BATCH option to remove the NMENU utility from memory, thus allowing you an extra 32KB of workstation memory for running applications. For example, when you load WordPerfect, you don't want to lose 32KB of memory to the menu system. You can use the BATCH option along with the CHDIR option, which brings you back to the menu and directory prior to calling an application using the BATCH and CHDIR options.

You use the SHOW option to display the name of the DOS command (in the upper left-hand corner of the screen) that you are running. This helps you keep better track of which command you are working on. The PAUSE option invokes DOS's PAUSE command, and also displays the "Press any key to continue" message. PAUSE stops the screen from changing until a key is pressed.

EXEC, SHOW, and LOAD Action Commands. The ITEM command comes with three commands that you can use to perform an action: EXEC, SHOW, and LOAD. The EXEC command is used to execute *.COM, *.BAT, and *.EXE files or it initiates DOS's COMMAND.COM (the command process) so you can run programs.

The EXEC command comes with three of its own commands that you can see in the *.SRC file of menu utility. These are EXEC EXIT, which closes the NMENU utility and places you at the network prompt; EXEC DOS, which keeps the NMENU utility open but still places you at the network prompt; and EXEC LOGOUT, which closes the NMENU utility and logs you out of the network. You can see EXEC EXIT and EXEC LOGOUT examples in our sample NMENU example.

The SHOW command allows you to run submenus that you create by using the MENU command and designating a menu number and title. Your NMENU menus can have up to 254 submenus. When a submenu comes up, it is offset a little to the right, but mostly covers the previous menu.

If having 254 submenus isn't enough, you can call other scripts as well through the LOAD command. Each new *.DAT file can give you another 254 submenus to work with. The scripts must also be run through the MENUMAKE program and be changed into a *.DAT file. When you call a new script through the LOAD command, the original menu will continue to display and the called menu will appear over the original menu, offset a little to the right.

GETO, GETR, and GETP (DOS Option Commands). When you want to give user input to an action command, you use the GETx commands. The GETx commands are GETO, GETR, and GETP. You must place the GETx commands before using the EXEC command to execute the program that is associated with the GETx commands. You can have up to 100 GETx commands in an ITEM command.

You use the GETO command when you want to get additional or optional input (hence the O in GETO). Once that input is entered, you press <F10> to run the command. If you have more than one place to store input, use the <Enter> key to move to the next place on the screen.

You use the GETR command when you require some input to move ahead with the command. If you don't type in something and you press <F10> to run the command, nothing will happen. So the program requires you to give input (hence the R in GETR).

The GETP command allows you to have more than one line of input per command, which is what you need with NetWare utilities such as NDIR and NCOPY. For those who have used the older version of the MENU utility, this command takes the place of the @1, @2, and @3 variable sets.

The GETx commands use the following format: GETx prompt, {prepend}, number of characters, default response between the commas (no spaces), SECURE (displays characters as asterisks), and {append}. The written format looks like this:

```
GETR Enter Drive and Filename (Enter then F10): { } 25,, {}
```

For this example, the GETR command requires that you enter some text into the box and prompts you to type in the drive and filenames you wish to copy from. The "Enter Drive and Filename" portion prompts you to specify the directory you wish to copy from and which file you wish to copy. After you type in the path and filename, press <Enter> and then <F10> to execute the command.

The first set of brackets is used if the command needs something between itself and its parameters. Since most commands need at least a space between the command and its parameters, place a space between the brackets. The number 25 shows the maximum number of characters you can type in to the places where you are prompted to type in. You can set this number up to 80, but you have to use some number; otherwise, the MENUMAKE program won't compile the *.SRC file into a *.DAT file. (We'll cover this later.)

You next use the commas to put in any default response that someone needs to make as they are typing. If everyone has to type it in, you can just put it in for them. You type in the default against both commas with no spaces. The SECURE command allows you to enter passwords and other items secretly without them being displayed. When you type in a password or response, you'll only see asterisks for each of the characters typed.

The last set of brackets you can use to append any value or parameter you want at the end of the GETx line. For example, if you are setting up the NDIR command, you can add such things as /SUB to show all the subdirectories or /C to continuously scroll through the screens of information.

We'll look at each of these options as we create our own personal menus, as described in the following pages.

Creating Your Own Menu

Now that you have the basics of commands for creating a menu utility, it's time to create your own menu. Let's call it the "What I Use" menu. In this example, you'll create the "What I Use" menu with five options. The first option enables access to the network prompt and DOS. The next option accesses a word processing program.

The third option takes the above NetWare menu that we began with and makes it a submenu of the "What I Use" window. The fourth option moves the "Logout" option

628

from the NetWare Menu's submenu to your "What I Use" menu window. And the fifth option is the Exit command for exiting from the menu. When you're finished, the "What I Use" menu utility will appear as shown in Figure E-2:

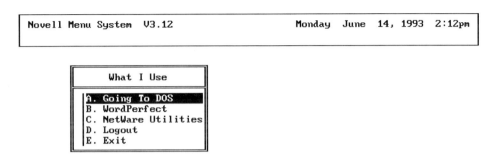

```
Novell Menu System  V3.12                    Monday  June  14, 1993  2:12pm
```

```
         What I Use
    A. Going To DOS
    B. WordPerfect
    C. NetWare Utilities
    D. Logout
    E. Exit
```

Figure E-2. How your customized menu will look when we begin making the menu

From any DOS text editor or word processor that allows you to save files in the DOS text format, bring in the MENU.SRC file (or whatever name you gave your customized .SRC file). The first window of our new menu should be the "What I Use" window. To change it to this, rename the MENU 01,Main Menu { } name to the following:

```
MENU 01,What I Use { }
```

The options you want to see in the "What I Use" window include "Going to DOS," "WordPerfect," "NetWare Utilities," "Logout," and "Exit." So beneath the MENU 01,What I Use { } line, type in the following parameters:

```
MENU 01,What I Use { }
    ITEM Going To DOS {BATCH}
       EXEC DOS
    ITEM WordPerfect {BATCH}
       EXEC WP
    ITEM NetWare Utilities { }
       SHOW 2
    ITEM Logout { }
       EXEC LOGOUT
    ITEM Exit { }
       EXEC EXIT
```

629

In the NMENU utility, order does matter, so place the items in the order that you wish to see them in the menu. Note that I indented the ITEM commands as well as the EXEC and SHOW commands. Although this is not necessary, it helps me better understand their relationship to one another.

The "Going to DOS" option can be invaluable for accessing the network prompt from the menu. When you select this option, NMENU places a "Type EXIT to return to the menu" signal, followed by the network prompt. Then, when you're through in DOS, simply type EXIT <Enter> to return to the menu.

Next, you want to set up access to your word processor, WordPerfect in this example. Under the "WordPerfect" option is EXEC WP. When you select this item, it echoes "Loading WordPerfect" (or whatever the title of the option you select) on the screen.

If you access WordPerfect from a search drive or a local directory designated through the PATH command, all you need to do is include the executable filename, such as WP for WP.EXE. Otherwise, you'll need to type in the directory path where the program resides. For example, if you are using WordPerfect's Text Editor (PE.EXE), located in a C:\PE directory, you would type EXEC C:\PE\PE { } <Enter> in the menu script.

Notice that the example uses the {BATCH} option when NMENU loads the WordPerfect program and when going to DOS. This takes 32KB of the menu out of memory so you can use that memory for applications and their data files. When you exit the application, you'll simply return to this menu.

Next, you want to make the original MAIN.SRC file a submenu of your "What I Use" window. To do this, place a SHOW command and number for calling the submenu beneath the "NetWare Menus" option, such as SHOW 2. Then place another MENU line, followed by the number and title, such as MENU 2,NetWare Utilities { }.

```
MENU 01.What I Use { }
    ITEM Going To DOS {BATCH}
     EXEC DOS
    ITEM Word Perfect {BATCH}
     EXEC WP
    ITEM NetWare Utilities { }
     SHOW 2
    ITEM Logout { }
       EXEC LOGOUT
    ITEM Exit { }
       EXEC EXIT
```

630

```
MENU 2,NetWare Utilities { }
    ITEM Session Management { }
        EXEC Session
    ITEM File Management { }
        EXEC Filer
    ITEM Volume Information { }
        EXEC VolInfo
    ITEM System Configuration { }
        EXEC SysCon
    ITEM Print Job Configurations { }
        EXEC PrintCon
    ITEM FirstMail Utility {BATCH CHDIR}
        EXEC MAIL
```

This example uses only the NetWare menu utilities you use most often. (Notice the addition of the FirstMail utility—see Appendix F for more information.) Set your options according to your preference, or leave them all in. Moving the "Logout" and "Exit" options to the "What I Use" menu means you won't have to go to a submenu to log out or exit the NMENU utility.

If you need to, you can also use the {BATCH CHDIR} options to ensure you have enough memory for running the utilities, as well as ensure you return to your default directory in case you end up in a different directory and NMENU gets lost along the way.

Setting Up Command-Line Utilities in Your Menus

You can also define the command-line utilities that you wish to run from the menu. Let's add another option, "Command Line Utilities," to the MAIN.SRC file. This option will set up another submenu so that a command-line utility can run in the menu environment. From any DOS text editor or word processor that allows you to save files in the DOS text format, bring in the NEWMENU.MNU file. Beneath the other options, place the following command:

```
MENU 01,What I Use { }
    ITEM Going To DOS {BATCH}
        EXEC DOS
    ITEM Word Perfect {BATCH}
        EXEC WP
    ITEM NetWare Utilities { }
        SHOW 2
```

```
ITEM NetWare Command-Line Utils { }
   SHOW 3
ITEM Logout { }
   EXEC LOGOUT
ITEM Exit { }
   EXEC EXIT
```

Go to the end of the "NetWare Menus" submenu in this file and type:

```
MENU 3,NetWare Command-Line Utils { }
   ITEM NCOPY {SHOW PAUSE}
       GETR Enter Drive and Filename: { } 30,, {}
       GETR Enter Destination (Enter then F10): { } 25,, {}
       EXEC NCOPY
   ITEM RIGHTS {SHOW PAUSE}
       GETO Enter Drive Letter or Path: { } 25,, {}
       EXEC RIGHTS
   ITEM NDIR {SHOW PAUSE}
       GETO Parameters?: { } 60,, {/sub /c}
       EXEC NDIR
```

Command Parameters in NMENU.

It usually takes more than simply typing the name of a command to use most DOS and NetWare utilities. For example, to use NCOPY, you need to know which files in which directories you wish to copy to which other directory, and you need to include that information when running the command.

NMENU allows you to designate those inputs by using the GETO, GETR, and GETP commands. Any message you give must not end with a semicolon (NMENU does not accept semicolons). Messages aren't necessary, but they serve as prompts so you know where you are during command execution. The {SHOW PAUSE} option at the end of the ITEM statement allows you to view what's being done before you return to MENU.

In the NCOPY example above, the GETx command used follows the syntax of GETx prompt, {prepend}, number of characters, default response between the commas (no spaces), and {append}. This written format is shown in the following line:

```
GETR Enter Drive and Filename: { } 30,, {}
GETR Enter Destination (Enter then F10): { } 25,, {}
```

In this case, the GETR command requires you to enter some text into the box and prompts you to type in the drive and filenames you wish to copy from. The "Enter Drive and Filename" prompts you to type in the directory you wish to copy from and which file you wish to copy.

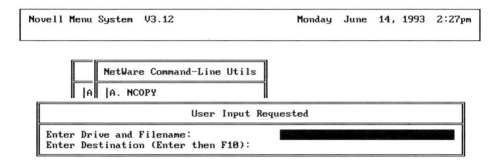

Figure E-3. The User Input Requested screen from the GETR command

After you type in the path and filename, press <Enter> to move to the second GETR command. The second GETR command asks which drive letter you wish to copy the file to. When that's completed, press <Enter> and then <F10> to execute the command.

You use the first set of brackets if the command needs something between itself and its parameters. Since most commands need at least a space between the command and its parameters, leave a space between the brackets. The number 25 shows the maximum number of characters you can type in. You can set this up to 80, but you have to have some number or the MENUMAKE program won't compile.

You next use the commas to put in any default response that needs to go into the command. You type in the default against both commas with no spaces. The last set of brackets you can use to append any value or parameter you want at the end of the GETx line. As in the case of NDIR, you can add such things as /SUB to show all the subdirectories or /C to continuously scroll through the screens of information.

Setting Up DOS Utilities

You can also define the DOS utilities that you wish to run from the menu. Let's add one last option, "DOS Utilities," to the MAIN.SRC file. This option will set up another submenu so that a DOS utility can run in the menu environment. Beneath the other options, place the following command (You can also move ITEM "Going To DOS" beneath the new DOS Commands ITEM):

```
MENU 01,What I Use { }
    ITEM Word Perfect {BATCH}
        EXEC WP
    ITEM NetWare Utilities { }
        SHOW 2
    ITEM NetWare Command-Line Utils { }
        SHOW 3
    ITEM DOS Commands { }
        SHOW 4
    ITEM Logout { }
        EXEC LOGOUT
    ITEM Exit { }
        EXEC EXIT
```

Go to the end of the "NetWare Menus" submenu in this file and type:

```
MENU 4,DOS Commands { }
    ITEM Going To DOS {BATCH}
        EXEC DOS
    ITEM XCOPY {SHOW PAUSE}
        GETR Enter Drive and Filename: { } 30,, {}
        GETR Enter Destination (Enter then F10): { } 25,, { }
        GETO Include Subdirectories? type S: {/} 1,, {}
        GETO Include Empty Subdirectories? type E: {/} 1,, {}
        GETO Verify File Sizes? type V: {/} 1,, {}
        EXEC XCOPY
    ITEM FORMAT {SHOW PAUSE}
        GETR Enter driveletter: { } 5,,{:}
        GETO Quick Format? type Q: {/} 1,, {}
        GETO System Format? type S: {/} 1,, {}
        GETO Delete Earlier Format Info? type U: {/} 1,, {}
        EXEC FORMAT
```

There really isn't anything different for the first two entries, other than moving the ITEM Going To DOS under this new menu screen. Also, XCOPY adds three options that allow you to add /S, /E, and /V parameters to the command (these will also work with

NCOPY). The front brackets supply the forward slash (/) so all you have to do is type in the designated letter. Also notice that the last bracket set at the end of the second GETR command has a space in it so the additional parameters won't crowd the destination directory.

The ITEM FORMAT allows you to type in the drive letter you wish to format (it adds the colon with its second bracket). You can then select such options as a quick format (if you are running MS DOS 5.0 and above), a system format, or whether you wish to retain earlier DOS format information (if you are running MS DOS 5.0 and above). If you don't want to select one of the options, simply press <Enter> twice to skip it, and then press F10 to run the command.

When you finish editing your script, exit from your editor and save the file as a DOS text file. Then type MENUMAKE MAIN.SRC <Enter> (or whatever name you called the file) to compile a .DAT file. Each part of the command structure is important in order for the MENUMAKE program to compile the .SRC file into a .DAT file for NMENU. If you receive errors when compiling, look at the messages that the MENUMAKE program gives you, and then go back into the text editor, bring up the .SRC file, look over your syntax, and fix it where necessary. Then try the MENUMAKE program again.

Once the MENUMAKE program turns the .SRC file into a .DAT file, type NMENU MAIN <Enter> to see your results. Your own menu will appear on the screen. You can then see if you made any mistakes that need correcting once you get out of the menu. If you have any mistakes, run the text editor again and bring up the .SRC file. Then, once you have finished editing the .SRC file, run the MENUMAKE program again. MENUMAKE will overwrite the old .DAT file with the newly compiled .DAT file.

One of the biggest problems you can face in NMENU is leaving the directory in which you initiated the menu. When this happens, you can put CHDIR in brackets ({CHDIR}) so NMENU can find its way back to your default directory.

Tips When Creating Your Own Menu

When creating your own menu utility, remember the following:

➤ For clarity's sake, write option names to the left margin and indent two or more spaces the commands for executing the options;

➤ Don't get your option lines too long or MENUMAKE won't compile; about 60 characters (including spaces) on a line seems to be the limit.

➤ Be sure to save the file as a DOS text file with a .SRC extension.

➤ Be sure to run MENUMAKE to change the .SRC file into a .DAT file so it will run with the NMENU utility.

➤ To use the new menu, type NMENU filename.DAT <Enter> in the directory containing the .DAT file.

There is certainly a lot more you can do with the NMENU utility and its options. To get the most out of this utility, feel free to experiment.

Using the FirstMail Package

NetWare 3.12 comes with a small electronic-mail (E-mail) package called FirstMail. The mail package is actually two products: NetWare Basic MHS and FirstMail. The supervisor uses the NetWare Basic MHS product to install the Message Handling Service, or MHS, portion of the mail package. Once installed, the NetWare Basic MHS lets you send mail messages to other users mail boxes on the same server (it does not extend to other servers).

Those wishing to extend their messaging capability will need to look into products such as NetWare Global MHS, which can send messages with LAN/WAN connectivity. NetWare Basic MHS is fully compatible with NetWare Global MHS. NetWare Global MHS also has connectivity capabilities for SNMP, X.400, and SNADS when using these protocol modules.

For the most part, the supervisor will use the NetWare Basic MHS product and set you up as a FirstMail user on your network. FirstMail is what you will be using to send and receive mail on this server and will be the focus of this appendix. Here I cover the basic operation of the FirstMail utility as well as some of the more advanced features of the utility. FirstMail comes with a USER.TXT file; it is located in the SYS:PUBLIC directory, and contains some of the more advanced features you can perform. To get a copy of this text file, type NPRINT Z:USER.TXT Q=queuename <Enter> at the network prompt. As with all NetWare utilities, take the time to use it until you are comfortable with what you can and can't do.

The FirstMail Utility

To run the FirstMail utility, type MAIL <Enter> at the network prompt. You'll see a screen similar to the one shown in Figure F-1.

FirstMail comes with seven options in the "Mail Options" window: check for New mail, Send a mail message, Browse mail messages, Change file server, Preferences, Edit a file, and Quit using FirstMail. To get around in FirstMail, use the Up arrow key to move the selector bar up an option; use the Down arrow key to move it down an option. To choose the selected option, press <Enter>. You can also select an option by typing the initial capital letter of the options, which are N, S, B, C, P, E, and Q. This selects the option without your having to press <Enter>.

```
              ═══ Mail Options ═══
      ┌───────────────────────────────┐
      │ N: check for New mail          │
      │ S: Send a mail message         │
      │ B: Browse mail messages        │
      │ C: Change file server          │
      │ P: Preferences                 │
      │ E: Edit a file                 │
      │ Q: Quit using FirstMail        │
      │                                │
      └───────────────────────────────┘
```

Press <F1> for help   NTS3/TED   Folder <Main>

Figure F-1. FirstMail's initial screen

To leave a screen that you don't wish to change the settings in, press <Esc>. You will see an "<Esc> key pressed" screen that confirms you wish to cancel or quit what you were doing. Pressing <Enter> selects the default of Yes and returns you to the screen prior to the one you were working in.

To exit from FirstMail, move the selector bar to the Quit using FirstMail option and press <Enter> or type the letter Q and press <Enter>. You can also press <Esc> at the "Mail Options" window, and then <Enter> to leave FirstMail. You are immediately placed at the network prompt.

FirstMail comes with on-line help that you can access by pressing the F1 key. Help is menu-screen sensitive, and the help changes to reflect the screen you are presently looking at. Also, pressing F1 again lists the special keys that are available to you.

Checking for New Mail

The first option, "check for New mail," displays the list of new mail messages you have received since the last time you used the program. If you have no new mail messages, you won't see this option when you bring up FirstMail. If you receive messages while in FirstMail, this option will appear as part of the "Mail Options" menu. If you have messages and you select this option, you'll see a screen similar to the one shown in Figure F-2.

```
┌───────────────── Folder <New Mail> (5 messages) ─────────────────┐
│      From                 Subject                 Date          + │
│ ┌──────────────────────────────────────────────────────────────┐ │
│ │ ED@NTS3              Don't say that!!         13 Jun 93 12:00 │ │
│   Ted E. Beara          Howsit going??          13 Jun 93 13:14   │
│   ED@NTS3               <None>                   13 Jun 93 13:39 Y │
│   Ted E. Beara          Re: new mail editor      13 Jun 93 15:49  │
│   Ted E. Beara          Re: rprint file          13 Jun 93 15:58  │
│ ─────────────────────────<     End of list     >───────────────── │
│                                                                   │
│                                                                   │
│                                                                   │
│                                                                   │
│                                                                   │
│                                                                   │
│                                                                   │
│                                                                   │
│                                                                   │
│ Attachments Copy Dos Forward Info Locate Move Order Print Reply Send eXtract │
│    KEYS: F10=Select folder   F5=(un)mark   Enter=Read   Del=Delete   Esc=Exit │
└───────────────────────────────────────────────────────────────────┘
```

Figure F-2. The messages you receive

The "New Mail" window lists the messages you have received since the last time you entered FirstMail. (New mail messages received while you are in FirstMail won't appear on the "New Mail" window until you exit and reenter the window.) The window contains three columns: From, Subject, and Date. The From column shows who sent you the message, and the Subject column tells you what a message is about. This can be useful if you are keeping certain conversations in selected folders. The Date column shows the date and time when the message was sent. Those messages with file attachments will have a "Y" mark to the right of the Date column.

To read a message, highlight the entry using the up/down arrow keys, and then press <Enter>. Use the up/down arrow keys to scroll through the message. We'll cover more on reading messages under the Enter=Read command. The bottom part of the "New Mail" window contains the following selections that cover what you can do in this window with the messages you receive. These are as follows:

Attachments. If you see a "Y" at the end of your new messages, you have received a file along with the message. Pressing the letter "A" displays an "Attached to this message" screen telling you the filename, the type of format the file is in, and the operating system that created the file. You can have up to 64 attachments to a message, which are deleted only when the message itself is deleted.

To save the attachment to the directory you are presently in (or the default directory you set up through the "Preferences" option), highlight the file and press <Enter>. You'll see a small screen that says "Extract filename to what file?" appear at the bottom of the screen, along with the name of the file as it was sent. Press <Enter> to drop the file into the directory you were in when you went into FirstMail, or to the default directory you set up through the "Preferences" option. Or you can type in a new directory path and filename, and then press <Enter>. The file will be copied to the destination directory and you'll return to the "Attached to this message" screen where you can extract other files (if any). Press <Esc> to return to the "New Mail" window.

Copy. Use the Copy command to copy the message and/or attachments to a folder. Folders are a means to store messages that are related. To place the message into a folder, highlight the folder and press <Enter>. You begin with a Main folder, but you can create new folders as well.

To add a new folder, press the <Ins> key. If you copy the messages you send to yourself, you will also see a Copies to Self folder. Long folder names can't be over 50 characters in length. It's best to also fill out the short name field (eight characters or less), which gives the directories where the messages are stored a name you can remember.

To delete a folder, press the <Del> key (however, you can't delete the Main Folder); to rename a folder, press the <Alt>+R keys at the same time. If you want to compress the files within the selected folder, press the F10 key.

DOS. Use the DOS command when you want to pass the name of the message file to a DOS command or to a DOS file. For example, if you were sending the name of the files to a DOS tracking file, you could type ECHO Received %s on July 4th, 1993 >>TRACKING.MSG <Enter> and DOS will redirect and append the message to the TRACKING.MSG file. The %s command allows you to tell DOS where you wish the name of the message file to go. You could also type COPY %s G: <Enter> to copy the message to whatever directory the G: letter is mapped to.

Forward. The Forward command allows you to pass the message along to another user. Type the letter "F" to bring up the "Forward message or file to" screen, in which you can then type the person's address or press F2 to bring up the directory list and <Enter> to select the person you wish to forward the message to. If you wish to alter the message before sending it, type Y in the "Edit before sending" field and press <Enter> and <Enter> again to the "Accept and continue?" screen. Then type in your changes and press <Ctrl>+<Enter> to send the message and <Enter> again to the "Accept and continue?" screen.

Info. The Info command shows you information about the message you have highlighted. When you press the letter "I," you'll see an "About this message" screen with information about who sent the message (From), the subject of the message (Subject), the date it was sent (Date), and those who were included in receiving the message (Cc). You can also see how many characters the message was (Size), if there were any files attached to the message (Attachments), and whether the person sending the message asked for a confirmation (Confirmation). This screen also indicates whether the message has been read (Read), whether there was a reply sent (Reply sent), or whether the message has been forwarded to someone else (Forwarded). Pressing any key drops the Information screen and returns you to the "New Mail" screen.

Locate. The Locate command allows you to locate a string of characters from within marked files or the file you have highlighted. (To mark files, press the space bar or the F5 key.) Pressing the letter "L" brings up the "Locate string in file(s)" screen with three options: Search for, Select files containing string, and Search in headers only.

For example, suppose you needed to know if any of the messages had an answer to your Ethernet Frame 802_3 problem. You could type *ETHERNET*FRAME*802_3* <Enter> in the Search for entry, and then answer Yes to the Select files containing string entry and No to the Search in headers only entry. Press <Enter> and then <Enter> again to the "Accept and continue?" screen. If there are any matches, FirstMail will display the file(s).

This search mechanism is an iffy proposition at best, for it depends on you to type in the syntax the way FirstMail wants to search for things. Otherwise, you'll see a "No Matches" screen even though the text string may be in one of the messages. FirstMail only looks for the string in one line, and won't find it if the string straddles two lines, so short string searches on key words may work best. It also depends on if you select to search in the files or the headers-only entry. You can also use wild card characters such as the asterisk (*) to designate a number of characters and the question mark (?) to designate any single character.

Move. The Move command moves the message and file to a folder and out of the "New Mail" window. To place the message into a folder, highlight the folder and press <Enter>. You begin with a Main folder, but you can create new folders as well.

Order. The Order command allows you to sort messages by Date, Name, Subject, or by Reverse date. For example, to sort messages by subject, type the letter "O" and then "S."

Print. The Print command controls how you wish to print your messages. To print a message, type "P" to bring up the "Print Settings" screen with its six entries: Print To, Filename, PostScript, PS font, Page length, and Print a Banner page. If you are using the CAPTURE command to send print jobs where you want them to go, press <Enter> to change the LPT1 entry to match the location you wish to print to.

You can also send the print job to a print queue on this file server (use the CAPTURE command to send print jobs to other servers and queues if necessary). Press <Enter> at the Print To entry, select the Queue option, type in the print queue name on this server, and then press <Enter>. Use the Down arrow key to finish out the fields and press <Enter> to the "Accept and continue?" screen.

You can also send the message to a file by pressing <Enter> at the Print To entry and selecting the File option. You then type in the name of the file and directory path (if needed) and press <Enter>. Then use the Down arrow key to finish out the fields and press <Enter> to the "Accept and continue?" screen.

Use the PostScript and PS Font entries when printing to a printer that can handle PostScript files. Highlight the PostScript entry and type "Y" and <Enter> to then change the printing font that's supported by the printer. Once you've chosen the proper font, press <Enter>, and then use the Down arrow key to finish out the fields and press <Enter> to the "Accept and continue?" screen. If you are printing to a dot matrix or laser printer, you can't change the Fonts entry (unless your laser printer also supports PostScript). The default is Courier type.

The Page Length entry defaults to 66 lines, which matches a standard 8.5 by 11-inch paper size. If you have longer paper, multiply 6 times the paper length (for 17-inch paper length, it's 6 times 17, or 102).

The Banner page entry allows you to send a banner along with the message. Type Y if you want the print job to have a banner page before the printed message. If you are already sending a banner with your print jobs through the CAPTURE command, leave this entry to No; otherwise, you'll get two banners. FirstMail can also create banner pages for PostScript printers.

When you press the Down arrow key at the end of the "Print Settings" screen, press <Enter> to the "Accept and continue?" screen, and your print job is on the way.

Reply. You can reply to a message sent to you by typing the letter "R" on the highlighted message entry. You will see the "Select reply format" screen with General options, Address options, and a Copy option. The General options allow you to include the message itself in the reply (default is No), to comment out the original message (if included) with your own personal comments (defaults to Yes), and to send the reply to all who received the message in the first place (defaults to No).

The Address options allow you to use the information found in the message to fill out the header information for the reply message. For example, type Y in the From Field entry to reply to the original sender (defaults to No). Type Y in the Reply Field entry if you want to reply to any reply-to address specified in the original message (defaults to Yes). Type Y in the Cc Field entry if you want to send to everyone who originally received the message (defaults to No). Leave the Sender Field entry set to No (the

642

default), for it doesn't apply to FirstMail and NetWare Basic MHS services. Type Y in the To Field entry is you want the sender of the original message to also receive the original message as well.

The last entry, Copy Cc Field, will also copy the message to those names found in the original message's Copy Cc field. This way, those who receive the original message will also get your response to the message (defaults to No). Once you have made your responses, press <Enter>, and then <Enter> again to the "Accept and continue?" screen.

Depending on your selections, you will either see the original message or you will see a new message screen with the fields you selected through the Reply command filled in. Since this is the same editing screen you see when you choose the "Send a mail message" option from FirstMail's initial window, we'll defer editing discussions to the "Sending a Mail Message" subheading later in this appendix. But once you have made your changes, press <Ctrl>+<Enter> to send the message, and then press <Enter> again to the "Accept and continue?" screen. You will return to the "New Mail" screen.

Send. Use the Send command when you want to send a message while in the "New Mail" screen. Since this is the same editing screen you see when you choose the "Send a mail message" option from FirstMail's initial window, we'll also defer editing discussions to the "Sending a Mail Message" subheading later in this appendix.

eXtract. The eXtract command allows you to copy the message to a DOS file by typing in the filename you wish to save the message in. DOS file naming convention allows you eight characters, followed by a period, and then three more characters following the period. You can press the <Tab> key to select which file you wish to append the message to. Before you type in a filename, press <Tab>, and you'll see a list of the files in your default directory or the directory you selected as your default directory through the "Preferences" option in FirstMail's initial "Mail Options" window.

You can then select one of those files through the up/down arrow keys and by pressing <Enter> on the highlighted file, and then pressing <Enter> again to append to the file. Depending on how you have set up your preferences, you may see a screen asking you to press Y to overwrite the existing file, press N to append to the existing file, or to press <Esc> to forget about the whole thing and return to the "New Mail" screen.

If the message also has a file attached, you'll see a screen asking if you wish to extract the file attachment, the same as you see under the Attachments command. Press <Enter> to include the file attachment; otherwise, type N and press <Enter>. If you select to add the attachment, you'll see the "Attached to this message" screen appear before you with the first file that is attached highlighted. If you have more than one file and you want to extract them all, use the F5 key or the space bar to mark those files for extraction, and then press <Enter> to start the extraction process.

The last line on the "New Mail" screen contains the keys you can use to perform a function. The keys include F10=Select folder, F5=(un)mark, Enter=Read, Del=Delete, and Esc=Escape.

F10=Select Folder. When you press F10, you select where you wish to place a message or attachments. To place the message into a folder, highlight the folder and press <Enter>. You begin with a Main folder, but you can create new folders as well.

To add a new folder, press the <Ins> key. If you copy the messages you send to yourself, you will also see a Copies to Self folder. Long folder names can't be over 50 characters in length. It's best to also fill out the short name field (eight characters or less), which gives the directories where the messages are stored a name you can remember.

To delete a folder, press the <Del> key (however, you can't delete the Main Folder); to rename a folder, press the <Alt>+R keys at the same time. If you want to compress the files within the selected folder, press the F10 key again.

F5=(un)mark. To mark messages, press the F5 key or the space bar and you'll see a star in front of the messages you selected. You can then use one of the other commands to place the marked messages with their attachments into folders. You can also use the F5 key to mark messages for string searches through the Locate command.

Enter=Read. To see the contents of a message, highlight the message and press <Enter>, you'll see a screen similar to the one shown in Figure F-3. To get around in a message, <PgDn> moves the cursor to the bottom of the present screen, and <PgUp> brings you to the top of the present screen. If the text contains more than one screenfull, press the <PgDn> or <PgUp> keys to see the next screenfull. If a message occupies more than a single screen and you want to move to the beginning, press <Ctrl>+<PgUp>; to move to the end of your message, press <Ctrl>+<PgDn>. You can also use the Up arrow key (8 on the numeric keypad) to move up one line, and the Down arrow key (2 on the numeric keypad) to move down one line.

When you're editing a message or creating a new message, you have still other ways of moving around. The left arrow key (6) moves you one cursor position to the left, and the right arrow key (4) moves you one cursor position to the right. To move a full word to the left, press the <Ctrl>+left arrow keys; to move one word to the right, press the <Ctrl>+right arrow keys. You can use the Home key (7) to go to the far left position, and the End key (1) to go to the far right of the line you're on. When you are finished viewing the message, press <Esc>.

Del=Delete. If you receive a message that you don't want to save, highlight the message and press the <Del> key. You'll see a "Delete this message?" screen with Yes highlighted. Press <Enter> to delete the message. If you have multiple files to delete, use F5 or the space bar to mark them, press the <Del> key, and then <Enter> to delete the messages.

644

Esc=Exit. When you are finished with the "New Mail" screen, press the <Esc> key to return to the "Mail Options" window. Press <Esc> again to exit from the FirstMail utility.

Sending a Mail Message

The second option, "Send a mail message," allows you to create and send mail messages to other users on this server. To go to the "Send Message: Editing Screen" window, highlight the option and press <Enter>. You'll see a screen similar to that shown in Figure F-3.

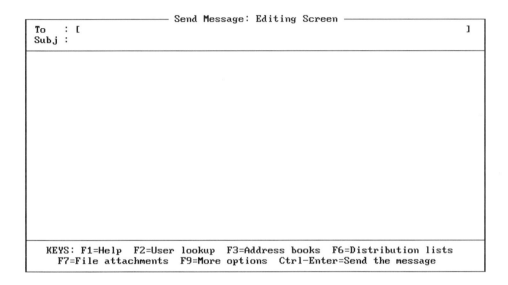

Figure F-3. The Editing screen allows you to compose and edit messages

The top of the "Send Message: Editing Screen" window contains a To: and Subj: entries. Use the To: entry to designate who should receive the message. You can type in the user's E-mail name if you know it, or you can use the F2, F3, or F6 keys to designate who should receive the message. For example, if you want to send the message to Rachel, press F2 to see the "SMF Directory List" window with the names of the users who can receive the message. Highlight Rachel and press <Enter>. You'll see the name added to the To: entry on the "Send Message: Editing Screen" window. Repeat the process if you want more than one person to receive the message.

645

You can also press F4 to see what users are presently logged in to the server. If you use F4, you can press <Alt>+S to send a brief message, just as if you were using the SEND command.

The Subj: entry can help you group messages into categories, or can be used as a one-line summary of topics. You can use the Subj: entries as a means to browse certain ideas through your conversations. Type in a concise idea, or you can leave this entry blank if you wish by pressing <Enter> to go to the editing screen.

The editing screen is where you type in your message. Each line defaults to 70 characters long (including spaces) and will break to the next line when that limit is reached. (You can change the default through the Editor and Keyboard Settings option under the "Mail Options" window's Preferences option.) Once you have finished composing your message, you can edit your message by using the following commands.

To get around in a message, <PgDn> moves the cursor to the bottom of the present screen, and <PgUp> brings you to the top of the present screen. If the text contains more than one screenfull, press the <PgDn> or <PgUp> keys to see the next screenfull. If a message occupies more than a single screen and you want to move to the beginning, press <Ctrl>+<PgUp>; to move to the end of your message, press <Ctrl>+<PgDn>. You can also use the Up arrow key (8 on the numeric keypad) to move up one line, and the Down arrow key (2 on the numeric keypad) to move down one line.

When you're editing a message or creating a new message, you have still other ways of moving around. The left arrow key (6) moves you one cursor position to the left, and the right arrow key (4) moves you one cursor position to the right. To move a full word to the left, press the <Ctrl>+left arrow keys; to move one word to the right, press the <Ctrl>+right arrow keys. You can use the Home key (7) to go to the far left position, and the End key (1) to go to the far right of the line you're on. If you press the <Ins> key, you'll overwrite text that is to the right of the cursor; otherwise, the text editor will move any text that is to the right of the cursor when you type in more text. To delete a line, type Home to go to the front of the line, and then press the <Ctrl>+End keys simultaneously. To see what other editing capabilities are available to you, press F1 for Help.

FirstMail's editor is similar to WordStar and Borland's Turbo editors. However, there are some differences. To learn about the commands you can use in FirstMail's editor, bring up the editor and press F1. You will see a small menu with six options: Introduction to the editor, Quick reference guide, Block and file commands (^K), Movement commands (^Q), Searching and replacing, and Other commands and features.

The Introduction to the editor option explains the changes or differences in the FirstMail editor over similar editors, as well as information to get back to change header information (F9) or how to paste entries from the address book into the current message (F3).

The Quick reference guide is exactly that—all the commands you can use with the FirstMail editor. The Block and file commands contains all the block commands supported by FirstMail, as well as a brief explanation of what the commands mean. The Movement commands option covers all the commands that are supported by FirstMail in order to move around in the editor, as well as a brief explanation of what the commands mean.

The Searching and replacing option covers all the commands that are supported by FirstMail to find and replace text in the editor, as well as an explanation of what the commands mean. The Other commands and features option covers all the additional commands available in the FirstMail editor that were not covered in the other options.

FirstMail's editing screen presents a line toward the bottom of the screen that contains two numbers separated by a colon. The first number reflects how many lines deep you are in the text and the second line shows the number of characters wide a particular line is, including spaces.

The bottom part of the "Send Message: Editing Screen" window contains the following keys that cover what you can do in this window with the messages you create. These are as follows:

F1=Help. If you need help at any point with a selection, press the F1 key.

F2=User Lookup. Use F2 to add who you wish to send the message to at the To: entry at the top of the screen. For example, if you want to send the message to Tim, press F2 to see the "SMF Directory List" window with the names of the users who can receive the message. Highlight that person's name and press <Enter>. You'll see the name added to the To: entry. Repeat the process if you want more than one person to receive the message.

F3=Address Books. You can also create address books for the users that you send most of your messages to. The address books become a place to look up information about users. When you press F3, you'll see the "Select an address book" screen with no entries. Press <Ins> to add a name to the address book. You can add a long and short name to the list. Long names can't be over 50 characters in length. It's best to also fill out the short name field (eight characters or less), which gives the directories where the messages are stored a name you can remember. To delete an address book, press the <Del> key; to rename an address book, press the <Alt>+R keys at the same time.

If you want to select an address book, highlight the entry and press <Enter>. You'll see the "Address book contents" screen with Key, Name, and Phone columns and entries underneath. To add information into an address book, press <Ins> and fill out the screen's information. This information includes the user's name, department, telephone and fax number, postal and street address, E-mail address, and any notes you wish to add. When you are through, press <Ctrl>+<Enter> and then <Enter> again to the "Accept and continue?" screen. You can save as many entries per address as you like.

To delete an entry, press the <Del> key, and then <Enter>. To search for a character string, press <Alt>+S, type in the character string, and then press <Enter>. If FirstMail can match the string, it will place you on that entry. To edit an entry that has changed, highlight the entry and press <Alt>+E, and then use the up/down arrow keys to bring you to the fields you wish to change. Press <Ctrl>+<Enter> when you are finished editing.

The F10-Options command in the "Address book contents" screen allows you to sort the entries in the address book by the name column, by the key column, or by the reindex book. Select one and press <Enter> to see the results.

When you are all finished with this address book, press <Ctrl>+<Enter> to return to the To: entry in the "Send Message: Editing Screen" window. You'll see the entry from which you left the "Address book contents" screen added to the To: entry.

F6=Distribution Lists (DLists). FirstMail also comes with the ability to group users together into distribution lists. For example, you can create a Lunch distribution list or a Rides Home list. Those users placed in the Distribution list will then receive the message. When you press F6, you'll see the "Select a distribution list" screen with a Supervisor entry. Press <Ins> to add a name to the distribution list. You can add a long and short name to the list. Long names can't be over 50 characters in length. It's best to also fill out the short name field (eight characters or less), which becomes the directory name (with a .PML extension) where the user's long names are stored for the distribution list.

Once you create a DList, you'll come to a screen showing the initial title name of the DList, which looks similar to the following:

```
\title  Rides Home
```

Beneath this line, type in the E-mail addresses of the users you wish to be a part of this DList. You can do this by pressing the F2 key to see a list of the users in the SMF directory. Use the F5 key to mark the users you want and press <Enter>. The user's E-mail addresses are added to the DList. When you are finished, press <Ctrl>+<Enter> to return to the "Select a distribution list" screen, and then press <Enter> again to place the DList directory path in the To: entry of the "Send Message: Editing Screen" window.

To delete a DList, highlight the list and press the <Del> key; to rename a DList, press the <Alt>+R keys at the same time, and then change the long name and short name if necessary.

F7=File attachments. IF you wish to send a file along with the message, press the F7 key to see the "Attached to this message" screen with the Filename, Format, and ASCII columns. Pressing <Ins> displays the "Enter attachment information" screen telling you to type in the filename and directory path (if needed). You can use wildcards as well.

Press <Enter> on the File Type entry to see which formats you can choose from. If you can't match a format, choose "Unknown." Then press <Enter> and then <Enter> again to the "Accept and continue?" screen. The files are added to the "Attached to this message" screen. To delete a file from the screen, highlight the file and press the <Del> key. You can have up to 64 attachments to a message. Press <Ctrl>+<Enter> when you are finished and the files are attached to the message.

F9=More options. Pressing F9 brings up the "Options for your message" screen with eight entry fields. The Cc (Carbon copy) and Bcc (Blind carbon copies) fields allow you to have others receive the message. Press F2 to see the list of users you wish to include from the SMF directory. Use the F5 key to mark the users you want and press <Enter>. The user's E-mail addresses are added to the Cc or Bcc fields. Use the Reply to: field if you want all replies to go to someone else, like your secretary or a committee chairperson.

The next five entries—Keep a copy, Confirm reading, Confirm delivery, Urgent message, and Omit signature—all default to No. If you want to use any of the entries, highlight the entry and type Y <Enter>. At the end of the list, press <Enter> and then <Enter> again to the "Accept and continue?" screen.

Ctrl+Enter=Send the message. When you are finished with the message, press <Ctrl>+<Enter> and then <Enter> again to the "Accept and continue?" screen. The message is on its way, and you'll return to FirstMail's initial "Mail Options" window.

Browsing Through the Mail Messages

To select Browse Mail Messages, highlight the option and press <Enter>. You'll see the mail messages that are stored in FirstMail's Main folder, similar to the folder shown in Figure F-4.

The Browse Mail Messages option gives the same options at the bottom as the Check For New Mail option, since there is little difference between a new mail message and one that you have sitting around in a folder (except that you haven't seen the new mail message before). To see how each command in the Browse Mail Message option works, go to the heading "Checking for New Mail" in this appendix. This part will focus on some of the jobs you will perform the most through the Browse option.

To view the messages that are located in another folder, type F10, select the folder you wish to view and press <Enter>. To move messages from one folder to another, press

F5 to mark the messages, press the letter "M" for the Move command, and then select the folder you wish to place the messages in and press <Enter>.

```
┌─────────────────── Folder Main folder (12 messages) ───────────────────┐
│    From                   Subject                  Date            ◆    │
├────────────────────────────────────────────────────────────────────────┤
│ √ ED@NTS3                 New Message              12 Jun 93 14:08       │
│ √ ED@NTS3                 glipcrap                 12 Jun 93 15:03       │
│ √ SUPERVISOR@NTS3         gurpl                    12 Jun 93 15:15       │
│ √ ED@NTS3                 attachment               12 Jun 93 17:02 Y     │
│ √ SUPERVISOR@NTS3         solution                 12 Jun 93 18:34       │
│ √ ED@NTS3                 hardy harhar             12 Jun 93 17:54       │
│ √ ED@NTS3                 glopnop                  12 Jun 93 19:53       │
│ √ Ted E. Beara           too many spoons          12 Jun 93 18:55       │
│ √ Ted E. Beara           Re: too many spoons      12 Jun 93 21:34       │
│ √ ED@NTS3                 (Forwarded) Whose idea was thi 13 Jun 93  8:40 Y│
│ √ ED@NTS3                 new mail editor          13 Jun 93 15:46       │
│ √ ED@NTS3                 rprint file              13 Jun 93 14:22 Y     │
│ ─────────────────────────< End of list    >───────────────────────────  │
│                                                                          │
│                                                                          │
│                                                                          │
│                                                                          │
├────────────────────────────────────────────────────────────────────────┤
│ Attachments Copy Dos Forward Info Locate Move Order Print Reply Send eXtract│
│    KEYS: F10=Select folder   F5=(un)mark   Enter=Read   Del=Delete   Esc=Exit│
└────────────────────────────────────────────────────────────────────────┘
```

Figure F-4. When you select the Browse option, you'll see the mail messages that are stored in FirstMail's Main folder

To copy messages to a floppy disk press F5 to mark the messages, press the letter "D" for the DOS command, and then type in the file path where you wish to copy the files to and press <Enter>. To delete unwanted messages, press F5 to mark the messages, press the <Del> key and then the <Enter> key.

To print a message, highlight the message and press the letter "P" for the Print command. Specify the way you want to print the file, use the Down arrow key to reach the end of the screen, and then press <Enter> to the "Accept and continue?" screen.

To extract an attachment from a message, highlight the message that has attachments (it has a Y at the far right of the entry), and press the letter "A" for Attachments. You'll see the "Attached to this message" screen with the list of attached files. Press <Enter> to extract a file into the directory from which you came into FirstMail, or into the working directory you designate through the Preferences option.

To forward a message to a distribution list, highlight the message, type the "F" letter to forward the message, and then press F2 to choose someone to send the message to. Next, answer Yes to the Edit before sending entry in the "Forward message of file to" screen. Once in the message, select F6 for the distribution list. Highlight the list and press

<Enter> and then <Ctrl>+<Enter> to bring up the "Accept and continue?" screen, and then <Enter> again to send the message.

Press <Esc> to exit from the Browse Mail Message option and return to the "Mail Options" window.

Changing to Another File Server

You use the Change File Server option to send messages to users on other servers who also have the FirstMail utility installed. FirstMail works only on one server at a time. Highlight the Change File Server option and press <Enter>. You'll see the "Select New Servers" screen with an asterisk by the servers you are presently attached to (see figure F-5). Highlight the server you wish to look at and press <Enter>. If successful, you will see a different server along with your username on that server at the bottom of the "Mail Options window. You can then perform the same functions that you did on your present server, such as viewing new mail, and creating and forwarding messages.

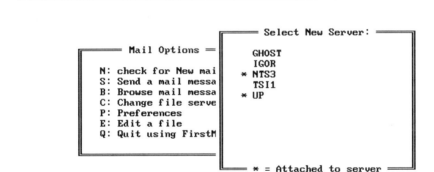

Figure F-5. Changing to a different file server

To see the correct mail service for you, you must log in as the person for which the mailbox was created. If you are attached to a server under a different name, highlight the Change File Server option and press <enter>, highlight the server you wish to log out from and press the <Del> key. Then press <Ins> to see the "Server servername" screen with the Username and Password entries. Type in the correct username and password, press <Enter> and then <Enter> again to the "Accept and continue" screen. You will see the bottom of the FirstMail screen change to reflect the new file server and username.

Again, the other file server must also be running Global MHS or Basic MHS for this opt ion to work.

Setting Your Preferences

Use the Preferences option to customize FirstMail for your environment. When you highlight the Preferences option and press <Enter>, you'll see a "Preferences Menu" screen with seven options. These options are Edit or create Signatures. (You can bring up the "Preferences Menu" screen at any time by pressing Shift+F10 simultaneously.)

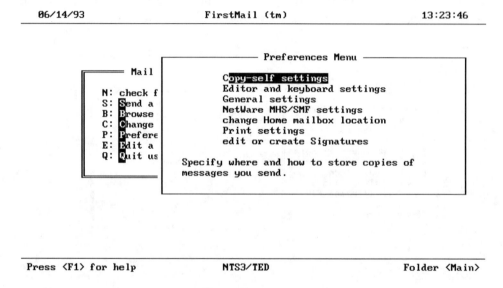

06/14/93   FirstMail (tm)   13:23:46

```
                                  ── Preferences Menu ──
          ═══ Mail
                              Copy-self settings
    N: check f                Editor and keyboard settings
    S: Send a                 General settings
    B: Browse                 NetWare MHS/SMF settings
    C: Change                 change Home mailbox location
    P: Prefere                Print settings
    E: Edit a                 edit or create Signatures
    Q: Quit us
                          Specify where and how to store copies of
                          messages you send.
```

Press <F1> for help   NTS3/TED   Folder <Main>

Figure F-6. Customize your FirstMail environment through the Preferences option

Copy-self settings. Use this option to specify where you want to store messages that you send or copy to yourself as well as to the person you are sending the message. Selecting the option brings up the "Copy-self Settings" screen with two entries: Folder for copies to self and Always prompt copy to self. You can type the folder name to be eight characters long, and the default folder name is COPYSELF. The Always prompt copy to self entry defaults to No, but if you change it to Yes, you will be asked if you want a copy of every message you send. If you wish to cancel your changes, press <Esc> and then <Enter> to return to the "Preferences Menu" screen.

Editor and keyboard settings. You can use a different editor for creating and modifying e-mail messages. The Editor and keyboard settings option allows you to specify how wide the margins should be, if you wish to use an external editor, how many spaces tabs should be set to, as well as general keyboard layout specifications. To perform these functions, highlight this option and press <Enter>. Then, at the "Editor Settings" screen, there are six entries: Default editor right margin, Default commenting string, Editor string, Scratch area, Always use external editor, and Keyboard layout.

Through the Default editor right margin entry, you can set how wide you want the right margin to be (the default is 70). Through the Default commenting string entry, you can add comments to mark your message replies with a unique comment.

Through the Editor string entry, you can specify your own word processor or text editor instead of using FirstMail's when creating and modifying messages. For example, if you wanted to use WordPerfect's Personal Editor (PE) for message creation, select the Editor string entry and type in the command you would use at the DOS prompt to bring up the program, such as PE <Enter>.

(However, in the beta release of FirstMail that I wrote this appendix about, when I chose an external editor and set up FirstMail to always use the external editor, FirstMail wouldn't allow me to read my new mail. You will have to experiment and see if you have the same problem or if the problem was fixed.)

If you use a word processor as your text editor, be sure to save your file as a DOS text file; otherwise, other users won't be able to read the file if they are using FirstMail as their file editor.

You use the Scratch area entry in conjunction with the external text editor. A scratch area is where the editor can store temporary files, so select a directory in which you have read and write rights.

The Always use external editor entry allows you to select which editor you can use. If you always want to use the external editor, change the N field to Yes. You can leave the field set to No, and then invoke the external text editor by holding down the <Ctrl> key and typing KE from within FirstMail's editor. The Keyboard layout entry is set to default and should not be changed by normal users.

Once you have made your changes, press <Enter> and then <Enter> again to the "Accept and continue?" screen. You will return to the "Preferences Menu" screen.

General Settings. The General settings option in the "Preferences Menu" screen allows you to give yourself a personal name, as well as set nine other general parameters.

For example, you can type in your full name, set up a default reply-to so that when others reply to your messages, they go to someone else, such as a secretary (but you better tell that person first).

The next three entries default to No, but you can change this by highlighting and typing Yes. You can require a password when you enter FirstMail. You can preserve deleted messages in a "Deleted Messages" folder while you are currently in FirstMail; however, this folder and files are deleted when you leave the FirstMail utility. You can set the Swap out when calling DOS entry to Yes if you want to place FirstMail into EMS (if you are running EMS) when you are performing DOS commands.

Through the Work directory entry, you can create a default working directory that FirstMail will go to when you start up the program.

The next four entries default to No, but you can change them by highlighting and typing Yes. You can use the Address only in browser entry to set it up so that the Browser only shows you MHS addresses and not personal names. If you have printing set up the way you like it, you can set the Suppress print dialog entry to Yes and not see the print dialog box when you are in the Browser utility.

You can also set up FirstMail to automatically open new mail when it starts up by setting the Automatically open new mail entry to Yes. You can also leave new mail that you have already read once in the New Mail folder by setting the Leave read new mail new entry to Yes. Once you have made your changes, press <Enter> and then <Enter> again to the "Accept and continue?" screen. You will return to the "Preferences Menu" screen.

NetWare MHS/SMF settings. The NetWare MHS/SMF settings option in the "Preferences Menu" screen allows you to customize NetWare SMF/MHS for your use. However, only change these settings if your network administrator tells you to. Otherwise, you might not be able to receive or send mail, or even bring up the FirstMail utility.

Selecting the option brings up the "NetWare MHS Settings" screen with four entries. The first entry, My SMF/MHS user name, allows you to change your MHS name to be something different from your login name. This is not necessarily preferred, however, so before changing anything, talk to your network administrator.

If you change your MHS name, you'll need to change the second entry, My SMF/ MHS mailbox name. Match the mailbox name to the directory within the MHS directory tree. You'll need to ask your network administrator what that directory name is. Again, this is not necessarily preferred, so before changing anything, talk to your network administrator.

The My application name entry (followed by FIRST) allows you to set how FirstMail scans MHS or other electronic mail directory structures under MHS. Unless your network administrator tells you to change this, use the default.

The last entry, Scan the MHS user dir, allows FirstMail to scan a "generic application" MHS directory for mail that might come in from different electronic mail packages. The default is Yes, which allows FirstMail to scan the generic application directory as well as your mail directory.

Once you have made your changes (and I strongly suggest you only change these parameters with the network administrator's permission), press <Enter> and then <Enter> again to the "Accept and continue?" screen. You will return to the "Preferences Menu" screen.

Change home mailbox location. Use the Change home mailbox location option to set up a different location for folders, messages, distributions lists and address books. For example, if volume SYS is running out of space and you are working out under VOL1, you can select this option and type in the directory path where you want your mailbox contents stored. You are then asked if you want to move the contents to the designated directory, and pressing <Enter> moves the mailbox contents. If you make a mistake and want to place the mailbox contents back, choose the option again, and erase the directory path; you will again be asked to move the contents, only this time it will be to your default mail directory. Press <Enter> to move everything back.

Print Settings. The Print settings entry allows you to set the way you want to print in all cases. Once this is in place, you can answer Yes to the Suppress print dialog entry under the General Preferences option. The "Print Settings" screen comes with six entries: Print To, Filename, PostScript, PS font, Page length (Lines @ 6LPI), and Print a Banner page.

If you are using the CAPTURE command to send print jobs where you want them to go, press <Enter> to change the LPT1 entry to match the CAPTURE statement you wish to use. You can also send the print job to a print queue on this file server (use the CAPTURE command to send print jobs to other servers and queues if necessary).

To change selections to print to a queue, press <Enter> at the Print To entry, and select the Queue option, type in the print queue name on this server, and then press <Enter>. Then use the Down arrow key to finish out the fields and press <Enter> to the "Accept and continue?" screen. You can also print messages to a file instead of to a printer by pressing <Enter> at the Print To entry and selecting the File option. You then type in the name of the file and directory path (if needed) and press <Enter>.

Use the PostScript and PS Font entries when you are printing to a printer that can handle PostScript files. Highlight the PostScript entry and type "Y" and <Enter> to then change the printing font that's supported by the printer. Once you've chosen the proper font, press <Enter>, and then use the Down arrow key to finish out the fields and press <Enter> to the "Accept and continue?" screen. If you are printing to a dot matrix or laser printer, you can't change the Fonts entry (unless your laser printer also supports PostScript). The default is Courier type face.

The Page Length entry defaults to 66 lines, which matches a standard 8.5 by 11-inch paper size. If you have longer paper, multiply 6 times the paper length (for 17-inch paper length, it's 6 times 17, or 102).

The Banner page entry allows you to send a banner along with the message. Type Y if you want the print job to have a banner page before the printed message. If you are already sending a banner with your print jobs through the CAPTURE command, leave this entry set to No; otherwise, you'll get two banners. FirstMail can also create banner pages for PostScript printers.

When you are finished setting up your printer specifications, press the Down arrow key at the end of the "Print Settings" screen, and press <Enter> to the "Accept and continue?" screen to accept the new print settings. You'll then return to the "Preferences Menu" screen.

Edit or create Signatures. You can use this option to create a small ending that FirstMail will plug on to all the messages you write. For example, you can put your name, title, phone number, and fax number into a file called MHSSIG.PMS under your current mailbox directory. When you are finished composing the ending, press <Ctrl>+<Enter> to return to the "Preferences Menu" screen. You can re-edit this file at any time.

When you are finished making changes in the "Preferences Menu" screen, press <Esc> to return to the "Mail Options" window.

Editing a File in FirstMail

The next option in the "Mail Options" window is Edit a file. The Edit a file option lets you edit DOS text files through FirstMail's editor. If you set up a default editor that is not FirstMail, you can use that editor as well.

To edit a file, highlight the Edit a file option and press <Enter>. You'll see an "Enter name of the file to edit" screen, which allows you to type in the directory path and filename of the file you wish to edit. For example, if you wanted to edit your MAINMENU.SRC file for the NMENU utility (see Appendix E) and the file was in your F:\PERSONAL\TED directory, you would type F:\PERSONAL\TED\MAINMENU.SRC and press <Enter>. You will then come up in FirstMail's editor.

To get around in FirstMail's editor, <PgDn> moves the cursor to the bottom of the present screen, and <PgUp> brings you to the top of the present screen. If the text contains more than one screenfull, press the <PgDn> or <PgUp> keys to see the next screenfull. If a message occupies more than a single screen and you want to move to the beginning, press <Ctrl>+<PgUp>; to move to the end of your message, press <Ctrl>+<PgDn>. You can also use the Up arrow key (8 on the numeric keypad) to move up one line, and the Down arrow key (2 on the numeric keypad) to move down one line.

When you're editing a message or creating a new message, you have still other ways of moving around. The left arrow key (6) moves you one cursor position to the left, and the right arrow key (4) moves you one cursor position to the right. To move a full word to the left, press the <Ctrl>+left arrow keys; to move one word to the right, press the <Ctrl>+right arrow keys. You can use the Home key (7) to go the far left position, and the End key (1) to go to the far right of the line you're on. If you press the <Ins> key, you'll overwrite text that is to the right of the cursor; otherwise, the text editor will move any text that is to the right of the cursor when you type in more text. To delete a line, type Home to go to the front of the line, and then press the <Ctrl>+End keys simultaneously. To see what other editing capabilities are available to you, press F1 for Help (see Figure F-7).

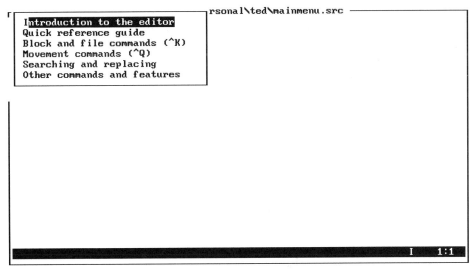

Figure F-7. When you pull up a file in FirstMail's editor, you can use the F1 key to assist in explaining the available commands.

FirstMail's editor is similar to WordStar and Borland's Turbo editors. There are some differences, however. To learn about the commands you can use in FirstMail's editor, bring up the editor and press F1. You will see a small menu with six options: Introduction

657

to the editor, Quick reference guide, Block and file commands (^K), Movement commands (^Q), Searching and replacing, and Other commands and features.

The Introduction to the editor option explains the changes or differences in the FirstMail editor over similar editors, as well as information to get back to change header information (F9) or how to past entries from the address book into the current message (F3).

The Quick reference guide is exactly that—all the commands you can use with the FirstMail editor. The Block and file commands contains all the block commands supported by FirstMail, as well as a brief explanation of what the commands mean. The Movement commands option covers all the commands that are supported by FirstMail in order to move around in the editor, as well as a brief explanation of what the commands mean.

The Searching and replacing option covers all the commands that are supported by FirstMail to find and replace text in the editor, as well as an explanation of what the commands mean. The Other commands and features option covers all the additional commands available in the FirstMail editor that were not covered in the other options.

When you are done editing the file, be sure to save your changes. To save changes through FirstMail's editor, press <Ctrl>+<Enter> and you'll return to the "Mail Options" window.

Quitting the FirstMail Utility

To exit from FirstMail, move the selector bar to the Quit using FirstMail option and press <Enter> or type the letter Q and press <Enter>. You can also press <Esc> at the "Mail Options" window, and then <Enter> to leave FirstMail. You are immediately placed at the network prompt.

Summary

The FirstMail utility offers NetWare 3.12 users a basic electronic mail package that can meet the rudimentary needs of most users. In this appendix, you learned how to view new mail, send mail messages, and look through old messages that you have saved. There may come a time, however, when users may want a more global E-mail package that is not so server-centric.

Index

Symbols

& AND operator 250
@ at sign 182, 183
\ backslash character 40, 183
^ carat 626
, comma 183
{} curly brackets 625
> DOS redirection symbol 313
. dot or period 313
"" double quotes 183
= equals 76
== equals 76
~ EXCLUSIVE OR operator 250
# external program execution 62, 68
/ frontslash character 40, 633
/ OR operator 250
* global wild card 38, 126, 250, 273
> is greater than 76
>= is greater than or equal to 77
< is less than 76
<= is less than or equal to 77
– minus key, 236, 252
!= not equals 76
<> not equals 76
not equals 76
^ NOT operator 250
% parameter prefix 79
% percent sign 183
+ plus key 236, 252
? single-character wild card 38, 127, 250, 274

A

Access Control rights 15, 317, 320, 332, 614
    deleting 113
Access control security right 13
Account Balance option 94
Account Disabled option 95
Account Has Expiration Date option 95
Account Reset Time 98
Account Restrictions option 94

Account Disabled 95
Account Has Expiration Date 95
Allow User to Change Password 95
Date Account Expires 95
Limit Concurrent Connections 95
Maximum Connections 95
Remaining Grace Logins 96
Require Password 96
Require Unique Passwords 96
Accounting 84–86
Activity option 215, 232
Allow User to Change Password option 95
ALLOW utility 253, 317–321, 591
    /ALL option 320
    /H command 318
    [PATH [TO INHERIT] [rightslist] 318,
    591–592
<Alt-F10> key combination 55, 173
<Alt>-<O> 251
AND operator (&) 250
And option 241
Applications 3
    accessible 41
    formatting capabilities 372
    interpretations of Netware security 17
    printing dumb applications 370
    printing later 372
    printing network applications 370
    printing smart applications 370
Apply Query To All option 241
Archive attribute 15
ASSIGN (DOS) command 36, 565
Asterisk (*) wild card 38, 126, 273
At sign (@) 182, 183
AT&T 166
Attach to a server 28
ATTACH command 28, 60, 62, 63, 264
ATTACH utility 253, 264–266, 592
    servername/username 265, 592
Attributes option 135
AUTO.VLM module 22
AUTOEXEC.BAT file 19
    COPY CON AUTOEXEC.BAT 459

679

X

Y

Z